D1226287

EVANS'
AMERICAN BIBLIOGRAPHY

1639–1800 A. D.

THE AMERICAN BIBLIOGRAPHY

OF

CHARLES EVANS

A CHRONOLOGICAL DICTIONARY OF ALL
BOOKS PAMPHLETS AND PERIODICAL PUBLICATIONS

Printed in the United States of America from the Genesis
of Printing in 1639 Down to and Including the
Year 1800 with Bibliographical and
Biographical Notes

Volume 13 • 1799–1800

BY CLIFFORD K. SHIPTON

AMERICAN ANTIQUARIAN SOCIETY
WORCESTER, MASSACHUSETTS
1955
REPRINTED, 1962

COPYRIGHT, 1955, BY
AMERICAN ANTIQUARIAN SOCIETY

REPRINTED, 1962 BY

PETER SMITH
WITH THE PERMISSION OF
AMERICAN ANTIQUARIAN SOCIETY

120872

PREFACE

In the entire history of bibliography there are few singlehanded exploits to compare with the *American Bibliography* of Charles Evans. Begun before modern techniques had been developed, it was far in advance of the general practice of its time, and is still, and long will be, in daily use in every great library. It is uniquely the product of the devotion of one man.

There was nothing in the background of Charles Evans to explain his love of books and the skill with which he handled them. The son of an immigrant mariner, and early an orphan, he was educated at the Boston Farm and Trades School. Without doubt his interests were influenced by Dr. Samuel Eliot, who placed him at the age of sixteen in the Boston Athenaeum, where he soon showed that genius for books without which one can no more be a good bibliographer than a tone-deaf man can be a good musician. At the age of twenty-two he went west to organize and head the Indianapolis Public Library, and in the next three decades he served in a similar way the Enoch Pratt Free Library, the Omaha Public Library, and the Newberry Library of Chicago.

In 1901, at the age of fifty-one, Mr. Evans decided to devote the remainder of his life to the great bibliographical project which he had in mind at least as early as 1880, when he began recording early American imprints. For the next thirty-five years this was his life. Food and drink were incidentals. It should be recorded that his wife, Lena Young, accepted this way of life with a sympathy and interest which sustained his spirits and his enthusiasm for the work when all else seemed to conspire against it. For the sake of economy and mobility he wrote his notes with a very fine pen on the backs of halved three-by-five library cards and packed them neatly into corset boxes which he could carry around under his arm. His travels carried him as far as London, where the inability of the custodians of the British Museum to find the volume of broadsides which contained the item which he suspected to be the *Freeman's Oath* gave him as tragic an hour as can be found in fiction.

In 1903 the first volume of the great work appeared, describing one-third more titles than any earlier bibliography in the field. Evans had already been in correspondence with the American Antiquarian Society, and in the preparation of volume two he visited the Library and was received with a helpfulness and interest which greatly impressed him. However, our real coöperation began with the coming of Clarence Brigham as librarian in 1908. Realizing that the future usefulness of this Library depended largely on specialization in the field in which Evans was working, Brigham in his first year bought four thousand titles which would be covered by the bibliography. He urged Evans to accept his help, and for years made the *American Bibliography* one of our chief activities.

This enthusiastic support reassured Charles Evans when he was faced by discouraging conditions. Finding the regular printing houses "throttled" by the labor unions which every year were forcing up prices, in 1910 he met the cost of manufacturing volume six only by hiring five printers and working as their foreman. He was office boy and messenger as well, and considered it normal to work an eighteen-hour day himself in order to keep his hired craftsmen busy. The election of Mr. Evans to the American Antiquarian Society in 1910 was one of the two great events in his life, the other being the award of an LL.D. from Brown, Mr. Brigham's college. There must have been times when his fond family thought that the Society was second to the bibliography in his affections. There were times when his loyal generosity to the Library was embarrassing to its officers, who rightly regarded his personal needs as more important than those of the institution. They were repeatedly amazed to find the sacrifices he made in order to carry on his work. Never, however, did he make the slightest complaint. Always witty and charming, he undervalued both himself and his accomplishments. With seeming gratitude he accepted our suggestions as to improvements in his bibliographical style, but he did little about them, probably because he had long ago recognized the same points but decided not to change his ways. He never regarded the mere mechanics of bibliography as particularly important. Until the pressure of years compelled him to hasten, he read the books which he described. The essays with which he prefaced his earlier volumes are good historical writing.

The First World War presented the *American Bibliography* with another crisis. The increased exactions of the printing unions sent up costs just as the loss of the German subscriptions cut sales below the break-even point. The officers of the Society rebuilt the list by buttonholing their friends and mercilessly selling subscriptions, but the time came when even an oversubscribed volume failed to meet the cost of manufacture. The reluctant raising of the subscription price from $15 to $25 a volume kept the work going for a few years more. One volume was financed by a personal loan from the Society to Mr. Evans, a transaction which exposed the extent to which he had previously drawn upon his own business credit. When, in the Thirties, the Society began to have its own financial difficulties, it went to the American Council of Learned Societies and obtained from it the means to finance two more volumes. Mr. Evans was very reluctant to accept these grants-in-aid, feeling that they partook of the nature of charity which, in spite of his own generosity, he would accept from no man. He was, as he used to say when for amusement he exaggerated the failings of the breed, very much a Calvin Coolidge Yankee. His charm came from the virtues which are found in the best men of every place or tribe, and it made his death, in harness, in 1935, saddening for those who worked with him.

Evans had originally proposed to carry his bibliography through the year 1820, but he finally lowered his sights to the year 1800. Only a single handful of his cards describe titles printed after that date. Naturally the Society became his literary executor. There was some question of the advisability of completing his work, even though it ended awkwardly with the letter M in the year 1799. Does not the future lie with smaller, more thorough bibliographies, like Alden's *Rhode Island*? The answer seemed to be that no one is proposing to Alden Massachusetts, New York, or Pennsylvania, and that librarians the world over seemed anxious to have Evans carried on if possible. So the Society decided to bring out the present volume, for which Evans had about one third of the titles, including scores of ghosts.

It is our present opinion that the mushrooming production of the American press after 1800 (our own imprint catalogue goes through 1820) can best be studied in small segments, preferably by individual city or press. The daily work on our own imprint catalogue, which now covers perhaps 70 per cent of the books and pamphlets printed in the first two decades of the nineteenth century, lays the foundations for such bibliographies.

Mr. Evans projected a final volume which would include titles omitted from their proper places in the series, all to be made readily available by a master index to the entire work. The index would be of great value in reducing the serious labor of examining the separate volumes, and would afford an opportunity to correct the greatest weakness in Evans — the entry of anonymous titles under peculiar author headings. Negotiations are now under way regarding the preparation of such a supplement and index.

Fifty years of daily work with the *American Bibliography* have convinced us that we should in this continuation make some changes in the Evans system in spite of the resulting inconsistency. Perhaps the most troublesome practice in which he and his contemporaries indulged was the description of items from advertisements. The editor of the present volume had to devote two years to the laying of ghosts created by such advertisements or by simple typographical errors. It has all too frequently been assumed that when a printer advertised a book as "just off the press" it bore his imprint and the date of that year, but comparison of the correspondence and the advertisements of a printer like Isaiah Thomas shows the rashness of such conclusions. Modern booksellers' catalogues have given rise to hundreds of ghosts in bibliographies and union catalogues. Check almost any catalogue of imprints against the *American Bibliography* and you will come up with several "not in Evans" items which are simple and inevitable typographical errors. In general we have not accepted for this volume titles known only by the descriptions in dealers' catalogues unless the titlepage was reproduced photographically.

The fact that 1800 is a good round number has caused hundreds of undated items to be entered under this year in the bibliographies. We have excluded all those which we cannot date with reasonable assurance by advertisements or other evidence. Like Evans, we have also excluded invitations, tickets, and circulars and forms which contain blanks to be filled in in manuscript.

The large majority of the titles described in this volume have been examined by the present editor. It seemed pedantry, however, to retrace the steps of competent and reliable bibliographers even though they might use a somewhat different system of describing pagination. Being ourselves very much in the business, we know how disrupting to a library it is to have a bibliographer arrive and demand to see all of its imprints of a certain year, or even all of its unique imprints of that year. We strongly advocate that bibliographers ask their questions of librarians by mail so that their queries can be processed in bunches when convenient. In this way the Library of Congress, the New York Historical Society, the New York Public Library, the New York State Library, the Henry E. Huntington Library, the Newberry Library, the Harvard College Library, the Historical Society of Pennsylvania, Yale, and scores of smaller institutions have contributed to this volume.

Evans caused great trouble in his volumes by not distinguishing between titles which he quoted accurately and those which he only described. In this volume titles which have not been seen by the editor or described by a careful bibliographer are put in brackets as a warning that the wording may be inaccurate. Whenever possible Evans placed anonymous works under author or institution where they are sometimes so effectively lost that even the best dealers quote them to us as "not in Evans." In this volume we have included the titles as cross references. The names of the authors of anonymous works we have placed in brackets. Pseudonymous works we have placed under title unless the pseudonym might be mistaken for an author.

Printing costs now make impossible the reprinting of long descriptive titlepages which Evans enjoyed. We have herein shortened titles, taking care to indicate omissions and to retain those portions which tell "who, what, why, where, and when." Imprints are quoted more fully and accurately than was his practice, but well-known addresses are sometimes omitted from them.

Like most bibliographers Evans used the symbols 4to, 8vo, etc., for the purpose of indicating size, but sometimes he used them to describe the fold. By 1800 paper sizes were various, and half sheets were frequently used. The result is that the number of leaves in the signature is no certain indication of the size of the book. The use of centimeter measurements is not satisfactory because a majority of the books herein described have been trimmed in rebinding. Moreover, books were commonly issued in two forms, one tall, with uncut pages, in boards, and the other sharply trimmed, in calf. Which should we describe? Nor can one rely on a library ruler marked off into sizes, for a book which obviously was originally a 4to is now frequently trimmed to 8vo. The solution we have followed in this volume is to disregard the present trim size of the copy before us, and to use the symbols 4to, 8vo, etc., as the publishers of 1800 did, to indicate size without regard to fold. In children's books, for example, these symbols meant, to the bookseller of 1800, a certain size and established price class regardless of whether or not the printer chanced to use whole or half sheets.

One of the great drawbacks to Evans' volumes was his habit of citing only one or two locations, or none at all, if by that omission he could save a line. The result has been an exaggeration of the rarity of the books, and a great hindrance to scholars. In this volume we have proposed to include all locations which might be useful to students or booksellers. Inevitably there is some unevenness depending upon the freedom with which our friends volunteered information or permitted themselves to be imposed upon.

Evans' use of library initials as location symbols became so confusing in his later volumes as to be one of the chief reasons for the development of the system of geographical symbols now in general use. In this volume we felt obliged to continue Evans' practice because some of his symbols represent different libraries in the geographical system. We have made a few obvious expansions (as BrU for BU and PrU for PU) because of our experience in confusion, and have added a few new symbols on the Evans plan. For other symbols used in earlier volumes see John C. Munger's list in the *Bulletin* of the New York Public Library for August, 1936.

The list of librarians who labored beyond any call of duty to assist in the preparation of this volume would be familiar to everyone who has done extensive research in the American field. The editor, old hand though he is, has been amazed and humbled by the kind assistance which he has received from every side, and will always be grateful for having been saved from the humiliation of presenting in print certain absurd errors. Those which survive in this volume are his, and his alone.

Clifford K. Shipton

LIST OF LOCATION SYMBOLS USED IN THIS VOLUME

AAS	American Antiquarian Society, Worcester, Mass.
ABHS	American Baptist Historical Society, Philadelphia.
AGS	American Geographical Society, New York City.
AHTS	Andover-Harvard Theological Library, Cambridge, Mass.
AML	Army Medical Library, Cleveland, Ohio.
APS	American Philosophical Society, Philadelphia.
BA	Boston Athenaeum, Boston.
BM	British Museum, London.
BMFA	Museum of Fine Arts, Boston.
BML	Boston Medical Library, Boston.
BPL	Public Library of the City of Boston.
BrA	Berkshire Athenaeum, Pittsfield, Mass.
BrU	Brown University, Providence.
BwC	Bowdoin College, Brunswick, Me.
CHS	Connecticut Historical Society, Hartford.
CL	Library of the American Congregational Association, Boston.
CLS	Charleston Library Society, Charleston, S. C.
CorU	Cornell University, Ithaca, N. Y.
CSL	Connecticut State Library, Hartford.
CTS	Columbia Theological Seminary, Columbia, S. C.
CU	Columbia University, New York City.
CU-T	Columbia University, Teachers College Library, New York City.
CVHS	Connecticut Valley Historical Society, Springfield, Mass.
DC	Dartmouth College, Hanover, N. H.
DeRGL	Wymberley Jones DeRenne Georgia Library, Savannah, Ga.
DHS	Delaware Historical Society, Wilmington.
DSA	Delaware State Archives, Dover.
EI	Essex Institute, Salem, Mass.
EPFL	Enoch Pratt Free Library, Baltimore.
FL	Friends Library, Haverford College, Haverford, Pa.
FLN	Forbes Library, Northampton, Mass.
GHS	Georgia Historical Society, Savannah.
GrL	Grosvenor Library, Buffalo.
GSL	Georgia State Library, Atlanta.

GSP   Pennsylvania German Society, Philadelphia.
GTS   General Theological Seminary of the Protestant Episcopal Church in the United
           States, New York City.
GU   Georgetown University, Washington, D. C.

HC   Harvard University, Cambridge, Mass.
HC-L   Harvard University, Law School Library.
HCBA   Hartford County Bar Association, Hartford, Conn.
HCC   Hamilton College, Clinton, N. Y.
HEH   Henry E. Huntington Library and Art Gallery, San Marino, Cal.
HFL   Huntington Free Library, New York City.
HPL   Hartford, Connecticut, Public Library.
HSP   Historical Society of Pennsylvania, Philadelphia.

JCB   John Carter Brown Library, Providence, R. I.
JCL   John Crerar Library, Chicago, Ill.

KyHS   Kentucky Historical Society, Frankfort.
KySL   Kentucky State Library, Frankfort.

LaHS   Lancaster Historical Society, Lancaster, Pa.
LaML   Lancaster Mercantile Library, Lancaster, Pa.
LCP   Library Company of Philadelphia.
LePL   Leominster Public Library, Leominster, Mass.
LHS   Litchfield Historical Society, Litchfield, Conn.
LIHS   Long Island Historical Society, Brooklyn, N. Y.
LOC   Library of Congress, Washington, D. C.

MA   Massachusetts Archives, Boston.
MdFM   Maryland Grand Lodge, Free and Accepted Masons, Baltimore.
MdHS   Maryland Historical Society, Baltimore.
MDL   Maryland Diocesan Library, Baltimore.
MdSL   Maryland State Library, Annapolis.
MeHS   Maine Historical Society, Portland.
MFM   Massachusetts Grand Lodge, Free and Accepted Masons, Boston.
MHS   Massachusetts Historical Society, Boston.
MinnHS   Minnesota Historical Society, St. Paul.
MMS   Massachusetts Medical Society Library, Boston.
MPL   Milton Public Library, Milton, Mass.
MsA   Mississippi State Archives, Jackson.
MSL   Massachusetts State Library, Boston.

NA   National Archives, Washington, D. C.
NBPL   New Bedford Public Library, New Bedford, Mass.

NCHC	North Carolina Historical Commission, Raleigh.
NCSL	North Carolina State Library, Raleigh.
NCU	North Carolina University, Chapel Hill.
NEHGS	New England Historic Genealogical Society, Boston.
NEMHS	New England Methodist Historical Society, Boston University.
NHHS	New Hampshire Historical Society, Concord.
NHS	Newport Historical Society, Newport, R. I.
NHSL	New Hampshire State Library, Concord.
NJHS	New Jersey Historical Society, Newark.
NJSL	New Jersey State Library, Trenton.
NL	Newberry Library, Chicago, Ill.
NLPL	New London Public Library, New London, Conn.
NPL	Newark Public Library, Newark, New Jersey.
NYAM	New York Academy of Medicine, New York City.
NYBA	Association of the Bar of the City of New York.
NYFM	New York Grand Lodge, Free and Accepted Masons, New York City.
NYHS	New York Historical Society, New York City.
NYLI	New York Law Institute, New York City.
NYML	Mercantile Library Association, New York City.
NYPL	New York Public Library, New York City.
NYSL	New York State Library, Albany.
NYSOC	New York Society Library, New York City.
OH&PS	Ohio Historical and Philosophical Society, Cincinnati.
OSL	Ohio State Library, Columbus.
OU	Ohio State University, Columbus.
PFM	Pennsylvania Grand Lodge, Free and Accepted Masons, Philadelphia.
PL	Pequot Library, Yale University.
PM	Mercantile Library, Philadelphia.
PPL	The Free Library of Philadelphia.
PrA	Providence Athenaeum Library, Providence, R. I.
PRO	Public Record Office, London.
PrPL	Providence Public Library, Providence, R. I.
PrU	Princeton University, Princeton, N. J.
PSL	Pennsylvania State Library, Harrisburg.
PTS	Princeton Theological Seminary Library, Princeton, N. J.
RIHS	Rhode Island Historical Society, Providence.
RIMS	Rhode Island Medical Society, Providence.
RISL	Rhode Island State Library, Providence.
RL	Redwood Library, Newport, R. I.
RU	Rutgers University, New Brunswick, N. J.

SCBHC	Samuel Colgate Baptist Historical Collection, Rochester, N. Y.
SCHS	South Carolina Historical Society, Charleston.
SCSL	South Carolina State Library, Columbia.
TCH	Trinity College, Hartford, Conn.
TnSL	Tennessee State Library, Nashville.
UOC	University of Chicago, Chicago, Ill.
UOG	University of Georgia, Athens.
UOIll	University of Illinois, Urbana.
UOK	University of Kentucky, Lexington.
UOMi	University of Michigan, Ann Arbor.
UOP	University of Pennsylvania, Philadelphia.
UOPi	University of Pittsburgh, Pittsburgh, Pa.
UOTx	University of Texas, Austin.
UOW	University of Wisconsin, Madison.
UTS	Union Theological Seminary, New York City.
VaHS	Virginia Historical Society, Richmond.
VaSL	Virginia State Library, Richmond.
VaU	University of Virginia, Charlottesville.
VtHS	Vermont Historical Society, Montpelier.
VtSL	Vermont State Library, Montpelier.
VtU	University of Vermont, Burlington.
WC	Williams College, Williamstown, Mass.
WiPL	Wilmington Public Library, Wilmington, Del.
WisHS	State Historical Society of Wisconsin, Madison.
WL	Watkinson Library, Trinity College, Hartford, Conn.
WLC	William L. Clements Library, Ann Arbor, Mich.
WorHS	Worcester Historical Society, Worcester, Mass.
WPL	Woburn Public Library, Woburn, Mass.
WRHS	Western Reserve Historical Society, Cleveland, Ohio.
WU	Wesleyan University, Middletown, Conn.
YC	Yale University, New Haven, Conn.
YHS	York Historical Society, York, Pa.
YLS	School of Law, Yale University, New Haven, Conn.

35855 [NANCREDE, Paul Joseph Guerard de]   1760–1841
    Boston, February 5, 1799. Proposals for publishing, by subscription, the History of the
    destruction of the Helvetic Union and Liberty. By J. Mallet du Pan. . . .
      [*Boston: Printed by Manning & Loring, 1799.*] Broadside.   RIHS.

35856 THE NASHVILLE Intelligencer.   1799
      Nashville: — Printed by John M'Laughlin. fol. weekly. For 1799: [UOC].

35857 NATIONAL magazine; or a political, historical, biographical, and literary repository, for
    June 1, 1799. . . . Number 1 [to Number 4]. — Volume 1. . . . By James Lyon. . . .
      Richmond, Virginia; Printed by and for the editor. 1799. pp. 397. 8vo.
    The third number was "printed for the editor, by H. Pace." Each number had printed
    wrappers and several pages of front and back matter which are not included in the volume
    pagination.   AAS, HC, JCB, LOC, MHS, NYHS, NYPL, NYSL, V*SL, YC.

35858 DER NEUE, gemeinnützige landwirthschafts Calender, auf das Jahr, nach der heilbringen-
    den geburt unsers Herrn Jesu Christi, 1800. . . .
      Lancäster, Gedruckt and zu haben bey Johann Albrecht und Comp. . . . pp. [44].
    sq. 8vo.
    The cover is a woodcut of a farming scene with the heading, "Neuer Lancästerche Calender,
    1800."   AAS, HSP, L*HS, LOC.

35859 DER NEUE Hoch-Deutsche Americanische Calender auf das Jahr Christi 1800. . . . Zum
    zehntenmal herausgegeben.
      Baltimore: Gedruckt un zu haben bey Samuel Saur. pp. [40]. 8vo.   HSP.

35860 DER NEUE Nord-Americanische Stadt und Land Calender, auf das Jahr Christi 1800. . . .
    Zum viertenmal herausgegeben.
      Hägerstaun [Maryland]: Gedruckt und zu haben den Johann Gruber. pp. [40],
    tables. 4to.   LOC, NYPL.

35861 DAS NEUE und verbesserte Gesangbuch. . . .
    See 36193.

35862 NEUE Unpartheyische Readinger Zeitung und Anzeigs-Nachrichten.   1789–1802
      Reading: Gedruckt bey Gottlob Jungmann und Comp. fol. weekly.
                 For 1799: [AAS], Berks Co. Hist. Soc., LOC.

35863 NEUER Hausswirthschafts Calender, auf das gnadenriche Jahr . . . 1800. . . . Zum drit-
    tenmal herausgegeben.
      Reading, Gedruckt und zu haben bey Gottlob Jungmann. . . . pp. [44]. sq. 8vo.
    The front cover is a cut of the "Südwestlicher Prospect von Reading."
                            AAS, HSP, LOC, PSL.

35864 NEUER Hauswirthschafts Calender, auf das Jahr, nach der heilbringenden geburt unsers
    Herrn und Heylandes Jesu Christi, 1800. . . .
      Philadelphia: Gedruckt und zu haben bey Henrich Schweitzer. . . . pp. [40].
    sq. 8vo.
    The imprint is taken from the cover which shows a large woodcut of a rural scene signed
    "F. Reiche."   AAS, HSP.

35865 [NEUER UNPARTHEYISCHER EASTONER BOTHE, UND NORTHAMPTONER KUNDSCHAFTER.   1793–1805
    Jacob Weygandt und Sohn . . . Easton.   fol.   weekly.]
            FOR 1799: NO COPY KNOWN.

35866 NEW BEDFORD. MASSACHUSETTS. SOCIAL SCHOOL.
    [REGULATION FOR THE GOVERNMENT OF SOCIAL SCHOOL, NEAR THE HEAD OF THE RIVER, IN NEW
    BEDFORD. . . . NOVEMBER 28TH, 1798.
        Printed by J. Spooner, New Bedford, January, 1799.   pp. 14.   16mo.]
            SABIN 52498.

35867 A NEW COLLECTION OF COUNTRY DANCES, FOR THE USE OF DANCING ASSEMBLIES: IN THE YEAR 1799.
    Printed at Leominster, (Mass.) 1799.   pp. 12.   48mo.   AAS.

35868 A NEW DISPLAY OF THE UNITED STATES.
    New Haven printed & sold wholesale by Amos Doolittle, August 14, 1799.   Broad-
    side.   fol.   MHS.

35869 THE NEW-ENGLAND ALMANACK. . . .
    See West, Benjamin, 1730–1813, and Daboll, Nathan, 1750–1818.

35870 THE NEW-ENGLAND PRIMER ENLARGED: OR, AN EASY AND PLEASANT GUIDE TO THE ART OF READING.
    ADORNED WITH CUTS. TO WHICH ARE ADDED, THE ASSEMBLY OF DIVINES CATECHISM, &c.
        Boston: Printed by E. Draper for James White, at Franklin's Head, Court-Street, 1799.
    pp. [80].   STONE

35871 THE NEW-ENGLAND PRIMER IMPROVED. FOR THE MORE EASY ATTAINING THE TRUE READING OF
    ENGLISH. TO WHICH IS ADDED THE ASSEMBLY OF DIVINES CATECHISM.
        Hartford: Printed by Nath. Patten, M,DCCXCIX.   pp.[62].   32mo.   STONE.

35872 — — — *New-York: Printed for Naphtali Judah, 1799.*   pp. [72].   24mo.   LOC.

35873 — — — *Norwich: Printed and sold by John Sterry. M,DCC,XCIX,*   pp. [72].   24mo.
            CHS.

35874 — — — *Suffield: Printed by Edward Gray, for Nathaniel Patten, Hartford. . . . MDCCXCIX.*
    pp. [48].   24mo.   MHS, NYPL.

35875 THE NEW-ENGLAND PRIMER IMPROVED, FOR THE MORE EASY ATTAINING THE TRUE READING OF
    ENGLISH. TO WHICH IS ADDED, THE ASSEMBLY OF DIVINES & EPISCOPAL CATECHISMS.
    New York: Printed for T. & J. Swords. 1799.   HEARTMAN, NO. 176.

35876 THE NEW-ENGLAND PRIMER; MUCH IMPROVED. CONTAINING, A VARIETY OF EASY LESSONS, FOR
    ATTAINING THE TRUE READING OF ENGLISH.
        Philadelphia: Printed by T. Dobson, at the Stone House, no. 41, S. Second Street. 1799.
    pp. [72].   24mo.   PL.

35877 THE NEW-ENGLAND PRIMER, OR, AN EASY AND PLEASANT GUIDE TO THE ART OF READING.
    ADORN'D WITH CUTTS. TO WHICH IS ADDED, THE ASSEMBLY OF DIVINES' CATECHISM.
        Printed at Albany, for Thomas, Andrews, & Penniman, 1799.   pp. [70].   12mo.
            PPL.

35878 THE NEW GAME OF CARDS. . . .
    Printed at Northampton [Mass., by William Butler]. 1799.   pp. 8.   16mo.   AAS.

35879 NEW HAMPSHIRE. STATE.
    A JOURNAL OF THE PROCEEDINGS OF THE HON. HOUSE OF REPRESENTATIVES OF THE STATE OF NEW-
    HAMPSHIRE . . . AT CONCORD, NOVEMBER, 1798.
        State of New-Hampshire: Portsmouth: Printed by John Melcher . . . 1799.   pp. 93.
    12mo.   AAS, LOC, YC.

35880 —— A Journal of the proceedings of the Hon. House of Representatives . . . at Concord, June, 1799. . . .
    Portsmouth: Printed by John Melcher, printer to the State, 1799.   pp. **78.**   8vo.
        AAS, LOC, NYHS, NYPL, NYSL.

35881 —— A Journal of the proceedings of the Honorable Senate of the State of New-Hampshire . . . at Concord, Nov. 1798.
    State of New-Hampshire: Portsmouth: Printed by John Melcher. . . . 1799.   pp. **72.**
12mo.   AAS, LOC, YC.

35882 —— A Journal of the proceedings of the Honorable Senate of the State of New-Hampshire . . . at Concord, June, 1799.
    State of New-Hampshire. Portsmouth: Printed by John Melcher . . . 1799.   pp. **47.**
12mo.   AAS, NYSL.

35883 —— The Laws of the State of New-Hampshire, passed at a session of the Honorable General Court, begun and holden at Concord, December, 1798. . . .
    Portsmouth — New-Hampshire: Printed by John Melcher . . . 1799.   pp. **[4],**
517–30. 8vo.   AAS, HEH, LOC.

35884 —— The Laws of the State of New-Hampshire, passed at a session of the Honorable General Court, begun and holden at Concord, June, 1799. . . .
    Portsmouth — New-Hampshire: Printed by John Melcher . . . 1799.   pp. **[4],**
531–41. 8vo.   AAS.

35885 —— State of New Hampshire. In the House of Representatives, December 26th, 1798. Resolved that the senators and representatives of this State, be . . . requested to use their best endeavors [to obtain amendments to the Constitution]. . . .
    [Portsmouth: Printed by John Melcher. 1799.]   pp. **[2]**   fol.   RISL.

35886 —— State of New-Hampshire. In the House of Representatives, Dec. 10, 1799. Whereas the Constitution of this State. . . .
    [Portsmouth, printed by John Melcher, 1799.]   Broadside.   fol.   AAS, LOC.

35887 —— State of Newhampshire. In the year of our Lord one thousand seven hundred and ninety nine. An Act to authorize Samuel Blodget, Esquire, to set up a lottery for the purpose of locking Amoskeag Falls.
    [Portsmouth?]   Broadside.   BPL.

35888 —— State of Newhampshire. In the year of our Lord, one thousand seven hundred and ninety nine. An Act to incorporate . . . the Third Turnpike Road in Newhampshire. . . . Approved, December 27, J. T. Gilman, governor. . . .
    [Portsmouth?]   Broadside.   fol.   UOM[1].

35889 New-Hampshire Association. Minutes . . . at . . . Wells. . . . June 12th and 13th. 1799.
    Portsmouth, N. H. Printed by Charles Peirce. 1799.   pp. **8.**   12mo.   AAS.

35890 THE NEW HAMPSHIRE Gazette.   **1756 ——**
    Portsmouth: (New-Hampshire) published . . . by John Melcher.   weekly   fol.
        For 1799: AAS, BA, DC, NHHS.

35891 NEW HAMPSHIRE Medical Society.
    Laws of the Eastern District of the Newhampshire Medical Society. (Published by direction of the Society.) . . . .
    From the Press of H. Ranlet, Water-Street, Exeter. 1799.   pp. **8.**   12mo.
        AAS, LOC, NHHS, NYHS.

35892 NEWHAMPSHIRE Sentinel.   Mar. 23, 1799 ——
    Keene: Printed by John Prentiss.   weekly.   fol.   For 1799: AAS.

35893 NEW JERSEY. STATE.
AN ACT FOR THE REGULATION OF THE MILITIA OF NEW-JERSEY, TOGETHER WITH THE ACT OF CONGRESS . . . ESTABLISHING AN UNIFORM MILITIA. . . .
Trenton: Printed by Sherman, Mershon & Thomas. 1799. pp. 48. 12mo.
JCB, LOC, NYPL.

35894 —— ACTS OF THE TWENTY-THIRD GENERAL ASSEMBLY. . . . A SESSION BEGUN AT TRENTON ON THE TWENTY-THIRD DAY OF OCTOBER, ONE THOUSAND SEVEN HUNDRED AND NINETY-EIGHT. . . . BEING THE SECOND SITTING.
Trenton: Printed by Gershom Craft . . . 1799. pp. [2], 425–510. fol.
HEH, LOC, NJHS, NJSL, NYPL.

35895 —— ACTS OF THE TWENTY-THIRD GENERAL ASSEMBLY. . . . A SESSION BEGUN AT TRENTON, ON THE TWENTY-THIRD DAY OF OCTOBER, ONE THOUSAND SEVEN HUNDRED AND NINETY-EIGHT. . . . BEING THE THIRD SITTING.
Trenton: Printed by Gershom Craft . . . 1799. pp. [2], 513–637.
HEH, LOC, NJHS, NJSL, NYPL.

35896 —— ACTS OF THE TWENTY-FOURTH GENERAL ASSEMBLY. . . . A SESSION BEGUN AT TRENTON, ON THE TWENTY-SECOND DAY OF OCTOBER, ONE THOUSAND SEVEN HUNDRED AND NINETY-NINE. . . .
Trenton: Printed by Sherman, Mershon & Thomas . . . 1799. pp. [2], 641–663. fol.
LOC, NJSL, NYPL.

35897 —— THE EVIDENCE. . . .
See Tatem, William.

35898 —— JOURNAL OF THE PROCEEDINGS OF THE LEGISLATIVE-COUNCIL . . . CONVENED . . . AT TRENTON, ON TUESDAY THE TWENTY-THIRD DAY OF OCTOBER, SEVENTEEN HUNDRED NINETY-EIGHT. BEING THE FIRST AND SECOND SITTINGS OF THE TWENTY-THIRD SESSION.
Trenton: Printed by Matthias Day . . . 1799. pp. 56. fol. NJSL, NYPL.

35899 —— JOURNAL OF THE PROCEEDINGS OF THE LEGISLATIVE-COUNCIL . . . CONVENED . . . AT TRENTON, ON TUESDAY THE TWENTY-THIRD DAY OF OCTOBER, SEVENTEEN HUNDRED NINETY-EIGHT, BEING THE THIRD SITTING OF THE TWENTY-THIRD SESSION.
Trenton: Printed by Sherman, Mershon & Thomas, for M. Day. 1799. pp. 42. fol.
NJHS, NJSL, NYPL.

35900 —— JOURNAL OF THE PROCEEDINGS OF THE LEGISLATIVE-COUNCIL. . . . CONVENED . . . AT TRENTON, ON TUESDAY THE TWENTY-SECOND DAY OF OCTOBER, SEVENTEEN HUNDRED NINETY-NINE. BEING THE FIRST SITTING OF THE TWENTY-FOURTH SESSION.
Trenton: Printed by Sherman, Mershon & Thomas . . . 1799. pp. 47. fol.
NJSL, NYPL.

35901 —— STATE OF NEW-JERSEY. AN ACT, TO REGULATE THE PRACTICE OF THE COURTS OF LAW.
[*Trenton?*] pp. 16.
Caption title.
NYHS.

35902 —— VOTES AND PROCEEDINGS OF THE TWENTY-THIRD GENERAL ASSEMBLY. . . . A SESSION BEGUN AT TRENTON ON THE TWENTY-THIRD DAY OF OCTOBER, SEVENTEEN HUNDRED AND NINETY-EIGHT. . . . BEING THE SECOND SITTING.
Trenton: Printed by Sherman, Mershon & Thomas, for M. Day. 1799. pp. 63. fol.
LOC, NJHS, NJSL, NYPL, PPL.

35903 —— VOTES AND PROCEEDINGS OF THE TWENTY-THIRD GENERAL ASSEMBLY . . . AT A SESSION BEGUN AT TRENTON ON THE TWENTY-THIRD DAY OF OCTOBER, SEVENTEEN HUNDRED AND NINETY-EIGHT. . . . BEING THE THIRD SITTING.
Trenton: Printed by Sherman, Mershon & Thomas, for M. Day. 1799. pp. 44 fol.
NJHS, NJSL, NYPL, PPL.

35904 —— Votes and proceedings of the twenty-fourth General Assembly . . . at a session begun at Trenton, on the twenty-second day of October, one thousand seven hundred and ninety-nine. . . .
   Trenton: Printed by Gershom Craft. . . . pp. 100. fol. NJHS, NJSL, NYPL, PPL.

35905 THE NEW-JERSEY and New-York Almanac.
   See Shoemaker, Abraham.

35906 THE NEW-JERSEY and Pennsylvania Almanac.
   See Shoemaker, Abraham.

35907 NEW-JERSEY Journal.   1786–1900
   Elizabeth-Town: Printed and published by Shepard Kollock. . . . weekly. fol.
                For 1799: [AAS], [NJHS].

35908 NEW-JERSEY State Gazette.   Mar. 5, 1799–1800
   Trenton — printed by Sherman & Mershom. . . . weekly. fol.
   This paper was a continuation of *The State Gazette, & New-Jersey Advertiser*. With the issue of Mar. 26, Isaiah Thomas, a nephew of Isaiah Thomas of Worcester, was admitted to the firm.   For 1799: [AAS], NJSL, [NYHS].

35909 —— The News-boy's address to the patrons of the New-Jersey State Gazette. January 1, 1799.
   [*Trenton — printed by Sherman & Mershom, 1799*] Broadside. fol. NYHS.

35910 NEW PENNSYLVANIA spelling-book; calculated for the use of children; in spelling and reading the English language with accuracy. Compiled by a Pennsylvanian.
   Norristown, printed and sold by David Sower, 1799. pp. 156. HSP, LCP.

35911 THE NEW pleasing instructor; or, young lady's guide. . . . Consisting of essays, relations . . . and poetry. . . . Extracted from the best modern authors. . . .
   Printed at Boston, by I. Thomas and E. T. Andrews, sold by . . . I. Thomas, Worcester; by Thomas, Andrews, & Penniman, Albany; and by Thomas, Andrews, & Butler, Baltimore. April, 1799. pp. 323. 12mo. AAS, HC, MHS, YC.

35912 THE NEW Testament of our Lord and Saviour Jesus Christ, newly translated out of the original Greek. . . .
   Octoraro: Printed by Francis Bailey, and to be sold at his bookstore, no. 116, High-street, Philadelphia. M,DCC,XCIX. pp. 312. 12mo. AAS.

35913 THE NEW Trade Directory for New-York anno 1800 . . . a complete list of all the occupations and trades . . . with the names and residences of those who follow each of them . . . in alphabetical order.
   New-York: Printed for the editor. pp. xii, 192. 16mo. HEH.

35914 THE NEW Trade Directory, for Philadelphia, anno 1800. . . . To which is added an alphabetical list of all the streets, alleys and lanes. . . .
   Philadelphia: Printed for the author by Way & Groff. 1799. pp. [2], xii, 216.
   12mo.   APS, UOP.

35915 [THE NEW-WINDSOR Gazette.   1797–1799
   New-Windsor [N. Y.], printed by Jacob Schultz & Abraham Lott. weekly. fol.]
   In December the printers removed to Newburgh where they established *The Orange Couny Gazette*.   For 1799: no copies known

35916 NEW YORK. State.
   An Act for the assessment and collection of taxes. Enacted . . . the 1st day of April . . . one thousand seven hundred and ninety-nine. . . .
   [*Albany:*] *Printed by Loring Andrews . . . 1799.* pp. 28. 8vo. LOC, NYPL, NYSL.

35917 —— An Act of incorporation of the Manhattan Company.
[*New York:*] *Printed by John Furman. . . . M,DCC,XCIX.* pp. 12. 4to.
HEH, NYHS.

35918 —— [An Act to amend an act entitled An act for regulating elections in the State of New York.
Albany: Printed by Loring Andrews. 1799. pp. 2. fol.] Evans.

35919 —— [An Act to organize the militia of this State. Passed the 9th of March, 1793. To which is added the amendments, passed since that period.
Poughkeepsie: Printed by Power and Southwick. 1799. pp. 22. 12mo.] Evans.

35920 —— An Act to raise a sum of money for the use of this State. . . . Passed the 3d of April, 1799. . . .
[*Albany?*] Broadside. fol. NYSL.

35921 —— Collection of penal laws, and laws concerning the state prison.
New-York Printed by Isaac Collins no. 189 Pearl-Street 1799. pp. 40. 8vo. HPL.

35922 —— Forms & directions for the assessors in the execution of the statute entitled "An Act for the assessment and collection of taxes."
Albany, 20th April, 1799. pp. 3. NYSL.

35923 —— Gentlemen. I now lay before you an authenticated copy of an act of Congress . . . entitled "An act respecting balances reported against certain States. . . ." John Jay. Albany, 25th February, 1799.
[*Albany.*] Broadside. fol. NYSL.

35924 —— Journal of the Assembly of the State of New-York; at their twenty-second session, second meeting, began . . . the second day of January, 1799.
Albany: Printed by Loring Andrews. . . . pp. 293. 4to.
LOC, NYHS, NYPL, NYSL, YC.

35925 —— Journal of the Senate of the State of New-York; at their twenty-second session, second meeting, began . . . the second day of January, 1799.
Albany: Printed by Loring Andrews. . . . pp. 129. 4to. AAS, LOC, NYHS, NYSL.

35926 —— Laws of the State of New-York, passed at the twenty-second meeting of the legislature, begun . . . the second day of January, 1799.
Albany: Printed by Loring Andrews. . . . 1799. pp. [2], [555]–844, [4]. 8vo.
HC, HEH, LOC, NYBA, NYPL, NYSL.

35927 —— Members composing the Senate of the State of New-York; with their respective districts, classes and places of abode. . . . Albany, January, 1799.
[*Albany.*] Broadside. fol. NYHS.

35928 —— Message from Governor Jay, of the 12th January, 1799, accompanying Resolutions from Virginia and Kentucky.
[*Albany: Printed by Loring Andrews.*] pp. 4. 8vo. NYSL.

35929 —— The Militia Act. . . . Enacted . . . the ninth day of March . . . one thousand seven hundred and ninety three. . . . Also, two other acts. . . .
Albany: Printed and sold, by Charles R. & George Webster. 1799. pp. 36. 12mo.
NYPL.

35930 —— Report of the Inspectors of the State-Prison. . . .
Albany: Printed by Loring Andrews. pp. 8, 3 folded leaves. 8vo.
Dated "1st Month 15, 1799" on p. 8. CU, NYHS, NYPL.

35931 —— Rules of the Supreme Court of the State of New-York. To which are added, the circuit courts. . . .
Albany: Printed by Charles R. & George Webster. . . . 1799.   pp. 38.   16mo.
HC.

35932 —— State of New York. In Senate. January 12, 1799. The following message from his excellency the Governor. . . .
[Albany:] Printed by Loring Andrews, printer to the State.   pp. 4.   fol.   NYSL.

35933 NEW YORK. State. Medical Society.
Report of the committee appointed by the Medical Society, of the State of New-York, to enquire into the symptoms, origin, cause, and prevention of the pestilential disease that prevailed in New-York during the summer and autumn of the year 1798.
From the office of the Daily Advertiser, no. 71, Pine Street, New York, 1799.   pp. [4], 47.   AAS, AML, LOC, NYAM, NYHS, NYPL, NYSL.

35934 NEW YORK. State. Republican Party.
New York, 9th April, 1799. Sir, we are appointed a committee by the Republican electors of New York, to inform the electors of the southern district, that Ezekeil Robins, of New York, and Pierre Van Courtlandt, junr. of West-Chester, have been nominated as candidates for the senate. . . .
[New York.]   Broadside.   8vo.   NYPL[ph].

35935 NEW YORK. State. Society for the Promotion of Agriculture, Arts, and Manufactures.
Transactions of the Society, instituted in the State of New-York, for the Promotion of Agriculture, Arts, and Manufactures. Part IV. . . .
Albany: Printed by Loring Andrews. . . . M,DCC,XCIX.   pp. [6], 178, 2 plates.
4to.   AML, BA, BM, HC, JCL, MHS, NYHS, NYPL, NYSL, UOC, UOP, UOW.

35936 NEW YORK. City.
At a Common Council held on Monday the 21st day of January, 1799 — the following report [on Pestilential Diseases] was read. . . . New York, 21st January, 1799.
[New York.]   Broadside.   NYSL.

35937 —— Funeral procession. New-York. Regulations, relative to the procession for rendering funeral honors to the deceased General Washington. . . . New-York, 29th Dec. '99.
[New-York.]   Broadside.   fol.   NYHS.

35938 —— Laws and ordinances, ordained and established by the Mayor, Aldermen, and Commonalty. . . . Published the 29th day of April, 1799. . . .
Printed by John Furman. . . .   pp. 70.   8vo.   NYSOC.

35939 —— —— The second edition, with additions and corrections.
Printed and re-printed, by John Furman. . . .   pp. 47.   8vo.   NYPL, NYSOC, YC.

35940 —— Order of the funeral procession the 31st of December, 1799. By direction of the committee of arrangements. . . . New-York, December 29, 1799.
[New York.]   Broadside.   fol.
Relating to the ceremonies after the death of Washington.   HSP, NYPL.

35941 —— Proceedings of the Corporation of New-York, on supplying the city with pure and wholesome water; with a memoir of Joseph Browne. . . .
[New York:] Printed by John Furman. 1799.   pp. 29.   8vo.
BM, LOC, NYAM, NYHS, NYPL, NYSL.

35942 NEW YORK. City. Committee on Health.
Record of death, or, an accurate list, of the names, places of abode, occupation, etc. of our fellow citizens who have fallen victims to the late fever. . . .
[New York:] Printed for John Hill, and Co. (Copy-right secured).   pp. 14.   8vo.
The deaths listed show that the pamphlet was printed after September, 1799.   NYAM.

35943 NEW YORK. City. Deutschen Gesellschaft.
    Gesetze und verfassung der Deutschen Gesellschaft im Staat von New-York; gestiftet
    am 9ten October, im Jahre 1784.
        New-York: Gedruckt bey T. und J. Swords, no. 99 Pearl-Strasse. 1799.   pp. 20.
    8vo.
    German and English text on opposite pages.   HC, NYHS.

35944 NEW YORK. City. Federalist Party.
    Impositions on the sixth and seventh wards detected. New-York, April 30. I am a
    peaceable man. . . .
        [From Lang's press, New York, 1799.]   Broadside.   fol.   WLC.

35945 NEW YORK. City. Free and Accepted Masons.
    [Order of the procession, on the 31st Dec. 1799, in commemoration of the death of their
    illustrious and much beloved brother, George Washington.
        New-York: Printed by brother J. Oram.   Broadside.   fol.]   Evans.

35946 NEW YORK. City. H. G. Rutgers & Co.
    Catalogue of books, for sale . . . January 12th. . . .
        Rutgers. Sold at 145 Pearl Street, New York.   Broadside.   fol.   NYPL.

35947 —— [A Large consignment of valuable books, per the Fair American, from London. . . . Sold
    at their auction room, New York, Apr. 26, 1799.]   McKay 142f.

35948 —— [A Large catalogue of books, comprising a general assortment, handsomely bound. Feb. 9,
    1799.]   McKay 142b.

35949 NEW YORK. City. Isaac Moses & Sons.
    [An Extensive and valuable collection of French books. . . . Sold at their auction room,
    New York, June 14, 1799.]   McKay 142i.

35950 NEW YORK. City. Manhattan Company.
    Report of Manhattan committee [on the best mode of procuring a supply of water,
    dated 4th mo. 22d. 1799].
        [New York:] Printed by John Furman.   pp. 37.   8vo.   CU, NYPL, NYSL.

35951 NEW YORK. City. St. Paul's Church.
    Sacred music, to be performed in St. Paul's Church, on Tuesday the 31st December, 1799,
    by the Anacreontic and Philharmonic societies, at the funeral ceremonies in honor
    of . . . Washington. . . .
        [New York.]   Broadside.   fol.   AAS, HEH.

35952 NEW YORK. City. Society for the Relief of Poor Widows with Small Children.
    Constitution of the ladies society, established in New-York, for the relief of poor
    widows with small children.
        New-York: Printed by J. Oram, no. 33 Liberty-street, 1799.   pp. 38.   16mo.   AAS.

35953 NEW YORK. City. The Society of the Lying-In Hospital.
    An Act to incorporate the Society of the Lying-In Hospital of the City of New-York.
    Together with the by-laws, rules and regulations for the government of said hospital.
        Brooklyn, Printed by T. Kirk.   pp. 23.   12mo.   AAS, BM, NYHS.

35954 —— Constitution of the New-York Lying-In Hospital.
        [New York:] Printed by John Furman, 102 Pearl-Street. . . . MDCCXCIX.   pp.
    13, 4.   8vo.
    The AAS copy has a four-page list of subscribers laid in.
        AAS, APS, HC, LCP, LOC, NYAM, NYHS, NYPL, NYSL.

35955 NEW YORK. City. William Prince.
       A Catalogue of fruit-trees, flowering-shrubs, and plants, for sale by William Prince, at
       Flushing-Landing . . . New-York, March 10, 1799.
            Printed by Hugh Gaine, at the Bible, no. 148, Pearl-Street.   Broadside.   fol.
                                                                                          MHS.

35956 [NEW YORK] Argus.
       The Carrier of the Argus most respectfully presents the following address to his
       patrons.
            [New York.]   Broadside.
       For the newspaper see 35115.   NYHS.

35957 [NEW YORK] Commercial Advertiser.
       [Carrier's address.]
            Reprinted in *The Spectator*, N. Y., Jan. 9, 1799. For the newspaper see 35332.

35958 [NEW YORK] Daily Advertiser.
       Address of the carrier of the Daily Advertiser: to his kind customers and patrons . . .
       January 1, 1799.
            [New York.]   Broadside.
       For the newspaper see 35373.   NYHS.

35959 THE NEW YORK Gazette and General Advertiser.   1795–1840
            Published (daily) by M'Lean & Lang. . . .   fol.   daily.
       With the issue of Mar. 21 John Lang became sole proprietor.   For 1799: [AAS], NYHS.

35960 NEW-YORK Price-Current.
            See Oram's New-York Price-Current.

35961 [NEWARK] Centinel of Freedom.
       Address presented by the carrier to the patrons of the Centinel of Freedom. With the
       compliments of the season. January 1, 1799.
            [Newark.]   Broadside.
       For the newspaper see 33504.   NYHS.

35962 NEWARK Gazette and New-Jersey Advertiser.   1797–1804
            Newark — printed by John H. Williams for the proprietors.   weekly.   fol.
       With the issue of May 7 the paper was published by Jacob Halsey who on May 21
       shortened the title to *The Newark Gazette*.   For 1799: [AAS], NJHS, RU.

35963 THE NEWBERN Gazette.   1798–1804
            Newbern, (North-Carolina:) printed for John C. Osborn & Co.   fol.   weekly.
                                                                             For 1799: [LOC].

35964 THE NEWBURYPORT Herald and Country Gazette.   1797–1902
            Published on Tuesdays and Fridays, by Angier March, at his office, Middle-Street.
       fol.   semi-weekly.   For 1799: AAS, EI, YC.

35965 —— The New Year. From the carrier of the Newburyport Herald, &c. to his generous
       customers. . . .
            [Newburyport.]   Broadside.   4to.   EI.

35966 NEWCOMB, Richard English.   1770–1849
       An Oration, spoken at Greenfield, on the anniversary of American independence. . . .
            Printed at Greenfield, Massachusetts, by Thomas Dickman, 1799.   pp. 15.   8vo.
                                                                             JCB, NYHS.

35967 NEWPORT. Rhode Island. Engine Company, Number V.
       Newport Engine Company, Number V. Whereas in the interest and good understanding
       of all societies. . . .
            Newport: Printed by H. & O. Farnsworth. 1799.   Broadside.   fol.   NHS.

35968 NEWPORT. Rhode Island. Marine Society.
Laws of the Marine Society. . . . Instituted at Newport, Dec. 5, A.D. 1752, under the title of the Fellowship-Club. . . .
Newport: [Printed by] Henry Barber, M,DCC,XCIX. pp. 16. 8vo. NHS.

35969 THE NEWPORT Almanac, for the year of our Lord, 1800. . . . Calculated for the meridian of Newport. . . .
Published at Newport, by Oliver Farnsworth. . . . pp. [24]. 12mo.
AAS, JCB, LOC, NHS, NYHS, RIHS.

35970 NEWPORT Insurance Company.
See Rhode Island.

35971 THE NEWPORT Mercury. 1758 ———
Newport (Rhode Island) published by Henry Barber. . . . fol. weekly.
For 1799: [AAS], [LOC], RIHS, RL.

35972 NICHOLAS, George 1754–1799
Correspondence between George Nicholas, Esq. of Kentucky, and the Hon. Robert G. Harper, member of Congress. . . .
Lexington: Printed by John Bradford, Main Street. 1799. pp. 26, viii. 8vo.
LOC, NL, UOC, UOK.

35973 —— A Letter from George Nicholas, of Kentucky, to his friend in Virginia. Justifying the conduct of the citizens of Kentucky. . . .
Lexington: Printed — Philadelphia: Reprinted, by James Carey, no. 16, Chestnut-street. 1799. pp. 39. 8vo.
AAS, APS, BM, BPL, HC, HEH, JCB, LCP, LOC, MHS, NYHS, NYPL, NYSL, UOC, VᵃU, YC.

35974 —— To the freemen of Kentucky. Considering myself as accountable to my fellow citizens for my political conduct. . . . Lexington, March 30th, 1799.
[Lexington: Printed by John Bradford.] Broadside. fol. LOC.

35975 NISBET, Richard
Numbers of poetry — serious and comic. . . . No. 1. The simple, soft Leylock. Once more I tune the vocal shell — Garrick.
[n. p.] pp. 4. 8vo. NYHS.

35976 —— —— No. II. The fruits of sermon-hunting: or, the expounder refuted. . . .
Printed for the author. pp. 16. 8vo. NYHS.

35977 NORCOM, James 1778–1850
An Inaugural thesis on jaundice. . . . Submitted to the . . . Medical Faculty of the University of Pennsylvania; on the 6th day of June, 1799, for the degree of doctor of medicine. . . .
Philadelphia: Printed by James Carey, for Mathew Carey, 118, Market-street. pp. 49, [1]. 8vo.
The final page contains errata. AAS, AML, HEH, HSP, LCP, MHS, NYAM, UOP.

35978 NORCOTT, John — 1676
Baptism discovered, plainly and faithfully according to the word of God. . . . A new edition.
Mount-Holly: Printed by Stephen C. Ustick, 1799. pp. [2], 52. 8vo. PPL.

35979 —— —— *Mount-Holley: Printed for Rev. Alexander M'Gowan, by S. C. Ustick.* pp. [2], 52. 8vo. ABHS.

35980 THE NORFOLK Herald. 1794–1861
Norfolk [Va.]: Published . . . by Willett & O'Connor. fol. tri-weekly.
For 1799: [LOC], VᵃU.

35981   [NORMAN, WILLIAM, EDITOR]
THE MUSICAL REPERTORY: BEING, A COLLECTION OF THE MOST MODERN & FAVORITE SONGS, AIRS, MARCHES, &C. . . . VOL. 1.
Boston, printed and sold by Wm. Norman no. 75 Newbury Street.   pp. 96.   4to.
Except for the index, this work consists of engraved plates. There may have been an issue with the title "The Musical Repository, containing a variety. . . ."   AAS.

35982   NORRISTOWN. PENNSYLVANIA. LIBRARY COMPANY.
THE ACT OF INCORPORATION, BYE-LAWS, AND CATALOGUE OF BOOKS, OF THE NORRISTOWN LIBRARY COMPANY.
Philadelphia: Printed by John Ormrod, no. 41, Chestnut-Street. 1799.   pp. 22.
8vo.   HSP.

35983   THE NORRISTOWN GAZETTE.   JUNE 15, 1799–1800
Norristown [Pa.]: Printed by David Sower.   4to.   weekly.
FOR 1799: [AAS], BERKS CO. HIST. SOC., [HSP].

35984   NORTH CAROLINA. STATE.
LAWS OF NORTH-CAROLINA. AT A GENERAL ASSEMBLY, BEGUN AND HELD AT THE CITY OF RALEIGH, ON MONDAY THE NINETEENTH DAY OF NOVEMBER IN THE YEAR OF OUR LORD ONE THOUSAND AND SEVEN HUNDRED AND NINETY-EIGHT. . . .
[Wilmington, printed by A. Hall, Printer to the State.]   pp. 27.   fol.
This edition is the supplement to James Iredell's revision, Evans 23641. The session-laws edition is Evans 34247.   HC-L, NCU.

35985   —— [THE MILITIA LAWS, NOW IN FORCE IN THE STATE OF NORTH CAROLINA. EXTRACTED FROM THE SEVERAL ACTS OF THE GENERAL ASSEMBLY. . . .
Salisbury: Francis Coupee, 1799.]   McMURTRIE 270.

35986   NORTH CAROLINA. FREE AND ACCEPTED MASONS.
AN ABSTRACT OF THE PROCEEDINGS OF THE GRAND LODGE OF NORTH-CAROLINA, IN THE YEAR A. L. 5799. A. D. 1799.
[Raleigh — Printed by Brothers Hodge & Boylan.]   pp. 28.   12mo.
Caption title; the imprint is from p. 28.   NYFM, PFM.

35987   NORTH CAROLINA. NEUSE BAPTIST ASSOCIATION.
MINUTES OF THE NORTH-CAROLINA NEUSE BAPTIST ASSOCIATION, HOLDEN AT POPLAR SPRING MEETING-HOUSE, FRANKLIN COUNTY. FRIDAY, OCTOBER 18, 1799.
[Colophon:] Raleigh: Joseph Gales, 1799.   pp. 8.   12mo.   ABHS.

35988   THE NORTH-CAROLINA JOURNAL.   1792–1814
Halifax [N. C.]: printed by Abraham Hodge.   fol.   weekly.
FOR 1799: JOHN G. WOOD OF EDENTON, [LOC].

35989   THE NORTH-CAROLINA MERCURY, AND SALISBURY ADVERTISER.   1798–1801
Salisbury: Published by Francis Coupee.   fol.   weekly.   FOR 1799: [DUKE].

35990   THE NORTH-CAROLINA MINERVA, AND FAYETTEVILLE ADVERTISER.   1796–1799.
Fayetteville: — published every Tuesday by Hodge & Boylan.   fol.
In May the press and paper were removed to Raleigh.   FOR 1799: [HC].

35991   THE NORTH-CAROLINA MINERVA, AND RALEIGH ADVERTISER.   1799–1803
Raleigh: Published by Hodge and Boylan.   fol.   weekly.   FOR 1799: [NCU].

35992   NORTHERN BUDGET.   1798–1927
Troy: — published every Tuesday . . . by Robert Moffitt & Co. . . .   fol.
weekly.   FOR 1799: AAS.

35993   NORTHERN CENTINEL.   1798–1804
Salem, Washington County, State of New-York: Published every Tuesday by Henry Dodd. . . .   fol.   weekly.   FOR 1799: [AAS].

35994 NORTHWEST TERRITORY.
    JOURNAL OF THE LEGISLATIVE COUNCIL. . . . BEGUN AND HELD AT CINCINNATI, ON MONDAY, THE SIXTEENTH DAY OF SEPTEMBER, A. D. ONE THOUSAND, SEVEN HUNDRED AND NINETY NINE.
        Cincinnati — from the press of Carpenter & Findlay.   pp. 103.   8vo.   OH&PS, OSL.

35995 THE NORWICH PACKET.   1773–1802
        Norwich (Connecticut). Published by John Trumbull a few rods west of the meeting-house. 1799.   fol.   weekly.   FOR 1799: [AAS], [HC].

35996 —— THE NEWSBOYS ANNUAL ADDRESS TO THE ESTEEMED PATRONS OF THE NORWICH-PACKET FOR THE NEW YEAR.
        [*Norwich: Printed by John Trumbull, Jan. 1, 1799.*]   Broadside.   fol.
        RITTER HOPSON GALLERIES, SALE NO. 14, Nov. 24, 1931, ITEM 165.

35997 NOTES ON THE FINANCES OF THE STATE OF SOUTH-CAROLINA. BY A MEMBER OF THE HOUSE OF REPRESENTATIVES.
        Charleston: Printed by W. P. Young. . . .   pp. xii, 32, 3 tables, errata.   8vo.
    The author was probably Henry William Desaussure, 1763–1839.   AAS, HSP, LOC, NYHS.

35998 NOURSE, G.
    THE HISTORY OF THE INDEPENDENTS OR, CONGREGATIONALISTS, A VERY NUMEROUS SECT OF CHRISTIANS IN THE EASTERN STATES. . . .
        Frankfort: Printed by Hunter and Beaumont. . . . *1799.*   pp. 12.   12mo.   UOC.

35999 NUGENT, HENRY PAUL
    MR. NUGENT'S VINDICATION OF HIS WRITINGS IN A LETTER TO MR. LILLY. WITH . . . REMARKS ON A VERDICT LATELY FOUND IN THE MAYOR'S COURT IN THE CITY OF ALBANY.
        [*Albany:*] *Printed for the author. 1799.*   pp. v, 40.   12mo.   AAS, NYHS.

36000 OBSERVATIONS, ON A LETTER FROM GEORGE NICHOLAS, OF KENTUCKY. . . . IN WHICH . . . THE LATE MEASURES OF THE GOVERNMENT, WHICH HAVE BEEN COMPLAINED OF IN KENTUCKY, ARE JUSTIFIED, BY AN INHABITANT OF THE NORTH-WESTERN TERRITORY.
        Cincinnati: Printed and sold by Edmund Freeman, Front Street. Feb. 14, M,DCC,XCIX.   pp. 46, [2].   8vo.   BA, BPL, OH&PS.

36001 OBSERVATIONS ON THE ALIEN & SEDITION LAWS OF THE UNITED STATES.
        Washington: (Penn.) Printed by John Colerick. 1799.   pp. 43.   8vo.   AAS.

36002 [THE OBSERVER.   MARCH TO AUGUST, 1799
        Knoxville, Tennessee: Printed by George Wilson, 1799.]
    No copy known. When the paper was combined with the *Knoxville Gazette* in August its title was given as *The Impartial Observer.*

36003 THE OBSERVER.   1798–1799
        Salem, New Jersey, published by William Black and Marcus (?) North.   weekly.   fol.   FOR 1799: [CAMDEN CO. HIST. SOC.]

36004 ODE ON ENDS; OR THE BOY'S ADDRESS, WHO CARRIES THE AMERICAN MERCURY. HARTFORD, JANUARY 1, 1799. . . .
        [*Hartford.*]   Broadside.   fol.   NYHS.

36005 [OGDEN, JOHN COSENS]   1751–1800
    FRIENDLY REMARKS TO THE PEOPLE OF CONNECTICUT, UPON THEIR COLLEGE AND SCHOOLS.
        [*Litchfield: Printed by Thomas Collier?*] *1799.*   pp. 42.   8vo.   AAS, BA, YC.

36006 —— A SHORT HISTORY OF THE LATE ECCLESIASTICAL OPPRESSIONS IN NEW-ENGLAND AND VERMONT. . . .
        Richmond: Printed by James Lyon, at the office of the National Magazine, 1799.
    pp. 19.   8vo.   AAS, BA, BM, HC, JCB, LOC, NYHS, NYPL, UOC, Vᵃ U, Vᵗ U.

36007 [——] A Tour, through Upper and Lower Canada. By a citizen of the United States. Containing, a view of the . . . settlements.
   Printed at Litchfield, (according to Act of Congress) [by Thomas Collier] 1799.
 pp. 119. 24mo.   AAS, BA, BPL, HC, HSP, JCB, LCP, LOC, NYHS, NYPL, WL, YC.

36008 [——] A View of the Calvinistic clubs in the United States.
   [Litchfield, printed by Thomas Collier, 1799?] pp. 23. 16mo.
                 AAS, BA, NYHS, NYPL, YC.

36009 [——] A View of the New-England illuminati: who are indefatigably engaged in destroying the religion and government of the United States. . . .
   Philadelphia: Printed by James Carey, no. 16, Chestnut-Street. 1799. pp. 20. 8vo.
 APS, BA, BM, CL, HC, HSP, JCB, LCP, LOC, MHS, MSL, NL, NYHS, NYPL, NYSL, PPL, PSL, WⁱˢHS, YC.

36010 [——] —— The second edition.
   Philadelphia: Printed by James Carey, no 16, Chestnut-Street. 1799. pp. 20. 8vo.
      AAS, CU, HC, HEH, HSP, JCB, LCP, LOC, MHS, NL, NYHS, YC.

36011 THE ONLY sure guide to the English tongue. . . .
 See Perry, William.

36012 THE ONTARIO Gazette.   1799–1803
   [Geneva and Canandaigua, published by Lucius Cary.] weekly fol.
 A continuation of the *Ontario Gazette* begun by Cary at Geneva in 1796 and removed to Canandaigua some time in 1799. Late in that year or early in 1800 the title was changed to *The Ontario Gazette, & Genesee Advertiser.*
             For 1799: [Univ. of Ill.], [Troy Pub. Lib.].

36013 ORACLE of Dauphin.   1792–1827
   Harrisburgh: Published by John Wyeth, 1799. fol. weekly.
             For 1799: HSP, NYHS.

36014 THE ORACLE of the Day.   1793–1799
   Printed and published every Saturday morning, by Charles Peirce . . . Portsmouth, New Hampshire. weekly. fol.
 Succeeded by *The United States Oracle of the Day.*   For 1799: AAS, BA, DC, NHHS.

36015 ORAM'S New-York Price-Current, and Marine Register.   1797–1817
   New-York: Published weekly by James Oram. 4to. weekly.
 With the issue of May 25, 1799, the name was changed to *New-York Price Current.*
                For 1799: NYHS.

36016 THE ORANGE County Gazette.   1799
   Newburgh [New York], printed and published, (every Tuesday morning) by J. Schultz, and J. E. Barber. fol. weekly.   For 1799: [NYPL].

36017 ORDER of procession for the funeral of the late Governor Sumner. . . .
   [Boston.] Broadside.   BPL, HC, MHS.

36018 ORIENTAL Trumpet. Or, the Town and Country Gazette.   1796–1800
   Portland (District of Maine) published by Rand and Burdick. fol. weekly.
             For 1799: [AAS], [HC].

36019 OSGOOD, David   1747–1822
 A Conclusive argument for the truth of the Gospel . . . a discourse . . . at the ordination of . . . Leonard Woods . . . in Newbury December 5, 1798. . . .
   Printed by Angier March, Newburyport, 1799. pp. 32. 8vo.
 Contains Woods' Address, the Right Hand of Fellowship by Joseph Russell of Princeton, and the Charge by Nathaniel Noyes of South Hampton.
       AAS, BA, BM, HC, JCB, LOC, NYHS, NYPL, NYSL, YC.

36020 —— The Devil let loose . . . a discourse delivered on the day of the national Fast, April 25. 1799.
        Boston: Printed for and sold by Samuel Hall . . . 1799.   pp. 16.   8vo.
        AAS, AHTS, BA, BM, BPL, CHS, EI, HC, HEH, HSP, JCB, LOC, MHS, NYHS, NYPL, WLC.

36021 OSGOOD, Nathan
    An Oration, delivered in Rutland, in the State of Vermont, on the anniversary of American independence, July, 4th, 1799. . . .
        Rutland: Printed by S. Williams. 1799.   pp. 16.   8vo.   NYHS, VᵗU.

36022 OTSEGO Herald: or, western advertiser.   1795–1821
        Cooperstown: Printed and published . . . by Elihu Phinney.   weekly.   fol.
        For 1799: Otsego Co. Hist. Soc., Cooperstown.

36023 PACKARD, Hezekiah   1761–1849
    Federal Republicanism . . . two discourses preached on the day of the State Fast at Chelmsford, and on the day of the national Fast at Concord, in April, 1799. . . .
        Boston, printed by John Russell, 1799.   pp. 35, [1].   8vo.
    The last page is an advertisement of books by the same author.
        AAS, AHTS, BA, BM, CL, EI, HC, HEH, JCB, MHS, NHSL, NYHS, NYPL, NYSL, PL, RU, YC.

36024 —— A Sermon preached on the death of Miss Sibyl Richardson. . . .
        Amherst, New-Hampshire: from the press of Samuel Preston, 1799.   pp. 28.   8vo.
        AAS, BM, EI, NYHS.

36025 THE PACKET.   Mar. 9–Aug. 29, 1799
        Catskill, (State of New-York): Printed by Mackay Croswell. 1799.   fol.   weekly.
        For 1799: Greene County Hist. Soc., Coxsackie, N. Y.

36026 PAGE, John   1744–1808
    An Address to the citizens of the District of York, in Virginia. By their Representative, John Page, of Rosewell.
        [Philadelphia.]   pp. 40.   8vo.   AAS, YC.

36027 —— Address to the freeholders of Gloucester County, at their election of a member of Congress . . . and of their delegates . . . in the General Assembly of . . . Virginia, April 24, 1799. . . .
        Richmond: Printed by John Dixon — 1799.   pp. [2], 44, [1].   8vo.
    The last leaf contains errata.   AAS, HC.

36028 PAINE, Clement   1769–1849
    An Oration on Masonry. Delivered at the request of the lodge at Athens, Luserne County, Pennsylvania, on the twenty-seventh of December, one thousand seven hundred and ninety-eight. . . .
        Charleston, South-Carolina: Printed by Freneau & Paine, no. 47, Bay. 1799.   pp. 14.
    12mo.   PFM.

36029 PAINE, Robert Treat
    See Paine, Thomas.

36030 PAINE, Thomas   1773–1811
    An Oration, written at the request of the young men of Boston, and delivered, July 17th, 1799, in commemoration of the dissolution of the treaties . . . between France and the United States. . . .
        Boston, printed by John Russell, 1799.   pp. 30.   8vo.
    Issued with and without errata on p. 30.
        AAS, BA, BM, BPL, CSL, HC, HEH, JCB, LOC, MHS, NYHS, NYPL, PL, RU, WLC.

36031 —— —— —— *Suffield [Conn.], printed by Edward Gray, 1799.*   pp. 16.   8vo.   AAS, HC, JCB, YC.

36032 —— SECOND EDITION.
Boston, printed by John Russell, 1799. pp. 30. 8vo.
AAS, BM, HC, LOC, NYHS, NYPL, NYSL, RIHS, UTS.

36033 —— To ARMS COLUMBIA. . . . WRITTEN FOR THE ANNIVERSARY OF THE MASSACHUSETTS CHARITABLE FIRE SOCIETY. . . . THE MUSIC COMPOSED BY P. A. VON HAGEN, JUN.
Boston, printed and sold at P. A. von Hagen & cos. Musical magazine, no. 3 Cornhill. Also by G. Gilfert New-York. pp. [2]. 4to. AAS, JCB.

36034 THE PALLADIUM: A LITERARY AND POLITICAL WEEKLY REPOSITORY. 1798–1816
Frankfort: Printed and published (weekly) by Hunter & Beaumont, Printers to the Commonwealth. fol. FOR 1799: UOC, W¹ˢHS.

36035 PANTHER, ABRAHAM, pseud.
A SURPRISING NARRATIVE OF A YOUNG WOMAN, DISCOVERED IN A CAVE IN THE WILDERNESS, AFTER HAVING BEEN TAKEN BY THE SAVAGE INDIANS. . . .
Leominster: Printed for Chapman Whitcomb, by Charles Prentiss. pp. 12. 12mo.
AAS, NYPL, YC.

36036 —— A SURPRISING NARRATIVE OF A YOUNG WOMAN, WHO WAS DISCOVERED IN THE GLOOMY MANSION OF A ROCKY CAVE. . . .
Fryeburgh, [Me., by Elijah Russell.] 1799. pp. 8. 16mo. AAS.

36037 PARISH, ELIJAH 1762–1825
AN ORATION DELIVERED AT BYFIELD JULY 4, 1799. By REV. ELIJAH PARISH, A. M.
Newburyport: Printed by Angier March. pp. 18. 8vo.
AAS, BA, HC, HEH, JCB, LOC, MHS, NL, NYHS.

36038 —— —— SECOND EDITION.
Printed by Angier March, Newburyport. pp. 14. 8vo.
AAS, BM, HC, NYHS, NYPL, NYSL.

36039 —— A SERMON OCCASIONED BY THE DEATH OF THE REV. JOHN CLEAVELAND . . . PREACHED TO THE BEREAVED PEOPLE, JUNE, 2, 1799. . . .
Newburyport: Printed by Angier March. pp. 28. 8vo.
AAS, BM, HC, HEH, JCB, LOC, NYPL, YC.

36040 PARK, JAMES ALAN 1763–1838
A SYSTEM OF THE LAW OF MARINE INSURANCES. WITH . . . CHAPTERS . . . ON INSURANCES ON LIVES; AND . . . AGAINST FIRE. . . . SECOND AMERICAN, FROM THE LATEST ENGLISH, EDITION.
Printed at Boston, for Thomas and Andrews . . . David West . . . and John West. . . . Aug. 1799. pp. xxvii, liv, 516 [i.e. 570]. 8vo. AAS, BPL, HC, LOC, NYPL, NYSL, YC.

36041 PARKINSON, RICHARD 1748–1815
THE EXPERIENCED FARMER, AN ENTIRE NEW WORK, IN WHICH THE WHOLE SYSTEM OF AGRICULTURE . . . IS EXPLAINED. . . . IN TWO VOLUMES. . . .
Philadelphia: Printed by Charles Cist, North Second-Street. 1799. pp. xx, 275; [2], 292. 8vo.
The text was printed in England, the titlepages, only, in the United States. The work is dedicated to Washington. AAS, BPL, HC, LCP, NYPL.

36042 PARTY SPIRIT EXPOSED.
See Fraser, Donald (in preceding volume).

36043 A PASTORAL LETTER, FROM A MINISTER IN THE COUNTRY, TO THOSE OF HIS FLOCK WHO REMAINED IN THE CITY OF PHILADELPHIA DURING THE PESTILENCE OF 1798.
Philadelphia: Printed by John Ormrod, no. 41, Chestnut-Street. 1799. pp. 12. 8vo. HSP, JCB, LOC, NYPL.

36044 PATRIOTIC Gazette.   Apr. 12, 1799–1800
         Northampton, Mass. Published by Andrew Wright.   fol.   weekly.
         For 1700: [aas], nypl.

36045 PATTERSON, Mrs.
         The Unfortunate lovers, and cruel parents. A very interesting tale, founded on fact. Written by Mrs. Patterson. Eighteenth edition.
         New-Haven: Printed by Read & Morse, 1799.   pp. 23.   12mo.   nypl, yc.

36046 PAWLET. Vermont. Pawlet Library.
         Constitution, and catalogue, of Pawlet Library.
         Bennington: Printed by Anthony Haswell. MDCCXCIX.   pp. [10].   24mo.
         aas, Vᵗsl.

36047 PAYNE, John
         New and complete system of universal geography. . . . To which is added, a view of astronomy. . . . In four volumes. Vol. IV.
         New-York: Printed for, and sold by John Low, book-seller, at the Shakespears Head, no. 332 Water-Street. 1799.   pp. 525, [1], 36, [4], 17, [11].   8vo.
         The supplements to this volume, which deals entirely with America, include a reprint of Charles Williamson's "Description of the Genesee Country" and a list of subscribers. The first volume was printed in 1798 and the second and third in 1800. There is an additional undated 8vo. atlas with the imprint of Low and Willis. The maps were engraved by A. Anderson and by Doolittle.   aas, ba, Dᵉrgl, loc, nl, nyhs, nypl.

36048 PAYNE, [William]
         Mr. Payne's game of draughts, containing twenty select games. . . .
         New York: Printed in the year 1799.   12mo.   pp. 32.   University Place Bookshop.

36049 PAYSON, Seth   1758–1820
         A Sermon preached at Concord, June 6th 1799, before . . . the Governor, the . . . Council, Senate, and House of Representatives. . . .
         Portsmouth: New-Hampshire, printed by John Melcher . . . 1799.   pp. 23.   8vo.
         aas, ba, bm, bpl, cl, ei, hc, heh, jcb, loc, mhs, nhhs, nl, nyhs, yc.

36050 PEABODY, Stephen   1741–1819
         A Sermon, delivered at the ordination of . . . Josiah Webster . . . in Ipswich, November 13th, 1799. . . . Together with the Charge by the Rev. Mr. Thayer, of Kingston, the Right Hand of Fellowship by the Rev. Mr. Frisbie of Ipswich, and an hymn composed on the occasion.
         Printed by Seth H. Moore, Haverhill.   pp. 35.   8vo.   aas, bpl, cl, hsp, jcb, yc.

36051 [PECK, John]   1735–1812?
         Facts and calculations respecting the population and territory of the United States of America.
         [Boston, Printed by Russell for John Peck.]   pp. 7, [1].   8vo.
         Title and imprint from verso of p. 7. Paper has watermark date "1799."   heh.

36052 PECK, William Dandridge   1763–1822
         Natural history of the slug worm. . . . By order of the Massachusetts Agricultural Society.
         Boston: Printed by Young & Minns. 1799.   pp. [1], 14, plate.   8vo.
         Frontispiece drawn by W. D. P. and engraved by S. Hill.
         aas, ba, bm, bpl, Bʳu, hc, jcb, lcp, loc, mhs, nyhs, nypl, wl, yc.

36053 [PEDDLE, Mrs.]
         Rudiments of taste, in a series of letters from a mother to her daughter.
         Reprinted at T. Collier's office in Litchfield.   pp. 142.   32mo.   yc.

36054 PEIRCE, John, Jr.
THE NEW AMERICAN SPELLING-BOOK, IMPROVED. IN THREE PARTS. . . . THE FOURTH REVISED
EDITION.
Philadelphia: Printed for . . . Joseph & James Crukshank, 1799.   pp. [4], 200.
12mo.   NYPL.

36055 PENDLETON, Edmund   1721–1803
AN ADDRESS . . . TO THE AMERICAN CITIZENS ON THE PRESENT STATE OF OUR COUNTRY.
Boston, Printed and sold by Benjamin Edes. . . . 1799.   pp. 20.   12mo.
AAS, BA, BPL, HC, JCB, LOC, MᶜHS, MHS, NHSL, NYHS, NYPL, NYSL, PʳU, VᵃSL, VᵃU, WⁱˢHS, YC.

36056 PENNSYLVANIA. STATE.
AN ACT FOR ESTABLISHING AN HEALTH OFFICE, FOR SECURING THE CITY AND PORT OF PHILADELPHIA,
FROM THE INTRODUCTION OF PESTILENTIAL AND CONTAGIOUS DISEASES.
Philadelphia: Printed at the office of the "True American." 1799.   pp. 28.   8vo.
AAS, AML, LOC.

36057 —— AN ACT FOR THE REGULATION OF THE MILITIA OF THE COMMONWEALTH OF PENNSYLVANIA,
APPROVED APRIL 9, 1799.
[Harrisburg?]   pp. 62.   16mo.   UOC.

36058 —— AN ACT TO REGULATE THE GENERAL ELECTIONS, WITHIN THE COMMONWEALTH OF PENNSYLVANIA.
Philadelphia: Printed by Francis and Robert Bailey. 1799.   pp. 40.   8vo.   HSP.

36059 —— ACTS OF THE GENERAL ASSEMBLY OF THE COMMONWEALTH OF PENNSYLVANIA, PASSED AT A
SESSION, WHICH WAS BEGUN AND HELD AT THE CITY OF PHILADELPHIA ON TUESDAY, THE
FOURTH DAY OF DECEMBER, IN THE YEAR ONE THOUSAND SEVEN HUNDRED AND NINETY-
EIGHT. . . .
Philadelphia: Printed by Hall and Sellers, no. 51, Market-street. M.DCC.XCIX.
pp. [2], [319]–527.   4to.   AAS, LOC, YC.

36060 —— THE DISSENT OF THE MINORITY OF THE HOUSE OF REPRETENTATIVES [SIC] OF . . . PENNSYLVANIA,
FROM THE ADDRESS TO THE PRESIDENT OF THE UNITED STATES, ADOPTED BY SAID HOUSE,
DECEMBER, 1798.
[Philadelphia: Printed by William Duane for Benjamin F. Bache, 1799.]   pp. [8].
8vo.   HC, HSP, JCB, LOC, NYPL.

36061 —— EXTRACT FROM THE ELECTION LAW OF PENNSYLVANIA, 1799. I. WHO MAY VOTE AT ELECTIONS.
1. CITIZENS OF THIS STATE. . . .
Broadside.   fol.   LOC.

36062 —— JOURNAL OF THE FIRST SESSION OF THE NINTH HOUSE OF REPRESENTATIVES OF THE COMMON-
WEALTH OF PENNSYLVANIA, WHICH COMMENDED AT PHILADELPHIA; ON TUESDAY, THE FOURTH
DAY OF DECEMBER, IN THE YEAR OF OUR LORD ONE THOUSAND SEVEN HUNDRED AND NINETY-
EIGHT. . . .
Philadelphia: Printed by Hall & Sellers, no. 51, Market-Street. MDCCXCIX.
pp. [2], 488, 61, 17, 8.
The three appendices contain the *Receipts and Expenditures* for 1798, the *Report of the
Register-General of the State of the Finances,* and the *Report of the Arrears of Taxes.*
Each has its own titlepage. For the Journal of the tenth House see 1800.
APS, HC, HSP, LCP.

36063 —— JOURNAL OF THE SENATE OF THE COMMONWEALTH OF PENNSYLVANIA, COMMENCING ON TUESDAY,
THE FOURTH DAY OF DECEMBER, IN THE YEAR OF OUR LORD ONE THOUSAND SEVEN HUNDRED
AND NINETY-EIGHT. . . . VOLUME IX.
Philadelphia: Printed by Zachariah Poulson. . . . 1798 [1799].   pp. 371, 8, 61, 17.
fol.
The appendices contain the *Report of the Arrears of Taxes,* the *Receipts and Expenditures,*
and the *Report of the Register General,* each with its own titlepage dated 1799.
APS, HSP, LCP, LOC.

36064 —— MEIN HERR, IN BEFOLGUNG DES ZEHNTEN ABSCHNITTS DES GESETZES VOM 4TEN APRIL 1792, HABE
ICH DE EHRE, DEM ACHTBAREN HAUSE DER REPRESENTANTEN EINE ANGABE VON DEN FINANZEN
DIESES STAATS . . . VORZULEGEN. . . . SAMUEL BRYAN. . . . DEN 13TEN JENNER, 1800. . . .
Broadside. 4to. HSP.

36065 —— PROCEEDINGS IN THE CASE OF FRANCIS JOHNSTON, ESQ., LATE RECEIVER-GENERAL OF THE LAND-OFFICE,
PROSECUTED FOR DELINQUENCIES IN THE SAID OFFICE.
Lancaster, Printed by Francis & Robert Bailey. 1799. pp. 27. 8vo.
APS, HSP, JCB, MHS, NYHS, WLC.

36066 —— RECEIPTS AND EXPENDITURES IN THE TREASURY OF PENNSYLVANIA FROM THE FIRST OF JANUARY
TO THE THIRTY-FIRST OF DECEMBER, 1798. . . .
Philadelphia: Printed by Zachariah Poulson, Junior. . . . 1799. pp. 61. fol.
This edition appeared in wrappers independent of the *Journals.* AAS, LCP, LOC.

36067 —— REPORT OF THE ARREARS OF TAXES DUE FROM THE SEVERAL COUNTIES OF THE COMMONWEALTH OF
PENNSYLVANIA. . . .
Philadelphia: Printed by Zachariah Poulson, junior. . . . pp. 8 fol.
Issued also bound in with the *Journal* of the Senate. LOC, NYPL, PPL.

36068 —— REPORT OF THE REGISTER GENERAL OF THE STATE OF THE FINANCES OF THE COMMONWEALTH OF
PENNSYLVANIA, FOR THE YEAR 1798.
Philadelphia: Printed by Zachariah Poulson, junior. . . . 1799. pp. 17. fol. LOC.

36069 —— [TAGEBUCH DES SENATS DER REPUBLIK PENNSYLVANIEN. 1798–1799.
Germantaun, Gedruckt bey Michael Billmeyer. 1799.]
Ordered printed by the Senate, but no copy has been found. The printed title may have
been *Journal des Senats.*

36070 PENNSYLVANIA. REPUBLICAN PARTY.
ADDRESS TO THE REPUBLICANS OF PENNSYLVANIA. BY PETER MUHLENBERG, SAMUEL MILES, A. J.
DALLAS, MICHAEL LEIB, WILLIAM PENROSE AND TENCH COXE. PHILADELPHIA, AUGUST 7TH,
1799.
Philadelphia: Printed by J. R. Kammerer and G. Hembold, jun. 1799. pp. 7.
8vo. EVANS.

36071 —— AN DIE REPUBLICANER DES STAATS VON PENNSYLVANIEN . . . EURE FREUNDE AND MITBÜRGER,
PETER MÜHLENBERG. . . . PHILAD. DEN 7TEN AUGUST, 1799.
Philadelphia: Gedruckt bey J. R. Kämmerer und G. Hembold, jun. . . . pp. [2].
fol. LOC.

36072 PENNSYLVANIA. WELSH SOCIETY.
CONSTITUTION AND RULES OF THE WELSH SOCIETY OF PENNSYLVANIA, FOR THE ADVICE AND ASSIST-
ANCE OF EMIGRANTS FROM WALES.
Mount-Holly: Printed by Stephen C. Ustick. 1799. pp. 12. 8vo. HSP.

36073 THE PENNSYLVANIA GAZETTE. 1728–1815
Philadelphia: Printed by Hall and Sellers. . . . fol. weekly.
FOR 1799: [AAS], [HC], LCP.

36074 THE PENNSYLVANIA HERALD, AND YORK GENERAL ADVERTISER. 1789–1800
York: Printed . . . by John Edie. fol. weekly.
FOR 1799: [YORK CO. HIST. SOC.]

36075 [THE PENNSYLVANIA, MARYLAND AND VIRGINIA ALMANACK, FOR THE YEAR 1800.
Frederick-Town, Maryland: Printed by Matthias Bartgis, 1799.] MINICK 530.

36076 THE PENNSYLVANIA, NEW-JERSEY, DELAWARE, MARYLAND AND VIRGINIA ALMANAC, FOR THE
YEAR OF OUR LORD, 1800. . . .
Philadelphia: Printed and sold by Peter Stewart, no. 34, South Second-Street.
pp. [40]. 16mo. AAS.

36077 PENNSYLVANISCHER Calender, auf das 1800ste jahr Christi, welches ein gemeines jahr von 365 tages ist. . . .
   York: — Gedruckt und zu haben bey Salomon Mayer. pp. [40]. sq.8vo. AAS.

36078 DIE PENNSYLVANISCHE Correspondenz.   1797–1800
   Herausgegeben von Henrich Schweitzer . . . Philadelphia. . . . fol. semi-weekly.
        For 1799: [Montgomery Co. Hist. Soc., Norristown].

36079 [DIE PENNSYLVANISCHE Wochenschrift.   1797–1805
   Hanover, Pa., published by W. D. Lepper and S. E. Stettinius.] weekly.
         For 1799: No copy known.

36080 PENROSE, Jonathan
   Philadelphia, March 4, 1799. By virtue of a writ of levari facias to me directed, will be sold by public vendue, at the Merchants Coffee-House . . . on Tuesday, the 26th of March. . . .
    [Caption title. Colophon:] Printed by D. Humphreys, no. 48, Spruce-street [Philadelphia]. Broadside. fol.
   Sheriff's sale of lands belonging to Robert Morris.   NYHS.

36081 PERRIN, John
   A Grammar of the French tongue, grounded upon the decisions of the French Academy. . . . The tenth edition, carefully revised.
    New-York: Printed by M. L. & W. A. Davis, for E. Duyckinck, T. S. Arden, S. Stephens, P. A. Mesier, and W. Falconer. 1799. pp. xii, 358. 12mo. BA, YC.

36082 PERRY, William
   [The Only sure guide to the English tongue, or new pronouncing spelling book. Twelfth Worcester edition.
    Printed at Worcester, Massachusetts, by Isaiah Thomas, Jun. . . . Sold also . . . by Thomas and Andrews . . . in Boston. MDCCXCIX.]
   Existence assumed from the sequence of editions.

36083 —— —— S. Hall's seventh Boston edition.
    Printed and sold by Samuel Hall, no. 53, Cornhill, Boston. 1799. pp. ix–180, front., 12 illus. 16mo. BMFA.

36084 PETERSBURG. Virginia. Theater.
   The Petersburg theatre. On Wednesday evening, November 13, 1799, will be presented. . . . The child of nature. . . .
    [Petersburg, Va.] Broadside.   NYHS.

36085 THE PHENIX.   1798–1804
   Staunton (Virginia) published . . . by John Wise. . . . fol. weekly.
         For 1799: [AAS], [UOC].

36086 PHILADELPHIA. Pennsylvania.
   An Answer to the joint committee of the Select and Common Councils of Philadelphia, on the subject of a plan for supplying the city with water. . . .
    [Philadelphia.] pp. 7. 8vo.
   Caption title. Dated Philadelphia, March 2d, 1799, and signed by B. H. Latrobe, engineer.
                    HSP.

36087 —— An Ordinance providing for the raising of a sum of money for supplying the city of Philadelphia with wholesome water. . . .
    Philadelphia: Printed by Zachariah Poulson, junior. . . . 1799. pp. 7. 8vo.
          AML, HSP, LOC, NYPL, PPL.

36088 —— Public notice. Notice is hereby given to the foremen of the place the general election will be held. . . . Jonathan Penrose, sheriff. September 26, 1799.
    [Colophon:] James Carey, printer. — no. 16, Chestnut-Street. Broadside. 4to.
                    HSP.

36089 —— Report of the joint committee of the Select and Common Councils, appointed to receive information on the subject of watering the city, and to employ agent . . . to promote that object. . . .
Philadelphia: Printed by Zachariah Poulson, junior. 1799. pp. 7. 8vo.
HSP, NYPL.

36090 —— Report of the joint committee of the Select and Common Councils, to estimate the sums necessary to meet expenses of the current year.
Philadelphia, 1799. pp. 20. HSP.

36091 —— Report to the Select and Common Councils, on the . . . Water Works, on the 24th. of November, 1799. Printed by order of the Corporation of Philadelphia.
Philadelphia: Printed by Zachariah Poulson, Junior, no. 106, Chestnut-street. 1799. pp. 44. 8vo. AAS, AML, HSP, LCP, LOC, NYHS, NYPL.

36092 —— To be sold, by public vendue; on Wednesday next, the 27th of February . . . sundry articles . . . seized for ground rent, by the guardians to the estate of Robert Nichol, deceased, and sold by George Gass and Richard Hunt, Constables. February 23d, 1799.
[Philadelphia:] Printed by Patterson & Cochran, no. 34, South Second-street. Broadside. 8vo. Mrs. Joseph Carson.

36093 PHILADELPHIA. Pennsylvania. Academy of Medicine.
Constitution of the Academy of Medicine of Philadelphia.
[Philadelphia.] pp. 4. 8vo. AML, NYPL.

36094 —— Laws of the Academy of Medicine of Philadelphia.
[Philadelphia.] pp. 7. 8vo. AML, NYPL.

36095 PHILADELPHIA. Pennsylvania. African Methodist Episcopal Church.
Articles of association of the African Methodist Episcopal Church, of the city of Philadelphia. . . .
Philadelphia: Printed by John Ormrod. . . . 1799. pp. 21. 12mo. LCP.

36096 PHILADELPHIA. Pennsylvania. Baptist Association.
Minutes of the Philadelphia Baptist Association, held at the Great Valley . . . October 1st, 2d, and 3d, 1798.
[Mount-Holly, Printed by Stephen C. Ustick, 1799.] pp. 8. 12mo.
BrU, NJHS, NYHS.

36097 PHILADELPHIA. Pennsylvania. Churches.
Mortality. An account of the baptisms and burials in the united churches of Christ Church and St. Peter's. . . . Also . . . baptisms . . . in various congregations in the city and suburbs of Philadelphia from Dec. 25, 1798 to Dec. 25, 1799.
Philadelphia: Printed by J. Ormrod. . . . Broadside. LCP.

36098 PHILADELPHIA. Pennsylvania. Edward Pole, & Co.
Sales at auction of horses & carriages. . . . Edward Pole, & Co. auctioneers. April 24, 1799.
Philadelphia: Printed by R. Aitken, no. 22 Market-Street. Broadside. fol. HSP.

36099 PHILADELPHIA. Pennsylvania. Fire Companies.
Return of the several fire companies. . . .
[Philadelphia.] Broadside. JCB.

36100 PHILADELPHIA. Pennsylvania. Library Company.
Fifth supplement to the catalogue of books belonging to the Library Company of Philadelphia. . . .
Philadelphia: Printed by Zachariah Poulson, junior . . . July 31, 1799. pp. 32. 8vo. LCP, NYPL, YC.

36101   PHILADELPHIA. Pennsylvania. New Theatre.
The Last night Mr. Reinagle's benefit. On Saturday evening, May 25th, will be presented . . . Lover's Vows. . . .
[Philadelphia: Printed by John Ward Fenno, 1799.]   Broadside.   fol.   LOC.

36102   —— On Wednesday evening, Feb. 27, will be presented (for the second time here) a celebrated comedy, called Cheap Living. . . .
[Philadelphia.]   Broadside.   fol.   NYPL.

36103   —— Resolutions and articles of agreement entered into and adopted by the proprietors of the building and lots of the New Theatre, in Philadelphia.
Philadelphia.   pp. 16.   16mo.
Includes a list of the proprietors.   HSP, MHS, WLC.

36104   PHILADELPHIA. Pennsylvania. Pennsylvania Hospital.
To the Senate and House of Representatives of the Commonwealth of Pennsylvania. The memorial and petition of the managers of the Pennsylvania Hospital.
Philadelphia: Printed by Z. Poulson, jun. no. 106, Chestnut-Street. December 17, 1799.
pp. 7.   fol.   AAS.

36105   PHILADELPHIA. Pennsylvania. Philadelphia Militia Legion.
Legionary orders. December 28th, 1799. Yesterday the commandant was honored by a communication. . . . John Hall, commandant. . . .
[Philadelphia.]   Broadside.   fol.   LOC.

36106   —— Legionary orders. The militia legion is notified, that they are to parade on Thursday morning next . . . in the State-House Yard, to attend the ceremonial of the interment of . . . Washington. . . . Dec. 24, 1799.
[Philadelphia.]   Broadside.   8vo.   LOC.

36107   PHILADELPHIA. Pennsylvania. Samuel Israel.
[The Valuable library of an English gentleman, in excellect condition. . . . Sold at his vendue store, Front Street, Philadelphia, July 20, 1799.]   McKay 142J.

36108   PHILADELPHIA. Pennsylvania. Scots Thistle Society.
Constitution of the Scots Thistle Society of Philadelphia. Instituted November 30, 1796.
Philadelphia: Printed by John Bioren. 1799.   pp. 28.   8vo.   LCP.

36109   PHILADELPHIA. Pennsylvania. Second City Troop of Horse.
Articles, or by-laws, for the government of the Second Philadelphia City Troop of Horse.
Philadelphia: Printed by Henry Tuckniss, 1799.   pp. 7.   8vo.   HSP.

36110   PHILADELPHIA. Pennsylvania. Society of Friends.
To our fellow citizens of the United States of North America . . . [respecting the evil of slavery]. Philadelphia, Nov. 11, 1799.
[Philadelphia.]   pp. 3.   LCP, PrU.

36111   PHILADELPHIA. Pennsylvania. Zion German Lutheran Church.
Arrangement of the music, to be performed at the German Lutheran Church . . .December 26, 1799 . . . in honor of General Washington.
[Philadelphia.]   pp. 6.   8vo.   AAS, MHS.

36112   THE PHILADELPHIA Directory.
See Stafford, Cornelius William.

36113   THE PHILADELPHIA Gazette & Universal Daily Advertiser.   1794–1802
[Published] By A. Brown.   fol.   daily.
With the issue of July 2 Samuel Relf was admitted to partnership.
For 1799: [AAS], BM, LCP, WⁱˢHS.

36114 THE PHILADELPHIA MAGAZINE AND REVIEW; OR, MONTHLY REPOSITORY OF INFORMATION AND AMUSEMENT: FOR JANUARY [–JUNE], 1799.
Philadelphia: Printed for Benjamin Davies, no. 68, High-Street. pp. 415, [3], front. 8vo.
There are pagination errors and variations between copies. The plate of Washington's resignation was engraved by A. Lawson after J. J. Barralet.
AAS, BA, BPL, HSP, LCP, LOC, NYPL, YC.

36115 PHILADELPHISCHE CORRESPONDENZ. 1798–1800
Alle Dienstag herausgegeben von Joseph R. Kämmerer, und Comp. fol. weekly.
George Helmbold, Jr., became one of the publishers as of May 14. The paper is a segment of the *Neue Philadelphische Correspondenz, 1790–1812.* FOR 1799: [HSP].

36116 PIDGIN, WILLIAM. 1772–1848
GREAT PLAINNESS NECESSARY IN DELIVERING THE GOSPEL-MESSAGE WITH A PROSPECT OF SUCCESS. ... DELIVERED AT THE INSTALLATION OF THE REV. SAMUEL TOMB ... IN NEWBURY, NOV. 28, 1798. ...
Newburyport: Printed by Edmund March Blunt. 1799. pp. 28. 8vo. AHTS, JCB, LOC.

36117 PILKINGTON, [MARY (HOPKINS)] 1766–1839
A MIRROR FOR THE FEMALE SEX. HISTORICAL BEAUTIES FOR YOUNG LADIES. ... DESIGNED PRINCIPALLY FOR THE USE OF LADIES' SCHOOLS. ...
Hartford: Printed by Hudson and Goodwin, for Oliver D. and I. Cooke. 1799.
pp. xxiv, 211, [1]. 12mo. AAS, BPL, CHS, HC, HEH, JCB, LOC, MHS, NYHS, NYPL, YC.

36118 PILLSBURY, EDMUND 1738–1816
THE LAW AND THE GOSPEL, OR, THE MINISTRY OF CONDEMNATION. ... DESIGNED AS A FRIENDLY REPLY, TO THE REV. S[AMUEL] SHEPARD'S LETTER. ...
Portsmouth, New Hampshire: Printed by Charles Peirce. ... 1799. pp. 37.
NEMHS.

36119 PILSBURY, AMOS
THE UNITED STATES' SACRED HARMONY. CONTAINING THE RUDIMENTS OF VOCAL MUSIC. ... ALSO, A LARGE NUMBER OF TUNES NEVER BEFORE PUBLISHED. ...
Printed, Typographically, at Boston, by Isaiah Thomas and Ebenezer T. Andrews. Sold by them ... and by the compiler, in Charleston, (South-Carolina.) Nov. 1799.
pp. 224. obl. 24mo.
There is some evidence that the copies printed for sale in Charleston had a special titlepage.
AAS, LOC, NL, YC.

36120 [PINCHARD, MRS.]
THE TWO COUSINS, A MORAL STORY, FOR THE USE OF YOUNG PERSONS. ... BY THE AUTHOR OF THE "BLIND CHILD," AND "DRAMATIC DIALOGUES". ...
New-York: Printed and sold by John Tiebout. ... 1799. pp. 130. 24mo. AAS.

36121 PINCKNEY, CHARLES 1758–1824
CASE OF JONATHAN ROBBINS, EXAMINED BY CHARLES PINCKNEY, ESQ. SENATOR IN CONGRESS FOR SOUTH CAROLINA. ...
Baltimore: Printed by Warner & Hanna. ... 1799. pp. 36. 12mo.
Pagination irregular. LCP, LOC, NYPL.

36122 —— THREE LETTERS ... WHICH HAVE LATELY APPEARED UNDER THE SIGNATURE OF "A SOUTH-CAROLINA PLANTER". ... ON THE CASE OF JONATHAN ROBBINS. ... ON THE RECENT CAPTURES OF THE BRITISH CRUISERS. ... ON THE CLAIMS OF THE BRITISH CREDITORS. ...
Charleston: Printed by T. C. Cox, Tradd-Street, Dec. 1799. pp. [1], 69. 8vo.
AAS, JCB, LOC, VᵃU.

36123 —— —— TO WHICH IS ADDED, AN APPENDIX, CONTAINING SUNDRY DOCUMENTS CONCERNING JONATHAN ROBBINS.
Charleston: Printed by T. C. Cox, Tradd-street, Dec. 1799. pp. [4], 69. 8vo.
AAS, CU, GU, JCB, LOC.

36124 — — — *Philadelphia: Aurora-office, 1799.*   pp. [1], 65.   8vo.
         AAS, BA, BM, BPL, CLS, HC, HEH, HSP, JCB, LOC, MHS, NL, NYPL, NYSL, YC.

36125   PISCATAQUA Association.
     A Prayer Book for the use of families; prepared by the association of ministers on
     Piscataqua-River. . . .
         Printed by Charles Peirce, at the Oracle-Press, no. 5, Daniel-Street, Portsmouth,
     N. H. . . . July 1799.   pp. 72.   16mo.   AAS, BM, CL, HEH, JCB, NHHS, NYPL, NYSL.

36126   THE PITTSBURGH Gazette.   1786–1876
         Pittsburgh: Printed by John Scull. . . .   fol.   weekly.
         For 1799: Carnegie Library, Pittsburgh.

36127   PLAIN sense: or, the history of Henry Villars and Ellen Mordaunt. A novel in two
     volumes. . . .
         Philadelphia: Printed for Mathew Carey. no. 118, Market-Street. October 1, 1799.
     pp. 211; 246, [6].   12mo.
     The final pages contain publisher's advertisements. An anonymous English novel first
     published in 1795.   HC, LOC, VᵃU, YC.

36128   PLAIN truth. . . .
     See Evans 35723.

36129   THE POETICAL flower basket, being a selection of approved and entertaining pieces of
     poetry, calculated for the improvement of young minds. First American edition.
         Printed at Worcester, by Isaiah Thomas, Jun. July — 1799.   pp. 71, front.   24mo.
                                      AAS, BPL, HC, JCB.

36130   A POLEMIC essay. . . .
     See 36739.

36131   POLITICAL Banquet, and Farmer's Feast.   1799–1800
         Exeter (New-Hampshire) printed and published by Henry Ranlet.   weekly.   fol.
     This was a continuation of the *Exeter Federal Miscellany.*   For 1799: [AAS], [LOC].

36132   THE POLITICAL Focus.   1798–Dec. 5, 1799
         Published every Thursday, by Charles & John Prentiss.   fol.   weekly.
     With the issue for Mar. 7 John Prentiss withdrew.   For 1799: [AAS], [HC], [MHS].

36133   THE POLITICAL green-house, for the year 1798. Addressed to the readers of the Con-
     necticut Courant, January 1st, 1799. . . .
         Hartford: Printed by Hudson & Goodwin.   pp. 24.   16mo.
     The authors were Richard Alsop, Lemuel Hopkins, and Theodore Dwight.
                                     AAS, BʳU, HC, HEH, NYHS, YC.

36134   THE POLITICAL repository: or, farmer's journal.   1798–1802
         Printed at Brookfield, Massachusetts, by Ebenezer Merriam & Co.   weekly.   fol.
         For 1799: AAS.

36135   POMEROY, Zadock   1774–1804
     Sign of the Indian queen. The subscriber takes this method. . . . Boston, June 1799. . . .
         [*Boston.*]   Broadside.   16mo.   MHS.

36136   POOR Richard revived; or, Barker & Southwick's Almanack: for the year of our Lord, 1799.
     . . . Calculated for the meridian of Albany. . . .
         Albany: Printed and sold by Barker and Southwick. . . .   pp. [40].   16mo.
     Omitted by Evans from the preceding volume because he had found no copy.   AAS, YC.

36137 POOR Richard revived: or, Barker & Southwick's almanack: for the year of our Lord, 1800. ... Calculated for the meridian of Albany. ...
> *Albany: Printed and sold by Barker and Southwick.* ...   pp. [34].   8vo.
G⸱L, NYPL.

36138 POOR Robin
No. II. The Farmer's, merchant's and mechanic's almanack, or the Register of Maine, for ... 1800. ...
> *Printed by Elezer A. Jenks, Portland.* ...   pp. [36].   12mo.   BPL, M⸱HS.

36139 POOR Will's Almanack, for the year of our Lord, 1800. ... Also a variety of essays in prose and verse.
> *Philadelphia: Printed for, and sold by, Joseph and James Crukshank, no. 87, High-Street.*   pp. [36].   12mo.   AAS, HC, NYPL.

36140 POOR Will's pocket Almanack, for the year 1800; being the fourth after bissextile or leap-year. ...
> *Philadelphia: Printed for, and sold by, Joseph & James Crukshank, no. 87, High-Street.*   pp. [48], interleaved.   32mo.   AAS, HSP, LOC.

36141 PORCUPINE'S Gazette.   1797–1799
> *Philadelphia: Published every evening, by William Cobbett.* ...   fol. and 12mo.
daily and weekly.   For 1799: [AAS], LCP, LOC, NYHS, NYSL.

36142 PORTER, Eliphalet   1758–1833
A Sermon delivered to the First Religious Society in Roxbury, June 16, 1799. Occasioned by the death of ... Increase Sumner. ...
> *Printed at Boston, by Young & Minns.* ... *1799.*   pp. 27.   8vo.
AAS, BA, BM, EI, HC, JCB, LOC, MHS, NYHS, NYPL, NYSL, WL, WLC, YC.

36143 PORTLAND Gazette.
See Jenk's Portland Gazette.

36144 POTOMACK Company.
Great Falls, July 2, 1799. Entrusted as we are, with the interests of the Potomack Company. ...
> [*Georgetown.*]   Broadside.   fol.   LOC.

36145 THE POTOMAK Guardian.   1792–1800
> *Martinsburg, Virginia: Printed and published ... by N. Willis.* ...   fol.   weekly.
For 1799: [Wvᵃ. Archives.]

36146 POTTS, John
[A Plain and concise table (particularly calculated for the use of importing merchants) of the duties payable by law on all goods ... imported ... after the last day of June 1797.
> *Petersburg: Printed by Ross & Douglas. 1799.*]
14th Virginia district copyright issued Oct. 1, 1799, to John Potts.

36147 THE POUGHKEEPSIE Journal. 1789–1844
> *Poughkeepsie, (Dutchess County), published by Power and Southwick.* ...   fol.
weekly.   For 1799: Adriance Lib., Poughkeepsie.

36148 POULSON'S town and Country Almanac, for the year of our Lord, 1800. ... The constellations ... and the manner in which they are said to govern the human body. ...
> *Philadelphia: Printed and sold by Zachariah Poulson, Junior, no. 106, Chestnut-street.* ...   pp. [48].   12mo.   AAS, LOC, NYHS, NYPL, NYSL.

36149   PRACTICAL EXERCISES IN GRAMMAR, PUNCTUATION AND RHETORIC.
          Printed by H. Ranlet, and sold at his book-store, Water-Street, Exeter. 1799.   pp.
          24.   12mo.   AAS, HEH, NYPL.

36150   A PRAYER BOOK, FOR THE USE OF FAMILIES. . . .
          See Piscataqua Association.

36151   PRENTICE, CALEB   1746–1803
          A SERMON DELIVERED BEFORE MOUNT MORIAH LODGE: AT READING . . . AT THE CELEBRATION OF
          ST. JOHN; JUNE 24TH, A. D. 1799. BY CALEB PRENTISS, A. M. PASTOR OF THE FIRST PARISH
          IN SAID TOWN. . . .
          Leominster, (Mass.) Printed by Brother Charles Prentiss for Mount Moriah Lodge.
          Anno Lucis 5799.   pp. 16.   8vo.   AAS, BA, HC, MFM, NYHS, NYPL.

36152   —— A SERMON PREACHED AT THE INSTALMENT OF . . . ELIAS HULL . . . IN SEABROOK — FEB. 6TH,
          1799. BY CALEB PRENTISS. . . .
          Printed at Newburyport by Edmund M. Blunt. M,DCC,XCIX.   pp. 22.   8vo.
          Includes the Charge by Elijah Parish of Byfield and the Right Hand of Fellowship by
          Andrew Beattie of Salisbury.   AAS, BPL, HC, JCB, NYHS, NYSL.

36153   PRENTISS, CALEB   1746–1803
          See Prentice, Caleb.

36154   PRENTISS, THOMAS   1747–1814
          A DISCOURSE DELIVERED AT MEDFIELD . . . JULY 4, 1799. BY THOMAS PRENTISS, A. M. PASTOR
          OF THE CONGREGATIONAL CHURCH. . . .
          Printed at the Minerva Press in Dedham, by Herman Mann, 1799.   pp. 22.   8vo.
          AAS, AHTS, BA, BPL, CL, HC, HEH, JCB, LOC, MHS, MSL, NYHS, NYPL, NYSL, WC, WLC.

36155   —— A SERMON, DELIVERED AT THE ORDINATION OF . . . THOMAS MASON . . . IN NORTHFIELD, NOVEM-
          BER 6, 1799. . . .
          Brattleboro': From the press of B. Smead. 1799.   pp. 24.   12mo.
                                                                      AHTS, BM, JCB, NYHS, YC.

36156   PRENTISS, THOMAS MELLEN   1773–1823
          THE MAINE SPELLING BOOK. . . . TO WHICH IS ANNEXED. A CONCISE GEOGRAPHICAL DESCRIPTION
          OF MAINE. . . .
          Leominster, Massachusetts: Printed by Charles & John Prentiss, for the author, 1799.
          pp. 123.   12mo.   HC, NYPL.

36157   —— —— [*Augusta, Peter Edes, Feb. 1799.*]   pp. 132.   16mo.
          Adv.; Williamson 8298; Maine copyright Dec. 9, 1799.

36158   PRESBYTERIAN CHURCH IN SOUTH CAROLINA.
          PASTORAL LETTER, OF THE PRESBYTERY OF CHARLESTON, TO THE CHURCHES OF THE PRESBYTERIAN
          DENOMINATION, WITHIN THEIR BOUNDS.
          Charleston: Printed by Benjamin F. Timothy. 1799.   pp. 14.   8vo.   BA, HC, HEH.

36159   PRESBYTERIAN CHURCH IN THE UNITED STATES OF AMERICA.
          ACTS AND PROCEEDINGS OF THE GENERAL ASSEMBLY OF THE PRESBYTERIAN CHURCH, IN THE
          UNITED STATES OF AMERICA, MAY 16TH, 1799.
          Philadelphia: Printed by William W. Woodward, no. 17, Chestnut Street, 1799.
          pp. 24.   8vo.   AAS, JCB, LOC, NYSL.

36160   PRIESTLEY, JOSEPH   1733–1804
          A COMPARISON OF THE INSTITUTIONS OF MOSES WITH THOSE OF THE HINDOOS . . . AND AN
          ADDRESS TO THE JEWS ON THE PRESENT STATE OF THE WORLD. . . .
          Northumberland [Pa.]: Printed for the author by A. Kennedy. MDCCXCIX.
          pp. xxvii, 428, [8].   8vo.
          The last pages contain "A catalogue of books, written by Dr. Priestley."
                                            AAS, BA, BPL, HC, HEH, HSP, NYHS, NYPL, YC.

36161 —— LETTERS TO THE INHABITANTS OF NORTHUMBERLAND AND ITS NEIGHBOURHOOD, ON SUBJECTS INTERESTING TO THE AUTHOR AND TO THEM. . . . PART. I. . . .
Northumberland [Pa.]: Printed for the author, by Andrew Kennedy. MDCCXCIX.
pp. 48. 8vo.
There are copies with the date printed MDCCLXLIX.

BA, BM, BPL, HC, HEH, HSP, LOC, NL, NYHS, NYPL, PPL, PSL, UOP.

36162 —— LETTERS TO THE INHABITANTS OF NORTHUMBERLAND. . . . PART II.
Northumberland [Pa.]: Printed for the author by Andrew Kennedy. MDCCXCIX.
pp. 42, [1]. 8vo.
Second title: Maxims of political arithmetic, applied to the case of the United States of America. First published in the Aurora for February 26 and 27, 1798. By a Quaker in politics. pp. 33–42. The final page contains the Contents. AAS, AHTS, BA, BM, HEH, JCB, NYPL.

36163 THE PRINCIPLES OF THE CHRISTIAN RELIGION: DIVIDED INTO LESSONS AND ADAPTED TO THE CAPACITIES OF CHILDREN.
Printed at Worcester: by Isaiah Thomas, Jun. . . . 1799. pp. 30, [1], illus.
32mo. AAS.

36164 PROCEEDINGS IN THE CASE OF FRANCIS JOHNSTON. . . .
See Pennsylvania.

36165 PROCEEDINGS OF THE GRAND LODGE OF CONNECTICUT, HOLDEN AT THE CITY OF NEW HAVEN, ON WEDNESDAY THE SEVENTEENTH DAY OF OCTOBER, ANNO LUCIS, FIVE THOUSAND SEVEN HUNDRED AND NINETY EIGHT, A. D. 1798.
Hartford: Printed by br. Elisha Babcock. 1799. pp. 8. 12mo.
See also Evans 35503. CHS.

36166 THE PRODIGAL DAUGHTER, OR A STRANGE AND WONDERFUL RELATION, SHEWING HOW A GENTLEMAN OF GREAT ESTATE IN BRISTOL, HAD A PROUD AND DISOBEDIENT DAUGHTER, WHO, BECAUSE HER PARENTS WOULD NOT SUPPORT HER IN ALL HER EXTRAVAGANCE, BARGAINED WITH THE DEVIL TO POISON THEM. . . . HOW SHE LAY IN A TRANCE FOUR DAYS; AND WHEN SHE WAS PUT INTO THE GRAVE, SHE CAME TO LIFE AGAIN, AND RELATED THE WONDERFUL THINGS SHE SAW IN THE OTHER WORLD.
Hartford: Printed for the Travelling Booksellers. 1799. pp. 12. 12mo.
AAS, CSL, JCB, LOC, YC.

36167 —— —— —— *New York: Printed for the Travelling Booksellers. 1799.* pp. 8. 16mo. JCB.

36168 THE PROMPTER; OR A COMMENTARY ON COMMON SAYINGS. . . .
See Webster, Noah.

36169 PROPOSALS FOR PRINTING BY SUBSCRIPTION, A SERMON ENTITLED THE ADVANTAGES AND PRAISES OF WISDOM. . . . BY THE REV. JOSEPH LYMAN. . . . GREENFIELD, JAN. 8TH, 1799. . . .
[Printed at Greenfield by Francis Barker, 1799.] Broadside. fol.
MRS. EDNA H. GREENWOOD.

36170 PROPOSALS FOR PUBLISHING BY SUBSCRIPTION . . . MEMOIRS AND TRAVELS OF MAURITIUS AUGUSTUS COUNT BENYOWSKY. . . . IN TWO VOLUMES OCTAVO. . . .
[William Spotswood, bookseller. Boston, 7th November, 1799.] Broadside. fol.
The imprint is from the heading of the broadside. AAS.

36171 PROTESTANT EPISCOPAL CHURCH IN MARYLAND.
JOURNAL OF A CONVENTION OF THE PROTESTANT EPISCOPAL CHURCH, IN THE STATE OF MARYLAND; HELD AT EASTON, IN WHITSUN-WEEK.
Easton: Printed by James Cowan. 1799. pp. 8. 8vo. MᵈHS, NYPL.

36172 PROTESTANT Episcopal Church in New Jersey.
Proceedings of a convention of the Protestant Episcopal Church in . . . New-Jersey. Held at New-Brunswick, the 5th and 6th of June, 1799.
Newark — New-Jersey — printed by Jacob Halsey, at the office of the Gazette — 1799.
pp. 8. 8vo. AAS, NYHS.

36173 —— Proceedings of a special convention of the Protestant Episcopal Church in . . . New-Jersey . . . in Perth-Amboy, the 16th and 17th Oct. 1799.
Elizabeth-town: Printed by Shepard Kollock — 1799. pp. 16. 8vo.
AAS, CU, NYHS, PᵣU, YC.

36174 PROTESTANT Episcopal Church in Pennsylvania.
Journal of the fifteenth convention of the Protestant Episcopal Church, in the State of Pennsylvania, held in Christ-Church, on . . . May 21st, 1799.
[Philadelphia.] pp. [2]. 8vo. AAS.

36175 PROTESTANT Episcopal Church in the United States.
The Book of Common Prayer . . . together with the Psalter, or Psalms of David.
Charleston: Printed for W. P. Young, 43 Broad-Street. 1799. pp. [368]. 12mo.
JCB, LOC.

36176 —— The Catechism of the Protestant Episcopal Church.
Philadelphia: Printed by John Ormrod. . . . 1799. pp. 8. 16mo. LCP.

36177 —— Journal of the proceedings . . . in a convention held in the city of Philadelphia, from . . . June the eleventh, to . . . June the nineteenth, 1799.
Philadelphia: Printed by John Ormrod, 41, Chestnut-Street M.DCC,XCIX. pp. 80.
8vo. AAS, GTS, HEH, HSP, JCB, LCP, LOC, MHS, NYPL, NYSL, NYSOC, YC.

36178 PROTESTANT Episcopal Church in Virginia.
Journal of a convention of the Protestant Episcopal church in Virginia, held at the Capitol in the city of Richmond, May 7, 1799.
Richmond: Printed by Thomas Nicholson, at the first house below the Capitol.
pp. 16. 8vo. NYPL.

36179 PROUDFIT, Alexander Moncrief 1770–1843
The Importance of family religion. A sermon. By Alexander Proudfit, A. M. Pastor of the Associate Reformed Congregation in Salem.
Salem [N. Y.]: Printed by Henry Dodd. 1799. pp. 23. 8vo. AAS, NYSL.

36180 PROVIDENCE. Rhode Island.
At a town-council holden in . . . Providence, this second Day of August, A.D. 1799. . . . Resolved that three hundred copies of the . . . act, entitled, "An Act to prevent the spreading of the small-pox". . . .
[Providence.] Broadside. fol. JCB.

36181 PROVIDENCE. Rhode Island. Association of Mechanicks.
To the Hon: General Assembly, June. The memorial of the Providence Association of Mechanicks for the support of free schools.
Newport: Farnsworth. 1799. RIHS.

36182 PROVIDENCE. Rhode Island. Providence Insurance Company.
Charter of the Providence Insurance Company.
Providence: Printed by Bennett Wheeler. 1799. pp. 10. RIHS.

36183 PROVIDENCE. Rhode Island. Providence Marine Society.
Charter, laws, &c. of the Providence Marine Society.
Printed at Providence, by Bennett Wheeler. 1799. pp. 22. 16mo.
AAS, JCB, NYPL, RIHS.

36184   THE PROVIDENCE Gazette.   1762–1825
[Providence, R. I.] Printed by Carter and Wilkinson. . . . fol. weekly.
With the issue of May 11, William Wilkinson retired and John Carter became sole publisher.   For 1799: AAS, BʳU, JCB, [LOC], RIHS, [RL].

36185   THE PROVIDENCE Journal, and Town and Country Advertiser.   1799–1801
Published . . . by John Carter, jun. . . . fol. weekly.
For 1799: AAS, [BA], BʳU, LOC, NYHS, NYPL, RIHS.

36186   PUTNEY Argus.   1797–1799
Published . . . by Cornelius Sturtevant, at Putney, Vermont. fol. Weekly.
For 1799: [AAS].

36187   QUARLL, Philip, *pseud.*
The English hermit; or, the adventures of Philip Quarll. Who was discovered by Mr. Dorrington, a Bristol merchant, upon an unhabited island. . . . Adorned with cuts.
Hartford, printed by John Babcock. 1799. pp. 95, [1]. 16mo.
The author was Peter Longueville.   AAS, CHS, YC.

36188   QUINCE, Peter
See Story, Isaac.

36189   RALEIGH Register, and North-Carolina Weekly Advertiser.   Oct. 22, 1799–
Raleigh: Printed by Joseph Gales. fol. weekly.   For 1799: [NCSL].

36190   RANLET'S Federal Miscellany.   1798 — Jan. 16, 1799
Exeter (New-Hampshire) printed and published by Henry Ranlet. weekly. fol.
On Jan. 16 the name was changed to the *Exeter Federal Miscellany.*
For 1799: [AAS], [HC], [LOC].

36191   A REAL treasure for the pious mind. Compiled by a lady of Connecticut. From the collections and writings of the Countess of Huntingdon, Mrs. Rowe, Miss Harvey, Dr. Watts, Mr. Perin, Mr. Smith, and others. Second edition. . . .
Hartford: Printed by John Babcock. 1799. pp. 96. 12mo.   AAS, GʳL, HC, YC.

36192   REFLEXIONES sobre el comercio de Espana con sus colonias en America, en tiempo de guerra. Por un espanol, en Philadelphia.
Philadelphia: En la imprenta de Jaime Carey. XDCCLXXXXIX. pp. 90, folded table. 8vo.
Attributed to Santiago Felipe Perglia.   JCB, LOC.

36193   REFORMED Church in the United States.
Das Neue und verbesserte gesangbuch, worinnen die Psalmen Davids samt einer sammlung. . . . 2. aufl.
Germantaun: Gedruckt bey Michael Billmeyer, 1799. pp. [4], 148, [8], 585, [9], 26, front. 16mo.   AAS, HEH, LOC, NL, NYSL.

36194   REINAGLE, Alexander   1756–1809
[The Music in the historical play of Columbus. Composed and adapted, for the piano forte, flute or violin. By Alexander Reinagle.
Philadelphia.]
223d Pennsylvania District copyright issued to Alexander Reinagle, as author, Feb. 22, 1799.

36195   RELIANCE Property Company.
Constitution of the Reliance Property Company, as adopted at an adjourned meeting, on the 12th day of June, 1799. . . .
Baltimore: Printed by John Hayes. . . . M,DCC,XCIX. pp. 12. 16mo.
This was a fire company.   HSP.

36196   [A REMARKABLE AND SURPRISING ACCOUNT OF THE ABANDONED LIFE, HAPPY CONVERSION, AND
         COMFORTABLE DEATH OF FANNY SIDNEY.
                  Troy: Printed for the Travelling Booksellers. 1799.   12mo.]   EVANS.

36197   THE REMARKABLE HISTORY OF AUGI: OR: A PICTURE OF TRUE HAPPINESS. TOGETHER WITH THE
         STORY OF THE DREAMER. SECOND WORCESTER EDITION.
                  Printed at Worcester, Massachusetts: by Isaiah Thomas, Jun. . . . 1799.   pp. 31,
         front.   32 mo.   AAS, JCB.

36198   THE REMARKABLE HISTORY OF TOM JONES, A FOUNDLING.
                  Salem: Printed and sold at Faust's Head, Essex Street. 1799.   pp. 29.   48vo.
         A variant of Evans 35481.   AAS.

36199   A REMARKABLE NARRATIVE OF THE CAPTIVITY AND ESCAPE OF MRS. FRANCES SCOTT, AN INHABITANT
         OF WASHINGTON COUNTY, VIRGINIA.
                  Newburyport: Printed and sold by Parker & Robinson.   pp. 14.   32mo.   AAS.

36200   REMARKS ON A SECOND PUBLICATION OF B. HENRY LATROBE, ENGINEER, SAID TO BE PRINTED BY ORDER
         OF THE COMMITTEE OF THE COUNCILS; (OF THE CITY) AND DISTRIBUTED AMONG THE MEMBERS OF
         THE LEGISLATURE.
                  [*Philadelphia.*]   pp. 7.   8vo.
         Attributed to William Smith, 1727–1803.   HSP, LOC, NYPL, NYSL.

36201   REMARKS ON THE ORGANIZATION AND CONSTITUTIONAL POWERS OF THE COUNCIL OF APPOINTMENT
         OF THE STATE OF NEW YORK . . . BY JUSTITIUS.
                  Albany: Printed by Barker & Southwick. . . . 1799.   15pp.   8vo.   LOC, NYHS.

36202   REMMEY, JOHN
              AN ACCOUNT OF THE PRESENT STATE OF EGYPT. . . . TO WHICH IS ADDED, AN APPENDIX, CONTAIN-
              ING AN . . . ACCOUNT OF THE LATE NAVAL ACTION IN THE ROAD OF ABOUKIR, WITH AN
              ACCURATE PLAN. . . . ILLUSTRATED BY A MAP OF EGYPT AND PART OF SYRIA. . . .
                  New York: Printed for John Reid, no. 106, Water Street, by M. L. & W. A. Davis.
         1799.   pp. 107, [1].   8vo.
         The two maps were engraved by Tanner.
                                            AAS, AHTS, BA, BM, CU, HC, LCP, LOC, NYHS, NYPL, NYSL, YC.

36203   RENSSELAERVILLE BAPTIST ASSOCIATION.
              THE MINUTES OF THE RENSSELAER-VILLE CONFERENCE, HELD AT THE HOUSE OF BROTHER SIMEON
              CHURCH, IN RENSSELAERVILLE, ON THE SEVENTEENTH AND EIGHTEENTH OCTOBER, ONE
              THOUSAND SEVEN HUNDRED AND NINETY-EIGHT.
                  Albany: Printed by Charles R. and George Webster. . . . 1799.   7, [1] pp.   8vo.
                                                                                              SCBHC.

36204   —— THE MINUTES OF THE RENSSELAER-VILLE ASSOCIATION, HELD AT THE HOUSE OF ELDER JOSIAH
              BAKER, IN RENSSELAER-VILLE, ON THE SIXTEENTH AND SEVENTEENTH OCTOBER, ONE THOUSAND
              SEVEN HUNDRED AND NINETY-NINE.
                  Albany: Printed by Barber and Southwick. . . . MDCCXCIX.   8 pp.   8vo.
                                                                                              SCBHC.

36205   REPORTS OF COMMITTEES IN CONGRESS TO WHOM WERE REFERRED CERTAIN MEMORIALS AND PETITIONS
              . . . CONCERNING THE ALIEN AND SEDITION LAWS. AND ON THE NAVAL ESTABLISHMENT. . . .
              ALSO AN ANSWER OF THE MASSACHUSETTS LEGISLATURE TO THE VIRGINIA RESOLUTIONS. . . .
                  Richmond, Printed by Thomas Nicolson, 1799.   pp. 20.   8vo.   LOC.

36206   [THE REPUBLICAN.   DEC. 1799–1827
                  Petersburg, Va., printed by Lyon & Field.   fol.   weekly.]
                                                                       FOR 1799: NO COPY KNOWN.

36207   THE REPUBLICAN CALENDAR FOR THE YEAR OF OUR LORD 1800. . . . CONTAINING . . . A LARGE AND
              CORRECT LIST OF ROADS, &C. . . .
                  Washington, (Penn.) Printed by John Israel, opposite the Court house. . . .   pp.
         [36].   12mo.   AAS.

36208   REPUBLICAN Journal.   1796–1800
          Danbury: compiled by Stiles Nichols for Douglas & Nichols. 1799.   weekly.   fol.
                                                                                          [AAS].

36209   THE REPUBLICAN Ledger.   Aug. 29? 1799–1803
          Portsmouth, (New-Hampshire). Printed by George Jerry Osborne, jun.   weekly.
        fol.   For 1799: [DC].

36210   [REPUBLICAN Star, or, Eastern Shore Political Luminary.   1799–1833
          *Easton, (Maryland): printed and published every Tuesday morning, by Thomas
        Perrin Smith, 1799.*   fol.   weekly.]   For 1799: no copy known.

36211   RESOUTIONS agreed to in Committee of the Whole, July 27, 1799. I. Resolved, that from
        the 8th to the 15th section inclusive. . . .
          [*Lexington, Ky., printed by John Bradford?*]   Broadside.   8vo.   LOC.

36212   RESOLUTIONS and proceedings in Committee of the whole, on the 29th day of July,
        1799. . . .
          [*Lexington: printed by John Bradford?*]   Broadside.   8vo.   LOC.

36213   RESOLUTIONS and proceedings in Committee of the whole, on the 1st day of August,
        1799. . . .
          [*Lexington: printed by John Bradford?*]   Broadside.   8vo.   LOC.

36214   RHODE Island. State.
          [An Act to incoporate Washington Lodge No. 3, of Free and Accepted Masons in the
        town of Warren.
          Warren: Printed by Nathaniel Phillips, 1799.]   Broadside.   fol.
        George Haile Free Library, Warren (not found 1951).

36215   — At the General Assembly . . . holden at East-Greenwich, on the last Monday of
        February, A. D. 1799. An Act to incoporate the Newport Insurance Company. . . .
          [*Colophon:*] *Newport: Printed by H. & O. Farnsworth.*   pp. 10.   16mo.
                                                                          AAS, NHS, RIHS.

36216   — By His Excellency Arthur Fenner, Esq; governor . . . a proclamation. Whereas the
        General Assembly . . . this fifth day of November . . . one thousand seven hundred
        and ninety-nine. . . .
          [*Providence:*] *Printed by John Carter.*   Broadside.   fol.   AAS, RIHS.

36217   — February, 1799. At the General Assembly of the State of Rhode Island . . . begun . . .
        at East-Greenwich . . . on the last Monday in February, in the year of Our Lord
        one thousand seven hundred and ninety-nine. . . .
          [*Colophon:*] *Newport, Printed by Oliver Farnsworth. . . .*   pp. 21.   4to.
                                          AAS, BʳU, CSL, HC, JCB, LOC, MSL, NYBA, NYPL, RIHS.

36218   — May 1799. At the General Assembly of the State of Rhode-Island . . . begun . . . at
        Newport . . . on the first Wednesday in May, in the year of Our Lord, one thousand
        seven hundred and ninety-nine. . . .
          [*Colophon:*] *Newport, Printed by Oliver Farnsworth. . . .*   pp. 22.   4to.
                                          AAS, BʳU, CSL, HSP, JCB, LOC, MSL, NYBA, NYPL, RIHS, RISL.

36219   — June, 1799. At a General Assembly of the State of Rhode-Island . . . begun . . . at
        Newport . . . on the second Monday in June, in the year of Our Lord one thousand
        seven hundred and ninety-nine. . . .
          [*Colophon:*] *Newport, Printed by Oliver Farnsworth. . . .*   pp. 16.   4 to.
                                          AAS, BʳU, CSL, JCB, LOC, MHS, MSL, NYBA, NYPL, RIHS, RISL.

36220   —— OCTOBER, 1798. AT THE GENERAL ASSEMBLY OF . . . THE STATE OF RHODE-ISLAND . . . BEGUN
         . . . ON THE LAST MONDAY IN OCTOBER, IN THE YEAR OF OUR LORD ONE THOUSAND SEVEN
         HUNDRED AND NINETY-EIGHT. . . .
                 [Colophon:] Newport: Printed by H. & O. Farnsworth. . . . M,DCC,XCIX.   pp.
         26.   4to.   AAS, CSL, HC, HSP, JCB, LOC, MSL, NYBA, RIHS, RISL.

36221   —— PUBLIC LAWS OF THE STATE OF RHODE-ISLAND AND PROVIDENCE PLANTATIONS, PASSED SINCE THE
         SESSION OF . . . JANUARY, A. D. 1798. . . .
                 Newport: Printed by H. & O. Farnsworth. . . .   pp. 18.   8vo.
         This printing includes the laws of February, 1799. See Alden 1644.
                                                         AAS, CSL, HC, JCB, MSL, RIHS.

36222   —— 1799. HIS EXCELLENCY ARTHUR FENNER, ESQ; GOVERNOR. THE HONOURABLE GEORGE BROWN,
         ESQ; DEPUTY-GOVERNOR. . . .
                 [Providence;] Printed by John Carter. jun.   Broadside.   8vo.   RIHS.

36223   —— 1799. HIS EXCELLENCY ARTHUR FENNER, ESQ; GOVERNOR. THE HONOURABLE SAMUEL J. POTTER,
         ESQ; DEPUTY-GOVERNOR. . . .
                 [Providence:] Printed by Carter and Wilkinson.   Broadside.   12mo.
         There are two settings of this broadside.   RIHS.

36224   —— 1799. JOHN BROWN, ESQ. GOVERNOR. THOMAS G. HAZZARD, ESQ; DEPUTY-GOVERNOR. . . .
                 [Newport:] Printed by O. Farnsworth.   Broadside.   8vo.   RIHS.

36225   —— SUPREME JUDICIAL COURT. LIME. FEES.
                 [Newport: Printed by Oliver Farnsworth.]   pp. 19–26.   8vo.
         Running title only. This is the continuation of the *Public Laws*, above, and contains the
         acts of the sessions of May and June, 1799.   AAS, CSL, HC, JCB, MSL, RIHS, RISL.

36226   RHODE ISLAND COLLEGE.
                 COMMENCEMENT OF RHODE-ISLAND COLLEGE, SEPTEMBER 4, 1799. ORDER OF THE EXERCISES. . . .
                 [Providence:] Printed by John Carter, jun.   Broadside.   4to.   BʳU.

36227   —— ILLUSTRISSIMO JABEZ BOWEN, ARMIGERO, COLLEGII RHOD. INSULAE QUOD PROVIDENTIAE EST. . . .
         DIE QUARTO SEPTEMBRIS, A. D. M,DCCXCIX.
                 Providentiae: Typis Johannis Carter, jun.   Broadside.   fol.   BʳU.

36228   RHODES, JOHN   1755–
                 THE SURPRISING ADVENTURES AND SUFFERING OF JOHN RHODES. . . . AN ACCOUNT OF HIS
         CAPTIVITY . . . WITH THE INDIANS. . . .
                 Newark, Printed by Pennington and Dodge, for R. Cotton, New York, 1799.
         pp. 268.   16mo.
         In other editions the name of the adventurer is given as John Roach.
                                           AAS, BA, JCB, LOC, NL, NYHS, NYPL, NYSL, PPL, YC.

36229   RICHARDS, GEORGE   –1814
                 SOLEMN DIRGE! (L. M.) BY THE REV. MR. RICHARDS. . . . MASONIC HYMN. (C. M.) BY THE
         REV. BROTHER RICHARDS. . . .
                 From the press of the Federal Observer [Portsmouth, N. H.]   Broadside.   fol.
         Washington memorial verse composed for the service at St. John's Chapel, December 31,
         1799.   AAS, HC.

36230   RICHARDSON, SAMUEL   1689–1761
                 THE HISTORY OF PAMELA; OR, VIRTUE REWARDED. ABRIDGED FROM THE WORKS OF SAMUEL
         RICHARDSON, ESQ.
                 Norristown: Printed and sold by David Sower. 1799.   pp. 156.   24mo.
                                                                           AAS, HSP, PPL.

36231   —— —— —— *Fairhaven (Vermont) printed by Judah P. Spooner, 1799.*   H. G. RUGG.

36232 [RICHARDSON, WILLIAM]   1742–1814
    THE CACIQUE OF ONTARIO, BEING AN ENTERTAINING, MORAL, AND INSTRUCTIVE HISTORY OF TWO
    LOVERS, FOUNDED UPON FACTS.
        Stonington-Port. Printed by Samuel Trumbull, and sold at his office, 1799.   pp. 24.
    16mo.
    An alteration of Richardson's *The Indians, a Tale.*   AAS, NYPL, YC.

36233 [RIGHTS OF MAN.   1794–1800
        Frederick-Town, (State of Maryland): Printed by John Winter . . . 1799.   fol.
    weekly.]   FOR 1799: NO COPY KNOWN.

36234 RIGHTS OF MAN.   FEB.–APR. 1799
        Nashville: — printed by John M'Laughlin.   fol.   weekly.   FOR 1799: [UOC].

36235 [THE RIGHTS OF MAN.   1799–1806
        Newburgh, N. Y., published by Benoni H. Howell, for Elias Winfield.   fol.
    weekly.]   FOR 1799: NO COPY KNOWN.

36236 [ROBERTSON, JOHN]   1712–1796
    TABLES OF DIFFERENCE OF LATITUDE AND DEPARTURE: CONSTRUCTED TO EVERY QUARTER OF A
    DEGREE. . . .
        Wilmington: Printed by Bonsal and Niles, for Zachariah Jess. M,DCCXCIX.   pp.
    [1], 91, [3], 60.   8vo.
    Usually found bound with Jess, *Compendious System of Practical Surveying.*
                                            AAS, DHS, JCB, LOC, NYPL, NYSL.

36237 ROBERTSON, WILLIAM   1721–1793
    THE HISTORY OF AMERICA, BOOKS IX. AND X. CONTAINING THE HISTORY OF VIRGINIA TO THE
    YEAR 1688; AND OF NEW ENGLAND TO THE YEAR 1652. . . .
        *Philadelphia: Printed from the London edition by James Humphreys, and sold by
    him. . . . 1799.*   pp. 196, [2].   8vo.
    The last leaf contains advertisements.   AAS, BPL, JCB, MHS, NYPL, NYSOC, PSL, RIHS, VᵃU, YC.

36238 ROBINSON, JAMES
    ROBINSON'S PHILADELPHIA REGISTER AND CITY DIRECTORY, FOR 1799. . . .
        Philadelphia: Printed by John Bioren . . . 1799.   pp. 16, 154, 17–50, 24.   12mo.
                                            APS, LCP.

36239 ROBISON, JOHN   1739–1805
    EXTRACTS FROM PROFESSOR ROBISON'S "PROOFS OF A CONSPIRACY," &C. WITH BRIEF REFLECTIONS
    ON THE CHARGES. . . .
        Boston: Printed by Manning & Loring. 1799.   pp. 30.   8vo.
    Signed "Cornelius" and dated "Massachusetts, Dec. 1798."   AAS, BA, HC, NYHS.

36240 ROCHE, REGINA MARIA   1764–1845
    [CHILDREN OF THE ABBEY; A TALE. BY REGINA MARIA ROCHE, AUTHOR OF THE MAID OF THE
    HAMLET, &C.
        New-York: Printed for H. Caritat . . . 1799.   4 vol. in two.   12mo.]   EVANS.

36241 RODGERS, JOHN   1773–1838
    [A GLORIOUS VICTORY BY ONE OF OUR "USELESS FRIGATES," AS THEY ARE SEDITIOUSLY TERMED BY
    THE INGRATES. [COPY OF A LETTER:] "ON BOARD THE PRIZE FRIGATE L'INSURGENTE, ST.
    CHRISTOPHERS, 15TH FEB. 1799. . . ."
        Baltimore, 1799.]   MINICK 537

36242 ROMAN CATHOLIC CHURCH. COUNCIL OF BALTIMORE.
    [ORDO DIVINI OFFICII RECITANDI . . . PRO ANNO DOMINI MDCCC.
        Baltimore.]   PARSONS 210.

36243 THE ROMANS IN GREECE.
    See 35160.

36244 ROOT, Erastus   1773–1846
      [An Introduction to arithmetic for the use of common schools. By Erastus Root.
            Printed by Thomas Hubbard for the author, Norwich, 1799.]   Bates 2576.

36245 ROSS, James   1744–1827
      [A Practical, new vocabulary, Latin and English . . . serving to exemplify and illustrate
      the rules . . . in the Latin grammar. . . .
            Chambersburg: Printed by Snowdon & M'Corkle.]
      228th Pennsylvania District copyright issued to James Ross on March 30, 1799. Advertised
      as for sale, but no copy seen.

36246 [ROWSON, Susanna Roswell]   1761–1824
      Captain Truxton or huzza! for the Constellation. Sung by Mr. Tyler at the theatre
      with the greatest applause.
            *New York. Printed at J. Hewitt's Musical Repository. . . . Sold also by B. Carr,
      Philadelphia & J. Carr, Baltimore. . . .*   pp. [2].   4to.
      The attribution to Mrs. Rowson is very dubious.   LOC.

36247 [——] Huzza for the Constellation. Sung by Mr. Fox at the theatre.
            *Printed & sold at B. Carr's Musical repository, Philadelphia; J. Carr's, Baltimore &
      J. Hewitt's, N. York. . . .*   pp. 3.   fol.
      Attribution to Mrs. Rowson very dubious.   LOC, MᵈHS, NL.

36248 —— Truxton's victory. A naval patriotic song. Sung by Mr. Hodgkinson. Written by Mrs.
      Rowson, of Boston.
            [*Boston: Printed by Thomas and Andrews. Published at P. A. von Hagen jun. and
      Co's.*]   pp. [2].   fol.   AAS.

36249 RUDIMENTS of taste. . . .
            See Peddle, Mrs.

36250 RULES and regulations for the Social Library in the town of Bath. Instituted 1st June, 1799.
            Broadside.   fol.   AAS.

36251 RUMFORD, Sir Benjamin Thompson, Count.   1753–1814
      Essays, political, economical, and philosophical. . . . The first American, from the third
      London, edition. Vol. II.
            *Boston: Printed by Manning & Loring, for David West. . . . Cornhill; by Ebenezer
      S. Thomas, Charleston, S. Carolina; and by Solomon Cotton & Co. Baltimore. August,
      1799.*   pp. [18], 496, 11 plates, 1 folding plate.   8vo.
      The first volume was printed in Boston in 1798 and the third in 1804.
                        AAS, AML, BA, BM, BPL, BʳU, HEH, LCP, LOC, NL, NYPL, NYSOC, YC.

36252 THE RURAL Magazine. Volume I. Number 47. Saturday, January 5, [to Number 52, Saturday,
      February 9, 1799]:
            Newark — Printed by John H. Williams. . . . 1799.   fol.
                                                    AAS, JCB, LOC, NJHS, NJSL, NYHS.

36253 RUSH, Benjamin   1745–1813
      Observations upon the origin of the malignant bilious, or yellow fever in Philadel-
      phia. . . .
            *Philadelphia: Printed by Budd and Bartram, for Thomas Dobson, at the Stone House,
      no. 41, South Second Street. 1799.*   pp. 28.   8vo.
                        AAS, AML, BA, BML, BPL, HSP, JCB, LCP, LOC, NYAM, NYHS, NYPL, PSL, RU, UOP, YC.

36254 —— A Second address to the citizens of Philadelphia, containing additional proofs of the
      domestic origin of the malignant bilious, or yellow fever. . . .
            *Philadelphia: Printed by Budd and Bartram, for Thomas Dobson, at the Stone
      House, no. 41, South Second Street. 1799.*   pp. 40.   8vo.   AML, BA, LOC, NYHS, PʳU, UOP, YC.

36255 — Three lectures upon animal life, delivered in the University of Pennsylvania. . . .
Philadelphia: Printed by Budd and Bartram, for Thomas Dobson, at the Stone House,
no. 41, South Second Street. 1799.   pp. viii, 84.   8vo.
AAS, AML, BPL, HSP, JCB, LCP, LOC, MFM, MHS, NYAM, NYHS, NYPL, PᵗU, UOP.

36256 RUSSELL, John Miller   1768–1840
The Pastoral songs of P. Virgil Maro. To which are added, poems, sentimental and
descriptive. . . .
Boston: Manning & Loring. 1799.   pp. 92.   12mo.   BA, BPL, BᵗU, NYHS.

36257 RUSSELL, Joseph   1775–1861
An Oration; pronounced in Princeton, Massachusetts . . . July 4, 1799. . . .
Printed at Worcester: by Isaiah Thomas, Jun. July — 1799.   pp. 29.   8vo.
AAS, BA, BPL, HC, JCB, NYPL, PL.

36258 J. RUSSELL'S Gazette. Commercial and political.   1798–1800
Published on Mondays and Thursdays, by John Russell, at his office, in Quaker-Lane,
Boston.   fol.   semi-weekly.   For 1799: AAS, BA, BPL, CHS, EI, LOC, MHS, NYPL.

36259 RUSSEL'S Echo.   1789–Jan. 11, 1799
Published by Elijah Russel, Fryeburg, District of Maine.   fol.   weekly.
For 1799: [HC].

36260 RUTHERFORD, Thomas   1712–1771
Institutes of natural law: being the substance of a course of lectures on Grotius De
Jure Belli et Pacis. . . . 3d. ed.
Whitehall: Printed for William Young, bookseller. . . . Philadelphia M,DCC,XCIX.
2 vol.   8vo.   BPL, BᵗU, HSP, LOC, PᵗU, UOP.

36261 RUTLAND County. Vermont.
See To the Representatives of the Freemen of the United States of America.

36262 THE RUTLAND Herald.   1794–1920
Printed at Rutland, (Vermont) by John Walker, jun. for S. Williams & Co. . . .
fol.   weekly.   For 1799: [VᵗSL].

36263 [S., R.]
Jachin and Boaz; or, an authentic key to the door of Free-Masonry. . . . Illustrated
with an accurate plan of the drawing on the floor of a lodge. . . . By a gentleman
belonging to the Jerusalem Lodge. . . .
Suffield: Printed by Edward Gray. M,DCC,XCIX.   pp. 60.   16mo.
The earlier editions contain an advertisement signed "R. S."   AAS.

36264 SACRED music, to be performed in St. Paul's Church. . . .
See New York. City. St. Paul's Church.

36265 SACRED to the memory of Mr. Ebenezer Jenckes, son of the late John Jenckes. . . . Died
at the island of St. Thomas . . . April 26, 1799. . . .
[Providence, printed by John Carter, jr.]   Broadside.   8vo.   AAS, JCB, RIHS.

36266 SAINT Pierre, [Jacques Henri Bernardin de]   1737–1814
Beauties of the studies of nature: selected from the works of Saint Pierre. . . .
London — printed, 1799. New-York: Re-printed for H. Caritat . . . by M. L. & W. A.
Davis. 1799.   pp. 332, [3].   8vo.
The last three pages contain the table of contents.   AAS, BPL, HC, JCB, NYPL, YC.

36267 — Paul and Virginia, an Indian story. Translated from the French. . . . By H[enry]
Hunter, D. D. . . .
Printed at Wrentham, (Mass.) by Nathl. and Benj. Heaton, for E. Goodale, Mendon;
and S. Warriner, Jun. Wilbraham. M,DCC,XCIX.   pp. 180.   24mo.
AAS, BA, HEH, JCB, LOC, MHS, NYPL, YC.

36268   SALEM, MASSACHUSETTS. JOHN DUTCH.
         [A LARGE COLLECTION OF BOOKS. . . . SOLD AT HIS OFFICE, COURT STREET, SALEM, MASS.,
         APR. 17, 1799.]   McKAY 142D.

36269   SALEM. MASSACHUSETTS. THEATRE WASHINGTON HALL.
         LAST NIGHT OF PERFORMING THIS SEASON, THEATRE WASHINGTON HALL, OF FRIDAY EVENING, JUNE
         14TH, WILL BE PERFORMED THE CELEBRATED COMEDY, OF THE SPOILED CHILD. . . .
                 [*Salem.*]   Broadside.   fol.   EI.

36270   SALEM, MASSACHUSETTS. WILLIAM LANG.
         [THE REMAINDER OF A LARGE CATALOGUE OF BOOKS; TO WHICH HAVE SINCE BEEN ADDED MANY
         WORTH ATTENTION. . . . SOLD AT HIS OFFICE, ESSEX STREET, SALEM, MASS., DEC. 31, 1799.]
                                                                            McKAY 142M.

36271   THE SALEM GAZETTE.   1790–1908
                 Published on Tuesdays and Fridays, by Thomas C. Cushing . . . Salem, Massachusetts.
         fol.   semi-weekly.   FOR 1799: AAS, BA, BPL, EI, HC, LOC, NYHS, NYPL, NYSL, YC.

36272   —— INTERESTING INTELLIGENCE. SALEM, TUESDAY, NOV. 26, BY CAPT. JOHN FAIRFIELD, WHO ARRIVED
         HERE THIS DAY FROM HAMBURG. . . .
                 [*Salem: Printed by Thomas C. Cushing.*]   Broadside.   EI.

36273   —— TO THE PATRONS OF THE SALEM GAZETTE, THE CARRIERS PRESENT THE COMPLIMENTS OF THE SEASON
         AND THE FOLLOWING ADDRESS. . . .
                 [*Salem: Printed by Thomas C. Cushing.*]   Broadside.   Printed on silk.   EI.

36274   SANDERS, CHARLOTTE
         THE LITTLE FAMILY. CONTAINING A VARIETY OF MORAL AND PHILOSOPHICAL MATTER. WRITTEN
         FOR THE AMUSEMENT AND INSTRUCTION OF YOUNG PERSONS. . . .
                 Printed at Haverhill, Massachusetts: by Moore & Stebbins, for David West . . .
         Boston. 1799.   2 vols. in 1.   pp. 143, [1], 140.   12mo.
                                                      AAS, BPL, EI, HC, LOC, NYPL, NYSL.

36275   [THE SARATOGA REGISTER: OR, FARMER'S JOURNAL.   1798–1800
                 Ballston Spa: Published by Increase & William Child.   weekly.   fol.]
                                                         FOR 1799: NO COPY KNOWN.

36276   SASSE, BERNHARD HENRICH
         GEISTLICHE LIEDER, VON BERNHARD HENRICH SASSE, EINEM IN KIRCH-LENGERN. ERSTE [UND
         ZWEYTE] SAMMLUNG. . . .
                 Minden gedruckt, 1781. Hägerstaun nach gedruckt, bey Joh. Gruber. 1799.   pp. 36,
         [2], 42.   24mo.   AAS, EPFL.

36277   SAUNDERS, RICHARD, *pseud.*
         POOR RICHARD IMPROVED: BEING AN ALMANACK AND EPHEMERIS . . . FOR THE YEAR OF OUR LORD
         1800. . . .
                 Philadelphia: Printed and Sold by Hall & Sellers — no. 51 — Market-Street.
         pp. [44].   12mo.   AAS, HEH.

36278   SAY, BENJAMIN   1756–1813
         AN ANNUAL ORATION PRONOUNCED BEFORE THE HUMANE SOCIETY OF PHILADELPHIA, ON THE
         OBJECTS & BENEFITS OF SAID INSTITUTION; THE 28TH DAY OF FEBRUARY, 1799. . . .
                 Whitehall: Printed for William Young . . . no. 52, South Second-Street, Philadelphia.
         M,DCC,XCIX.   pp. 50.   8vo.
         With the Charter of incorporation of the Society and directions for recovering persons
         who are supposed to be dead from drowning, pp. 27–49.   AAS, AML, APS, HSP, JCB, NYPL, YC.

36279   SCHENECTADY, APRIL 13TH, 1799. IN COMMITTEE. . . . SIR, IT IS THE OPINION OF A GREAT MANY
         OF THE RESPECTABLE ELECTORS OF THE CITY OF SCHENECTADY. . . .
                 Broadside.   8vo.
         Solicits votes for the election of Jeremiah Van Rensselaer to the legislature.   NYHS.

36280 SCHENECTADY GAZETTE. 1799–1802
    Schenectady, (State of New-York) printed by John L. Stevenson. . . . fol.
weekly. FOR 1799: [HC].

36281 SCOTT, J[OHN], OF ISLINGTON, ENGLAND.
    WAR INCONSISTENT WITH THE DOCTRINE AND EXAMPLE OF JESUS CHRIST. . . . BY I. SCOTT.
    Printed by W. W. Woodward, no. 17, Chestnut Street, Philadelphia. 1799. pp. 26.
16mo.
This tract is sometimes attributed to Job Scott, 1751–1793, but the author is identified
in the 2nd London edition, 1817, of tract no. 2 of the Society for the Promotion of
Permanent and Universal Peace. AAS, HSP.

36282 SCOTT, JOSEPH
    THE NEW AND UNIVERSAL GAZETTEER; OR, MODERN GEOGRPHICAL DICTIONARY. . . . ILLUSTRATED
    WITH TWENTY-FIVE MAPS, AN ARMILLARY SPHERE, AND SEVERAL DIAGRAMS. . . . IN FOUR
    VOLUMES. . . .
    Philadelphia: Printed by Francis & Robert Bailey. . . . 1799. pp. xxxviii, [410],
6 maps; [436], 4 maps. 8vo.
Volumes 3 and 4 were published in 1800.
        AAS, BPL, EPFL, HSP, LOC, NYHS, NYPL, NYSL, PᵣU, UOP.

36283 SCOTT, WILLIAM, *of Edinburgh*
    LESSONS IN ELOCUTION: OR, A SELECTION OF PIECES IN PROSE AND VERSE . . . WITH AN APPENDIX
    CONTAINING . . . ENGLISH GRAMMAR. . . .
    New-Haven: Printed by George Bunce. M,DCC,XCIX. pp. 322, [84]. 12mo.
Appended, with signatures continuous but without pagination, is the "Elements of Gesture"
illustrated with cuts. AAS, RU, YC.

36284 —— —— TO THIS EDITION ARE PREFIXED, ELEMENTS OF GESTURE, ILLUSTRATED BY FOUR PLATES. . . .
    New-York: Printed by Thomas Kirk. 1799. pp. [1], 396, 4 plates. 12mo. AAS.

36285 —— —— THE EIGHTH AMERICAN, FROM THE FIFTH BRITISH EDITION. TO WHICH IS PREFIXED,
    ELEMENTS OF GESTURE, ILLUSTRATED BY FOUR ELEGANT COPPER PLATES. . . .
    *Whitehall: printed for William Young, bookseller and stationer, N. 52 South Second-
Street, Philadelphia. M,DCC,XCIX.* pp. viii, [13]–436, 4 plates. 12mo. AAS.

36286 THE SECRET HISTORY OF ELIZABETH, QUEEN OF ENGLAND, AND THE EARL OF ESSEX. TO WHICH
    IS ADDED, AN ACCOUNT OF THE SUFFERINGS, TRIAL AND BEHEADING OF MARY, QUEEN OF SCOT-
    LAND, BY QUEEN ELIZABETH. . . .
    Rutland, [Vermont:] Printed for S. Williams, Esq. 1799. pp. 80. 16mo. AAS.

36287 SELECT PAMPHLETS RESPECTING THE YELLOW FEVER, VIZ. I. A SHORT ACCOUNT OF THE MALIGNANT
    FEVER, PREVALENT IN PHILADELPHIA . . . IN . . . 1793. . . . BY MATHEW CAREY. II. AN
    ENQUIRY INTO . . . THE CAUSES AND EFFECTS OF THE EPIDEMIC . . . IN PHILADELPHIA. . . .
    BY JEAN DEVEZE. . . . III. A TREATISE OF THE SYNOCHUS ICTEROIDES, OR YELLOW FEVER. . . .
    BY WILLIAM CURRIE. . . . IV. A SHORT HISTORY OF THE YELLOW FEVER. . . . BY RICHARD
    FOLWELL. V. HISTORY OF THE PESTILENCE. . . . BY THOMAS CONDIE AND RICHARD FOLWELL.
    Philadelphia: Published by Mathew Carey, no. 118, Market Street. (price two dollars.)
pp. [2], 160; vii, [8], 145; [iv], 6–[viii], 85; 64, [16]; 108, xxxii, [67]. 8vo.
The pamphlets are described separately as Evans 26736, 26873, 26837, 26747, 33742, 35335.
Different issues of the pamphlets included cause variant pagination. JCB, NYAM, NYPL.

36288 [SERLE, AMBROSE] 1742–1812
    THE CHRISTIAN REMEMBRANCER. . . . SECOND AMERICAN EDITION. . . .
    Chambersburg: From the press of Snowden & M'Corkle. March 30, 1799.
pp. iv, 272. 16mo.
Contains a seven-page list of subscribers. AAS, HEH.

36289   —— HORAE SOLITARIAE; OR, ESSAYS UPON SOME REMARKABLE NAMES AND TITLES OF JESUS CHRIST.
        . . . VOL. I. FIRST AMERICAN, FROM THE SECOND LONDON EDITION.
            Philadelphia: Printed by Patterson & Cochran, no. 108, Race-Street.   pp. [2], 430.
        8vo.
        An inserted page of recommendations which is missing in some copies in original bindings
        is dated June, 1799. The second volume appeared in 1801.   AAS, JCB, NYPL, NYSL, YC.

36290   SERMONS ON VARIOUS IMPORTANT DOCTRINES. . . .
            See Hampshire County, Massachusetts, Northern Association, in previous volume.

36291   SEVEN CHAMPIONS OF CHRISTENDOM.
            THE ILLUSTRIOUS AND RENOWNED HISTORY OF THE SEVEN FAMOUS CHAMPIONS OF CHRISTEN-
        DOM. . . .
            Amherst, New Hampshire: Printed by Samuel Preston. 1799.   pp. 120.   12mo.
            This work is attributed to Richard Johnson, 1573–1659.   AAS.

36292   SEWALL, DANIEL   1755–1842
            AN ASTRONOMICAL DIARY, OR ALMANAC, FOR THE YEAR OF CHRISTIAN AERA, 1800. CALCULATED FOR
            THE MERIDIAN OF PORTSMOUTH, NEW-HAMPSHIRE. . . .
                *Portsmouth, New-Hampshire: Printed by Charles Peirce, no. 5, Daniel-street; sold by
            him . . . also, by the author at his office in York. . . .*   pp. [24].   12mo.   AAS.

36293   [——] BICKERSTAFF'S ALMANACK; FOR THE YEAR OF CHRISTIAN AERA, 1800. CALCULATED FOR THE NEW
            ENGLAND STATES. . . .
                *Printed for, and sold by, the booksellers in Boston, and the country traders [by
            Charles Peirce, Portsmouth, N. H.]*
            The text is identical with that of the Weatherwise almanac which also has Peirce's
            colophon.   AAS, BPL.

36294   SEWALL'S SHEET ALMANAC, FOR 1800. . . .
                *Portsmouth, (New-Hampshire,) printed at Oracle-Press, by Charles Peirce, sold by
            him . . . and by the booksellers in Boston, Salem, Newburyport, &c. &c.*   Broadside.
            fol.   AAS.

36295   SHAFTSBURY BAPTIST ASSOCIATION.
            MINUTES OF THE SHAFTSBURY ASSOCIATION; HOLDEN AT [STEPHENTOWN] . . . JUNE, 5TH & 6TH
            1799. . . .
                Pittsfield: Printed by Chester Smith. . . . 1799.   pp. 12.   8vo.   AAS.

36296   SHARP, JOSHUA
            CITIZEN AND FARMER'S ALMANAC FOR THE YEAR 1800. . . . CONTAINING . . . ASTRONOMICAL CAL-
            CULATIONS BY JOSHUA SHARP. . . .
                Philadelphia: Printed and sold by John M'Culloch, no. 1. North Third Street.
            pp. [36].   12mo.   AAS, LOC.

36297   —— FATHER TAMMANY'S ALMANAC, FOR THE YEAR 1800. . . . CONTAINING . . . ASTRONOMICAL CAL-
            CULATIONS, BY JOSHUA SHARP. . . .
                *Philadelphia: Printed for William Young, no. 52, the Corner of Chestnut and Second
            Street.*   pp. [36].   12mo.   AAS.

36298   —— —— —— *Philadelphia: Printed for David Hogan, no. 222, South Third-Street.*   pp. [36].
            12mo.   LOC.

36299   SHAW, ROBERT G.
            [A LARGE, VALUABLE AND WELL CHOSEN ASSORTMENT OF BOOKS, INTIRELY NEW, IN THE SEVERAL
            BRANCHES OF USEFUL AND POLITE LITERATURE. . . . SOLD AT HIS OFFICE, BOSTON, SEPT. 19,
            1799.]   McKAY 142K.

36300   SHAW, WILLIAM   1741–1816
            THE RESURRECTION OF GOOD MEN . . . A DISCOURSE, DELIVERED AT PLYMOUTH, JULY 14, 1799 . . .
            AFTER THE DEATH . . . OF . . . CHANDLER ROBBINS. . . .
                Printed by Samuel Hall, no. 53, Cornhill, Boston. 1799.   pp. 24.   8vo.
                                AAS, AHTS, BA, BPL, CL, HC, JCB, NYHS, WL, YC.

36301 [SHERMAN, Thomas]
See Divine breathings, Evans 35412.

36302 SHOEMAKER, Abraham
The New-Jersey and New-York Almanac, for the year 1800. Being the fourth after leap year. . . .
Newark: Printed by Matthias Day, for Cornelius Davis . . . New York. pp. [36]. 12mo.
Includes "The way to make money plenty in every man's pocket. — By Dr. Franklin," and "A Profound Meditation upon a Broomstick. By Dean Swift." AAS, RU.

36303 —— —— —— *Newark: Printed by Matthias Day, for Parkhurst & Pennington.* pp. [36]. 12mo.
NJHS, NYPL.

36304 —— —— —— *Newark: Printed and sold by Jacob Halsey & Co.* pp. [36]. 12mo. LOC.

36305 —— The New-Jersey and Pennsylvania Almanac, for the year 1800. Being the fourth after leap-year. . . . Calculated for . . . Philadelphia. . . .
Trenton: Printed and sold . . . by Sherman, Hershon & Thomas, at their office, opposite the Indians-Queen Tavern. pp. [36]. 12mo.
AAS, HSP, LOC, NYHS, NYPL, NYSL, PʳU.

36306 —— —— Same, without the printers' address. AAS.

36307 —— The Town and country almanack, for . . . 1800. . . .
New York: Printed for and published by Longworth and Wheeler. . . . [From the press of J. C. Totten & Co.] pp. 36. 12mo. LOC, NJHS, RU.

36308 A SHORT history of late ecclesiastical oppressions. . . .
See Odgen, John Cosins.

36309 A SHORT introduction to Latin grammar, for the use of the university and academy of Pennsylvania, in Philadelphia. . . . Sixth edition. . . .
Philadelphia: Printed by Charles Cist, in Second-Street, near Race-Street, M,DCC,XCIX. pp. iv, 116. 12mo. AAS, NYPL.

36310 SIERRA Leone Company.
Substance of the reports delivered by the court of directors of the Sierra Leone Company. . . . To which is prefixed memoirs of Naimbanna, an African prince.
Philadelphia: Printed for Thomas Dobson, at the Stone-House. no. 41, South Second Street. 1799. pp. 22, [2], 168, 24, map. 12mo.
The map and the two reports are those published by Dobson in 1795 and described as Evans 29513 and 29514. AAS, LCP, NYPL, VªU.

36311 SIR, BEING a candidate for the office of assistant clerk to the House of Representatives of the State of Pennsylvania. . . . Your obedient servant [Thomas Lloyd].
Broadside. 8vo. NYHS.

36312 SIXTH Massachusetts Turnpike Corporation.
See Evans 35803.

36313 SKINNER, Ichabod L[ord] 1767–1852
A Farewell discourse, delivered at North-Coventry, November 11, 1798.
Hartford: Printed by Hudson & Goodwin. 1799. pp. 16. 8vo. CHS, YC.

36314 SLENDER, Robert, *pseud.*
See Freneau, Philip.

36315   A SMALL COLLECTION OF QUESTIONS & ANSWERS, FROM VARIOUS AUTHORS.
        Litchfield: Printed by Thomas Collier, 1799.   pp. 15.   16mo.   WL.

36316   SMITH, CHARLOTTE (TURNER)   1749–1806
        THE ROMANCE OF REAL LIFE. . . .
                Philadelphia: Printed by J. Carey, 16, Chestnut-Street. 1799.   pp. [2], 333, [1].
        24mo.
        The book consists of adaptations from *Les Causes Célébres* of Gayot de Pitaval.
                                                          AAS, HC, HSP, LCP, VᵃU.

36317   SMITH, JAMES   1737–1812
        AN ACCOUNT OF THE REMARKABLE OCCURRENCES IN THE LIFE AND TRAVELS OF COL. JAMES
        SMITH. . . .
                Lexington: Printed by John Bradford, on Main Street, 1799.   pp. 88.   8vo.
                                        HC, HEH, LOC, NL, NYHS, NYPL, UOP¹, WˡˢHS.

36318   SMITH, JOHN, *of Suffield, Conn.*
        AN ORATION PRONOUNCED JULY 4TH, 1799, AT THE REQUEST OF THE CITIZENS OF THE TOWN OF
        SUFFIELD. . . .
                Printed at Suffield, by Edward Gray, July, 1799.   pp. 15.   12mo.
                                                     AAS, CHS, JCB, LOC, NYPL.

36319   SMITH, JOSHUA   –1731
        DIVINE HYMNS, OR SPIRITUAL SONGS . . . A COLLECTION BY JOSHUA SMITH — AND OTHERS. NINTH
        EDITION WITH A LARGE ADDITION OF HYMNS NEVER BEFORE PUBLISHED. BY WILLIAM NORTHUP,
        V. D. M.
                Norwich: Printed and sold by John Sterry. 1799.   pp. 214.   12mo.   AAS, UTS.
36320   —— —— LATEST AND LARGEST EDITION.
                Portsmouth, N. H.: 1799.   pp. 168.   12mo.   HC.

36321   SMITH, SAMUEL   –1799
        LAST WORDS AND DYING SPEECH OF SAMUEL SMITH, WHO WAS EXECUTED AT CONCORD . . . THE
        26TH OF DECEMBER, A. D. 1799, FOR THE CRIME OF BURGLARY. . . .
                *To be sold at Mr. Reuben Bryant's Book-Store, Concord.—Also at Edes's Printing-
        Office, Kilby-Street, Boston.*   Broadside.   fol.
        The AAS has copies with and without a coffin in the upper right hand corner.   AAS, NYHS.

36322   SMITH, SAMUEL STANHOPE   1750–1819
        SERMONS, BY SAMUEL STANHOPE SMITH, D. D. PRESIDENT OF THE COLLEGE OF NEW-JERSEY.
        CORRECTED AND REVISED BY THE AUTHOR. . . .
                Newark, New-Jersey: Printed and sold by Jacob Halsey and Co. . . . 1799.   pp. viii,
        [2], 437, [9].   8vo.
        The pagination in the different copies varies because of the presence or absence of the
        list of subscribers, and similar irregularities.
                AAS, BPL, BʳU, CU, HC, HEH, JCB, LCP, LOC, NJHS, NPL, NYPL, NYSL, PPL, PʳU, YC.

36323   SMITH, WILLIAM   1754–1821
        A LETTER FROM CONNECTICUT TO ELDER ELIAS LEE, ANABAPTIST TEACHER IN THE VICINITY OF
        BALLSTOWN, STATE OF NEW-YORK.
                [*New Haven.*]   pp. 4.   8vo.
        Dated Norwalk, November 16th, 1799.   CU.

36324   [——] THE MASONIC BURIAL-OFFICE, AS OBSERVED BY THE GRAND LODGE OF THE STATE OF RHODE-
        ISLAND. . . .
                *Bennington, re-printed by Br. Anthony Haswell, for Br. Sampson Simans, an infirm,
        but deserving member of the Fraternity.*   pp. 8.   8vo.
        The author is identified in the votes of the Grand Lodge of Rhode Island of June 26, 1797,
        and June 27, 1798. For the first edition see Evans 35509.   AAS.

36325   —— AN OFFICE OF INDUCTION, ADOPTED BY THE BISHOP AND CLERGY OF THE DIOCESE OF CONNECTICUT,
        IN CONVOCATION, AT DERBY, NOV. 20TH, 1799. . . .
                Printed at New-Haven, by Thomas Green and Son.   pp. 8.   8vo.   CU, GTS, NYHS.

36326 SMITH, William [Moore]   1759–1821
 The Flowret. A collection of poems, written by William Smith, Esq. Attorney at law,
 Philadelphia. . . . The third edition.
  *First American edition printed by E. S. in Philadelphia. — Reprinted in London and
  now Baltimore, printed and sold by E. Story. 1799.*   pp. 141, [2], frontispiece.   12mo.
 The frontispiece represents a bust of the author.   LCP, NYHS.

36327 —— To the claimants under the Sixth Article of the Treaty of amity, commerce and naviga-
 tion, concluded between His Britannic Majesty and the United States of America.
 [Philadelphia.]   pp. 8.   4to.
 No titlepage. Dated, Philadelphia, January 8th, 1799.   JCB, NYPL.

36328 SMYTH, James Carmichael   1741–1821
 The Effect of the nitrous vapour, in preventing and destroying contagion. . . .
  *Philadelphia: Printed by Budd and Bartram, for Thomas Dobson, at the Stone
  House, no. 41, South Second Street. — 1799.*   pp. 174, 1 table.   8vo.
                             AAS, AML, APS, BML, CU, HC, LOC, NYAM, NYPL, YC.

36329 SOBERSIDES, Solomon, pseud.
 Christmas tales, for the amusement and instruction of young ladies and gentlemen in
 winter evenings. . . .
  Philadelphia: Printed by Robert Johnson, for B. and J. Johnson . . . 1799.   pp.
 144+, illust.   32mo.   HSP.

36330 THE SOCIAL companion, and songster's pocket book, a choice collection of new songs.
  *Portsmouth, N. H. Printed for and sold by Samuel Larkin, at the Portsmouth book-
  store, 1799. [Colophon:] Printed at the Oracle Press, in Portsmouth, September 1799.*
 pp. 60.   24mo.   AAS.

36331 SOCIAL harmony; containing first The Rudiments of psalmody made easy. Second, A
 Collection of modern music. . . . By Asahel Benham. . . . Published according to
 act of Congress.
  [Preface dated:] Wallingford, September 6, 1799.   pp. 56, [4].   obl. 12mo.
                                                                              AAS, WLC, YC.

36332 SOCIAL Library in the town of Bath.
 See Rules.

36333 SOCIETY for the Relief of Poor Widows with Small Children.
 See New York.

36334 SOME advice to governesses and teachers. Written by the author of The Evidence of the
 Existence of God. Supposed to be translated by Bishop Barclay.
  New-York: Printed by Isaac Collins, no. 189, Pearl-Street. 1799.   pp. 12.   12mo.
                                                                              BA, HC.

36335 SONGS and lullabies of the good old nurses. . . . Embellished with cuts; and illustrated
 with notes and maxims. . . . First Worcester edition.
  Printed at Worcester: Massachusetts, by Isaiah Thomas, Jun. . . . 1799.   pp. 29,
 [2], cuts.   32mo.   AAS, PPL.

36336 SOUTH Carolina. State.
 Acts and resolutions of the General Assembly, of the State of South-Carolina. Passed
 in December, 1798.
  Charles-ton: Printed by Young and Faust, printers to the State. M.DCC.XCIX.
 pp. 44, [2], 46, [1].   fol.   HC, HEH, JCB, NYBA.

36337 —— In the House of Representatives, November 29, 1799. Resolved, that 150 copies of the
 governor's message No. 2 . . . be printed. . . .
  [Colophon:] Columbia: Printed by Freneau & Paine, printers to the State.   pp. [3].
 fol.   LOC.

36338 SOUTH CAROLINA. FREE AND ACCEPTED MASONS.
    GRAND LODGE, ANTIENT YORK MASONS, OF THE STATE OF SOUTH CAROLINA, ASSEMBLED IN DUE
    FORM, THE 8TH DAY OF NOVEMBER, 1799.
            pp. [2].   8vo.   LIBRARY OF THE SUPREME COUNCIL OF THE 33°, WASHINGTON, D. C.

36339 THE SOUTH-CAROLINA & GEORGIA ALMANAC, FOR THE YEAR 1799. . . . THE SECOND EDITION. . . .
        Charleston: Printed by Freneau & Paine, no. 47, Bay.   pp. [46].   8vo.
    "With some alterations and additions made since the meeting of the Legislature," dated
    Feb. 12, 1799.   CLS.

36340 THE SOUTH CAROLINA & GEORGIA ALMANAC, FOR THE YEAR OF OUR LORD 1800. . . . ALSO A FRENCH
    AND A HEBREW CALENDAR. . . .
        Charleston: Printed by Freneau & Paine, no. 47, Bay.   pp. [40].   8vo.
                                                       AAS, LOC.

36341 —— —— SECOND EDITION.   LOC.

36342 THE SOUTH-CAROLINA STATE GAZETTE, AND GENERAL ADVERTISER.   1795–1830
        Columbia, South-Carolina. Published by Daniel Faust & Company.   fol.   weekly.
    With the issue of Nov. 29, William P. Young retired from the company, Faust became
    sole publisher, and the title was changed to *The South-Carolina Gazette, and Columbian
    Advertiser.*   FOR 1799: [HC].

36343 SOUTH-CAROLINA STATE GAZETTE, AND TIMOTHY'S DAILY ADVERTISER.   1794–1802
        [Charleston, printed and published by Benjamin Franklin Timothy.]   fol.   daily.
                                                 FOR 1799: AAS, [CLS].

36344 SOUTHERN CENTINEL.   1793–1799
        Augusta: [Ga.] Printed by Alexander M'Millan, printer to the State.   fol.   weekly.
                                                 FOR 1799: [GHS].

36345 SOUTHEY, ROBERT   1774–1843
    POEMS BY ROBERT SOUTHEY. . . . FIRST AMERICAN EDITION.
        Boston: Printed by Manning & Loring, for Joseph Nancrede, no. 49, Marlbro'-Street.
    1799.   pp. 132.   12mo.
    It is probable that some copies were issued without the advertising pages [126]–32.
               AAS, BPL, EI, HC, HSP, JCB, LCP, LOC, MHS, NYPL, NYSL, PᵗU, YC.

36346 SPALDING, JOHN   1765–1795
    SOME ACCOUNT OF THE CONVINCEMENT, AND RELIGIOUS PROGRESS OF JOHN SPAULDING; LATE OF
    READING. WITH HIS REASONS FOR LEAVING THE NATIONAL ESTABLISHED MODE OF WORSHIP.
        Philadelphia: Printed by Benjamin & Jacob Johnson, no. 147, High Street. 1799.
    pp. 70.   8vo.   AAS, HC, HSP, LOC, NYHS, PSL, YC.

36347 SPALDING, LYMAN   1775–1821
    A NEW NOMENCLATURE OF CHEMISTRY, PROPOSED BY MESSRS. DE MORVEAU, LAVOISIER, BERTHOLLET,
    AND FOURENOY: WITH ADDITIONS AND IMPROVEMENTS, BY LYMAN SPALDING, M. B. LECTURER
    IN CHEMISTRY IN DARTMOUTH UNIVERSITY.
        Hanover, (N. H.) Printed by Moses Davis. 1799.   pp. 16.   4to.
                                AML, HC, LOC, MHS, NYAM, NYHS.

36348 THE SPECTATOR.   1797–1879
        New-York . . . published (Wednesdays and Saturdays) by George F. Hopkins. . . .
    fol.   semi-weekly.
    In July Noah Webster, Jr., retired from the business, his place being taken by Ebenezer
    Belden, and the firm name was changed to E. Belden & Co.
            FOR 1799: AAS, BPL, CHS, LOC, MHS, NYHS, NYPL, NYSL, WᴵᴬHS, WLC, YC.

36349 SPIEGEL FÜR ALLE MENSCHEN. . . .
    See 35202.

36350 SPINDLESHANKS, PETER, *pseud.*
THE BATTLE OF THE TWO TAYLORS. AN EPIC POEM. . . .
Printed in the year 1799. pp. 12. 12mo. AAS.

36351 SPOONER'S VERMONT JOURNAL. 1783–
Windsor: Printed and published by Alden Spooner. . . . fol. weekly.
FOR 1799: AAS, VᵗSL.

36352 SPRINGER'S WEEKLY ORACLE. 1795–1800
Printed and published by James Springer, on the Parade, New-London. 1799. fol.
weekly. FOR 1799: [AAS], [HC].

36353 STAFFORD, CORNELIUS WILLIAM
THE PHILADELPHIA DIRECTORY, FOR 1799, CONTAINING THE NAMES, OCCUPATIONS, AND PLACES OF
ABODE OF THE CITIZENS . . . ALSO A REGISTER OF . . . THE UNITED STATES. . . .
Printed for the Editor, by William W. Woodward . . . *1799.* pp. 159, 78, [2]. 8vo.
LCP, LOC, YC.

36354 STAFFORD, H[OSEA], *pseud.*
AN ASTRONOMICAL DIARY, CALENDAR, OR ALMANACK, FOR . . . 1800. . . . CALCULATED FOR THE
MERIDIAN AND HORIZON OF NEW-HAVEN. . . .
New-Haven, printed & sold by T. Green & Son. pp. [24]. 12mo.
These almanacs are attributed by Dexter to Nehemiah Strong (1729–1807).
AAS, BPL, CHS, LOC, NYHS, NYPL, NYSL, YC.

36355 STANFORD, JOHN 1754–1834
A COLLECTION OF HYMNS. IN THREE PARTS. . . .
New-York: Printed by T. and J. Swords, 1799[–1806]. 3 v. in 1. 24mo.
Contains Stanford's *Collection of Evangelical Hymns,* 1793, *Collection of Society Hymns,*
1797, and *Collection of Hymns for Youth,* 1806. NYPL.

36356 —— THE GOODNESS OF GOD IN THE CONVERSION OF YOUTH: A SERMON ON THE DEATH OF CHARLES I. S.
HAZZARD . . . AN ACCOUNT OF HIS VERY EARLY ENJOYMENT OF THE GRACE OF GOD. . . .
TRANSCRIBED FROM THE DIARY WRITTEN WITH HIS OWN HAND. . . .
New-York: Printed by T. & J. Swords . . . *1799.* pp. 60. 12mo.
GTS, LOC, NYHS, NYSOC.

36357 THE STARRY CALCULATOR; BEING AN ALMANAC FOR THE YEAR OF OUR LORD, 1800. BEING A
CENTURIAL YEAR, AND NOT BISSEXTILE. . . .
Lancaster, printed by Henry and Benjamin Grimler. pp. [36]. 12mo. AAS.

36358 THE STATE GAZETTE, AND LOUISVILLE JOURNAL. 1798–1811
Louisville, Georgia. Published by Elisha H. Waldo. fol. weekly.
This is the paper recorded under its later title as Evans 35742. FOR 1799: [UOG].

36359 THE STATE GAZETTE & NEW-JERSEY ADVERTISER. 1796–FEB. 26, 1799
Printed by Matthias Day, Trenton. weekly. fol.
After the issue of Feb. 26, Day sold out to Sherman & Mershon who discontinued the
State Gazette and began the *New-Jersey State Gazette.* FOR 1799: [AAS], NJHS.

36360 STATE GAZETTE OF NORTH-CAROLINA. 1788–1799
Edenton [N. C.]: printed by James Wills. fol. weekly.
In March the title was changed to *The Herald of Freedom.* FOR 1799: [AAS].

36361 —— THE NEWS-BOY'S ADDRESS TO THE PATRONS OF THE STATE GAZETTE.
[Trenton] January 1, 1799. 4to. NYHS.

36362 A STATISTICAL TABLE FOR THE UNITED STATES OF AMERICA, FOR A SUCCESSION OF YEARS, COMPILED
CHIEFLY FROM OFFICIAL DOCUMENTS.
[Philadelphia.] Broadside. obl. 8vo. NYPL.

36363 STAUNTON, George   1737–1801
    An authentic account of an embassy from the King of Great Britain to the Emperor of
    China. . . . In two volumes. . . .
        Philadelphia: Printed for Robert Campbell, by John Bioren. 1799.   pp. xxiii, [1],
    297, 2 plates; 267, xxiv, 6 plates and folded table.   8vo.
    Although the two volumes have independent signature series they were issued bound in
    one. The engravings are by Seymour.
              AAS, BA, BPL, BʳU, HC, HEH, JCB, LCP, LOC, PSL, NYPL, NYSL, PʳU, WC, YC.

36364 STEARNS, Charles   1753–1826
    Principles of religion and morality. In three parts. . . . In the form of dialogues;
    adapted to schools. . . . Second edition. . . .
        Amherst, New Hampshire, printed by Samuel Preston — for the author. 1799.
    pp. 72.   12mo.   AAS, LOC, NYPL.

36365 STEELE, Eliphalet   1742–1817
    A Discourse on psalmody: delivered at Paris [N. Y.], March 1799, at the close of a
    singing school. . . .
        .Utica: [Printed by William M'Lean?]. M,DCC,XCIX.   pp. 15.   16mo.   WL.

36366 STEVENS, John   1750–1799
    A Posthumous publication, of some of the writings of the late Rev. John Stevens,
    pastor of the Second Church in New-Marlborough. . . . To which is added, a sketch
    of the life of the author.
        Hartford: Printed by Hudson & Goodwin. 1799.   pp. 35.   8vo.
    The sketch was probably by Jacob Catlin, the editor.   CHS, CSL, LOC, NYHS, PʳU, UTS.

36367 STEWART'S Kentucky Herald.   1795–1803
        Lexington: Printed by James H. Stewart.   fol.   weekly.   For 1799: [UOC].

36368 STILES, Ezra   1727–1795
    A Discourse on the Christian union . . . delivered before the . . . convention of the
    Congregational clergy in . . . Rhode-Island; assembled at Bristol. April 23, 1760. . . .
        Printed at Brookfield, (Massachusetts,) September, 1799.   pp. 163, [1].   12mo.
    The last page contains errata.   AAS, HC, HEH, JCB, NL, NYHS, NYPL, YC.

36369 STILLMAN, Samuel   1738–1807
    A Sermon, preached at Boston, April 25, 1799; the day . . . for a national fast. . . .
        Boston: Printed by Manning & Loring, Spring-Lane. 1799.   pp. 23.   8vo.
        AAS, BA, BPL, CL, EI, HC, HEH, JCB, LOC, MHS, NL, NYHS, NYPL, PL, RIHS, WLC, YC.

36370 STODDARD, A[mos]   1762–1813
    An Oration, delivered before the citizens of Portland, and the Supreme Judicial Court
    of . . . Massachusetts, on the fourth day of July, 1799. . . .
        Portland: Printed and sold by E. A. Jenks. 1799.   pp. 30.   8vo.
        AAS, BA, BPL, JCB, LOC, MHS, NYHS, NYPL, WLC.

36371 —— An Oration, delivered in the meeting house of the First Parish of Portland . . . June
    24th, 5799. At the request . . . of the Portland Lodge of Free and Accepted Masons,
    in celebration of the . . . festival of St. John the Baptist. By Brother Amos
    Stoddard, captain in the artillery of the United States.
        Portland: Printed by Baker and George — 1799.   pp. 14.   sm. 4to.
        AAS, BA, HC, JCB, MFM, NYPL.

36372 STODDARD'S diary: of the Columbia almanack, for the year of our Lord 1800. . . . By
    Andrew Beers, Philom.
        Hudson: Printed and sold by Ashbel Stoddard. . . .   pp. [36].   12mo.   AAS.

36373 STONE, Eliab   1737–1822
    A Discourse, delivered at Reading, on the day of the national fast, April 25, 1799. . . .
        Boston: Printed by Manning & Loring. 1799.   pp. 29.   8vo.
        AAS, BA, BPL, HC, JCB, MHS, NHHS, NYPL, UTS.

36374 STONINGTON ASSOCIATION.
 MINUTES OF THE STONINGTON ASSOCIATION, HELD AT COLCHESTER, OCTOBER 15 AND 16, 1799.
  Norwich: Printed by John Sterry. 1799. pp. 8. 8vo.   AAS.

36375 STORACE, [STEPHEN]
 SWEET LITTLE BARBARA. A FAVORITE DUETT IN THE IRON CHEST. COMPOSED BY STORACE. PRICE
 32 CENTS.
  Printed and sold at B. Carr's musical repository, Philadelphia; J. Carr's Baltimore &
  J. Hewitt's New York. pp. 3. fol.
 Advertised in March, 1799, as shortly to be published.   NL, NYPL.

36376 [STORY, ISAAC   1774–1803
 CONSOLATORY ODES, DEDICATED WITH CHRISTIAN PIETY TO THOSE UNFORTUNATE BEINGS WHO LABOR
 UNDER THE MALIGNANT INFLUENCE OF THE DEMOCRATIC MANIA. BY PETER QUINCE.
  New York, 1799. 12mo.]
 Listed in the NYSL catalogue of 1855.   SABIN 92278.

36377 THE STORY OF JOSEPH
  Printed for John G. Ustick, no. 79, North Third-street, Philadelphia. 1799. pp. 39.
  32mo.   AAS.

36378 THE STORY OF THE INNOCENT AMELIA; OR THE TREACHEROUS BROTHER. IN A SERIES OF LETTERS.
 BEING A FACT.
  Putney, Ver.—Printed for, and sold by J. Hinds, Walpole, New Hampshire. 1799.
 pp. 59. 32mo.   AAS.

36379 STRONG, CYPRIAN   1743–1811
 A DISCOURSE, DELIVERED AT HEBRON . . . JULY 4TH, 1799. BY CYPRIAN STRONG, A. M. PASTOR
 OF THE FIRST CHURCH IN CHATHAM.
  Hartford: Printed by Hudson and Goodwin. 1799. pp. 18. 8vo.
           AAS, BA, CHS, JCB, LOC, NYHS, YC.

36380 —— THE KINGDOM IS THE LORD'S. A SERMON, PREACHED AT HARTFORD, ON THE DAY OF THE ANNIVER-
 SARY ELECTION, MAY 9, 1799. . . .
  Hartford: Printed by Hudson and Goodwin. 1799. pp. 46. 8vo.
    AAS, BA, BPL, CHS, HC, HEH, HSP, JCB, LOC, MHS, NL, NYHS, NYPL, NYSL, YC.

36381 STRONG, NATHAN   1748–1816
 POLITICAL INSTRUCTION. . . . A SERMON PREACHED ON THE STATE THANKSGIVING, NOVEMBER 29,
 1798. . . .
  Hartford, printed: New-York, Reprinted by G. Forman, for C. Davis. 1799. pp. 24.
 8vo.   AAS, AHTS, BPL, CHS, GʳL, HEH, JCB, LOC, NL, NYPL, NYSL, UTS, WC, YC.

36382 STRONG, NATHAN, ETC.
 THE HARTFORD SELECTION OF HYMNS. FROM THE MOST APPROVED AUTHORS. . . . COMPILED BY
 NATHAN STRONG, ABEL FLINT, AND JOSEPH STEWARD. . . .
  Hartford: Printed by John Babcock. 1799. pp. 333, [1]. 24mo.
         AAS, BʳU, CHS, CU, GʳL, HC, LOC, NYSL, YC.

36383 STRONG, NEHEMIAH   1729–1807
 AN ASTRONOMICAL DIARY, CALENDAR, OR ALMANACK, FOR . . . 1800. . . . CALCULATED FOR THE
 HORIZON AND MERIDIAN OF HARTFORD. . . .
  Hartford: Printed by Elisha Babcock. 12mo. pp. [36].
 "To the reader" is dated New-Milford, July 19, 1799. AAS, BPL, CHS, LOC, NYPL, YC.

36384 —— THE CONNECTICUT POCKET ALMANAC, FOR . . . 1800. . . . CONTAINING . . . THE LAWYER'S AND
 JUSTICE'S CALENDAR FOR THE NEW-ENGLAND STATES. . . .
  Hartford: Printed by John Babcock, for E. & J. Babcock. pp. [47]. 28mo.
 Contains also "An Historical account of a most extraordinary duel," an "Unfortunate
 disaster on a wedding day," cookery receipts, etc. AAS, BM, BPL, CHS, LOC, YC.

36385 — — — *Hartford: Printed for Henry Dwier, ten rods north of the Court-House.*   pp. 47.
       12mo.   BPL.

36386 — [SHEET ALMANACK FOR 1800.
             Hartford: Elisha Babcock.]   Broadside.
       Advertised in the *American Mercury* of Oct. 31, 1799. *See also* Stafford, Hosea, a pseudonym
       used by Strong.

36387 THE SUN. DOVER GAZETTE, AND COUNTY ADVERTISER.   1795–1818
             Published on Wednesdays by Samuel Bragg, jun. at his printing-office, Dover.
       weekly.   fol.   FOR 1799: [AAS], [HC].

36388 THE SUNBURY AND NORTHUMBERLAND GAZETTE.   1793–1817
             Northumberland — printed by George Schusler.   fol.   weekly.   FOR 1799: [LOC].

36389 SUNDRY LETTERS AND PETITIONS ADDRESSED TO HIS EXCELLENCY JAMES GARRARD, ESQ. GOVERNOR
       OF KENTUCKY: RELATIVE TO THE CASE OF HENRY FIELD.
             [Imprint missing: dated Sept. 4, 1799.]   pp. vi, 32.   12mo.   WᶦˢHS.

36390 SUPLEE, NATHAN
             TO THE ELECTORS OF PENNSYLVANIA. WHEN THE CHARACTER OF A WORTHY CITIZEN IS TRADUCED. . . .
       BLOCKLEY, OCTOBER 3D. 1799. . . . NATHAN SUPLEE.
             pp. 2.   fol.   HSP.

36391 [SURPRIZING ACCOUNT OF THE CAPTIVITY OF MISS HANNAH WILLIS, WHO WAS TAKEN BY THE
       INDIANS ON THE 30TH JULY 1791. . . . TO WHICH IS ADDED AN AFFECTING HISTORY, OF . . .
       FREDERIC MANHEIM'S FAMILY, WHO WAS TAKEN . . . IN 1779.
             Stonington-Port, printed by S. Trumbull. 1799.   pp. 15, [1].   12mo.]
                                                                                       BATES 2658.

36392 SYMMES, THOMAS   1678–1725
             THE HISTORY OF THE FIGHT OF THE INTREPID CAPTAIN JOHN LOVELL, WHICH TOOK PLACE ON THE
       EIGHTH DAY OF MAY, 1725. . . .
             Printed at Fryeburg, by and for Elijah Russel. 1799.   pp. 60.   12mo.
                                                                             AAS, MHS, NHHS, NYPL.

36393 A SYSTEM OF SEAMANSHIP, AND NAVAL TACTICS. EXTRACTED FROM THE ENCYCLOPAEDIA, PUBLISHED
       BY THOMAS DOBSON. ILLUSTRATED WITH COPPER-PLATES.
             *Philadelphia: Printed for Thomas Dobson, at the Stone-House, no. 41, South Second
       Street. 1799.*   pp. 192, 8 folding plates.   8vo.
       The plates were engraved by B. Jones and by Bowes. According to the edition printed
       at Philadelphia in 1807, the author was John Clerk (1728–1812).   AAS.

36394 TABLES OF DIFFERENCE OF LATITUDE AND DEPARTURE. . . .
             See Robertson, John.

36395 DIE TÄGLICHEN LOOSUNGEN UND LEHRTEXTE DER BRÜDERGEMEINE, FÜR DAS JAHR 1800.
             Lancäster: Gedruckt bey Johann Albrecht und Comp. . . . 1799.   pp. 126.   16mo.
                                                                                             HSP.

36396 TATEM, WILLIAM
             THE EVIDENCE IN A CAUSE DEPENDING IN THE COURT OF CHANCERY OF . . . NEW JERSEY,
       BETWEEN WILLIAM TATEM, ESQUIRE, AND OTHERS, COMPLAINANTS, AND JEFFERY CHEW. . . .
             Trenton: Printed by Gershom Craft, 1799.   pp. 136, folding table.   4to.   PʳU.

36397 TATHAM, WILLIAM   1752–1819
             THE POLITICAL ECONOMY OF INLAND NAVIGATION, IRRIGATION AND DRAINAGE . . . INTO THE
       REMOTEST INTERIOR OF GREAT BRITAIN AND OF FOREIGN PARTS.
             Philadelphia: Printed for the author. 1799.   pp. xvi, 500, [3].   4to.
       In the APS copy "Philadelphia" is struck out and a note, probably in the hand of
       librarian John Vaughn, reads: "N. B. Should be London." The London, 1799, edition has
       the same pagination.   APS.

36398 TATTLE, Tom, *pseud.*
  Father Abraham's Almanac, for the year of our Lord, 1800. . . . The astronomical calculations, by Tom Tattle. . . .
    Philadelphia: Printed and sold by Peter Stewart, no. 34. South Second-street.
  pp. [40]. 12mo.   loc.

36399 THE TEARS of America How are the mighty fallen and the weapons of war perished: — The path of glory leads but to the grave. . . .
    Broadside. fol.
  A memorial to Washington, printed on cotton.   aas.

36400 THE TELEGRAPHE and Daily Advertiser.   1795–1807.
    Baltimore — printed by Thomas Dobbin, 1799. fol. daily. For 1799: M^dHS.

36401 TELLTRUTH, Timothy, *pseud.*
  The Collected wisdom of ages, the most stupendous fabric of human invention, the English constitution. A true copy from the original, in the possession of William Pitt, & Co. . . .
    Philadelphia: Printed by James Carey, no. 7, South Front-Street. 1799. . . . pp. 47.
  8vo.   aas, heh, hsp, jcb, lcp, loc, mhs, nypl, p^ru, psl.

36402 TENNESSEE. State.
  Acts passed at the first session of the third General Assembly of the State of Tennessee, begun and held at Knoxville, on Monday the sixteenth day of September, one thousand seven hundred and ninety-nine.
    Knoxville: Printed by Roulstone & Wilson. . . . 1799. pp. 136. 8vo.
  Pages 85–91 are misnumbered.   hc, loc, nyhs, nypl.

36403 —— Acts passed at the second session of the second General Assembly of the State of Tennessee. Begun and held at Knoxville, on Monday the third day of December [sic]. one thousand seven hundred and ninety eight.
    Knoxville: Printed by Roulstone & Parrington. . . . MDCCXCVIII [1799]. pp. 70.
  8vo.
  Despite the imprint date the session ran to Jan. 5, 1799.   hc, loc, nypl.

36404 —— The Constitution of the United States of America. To which is prefixed the Constitution of the State of Tennessee.
    Knoxville: Printed by Roulstone & Parrington, printers to the State. M,DCC,XCIX.
  pp. 30. 8vo.   nyba, tⁿsl.

36405 THACHER, Peter   1752–1802
  A Sermon preached June 12, 1799, before . . . the . . . Council, Senate and House of Representatives of . . . Massachusetts, at the interment of . . . Increase Sumner. . . .
    Boston: Printed by Young & Minns. . . . pp. xviii. 8vo.
  aas, ba, bm, bpl, hc, heh, hsp, jcb, loc, mhs, nl, nyhs, nypl, nysl, w^{is}hs, yc.

36406 THAYER, Ebenezer   1734–1792
  Family worship. Two sermons of the late Rev. Ebenezer Thayer, A. M., pastor of the church in Hampton. . . .
    Printed at Newburyport by Edmund M. Blunt. M.DCC.XCIX. pp. 32. 8vo.
                        heh, jcb, loc.

36407 [THAYER, Nathaniel]   1769–1840
  Anthems and hymns, to be sung at the installation of the reverend Mr. [William] Emerson, on Wednesday the 16th of October, 1799.
    [*Boston: Printed by Samuel Hall.*] Broadside.   hsp.

36408 —— The Preaching and practice of the apostles. . . . Preached at the ordination of . . . Elihu Whitcomb . . . in Pepperellborough, on the 3d of July, 1799. . . .
    Printed at Portland, by B. Titcomb, 1799. pp. 22. 8vo.
             aas, ba, bpl, jcb, loc, m^ehs, pl, yc.

36409 — A Sermon, preached at the installation of . . . William Emerson . . . in Boston, on the 16th of October, 1799.
Printed by Samuel Hall, in Boston. 1799. pp. 30. 8vo.
Includes the Charge by Ezra Ripley of Concord and the Right Hand of Fellowship by Peter Thacher of Boston.
AAS, BA, BM, BPL, CL, HC, HSP, JCB, LOC, MHS, NL, NYHS, NYPL, NYSL, PL, YC.

36410 THE THEOLOGICAL magazine, or synopsis of modern religious sentiment. On a new plan. . . . Vol. III [No. 1, October. 1797, to No. 6, February, 1799].
New-York; Printed for Cornelius Davis, no. 94 Water-Street. 1799. pp. [4], 474, [2].
8vo. AAS, BA, BPL, HC, JCB, LOC, MHS, NYHS, NYPL, NYSL, YC.

36411 THEOPHILANTHROPY: or the spirit of genuine religion . . . published for the considera-tion of all rational and liberal minds. . . . By a layman.
Lancaster, [Pa.]: Printed by Wm. Hamilton — M,DCC,XCIX. pp. 23. 12mo.
AAS, BA, HEH, WⁱˢHS, YC.

36412 THERMOMETRICAL navigation.
See Williams, Jonathan.

36413 THOMAS, Isaiah   1749–1831
Isaiah Thomas's Massachusetts, Connecticut, Rhode Island, Newhampshire & Vermont Almanack . . . for . . . 1800. . . .
Printed at Worcester, Massachusetts, by Isaiah Thomas. Sold by him, and by I. Thomas, jun. in Worcester; by Thomas & Andrews, S. Hall, West & Greenleaf, E. Larkin, J. Boyle, W. Spotswood, C. Bingham . . . in Boston; by Thomas and Thomas, Walpole; by T. C. Cushing, Salem. . . . AAS, LOC, NYHS, NYPL, NYSL.

36414 THOMAS, Robert B[ailey]   1766–1846
No. VIII. The Farmer's Almanack . . . for . . . 1800. . . . Containing . . . a variety . . . of new, useful, and entertaining matter. . . .
Boston: Printed by Manning & Loring, for John West, proprietor of the copy-right. . . . Sold also . . . by the author at Sterling, and at various other places. . . . pp. [48]. 12mo.
There are two issues with varying advertisements on the last page. Probably that headed "Books" is the later issue. AAS, HEH, LOC, MHS, NYPL, NYSL, YC.

36415 THOMAS, William
Hodge & Boylan's North-Carolina Almanack, for the year of our Lord 1800. . . . Cal-culated for the State of North-Carolina. . . .
Halifax: Printed and Sold by Abraham Hodge. pp. [48]. 16mo. AAS.

36416 THOMAS & ANDREWS. Catalogue of books. (American editions) for sale at the bookstore of Thomas & Andrews, Faust's Statue, n. 45, Newbury-Street, Boston. . . .
Printed at Boston, for Thomas and Andrews, Feb. 1799. pp. 36. EI.

36417 THOMAS'S Massachusetts Spy: or, the Worcester Gazette.   1775–1904
Printed at Worcester, (Massachusetts) by Leonard Worcester . . . for . . . Isaiah Thomas. . . . fol. weekly.
With the issue for Mar. 6 Worcester withdrew, and the *Spy* was printed by Isaiah Thomas, Jr., for Isaiah Thomas and Son.
For 1799: AAS, APS, BA, BM, BPL, LOC, MHS, MSL, NYHS.

36418 THOMPSON, Thomas [White]   1766–1821
An Oration pronounced the 4th day of July, 1799, at Salisbury, in the State of New-Hampshire. . . .
Printed at Concord [N. H.], by Geo Hough. 1799. pp. 16. 12mo.
AAS, HEH, LOC, NYHS.

36419 TICHENOR, Isaac, *etc.*
  The Illustrious and beloved General Washington, has departed. . . . The citizens of Bennington and vicinity are requested to meet at the Court-House on Friday the 27th inst. . . .
    [*Bennington.*] Broadside. 4to.   AAS.

36420 THE TIMES. Alexandria Advertiser.   1797–1802
    Printed daily by Thomas and Wescott . . . Alexandria. fol. daily.
  With the issue of Apr. 17 the title was changed to *The Times; and District of Columbia Daily Advertiser,* John V. Thomas retired, and the publishers became John and James D. Wescott.   For 1799: [LOC], [Wⁱ•HS].

36421 TO THE citizens of Pennsylvania.
    [*Philadelphia.*] pp. 16. 8vo.
  A tract in support of Thomas McKean for governor, signed, An Elector.   LOC.

36422 TO THE citizens of the County of Philadelphia. Friends and fellow citizens . . . you have been addressed by the committee, appointed to promote the election of James Ross.
    [*Philadelphia.*] Broadside. fol.
  This address, signed "Franklin," opposes the election of Ross.   LOC.

36423 TO THE electors of Pennsylvania. Take your choice! Thomas M'Kean — or — James Ross. Now or never!
    [*Philadelphia.*] Broadside. 4to.
  This address favors the election of M'Kean.   LOC.

36424 TO THE electors of Pennsylvania. When a candidate for the highest office in the State is presented for the public opinion. . . .
    [*Philadelphia.*] pp. 8. 8vo.
  This tract, signed "A Pennsylvanian," opposes the election of Thomas M'Kean. HSP.

36425 TO THE electors of Pennsylvania. When the character of a worthy citizen is traduced. . . . Blockley, October 3d. 1799. . . .
    pp. 2. fol.
  An attack on M'Kean.   HSP.

36426 TO THE electors of Philadelphia County. . . .
    [*Philadelphia.*] pp. 7. 8vo.
  Signed by Matthew Huston, chairman of the Committee to Promote the Republican Ticket.   LOC.

36427 TO THE electors of the City of New York. Fellow-citizens. The aristocratic prints have teemed with abuse and misrepresentation. . . .
    Broadside. fol.   NYHS, NYPL.

36428 TO THE electors of the Kennebec and Somerset district. . . .
    [*Augusta, Me., printed by Peter Edes at the office of the Kennebunk Intelligencer and probably issued as a supplement to that paper for January 12, 1799.*] Broadside. fol. pp. [2].   AAS.

36429 TO THE foremen of the Northern-Liberties. Fellow-citizens, the young men of our district have been addressed by an anonymous incendiary. . . . Brutus.
    [*Philadelphia.*] Broadside. fol.   LOC.

36430 TO THE free and independent electors of the County of Ulster. . . .
    [*Catskill, Apr. 24, 1799.*] Broadside. fol.
  This broadside has been reprinted in facsimile.   NYPLᵖʰ.

36431   TO THE FRIENDS OF FREEDOM AND PUBLIC FAITH, AND TO ALL LOVERS OF THEIR FELLOW-MEN.
    [*Philadelphia?*] pp. 8. 8vo.
    A memorial of natives of Ireland to Congress protesting the Alien and Sedition Act.
    Accompanying comment is signed "A Native American."   BPL, LOC.

36432   TO THE INDEPENDENT ELECTORS OF PENNSYLVANIA. . . .
    [*Philadelphia.*] pp. 11. 8vo.
    Advocates the election of M'Kean as governor; signed, "An American."   LOC.

36433   TO THE PUBLIC. WE THE UNDERSIGNED HAVING SEEN A PUBLICATION IN THE PHILADELPHIA GAZETTE,
    OF THE 5TH INST. SIGNED NATHAN SUPLEE. . . . SIGNED BY EDWARD HESTON. . . . BLOCKLEY,
    OCT. 7TH, 1799.
      [*Philadelphia?*] Broadside. 4to.   LOC.

36434   TO THE REPRESENTATIVES OF THE FREEMEN OF THE UNITED STATES OF AMERICA; IN CONGRESS
    ASSEMBLED: THE MEMORIAL OF THE UNDERSIGNED FREEMEN OF THE COUNTY OF RUTLAND,
    AND STATE OF VERMONT [FOR THE REPEAL OF THE ALIEN AND SEDITION ACTS]. . . . JANUARY
    1799.
      Broadside. fol.   AAS.

36435   TO THE REPUBLICANS OF PENNSYLVANIA.
    [*Philadelphia?*] pp. 8. 8vo.
    Signed by John Peter Gabriel Muhlenberg (1746–1807) and others.   APS, HC, LOC.

36436   TODD, TIMOTHY   1758–1806
    AN ODE FOR THE FOURTH OF JULY, 1799. WRITTEN BY TIMOTHY TODD ESQ. SET TO MUSIC BY
    THE REV. CHAUNCEY LEE.
      Hudson, engraved & sold by G. Fairman. Broadside.   AAS.

36437   TOMB, SAMUEL   1766–1832
    THE DUTIES OF GOSPEL-MINISTERS . . . TWO DISCOURSES, DELIVERED DECEMBER 2D. 1798 . . . IN
    NEWBURY. . . .
      Printed at Newburyport by Edmund M. Blunt — 1799. pp. 34. 8vo.
          AAS, BM, JCB.

36438   [TORREY, WILLIAM
    AN ANNUAL HISTORY OF THE LEGISLATIVE PROCEEDINGS OF THE STATE OF NEW-YORK. . . . VOL. I.
    CONTAINING THE PROCEEDINGS AND LAWS IN 1799.
      New York: 1799.]
    79th New York District copyright issued to William Torrey as proprietor, May 11, 1799.

36439   THE TORY LIE DETECTED! TO THE REPUBLICAN ELECTORS OF THE CITY OF NEW-YORK. . . . EDWARD
    LIVINGSTON, PETER R. LIVINGSTON. MAY 1, 1799.
      Broadside. fol.   WLC.

36440   A TOUR, THROUGH UPPER AND LOWER CANADA. . . .
    See Ogden, John Cosins.

36441   THE TOWN AND COUNTRY ALMANACK, FOR . . . 1800. . . .
    New York: Printed for and published by Longworth and Wheeler. . . . pp. 36.
          NJHS, RU.

36442   THE TOWN AND COUNTRY ALMANAC, FOR . . . 1800. . . . CONTAINING . . . A GREAT VARIETY OF
    INSTRUCTING, ENTERTAINING, AND USEFUL MATTER IN PROSE AND VERSE.
      Wilmington: Printed and sold by Bonsal & Niles. pp. [48]. 16mo. AAS, LOC, YC.

36443   TOWN & COUNTRY ALMANAC, (REVIVED) CALCULATED FOR VIRGINIA, PENNSYLVANIA, DELAWARE,
    MARYLAND AND KENTUCKY — FOR THE YEAR OF OUR LORD, 1800. . . .
      Baltimore: Printed for Thomas, Andrews & Butler . . . by W. Pechin. . . . pp. [34].
    12mo.   LOC, MᵈHS.

36444   EIN TRAUER GEDICHT ÜBER EINE GRAUSAME MORDTHAT. . . .
      Reading: Gedmekt by J. Schneider u. Co. für William Bradley, im jahr 1799.   pp. 8.
      8vo.   PGS.

36445   TRAVELS OF ROBINSON CRUSOE. WRITTEN BY HIMSELF. FIRST NEWPORT EDITION.
      Newport: Printed by H. & O. Farnsworth. 1799.   pp. 26.   32mo.   AAS, NHS.

36446   TRENCK, FRIEDRICH, FREIHERR VON DER,   1726–1794
      THE LIFE OF BARON FREDERICK TRENCK. CONTAINING HIS ADVENTURES . . . DURING TEN YEARS
      IMPRISONMENT. . . . TRANSLATED . . . BY THOMAS HOLCROFT.
      Philadelphia: Printed by Robert Johnson, for B. & J. Johnson No. 147, High Street.
      1799.   pp. 198, portrait.   32mo.   AAS, NYPL.

36447   —— —— *New York: Printed for William Falconer. 1799.*   pp. 144.   12mo.   NYPL.

36448   TRENTON. NEW JERSEY.
      ACTS AND ORDINANCES OF THE CITY OF TRENTON, TO WHICH IS PREFIXED, THE ACT OF INCORPORA-
      TION. PUBLISHED BY ORDER OF THE COMMON-COUNCIL.
      Trenton: Printed by Sherman, Mershon & Thomas, printers to the City. 1799.
      38 numbered leaves.   8vo.   LOCᴾʰ.

36449   TRIBUTE TO THE MEMORY OF WASHINGTON. . . .
      See Salem, Mass.

36450   THE TRIFLE-HUNTER: OR, THE ADVENTURES OF PRINCE BONBENNIN. A CHINESE TALE, FIRST
      NEWPORT EDITION.
      Newport: Printed by O. Farnsworth. 1799.   pp. 29, [2].   32mo.   AAS, NHS.

36451   [THE TRUE AMERICAN.   1798–1800
      Leesburg, (Virginia) published by Patrick M'Intyre.   fol.   weekly.]
                                     FOR 1799: NO COPY KNOWN.

36452   THE TRUE AMERICAN AND COMMERCIAL ADVERTISER.   1798–1818
      [Philadelphia: published] By Samuel F. Bradford. . . .   fol.   daily.
                                 FOR 1799: [AAS], [HC], HSP.

36453   — AN ELEGIAC POEM ON THE DEATH OF GENERAL GEORGE WASHINGTON . . . DEDICATED TO THE
      PATRONS OF THE TRUE AMERICAN AT THE COMMENCEMENT OF THE YEAR 1800.
      [Philadelphia: Samuel F. Bradford.]   Broadside.   fol.
      By Charles Caldwell.   NYHS.

36454   [TRUMBULL, BENJAMIN?]   1735–1820
      AN APPEAL TO THE CANDID, UPON THE PRESENT STATE OF RELIGION AND POLITICS IN CONNECTICUT.
      [New Haven.]   pp. 23.   12mo.   YC.

36455   — TWELVE DISCOURSES, COMPRISING A SYSTEMATICAL DEMONSTRATION OF THE DIVINE ORIGIN OF THE
      HOLY SCRIPTURES. . . . PUBLISHED ACCORDING TO ACT OF CONGRESS.
      Hartford: Printed by Hudson and Goodwin. 1799.   pp. x, 305.   12mo.
      Contains a long list of names of subscribers.
                   AAS, BM, CHS, HC, JCB, LOC, NYPL, NYSL, PʳU, UTS, VᵃU, WC, YC.

36456   TRUMBULL, JOHN   1750–1831
      M'FINGAL: A MODERN EPIC POEM, IN FOUR CANTOS. . . . WITH EXPLANATORY NOTES. . . .
      Boston: Printed by Manning & Loring, for Ebenezer Larkin, no. 47, Cornhill. 1799.
      pp. 141, [3].   16mo.   AAS, BA, BPL, BʳU, EI, HC, JCB, LOC, MHS, NYHS, NYPL, WLC, YC.

36457 [TUCKER, St. George] 1752–1828
A Letter to a member of Congress; respecting the Alien and Sedition Laws.
pp. 48. 8vo.
Caption title; signed and dated June 6, 1799. HC, LOC.

36458 TULLAR, Martin 1753–1813
The Virtues of a prudent wife . . . a sermon delivered at Royalton, Vermont, on the anniversary Thanksgiving, December 5, A. D. 1799, by the Rev. Martin Tullar . . . soon after the death of his wife. . . .
Printed at Hanover, (N. H.) by Moses Davis. pp. 26, [2]. 8vo.
Errata on p. 26 followed by two pages of verse. AAS, UTS.

36459 TURNER, George
Memoir on the extraneous fossils, denominated mammoth bones; principally designed to shew, that they are the remains of more than one species. . . .
Philadelphia: Printed for Thomas Dobson, at the Stone House, no. 41 South Second Street. 1799. pp. 11. 4to.
Read before the American Philosophical Society on July 21, 1797. BM, LOC, MHS, PPL.

36460 TWENTY four fashionable country dances for the year 1799, with their proper figures as performed at Court, Bath. And all public assemblys.
London printed Boston reprinted & sold by W. Norman no. 75 Newbury Street. pp. [14]. obl. 32mo.
Music engraved by John Norman, with text beneath. AAS, NYPL.

36461 THE TWO cousins. . . .
See Pinchard, Mrs.

36462 TWO SONGS for the celebration of the 4th of July, 1799.
Broadside. NYHS.

36463 TYLER, John 1742–1823
A Discourse delivered in the city of New-London: before an assembly of Free and Accepted Masons . . . June 25th, in the year of light 5799.
New-London: Printed by Brother Samuel Green, 1799. pp. 20. 8vo. HSP, LOC.

36464 — A Discourse, delivered in the meeting-house of the Society in Lebanon, before an assembly of Free and Accepted Masons, convened for the installation of a lodge in that town. On Wednesday the 21st of November, in the year of light, 5798.
Norwich, John Trumbull, 1799. pp. 14. 8vo. AHTS.

36465 TYTLER, James 1747–1805
A Treatise on the plague and yellow fever. With an appendix, containing histories of the plague. . . . Published according to act of Congress.
Salem: Printed by Joshua Cushing, for B. B. Macanulty. 1799. pp. [4], 568, [1], folding table. 8vo.
The last leaf contains Errata.
AAS, AML, BA, BM, BPL, EI, HC, JCB, LOC, NYAM, NYHS, NYPL, NYSL, UOP, YC.

36466 ULSTER County Gazette. 1798–1803
Published at Kingston [N. Y.] (Ulster County) by Samuel Freer and Son. Weekly. fol.
For a period the title was *Ulster and Delaware Gazette.* For 1799: [LOC], [NYHS].

36467 UNITED States.
Abstract of cases transmitted to the Secretary of the Treasury, pursuant to the . . . Act . . . "Further to suspend the commercial intercourse between the United States and France. . . ." passed on the ninth day of February 1799.
[*Philadelphia?*] pp. [1], 7 folded tables. 8vo. AAS, BA, LOC, NYPL, YC.

36468 — An Account of the receipts and expenditures of the United States, for the year 1798. . . . Published by order of the House. . . .
　　Philadelphia: Printed by John Ward Fenno, no 119, Chestnut-Street. [*Nov. 20, 1799.*]
　　pp. iv, 10 tables, 11–76, table, 77–78, xii, table.　　fol.　　　　AAS, HC, JCB, LOC, NYPL.

36469 — Accounts of the Treasurer of the United States, of payments and receipts of public monies, commencing the first of January and ending the thirty-first of December, 1798. . . . Printed by order of the House. . . .
　　[*Philadelphia?*]　　pp. 15.　　8vo.
　　In spite of the title, this item contains only the accounts of the first quarter submitted under a covering letter dated May 11, 1798.　　　　AAS, LOC.

36470 — An Act, for the better organizing of the troops of the United States, and for other purposes.
　　[*Philadelphia.*]　　pp. 22.　　12mo.
　　The date of the imprint is assumed from the fact that this is the Act of Mar. 2, 1799.
　　　　　　　　　　JCB.

36471 — An Act for the government of the navy of the United States. . . . Approved March 2d, 1799. . . .
　　[*Philadelphia.*]　　pp. 16.　　8vo.　　　　　　NYHS, PPL.

36472 — An Act in addition to "An Act for the relief of sick and disabled seamen." Section 1. Be it enacted. . . . Approved — March 2, 1799. John Adams. . . .
　　[*Philadelphia?*]　　Broadside.　　fol.　　　　　　LOC.

36473 — An Act providing for salvage in cases of re-capture. . . .
　　[*Philadelphia.*]　　pp. [3].　　fol.　　　　　　LOC.

36474 — An Act providing for the enumeration of the inhabitants of the United States. . . . December 27th, 1798. Passed by the House. . . .
　　[*Philadelphia:*] *Printed by John Ward Fenno.*　　pp. 6.　　fol.　　　　LOC.

36475 — An Act respecting quarantines and health laws. Section 1. Be it enacted by the Senate. . . . Approved — February 25, 1799. John Adams. . . .
　　Broadside.　　fol.　　　　　　LOC.

36476 — An Act to establish the post-office of the United States. . . . Approved, March 2, 1799. . . .
　　[*Philadelphia.*]　　pp. 23.　　12mo.　　　　　　LOC.

36477 — An Act to regulate the collection of duties on imports and tonnage: passed at the third session of the fifth Congress. . . .
　　Philadelphia: Printed by W. Ross, in Locust-Street, near the corner of South Ninth-Street.　　pp. 171, [1], 12.　　8vo.
　　Second title: An Act to Establish the Compensations of the Officers Employed in the Collection of the Duties on Imports and Tonnage. . . . Passed at the Third Session of the Fifth Congress. . . .　　[Same imprint.]　　pp. 12.　　　　AAS, NYPL.

36478 — An Act to regulate the collection of duties on imports and tonnage. Passed March 2, 1799.
　　[*Charleston: Printed by Freneau and Paine.*]　　pp. 76.　　4to.
　　Issued in paged, unfolded, sheets with the *City Gazette* from May 17 to June 29, 1799.
　　　　　　　　　　CLS.

36479 — Acts passed at the third session of the fifth Congress of the United States [. . . Begun . . . at . . . Philadelphia . . . the third of December, one thousand seven hundred and ninety-eight].
　　[*Philadelphia.*]　　pp. [2], [242]–561, 26, iv, 48.　　8vo.
　　Appended are the Constitution, the Table of Contents, and the Index. There is evidence that this is the original edition. There are two issues, one with the half title between rules and one without rules. Of these the former is apparently the earlier.
　　　　　　　　　　AAS, HEH, JCB, MHS, MSL, RU, VªSL, WC.

36480 — — — *Supplement to the North-Carolina Journal, no. 357. Halifax: Printed by A. Hodge.*
pp. 123, [1]. fol. AAS, HC.

36481 — — — *State of Kentucky, Lexington. Printed by John Bradford. . . . 1799.* pp. 136.
8vo. LOUISVILLE LAW COLLEGE.

36482 — — — *New-London-(Connecticut,) printed by Samuel Green, 1799.* pp. 188, [2]. 8vo.
AAS, CSL.

36483 — — — *Philadelphia. Printed by Richard Folwell, no. 33, Carter's-Alley.* pp. [2], [243]–
561, [1], [1]–26, iv, 48. AAS.

36484 — — — *Pittsburgh; Printed by John Scull.* pp. 168. 8vo.
Printed, by authorization of the Secretary of State, serially as pages 3 and 4 of the *Pittsburgh Gazette,* in such a way that these pages in each issue could be folded into an 8-page
signature. JCB.

36485 — — — *District of Maine: Portland, printed by Elezer Alley Jenks. 1799.* pp. 202, [2].
8vo.
Issued serially with *Jenks' Portland Gazette.* AAS, NYPL.

36486 — — — *Providence, Printed by John Carter, jun. 1799.* pp. 202, [2]. 8vo.
Issued as a supplement of the *Providence Journal* from Apr. 17 to Oct. 2.
BᵞU, JCB, NYPL, RIHS.

36487 — — — *Richmond: Printed by Meriwether Jones . . . 1799.* pp. 140, 4, 15.
Appended are the Treaty with the Cherokees and the Constitution. NYPL, VᵃU.

36488 — — — *[Rutland: Printed by Samuel Williams, 1799.* pp. 202, [2]. 8vo.]* GILMAN.

36489 —— ALTERATIONS TO BE MADE IN THE BILL REPORTED BY THE POST-MASTER GENERAL "TO ESTABLISH
THE POST-OFFICE OF THE UNITED STATES. 7TH FEBRUARY, 1799. (PUBLISHED BY ORDER OF
THE HOUSE. . . .)
[Philadelphia: Printed by William Ross.] pp. [3]. 8vo. AAS, BA, NYPL.

36490 —— AMENDMENTS AGREED TO IN THE COMMITTEE OF THE WHOLE HOUSE TO THE BILL FOR ESTABLISHING
AN UNIFORM SYSTEM OF BANKRUPTCY THROUGHOUT THE UNITED STATES (PUBLISHED BY ORDER
OF THE HOUSE OF REPRESENTATIVES [JANUARY 8, 1799])
[Philadelphia.] pp. 7. 8vo. BA.

36491 —— ARTICLES OF A TREATY BETWEEN THE UNITED STATES OF AMERICA AND THE CHEROKEE INDIANS . . .
BY MESSAGE OF THE PRESIDENT . . . ON THE XVTH OF JANUARY, M,DCC,XCIX, AND
ORDERED TO BE PRINTED FOR THE USE OF THE SENATE.
Philadelphia: Printed by John Ward Fenno. pp. 8. 8vo. BA, LOC, NYPL.

36492 — — — *[Halifax, 1799.]*
Anderson catalogue 1912, no. 365; McMurtrie 272.

36493 —— AT A MEETING OF THE BOARD OF COMMISSIONERS, FOR THE STATE OF MASSACHUSETTS, BEGUN AND
HELD AT BOSTON, ON THE 24TH DAY OF APRIL, 1799, IN PURSUANCE OF THE ACT OF THE
UNITED STATES. . . .
[Boston.] Broadside. MA.

36494 —— AT A MEETING OF THE BOARD OF COMMISSIONERS FOR THE VALUATION OF LANDS AND DWELLING-
HOUSES, IN THE STATE OF MASSACHUSETTS, JUNE, 1799.
[Boston.] Broadside. MA.

36495 —— AT A TREATY HELD WITH THE ONEIDA NATION. . . . AT THEIR VILLAGE IN THE STATE OF NEW YORK, ON THE FIRST DAY OF JUNE IN THE YEAR ONE THOUSAND SEVEN HUNDRED AND NINETY-EIGHT. . . .
[*Philadelphia*.]   pp. 3.   8vo.   LOC, NYPL.

36496 —— A BILL FOR THE GOVERNMENT OF THE NAVY OF THE UNITED STATES. 23D JANUARY, 1799. . . . (PUBLISHED BY ORDER OF THE HOUSE. . . .)
[*Philadelphia: Printed by William Ross*.]   pp. 18.   8vo.
AAS, BA, LOC, NYHS, NYPL.

36497 —— BY THE PRESIDENT OF THE UNITED STATES OF AMERICA. A PROCLAMATION. AS NO TRUTH IS MORE CLEARLY TAUGHT. . . . I . . . RECOMMEND . . . THAT . . . THE 25TH DAY OF APRIL NEXT BE OBSERVED . . . AS A DAY OF SOLEMN HUMILIATION, FASTING AND PRAYER. . . .
[*Philadelphia*.]   Broadside.   fol.   AAS, JCB, NYHS, UOC.

36498 —— BY THE PRESIDENT OF THE UNITED STATES OF AMERICA, A PROCLAMATION. WHEREAS BY AN ACT OF CONGRESS . . . PASSED ON THE NINTH DAY OF FEBRUARY LAST, ENTITLED "AN ACT FURTHER TO SUSPEND THE COMMERCIAL INTERCOURSE BETWEEN THE UNITED STATES AND FRANCE". . . . GIVEN . . . AT PHILADELPHIA, THE TWENTY-SIXTH DAY OF JUNE . . . 1799. . . .
Broadside.   fol.   EI, LOC.

36499 —— BY THE PRESIDENT OF THE UNITED STATES OF AMERICA. A PROCLAMATION. WHEREAS BY AN ACT OF THE CONGRESS . . . PASSED THE NINTH DAY OF FEBRUARY LAST, ENTITLED. . . . GIVEN . . . AT PHILADELPHIA, THIS 17TH DAY OF JULY, A. D. 1799.
Broadside.   fol.   LOC.

36500 —— [BY THE PRESIDENT OF THE UNITED STATES OF AMERICA. A PROCLAMATION. WHEREAS THE CONGRESS OF THE UNITED STATES "IN HONOUR OF THE MEMORY OF GEN. GEORGE WASHINGTON". . . .
[*Philadelphia*.]   Broadside.   fol.]   EVANS.

36501 —— CIRCULARS TO COLLECTORS, NAVAL OFFICERS AND SURVEYORS. TREASURY DEPARTMENT, COMPTROLLER'S OFFICE, MAY 27, 1799. . . .
Broadside.   8vo.   LOC.

36502 —— (CIRCULAR.) TREASURY DEPARTMENT, MARCH 30TH, 1799. I . . . TRANSMIT AN ACT OF CONGRESS PASSED ON THE 28TH DAY OF FEBRUARY, 1799 . . . "TO PROVIDE FOR THE VALUATION OF LANDS. . . ."
pp. [2].   8vo.   MHS.

36503 —— THE CLAIM AND ANSWER WITH THE SUBSEQUENT PROCEEDINGS IN THE CASE OF ANDREW ALLEN, ESQUIRE, AGAINST THE UNITED STATES. . . .
Philadelphia: Printed by James Humphreys, opposite the Bank of the United States. 1799.   pp. 50.   sq. 8vo.   AAS, APS, BA, MHS, NYPL.

36504 —— THE CLAIM AND ANSWER WITH THE SUBSEQUENT PROCEEDINGS, IN THE CASE OF THE RIGHT REVEREND CHARLES INGLES, AGAINST THE UNITED STATES. . . .
Philadelphia: Printed by R. Aitken, no. 22, Market-Street. MDCCXCIX.   pp. 110, [1], 40.   sq. 8vo.
The first portion was also issued without the continuation, which has no titlepage but independent signature numbering.   AAS, BA, HEH, JCB, LOC, MHS, NHS, NYHS, NYPL.

36505 —— THE COMMITTEE TO WHOM WAS REFERRED THE BILL AUTHORIZING THE ACCEPTANCE, FROM THE STATE OF CONNECTICUT, OF A CESSION OF THE JURISDICTION OF THE TERRITORY WEST OF PENNSYLVANIA. . . .
[*Philadelphia*.]   pp. 24.   8vo.   LOC.

36506 —— DIE CONSTITUTION DER VEREINIGTEN STAATEN VON AMERICA . . . 1787. NEBST DEN VERBESSERUNGEN ZU BESAGTER CONSTITUTION. . . .
Hägerstown: Gedruckt bey Johann Gruber. . . . 1799.   pp. 22.   12mo.   UOP.

36507   —— The Constitution of the United States of America.
          New-London: Printed by Samuel Green, 1799.   pp. 16.   8vo.   HC, NYPL, YC.

36508   —— The Constitution of the United States of America; as proposed by the convention held at Philadelphia, September 17, 1787, and since ratified by the several States. (With the several Amendments thereto.) (Published by order of the House of Representatives.)
          Philadelphia: Printed by John H. Oswald. 1799.   pp. 27.   12mo.
     Issued interleaved.   AAS, APS, BPL, HC, HEH, JCB, LOC, NYPL, PSL, WC, WLC.

36509   —— —— —— *Philadelphia: Printed by John Ward Fenno — M,DCC,XCIX.*   pp. 48.   18mo.
     Two hundred interleaved copies were printed by order of the Senate.
                                          HC, JCB, LOC, MᵈHS, PʳPL.

36510   —— The Constitution of the United States of America, with all the amendments: and Gen. Washington's paternal address · . . . on resigning the presidency. . . .
          Baltimore: Printed for Thomas Herty, by Warner and Hanna, M,DCC,XCIX.
     pp. 34.   12mo.   NYPL.

36511   —— [The Constitution of the United States, with the amendments.
          Elizabeth (Hager's) Town: Printed by Thomas Grieves.]   Minick 545.

36512   —— [Copies of the communications relative to our affairs with France, with a report of the Secretary of State, submitted to Congress January, 1799.
          [Philadelphia.]   pp. 168.   8vo.]   Evans.

36513   —— Copy of an indictment. No. I [–II]. In the Circuit Court of the United States in and for the Pennsylvania district of the middle circuit.
          [Philadelphia.]   pp. [4]; [3].   8vo.
     Indictment of William Duane on a charge of libeling the government of the United States.
                                          LOC.

36514   —— The Declaration of American independence.
          Richmond, Virginia. Printed by Jones and Dixon. . . . 1799.   pp. 40.   16mo.
                                          VᵃU.

36515   —— Duties payable on goods, wares, and merchandize imported into the United States . . . after the 30th Sept. 1797. . . . Also rates of coins. . . . And sundry forms for the direction of merchants. . . .
          Boston: Printed for E. Larkin, no. 47, Cornhill. 1799.   pp. 43.   8vo.
                                   AAS, JCB, NYHS, NYPL.

36516   —— Fifth Congress — Third session. A list of the names, and places of residence, of the members of the Senate and the House of Representatives. . . .
          [Philadelphia.]   Broadside.   fol.
     The names in this directory show that this edition was printed after December 19, 1798, and before January 24, 1799. For the directory of the Sixth Congress see *List of* below.
                                          AAS.

36517   —— French originals of all the documents, translations of which accompanied the Message of the President . . . 18th January, 1799, relative to the affairs of the United States with the French Republic.
          Philadelphia: Printed by Charles Cist. M,DCC,XCIX.   pp. [2], 58.   8vo.
                       AAS, HEH, HSP, JCB, LCP, LOC, NYSL, WLC.

36518   —— Further report of the committee of revisal and unfinished business. . . . 24th December, 1799. . . . (Published by order of the House. . . .)
          [Philadelphia: Printed by William Ross.]   pp. 8.   8vo.
                       AAS, BA, JCB, LOC, NYPL, NYSL, WLC.

36519 —— Journal of the House of Representatives of the United States, at the third session of the fifth Congress. . . .
Philadelphia: Printed by W. Ross, in Locust-Street. . . . 1798 [1799]. pp. 266, [24].
8vo. AAS, APS, BA, BᵣU, CSL, HC, JCB, LOC, NYHS, NYPL, PPL, YC.

36520 —— A Journal of the proceedings of the third session of the fifth Congress of the United States. . . .
New-London, (Connecticut) Printed and published by Samuel Green. 1798–99.
pp. 549. 8vo.
Apparently issued in sections. AAS, NYPL, YC.

36521 —— Journal of the Senate of the United States of America, being the third session of the fifth Congress. . . .
Philadelphia: Printed by John Ward Fenno, no. 119, Chestnut-Street. pp. 222,
vi, xiv. 8vo. AAS, BA, BᵣU, JCB, MHS, LOC.

36522 —— [Law of the United States. By authority. Fifth Congress. Third session. 3 December, 1798. An Act further to suspend intercourse with France. Approved February 9, 1799.
Broadside. fol.] Evans.

36523 —— The Laws of the United States of America. In four volumes. Vol. IV. Published by authority.
Philadelphia: Printed by Richard Folwell. . . . 1799. pp. 240, vii, [241]–561, 26,
iv, [48]. 8vo.
This is the *Acts . . . of the Fifth Congress, q. v.,* with the above title added to continue the Folwell series. LOC, WC.

36524 —— The Laws of the United States of America. Vol. IV. . . .
Philadelphia: Printed for M. Carey, W. M'Culloch, printer, 1799. pp. 240, vii, [241]–
561, 26, iv, [48]. 8vo. HEH.

36525 —— Letter from the commissioners of the City of Washington, to the President . . . with an account of the present state of the public buildings in that city. . . . 5th December, 1799. (Published by order of the House. . . .)
[Philadelphia: Printed by William Ross.] pp. 9, 2 folding tables. 8vo.
AAS, BA, JCB, LOC, NL, NYPL.

36526 —— Letter from the Post-Master-General, accompanying draughts of two bills . . . also, his Report on the Petition of Ezekiel Williams. . . . 8th January, 1799. . . . (Published by order of the House. . . .)
[Philadelphia: Printed by William Ross.] pp. 48. 8vo. AAS, BA, LOC, NYHS, NYPL.

36527 —— Letter from the Secretary, inclosing sundry statements . . . of the comptroller of the Treasury, in pursuance of . . . "An Act establishing a mint. . . ." January 31st, 1799. . . . Published by order of the House. . . .
[Philadelphia:] Printed by Way & Groff, no. 48, North Third-Street. pp. [4],
3 folded tables, [2], 2 folded tables. 8vo. AAS, BA, JCB, LOC, NYHS, NYPL, NYSL.

36528 —— Letter from the Secretary of the Navy accompanying sundry statements relative to the vessels of war. . . . 26th December, 1798. . . . Published by order of the House. . . .
Philadelphia: Printed by J. Gales, no. 23, South Third-street. pp. 30, folded table.
8vo. AAS, BA, HSP, JCB, NYHS.

36529 —— Letter from the Secretary of the Navy, to the chairman of the committee, appointed on so much of the President's speech as relates to the naval establishment, inclosing a Bill, fixing the pay. . . . 12th February, 1799. . . . (Published by order of the House. . . .)
[Philadelphia: Printed by William Ross.] pp. 4, folding table. 8vo.
AAS, BA, HSP, JCB, LOC, NYHS, NYPL.

36530 —— LETTER FROM THE SECRETARY OF THE NAVY, TO THE CHAIRMAN OF THE COMMITTEE, ON THE NAVAL
ESTABLISHMENT. . . . 2D OF JANUARY, 1799. (PUBLISHED BY ORDER OF THE HOUSE. . . .)
[Philadelphia: Printed by William Ross.]   pp. 16.   8vo.
AAS, APS, BA, HEH, HSP, JCB, LOC, NYHS, NYPL, NYSL.

36531 —— LETTER FROM THE SECRETARY OF STATE, ACCOMPANYING HIS REPORT ON THE CLAIM OF JOHN
BROWN CUTTING. . . . 27TH FEBRUARY, 1799. . . . PRINTED BY ORDER OF THE HOUSE. . . .
Philadelphia: Printed by Way & Groff, no. 48, North Third-Street.   pp. 23.   8vo.
AAS, APS, BA, HSP, JCB, LOC, NL, UOC, WLC.

36532 —— LETTER FROM THE SECRETARY OF STATE, INCLOSING ABSTRACTS OF ALL THE RETURNS . . . OF
REGISTERED AND IMPRESSED SEAMEN; TOGETHER WITH A REPORT . . . FROM THE AGENTS. . . .
10TH DECEMBER, 1799. . . .
Printed by W. Ross, in Locust-Street, between Walnut and Spruce.   pp. 20, 3 folded
tables, 16, 5 folded tables.   8vo.   AAS, BA, JCB, LOC, NYPL, NYSL.

36533 —— LETTER FROM THE SECRETARY OF THE TREASURY, ACCOMPANIED WITH A REPORT AND ESTIMATES OF
THE SUMS NECESSARY TO BE APPROPRIATED FOR THE SERVICE OF THE YEAR 1800. . . . 18TH. OF
DECEMBER, 1799. . . . PUBLISHED BY ORDER OF THE HOUSE. . . .
Philadelphia: Printed by Zachariah Poulson, Junior, no. 106, Chestnut-street. 1799.
pp. 117.   8vo.   AAS, BA, HSP, JCB, LOC, NYHS, NYPL, NYSL, RU, WLC.

36534 —— LETTER FROM THE SECRETARY OF THE TREASURY, INCLOSING A LETTER FROM THE COMPTROLLER,
WITH AN ABSTRACT OF THE OFFICIAL EMOLUMENTS OF THE OFFICERS OF THE CUSTOMS. . . .
16TH FEBRUARY, 1799. . . . PUBLISHED BY ORDER OF THE HOUSE. . . .
[Philadelphia:] Printed by W. Ross.   pp. [4], 2 folded tables, [3].   fol.
AAS, BA, LOC, NYPL, NYSL.

36535 —— LETTER FROM THE SECRETARY OF THE TREASURY, INCLOSING A STATEMENT OF THE TONNAGE OF
THE SHIPPING OF THE UNITED STATES, AT THE CLOSE OF THE YEAR 1797. 7TH FEBRUARY,
1799. . . . (PUBLISHED BY ORDER OF THE HOUSE. . . .)
[Philadelphia:] Printed by John H. Oswald.   pp. [3], folded table.   fol.
AAS, BA, LCP, LOC, NYPL, NYSL.

36536 —— LETTER FROM THE SECRETARY OF THE TREASURY, TO THE CHAIRMAN OF THE COMMITTEE OF WAYS
& MEANS, ACCOMPANYING A PLAN FOR DIGESTING . . . DUTIES ON SPIRITS. . . . [7TH JANUARY,
1799.] (PUBLISHED BY ORDER OF THE HOUSE. . . .)
[Philadelphia: Printed by William Ross.]   pp. 39.   8vo.
AAS, BA, HC, LOC, NYHS, NYPL, WLC.

36537 —— LETTER FROM THE SECRETARY OF THE TREASURY, TRANSMITTING A STATEMENT OF GOODS . . .
EXPORTED. . . . 7TH FEBRUARY, 1799. . . . PUBLISHED BY ORDER OF THE HOUSE. . . .
[Philadelphia:] Printed by W. Ross.   pp. [4], folded table.
AAS, BA, LOC, NYPL, NYSL.

36538 —— LETTER FROM THE SECRETARY OF THE TREASURY, TRANSMITTING A STATEMENT OF THE OFFICIAL
EMOLUMENTS OF THE OFFICERS EMPLOYED IN THE COLLECTION OF THE INTERNAL REVENUES. . . .
1ST MARCH, 1799. . . .(PUBLISHED BY ORDER OF THE HOUSE. . . .)
[Philadelphia:] Printed by John H. Oswald.   pp. [4], 6 folded tables.   fol.
AAS, BA, HC, JCB, LOC, NYPL, PPL, WLC.

36539 —— LETTER FROM THE SECRETARY OF THE TREASURY, TRANSMITTING COPIES OF TWO LETTERS FROM THE
COMMISSIONERS OF THE CITY OF WASHINGTON. . . . 5TH DECEMBER, 1799. . . .
[Philadelphia:] Printed by W. Ross, in Locust-Street, between Walnut and Spruce.
pp. 18, 4 folded tables.   8vo.   AAS, BA, JCB, LCP, LOC, PⁱU.

36540 —— LETTER FROM THE SECRETARY OF THE TREASURY, TRANSMITTING TWO STATEMENTS; ONE EXHIBITING
THE VALUE OR QUANTITIES OF THE GOODS, WARES AND MERCHANDIZE, IMPORTED INTO THE
UNITED STATES. . . . 30TH JANUARY, 1799. . . . PUBLISHED BY ORDER OF THE HOUSE. . . .
[Philadelphia:] Printed by W. Ross.   pp. [4], 2 folded tables.   fol.
AAS, BA, JCB, LOC, NYPL, NYSL.

36541 —— Letter from the Treasurer of the United States, transmitting the account of the receipts and expenditures in the Treasury Department for the quarter ending September 30, 1798 [House document, February 11, 1799].
[*Philadelphia*]. pp. 27. 8vo. AAS.

36542 —— List of the names, and places of residence, of the members of the Senate and House of Representatives of the United States.
[*Philadelphia*.] Broadside. fol.
The names included show that the list must have been printed after December 5, 1799, and before January 10, 1800. For the preceding address list see *Fifth Congress* above.
AAS, JCB, NYPL.

36543 —— Manual of exercise and evolutions of the cavalry. As practiced in the late American army. Materially corrected and amended.
East Windsor: Printed by Luther Pratt. . . . 1799. pp. 36. 18mo.
NYPL.

36544 —— Marine rules and regulations.
Boston: Printed by Manning & Loring, for William T. Clap. . . . 1799. pp. 64.
8vo. AAS, BPL, HC, HEH, LOC, NYPL, NYSL, WⁱˢHS.

36545 —— Message from the President of the United States accompanying an extract of a letter from the minister . . . at London to the Secretary of State, dated the 16th of November, 1798, and an edict . . . of the . . . Directory of the French Republic, of the 29th of October, 1798. 28th January, 1799. . . .
Philadelphia: Printed by John Ward Fenno. 1799. pp. 8. 8vo.
AAS, BA, LOC, NYHS, NYPL, PPL, WLC.

36546 —— Message from the President of the United States accompanying a Report of the Secretary of State, containing observations on some of the documents, communicated by the President, on the eighteenth instant. 21st January, 1799. . . . Published by order of the House. . . .
Philadelphia: Printed by John Ward Fenno. 1798 [!]. pp. [2], 45. 8vo.
AAS, BA, HC, JCB, LOC, NYHS, NYSL, NYSOC, WLC.

36547 —— —— *Philadelphia: Printed by John Ward Fenno. 1799.* pp. [2], 45, [2]. 8vo.
Copies were circulated without the titlepage, which is tipped on, and without the final leaf, which contains Timothy Pickering's errata note, dated January 24. There are two forms of the Pickering note, one addressed to the President of the Senate and the other to the Speaker of the House.
AAS, APS, BA, BM, CL, HC, HEH, HSP, JCB, LOC, NHHS, NYSL, VᵃU, WⁱˢHS, YC.

36548 —— —— *Published by order of the House of Representatives by John W. Fenno. . . .* pp. 16.
8vo.
This is not the official printing but a pamphlet made by repaging a newspaper printing of the Message under the above heading. AAS, BA, NYHS.

36549 —— Message from the President of the United States, accompanying a Report to him, from the Secretary of War, of the 24th instant, relative to the military establishment. 31st December, 1798. . . . (Published by order of the House. . . .)
[*Philadelphia*.] pp. 27. 8vo. AAS, BA, JCB, NYHS, YC.

36550 —— Message from the President of the United States, accompanying his annual account of the application of grants made by Congress for the contingent charges of government. . . . 8th January, 1799. . . . Published by order of the House. . . .
Philadelphia: Printed by J. Gales, no. 23, South Third-Street. pp. 7. 8vo.
AAS, BA, LOC, NYHS, NYPL, WLC.

36551 —— Message from the President of the United States, accompanying sundry papers relative to the affairs of the United States, with the French Republic. 18th January, 1799. Published by order of the House. . . .
[*Philadelphia: Printed by William Ross.*]   pp. 123.   8vo.
AAS, BA, HC, HEH, HSP, JCB, LOC, NYHS, NYPL, NYSL, PPL, W¹ˢHS, WLC, YC.

36552 —— —— 22d January, 1799. Published by order of the Senate.
[*Philadelphia: Printed by William Ross.*]   pp. 123.   8vo.   AAS, BA, HC, LOC, YC.

36553 —— Message from the President of the United States, accompanying sundry papers relative to the impressment of American seamen. . . . 8th January, 1799. . . . Published by order of the House. . . .
Philadelphia: Printed by J. Gales, no. 23, South Third-street.   pp. 8.   8vo.
AAS, BA, HEH, JCB, LOC, NYHS, NYPL, YC.

36554 —— Message from the President of the United States, communicating to the House such information as he has received touching a suspension of the arrete of the French Republic. . . . Made in pursuance of a resolution of this House, of yesterday. [Feb. 15, 1799.]
Philadelphia: Printed by John Ward Fenno.   pp. 6.   8vo.
AAS, LOC, MᵈHS, NYPL, NYSL, WLC, YC.

36555 —— Message from the President of the United States, inclosing a Report to him, from the Director of the Mint. . . . 31st January, 1799. . . . Published by order of the House. . . .
[*Philadelphia:*] *Printed by Way & Groff, no. 48, North Third-Street.*   pp. 7   8vo.
AAS, BA, JCB, LOC, NYHS, NYPL.

36556 —— Message from the President of the United States transmitting a statement of the vessels with their tonnage, warlike force and complement of men to which commissions, as private armed vessels, have been issued since the ninth of July last. . . . Department of State, March 1, 1799. . . .
[*Philadelphia.*]   Broadside.   fol.   AAS, BA, LOC, NYPL.

36557 —— Message from the President of the United States transmitting certain documents on the subjects of the insurrection in Pennsylvania; the renewal of commerce with St. Domingo; and the mission to France. 5th December, 1799. . . . (Published by order of the House. . . .)
[*Philadelphia: Printed by William Ross.*]   pp. 42.   8vo.
AAS, BA, JCB, LCP, LOC, NL, NYHS, NYPL, YC.

36558 —— Message from the Senate, communicating a copy of the plea, filed . . . in behalf of William Blount, 26th December, 1798. . . . (Published by order of the House. . . .)
[*Philadelphia.*]   pp. 4.   8vo.   LOCᵖʰ

36559 —— Mr. Abiel Foster's Motion for an Amendment to the Constitution of the United States. 16th February, 1799. . . . (Published by order of the House. . . .)
[*Philadelphia: Printed by William Ross.*]   pp. [3].   8vo.   AAS, BA, JCB.

36560 —— The Proceedings of the House of Representatives of the United States, with respect to the petitions praying for a repeal of the Alien and Sedition Laws . . . and the speeches of Messrs. Gallatin and Nicholas. . . .
Philadelphia: Printed by Joseph Gales. 1799.   pp. 34.   8vo.
AAS, BPL, HC, LOC, NYSL, PʳU.

36561 —— Proceedings on the impeachment of William Blount . . . for high crimes and misdemeanors.
Philadelphia: Printed by Joseph Gales. 1799.   pp. 102.   8vo.
AAS, BM, CLS, HC, HEH, HSP, JCB, LOC, MHS, NYHS.

36562 —— Report. From the committee to whom was referred, the Bill, sent from the Senate, intituled, "An Act, for the relief of persons imprisoned for debt." 23d December, 1799. . . . Published by order of the House of Representatives.
[*Philadelphia: Printed by William Ross.*]   pp. 4.   8vo.   AAS, LOC.

36563 —— Report (in part) of the committee to whom was referred so much of the President's speech as relates to the "Naval establishment. . . ." 17th January, 1799. . . . (Published by order of the House. . . .)
[*Philadelphia: Printed by William Ross.*]   pp. 37.   8vo. AAS, BA, JCB, LOC, NYPL, YC.

36564 —— Report of the commissioners of the sinking fund, inclosing a report to them, from the Secretary of the Treasury. . . . 11th December, 1799. . . . Printed by order of the House. . . .
Philadelphia: Printed by Way & Groff, no. 48, North Third-street.   pp. 14, folded table.   8vo.   AAS, BA, LOC, NL, NYPL, NYSL, PrU, WLC, YC.

36565 —— Report of the committee appointed on the fourth instant to prepare an Address to both Houses of Congress. 6th December, 1799. . . .
Printed by W. Ross, in Locust-Street, between Walnut and Spruce.   pp. 7.   8vo.
AAS, BA, JCB, LOC, NL, NYHS, NYPL, NYSL, WLC, YC.

36566 —— Report of the committee of claims, on the memorials and petitions. . . . 17th April, 1798, ordered to lie on the table. 23d April, 1798, committed. . . . 15th January, 1799, committed. . . . (Published by order of the House. . . .)
[*Philadelphia: Printed by William Ross.*]   pp. 4.   8vo.   AAS, LOC, NYPL.

36567 —— Report of the committee of claims, on the petition of Stephen Sayre, presented the 29th March, 1796. 15th January, 1798, ordered to lie on the table. 17th January, 1798. . . . 25th January, 1799. . . . (Published by order of the House. . . .)
[*Philadelphia: Printed by William Ross.*]   pp. 14.   8vo.   AAS, BA, LOC, NYPL.

36568 —— Report of the committee of claims, to whom was recommitted, on the 24th ultimo, the petition of Comfort Sands. . . . 12th February, 1799. . . . (Published by order of the House. . . .)
[*Philadelphia: Printed by William Ross.*]   pp. 16.   8vo.
AAS, BA, HEH, LOC, NYPL, NYSL, PPL, WLC.

36569 —— Report of the committee of claims, to whom was referred, on the 7th instant, the petition of John Vaughan. . . . 21st February, 1799. . . . Published by order of the House of Representatives.
[*Philadelphia: Printed by William Ross.*]   pp. 4.   8vo.   AAS, LOC, NYPL, YC.

36570 —— —— 17th December, 1799, committed to . . . the whole House. . . . Published by order of the House. . . .
[*Philadelphia: Printed by William Ross.*]   pp. 4.   8vo.
Pages 3 and 4 are reversed.   AAS, BA, LOC, NL, NYPL, NYSL, WLC.

36571 —— Report of the committee of claims, to whom was referred, on the twenty-first ultimo, the petition of John Carr, presented the 21st of February, 1794. . . . 17th January, 1798, committed. . . . 17th January, 1799, committed. . . . (Published by order of the House. . . .)
[*Philadelphia: Printed by William Ross.*]   pp. 7.   8vo.   AAS, LOC, NYPL, WLC.

36572 —— Report of the committee of claims, to whom was referred on the 28th ult. the petition of Moses White. . . . 4th February, 1799. . . .
[*Philadelphia: Printed by William Ross.*]   pp. 5.   8vo.   AAS, BA, LOC, NYPL, WLC.

36573 —— Report of the committee of revisal and unfinished business, on bills, and reports, depending. . . at the last session of Congress. 10th December, 1799. . . . (Published by order of the House. . . .)
[*Philadelphia: Printed by William Ross.*]   pp. 6.   8vo.
AAS, BA, LOC, NYPL, NYSL, WLC.

36574 —— Report of the committee of ways and means, instructed, by a resolution of the ninth instant, "to enquire into the . . . duties on stamped . . . paper. . . ." 21st January, 1799. . . . (Published by order of the House. . . .)
[*Philadelphia: Printed by William Ross.*]   pp. 12, 2 folded tables.   8vo.
AAS, BA, BPL, JCB, LOC, NYPL, WLC.

36575 —— Report of the committee of ways and means, instructed on the ninth instant, to enquire and report . . . whether any and what amendments are necessary in the "Act to provide for the valuation of lands and dwelling-houses," and the "enumeration of slaves within the United States." 21st January, 1799. . . . (Published by order of the House. . . .)
[*Philadelphia: Printed by William Ross.*]   pp. 8.   8vo.
AAS, BA, LOC, NYPL, NYSL, PPL, WLC.

36576 —— Report of the committee of ways and means, to whom was referred, on the twenty-fifth instant, the petition of sundry distillers in the counties of Rockingham and Augusta, in the State of Virginia. 28th January, 1799. . . . (Published by order of the House. . . .)
[*Philadelphia: Printed by William Ross.*]   pp. 4.   8vo.   AAS, LOC, NYPL, PPL.

36577 —— Report of the committee to whom was recommitted the bill sent from the Senate, intitled, "An Act for the relief of persons imprisoned for debt." 30th December, 1799. . . . (Published by order of the House. . . .)
[*Philadelphia.*]   pp. 4.   8vo.   LOC, NYHS.

36578 —— Report of the committee to whom was referred, on the 19th of December last, a resolution for causing a publication of the Constitution of the United States. . . . 21st February, 1799. . . . (Published by order of the House. . . .)
[*Philadelphia: Printed by William Ross.*]   pp. 6.   8vo.   AAS, BA, LOC, NYPL.

36579 —— Report of the committee to whom was referred the Bill authorizing the acceptance from the State of Connecticut of a cession of the jurisdiction of the territory west of Pennsylvania, commonly called the Western Reserve of Connecticut. February 15, 1799.
[*Philadelphia.*]   pp. 24.   8vo.   AAS, NYPL.

36580 —— Report of the committee to whom was referred, the Bill sent from the Senate, intituled "An Act, for relief of persons imprisoned for debt." 23d December, 1799. . . . (Published by order of the House. . . .)
[*Philadelphia.*]   pp. 4.   8vo.   LOC, NYHS.

36581 —— Report of the committee to whom were referred, on the 12th instant, certain memorials & petitions complaining of the Act, intituled "An Act concerning aliens". . . . 21st February, 1799. . . . (Published by order of the House. . . .)
[*Philadelphia: Printed by William Ross.*]   pp. 15.   8vo.
AAS, BA, HC, JCB, LOC, NYHS, NYSL, NYSOC, PPL, WLC.

36582 —— Report of the Secretary of the Navy on the petition of sundry French officers confined in the prison of Burlington, State of New-Jersey. 27th December, 1799. . . . (Published by order of the House. . . .)
[*Philadelphia: Printed by William Ross.*]   pp. 4 [i. e. 3].   8vo.   AAS, BA, JCB, LOC.

36583 —— Reports of committees in Congress to whom were referred certain memorials and petitions complaining of the acts of Congress, concerning the Alien and Sedition Laws. And on the naval establishment. . . . Also an answer of the Massachusetts legislature to the Virginia Resolutions. . . .
Richmond, Printed by Thomas Nicolson, 1799. pp. 20. 8vo. LOC.

36584 —— Rules and regulations respecting the recruiting service.
[Philadelphia.] pp. 14, [4], 2 blank forms. 16mo.
The second of the forms is dated 1799. NYPL.

36585 —— 16th December, 1799. Read the first and second time, and committed to a committee of the whole House on Thursday next. A bill providing for salvage in cases of recapture. . . .
[Philadelphia.] pp. [3]. fol. LOC.

36586 —— 16th December, 1799. Read the first and second time, and committed to a committee of the whole house, on Thursday next. A bill providing for the enumeration of the inhabitants of the United States.
[Philadelphia.] pp. 7. fol. LOC.

36587 —— 16th December, 1799. Read the first and second time, and committed to a committee of the whole House on Wednesday next. A bill for the preservation of peace with the Indian tribes. . . .
[Philadelphia.] pp. [2]. fol. LOC.

36588 —— Speech of Mr. Gallatin in the House of Representatives . . . on the bill for augmenting the navy establishment, delivered on Monday, February 11th, 1799.
[Philadelphia.] pp. 12. 8vo. LOC.

36589 —— Speech of the President of the United States to both Houses of Congress. 3d. December, 1799. . . .
[Philadelphia:] Printed by W. Ross. pp. 7. 8vo. AAS, LOC, MᵉHS, NYHS, PPL, WLC.

36590 —— Standing rules and orders of the House of Representatives of the United States.
Philadelphia: Printed by John H. Oswald, 1799. pp. 22. 16mo.
AAS, HSP, JCB, NHHS, NHS.

36591 —— Sundry resolutions and proceedings, in cases before the Board of Commissioners, for carrying into effect the sixth article of the treaty . . . between His Britannic Majesty and the United States of America.
Philadelphia: Printed by R. Aitken, no. 22, Market Street. 1799. pp. 123. sq. 8vo.
AAS, BA, BPL, HSP, JCB, LCP, LOC, MHS, NYHS, NYPL.

36592 —— To the President of the United States, The Secretary of State respectfully submits the following Report on the transactions relating to the United States and France. . . . January 18, 1799.
Most copies of this Report have a tipped on titlepage reading *Message from the President of the United States, Accompanying a Report of the Secretary of State*, which see.

36593 —— Translation of the edict of the executive directory of the French Republic of 29th of October, 1798; referred to in the message of the President of the United States, of the 28th January, 1799. Printed by order of the Senate of the United States.
Philadelphia: Printed by John Ward Fenno. 1799. pp. 4. 8vo. AAS, LOC, NYSL.

36594 —— Treasury Department, Comptroller's Office. May 27, 1799. Circular to collectors, naval officers and surveyors. . . .
[Philadelphia.] Broadside. fol. LOC.

36595   —— Treasury of the United States, February 11th, 1799. Sir, My account of receipts and expenditures. . . . Samuel Meredith, Treasurer of the United States. . . .
[*Philadelphia.*]   pp. 27.   8vo.   AAS, HEH, LOC, NYPL, YC.

36596   —— Treasury United States. December 6th, 1799. Sir, My specie, war and navy accounts ending . . . September 30th, 1799. . . .
[*Philadelphia.*]   pp. [8].   8vo.   LOC.

36597   —— Treaty of amity and commerce, between his majesty the King of Prussia, and the United States of America. Printed by order of the Senate. . . .
Philadelphia: Printed by Way and Groff. . . . 1799.   pp. 19.   8vo.   LOC.

36598   —— Uniform for the army of the United States. The uniform of the commander in chief, to be a blue coat. . . . Given at the War Office of the United States, in Philadelphia, this 9th day of January, 1799. . . .
Broadside.   fol.   LOC.

36599   THE UNITED States Almanac, for the year of our Lord 1800. . . .
Elizabeth-town printed by Shepard Kollock for David Dunham.   pp. [26].   HEH.

36600   UNITED States Chronicle.   1784–1804
Published by B. Wheeler, at . . . Providence.   fol.   weekly.
For 1799: AAS, BʳU, HC, LOC, NYPL, RIHS, YC.

36601   UNITED States court kalendar, and gentleman's complete pocket-companion, for. . . 1800. . . .
New-York, Published by William Cobbett.   pp. [134].   NYHS, NYPL.

36602   THE UNIVERSAL Gazette.   1797–1800
Philadelphia: Printed by Samuel Harrison Smith.   fol.   weekly.
For 1799: AAS, BA, HSP, LOC, PPL.

36603   —— (Circular) Philadelphia, July 27, 1799. Sir. . . . I am with esteem, Samuel H. Smith.
[*Philadelphia: Printed by Samuel Harrison Smith.*]   Broadside.   fol.   HSP.

36604   THE UNIVERSAL right of sufferage is in danger from the Bryan's Station Ticket.
[*Kentucky.*]   Broadside.   UOC.

36605   UNPARTHEYISCHE Harrisburg Morgenröthe Zeitung.   Mar. 12, 1799–1840
Harrisburgh, Pennsylvania. Gedruckt bey B. Mayer und C. Fahnestock.   fol.
weekly.
With the issue of August 6 Conrad Fahnestock dropped out of the partnership.
For 1799: PSL.

36606   DER UNPARTHEYISCHE Readinger Adler.   1796–1913
Herausgegeben von Jacob Schneider und Comp. . . Reading. . . .   fol.   weekly.
For 1799: AAS, Berks Co. Hist. Soc.

36607   [DIE UNPARTHEYISCHE York Gazette.   1796–1804
York, Pa., published by Salomon Mayer.   weekly.]   For 1799: NO COPY KNOWN.

36608   VANDIKE, John, *pseud.*
A Narrative of the captivity of John Vandike who was taken by the Algerines in 1791; an account of his escape, bringing with him a beautiful English lady, that was taken in 1790; the ill usage she received from her master. The whole in a letter to his brother in Amsterdam. Tr. into English, by Mr. James How, of Holland.
Hanover, Printed, for the purchaser, 1799.   pp. 32.   12mo.   LOC.

36609 [VAUGHAN, John] 1775–1807
 Chemical Syllabus.
  [Wilmington: Bonsall & Niles, Printers.]   pp. 21.   12mo.
  Dedication dated November 20, 1799, on p. 2. The imprint is from p. 21.
  APS, BA, LCP, LOC, NYPL, WLC.

36610 DER VEREINIGTEN Staaten Calender, auf das jahr Jesu Christi, 1800. Ein gemeines jahr
 von 365 tagen.
  Philadelphia: Gedruckt bey Joseph R. Kämmer und G. Helmbold, jun . . .   pp.
  [42].   8vo.
  Cover-title with a cut of Philadelphia.   HSP.

36611 THE VERGENNES Gazette and Vermont and New-York Advertiser. 1798–1801
  Vergennes, State of Vermont: Printed . . . for Samuel Chipman, jun. . . .   fol.
 weekly.   For 1799: [DC], [VᵗSL].

36612 VERMONT. Memorial meeting.
 The Illustrious and beloved General Washington. . . .
  See 36419.

36613 VERMONT. State.
 Acts and laws passed by the legislature of the State of Vermont. At their session holden
  at Vergennes, October one thousand seven hundred and ninety eight.
  Bennington: Printed by Anthony Haswell. 1799.   pp. 141, [4].   8vo.
  AAS, BM, HC, LOC, NYBA, NYPL, VᵗU, VᵗSL.

36614 VERMONT. State.
 Acts and laws, passed by the legislature of the State of Vermont, at their session
  holden at Windsor, in October, A. D. one thousand seven hundred & ninety nine.
  Rutland, Printed by order of the legislature.   pp. 133.   8vo.
  AAS, BM, CU, HC, HEH, LOC, NYBA, NYPL, NYSL, VᵗSL, VᵗU.

36615 VERMONT. State.
 [His excellency Governor Isaac Tichnor's speech, to both Houses of the General
  Assembly.
  Windsor: Printed by Alden Spooner. 1799.]
  Advertisement.

36616 VERMONT. State.
 Journal of the General Assembly of the State of Vermont. Begun and holden at
  Windsor, October tenth, one thousand seven hundred and ninety nine.
  Rutland, Printed by order of the legislature. 1799.   pp. 157.   4to.
  AAS, NYPL, VᵗSL, VᵗU

36617 VERMONT. State.
 State of Vermont. In General Assembly, Windsor, November 5th, 1799. Resolved, that
  the senators and representatives of this State . . . propose . . . the following amendment to the Constitution of the United States. . . .
  [Windsor.]   Broadside.   fol.   AAS, RISL.

36618 THE VERMONT Almanac and Register. . . .
  See Williams, Samuel, 1743–1817.

36619 THE VERMONT Gazette. 1783–1847
  Printed and published at Bennington, by Anthony Haswell.   fol.   weekly.
  For 1799: VᵗSL.

36620 VERSES, COMPOSED AND SUNG AT TRENTON. . . .
        See 38668.

36621 VERSES, WRITTEN ON THE DEATH OF MR. BENJAMIN TUBBS, OF HEBRON — WHO DIED OF A CANCER, JANUARY 15TH, 1799.
        Narrow folio broadside.
        On the same sheet is printed "Thoughts on attending the funeral of a little child of nine weeks old; who died at Hebron." NYPL.

36622 A VIEW OF THE CALVINISTIC CLUBS IN THE UNITED STATES. . . .
        See Ogden, John Cosens.

36623 A VIEW OF THE NEW-ENGLAND ILLUMINATI. . . .
        See Ogden, John Cosens.

36624 VILLAGE MESSENGER.   1796–1801
        Samuel Preston, printer. — Amherst, New-hampshire. fol. weekly.
                FOR 1799: [AAS], AMHERST PUB. LIB.

36625 VIRGILIUS MARO, PUBLIUS
        THE PASTORAL SONGS OF P. VIRGIL MARO. TO WHICH ARE ADDED, POEMS SENTIMENTAL AND DESCRIPTIVE. BY JOHN MILLER RUSSELL, A. M. . . .
        Boston. Printed by Manning & Loring. 1799. pp: [4], 92. 12mo.
                AAS, BA, BPL, BʳU, LOC, MSL, NYPL.

36626 VIRGINIA. STATE.
        [AN ACT CONCERNING ELECTIONS.
        Richmond. Jones & Dixon. 1799.]   SWEM 7912.

36627 —— [AN ACT IMPOSING CERTAIN TAXES ON LAW PROCESS.
        Richmond. Jones & Dixon. 1799.]   SWEM 7914.

36628 —— [AN ACT LAYING TAXES FOR THE SUPPORT OF GOVERNMENT.
        Richmond. Jones & Dixon. 1799.]   SWEM 7920.

36629 —— ACTS PASSED AT A GENERAL ASSEMBLY OF THE COMMONWEALTH OF VIRGINIA: BEGUN AND HELD AT THE CAPITOL, IN THE CITY OF RICHMOND, ON MONDAY, THE THIRD DAY OF DECEMBER, ONE THOUSAND SEVEN HUNDRED AND NINETY-EIGHT.
        Richmond: Printed by Meriwether Jones & John Dixon. . . . 1799. pp. 36. fol.
           HC, HEH, HSP, JCB, LOC, MSL, NYBA, NYPL, VᵃSL.

36630 —— [ADDRESS OF THE CITIZENS OF GREENBRIER AND MUNROE COUNTIES, TO THE MEMBERS OF THE HONORABLE ASSEMBLY OF VIRGINIA.
        Staunton, printed by John Wise. . . . M,DCC,LXLIX [sic.]. pp. 32.]
        James Lewis Hook, cat. 30, Sept. 1940, no. 1.

36631 —— ADDRESS OF THE FIFTY-EIGHT FEDERAL MEMBERS OF THE VIRGINIA LEGISLATURE TO THEIR FELLOW-CITIZENS, IN JANUARY, 1799.
        Augusta, (District of Maine). Printed by Peter Edes. 1799. pp. 32. sm. 8vo.
           BA, HEH, LOC, MᵉHS.

36632 —— —— —— [*Philadelphia: Printed by John Fenno?*] pp. 12. 8vo.   LOC.

36633 —— [ADDRESS OF THE GENERAL ASSEMBLY TO THE PEOPLE OF THE COMMONWEALTH OF VIRGINIA.
        Richmond: Jones & Dixon. 1799.]   SWEM 7922.

36634 —— The Address of the legislature of Virginia to the people; with resolutions respecting the Alien & Sedition Laws, etc.
  [Norfolk:] Printed for the Constitutional Society, March 28, 1799.   pp. 26.   16mo.
  LOC.

36635 —— The Address of the minority of the Virginia legislature to the people of that State; containing a vindication of the constitutionality of the Alien and Sedition laws.
  [Richmond: A. Davis.]   pp. 16.   8vo.
  Attributed to Henry Lee.
  AAS, BA, BM, HC, JCB, LCP, LOC, NYHS, NYPL, NYSL, PʳU, VᵃU, WⁱˢHS.

36636 —— —— —— *[Colophon:] Albany: Printed by Loring Andrews.*   pp. 20.   8vo.
  NL, NYHS, NYPL, NYSL.

36637 —— The Address of the minority of the legislature of Virginia, to their fellow citizens.
  Petersburg: Printed by William Prentis. 1799.   pp. 16.   8vo.   DUKE UNIVERSITY.

36638 —— The Awful crisis which has arrived. . . . Extract from the Journal of the House of Delegates, Friday, January 4, 1799.
  [Richmond: Printed by Thomas Nicolson.]   pp. [4].   fol.
  This is another edition of *The Address of the Minority*.   LOC.

36639 —— The Communications of the several States, on the resolutions of the legislature of Virginia, respecting the Alien and Sedition Laws.
  Richmond.   pp. 20.   12mo.
  Ordered printed on December 25, 1799.   LOC.

36640 —— The Declaration of American independence. . . . Alien and Sedition Laws. . . . Proceedings of the legislature of this Commonwealth thereupon. . . .
  Richmond, Virginia: Printed by Jones and Dixon. . . . 1799.   pp. 40.   12mo.
  JCB, LOC, NL, VᵃSL, WLC.

36641 —— In the House of Delegates, Friday, January 11, 1799. The General Assembly of Virginia. . . . January 16th, 1799, agreed to by the Senate. . . .
  [Richmond: Printed by M. Jones and J. Dixon.]   Broadside.   8vo.
  Resolutions relative to the eligibility of aliens to sit in Congress.   JCB, LOC.

36642 —— Journal of the House of Delegates of the Commonwealth of Virginia: begun and held at the Capitol, in the City of Richmond, on Monday, the third day of December, one thousand seven hundred and ninety-eight.
  Richmond: Printed by Meriwether Jones and John Dixon, printers to the Commonwealth. 1798 [i. e. 1799].   pp. 104.   fol.   JCB, VᵃSL.

36643 —— [Journal of the Senate of the Commonwealth of Virginia, begun and held at the Capitol, in the City of Richmond, on Monday, the third day of December, one thousand seven hundred and ninety-eight.
  Richmond: Printed by Thomas Nicolson. 1798 [i. e. 1799].]   SWEM 7903.

36644 —— List of pensioners, continued by the honorable the Executive, for the year 1798. . . . Auditor's-Office, 5th January, 1799.
  [Richmond: Printed by Jones and Dixon.]   Broadside.   fol.   LOC, NYPL.

36645 —— Militia law. An Act to amend an Act entitled "An Act to amend and reduce into one Act, the several Acts . . . for regulating the militia. . . . Passed January 23, 1799.
  [Richmond: Printed by Jones & Dixon.]   pp. [2].   fol.   LOC.

36646 —— [Report of the committee on the state of the business in the High Court of Chancery.
  Richmond: Printed by Meriwether Jones.]   SWEM 7963.

36647 —— [Resolutions that the General Assembly of Virginia will cooperate with the authorities of the United States. . . .
   Richmond: Nicolson, Jan. 10, 1799.]   Swem 7916.

36648 VIRGINIA. United Baptist Churches.
 Minutes of the Baptist General Committee. Held at Waller's meeting-house, in Spottsylvania County. May 1799.
   Richmond: Printed by Samuel Pleasants, junior.   pp. 8.   4to.   NYPL.

36649 [THE VIRGINIA Almanac. . . .
   Richmond: Printed by Thomas Nicolson, 1800.]
   Title page lacking; printer assumed from notice on the last page.   VᵃSL.

36650 THE VIRGINIA Almanac, for the year of our Lord 1800. . . . Containing . . . a new and beautiful dissertation on the married life. . . .
   Fredericksburg: Printed by T. Green, for the Rev. Mason L. Weems.   pp. [36].
 12mo.   AAS, JCB.

36651 THE VIRGINIA & North Carolina Almanac, for the year of our Lord 1800. . . . Containing . . . a new and beautiful dissertation on the married life. . . .
   Fredericksburg: Printed by T. Green, for the Rev. Mason L. Weems.   pp. [36].
 12mo.   AAS.

36652 THE VIRGINIA & North Carolina almanack . . . the astronomical part by Isaac Briggs. The editorial part by Americanus Urban. . . .
   Petersburg: Published by Ross & Douglas, booksellers and stationers.   pp. [20].
 16mo.
 For another edition see Evans 35239.   BM, WⁱˢHS.

36653 THE VIRGINIA Argus.   1796–1816
   Richmond:—Printed . . . by Samuel Pleasants jun. . . .   fol.   semi-weekly.
                     For 1799: [Loc.].

36654 THE VIRGINIA Federalist.   1799–1800
   Richmond: Printed . . . by W. A. Rind. . . .   fol.   semi-weekly.
                     For 1799: [HC].

36655 THE VIRGINIA Gazette, and General Advertiser.   1790–1809
   Richmond: Printed by Aug. Davis. . . .   fol.   semi-weekly.   For 1799: Loc.

36656 VIRGINIA Gazette and Petersburg Intelligencer.   1786–1800
   Published . . . by William Prentis. . . .   fol.   semi-weekly.
 Early in 1799 Prentis took Tarlton W. Pleasants into partnership and changed the firm name accordingly.   For 1799: [Loc], [NYPL], [VᵃHS], [VᵃSL], [VᵃU].

36657 THE VIRGINIA Herald.   1787–1875
   Fredericksburg (Va.) published . . . by T. Green.   fol.   semi-weekly.
                     For 1799: [Loc].

36658 [VISCARDO y Guzman, Juan Pablo]
 Lettre aux Espagnols & Americains. Par un de leurs compatriotes. Vincet amor patriae. . . .
   A Philadelphie. MDCCXCXIX [sic].   pp. [2], 41.   8vo.
   Probably a fictitious imprint.   JCB, WLC.

36659 DER VOLKS-BERICHTER; ein Yorker Wochenblatt.   July 25, 1799–1803
   York [Pa], gedruckt bey Andreas Billmeyer. . . .   fol.   weekly.   For 1799: AAS.

36660 VOLLSTÄNDIGES Marburger gesang-buch, zur uebung der gottseligkeit, in 615 Christli-
chen. . . psalmen. . . Martin Luthers. . . .
Philadelphia: Gedruckt bey Carl Cist, num. 104, in der Zwenten-Strasse . . . 1799.
pp. 262, front. 12mo. AAS, LCP.

36661 VOLNEY, C[onstantin] F[rançois Chasseboeuf, comte de] 1755–1820
The Ruins: or a survey of the revolutions of Empires. . . . A new translation from the
French. . . .
Philadelphia: Printed by James Lyon, and sold at his bookstore, Richmond. . . . 1799.
pp. xxiv, 406, 45, front., fold. plate, fold. map. 8vo.
AAS, BPL, HEH, HSP, JCB, PᴿU, WLC, YC.

36662 [THE VOLUNTEER Songster, or vocal remembrancer: for 1799. Containing the newest and
most approved songs now extant. . . .
Baltimore: Printed by Thomas Dobbin? 1799.] MINICK 547.

36663 THE VOYAGES and adventures of Captain Robert Boyle. . . .
See Chetwood, W. R.

36664 WAKEFIELD, Priscilla (Bell) 1751–1832
Mental improvement: or the beauties and wonders of nature and art. In a series of
instructive conversations. . . . First American, from the third London edition.
New-Bedford: Printed by Abraham Shearman, Jun. for Caleb Greene & Son. 1799.
pp. 264. 12mo. AAS, HEH, JCB, NL, WC, YC.

36665 WALKER, Timothy P.
[The Flaming sword, or a sign from Heaven. Being a remarkable phenomenon, seen
in the State of Vermont.
Norwich [Connecticut], printed 1799. pp. 12. 16mo.] BATES 2891.

36666 WARD, Jonathan 1769–1860
A Brief statement . . . of the sentiments of the Weslean Methodists. . . . By Jonathan
Ward, A.M. Pastor of the Church in New-Milford.
Hallowell (District of Maine.) Printed by Peter Edes. 1799. pp. 32. 8vo.
AAS, HEH, LOC.

36667 WARREN. Rhode Island.
An Address of a school-master to his scholars, pronounced at an exhibition on the close
of his school. . . .
Warren (R. I.): Printed by Nathaniel Phillips. M,DCC,XCIX. pp. 7. 12mo.
NYHS.

36668 WARREN. Rhode Island. Library Society.
The Charter and by-laws for the regulation of the Warren Library Society in the town
of Warren, and State of Rhode Island.
Warren (R. I.): Printed by Nathaniel Phillips, M,DCC,XCIX. pp. 31. 16mo.
Contains a catalogue of books and a list of members. AAS, BᴿU, JCB, NHS, RIHS.

36669 WARREN Association.
Minutes of the Warren Association held at the South Baptist Meeting-House in Middle-
borough, September 10 and 11, 1799.
Boston: Printed by Manning and Loring. MDCCXCIX. pp. 11. 8vo.
AAS, JCB, NYPL.

36670 WASHINGTON, Bushrod 1762–1829
Reports of cases argued and determined in the Court of Appeals of Virginia. . . . Vol. II.
Richmond: Printed by Thomas Nicolson, M,DCC,XCIX. pp. viii, 302, [1], 19.
8vo.
Volume 1 was published at Richmond in 1798.
AAS, BM, HC, HEH, JCB, PSL, NYPL, VᴬSL, VᴬU, YC.

36671 [WATERMAN, Foster]
  The Child's instructor: consisting of easy lessons for children. . . . By a teacher of little children in Philadelphia. The second Connecticut edition. . . .
    Newfield: Printed by Lazarus Beach. 1799. pp. 108. 12mo.
  Also attributed to John Ely, 1758–1847.   AAS, WL.

36672 WATERVLIET, Berne, and Bethlehem. New York.
  At a meeting of . . . freeholders of Watervliet, Bern and Bethlehem, held in . . . Albany on the 18th day of April, 1799. . . .
      [Albany ?] Broadside. 4to.   NYSL.

36673 WATKINS, Robert
  An examination of the executive proceeding against a member of the late convention; containing a recent correspondence with Governor Jackson. . . .
    Augusta [Ga.]. Printed by John Erdman Smith. MDCCXCIX. pp. 30. 8vo.
                      AAS, NYHS, NYPL.

36674 WATTS, Isaac   1674–1748
  Discourses on the love of God, and its influence on all the passions . . . also, a devout meditation annexed to each discourse. . . .
    William W. Woodward, printer. Sold at his book store Philadelphia, no. 17, Chestnut Street. 1799. pp. 224. 12mo.   AAS, NYPL, YC.

36675 —— Divine & moral songs, attempted in easy language for the use of children. Revised and corrected. . . .
    Printed and sold by Samuel Hall, no. 53, Cornhill, Boston.—1799. pp. 70, front.
  sq. 32mo.   AAS, BPL, CU.

36676 —— Divine hymns. In verse, for children. . . . The thirteenth edition with moral songs, sacred hymns, etc. . . By other eminent divines.
    Baltimore: Printed by W. Corbet, at R. Wilde's. . . . 1799. pp. 72. 24mo. AAS.

36677 —— Divine songs, attempted in easy language, for the use of children. . . . The ninety fourth edition.
    Medford, (Massachusetts.) Printed and sold by Nathaniel Coverly. 1799. . . . pp. 30.
  16mo.   AAS, LOC, MHS.

36678 WATTS, Washington, *of Virginia.*
  An inquiry into the causes and nature of the Yellow Fever; submitted to the examination of . . . the trustees and medical professors of the University of Pennsylvania, on the sixth day of June, 1799. . . .
    Philadelphia: Printed by John Ormrod. . . . 1799. pp. 42. 8vo.
          AML, BML, HEH, HSP, LCP, LOC, NYAM, NYPL, PPL, UOP.

36679 WEATHERWISE, Abraham, *pseud.*
  The Astronomical repository; or the family calendar for . . . 1800, calculated for the town of Boston. . . .
    Boston, printed and sold by Benjamin Edes, in Kilby-Street. pp. 24. 16mo. AAS.

36680 WEATHERWISE, J., *pseud.*
  The Farmer's Almanack, for . . . 1800. . . . Calculated for the meridian of Norwich. . . .
  Wherein are contained . . . a number of useful receipts, entertaining stories, &c. . . .
    Printed and sold by John Trumbull, in Norwich. . . . pp. [24]. 16mo.
                AAS, CHS, LOC, NYPL, NYSL, WL.

36681 WEATHERWISE's Almanac, for the year of Christian aera, 1800. Calculated for the New-England States. . . .
    Printed for, and sold by the booksellers in Boston, Salem, Newburyport, Portsmouth, and by most of the country Traders. pp. [4], 12, [8]. 16mo.
  Probably printed by Charles Peirce of Portsmouth, New Hampshire, whose advertisement appears on the last leaf. This is Daniel Sewall's almanac with a different titlepage. AAS.

36682 WEBSTER, Noah   1758–1843
AN AMERICAN SELECTION OF LESSONS IN READING AND SPEAKING. . . . BEING THE THIRD PART OF A
GRAMMATICAL INSTITUTE. . . . THOMAS AND ANDREWS' ELEVENTH EDITION. . . .
*Printed at Boston, by Isaiah Thomas and Ebenezer T. Andrews. . . . Sold. . . at their
bookstore; by said Thomas, in Worcester; by Thomas, Andrews, & Penniman, in Albany;
and by Thomas, Andrews & Butler, in Baltimore. 1799.*   pp. 240, portrait frontispiece.
12mo.
There were other issues of the eleventh edition in 1797 and 1800.   AAS, EI, HC.

36683 — — THE FOURTEENTH EDITION.
Hartford: Printed by Hudson & Goodwin.   pp. 240, [2].   12mo.
AAS, BPL, CHS, CSL, LOC, NYPL, WL, WRHS.

36684 — THE AMERICAN SPELLING BOOK. . . . BEING THE FIRST PART OF A GRAMMATICAL INSTITUTE. . . .
THOMAS & ANDREWS' TWENTIETH EDITION. . . .
*Printed at Boston, by Isaiah Thomas and Ebenezer T. Andrews . . . sold . . . at their
bookstore; by said Thomas, in Worcester; by Thomas, Andrews & Penniman, in Albany;
and by Thomas, Andrews & Butler, in Baltimore. 1799.*   pp. 156, portrait frontispiece.
12mo.   AAS.

36685 — — [THOMAS & ANDREWS' TWENTY-FIRST EDITION.]
Assumed from sequence of editions.

36686 — — TWENTY-FIRST CONNECTICUT EDITION.
Hartford: Printed by Hudson & Goodwin.   pp. 165, [1].   12mo.
Date supplied from p. 119. Illustrations engraved by Z. Howe and W. Wadsworth.
CSL, NYHS, NYPL.

36687 — A BRIEF HISTORY OF EPIDEMIC AND PESTILENTIAL DISEASES. . . AND OBSERVATIONS DEDUCTED FROM
THE FACTS STATED. IN TWO VOLUMES. . . .
*Hartford: Printed by Hudson & Goodwin. 1799. (Published according to Act of Con-
gress.)*   2 vols.   pp. xii, [9]–348; [4], 352.   8vo.
AAS, AML, BM, BPL, CHS, HEH, JCB, LOC, MHS, NL, NYAM, NYHS,
NYPL, NYSL, NYSOC, RU, VªU, WC, YC.

36688 [—] THE PROMPTER; OR A COMMENTARY ON COMMON SAYINGS & SUBJECTS, WHICH ARE FULL OF COM-
MON SENSE, THE BEST SENSE IN THE WORLD. . . .
Printed for, and sold by the book-sellers. Dec. 1799.   pp. 72.   12mo.
AAS, BPL, BʳU, JCB, NYPL, WLC, YC.

36689 THE WEEKLY ADVERTISER, OF READING, IN THE COUNTY OF BERKS.   1796–1816
Published . . . by Gottlob Jungmann and Company . . . of Reading. . . .   4to.
weekly.   FOR 1799: AAS, BERKS CO. HIST. SOC.

36690 WEEKLY COMPANION; AND THE COMMERCIAL CENTINEL.   1798 — APR. 6, 1799
Newport, Rhode-Island: Printed by H. & O. Farnsworth.   fol.   weekly.
FOR 1799: [AAS], [RIHS].

36691 THE WEEKLY MAGAZINE OF ORIGINAL ESSAYS, FUGITIVE PIECES, AND INTERESTING INTELLIGENCE. . . .
VOL. III [No. 31, FEB. 9, 1799, TO VOL. IV, No. 50, JUNE 18, 1799].
[Philadelphia: Published by Ezekiel Forman.]   pp. [129]–422.   8vo.
This magazine was originally published by James Watters and discontinued on Aug. 25,
1798, shortly after his death. Most files of this continuation end with June 1, 1799.
AAS, BPL, HC, HSP, LCP, LOC, NYHS. NYPL, NYSL, YC.

36692 WEEKLY MUSEUM.   1788–1817
New-York: Printed and published by John Harrisson. . . .   4to.   weekly.
FOR 1799: AAS, HC, LOC, NYHS, NYPL.

36693   —— ADDRESS OF THE CARRIER OF THE WEEKLY MUSEUM TO HIS PATRONS WITH THE COMPLIMENTS OF THE SEASON. . . . NEW-YORK, JANUARY 1, 1799.
        [*New-York: Printed and published by John Harrison, 1799.*]   Broadside.   4to.
                                                                         NYHS, NYPL.

36694   WEEMS, MASON LOCKE.   1759–1825
      THE PHILANTHROPIST; OR, A GOOD TWELVE CENTS WORTH OF POLITICAL LOVE POWDER, FOR THE FAIR DAUGHTERS AND PATRIOTIC SONS OF VIRGINIA. . . .
        pp. [2], 30.   MᵈHS.

36695   —— —— *Alexandria: Printed by John & James D. Westcot. MDCCXCIX.*   pp. 30.   12mo.
                                                                              VᵃSL.

36696   —— —— *Printed by J. May. MDCCXCIX.*   pp. 31.   NYSL.

36697   —— THE PHILANTHROPIST; OR, A GOOD TWENTY-FIVE CENTS WORTH OF POLITICAL LOVE POWDER . . . WITH THE . . . RECOMMENDATION BY GEORGE WASHINGTON. . . .
        [*Dumfries?*]   pp. [6], 4–30.   8vo.
      There are at least three issues of this edition. In the AAS copy a leaf containing an address to Washington is inserted between the title-page and the first page of text.
               AAS, BPL, HEH, HSP, JCB, LCP, LOC, MᵈHS, NYPL, NYSL, PʳU, YC, WLC.

36698   —— —— *Charleston: Re-printed by W. P. Young.*   pp. [2], 31, [1].   8vo.   HSP, SCHS.

36699   WELD, EZRA   1736–1816
      A DISCOURSE DELIVERED APRIL 25, 1799; BEING THE DAY OF FASTING AND PRAYER THROUGHOUT THE UNITED STATES OF AMERICA. . . .
        Boston: Printed by Manning & Loring, Spring-Lane. 1799.   pp. 31.   8vo.
            AAS, BA, BPL, CHS, HC, HEH, JCB, LOC, MHS, NYHS, NYPL, NYSL, RU, YC.

36700   [WEST, BENJAMIN]   1730–1813
      THE NEW-ENGLAND ALMANACK, OR LADY'S AND GENTLEMAN'S DIARY, FOR THE YEAR OF OUR LORD CHRIST 1800. . . . BY ISAAC BICKERSTAFF. . . .
        Printed at Providence (R. I.) by John Carter, opposite the Market. . . .   pp. [24].
      16mo.
                                          AAS, HSP, LOC, NYPL, RIHS.

36701   WEST, DAVID   1765–1810
      CATALOGUE OF BOOKS, PRINTED AND PUBLISHED IN AMERICA, AND FOR SALE AT THE BOOKSTORE OF DAVID WEST, NO. 56, CORNHILL, BOSTON. . . .
        Printed at Boston, for David West, no. 56, Cornhill. 1799.   pp. 36.   12mo.   EI.

36702   WEST, JOHN   1770–1827
      A CATALOGUE OF BOOKS; PUBLISHED IN AMERICA, AND FOR SALE AT THE BOOKSTORE OF JOHN WEST, NO. 75, CORNHILL, BOSTON. . . .
        Printed at Boston, for John West. . . . *1799.*   pp. 36.   12mo.   MHS.

36703   [THE WESTERN ALMANACK, FOR THE YEAR OF OUR LORD 1800.
        Pittsburgh: Printed by John Scull. 1799.]
      Advertised in the *Pittsburgh Gazette* of Nov. 16, 1799.

36704   [WESTERN CENTINEL.   1794–1800
        Whitestown, N. Y. Printed by Lewis & Webb.   fol.   weekly.]
                                        FOR 1799: NO COPY KNOWN.

36705   THE WESTERN SPY, AND HAMILTON GAZETTE.   MAY 28, 1799–1822
        Cincinnati: Published by Joseph Carpenter.   fol.   weekly.
      With the issue of Dec. 10 Jonathan S. Findlay was taken into partnership.
                                        FOR 1799: [AAS], [OH&PS].

36706   THE WESTERN STAR.   1789–1806
             Printed at Stockbridge, (Mass.) by Benjamin Rosseter.   fol.   weekly.
         With the issue for Aug. 19 Rosseter sold out to a group of proprietors, and the *Star* was
         printed by Heman Willard for Horatio Jones & Co.   FOR 1799: [HC].

36707   [THE WESTERN TELEGRAPHE, AND WASHINGTON ADVERTISER.   1795–1811
             Washington (Pennsylvania): printed by John Colerick.   fol.   weekly.]
                                                                     FOR 1799: NO COPY KNOWN.

36708   [DIE WESTLICHE CORRESPONDENZ.   1795–1825
             Hagerstaun, Maryland. Gedruckt bey Johann Gruber, 1799.   fol.   weekly.]
                                                                     FOR 1799: NO COPY KNOWN.

36709   WESTON, WILLIAM   1752?–1833
             REPORT. . . ON THE PRACTICABILITY OF INTRODUCING THE WATER OF THE RIVER BRONX INTO THE
         CITY OF NEW YORK. . . .
             [New York:] No. 102, in Pearl Street, printed by John Furman. M,DCC,XCIX.
         There are copies with the imprint dated "M,DCC,XIX."
                                      AAS, BA, BM, HC, HSP, LOC, NYHS, NYPL, NYSL, YC.

36710   WHEATON, HANNAH
             THE AUTHOR . . . NOW CASTS HER MITE, TO THE MEMORY OF THAT WORTHY PERSON [WASHING-
         TON], WHOSE LOSS WE SEVERELY FEEL. . . .
             [Boston.]   Broadside.   fol.   HEH.

36711   —— [ON TAKING AN AFFECTIONATE FAREWELL OF MY KIND BENEFACTORS IN BOSTON. . . .
             [Boston: 1799.]   Broadside.]   EVANS, FORD.

36712   WHIPPLE, ENOCH   1755–c. 1840
             THE IMPORTANCE OF EARLY PIETY; SET FORTH IN A SERMON, DELIVERED IN THE ACADEMY AT GIL-
         MANTON, NOVEMBER 11TH, 1799. . . .
             Printed at Gilmanton, by Elijah Russel for the subscribers.   pp. 13.   8vo. LOC, NYHS.

36713   WHITE, WILLIAM   1748–1836
             A SERMON ON THE DUTY OF CIVIL OBEDIENCE. . . . DELIVERED IN CHRIST CHURCH AND ST. PETER'S,
         APRIL 25, 1799, BEING A DAY OF GENERAL HUMILIATION. . . .
             Philadelphia: Printed by John Ormrod, no. 41, Chestnut-street, 1799.   pp. 26   8vo.
                                      AAS, BA, HC, HSP, JCB, LCP, LOC, NYHS, WLC, YC.

36714   WHITEHAVEN PARISH. NORTH CAROLINA.
             AN INTRODUCTION TO THE KNOWLEDGE OF THE CHRISTIAN RELIGION. PUBLISHED FOR THE USE OF
         THE PROTESTANT EPISCOPAL CHURCH OF WHITEHAVEN PARISH. BY ROBERT JOHNSTON MIL-
         LER, R. P.
             Salisbury: Printed, by John M. Slump, at Michael Brown's Printing-Office. MDCC-
         XCIX.   pp. 50.   16mo.   MR. BRUCE COTTEN.

36715   WHITESTOWN GAZETTE. AND CATO'S PATROL.   1798–1803.
             Utica [N. Y.]: Published by William M'Lean. 1799.   weekly.   fol.
                                                                         FOR 1799: [UOI¹¹].

36716   WILBERFORCE, WILLIAM   1759–1833
             A PRACTICAL VIEW OF THE PREVAILING RELIGIOUS SYSTEM OF PROFESSED CHRISTIANS. . . . SECOND
         AMERICAN EDITION.
             Boston: Printed by Manning & Loring, for Ebenezer Larkin, no. 47, Cornhill. Sold by
         him; by Cornelius Davis, New-York; and by Hudson & Goodwin, Hartford. 1799.
         pp. 300.   12mo.
         There are copies without the Davis and Hudson & Goodwin imprint, and others with
         "London printed" before the imprint.   AAS, BPL, HC, JCB, LOC, MHS, NYPL, NYSL, WC, YC.

36717 WILDE, Samuel S[umner] 1771-1855
An Oration, delivered at Pownalborough, before the Lincoln Lodge of Free and Accepted Masons . . . June 24th, 5799. . . .
Wiscasset [Me.]: Printed by Henry Hoskins 1799. pp. 20. sm. 4to. AAS, MFM.

36718 WILKESBARRE. Pennsylvania.
Sheriff's sale. By virtue of a writ of venditioni exponas, issued out of the Supreme Court of. . . Pennsylvania. . . will be exposed to sale by public vendue at the Court-House in Wilkesbarre. . . the 21st of August. . . the following described tracts or parcels of land. . . . Seized and taken in execution of the property of Walter Stewart . . . Wilkesbarre, July 3, 1799. . . .
Broadside. fol. Mrs. Joseph Carson.

36719 WILKESBARRE Gazette, and Luzerne Advertiser. 1797-1801
Wilkesbarre: Published for the proprietor, T. Wright. fol. weekly.
From April to September the paper was published by Joseph Wright.
For 1799: Wyoming Hist. Soc., Wilkes-Barré.

36720 WILKINSON, Eliab, *of Smithfield*
The New-England Calendar, and ephemeris, for the year of our Lord 1800. . . . Calculated for the latitude and longitude of Newport. . . .
Printed at Warren, by Nathaniel Phillips. . . . pp. [24]. 12mo.
AAS, BʳU, RIHS.

36721 ——— ——— *Printed [at Warren, by Nathaniel Phillips] for Jacob Richardson, of Newport.*
pp. [24]. 12mo. AAS, BʳU, LOC, RIHS.

36722 [WILLIAMS, Jonathan] 1750-1815
Thermometrical navigation. . . . Extracted from the American Philosophical Transactions Vol. 2 & 3. With additions and improvements. . . .
Philadelphia: Printed and sold by R. Aitken, no. 22, Market Street. 1799. pp. xii, 98, [3], folding map. 8vo.
AAS, APS, BA, BM, BPL, HC, HSP, JCB, LCP, LOC, MHS, NYHS, NYPL, PPL, YC.

36723 [WILLIAMS, Samuel] 1743-1817
The Vermont Almanac and Register, for the year of our Lord 1800. . . . Fitted to the latitude and longitude of Rutland. . . .
Printed at Rutland, Vermont; and sold wholesale and retail at the printing office.
pp. [36]. 16mo. AAS, BM, NYPL.

36724 WILLIAMS College.
Catalogue of students in Williams College, Nov. 1799. . . .
Pittsfield: Printed by Chester Smith [1799]. Broadside. fol. MHS, WC.

36725 —— Catalogus, senatus academici, et eorum qui munera et officia accademica gesserunt, quique alicujus gradus laurea exornati fuerunt. . . .
Apud Pittsfield, typis Chester Smith, 1799. Broadside. fol. MHS, NYHS, WC.

36726 —— Commencement at Williams College, September 4, 1799. Order of exercises. . . .
[Colophon:] Pittsfield: Printed by Chester Smith. Broadside. 4to. WC.

36727 [WILLIAMSON, Charles] 1757-1808
Description of the settlement of the Genesee country, in the State of New-York. In a series of letters. . . .
New-York: Printed by T. & J. Swords. . . . *1799.* pp. 63, folding map. 8vo.
See the bibliographical note under Vail 1221.
AAS, AHTS, BA, BPL, HC, HEH, HSP, LOC, MHS, NL, NYHS, NYPL, WᴵˢHS, WL. WLC.

36728 WILLISTON, Seth 1770-1851
An Address to parents, upon the importance of religiously educating their children. . . .
Printed at Suffield [Conn.], by Edward Gray, M,DCC,XCIX. pp. 96. 12mo.
Errata at foot of p. 96. AAS, CHS, CL, HEH, NYPL, PL, WC, YC.

36729 THE WILMINGTON GAZETTE. 1799–1816
Wilmington, N. C. published by Allmand Hall. fol. weekly.
A continuation of *Hall's Wilmington Gazette.* FOR 1799: [HC].

36730 WINCHESTER GAZETTE. THE CENTINEL. 1788–1825
Winchester (Virginia) printed and published. . . by Richard Bowen. . . . fol.
weekly. FOR 1799: UOC.

36731 [WINCHESTER TRIUMPH OF LIBERTY. 1799–1803
Winchester, Va., published by Trisler & Haff. fol. weekly.]
FOR 1799: NO COPY KNOWN.

36732 WINDHAM HERALD. 1791–1816
Windham: Printed by John Byrne, in the lower room of the Court-House. 1799.
fol. weekly. FOR 1799: AAS, CHS, [HC], [LOC], [NYHS].

36733 WISCASSET TELEGRAPH. 1796–1799
Published by Henry Hoskins, Wiscasset, Maine. fol. weekly.
FOR 1799: [McHS].

36734 WITTER, EZRA 1768–1833
See Evans 35134.

36735 DER WOHLERFAHRNE BAUM-GÄRTNER, ODER GRÜNDLICHE ANWEISUNG ZUR BEHANDLUNG DER
OBST-BÄUME. . . .
Libanon [Pa.], gedruckt bey Jacob Schnee. pp. [2], 16. 8vo. HSP.

36736 WOODBRIDGE, [WILLIAM] 1755–1836
A PLAIN AND CONCISE VIEW OF THE SYSTEM OF EDUCATION, AS TAUGHT BY MR. WOODBRIDGE, AT HIS
PRIVATE ACADEMY IN MIDDLETOWN. . . .
Middletown: Printed by Tertius Dunning. 1799. . . . pp. 8. 8vo.
Issued bound with his *Plain and Concise Grammar,* Middletown, 1800. NYPL.

36737 WOODS, LEONARD 1774–1854
A CONTRAST BETWEEN THE EFFECTS OF RELIGION, AND THE EFFECTS OF ATHEISM. AN ORATION,
DELIVERED AT COMMENCEMENT, HARVARD UNIVERSITY . . . JULY 17TH, 1799. . . .
Boston, printed by John Russell, 1799. pp. 20. 8vo.
There are copies with and without an errata note on p. 20.
AAS, BA, BPL, CL, EI, HC, HEH, JCB, LOC, MA, McHS, MHS, NYPL, NYSL, WC.

36738 —— TWO SERMONS ON PROFANE SWEARING, DELIVERED APRIL 4, 1799; THE DAY APPOINTED BY THE
GOVERNOR OF MASSACHUSETTS FOR HUMILIATION. . . .
Printed by Angier March, Newburyport. MDCCXCIX. pp. 39. 8vo.
AAS, BA, BM, HC, HEH, NYSL, YC.

36739 [WORCESTER, NOAH] 1758–1837
A POLEMIC ESSAY: CONTAINING REMARKS ON A DIALOGUE, WRITTEN, IN TWO PARTS. . . . IN DEFENCE
OF THE DOCTRINE OF ELECTION. . . .
Newark: Printed by O. Pennington and Dodge, 1799. pp. 42. 8vo. NYHS.
Authorship dubious.

36740 WORKMAN, BENJAMIN, *A. M.*
ELEMENTS OF GEOGRAPHY. . . . THE SEVENTH EDITION. ILLUSTRATED. . . .
*Philadelphia: Printed and sold by John M'Culloch, No. 1, North Third-Street.
1799. . . .* pp. 180, 7 maps. 24mo. AAS, HSP, YC.

36741 YALE COLLEGE.
CATALOGUE OF THE MEMBERS OF YALE COLLEGE, IN NEW-HAVEN, NOVEMBER 1799. . . .
[New Haven.] Broadside. fol. AAS, HC, MHS, YC.

36742 —— Catalogus senatus academici, et eorum qui munera et officia academica gesserunt, quique aliquovis gradu exornati fuerunt in Collegio Yalensi. . . .
Novi-Portus: excudebant Thomas et Thomas Green, universitatis typographi.
pp. 38. 8vo. AAS, AML, BA, BM, BPL, HC, JCB, NYHS, NYPL, YC.

36743 —— Scheme of the exercises at the public commencement. Yale-College, Sept. 11, 1799.
[*New Haven.*] Broadside. YC.

36744 DIE YORK Gazette.
See *Unpartheyische York Gazette.*

36745 YORK. Pennsylvania. Republican Party.
[A mutilated account of a meeting in favor of Thomas M'Kean, signed:] A friend of truth.
York [Pennsylvania]: August 12th, 1799. Broadside. fol.
One of the resolutions calls for the printing of a German edition. AAS.

36746 YOUNG, Edward 1683–1765
Resignation: in two parts. To which is added a postscript addressed to Mrs. B[oscawen]. . . . Second Worcester edition.
Printed at Worcester: by Isaiah Thomas, Jun. August — 1799. pp. 55, [1]. 12mo.
AAS, HC, JCB, MHS, NYPL.

36747 YOUNG Jemmy is a pleasing youth. A favorite song.
Boston, printed & sold at P. A. von Hagen, junr. & cos. musical magazine, no. 3, Cornhill: also by G. Gilfert, New York. . . . pp. [2]. fol.
Advertised in June, 1799. BPL, JCB.

36748 THE YOUTH'S Monitor: or a collection of thoughts on civil, moral, and religious subjects: selected from different authors. . . .
Leominster: Printed for the purchaser. 1799. pp. 48. 12mo. AAS, HEH, JCB, NYPL.

36749 ZENGER, John Peter 1680–1746
A Brief narrative of the case and tryal of John Peter Zenger, printer of the New-York Weekly Journal. . . .
[*Colophon:*] *Reprinted and sold at the Bible and Heart, Cornhill, Boston. MDCCXCIX.* pp. 48. 8vo.
AAS, BA, JCB, LOC, MHS, NL, NYHS, NYPL, NYSL.

36750 ZIMMERMANN, J[ohann] G[eorg] 1728–1795
Essay on national pride. To which are prefixed, Memoirs of the author's life and writings. Translated from the original German of the late celebrated Dr. J. G. Zimmermann, aulic counsellor and physician to his Britannic Majesty at Hanover. By Samuel H. Wilcocke.
New York: Printed by M. L. & W. A. Davis, for H. Caritat. . . . *1799.* pp. 300, [25]. 8vo.
The last section contains the Index and a list of Caritat's new publications.
AAS, BA, HC, HEH, JCB, NYAM, NYPL, NYSL, PPL, VᵃSL, WC.

1800

36751 ABBOT, ABIEL 1770–1828
AN EULOGY ON . . . GEORGE WASHINGTON . . . DELIVERED BEFORE THE INHABITANTS OF THE TOWN OF HAVERHILL ON HIS BIRTHDAY, 1800. . . . AND THE INVALUABLE LAST ADDRESS OF PRESIDENT WASHINGTON TO THE CITIZENS. . . .
Haverhill. Printed by Seth H. Moore. pp. 27, 21. 8vo.
AAS, BA, BPL, CL, EL, HC, HEH, JCB, MHS, NL, NYPL, NYSL, WˡˢHS.

36752 THE ACCIDENTAL DEATH OF NATHAN THOMPSON. . . . EIGHTEEN HUNDRED WAS THE YEAR. . . . THIRD OF DECEMBER WAS THE DAY. . . .
Broadside. 4to. AAS.

36753 AN ACCOUNT OF LOUISIANA, BEING AN ABSTRACT OF DOCUMENTS, IN THE OFFICES OF THE DEPARTMENTS OF STATE, AND OF TREASURY.
Published by John Conrad, & Co. . . Philadelphia; M. & J. Conrad, & Co. . . Baltimore; Rapin, Conrad, & Co. Washington City; Somervell & Conrad, Petersburg; and Bonsal, Conrad, & Co. Norfolk. November, 1800. pp. 50. 12mo. NYSL.

36754 ADAMS, DANIEL 1773–1864
AN ORATION SACRED TO THE MEMORY OF GEN. GEORGE WASHINGTON. DELIVERED AT LEOMINSTER, FEB. 22, 1800. . . .
Leominster, (Mass.) Printed by Adams & Wilder. 1800. pp. 25. 8vo.
AAS, BA, BM, BPL, HC, HEH, JCB, LOC, MHS, NYHS, NYPL, NYSL.

36755 [ADAMS, ELIPHALET] 1677–1753
A SERMON, PREACHED AT WINDHAM, A. D. 1721, ON A DAY OF THANKSGIVING . . . OCCASIONED BY A REMARKABLE REVIVAL OF RELIGION. . . . BY SAMUEL WHITING. . . .
New-London: Printed 1721. Windham: Re-printed, by John Byrne. 1800. pp. 35. 8vo.
The titlepage of the 1721 edition of this sermon names Adams as the author, and the wording of the preface supports this attribution. AAS, BPL, CHS, HEH, NYPL, NYSL, UTS, YC.

36756 ADAMS, GEORGE 1750–1795
ASTRONOMICAL & GEOGRAPHICAL ESSAYS. . . . BY THE LATE GEORGE ADAMS. . . 4TH ED. WITH THE AUTHOR'S LAST IMPROVEMENTS. . . .
Whitehall: Printed for William Young. . . Philadelphia. 1800. pp. xvi, 194, [4], 238, [9]–148, 16 fold. pl. 8vo.
Some of these essays are attributed to the elder George Adams (d. 1773).
BPL, HSP, LOC, PʳU, UOC, VᵗU.

36757 —— AN ESSAY ON THE USE OF THE CELESTIAL AND TERRESTRIAL GLOBES. . . . BY THE LATE GEORGE ADAMS, MATHEMATICAL INSTRUMENT MAKER TO HIS MAJESTY. . . . FOURTH EDITION. . . . ILLUSTRATED WITH COPPER-PLATES.
Whitehall: Printed for William Young . . . n. 52 South 2d. Street, Philadelphia. 1800. pp. [1], 238, 2 plates.
The plates are signed "R. Scott sc. I. D." AAS, HC, HSP, JCB, NYPL, VᵃU, YC.

36758   THE ADAMS Centinel.   Nov. 12, 1800–
        Gettysburg, Pennsylvania. Published by Robert Harper.   fol.   weekly.
                                          For 1800: Gettysburg Times office

36759   ADDERLY, Thomas
        Table of an analytical system of human knowledge. . . . By Thomas Adderly, lecturer on
        the belles-lettres. New York, December, 1800. . . . Price 25 cents.
        Printed by T. & J. Swords, no. 99 Pearl-Street.   Broadside.   fol.   nyhs.

36760   ADDISON, Alexander   1756–1807
        Analysis of the report of the committee of the Virginia Assembly on the proceedings of
        sundry of the other States in answer to their resolutions. . . .
                Philadelphia: Printed by Zachariah Poulson, Junior, no. 106, Chestnut-street. 1800.
        pp. 54.   12mo.   aas, ba, bpl, hc, hsp, jcb, loc, nl, nypl, uop, vªsl, vªu, yc.

36761   — — — *Raleigh: Printed by Hodge and Boylan. 1800.*   pp. 54.   12mo.   nypl.

36762   — Liberty of speech and of the press. A charge to the grand juries of the county courts
        of . . . Pennsylvania. . . .
                Albany, printed by L. Andrews.   pp. 16.   8vo.   loc.

36763   — Reports of cases in the county courts of the fifth circuit, and in the high court of errors
        & appeals, of the State of Pennsylvania. And charges to the grand juries. . . .
                *Washington: Printed by John Colerick. and may be had of the booksellers in Phila-
        delphia. 1800.*   pp. x, 396, xxiv, vi, [1], 318.   8vo.
        The Charges have separate titlepage, pagination, and signature marks, but are called for by
        the catchword on the last page of the Reports.   aas, lcp, msl, ppl, pʳu, psl, vªu.

36764   — — Copyright, 254th Pennsylvania District, July 10, 1800.
                [*Same imprint.*]   pp. 714.   8vo.   bm, hc.

36765   ADDRESS of the committee for improving the condition of the free blacks, to the members
        of the Pennsylvania Abolition Society, and to the public in general.
                Philadelphia: Printed by J. Ormond. . . . 1800.   pp. 8.   8vo.   pʳpl.

36766   ADDRESS of the Federal Republicans of the State of New-Jersey, recommending the choice
        of . . . representatives in the Seventh Congress of the United States. By a com-
        mittee, appointed at the State-house in Trenton, on the 13th November, 1800.
                Trenton: Printed by Sherman, Mershon, & Thomas. 1800.   pp. 17, [1].   8vo.
                                          heh, lcp, loc, nyhs, nypl.

36767   ADDRESS of the Republican committee of the county of Gloucester, New-Jersey. Friends and
        fellow-citizens. . . . James Sloan, chairman. . . . December 15, 1800. . . .
                Broadside.   fol.   hsp, loc.

36768   ADDRESS to the citizens of Kent, on the approaching election. At a numerous and respecta-
        ble meeting of the Republicans of Kent County convened at the house of Capt. Philip
        Chaplin, in Chester-Town, on the 25th July. . . .
                [*Wilmington: Printed at the Franklin Press, by James Wilson.*]   pp. 14.   8vo.
                                                                                       ba, loc.

36769   ADDRESS to the citizens of South Carolina, on the approaching election. . . .
        See Desausseur, Henry William.

36770   AN ADDRESS to the citizens of the county of Morris. . . .
                [*Morristown: Printed by Jacob Mann.*]   Broadside.   12mo.
        Published December 16, 1800, as an extraordinary sheet of the *Genius of Liberty.*   nypl.

36771 ADDRESS to the Federal Republicans of Burlington County. . . . By a committee, appointed at the Court-House, on the 30th August, 1800.
  Trenton: Printed by Sherman, Mershon, & Thomas. M,DCCC. pp. 36. 8vo.
                         AAS, LCP, LOC, NYPL.

36772 ADDRESS to the people of the United States; with an epitome and vindication of the public life and character of Thomas Jefferson. . . .
  See Beckley, John James.

36773 AN ADDRESS to the voters for electors of president and vice-president of the United States, in the state of Virginia. . . . The American Republican ticket. . . . William Austin, secretary.
  Alexandria — Printed by Wm. Fowler. Broadside. fol.   LOC.

36774 —— —— [*Richmond: 1800.*] Broadside. fol.   LOC.

36775 [ADGATE, Matthew]
  A Northern light; or a new index to the Bible. . . . By a citizen of New-York.
  Troy: Printed by R. Moffitt & Co. 1800. pp. 101, v. 12mo. AAS, NYPL, NYSL, YC.

36776 —— —— *Albany: Printed by Barber & Southwick. 1800.* pp. 108. 8vo.   EVANS.

36777 "ADMONUERE plusquam mordere," Erasmus. To a wise man of Albany. . . . Apollos. Albany, June 4, 1800.
  Broadside. fol.   NYSL, WᴵˢHS.

36778 THE AFFECTING History of the children in the wood. Embellished with cuts. . . .
  Stonington-port: Printed by S. Trumbull, 1800. pp. [24]. 12mo. PPL.

36779 AFFECTING history of the dreadful distresses of Frederic Manheim's family. . . the sufferings of John Corbly's family. . . . Adventures of Capt. Isaac Stewart. — Deposition of Massy Herbeson. — Adventures. . . of Peter Wilkinson. — Remarkable adventures of Jackson Johonnot. With an account of the destruction of the settlements at Wyoming.
  Philadelphia: Printed by Henry Sweitzer, for Mathew Carey. . . . 1800. . . . pp. 48, frontispiece. 8vo.
  The frontispiece was drawn by S. Folwell and engraved by P. R. Maverick.
                 AAS, BA, HEH, LOC, MHS, NL, NYPL, PSL.

36780 AGNEW, James   –1840
  An Inaugural dissertation on perspiration; submitted to the examination of the . . . medical faculty of the University of Pennsylvania, for the degree of Doctor of Medicine, on the thirty-first day of May, 1800. . . .
  Philadelphia: Printed for Mathew Carey. From the press of D. Hogan, no. 51, South Third-street. . . . 1800. pp. 46. 8vo.
    AAS, AML, BA, BPL, HC, HEH, HSP, LCP, LOC, MSL, NYAM, NYPL, RU, UOP, YC.

36781 AGRICULTURAL Society
  See Massachusetts Society for Promoting Agriculture.

36782 AIKIN, John   1747–1822
  The Calendar of nature; designed for the instruction and entertainment of young persons.
  Samuel Wood & Sons. . . New York, 1800. pp. 104. illus.
  Woodcuts by Dr. Alexander Anderson, dated 1784.   EI.

36783 —— [Letters from a father to his son, on various topics, relative to literature and the conduct of life. . . .
  Philadelphia: James Carey, 1800.]
  "This Day is Published, By James Carey, No, 7, South Front-street (Printed on superfine wove paper,) Letters from a father to his son. . . . By the celebrated Dr. Aikin": *Philadelphia Constitutional Diary and Evening Advertiser,* January 23, 1800. In 1796 Carey made three issues of this work with the text on wove paper.

36784 ALBANY. New York.
           The Charter of the City of Albany; and the laws and ordinances, ordained and established
               by the ... Common Council. ...
                   Albany: Printed by Barber & Southwick. ... M,DCCC.   pp. 158, [2].   sq. 8vo.
               The last leaf contains the table of contents.   AAS, NYHS, NYSL.

36785 ALBANY. New York. North Dutch Church
           Order of divine service in the North Dutch Church, February 22d, 1800; the day recom-
               mended by Congress to pay to the memory of Washington, a national tribute of
               respect. ...
                   [*Albany: Loring Andrews.*]   Broadside.   fol.   AAS, BrU, HEH, NYHS.

36786 THE ALBANY Centinel.   1797–1806
                   Published ... by Loring Andrews. ...   fol.   semi-weekly.   For 1800: [AAS], HC.

36787 THE ALBANY Gazette.   1784–1822
                   Printed ... by Charles R. and George Webster. ...   fol.   semi-weekly.
                                                                                          For 1800: [AAS].

36788 THE ALBANY Register.   1788–1822
                   Published by Barber & Southwick. ...   fol.   semi-weekly.
               Solomon Southwick retired from the partnership with the issue of Sept. 5.
                                                                       For 1800: [AAS], [NYPL], [NYSL].

36789 ALDEN, Abner   1758–1820
           An Introduction to spelling and reading. In two volumes. Being the first and second parts
               of a Columbian exercise. ... Vol. I. ... Second edition. ...
                   *Printed at Boston, by I. Thomas and E. T. Andrews. Sold by ... I. Thomas, at Wor-
                   cester; by Thomas, Andrews & Penniman, at Albany; and by Thomas, Andrews & Butler,
                   at Baltimore. December, 1800.*   pp. 108.   12mo.   AAS, HC, JCB, RIHS.

36790 ALDEN, Timothy   1771–1839
           A Sermon, delivered at the South Church in Portsmouth, on the V January, M,DCCC.
               Occasioned by the ... death of George Washington. ...
                   *Portsmouth, (New-Hampshire,) Printed at the United States' Oracle-Office, by Charles
                   Peirce, January, 1800.*   pp. 24.   8vo.
                               AAS, BPL, HEH, HC, HSP, JCB, LCP, LOC, MHS, NYHS, NYPL, NYSL.

36791 —— —— *Portsmouth, New-Hampshire, printed at the United States' Oracle-office, in January,
               and re-printed in February, MDCCC: by Charles Peirce.*   pp. 23, [1].   8vo.
               If the entry in Sabin, 708, is accurate, there was a third edition.
                                                                   AAS, HC, HEH, LOC, MHS, NYPL, YC.

36792 ALEXANDER, Caleb   1755–1828
           The Columbian dictionary of the English language. ... To which is prefixed, a prosodial
               grammar. ... To the whole is added ... a classical pronouncing dictionary. ...
                   *Printed at Boston. By Isaiah Thomas and Ebenezer T. Andrews. Sold by them and ...
                   I. Thomas, in Worcester; by Thomas, Andrews & Penniman, in Albany; and by Thomas,
                   Andrews & Butler, in Baltimore. Aug. 1800.*   pp. 556.   sq. 24mo.
                                                                       AAS, JCB, LOC, NYPL, YC.

36793 —— A Sermon; occasioned by the death of ... George Washington. ... By Caleb Alexander,
               A.M. Pastor of the Church in Mendon. ...
                   Printed by Samuel Hall, no. 53, Cornhill, Boston. 1800.   pp. 23.   8vo.
                               AAS, BA, BM, BPL, CSL, HEH, JCB, LOC, NYHS, NYPL, NYSL, WᶦˢHS, WLC.

36794 ALEXANDRIA. Virginia.
           Laws of the mayor and commonalty of the town of Alexandria to which are prefixed,
               Acts of the legislature of Virginia respecting the town. ...
                   Alexandria, Printed by John and James D. Wescott. ...   pp. 37, [1].   fol.
                                                                                          LOC, NYPL.

36795 ALEXANDRIA. Virginia. Washington Society.
Constitution of the Washington Society. Instituted the 28th of January, 1800. . . . G. Deneale, Sec'ry.
Broadside. fol. LOC.

36796 ALEXANDRIA Advertiser and Commercial intelligencer. Dec. 8, 1800–1808
Alexandria: Printed daily by S. Snowden & Co. . . . fol. daily. For 1800: AAS.

36797 [THE ALEXANDRIA political and commercial pocket Almanac, for the year 1801; containing a complete calendar . . . civil and military officers of the town of Alexandria; biographical sketches, &c.
Alexandria: Printed by Cottom and Stewart.]
"Just published by Cottom and Stewart": *Alexandria Advertiser*, Dec. 22, 1800.

36798 ALFRED, an historical poem. . . .
See Hasell, William Soranzo.

36799 ALLEN, John
The Door of knowledge opened . . . or the operation of war divinely improved. . . .
Worcester: Printed by Mower & Greenleaf, for James Wilson. 1800. pp. 120. 12mo.
"The Northampton letter on Godly zeal" by John Ryland fills pp. 85–120. AAS, BPL, JCB.

36800 ALLEN, Joseph 1772–1806
An Oration on the character of the late Gen. George Washington . . . before . . the town of Western . . . the 22d of February, 1800. . . .
Printed at Brookfield, Massachusetts, by E. Merriam & Co. March, 1800. pp. 12.
12mo.
AAS, BA, HEH, JCB, LOC, NYPL.

36801 ALLEN, Paul 1775–1826
An Oration, on the principles of taste, delivered before the Federal Adelphi, on the Fourth of September, A. D. 1800, at the Baptist Meeting-House in Providence. . . .
Providence: Printed by Bennett Wheeler. 1800. pp. 14. 8vo.
AAS, BA, BPL, HC, JCB, LOC, RIHS, YC.

36802 ALLISON, Patrick 1740–1802
A Discourse, delivered in the Presbyterian church, in the city of Baltimore, the 22d of February, 1800 . . . to the memory of Gen. George Washington. . . .
Baltimore, Printed by W. Pechin — for the Editor of the American. pp. 24. 8vo.
LOC, MFM, MᵈHS, NYPL, PPL, WRHS.

36803 ALLYN, John 1767–1833
A Sermon preached at Hanover, October 30th, 1799, by John Allyn, minister of Duxboro'. . . .
Boston: Printed by John & Thomas Fleet, Cornhill. 1800. pp. 21. 8vo.
AAS, BA, BPL, HC, JCB, LCP, LOC, NYPL, YC.

36804 AN ALMANACK, for the year 1801; containing, besides the usual astronomical calculations . . . . The Gardner's Calendar. . . .
Frankfort: (K.) Printed by William Hunter. . . . pp. [16]. 24mo.
Louisville Free Public Library

36805 AN ALPHABET in prose. . . . To which is added Tom Noddy and his Sister Sue. . . . Also some account of the Society of Cuzes. Second Worcester edition.
Worcester: Printed by Isaiah Thomas, Jun. . . . *1800.* pp. 31. 32mo. AAS.

36806 ALSOP, Richard 1761–1815
A Poem; sacred to the memory of George Washington. . . . Adapted to the 22d of Feb. 1800. . . .
Hartford: Printed by Hudson and Goodwin. 1800. pp. 23. 8vo.
In part of the edition the lines "In swelling phrase and terms unmeaning veils Her hellish plots, her dark designs conceals" have been deleted from p. 20.
AAS, BA, BM, BʳU, CHS, CL, CSL, HC, HEH, JCB, LOC, MHS, NL, NYHS, NYPL, UOTˣ, WˡˢHS, WLC, YC.

36807   [AMBROSE, ISAAC]   1604–1664
CHRIST IN THE CLOUDS, COMING TO JUDGMENT; OR, THE DISSOLUTION OF ALL THINGS. . . . THE
SUBSTANCE OF A SERMON PREACHED BY THAT REVEREND DIVINE DR. [WILLIAM] BATES.
Norwich: Printed by J. Trumbull. 1800.   pp. 22.   12mo.
The text is taken from the collected works of Ambrose and is ascribed to him in the Boston
edition of 1752.   CHS.

36808   THE AMERICAN ALMANAC, FOR THE YEAR OF OUR LORD, 1801. . . . CALCULATED TO SERVE EITHER OF
THE MIDDLE STATES, WITHOUT ANY SENSIBLE VARIATION. . . .
New Brunswick: Printed and sold by Abraham Blauvelt.   pp. [36].   12mo.
AAS, LOC, NJHS.

36809   AMERICAN. AND DAILY ADVERTISER.   1799+
Baltimore: published by Alex. Martin, 1800.   fol.   daily.
There was also a tri-weekly country issue.   FOR 1800: [MᵈHS].

36810   AMERICAN CITIZEN AND GENERAL ADVERTISER.   MAR. 10, 1800–1810
[New York:] Published daily by D. Denniston. . . .   fol.   FOR 1800: NYHS.

36811   THE AMERICAN CONSTELLATION.   Nov. 15, 1800–1801
Union [N. Y.]. Published by D. Cruger, jun.   fol.   weekly.   FOR 1800: [NYSL].

36812   AMERICAN COPPER-MINES.
See Latrobe, Benjamin Henry.

36813   AMERICAN EAGLE.   1799–1805.
Easton, Pennsylvania. Published by Samuel Longcope.   fol.   weekly.
FOR 1800: EASTON PUB. LIB.

36814   AMERICAN FARMER, AND DUTCHESS COUNTY ADVERTISER.   1798 — JULY 22, 1800
Poughkeepsie, (State of New York) printed by John Woods. . . .   fol.   weekly.
FOR 1800: NJHS.

36815   THE AMERICAN JEST BOOK: CONTAINING A CHOICE SELECTION OF JESTS, ANECDOTES, BONMOTS,
STORIES . . . &C. A NEW EDITION. . . .
*Wilmington, printed and sold by Bonsal & Niles — also sold at their bookstore . . .
Baltimore. 1800.*   pp. 120.   12mo.   LOC.

36816   THE AMERICAN LADIES AND GENTLEMEN'S POCKET ALMANAC AND ELEGANT BELLES LETTRES REPOSI-
TORY FOR ANNO DOMINI 1801. DECORATED WITH ENGRAVINGS. . . .
*New York. Published at the Shakspeare Gallery, by David Longworth. Harrison
sculpt.*   pp. 74.   48mo.
Colophon: "From the Press of T. & J. Swords."   AAS, HC, HEH, NYPL.

36817   AMERICAN MERCURY.   1784–1833
Published by Elisha Babcock — Hartford. 1800.   fol.   weekly.
FOR 1800: AAS, CHS, [HC], LOC, NYPL, YC.

36818   —— PROGRESS OF TRUTH AND GENIUS, THROUGH THE EIGHTEENTH CENTURY: OR THE BOY'S ADDRESS WHO
CARRIES THE AMERICAN MERCURY. . . .
[Hartford.]   Broadside.   fol.   NYHS.

36819   AMERICAN MONTHLY MAGAZINE AND REVIEW.
See Monthly Magazine and American Review.

36820 [THE AMERICAN MUSEUM, OR REPOSITORY OF ANCIENT AND MODERN FUGITIVE PIECES . . . PROSE
AND POETICAL. VOL. X.
Mount Holly, N. J.: Stephen C. Ustick, 1800.]
A reprint mentioned in the Carey correspondence; see Gaskill 95.

36821 THE AMERICAN MUSICAL MAGAZINE. VOL. I. OCTOBER 1800. No. I. . . . PUBLISHED UNDER THE
DIRECTION OF THE HAMPSHIRE MUSICAL SOCIETY.
Printed, (Typographically,) at Northampton, by Andrew Wright. pp. 24, printed
wrappers. obl. 12mo. AAS, NYPL.

36822 THE AMERICAN SONGSTER; OR, FEDERAL MUSEUM OF MELODY AND WIT. IN FOUR PARTS, CONTAINING
A COLLECTION OF MUCH ADMIRED SONGS. . . .
Baltimore: Printed and sold by Warner & Hanna. . . . 1800. pp. 245. 16mo.
LOC, NYHS, NYPL.

36823 AMERICAN TELEGRAPHE. 1795–1804
*Newfield near Fairfield: Printed and published by Lazarus Beach, opposite Mr. Hin-
man's Inn. 1800.* fol. weekly.
Newfield having been incorporated as Bridgeport, the imprint was changed on the issue of
Nov. 5, 1800. FOR 1800: CSL, [YC].

36824 THE AMERICAN TUTOR'S ASSISTANT; OR, A COMPENDIOUS SYSTEM OF PRACTICAL ARITHMETIC. . . .
BY SUNDRY TEACHERS. . . . THE FOURTH EDITION.
Philadelphia: Printed and sold by Zachariah Poulson, Junior. . . . 1800. pp. [4], 200.
12mo.
The preface is signed by John Todd, Zachariah Jess, William Waring, and Jeremiah Paul.
AAS, HC, HSP, PSL, UOP.

36825 DER AMERICANISCHE STAATSBOTHE, UND LANCASTER ANZEIGS-NACHRICHTEN. 1800–1821
Lancaster: gedruckt bey Johann Albrecht und Co. fol. weekly. FOR 1800: LᴬHS.

36826 AMERICANISCHER STADT UND LAND KALENDER AUF DAS 1801ST JAHR CHRISTI, WELCHES EIN
GEMEINES JAHR IS VON 365 TAGEN.
Philadelphia: Gedruckt und zu haben ben Carl Cist. . . . pp. [48]. sq. 8vo.
AAS, LOC.

36827 AMERICA'S LAMENTATION ON THE DEATH OF GEN. WASHINGTON. HOW SAD ARE THE TIDINGS THAT
SOUND IN MY EARS. . . .
Broadside. fol. HEH.

36828 AMES, FISHER 1758–1808
AN ORATION ON THE SUBLIME VIRTUES OF GENERAL GEORGE WASHINGTON, PRONOUNCED AT THE
OLD SOUTH MEETING-HOUSE IN BOSTON, BEFORE . . . THE LEGISLATURE . . . ON . . . THE 8TH
OF FEBRUARY, 1800. . . .
Boston: Young & Minns, printers to the State. pp. 31. 8vo.
AAS, BPL, HC, HEH, JCB, LOC, MHS, MSL, NEHGS, NYHS, NYPL, NYSL, WC. YC.

36829 — — — *Boston: Printed for Young & Minns, and Manning & Loring.* pp. 31. 8vo.
AAS, BPL, HEH, JCB, LOC, NYPL, WLC, YC.

36830 — — — *Dedham: Printed by H. Mann — 1800.* pp. 29. 12mo. BA, HC, MHS, NYHS.

36831 — — — *New-York: Printed and sold by George Folliott Hopkins . . . 136, Pearl-Street. 1800.*
pp. 48. 8vo.
Also issued bound under a common half-title with John M. Mason, *A Funeral Oration on
Gen. Washington.* AAS, BA, BPL, HC, HEH, LOC, MᵈHS, NYPL, NYSL, YC.

36832 — — — *New-York: Printed for Charles Smith and S. Stephens. 1800.* pp. 31. 8vo.
BA, HEH, JCB, LOC, NYHS, NYPL, NYSL, WRHS.

36833 — — — *Philadelphia: Printed by John Ormrod, no. 41, Chestnut-Street. 1800.* pp. 51.
8vo. AAS, BPL, HC, HEH, JCB, LOC, MHS, NL, NYPL, RU, WLC, YC.

36834 THE AMOROUS SONGSTER. COMPARED WITH THIS VIGOROUS VOLUME, THE FRISKY SONGSTER IS A LIFELESS CHAP.
New York, Printed for the Sporting Club, 1800. pp. 96. 24mo. GrL.

36835 ANCIENT AND HONOURABLE COMPANY OF ARTILLERY.
See Massachusetts.

36836 ANDERSON, JOHN 1767–1835
VINDICIAE CANTUS DOMINICI. IN TWO PARTS: I. A DISCOURSE ON THE DUTY OF SINGING THE BOOK OF PSALMS IN SOLEMN WORSHIP. II. A VINDICATION OF THE DOCTRINE TAUGHT IN THE PRECEDING DISCOURSE. . . .
Philadelphia: Printed and sold by David Hogan, no. 51, South Third-street. . . . 1800.
pp. 403, viii. 16mo.
The last pages contain a list of subscribers. AAS, BPL, BrU, HEH, NL, NYSL.

36837 ANDREWS, BENAJAH
A NARRATIVE OF MRS. ELIZABETH ANDREWS, CONTAINING AN ACCOUNT OF HER CONVERSION, SICKNESS & DEATH. . . .
Stockbridge: Printed by Heman Willard, at the office of Horatio Jones & Co. 1800.
pp. 40. 12mo. AAS, LOC, NYHS, PrU.

36838 ANDREWS, ELISHA 1768–1840
A CANDID REPLY TO THE ARGUMENTS OF THE LATE REV. ELHANAN WINCHESTER, CONTAINED IN A WORK, ENTITLED, "THE UNIVERSAL RESTORATION. . . ."
Boston: Printed by Manning & Loring, 1800. pp. 91, [1]. 12mo.
AAS, CL, HC, JCB, LOC, NYSL.

36839 ANDREWS, JOHN 1764–1846
AN EULOGY ON GENERAL GEORGE WASHINGTON. . . . DELIVERED BEFORE THE FIRST RELIGIOUS SOCIETY, IN NEWBURYPORT, FEBRUARY 22D. 1800. . . .
From the press of Angier March. Sold at his bookstore, north side of Market-Square, Newburyport. pp. 21. 8vo.
AAS, BA, BPL, HC, HEH, HSP, JCB, MHS, NYHS, NYPL, NYSL, YC.

36840 ANGELS EVER BRIGHT AND FAIR. SUNG AT THE FUNERAL CEREMONIES IN HONOR TO THE MEMORY OF THE LATE GENERAL WASHINGTON.
New York, printed & sold by G. Gilfert, no. 177 Broadway. Broadside. fol.
NYPL.

36841 ANIMADVERSIONS ON JAMES HOLLAND'S STRICTURES ON GENERAL JOSEPH DICKSONS CIRCULAR LETTER, OF THE FIRST OF MAY 1800.
Lincolnton: N. C. Printed, by John Martin Slump. . . . 1800. pp. 15. 12mo.
Signed: A True Republican Federalist. NCU.

36842 THE ANNUAL VISITOR, OR ALMANAC, FOR THE YEAR OF OUR LORD, 1801. CALCULATED FOR THE MERIDIAN OF BALTIMORE. . . .
Baltimore, printed for Thomas, Andrews & Butler, no. 184, Market-Street. pp. [36].
12mo. AAS, HSP, LOC, MdHS.

36843 ANSWER TO A DIALOGUE BETWEEN A FEDERALIST AND A REPUBLICAN. . . .
See Desaussure, Henry William.

36844 AN ANSWER TO ALEXANDER HAMILTON'S LETTER CONCERNING THE PUBLIC CONDUCT AND CHARACTER OF JOHN ADAMS. . . .
See Cheetham, James.

36845 ANTHING, [Johann] Friedrick   1753–1805
      History of the campaigns of Prince Alexander Suworow Rymnikski. . . . To which is
      added a . . . history of his Italian campaign. . . .
         New-York: Printed by C. and R. Waite, for Wm. Cobbett. 1800.   2 vol. in 1.   pp.
      192; 219, portrait frontispiece.   8vo.
      The "History of the Campaign in Italy" is by William Cobbett and has a separate titlepage.
      The frontispiece is signed by T. Clarke.   AAS, EI, HC, HEH, NYPL, NYSL, PᵗU, VᵃSL, WC.

36846 ANTOINETTE Percival. . . .
      See Plumptre, Anne.

36847 ARGUS. Greenleaf's new daily advertiser.   1795 — Mar. 8, 1800
         New-York — printed and published (every morning) by Ann Greenleaf. . . .   daily.
      fol.
      With the issue of Mar. 8 the paper was sold to David Denniston who established the
      American Citizen in its place.   For 1800: NYHS, WⁱˢHS.

36848 ARMSTRONG, John
      Sermon on the death of General Washington preached [on January 12, 1800] . . . at
      Pottstown. Published by the request of the committee.
         Reading: Printed by Jungmann & Bruckmann. 1800.   pp. 43.   8vo.   HEH, MFM.

36849 ARRANGEMENTS to be observed. . . .
      See Haverhill. Massachusetts.

36850 THE ART of speaking. . . .
      See Burgh, James.

36851 ASH, John   1724?–1779
      Grammatical institutes: or, an easy introduction to Dr. Lowth's English grammar. . . .
      A new edition. . . .
         Printed for Mathew Carey. . . Philadelphia, by Stephen C. Ustick, Mount-Holly. 1800.
      pp. 76.   12mo.   HEH.

36852 AT A MEETING of a number of freeholders of the city of Albany, at Wendell's Hotel, on
      Saturday the 12th day of April, 1800. . . . Robert Yates, Esq. being nominated. . .
      Albany, April 14, 1800.
         Broadside.   8vo.   NYHS.

36853 AT A MEETING of a number of freeholders of the city of Albany, at Wendell's Hotel, on
      Saturday the 12th day of April, 1800. . . . Robert Yates and Stephen Lush, Esqrs.
      being nominated. . . . Albany, April 14, 1800.
         Broadside.   8vo.   NYHS.

36854 AT A MEETING of. . . Republican citizens, from. . . the county of Morris, on. . . the 17th
      of December, at the house of George O'Hara. . . .
         [*Morristown, Printed by Jacob Mann.*]   Broadside.   fol.
      Published as an extraordinary sheet of the *Genius of Liberty.*   NYPL.

36855 AT A MEETING of the General Association of the State of Connecticut. . . .
      See Congregational Church in Connecticut.

36856 AT A MEETING of the Republican citizens of the county of Burlington, at the house of
      Joshua Rainear in Springfield, the 20th September, 1800. . . .
         [*S. C. Ustick; Printed at Mount-Holly.*]   pp. 16.   8vo.   E. T. Hutchinson.

36857 AT A NUMEROUS meeting of committees and electors, from ten towns in the county of
      Washington, at Hartford, on the 22d of Aril [sic], 1800. . . .
         Broadside.   fol.   NYHS.

36858   ATHERTON, Charles Humphrey   1773–1853
        Eulogy on Gen. George Washington. . . delivered at Amherst, N. H. before the inhabit-
        ants. . . and the Benevolent Lodge, on the 22d day of February, 1800. . . .
            From the press of Samuel Preston, Amherst [N. H.]. 1800.   pp. 23.   8vo.
                                                AAS, BA, HC, HEH, JCB, LOC, NHSL, NYHS, NYPL.

36859   —— A Selection of orations and eulogies, pronounced in different parts of the United States,
        in commemoration of. . . Washington. . . .
            Amherst [N. H.]: printed by Samuel Preston. 1800.   pp. 165, [2].   12mo.
        Includes orations by Henry Lee, Fisher Ames, Jeremiah Smith, Benjamin Orr, G. R. Minot,
        C. H. Atherton, Thomas (R. T.) Paine, and Jacob MaGaw, and Washington's Farewell
        Address. The AAS has a presentation copy signed by the editor.
                                                AAS, BPL, BʳU, HEH, JCB, LOC, NYPL.

36860   ATWELL, Amos Maine   1765–1815
        See Clarke, Abraham Lynsen.

36861   [AUBIN, Penelope]
        The Noble slaves. Being an entertaining history of the. . . deliverances from Algerine
        slavery, of several Spanish noblemen. . . .
            New-York: Printed and sold by John Tiebout. . . 1800.   pp. 139.   24mo.   AAS, YC.

36862   AUGUSTA Herald.   1799–1822
            Printed by George F. Randolph & William J. Bunce [Augusta, Georgia.]   fol.
        weekly.   For 1800: [UOG].

36863   AULNOY, Marie, *comtesse d'*   1650?–1705
        The History of the tales of the fairies. Newly done from the French. . . .
            Wilmington, Printed by P. Brynberg, 1800.   pp. 141.   24mo.
                                                                          WⁱPL.

36864   AURORA, for the Country.   1800–1817
            Philadelphia: published (tri-weekly) by William Duane.   fol.
        A continuation of *The Philadelphia Aurora.*   For 1800: AAS, NYPL, PSL.

36865   AURORA. General Advertiser.   1794–1834
            Published (daily) for the heirs of Benj. Franklin Bache . . . Philadelphia.   fol.
        With the issue of Mar. 8 William Duane, the editor, became the publisher.
                                                For 1800: AAS, BM, HSP, LCP, LOC, PPL, PSL.

36866   AUSTIN, David   1759–1831
        See Dickinson, Jonathan.

36867   [——] The Dawn of day, introductory to the rising sun, whose rays shall gild the clouds. . . .
        In nine letters. . . .
            New-Haven: Printed by Read and Morse. 1800.   pp. 32.   8vo.
        There are three lines of errata on p. 32.   AAS, CHS, HEH, NYPL, NYSL, UOMⁱ, WL, YC.

36868   —— A Discourse . . . on occasion of the death of George Washington . . . in compliance
        with the request of . . . the borough of Elizabeth, December 25, 1799. Also, sketches
        of a running discourse, delivered to the Union brigade, on the same occasion . . .
        December 26, 1799. With an address to the throne of grace, offered at . . . the
        cantonment on Green Brook, February 22. . . .
            New-York: Printed by G. F. Hopkins. 1800.   pp. 35, [1], allegorical plate.   8vo.
                                                CHS, HEH, LOC, NYHS.

36869   —— Masonry in its glory. . . . By David Austin, Junr: citizen of the world. Published agree-
        ably to act of Congress.
            Printed at East-Windsor, (Connecticut) by Luther Pratt. 1800.   pp. 35.   16mo.
                                                AAS, WⁱˢHS.

36870 AUSTIN, Samuel   1760–1830
The Evangelical preacher. . . . Delivered at the ordination . . . of. . . Leonard Worces-
ter to the . . . church in Peacham, Vermont, October 30th, 1799. . . .
Peacham, Vermont, Printed by Farley & Goss. 1800. pp. 32. 8vo.
"The Charge, by the Rev. Noah Worcester, of Thornton," pp. 27–30, and "The Right
Hand of Fellowship, by the Rev. Thomas Worcester, of Salisbury," pp. 30–2.
AAS, BM, CL, HC, HEH, JCB, NHHS, NYHS, NYPL, NYSL, PTS, VᵗHS.

36871 BACHE'S Philadelphia Aurora.   1797–1800
Published (tri-weekly) for the heirs of Benj. Franklin Bache. fol.
With the issue of Mar. 10 the title was changed to *The Philadelphia Aurora*, and with
that of Nov. 7 it became *Aurora, for the Country.*
For 1800: AAS, [LOC], [NYPL], [PSL].

36872 BACKUS, Charles   1749–1803
The Scripture doctrine of Regeneration considered, in six discourses. By Charles Backus,
A. M. Pastor of a church in Somers. . . .
Hartford: Printed by Hudson and Goodwin, for Oliver D. and I. Cooke. 1800.
pp. 180. 16mo.
AAS, BM, BPL, CHS, CL, HC, JCB, LOC, NL, NYPL, NYSL, PʳU, UOC, VᵃU, YC.

36873 BAKER, Joseph   1779–1800?
The Confession of Joseph Baker, a Canadian by birth, who, for murder & piracy committed on the high seas, on board the schooner Eliza, Captain Wm. Wheland. . . .
was tried on the 25th of April, 1800 . . . and now under sentence of death, in . . .
Philadelphia. . . .
[Philadelphia:] Printed by Richard Folwell, no. 63, North Front-Street. pp. 8.
8vo. PM, WLC.

36874 BALDWIN, Thomas   1753–1825
The Approved workman. . . . Delivered at Templeton, October 16, 1800, at the installation
of . . . Elisha Andrews, to the . . . Baptist church. . . .
Boston: Printed by E. Lincoln, Water-Street. 1800. pp. 24. 8vo.
"The Charge. By the Rev. George Robertson," pp. 23–4.
AAS, BA, BM, BPL, HC, HEH, JCB, MHS, NYPL, YC.

36875 [——] A Brief account of the late revivals of religion, in a number of towns in the New
England States, and also in Nova-Scotia. . . .
Windsor [Vt.]: Re-printed by Alden Spooner. 1800. pp. 24. 12mo.
AAS, CSL, WC.

36876 —— Glorious news. A brief account of the late revivals of religion in a number of towns
in the New-England states, and also in Nova-Scotia. . . .
*[Mount Holly:] Printed by S. C. Ustick, and sold at no. 79, North Third Street,
Philadelphia, Jan. 1800.* pp. 28. 12mo. NYPL.

36877 —— A Sermon, delivered to the Second Baptist Society in Boston . . . December 29, 1799.
Occasioned by the death of . . . Washington. . . .
Boston: Printed by Manning & Loring, Spring-Lane. pp. 28. 8vo.
AAS, BA, BM, BPL, CL, HC, HEH, HSP, NYPL, NYSL, WLC.

36878 BALL, Edward I., ed.
Duties payable on goods, wares, and merchandize, imported into the United States of
America. . . . With extracts from the revenue laws, and sundry forms for the di-
rection of merchants. . . .
New-York: Printed by James Oram, no. 102, Water-Street, 1800. pp. 43, [1], forms,
tables. 8vo. NYPL.

36879 BALL, Heman   1764–1821
A Sermon delivered at Rutland . . . January 1st, 1800 . . . to publicly mourn the death
of General George Washington. . . .
Rutland [Vt.], printed for S. Williams, Esq. pp. 27. 8vo.
AAS, CHS, CL, HEH, JCB, LOC, MFM, NYPL, VᵗU.

36880   BALL, Isaac, *of New York*
Broadside.   fol.
Inscribed to the memory of the American Fabius, by Doctor Isaac Ball, of New York.
AAS.

36881   BALTIMORE. Maryland.
Extracts from an ordinance to mitigate the distress occasioned by the late prevailing fever. . . . Approved November 18, 1800. James Calhoun, mayor.
[*Baltimore*:] *Printed by John Hayes.*   Broadside.   fol.
MᵈHS.

36882   BALTIMORE. Maryland. Bentalou & Dorsey, auctioneers
[Catalogue of a choice collection of well bound new books to be sold at auction Friday evening, May 23, 1800, at Mr. David Fulton's. . . .
Baltimore: Printed by Thomas Dobbin ?]
Minick 564

36883   —— [Catalogue of scarce and valuable books to be sold at auction, Thursday evening, May 15, 1800, at David Fulton's tavern, Baltimore.]
Minick 559.

36884   BALTIMORE. Maryland. Female Humane Association
A Plan of the Female Humane Association charity school.
[*Baltimore: Printed by Warner & Hannah ?*]   Broadside.   fol.
MᵈHS.

36885   [BALTIMORE Postbote.   1799–1800
Baltimore, published by Samuel Saur.   tri-weekly.]   For 1800: No copy known.

36886   THE BALTIMORE Repository, for the year 1801: containing an Almanac; a Bill to establish an uniform system of bankruptcy throughout the U. States, abstract of the revenue law. . . .
Baltimore: Printed for and sold by Michael & John Conrad, & Co. . . .   pp. [156].
24mo.
Bound as a pocket book. The almanac is interleaved.
LOC, MᵈHS.

36887   THE BALTIMORE Weekly Magazine. . . .   Saturday, April 26, 1800. . . .
[*Colophon*:] *Printed by J. B. Colvin, at Pechin's printing-office . . .* [*Baltimore*].
4to.
The issue of May 27, 1801, contains a notice of cessation. The remainders were bound up with a titlepage bearing William Pechin's imprint and the date of June 10th, 1801.
AAS, EPFL, LOC, NYHS, NYPL, PPL, YC.

36888   BANCROFT, Aaron   1755–1839
An Eulogy on the character of the late Gen. George Washington. Delivered before the inhabitants of the town of Worcester . . . the 22d of February 1800. . . . Printed according to a vote of said town, requesting a copy for the press, and directing that each head of a family should be furnished with one.
Worcester: Printed by Isaiah Thomas, Jun. March — 1800.   pp. 21.   8vo.
AAS, BA, BM, BPL, HC, HEH, HSP, JCB, LOC, MHS, MSL, NL, NYPL, NYSL, YC.

36889   BANGS, Edward   1756–1818
An Oration on the anniversary of American independence, pronounced at Worcester, July 4, 1800. . . .
Printed at Worcester, By Isaiah Thomas, Jun. July — 1800.   pp. 30, [1].   8vo.
An errata slip is pasted on the last leaf.
AAS, BM, BPL, HC, HEH, JCB, LOC, MHS, NL, NYHS, NYPL, NYSL, YC.

36890   [BARBAULD, Anna Letitia (Aikin)]   1743–1825
Lessons for children, part II. From four to five years old. Adorned with cuts engraved by James Akin.
Wilmington, Del. Printed and sold wholesale and retail by James Wilson . . . 1800.
pp. 44.   24mo.
AAS.

36891   [——] Lessons for children, from five to six years old. Volume II.
Boston: Printed and sold by S. Hall, no. 53, Cornhill. 1800.   pp. 118.   32mo
BA, BPL.

36892 BARKER, JOSEPH 1751–1815
THE CHARACTER AND BLESSEDNESS OF THE UPRIGHT MAN. . . . PREACHED JANUARY 12, 1800, IN
MIDDLEBOROUGH, OCCASIONED BY THE FUNERAL OF DEACON BENJAMIN THOMAS. . . .
Printed by Samuel Hall, in Cornhill, Boston. 1800. pp. 21. 8vo.
AAS, AHTS, JCB, MᶜHS.

36893 BARLOW, JOEL 1754–1812
JOEL BARLOW TO HIS FELLOW CITIZENS OF THE UNITED STATES OF AMERICA. A LETTER ON THE
SYSTEM OF POLICY HITHERTO PURSUED BY THEIR GOVERNMENT. . . .
Philadelphia: Re-printed, at the Aurora Office, March 8, 1800. pp. 27. 8vo.
Caption title. Imprint from the colophon. LOC, NYPL, PPL, UOC, YC.

36894 — JOEL BARLOW TO HIS FELLOW CITIZENS, OF THE UNITED STATES OF AMERICA. LETTER I. ON THE
SYSTEM OF POLICY HITHERTO PURSUED BY THEIR GOVERNMENT. . . .
[Philadelphia: Printed by William Duane ?] pp. 32. 8vo.
AAS, HC, LOC, NL, WⁱˢHS, YC.

36895 [BARNARD, *Sir* JOHN] 1685–1764.
A PRESENT FOR AN APPRENTICE: OR, A SHURE GUIDE TO GAIN BOTH ESTEEM AND ESTATE. . . .
BY A LATE LORD MAYOR OF LONDON.
*Glasgow: Printed. Philadelphia: Reprinted by Charles Cist, no. 104, North Second-
Street. M,DCCC.* pp. [8], [1]–112. 24mo. AAS, LCP.

36896 BARNARD, THOMAS 1748–1814
A SERMON, PREACHED DECEMBER 29, 1799, IN THE NORTH MEETING HOUSE, SALEM . . . AFTER . . .
THE DEATH OF GENERAL GEORGE WASHINGTON. . . .
Salem: Printed by Thomas C. Cushing, at the Bible & Heart. pp. 27. 8vo.
AAS, BA, BM, CHS, EI, HC, HEH, JCB, LOC, MᵈHS, MFM, MHS, NL, NYHS, NYPL, NYSL, YC.

36897 BARNES, DAVID 1731–1811
DISCOURSE DELIVERED AT SOUTH PARISH IN SCITUATE, FEBRUARY 22, 1800. . . . TO MOURN THE
DECEASE . . . OF GENERAL GEORGE WASHINGTON. . . .
Boston: Manning & Loring, Printers, near the Old South Meeting-House. pp. 16.
8vo. AAS, BA, BPL, HC, HEH, JCB, LOC, MHS, MSL, NYHS, NYPL, NYSL, WLC, YC.

36898 BARRINGTON, GEORGE 1755–
A VOYAGE TO NEW SOUTH WALES; WITH A DESCRIPTION OF THE COUNTRY. . . . BY GEORGE BAR-
RINGTON, NOW SUPERINTENDANT OF THE CONVICTS AT PARAMATTA.
Philadelphia: Published by P. Stewart 1800. pp. xi, 150. 16mo. AAS.

36899 BARRY, JOHN 1745–1803
A SET OF SIGNALS PRESENTED TO THE NAVY OF THE UNITED STATES OF AMERICA BY JOHN BARRY,
ESQ. SENIOR OFFICER.
Norfolk, Virginia. Printed by Willett & O'Connor, 1800. WILLIAM DAVIS MILLER

36900 BARTGIS'S FEDERAL GAZETTE, OR THE FREDERICK-TOWN AND COUNTY, WEEKLY ADVERTISER.
1794–1800
*Printed every Wednesday, by Matthias Bartgis . . . Frederick-Town [Maryland],
1800.* fol. weekly. FOR 1800: [HC].

36901 [BARTGIS'S REPUBLICAN GAZETTE. 1800–1826
*Printed every Wednesday, by Matthias Bartgis, at . . . Frederick-Town [Maryland]
. . . 1800.* fol. weekly.] FOR 1800: NO COPY KNOWN.

36902 BARTLETT, JOSIAH 1759–1820
AN ORATION ON THE DEATH OF GENERAL GEORGE WASHINGTON, DELIVERED . . . BEFORE THE IN-
HABITANTS OF CHARLESTOWN . . . FEB. 22, 1800. . . .
Charlestown [Mass.]: Printed by Samuel Etheridge. M,DCCC. pp. 15. 8vo.
AAS, BA, BPL, HC, HEH, JCB, LOC, MHS, MSL, NYAM, NYPL, NYSL

36903   BARTON, Benjamin Smith   1766–1815
         A Memoir concerning the disease of goitre, as it prevails in different parts of North-
         America. . . .
                  Philadelphia: Printed for the author, by Way & Groff, no. 48, North Third-Street. 1800.
         pp. viii, 94.   8vo.   AAS, AML, BPL, HSP, LOC, MHS, NYAM, RIMS.

36904   [——] Supplement to a memoir concerning the fascinating faculty which has been ascribed to
         the Rattle-snake. . . . In a letter to Professor Zimmermann, of Brunswick, in Ger-
         many.
                  [*Philadelphia.*]   pp. 40.   8vo.   AAS, AML, BA, BM, BPL, HEH, LOC, MHS, WLC.

36905   BARTON, Titus Theodore   1766–1827
         A Sermon, preached at Tewksbury, February, 22, 1800. On account of the death of General
         George Washington. . . .
                  Printed at Medford, (Massachusetts.) 1800.   pp. 8.   8vo.
                                                        AAS, AHTS, BA, BʳU, HEH, JCB, NEHGS, NYHS.

36906   BASCOM, Jonathan   1740–1807
         An Oration delivered February 22, 1800. The day of public mourning for the death of
         George Washington. . . .
                  Printed by Samuel Hall, no. 53, Cornhill, Boston. 1800.   pp. 15.   8vo.
                                                        AAS, BA, BPL, HC, JCB, LOC, NYHS, NYPL.

36907   BASCOMB, Ezekiel L[ysander]   1779–1841
         A Masonic discourse, spoken at Greenfield, Massachusetts. . . January 1st, A. L. 5800. . .
                  Printed at Greenfield, (Mass.) by T. Dickman. 1800.   pp. 14.   8vo.   MFM, PFM.

36908   BATES, Rev. Dr.
                  See Ambrose, Isaac

36909   BATES, Issachar
         New songs, on different subjects. Composed by Issachar Bates. . . .
                  Salem: New-York: Printed by Henry Dodd. MDCCC.   pp. 16.   12mo.
                                                        AAS, NYHS, NYPL.

36910   BAXTER, Richard   1615–1691
         The Saints' everlasting rest. . . . Extracted from the works of Mr. Richard Baxter, by
         John Wesley, M. A. late fellow of Lincoln College, Oxford.
                  Philadelphia: Printed by Henry Tuckniss, for Ezekiel Cooper, no. 118, north Fourth
         Street. . . . 1800.   pp. 399, [1].   16mo.   AAS.

36911   BAYARD, Samuel   1767–1840
         A Funeral oration, occasioned by the death of Gen. George Washington; and delivered on
         the first of January, 1800. In the Episcopal Church, at New-Rochelle. . . .
                  New-Brunswick [N. J.]: Printed by Abraham Blauvelt. 1800.   pp. 24.   8vo.
                  AAS, BA, BM, BPL, CL, HC, HEH, JCB, LCP, LOC, NJHS, NYHS, NYPL, NYSL, PʳU, YC.

36912   BEALL, Isaac
         A Funeral discourse, delivered before the worshipful Master, Wardens, and Brethren of
         Center Lodge, at Rutland, on the 24th day of June, 1800. . . in memory of the Hon.
         Samuel Williams, Esq. . . .
                  Vergennes: Printed by Chipman & Fessenden.   pp. 19.   8vo.   MFM.

36913   BEAR ye one another's burdens. . . .
                  See Cheap repository no. 26.

36914   THE BEAU metamorphized. . . .
                  See Murdock, John.

36915   BEAUVOIS, A. M. F. J.
         [Catalogue raisonne du museum de Mr. C. W. Peale.
                  Philadelphia, 1800.   8vo.]   Sabin 4211.

36916 BECK, John
[The Doctrine of perpetual bondage reconcilable with the infinate justice of God, a truth plainly asserted in the Jewish and Christian Scriptures. . . .
Savannah: Printed by Seymour and Woolhopter. 1800. pp. 24. 8vo.] Evans.

36917 [BECKLEY, John James] 1757–1807
Address to the people of the United States; with an epitome and vindication of the public life and character of Thomas Jefferson.
Philadelphia: Printed by James Carey, no. 109 N. Sixth-Street. 1800. pp. 32. 8vo.
AAS, APS, BA, BPL, HEH, HSP, LOC, NYHS, NYPL, NYSL, VᵃU, WⁱˢHS, YC.

36918 — — — *Newport: Printed by Oliver Farnsworth. 1800.* pp. 31. 8vo. NHS, NYPL, RIHS.

36919 — — — *Philadelphia—Printed: Newport: Re-Printed by Oliver Farnsworth. 1800.* pp. 31.
8vo. AAS, BʳU, NHS, NYPL, YC.

36920 — — — *Richmond: Printed by Meriwether Jones. . . . 1800.* pp. 38. 8vo. LOC, NYHS.

36921 — An Epitome of the life & character of Thomas Jefferson.
[*Wilmington, printed by J. Wilson, at the Franklin press, 1800.*] pp. 8. 8vo.
Reprinted from Beckley's *Address*, above. DHS, LOC.

36922 BEDFORD, Gunning 1747–1812
A Funeral oration upon the death of. . . Washington, prepared at the request of the Masonic Lodge, No. 14, of Wilmington. . . and delivered. . . the 27th of December, anno lucis 5799. . . .
Wilmington: Printed at the Franklin Press, by James Wilson. 1800. pp. 19. sm. 4to.
Reprinted in *Washingtonia*, Lancaster, 1802. MFM.

36923 THE BEE. 1797–1802
New-London: Printed and Published by Charles Holt. 1800. fol. weekly.
For 1800; AAS, LOC, [NYHS], YC.

36924 BEERS, Andrew 1749–1824
Beers's Almanac for the year of Our Lord 1801. . . . Calculated for the meridian of Hartford. . . .
Hartford: Printed by Hudson and Goodwin. pp. [36]. 16mo.
AAS, CHS, HC, LOC, NYPL, YC.

36925 — The Farmers Almanac, for the year of our Lord Christ 1801. . . . Containing a great variety of useful and entertaining matter. . . .
Danbury: Printed. . . by Nicholas & Rowe. pp. 24. 16mo. AAS, YC.

36926 — Franklin's legacy: or, the New-York and Vermont Almanac, for the year of our Lord, 1801. . . . Calculated for the meridian of Troy. . . .
Troy: Printed and sold by R. Moffitt & Co. Sold also by the several post-riders from their office. . . . . pp. [36]. 12mo. AAS, LOC, NYPL, NYSL.

36927 — Hutchins improved: an Almanac, for the year of our Lord 1801. . . . Containing. . . a great variety of other matter. . . .
Elizabeth-town: Printed and sold by John Woods. pp. [36]. 12mo.
AAS, LOC, NL, NYPL

36928 — Hutchins improved: being an Almanack and ephemeris . . . for the year of our Lord 1801. . . .
New-York: Printed for and sold by the principal Booksellers in the city. . . . pp. [36]. 12mo. AAS, NYHS, NYSL, YC.

36929 — — — *New York: Printed for and sold by Evert Duyckinck, no. 110, Pearl Street, corner of the Old Slip. . . .* pp. [36]. 12mo. AAS.

36930   — — — *Kingston (Ulster County) Printed by Samuel Freer & Son. . . .*   pp. [36].   12mo.
       R. R. Hoes.

36931   — — — *Newburgh: Printed for Elias Winfield. . . .*   pp. [36].   12mo.   NYPL, NYSL.

36932   — — — *New-York: Printed for and sold by John Harrison. . . .*   pp. [34].   12mo.   NYHS.

36933   — Phinney's Calendar, or, Western Almanac for the year of Our Lord 1801. . . calculated for the meridian of Albany. . . .
       Cooperstown: Printed by Elihu Phinney. . . .   pp. [24].   16mo.   NYHS, NYSL.

36934   — The United States Almanac, for the year of our Lord 1801: being the commencement and first year of the 19th century. . . .
       Elizabeth-town: Printed and sold by Shepard Kollock. . . .   pp. [32].   16mo.
       AAS, NJHS.

36935   — Webster's calendar: or, the Albany Almanack, for the year of our Lord 1801. . . .
       Albany: Printed by Charles R. and George Webster, at their Bookstore, corner of State & Pearl streets. . . .   pp. [36].   12mo.   AAS, HC.

36936   BEERS, William Pitt   1766–1810
       An Oration, on the death of General Washington; pronounced before the citizens of Albany. . . January 9th, 1800. . . .
       Albany: Printed by Charles R. and George Webster.   pp. 17.   8vo.
       BA, BPL, CL, HC, HEH, JCB, LOC, MHS, NYHS, NYPL, NYSL, PPL, WLC, YC.

36937   [BELCHER, Joseph]   1669–1723
       A Copy of a letter found in the study of the Reverend Mr. Joseph Belcher, late of Dedham, since his decease. . . .
       [Printed by Charles Holt, New London.]   pp. 8.   16mo.
       The "Letter" is a reprint of a 1725 edition not recorded by Evans; it is also attributed to Joseph Eliot, 1638–94. In the 1800 ed. pp. 5–8 are occupied by "Mr. Joseph Alleine's rules for self-examination."   AAS.

36938   BELDEN, Jonathan   1774–1844
       An Oration, pronounced at Winthrop, February 22, 1800, commemorating the virtues of the late General Washington. . . .
       Hallowell (District of Maine.) Printed by Peter Edes. 1800.   pp. 20.   sm. 4to.
       HEH.

36939   BELKNAP, Daniel   1771–1815
       The Evangelical harmony. A great variety of airs, suitable for divine worship: besides a number . . . chiefly original. . . .
       Printed . . . at Boston, for the author, by Isaiah Thomas and Ebenezer T. Andrews . . . Sept. 1800.   pp. 79, [1].   obl. 8vo.
       The preface, dated at Framingham, August, 1800, contains a list of subscribers' names.
       AAS, BPL, HC, JCB, LOC, MHS, NL, NYPL, NYSL, UTS, YC.

36940   BELL, William   1731–1816
       A Practical enquiry into the authority, nature, and design of the Lord's Supper. . . .
       Cambridge, Re-Printed by William Hilliard, for F. Nichols — Boston. 1800.   pp. 33, [1].   16mo.
       The endpaper pasted against the back cover contains an advertisement of the book offerings of Nichols.   AAS, BA, BM, CL, HC, JCB, LOC, MHS, NYPL.

36941   BENJAMIN, Asher
       The Builder's assistant. . . . Correctly engraved on thirty seven copper-plates, with a printed explanation to each. . . . Third edition.
       Greenfield: Printed by Thomas Dickman. 1800.   pp. [34], frontispiece, 37 plates.
       8vo.   AAS, NYHS, PPL.

36942 BERKELEY, ROBERT, *of Virginia*
  AN INQUIRY INTO THE MODUS OPERANDI OF. . . SEDATIVES: SUBMITTED, AS AN INAUGURAL DISSERTA-
  TION TO THE EXAMINATION OF. . . THE MEDICAL FACULTY OF THE UNIVERSITY OF PENNSYLVANIA,
  ON THE THIRTY-FIRST OF MAY 1800. . . .
      Philadelphia: Printed by Way & Groff, no. 48, North Third-Street. 1800.   pp. 34.
  8vo.   AAS, AML, BM, HSP, JCB, LCP, LOC, NYAM, RU, UOP, YC.

36943 THE BERKELEY INTELLIGENCER.   1799–1809
      Martinsburg, Virginia. Printed by John Alburtis.   fol.   weekly.
                                          FOR 1800: [WVA. DEPT. ARCHIVES].

36944 BERKSHIRE GAZETTE.   1798 — FEB. 11, 1800
      Published by Chester Smith, Pittsfield, Massachusetts.   fol.   weekly.
                                                  FOR 1800: [HC].

36945 [BERINGTON, SIMON]   1680–1755
  THE ADVENTURES OF SIGNOR GAUDENTIO DI LUCCA. . . . GIVING AN ACCOUNT OF AN UNKNOWN
  COUNTRY IN THE MIDST OF THE DESARTS OF AFRICA. . . . WITH CRITICAL NOTES BY THE LEARNED
  SIGNOR RHEDI. . . .
      Wilmington, Printed and sold by Bonsal & Niles, 1800.   pp. 234.   16mo.
                                              AAS, LOC, NYPL, YC.

36946 — — — *Baltimore, Bonsal & Niles, 1800.*   pp. 234.   16mo.   LOC, MᵈHS, NYPL, NYSL, PPL.

36947 [BERQUIN, ARNAUD]
  THE LOOKING-GLASS FOR THE MIND. . . . BEING AN ELEGANT COLLECTION OF THE MOST DELIGHTFUL
  LITTLE STORIES. . . .
      New York: Published and printed by D. Longworth, 1800.   pp. 255.   12mo.
  No. 1 in the Youth's Library. Illustrations by A. Anderson. Translation by Samuel Cooper.
                                              HSP, NL, NYHS, NYPL.

36948 BEST, W[ILLIAM, M. A.]
  A DISSERTATION UPON ORATORY; AND PHILOLOGICAL INQUIRY INTO THE BEAUTIES AND DEFECTS OF
  THE ENGLISH LANGUAGE. . . .
      Charleston, South-Carolina, Printed by T. B. Bowen, 1800.   pp. 91.   8vo.
                                          COLLEGE OF CHARLESTON, NYPL.

36949 BETHEL ASSOCIATION.
  MINUTES OF THE BETHEL ASSOCIATION, OF BAPTIST CHURCHES, MET AT BETHLEHEM MEETING-
  HOUSE, AUGUST 9, 1800, IN SPARTANBURGH DISTRICT, SOUTH CAROLINA.
      pp. 8.   8vo.   WAKE FOREST COLLEGE LIBRARY.

36950 BIBLIA.
  DR. WATTS'S IMITATION OF THE PSALMS OF DAVID, SUITED TO CHRISTIAN WORSHIP IN THE UNITED
  STATES. AND ALLOWED BY THE SYNOD OF NEW-YORK AND NEW-JERSEY, TO BE USED IN ALL THE
  CHURCHES. . . .
      New-York — Printed by William Durell. . . for Thomas S. Arden. 1800.   pp. 304.
  24mo.   AAS, NYPL.

36951 — — — [*New York: Printed by William Durell, no. 106, Maiden-Lane. 1800.*]   pp. 304.
  24mo.
  This imprint is from Watts' *Hymns and Spiritual Songs* which is annexed. The titlepage is
  missing from the two copies seen, but one has a frontispiece engraving of David by Scoles.
                                                          AAS.

36952 — H KAINH ΔIAΘHKH. NOVUM TESTAMENTUM. JUXTA EXEMPLAR JOANNIS MILLII ACCURATISSIME
  IMPRESSUM. EDITO PRIMA AMERICANA.
      Wigorniae, Massachusettensi: Excudebat Isaias Thomas, Jun. . . . April, 1800.   pp.
  478, [2].   12mo.
  Edited by Caleb Alexander. The last leaf contains advertising matter.
      AAS, BA, BPL, CL, HC, HEH, NL, NYHS, NYPL, NYSL, LCP, UOC, VᴬU, VᵗU, WC, WLC, YC.

36953 —— Holy Bible abridged or, the history of the Old and New Testament. Illustrated with notes and adorned with cuts for the use of children. . . .
New-York: Printed by W. Durell, for Stephen Stephens and W. Falconer. 1800.
pp. 108.   24mo.   AAS.

36954 —— The Holy Bible, containing the Old and New Testaments. . . .
New-York: Printed and sold by Hugh Gaine, at his book-store and printing-office, at the Bible, in Hanover-Square, M,DCCC.   pp. [696].   12mo.
Second title: The New Testament of our Lord and Saviour Jesus Christ, newly translated out of the original Greek. . . .
[*Imprint as above.*]   pp. [192].   12mo.   AAS (N. T. ONLY), LOC, PᴿU, YC.

36955 —— The Holy Bible, containing the Old and New Testaments. . . .
United States of Columbia. Printed at Worcester, Massachusetts. By Isaiah Thomas. Sold by him in Worcester, by wholesale. . . . Also by said Thomas and Andrews, in Boston, and by the booksellers in the United States of Columbia. 1800.   pp. [676]; [290].   12mo.
Second title: The New Testament. . . .
[*Imprint as above.*]   pp. [290].   12mo.
This is a reissue of Thomas' standard duodecimo edition with only the title-pages changed.
AAS, HC, JCB, LCP, NYPL, YC.

36956 —— Das Neue Testament unsers Herrn und Heylandes Jesu Christi, nach der Deutschen uebersetzung d. Martin Luthers. . . .
Harrisburg: Gedruckt bey Benjamin Mayer. 1800. Second edition.   pp. [2], 523, [3].
12mo.   LOC, PSL.

36957 —— The New Testament of Our Lord and Saviour Jesus Christ, newly translated out of the original Greek. . . .
New-York: Printed and sold by Benjamin Gomez. . . no. 97, Maiden-Lane. 1800.
pp. [360].   16mo.   AAS.

36958 —— The Psalms of David, according to the version approved by the Church of Scotland. . . .
New-York: Printed by G. and R. Waite. 1800.   pp. 360.   12mo.   NYHS.

36959 —— The Testament abridged: or the history of the New Testament. Adorned with cuts. For the use of children. . . .
New-York: Printed by William Durell, no. 106, Maiden-Lane. 1800.   pp. 63.   32mo.
AAS.

36960 —— The Whole Book of Psalms, in metre; with Hymns, suited to the feasts and fasts of the Church, and other occasions of public worship.
Printed at Boston, by I. Thomas and E. T. Andrews. Sold by them and other Booksellers in Boston; by I. Thomas, in Worcester; by Thomas, Andrews, & Penniman, in Albany; and by Thomas, Andrews, & Butler, in Baltimore. Oct. 1800.   pp. 70, [2], 24.
12mo.
Probably issued only bound with the Thomas and Andrews edition of the *Book of Common Prayer.*   AAS, JCB, LOC, NYSL.

36961 BICKERSTAFF, Isaac, *pseud.*
An Astronomical Diary: or Almanack, for the year of our Lord 1800. . . . Calculated for the meridian of Boston. . . .
Boston: Printed for and sold by the following and other Booksellers. . . E. & S. Larkin, S. Hall, Thomas and Andrews, W. P. & L. Blake.   pp. [24].   12mo.   AAS, LOC.

36962 —— The New-England Almanack, or lady's and gentleman's diary, for the year of our Lord Christ 1801. . . .
Printed at Providence (R. I.) by John Carter, opposite the Market.   pp. [24].
12mo.
Attributed to Benjamin West (1730–1813).
AAS, BᴿU, HSP, LOC, NHS, NYHS, NYPL, NYSL, RIHS, WLC.

36963 BICKERSTAFF'S Almanac, for the year of Christian aera, 1801. . . . Calculated for the four New-England states.
    Printed for, and sold by the Booksellers. . . . [By Charles Peirce, Portsmouth, N. H.] pp. [24].   12mo.   AAS.

36964 BIELBY, Lord Bishop of London.
    See Porteus, Bielby.

36965 BIGELOW, Timothy   1767–1821
    An Eulogy on. . . George Washington. . . pronounced before the. . . Masons. . . at the Old South Meeting-House, Boston. . . Feb. 11, 1800. . . . To which are added, two addresses to the deceased . . . and his answers: Together with — the letter of condolence of the Grand Lodge to Mrs. Washington, and her answer. . . .
    Boston. Printed by I. Thomas and E. T. Andrews, no. 45, Newbury-Street.   pp. 26.
    8vo.   AAS, BA, BM, BPL, EI, HC, HEH, JCB, LOC, MHS, NL, NYHS, NYPL, PM, VtU, YC.

36966 BIGLOW, William
    The Child's library. Part first. Containing, lessons for spelling and reading, stops and marks, numbers, &c. . . .
    Salem: Printed by Joshua Cushing, 1800. Sold at the Book Stores of J. C. Cushing and B. B. Macnulty.   pp. 83.   24mo.   EI.

36967 —— The Child's library. Part second. Containing a selection of lessons for spelling, reading and speaking. . . .
    Salem: Printed by Joshua Cushing, 1800. Sold at the Book Stores of T. C. Cushing, and B. B. Macnulty.   pp. 108.   24mo.   AAS.

36968 BILLINGS, William, and Pitman, Thomas
    See Thomas, Eliza.

36969 BINGHAM, Caleb   1757–1817
    The American preceptor; being a new selection of lessons for reading and speaking. . . .
    New-York, Printed by John Furman, 1800.   pp. 228.   16mo.   NL.

36970 ——— [*The eighth edition. . . . Boston: Printed by Manning and Loring, for the author. 1800.* pp. 228.   12mo.]
    The seventh Boston edition was printed in 1799 and the ninth in 1801.

36971 —— An Astronomical and geographical catechism. For the use of children. . . . The fifth edition. . . .
    Boston: Printed by S. Hall, for the author, and sold at their respective book-stores in Cornhill. 1800.   pp. 35.   24mo.   AAS.

36972 —— The Columbian orator: containing a variety of original and selected pieces; together with rules. . . in the. . . art of eloquence. . . . Third edition.
    Boston: Printed by Manning & Loring, for the author; and sold at his Book-Store. . . .
    Sept. 1800.   pp. 300.   12mo.   AAS, BPL, HC, JCB, NYHS, NYSL, PrPL.

36973 BIOGRAPHICAL memoirs of the illustrious Gen. G. Washington. . . .
    See Condie, Thomas.

36974 BIRD, Jonathan   1746–1813
    A Discourse on friendship. . . .
    Hartford: Printed by Hudson and Goodwin. 1800.   pp. 19.   8vo.
    AAS, BM, CHS, CL, NYHS, NYPL, UTS, YC.

36975 BISCO, Abijah   D. 1801
    [An Address delivered to the scholars at the Academy in Westfield, Sept. 28th, 1800.
    Westfield?.   pp. 23.   8vo.]   Evans.

36976　BISHOP, Abraham　　　　　　　　　　　　　　　　　　　1763–1844
　　　Connecticut Republicanism. An oration . . . delivered in New-Haven, on the evening
　　　preceding the public Commencement, September, 1800. . . .
　　　　　[*New Haven?*] *1800.*　　pp. [4], 64, xi.　　8vo.
　　　　　　　　AAS, BPL, BʳU, CHS, CSL, HC, JCB, LOC, NYHS, NYPL, NYSL, RU, WC, YC.

36977　—— —— —— *Philadelphia: Printed for Mathew Carey, Nov. 13, 1800.*　　pp. 80.　　8vo.
　　　　　　　　AAS, APS, BA, BM, EI, HC, HEH, JCB, LOC, MSL, NL, NYHS, NYPL, WRHS, YC.

36978　—— —— —— *Philadelphia: Printed for Mathew Carey, no. 118, High-street. Nov. 13, 1800.*　　pp. 80.
　　　8vo.　　　　　　　AAS, BM, HC, LOC, NYHS, NYPL, NYSL, VᵗU, WⁱˢHS, WRHS, YC.

36979　—— —— —— [*Bennington or New Haven?*]　　pp. 68, xi.　　8vo.　　　　　HEH, NYHS.

36980　—— An Oration on the extent and power of political delusions. Delivered in New-Haven, on
　　　the evening preceding the public Commencement, September, 1800. . . . The second
　　　edition. . . .
　　　　　Newark: Printed by Pennington and Gould, M,DCCC.　　pp. 71.　　8vo.
　　　There are copies with the word "delusion" in the title broken and with several pages mis-
　　　numbered.　　　　AAS, BPL, CU, HEH, HSP, LOC, NJHS, NYHS, NYPL, NYSL, UOC, VᵃU, YC.

36981　BISHOP, Samuel G.
　　　An Eulogium on the death of Gen. George Washington. . . . Pronounced February 22d,
　　　A. D. 1800, at Pittsfield. . . New Hampshire. . . .
　　　　　Printed at Gilmanton, by E. Russell, for the author, March, 1800.　　pp. 15.　　12mo.
　　　　　　　　　　　　　　　　　　　　　　　　　AAS, HEH, LOC, NYPL.

36982　BLAIR, Hugh　　　　　　　　　　　　　　　　　　　　　1718–1800
　　　[Lectures on rhetorick and belles lettres. . . . Vol. 1.
　　　　　Mount Holly, N. J.: Stephen C. Ustick, 1800.]　　　　　GASKILL 94.

36983　BLAIR, John D[urbarrow]　　　　　　　　　　　　　　　　1759–1823
　　　A Sermon on the death of. . . Washington, delivered in the capitol in Richmond. . . .
　　　　　[*Richmond:*] *Printed by Meriwether Jones. . . . January — 1800.*　　pp. 18.　　12mo.
　　　　　　　　　　　　　　　　　　　　　　　　　HEH, LOC, NYPL.

36984　BLAKE, George　　　　　　　　　　　　　　　　　　　　1769–1841
　　　A Masonic eulogy, on. . . George Washington, pronounced before the brethren of St.
　　　John's Lodge, on. . . 4th Feb. 5800. . . .
　　　　　Boston, printed by brother John Russell. 5800.　　pp. 23.　　8vo.
　　　　　　　AAS, BA, BM, BPL, HC, HEH, JCB, LOC, MHS, NYFM, NYHS, NYPL, NYSL, WⁱˢHS.

36985　—— —— Second edition.
　　　　　Boston, printed by brother John Russell. 5800.　　pp. 23.　　8vo.
　　　　　　　　　　　AAS, BA, BPL, HC, HEH, JCB, LOC, MHS, NYPL, PFM.

36986　BLAKSLEE, Solomon　　　　　　　　　　　　　　　　　　1762–1835
　　　An Oration, delivered at East-Haddam, Feb. 22, 1800. . . on the death of. . . Washing-
　　　ton. . . .
　　　　　Hartford: Printed by Hudson and Goodwin, 1800.　　pp. 15.　　8vo.
　　　　　　　　　　　　　　　　　　　　CHS, HEH, LOC, MHS, NYPL.

36987　BLANCHET, François
　　　Reserches sur la médicine, ou l'application de la chimie à la médicine.
　　　　　New York: Claude Parisot. 1800.　　pp. xxiii, 246.　　8vo.
　　　　　　　　　　　　　　　　　　AML, BA, NYAM, NYHS, NYSOC, PPL.

36988　THE BLOSSOMS of morality. . . .
　　　　　See Cooper, Samuel.

36989 BLUNT, Edmund M.
      See Furlong, Lawrence.

36990 BLYTH, Joseph
      An Oration, on the death of. . . Washington, delivered at the chapel in All Saint's parish, on the 22d of February, 1800, at the desire of the officers and privates of Capt. Ward's company. . . .
          Georgetown, (S. C.) Printed by John Burd.   1800.   pp. 22.   12mo.
      Reprinted in *Eulogies and Orations*, Boston, 1800.   BA, HEH, LOC.

36991 BODDILY, John   1755–1802
      A Sermon delivered at Newburyport, on the 22d February, 1800. By Rev. John Boddily, minister of the second Presbyterian society. . . .
          Printed at Newburyport, by Edmund M. Blunt, 1800.   pp. 15.   8vo.
                  AAS, CL, HC, HEH, JCB, LOC, MFM, NYHS, NYPL, NYSL, RU.

36992 BONNET, [Charles]   1720–1793
      Conjectures concerning the nature of future happiness, translated from the French of Mons. Bonnet of Geneva.
          Charleston: Printed by John Dixon Nelson, no. 3, Broad-Street. 1800.   pp. 32.
      16mo.   AAS, CLS.

36993 BONSAL and Niles' town and country Almanac, for the year of our Lord, 1801. . . .
          Baltimore: Printed and sold by Bonsal and Niles, no. 173, Market-Street.   pp. [48].
      12mo.   AAS, BM, LOC.

36994 BOOK of Common Prayer. . . .
      See Protestant Episcopal Church.

36995 BOSTON. Massachusetts.
      The Board of Health, to their constituents. On Wednesday, the 2d day of April next, the powers of the present Board of Health will cease. . . . Paul Revere, President, Boston. March 12, 1800. . . .
          [*Boston.*]   Broadside.   fol.   BPL, MHS, NYPL.

36996 —— Boston, January 6, 1800. The committee chosen by the town to adopt such measures as may indicate the public sensibility on the. . . death of. . . Washington. . . .
          [*Boston.*]   Broadside.   fol.
      Signed by Charles Bulfinch as chairman of the committee.   BA, EI, HEH, NYPL.

36997 —— Names of the streets, lanes and alleys in the town of Boston. With an index directing to the page where the streets, &c. may be found.
          Boston: Printed by Benjamin Edes & Son, Temple-Street, MDCCC.   pp. 19.
      24mo.
      Reprinted in the Boston Directory of 1860.   AAS.

36998 —— Notification. The freeholders and other inhabitants of the town of Boston qualified to vote for representatives. . . . October 27, 1800.
          [*Boston.*]   Broadside.   32mo.   AAS, BPL.

36999 —— Order of performances. Instrumental dirge. Prayer, by Rev. Dr. Eckley. Hymn, written at the request of the committee of arrangements, by Rev. John S. J. Gardiner. . . . Eulogy, by the Hon. George Richards Minot, Esq. . . . Music by Mr. Holden.
          [*Boston.*]   Broadside.   fol.
      This is the program of the proceedings in memory of Washington, Jan. 9, 1800.   BA, HEH.

37000 BOSTON. Massachusetts. Blake's Circulating Library.
      Catalogue of W. P. & L. Blake's circulating library, at the Boston Bookstore, no. 1, Cornhill. . . .
          Boston: Printed for William P. and Lemuel Blake. 1800.   pp. 48.   16mo.   BA.

37001   BOSTON. Massachusetts. Boston Library Society.
        Catalogue of books in the Boston Library. March 1, 1800. . . .
                [*Boston.*]   pp. 24, printed wrappers.   12mo.
                Caption title. The "Rules and Regulations of the Boston Library Society" are appended.
                                                                                        AAS.

37002   BOSTON. Massachusetts. Brattle Street Church.
        To be performed at the Brattle-Street Church, on Wednesday February 19, 1800. Ode.
                I. . . . Ode II. . . .
                From the Chronicle-Press, by E. Rhoades [*Boston.*]   Broadside.   8vo.
                                                                        BPL, JCB, MHS, WLC.

37003   BOSTON. Massachusetts. Carpenters.
        The Rules of work, of the carpenters, in the town of Boston. . . . Published agreeably
                to Act of Congress.
                Printed [*by Samuel Etheridge at Charlestown*], *for the proprietors, 1800.*   pp. 34.
                24mo.   AAS, BA, BPL, HC, JCB, NYHS, NYPL.

37004   BOSTON. Massachusetts. Daniel Wild.
        [A Large and general assortment of new and valuable books. . . . Sold at his office, Bos-
                ton.   Oct. 23, 1800.]   McKay 143k

37005   —— [A Large and general assortment of valuable books, (all new). . . . Sold at his office, Bos-
                ton.   Nov. 15, 1800.]   McKay 143l

37006   —— [A Large, and well assorted collection of books (all new, and in handsome bindings). . . .
                Sold at his office, Boston. May 29, 1800.]   McKay 143g

37007   —— [A Small, but very valuable collection of new books, in the various departments. . . . Sold
                at his office, Boston. July 2, 1800.]   McKay 143h

37008   BOSTON. Massachusetts. First Universalist Church.
        Ode performed at the First Church of the Universalists in Boston, on the day devoted to
                funereal testimonies of . . . George Washington. . . . January 12, 1800.
                [*Boston.*]   Broadside.   4to.   AAS.

37009   BOSTON. Massachusetts. King's Chapel.
        Funeral dirge on the death of General Washington, as sung at the Stone Chapel, the
                music composed by P. A. von Hagen Organist of said church.
                *Boston, printed & sold by P. A. von Hagen & Cos. Musical Magazine, no. 3, Cornhill,
                and to be had of G. Gilfert New York.* . . .   4to sheet of music with words.
                Advertised in the *Columbian Centinel* of Jan. 11, 1800, as published on Jan. 4.   HEH, NYPL.

37010   BOSTON. Massachusetts. Mechanic Association.
        Order of performances, at the Old South Meeting-House, February 22, 1800. Before the
                mechanics of Boston. . . .
                [*Boston.*]   Broadside.   4to.   AAS, HSP.

37011   BOSTON. Massachusetts. Old South Church.
        To be performed at the Old-South, on Saturday, February 8, 1800. Ode 1. . . . Ode 2. . . .
                Young & Minns, printers [*Boston.*]   Broadside.   8vo.   BPL, HEH, HSP, NYPL.

37012   BOSTON. Massachusetts. R. G. Shaw & Co.
        [Spottswood, William, bookseller (Boston). Stock of new books. . . . Sold at 22 Marlboro'
                Street, Boston. Dec. 9, 1800.]   McKay 143m.

37013   —— [Valuable books. . . . Sold at their office, Boston. Dec. 24, 1800.]   McKay 143n.

37014 —— [A VALUABLE COLLECTION OF BOOKS. . . . SOLD AT THEIR OFFICE, BOSTON. FEB. 27, 1800.]
McKAY 143A.

37015 BOSTON. MASSACHUSETTS. ROMAN CATHOLIC CHURCH.
ANTHEMS, HYMNS, &C. USUALLY SUNG AT THE CATHOLICK CHURCH IN BOSTON.
Boston: Printed by Manning & Loring. '1800. pp. 72. 16mo.
BA, BPL, CL, GU, HC, NYPL.

37016 BOSTON. MASSACHUSETTS. SAMUEL CLAP.
[A LARGE COLLECTION OF BOOKS. . . . THE BEST THAT WAS EVER OFFERED AT PUBLIC SALE. . . .
SOLD AT HIS OFFICE, BOSTON. APR. 8, 1800.] McKAY 143B.

37017 —— [A VALUABLE COLLECTION OF BOOKS, BELONGING TO THE ESTATES OF TWO GENTLEMEN, LATE DE-
CEASED. . . . SOLD AT HIS OFFICE, BOSTON. OCT. 21, 1800.] McKAY 143J.

37018 BOSTON. MASSACHUSETTS. SCOTS' CHARITABLE SOCIETY.
RULES AND REGULATIONS OF THE SCOTS' CHARITABLE SOCIETY. INSTITUTED AT BOSTON, 1684.
RENEWED 1786.
Boston. pp. 8. 8vo. NYHS.

37019 BOSTON. MASSACHUSETTS. THOMAS CLARK.
[A LARGE, VALUABLE AND EXTENSIVE COLLECTION OF BOOKS, THE WHOLE OF WHICH ARE NEW. . . .
SOLD AT HIS OFFICE, BOSTON, FEB. 6, 1800.] McKAY 142N.

37020 BOSTON. MASSACHUSETTS. THOMAS JONES.
TEAS AT AUCTION. THIS DAY, THURSDAY, AUGUST 7, 1800, WILL BE SOLD BY PUBLIC AUCTION —
AT . . . LONG WHARF. . . . THOM[AS] JONES, AUCT.
[*Boston.*] Broadside. 4to. MHS.

37021 BOSTON. MASSACHUSETTS. WEST BOSTON BRIDGE COMPANY.
CONCISE VIEW OF THE FACTS, ETC.
[*Boston.*] pp. 8. 12mo.
Dated by the fact that the tolls are reported through December 31, 1799. MHS.

37022 BOSTON. MASSACHUSETTS. WILLIAM EUSTIS.
[A NEW AND VALUABLE ASSORTMENT OF BOOKS, ENTIRELY NEW, IN THE VARIOUS DEPARTMENTS OF
LITERATURE. . . . SOLD AT HIS OFFICE, BOSTON, MAY 8, 1800.] McKAY 143E.

37023 BOSTON. MASSACHUSETTS. WILLIAM RICHARDSON.
WILLIAM RICHARDSON, IMPORTS DIRECTLY FROM THE MANUFACTURERS . . . A LARGE ASSORTMENT
OF LUSTRINGS. . . . AT NO. 65, CORNHILL, BOSTON.
[*Boston.*] Broadside. 16mo. MHS.

37024 THE BOSTON DIRECTORY. CONTAINING THE NAMES OF THE INHABITANTS, THEIR OCCUPATIONS. . . .
ILLUSTRATED BY A PLAN OF THE TOWN. . . .
Boston, printed by John Russell, for John West, no. 75, Cornhill. 1800. pp. 149,
map. 12mo.
The directory is prefixed by a description of the town taken from Morse's *Gazetteer*. The
map is from the survey made by Osgood Carlton in 1796.
AAS, BPL, HSP, LCP, MHS, NEHGS, PPL, PʳU.

37025 BOSTON GAZETTE, COMMERCIAL AND POLITICAL. 1800–1840
Published on Mondays and Thursdays, by John Russell & James Cutler, Boston. 1800.
fol. semi-weekly.
A continuation of *Russell's Gazette*, the change of name occuring on October 9, 1800.
FOR 1800: AAS, BA, BPL, CHS, EI, [HC], HEH, LOC, MHS, NYHS, [NYPL].

37026 —— BOSTON, JANUARY 1ST. 1800. THE CARRIERS' OF THE BOSTON COMMERCIAL GAZETTE, AS CUSTOM
DICTATES, THUS ADDRESSES ITS READERS AND PATRONS. . . .
[*Boston.*] fol. Broadside. WLC.

37027 BOWDOINHAM Association.
MINUTES OF THE BOWDOINHAM ASSOCIATION, HELD AT THE BAPTIST MEETING-HOUSE IN GREEN, AUGUST 27 AND 28, 1800.
Portland: Printed by Elezer Alley Jenks. pp. 8. 8vo. HEH, NYPL, SCBHC.

37028 BOWERS, JAMES −1830
A DISCOURSE, ON OCCASION OF THE DEATH OF . . . WASHINGTON, DELIVERED IN ST. ANN'S CHURCH, PITTSTON, ON SATURDAY, 22D FEBRUARY, 1800. . . .
Hallowell (District of Maine) Printed by Peter Edes. 1800. pp 18. 8vo.
BA, HEH, JCB, LOC, MFM.

37029 —— —— —— [*Hallowell, (District of Maine.) Printed by E. Goodale. 1800.* pp. 18. 12mo.]
WILLIAMSON 1531.

37030 BOYD, ADAM 1738–1803
A DISCOURSE, SACRED TO THE MEMORY OF GEORGE WASHINGTON. . . . IN NASHVILLE, ON THE 22D OF FEBRUARY, 1800. BY THE REV. ADAM BOYD, LATE CHAPLAIN TO A CONTINENTAL BRIGADE. . . .
Nashville (Tennessee): Printed for the author. 1800. pp. 22. 8vo. LOC.

37031 [BRACKENRIDGE, HUGH HENRY] 1748–1816
[AN ODE IN HONOR OF THE PENNSYLVANIA MILITIA, AND A SMALL BAND OF REGULAR TROOPS UNDER THE COMMAND OF GENERAL GEORGE WASHINGTON. . . .
Albany, 1800. pp. 10. 12mo.] SABIN 56702, WEGELIN 874.

37032 BRADFORD, ALDEN 1765–1843
AN EULOGY . . . OF GENERAL GEORGE WASHINGTON . . . PRONOUNCED IN WISCASSET, FEBRUARY, 22D, 1800. . . .
Wiscasset: Printed by Henry Hoskins. 1800. pp. 16. 8vo.
AAS, BA, HEH, JCB, LOC, NYHS, NYPL, PFM.

37033 — A SHORT CATECHISM FOR CHILDREN. . . .
Wiscasset: Printed by Henry Hoskins. 1800. pp. 12. 16mo. AAS.

37034 BRADFORD, JOHN 1749–1830
THE GENERAL INSTRUCTOR: OR, THE OFFICE, DUTY, AND AUTHORITY OF JUSTICES OF THE PEACE, SHERIFFS, CORONERS AND CONSTABLES, IN THE STATE OF KENTUCKEY. . . .
Lexington: Printed by John Bradford. . . . 1800. pp. xii, 252. 12mo.
HC, HEH, KᴊHS, KᴊSL, OH&PS, UOC.

37035 BRAINARD, J[EREMIAH GATES] 1759–1830
AN ORATION, COMMEMORATIVE OF . . . WASHINGTON; SPOKEN IN THE PRESBYTERIAN CHURCH . . . NEW-LONDON, FEBRUARY 22D, 1800. . . .
New-London: Printed by Samuel Green. 1800. pp. 14. 8vo.
BPL, CHS, HEH, LOC, NYPL.

37036 BRAMAN, ISAAC 1770–1858
AN EULOGY ON THE LATE GENERAL GEORGE WASHINGTON. . . . DELIVERED AT ROWLEY, SECOND PARISH, FEBRUARY 22, 1800. . . .
Haverhill. From the press of Seth H. Moore. pp. 24. 8vo.
AAS, BA, BPL, CL, EI, HEH, JCB, LOC, MFM, NYPL, NYSL.

37037 BRAY, THOMAS WELLS 1738–1808
THE DUTY OF LIVING. . . . A SERMON DELIVERED AT THE FUNERAL OF THE REV. AMOS FOWLER, A. M. PASTOR OF THE FIRST CHURCH IN GUILFORD. . . .
Middletown [Conn.]: Printed by T. & J. B. Dunning. 1800. pp. 20. 8vo.
AAS, BM, CHS, HC, JCB, NYHS, NYSL, YC.

37038 A BRIEF ACCOUNT OF THE LATE REVIVALS OF RELIGION. . . .
See Baldwin, Thomas

37039 A BRIEF NARRATIVE OF THE TRIAL FOR THE BLOODY AND MYSTERIOUS MURDER OF THE UNFORTUNATE YOUNG WOMAN, IN THE FAMOUS MANHATTAN WELL. . . .
  [New York?] pp. 16. 8vo.   HC, NYHS.

37040 A BRIEF STATEMENT OF OPINIONS. . . .
  See Fitzsimmons, Thomas

37041 BRIGGS, ISAAC
  THE GEORGIA AND SOUTH-CAROLINA ALMANAC, FOR THE YEAR OF OUR LORD, 1801. . . . ALSO, THE CONSTITUTION OF THE UNITED STATES. . . .
    Augusta: Printed by John Erdman Smith, near the Market. pp. [46]. 8vo.
        D^eRGL.

37042 —— PALLADIUM OF KNOWLEDGE: OR, THE CAROLINA AND GEORGIA ALMANAC FOR THE YEAR OF OUR LORD, 1801. . . .
    Charleston: Printed and Sold by W. P. Young . . . also by T. C. Cox. . . . pp. [48].
  12mo.   AAS, D^eRGL.

37043 —— —— —— *[Second edition. Charleston.]*

37044 —— —— —— *Third edition. . . . Charleston: Printed and sold by W. P. Young . . . also by T. C. Cox. . . .* pp. [46]. 12mo.   CLS.

37045 —— THE VIRGINIA ALMANACK, OR EPHEMERIS FOR THE YEAR 1801. . . . ADAPTED TO THE LATITUDE AND MERIDIAN OF RICHMOND IN VIRGINIA.
    Richmond: Printed and sold . . . by Samuel Pleasants, junior. pp. [16]. 8 vo.
        LOC.

37046 —— THE VIRGINIA & NORTH CAROLINA ALMANACK FOR THE YEAR 1801. . . . THE ASTRONOMICAL PART BY ISAAC BRIGGS; THE EDITORIAL PART BY AMERICANUS URBAN. . . .
    Petersburg: Published by Ross & Douglas, Booksellers and Stationers. pp. [48].
  12mo.   AAS, BM, BPL, HEH, LOC, NYPL, W^{1s}HS.

37047 BRIGGS, JOHN   1765–1811
  AN ORATION, DELIVERED, AT THE NORTH MEETING-HOUSE, IN TIVERTON, ON THE 11TH OF FEBRUARY, A. D. 1800, ON THE DEATH OF . . . WASHINGTON. . . .
    Newport: Printed by Henry Barber, M,DCCC. pp. 10. 8vo. HEH, NHS, NYPL.

37048 BRISTOL. RHODE ISLAND. FIRST CHURCH.
  BRISTOL CHURCH LOTTERY. THE HONOURABLE GENERAL ASSEMBLY OF THE STATE OF RHODE-ISLAND, &C. HAVING GRANTED TO THE CHURCH IN BRISTOL. . . . JUNE 21, 1800.
    [Providence:] Printed by J. Carter. Broadside. 4to.   STREETER.

37049 BRISTOL. RHODE ISLAND. POTTER LIBRARY COMPANY.
  THE BY-LAWS AND CATALOGUE OF THE POTTER LIBRARY COMPANY, IN THE TOWN OF BRISTOL, AND STATE OF RHODE ISLAND.
    Warren (R. I.) Printed by Nathaniel Phillips, M,DCCC. pp. 24. 16mo. NYHS.

37050 BROOKS, JOHN   1752–1825
  AN EULOGY ON GENERAL WASHINGTON; DELIVERED BEFORE THE INHABITANTS OF THE TOWN OF MEDFORD . . . THE 13TH OF JANUARY, 1800. . . .
    Printed by Samuel Hall, no. 53, Cornhill, Boston. 1800. pp. 15. 8vo.
  AAS, BA, BM, BPL, HC, HEH, JCB, LCP, MFM, MHS, NEHGS, NL, NYHS, NYPL, NYSL, PFM, WLC, YC.

37051 THE BROTHER'S GIFT, OR THE NAUGHTY GIRL REFORMED.
    New-York: Printed by William Durell, for John Scoles. 1800. pp. 31. 48mo.
        AAS.

37052   — — — *New York: Printed by William Durell, for T. & J. Swords.*   pp. 31.   48mo.

                                                                                                    AAS.

37053   [BROWN, CHARLES BROCKDEN]   1771–1810
               ARTHUR MERVYN; OR, MEMOIRS OF THE YEAR 1793. SECOND PART. . . .
                   New-York: Printed and sold by George F. Hopkins. . . . 1800.   pp. 243.   12mo.
               The first volume was printed in Philadelphia in 1799.   HEH, HSP, UOP, YC.

37054   — EDGAR HUNTLEY; OR, MEMOIRS OF A SLEEPWALKER. TO WHICH IS ANNEXED, THE DEATH OF
               CICERO. . . . VOL. III.
                   Philadelphia: Printed by H. Maxwell . . . and sold by Thomas Dodson, Asbury
               Dickens, and the principal booksellers. 1800.   pp. 193, 48.   16mo.
               Some copies of vol. III have a 1799 imprint.   NYPL, PPL, YC.

37055   BROWN, CLARK   1771–1817
               A SERMON, ON THE GOSPEL'S GLAD TIDINGS . . . DELIVERED IN STONINGTON-PORT, CONNECTICUT
               . . . JANUARY 12TH, 1800. . . .
                   Stonington-Port, (Connecticut,) printed by Samuel Trumbull. . . . 1800.   pp. 15.
               16mo.   BA, CHS, MHS, NYPL.

37056   — A SERMON, PREACHED ON THE DEATH OF GEORGE WASHINGTON . . . DELIVERED IN STONINGTON-
               PORT, CONNECTICUT, ON . . . JANUARY 14TH, 1800. . . .
                   Stonington-Port, Printed by Samuel Trumbull . . . January, 1800.   pp. 14.   8vo.
                                                                                                    BPL, JCB.

37057   BROWN, ELIJAH
               [AN ORATION DELIVERED . . . PETERSBURGH FEBRUARY 22D, 1800, IN COMMEMORATION OF THE DEATH
               OF . . . WASHINGTON.
                   Troy: R. Moffitt & Co.   pp. 11.]   EVANS.

37058   BROWN, SAMUEL   1769–1830
               A TREATISE ON . . . YELLOW FEVER . . . AN ACCOUNT OF THE DISEASE IN SEVERAL OF THE
               CAPITALS OF THE UNITED STATES; BUT MORE PARTICULARLY . . . IN BOSTON. . . .
                   Boston: Printed by Manning & Loring. April, 1800.   pp. 112.   8vo.
                   AAS, AML, BA, BPL, HC, HEH, HSP, JCB, LCP, LOC, MHS, NYAM, NYHS, NYPL, PʳU, UOC.

37059   BROWN UNIVERSITY.
               See Rhode Island College.

37060   BRYAN, SAMUEL
               See, A Statement of the measures contemplated. . . .

37061   BUCKMINSTER, JOSEPH   1751–1812
               A DISCOURSE DELIVERED IN THE SOUTH, AND IN THE NORTH CHURCH IN PORTSMOUTH, DECEMBER
               14, 1800: THE ANNIVERSARY OF THE DEATH OF GEORGE WASHINGTON. . . .
                   Portsmouth, New-Hampshire, printed at the United States' Oracle-office by Charles
               Peirce. December 1800.   pp. 21.   8vo.   AAS, BPL, CHS, HC, HEH, JCB, LOC, NL, NYHS.

37062   — DOMESTIC HAPPINESS, A SERMON DELIVERED AT THE SOUTH CHURCH IN PORTSMOUTH, LORD'S-DAY,
               FEBRUARY 23, 1800. . . .
                   Portsmouth [N. H.], printed by William Treadwell.   pp. 24.   8vo.
                                                                                       AAS, BPL, HC, NYHS, YC.

37063   — RELIGION AND RIGHTEOUSNESS. . . . PREACHED TO THE NORTH AND SOUTH PARISHES IN PORTS-
               MOUTH . . . 22D FEBRUARY, 1800 . . . TO PAY TRIBUTARY RESPECT TO THE MEMORY OF GEN.
               WASHINGTON. . . .
                   Portsmouth, New-Hampshire, printed at the United States' Oracle-office, by Charles
               Peirce, 1800.   pp. 28.   8vo.
                   AAS, BM, BPL, HC, HEH, JCB, LOC, NHSL, NYHS, NYPL, NYSL, YC.

37064 —— A Sermon, delivered in the First Church in Portsmouth, on the Lord's day after the melancholy tidings of the death of George Washington. . . .
Second title: A Sermon, delivered in the First Church in Portsmouth, January 5th, 1800. The house being dressed in mourning in token of respect to the memory of General Washington. . . . [pp. 19–29.]
Third title: A Second sermon, delivered Lord's day, January 5, 1800. . . . [pp. 32–45.]
Portsmouth, printed by John Melcher, 1800.   pp. 45.   8vo.
AAS (pt. 1), BA, BPL, HC, HEH, JCB, NHSL, NL, NYPL, NYSL, WLC.

37065 BULLARD, Samuel
The Universal Almanack, for the year of our Lord 1801. . . . Calculated for . . . Boston. . . .
Boston, Printed and Sold by Benjamin Edes, in Temple-Street. . . .   pp. [24].
12mo.   AAS, LOC.

37066 BUNYAN, John   1628–1688
The Pilgrim's progress. . . . Embellished with cuts. . . . Wherein are set forth, I. The manner of his setting out. II. His dangerous journey. III. His safe arrival at the desired country. . . .
Boston: Printed for Joseph Bumstead. Sold by him at no. 20, Union-Street: Thomas and Andrews, Newbury-Street; by D. West, E. Larkin, W. Pelham, Wm. P. and L. Blake, Cornhill; and J. Nancrede, Marlborough-Street. 1800.   pp. 324.   12mo.
AAS, BPL, CL, HC, HSP, LOC, NYPL.

37067 BURGES, Tristam   1770–1853
The Spirit of independence . . . delivered before the Providence Association of Mechanics and Manufacturers, at their annual election, April 14, 1800. . . .
Printed by B. Wheeler, Providence. 1800.   pp. 28.   8vo.
"Odes [composed by Paul Allen], performed at the anniversary election" occupy pp. 25–8.
AAS, EI, HC, HEH, JCB, MᶜHS, MHS, MSL, NYHS, NYPL, NYSL, RIHS.

37068 [BURGH, James]   1714–1775
The Art of speaking. Containing, I. An Essay; in which are given rules for expressing properly the principal passions. . . .
Philadelphia: Printed by Charles Cist. . . . MDCCC.   pp. [4], 336, [1].   12mo.
AAS, AHTS, BPL, HSP, LOC, NYPL, WRHS, YC.

37069 BURNET, George Whitefield
[An Oration, delivered before Nova Caesaria Lodge, on the anniversary of St. John the Evangelist, December 27th, A. L. 5799. . . .
Cincinnati, 1800?]
W. P. A., *Ohio Imprints*, 9. Advertised as for sale in the *Western Spy*, May 29, 1802.

37070 BURRILL, George R[awson]   1770–1818
An Oration pronounced at the Baptist Meeting-House in Providence . . . the seventh of January, 1800 . . . on the death of Gen. George Washington. . . .
Providence: Printed by John Carter.   pp. 15.   8vo.
AAS, BA, HC, HEH, JCB, LOC, MHS, NYHS, NYPL, NYSL, RIHS, WL, WLC, YC.

37071 BURROUGHS, Peleg   D. 1800
An oration. . . . Pronounced at the Congregational meeting-house, in Tiverton, on the 22d day of February, A. D. 1800, at the funeral ceremony on the death of . . . Washington. . . .
Newport: Printed by Henry Barber, M,DCCC.   pp. 13, [2].   12mo.
HEH, JCB, LOC, NHS, NYPL.

37072 BURTON, Asa   1752–1836
A Sermon, preached at the ordination of the Rev. Timothy Clark . . . in Greenfield, January 1, 1800. . . .
Printed at Windsor, Vermont, By Alden Spooner. 1800.   pp. 24.   8vo.
AAS, AHTS, BA, BM, CL, HC, JCB, LCP, LOC, NL, NYPL, PTS, VᵗU, YC.

37073 BYBERRY LIBRARY COMPANY.
    CONSTITUTION, BY-LAWS AND CATALOGUE OF BOOKS BELONGING TO BYBERRY LIBRARY COMPANY
    INSTITUTED THE 29TH OF 12TH MONTH 1794.
        Philadelphia, Printed by John Ormrod. . . . 1800.   pp. 9.   12mo.   JCB.

37074 BYSTANDER; OR A SERIES OF LETTERS ON . . . THE "LEGISLATIVE CHOICE" OF ELECTORS IN MARYLAND:
    IN WHICH THE CONSTITUTIONAL RIGHT TO A LEGISLATIVE CHOICE IN THAT STATE, AND THE
    NECESSITY OF ADOPTING IT . . . IN ORDER TO COUNTERACT THE ARTIFICES OF THE ANTI-FEDERALISTS
    IN VIRGINIA AND OTHER STATES, AND TO PREVENT A PRESIDENT FROM BEING ELECTED BY THE
    MINORITY. . . .
        Baltimore: Printed by Yundt and Brown. . . . M,DCCC.   pp. 30.   12mo.
    Attributed to Robert Goodloe Harper.   BA, LOC, MᵈHS, NYPL.

37075 THE CABINET.   AUG. 26, 1800–1801
        [*Georgetown:*] *District of Columbia. Published by James Lyon.*   fol.   tri-weekly
    and daily.   FOR 1800: [NYSL].

37076 CAIUS, *pseud.*
    See Pinkney, William.

37077 CALDWELL, CHARLES   1772–1853
    AN ELEGIAC POEM ON THE DEATH OF GENERAL WASHINGTON. BY CHARLES CALDWELL, A. M., M. D.
        Philadelphia: Printed at the office of "The True American" [by Samuel F. Bradford].
    1800.   pp. [4], 12.   8vo.
                    AAS, BA, BPL, BʳU, HEH, HSP, JCB, LCP, LOC, MᵈHS, NYHS, NYPL.

37078 [——] AN ELEGIAC POEM ON THE DEATH OF GEORGE WASHINGTON, COMMANDER IN CHIEF OF THE
    ARMIES OF THE UNITED STATES.
        Springfield: Printed by Ashley & Brewer. 1800.   pp. 11.   12mo.   NYHS.

37079 [——] AN ELEGIAC POEM ON THE DEATH OF GENERAL GEORGE WASHINGTON. . . . DEDICATED TO THE
    CITIZENS OF THE UNITED STATES.
        [*Philadelphia:*] *printed by R. Aitken, January 1, 1800.*   Broadside.   fol.
    Printed on silk.   BPL, HC, HEH.

37080 [——] AN ELEGIAC POEM ON THE DEATH OF GENERAL GEORGE WASHINGTON . . . DEDICATED TO THE
    PATRONS OF THE TRUE AMERICAN. AT THE COMMENCEMENT OF THE YEAR 1800.
        [*Philadelphia: Printed by Samuel F. Bradford.*]   Broadside.   fol.
                                                            HC, HEH, LOC, NYPL.

37081 CALDWELL, JOSEPH
    EULOGY ON GENERAL WASHINGTON, PRONOUNCED IN PERSON-HALL, AT THE UNIVERSITY OF NORTH-
    CAROLINA, ON THE TWENTY-SECOND OF FEBRUARY, 1800. . . . BY THE REV. JOSEPH CALDWELL,
    A. M. PROF. MATH. . . .
        Raleigh: Printed by J. Gales. 1800.   pp. 34.   12mo.   NCU.

37082 CALET, JEAN JAQUES
    A TRUE AND MINUTE ACCOUNT OF THE DESTRUCTION OF THE BASTILLE. BY JEAN JAQUES CALET. . . .
    WHO HAD BEEN A PRISONER, THERE UPWARDS OF TWENTY YEARS. . . .
        Printed at Medford, (Massachusetts.) For William Hunt. 1800.   pp. 34.   12mo.
                                                            AAS, BM, BPL, EI, HC, NYPL.

37083 [CALLENDER, JAMES THOMSON]   1758–1803
    THE PROSPECT BEFORE US. VOLUME I. . . .
        Richmond, — Virginia: printed for the author, and sold by M. Jones, S. Pleasants, jun.
    and J. Lyon. — 1800.   pp. 184.   12mo.
    One line of errata on p. 184.
            AAS, BA, BPL, HC, HEH, JCB, LOC, MSL, NYHS, NYPL, NYSL, UOTˣ, WⁱˢHS, YC.

37084 [——] The Prospect before us. Vol. II. Part I. . . .
Richmond: Printed and sold by M. Jones . . . by S. Pleasants, jun . . . by T. Field,
Petersburg; and by the author, in the jail of Richmond . . . M,D,CCC. pp. 152. 8vo.
AAS, BA, BPL, HC, HEH, HSP, JCB, LOC, MSL, NYHS, NYPL, NYSL, UOTˣ, VᵃU, WⁱᵃHS, YC.

37085 CAMDEN, William 1551–1623
A Grammar of the Greek language: originally composed for the college-school, at
Gloucester. . . . First American from the third London edition. . . .
Printed at Boston, by I. Thomas and E. T. Andrews. Sold by them in Boston, by
Thomas, Andrews & Penniman, Albany; by Thomas, Andrews & Butler, Baltimore; by
I. Thomas, Worcester. . . . April, 1800. pp. [4], 223, [1]. 12mo.
Edited by John Snelling Popkin (1771–1852).
AAS, BPL, HC, JCB, NYPL, NYSL, PʳU, RU, UOC, VᵗU, WL, YC.

37086 CAMERON, Duncan
[Reports of cases determined by the Judges of the Superior Courts of law and the Court
of Equity of the State of North Carolina, at their meeting on the 10th of June,
A. D. 1800. . . .
Raleigh: Hodge & Boylan, Printers to the State. 1800. pp. 108. 8vo.]
Entry from Evans' notes. He evidently saw a copy, for he noted differences between the
above title and that recorded in the copyright entry.

37087 CAMPBELL, Thomas 1777–1844
The Pleasures of hope; with other poems. . . .
Edinburgh, Printed: New-York, re-printed by John Furman . . . for Jones Bull. 1800.
pp. 120. 16mo. AAS, BPL, HC, NYPL, NYSL, PPL.

37088 —— —— To which is added the Nurse. . . .
New-York: Printed by W. Durell, no. 106 Maiden-Lane, For the Book-Sellers. 1800.
pp. 164, 1 plate. 12mo.
The engraved frontispiece is marked "Scoles sculp." AAS, HC, LOC, NYPL, NYSL.

37089 —— —— —— *New-York: Printed by William Durell, for Evert Duyckinck. 1800.* pp. 164, plate.
12mo.
Frontispiece by Scoles. AAS, NYPL.

37090 —— —— —— *New-York: Printed by W. Durell . . . for Thomas S. Arden, 1800.* pp. 164, plate.
12mo. TCH.

37091 —— —— —— *New-York: Printed by W. Durell, for George F. Hopkins. 1800.* pp. 164, plate.
8vo. NYPL.

37092 —— —— The third American edition.
Wilmington: Printed at the Franklin Press, by James Wilson. 1800. pp. 56. 16mo.
AAS, DHS, LOC.

37093 A Candid address, to the freemen of the State of Rhode Island, on the subject of the ap-
proaching election. . . .
Providence: — Printed by J. Carter, jun. Broadside. fol.
In the support of Adams in the election of 1800. BʳU.

37094 CAPTAIN James. Who was hung and gibbeted in England, for starving to death his cabin-
boy. Second Newburyport edition.
[Newburyport:] Printed [by Angier March] for, and sold to the Travelling Stationers.
. . . Sold also at no. 4, Middle Street. . . . Broadside. EI.

37095 CAREY, Mathew 1760–1839
[The American primer; or an easy introduction to spelling and reading.
Philadelphia: Printed for Mathew Carey. . . . 1800.]
256th Pennsylvania District Copyright, issued to Mathew Carey as author, July 15, 1800.

37096 —— CAREY'S AMERICAN ATLAS; CONTAINING 20 MAPS AND ONE CHART. . . .
Philadelphia: Engraved for and published by Mathew Carey. . . . December 2, 1800.
fol. WᴵˢHS.

37097 —— CAREY'S GENERAL ATLAS. . . .
Ppiladelphia [!]: *Published by Mathew Carey. September 9, 1800.* 49 maps. fol.
There are copies with the imprint dated June 9, 1800. AAS, BA, NYHS, RU, UOPᴵ.

37098 —— [THE CHILD'S GUIDE TO SPELLING AND READING, OR AN ATTEMPT TO FACILITATE THE PROGRESS OF
SMALL CHILDREN WHEN FIRST SENT TO SCHOOL.
Philadelphia: Printed for Mathew Carey.]
255th Pennsylvania District Copyright issued to Mathew Carey as author, July 15, 1800.

37099 [——] THE SCHOOL OF WISDOM; OR, AMERICAN MONITOR. CONTAINING . . . EXTRACTS FROM THE MOST
EMINENT WRITERS. . . .
*Philadelphia: Printed for Mathew Carey, no. 118, Market-Street. 1800. (Copy-right
secured.)* pp. xii, [5]–304. 16mo. AAS, BPL, HSP, JCB, LCP, LOC, NYPL, PPL, WLC, YC.

37100 CAREY'S FRANKLIN ALMANAC, FOR THE YEAR 1801, CALCULATED FOR NEW JERSEY, PENNSYLVANIA,
DELAWARE, MARYLAND, AND VIRGINIA.
Philadelphia, printed for Mathew Carey, no. 118, Market-Street, — 1801 [*1800*]. *By
John Bioren.* pp. [50]. 12mo.
There are copies which show signature C partly reset. AAS, BM, LOC, VᵃSL, YC.

37101 CARLE, JOHN I.
A FUNERAL SERMON, PREACHED AT ROCKAWAY, DECEMBER 29, 1799, ON THE MUCH LAMENTED
DEATH OF GENERAL GEORGE WASHINGTON. . . .
Morris-Town: Printed by Jacob Mann. 1800. pp. 22. 12mo. NJHS.

37102 THE CAROLINA GAZETTE. 1798–1840
Charleston: Published by Freneau and Paine. fol. weekly. FOR 1800: AAS, WᴵˢHS.

37103 CARPENTER, T[HOMAS]
A REPORT OF AN ACTION FOR A LIBEL, BROUGHT BY DR. BENJAMIN RUSH, AGAINST WILLIAM
COBBETT, IN . . . 1799. . . . TAKEN IN SHORTHAND BY T. CARPENTER.
Philadelphia: Printed by W. W. Woodward, no. 17, Chestnut Street. 1800. pp. [70].
8vo. AAS, AML, BPL, CSL, HC, JCB, LOC, NYAM, NYPL, NYSL, RU, UOP.

37104 —— THE TWO TRIALS OF JOHN FRIES . . . TOGETHER WITH A BRIEF REPORT OF THE TRIALS OF SEVERAL
OTHER PERSONS, FOR TREASON AND INSURRECTION . . . IN THE CIRCUIT COURT OF THE UNITED
STATES, BEGUN AT . . . PHILADELPHIA, APRIL 11, 1799. . . .
Philadelphia: Printed and sold by William W. Woodward, no. 17 Chesnut . . . 1800.
pp. 4, 226, 51. 8vo.
AAS, BA, BPL, HC, HSP, JCB, LCP, MHS, MSL, NL, NYHS, NYPL, NYSL, WᴵˢHS, YC.

37105 CARR, BENJAMIN 1769–1831
DEAD MARCH & MONODY. PERFORMED IN THE LUTHERAN CHURCH, PHILADELPHIA . . . THE
26TH, DECEMBER 1799 BEING PART OF THE MUSIC SELECTED FOR FUNERAL HONOURS TO . . .
WASHINGTON. . . .
[*Colophon:*] *Printed by J. Carr, Baltimore. Copyright secured.* Two sheets, each
printed on one side. HEH, HSP.

37106 CARR, BENJAMIN, ed.
THE MUSICAL JOURNAL FOR THE FLUTE, OR VIOLIN. SOLD AT THE FOLLOWING MUSICAL REPOSITORIES,
J. CARR'S, BALTIMORE; J. CHALK'S, PHILADELPHIA AND J. HEWITT'S, NEW YORK.
[*Baltimore: Published by Joseph Carr.*] pp. 48. 8vo. LOC.

37107 —— THE MUSICAL JOURNAL FOR THE PIANO-FORTE. . . . SELECTED AND ARRANGED BY BENJAMIN CARR.
. . . VOL. 1.
[*Baltimore: Published by Joseph Carr.*] 29 numbers. fol.
EPFL, JCB, LOC, MᵈHS, NYPL, YC.

37108 CARROLL, John   1735–1815
    A Discourse on General Washington; delivered in the Catholic church of St. Peter, in
    Baltimore. — Feb. 22d 1800. . . .
        Baltimore: Printed by Warner & Hanna.   pp. 24.   8vo.
                            BA, BPL, GU, HC, HEH, HSP, LOC, MFM, MdHS, NYPL, OH&PS, PPL.

37109 CASTINE Journal and the Eastern Advertiser.   1799–1801
        Castine. Printed by David J. Waters.   fol.   weekly.   For 1800: [HC].

37110 CATHRALL, Isaac   1764–1819
    Memoir on the analysis of the black vomit, ejected in the last stage of the yellow
    fever. . . .
        Philadelphia: from the press of R. Folwell, no. 63, North Front-street. 1800.   pp. 32.
    8vo.   AAS, AML, LCP, LOC, UOP, PrU.

37111 CATLIN, Jacob   1758–1826
    The Gentiles' inheritance of the blessing of Abraham, through Jesus Christ . . . A
    sermon, delivered at New-Marlborough, in . . . 1798. . . .
        Greenfield: T. Dickman, printer. 1800.   pp. 31.   8vo.   CL.

37112 THE CENTINEL, & Country Gazette.   1796 — Nov. 1800
        From the press of Green, English & Co. George-town . . . 1800.   fol.   weekly.
    This was the country edition of *The Centinel of Liberty.*   For 1800: [HC].

37113 THE CENTINEL of Freedom.   1796–1909
        *Newark (New-Jersey) — printed and published . . . by Samuel Pennington & Stephen
    Gould. . . .   weekly.   fol.*   For 1800: AAS, NJHS.

37114 —— The News-carrier's address to the patrons of the Centinel . . . January 1, 1800.
        [Newark.]   Broadside.   NJHS, NYHS.

37115 THE CENTINEL of Liberty, or Georgetown and Washington Advertiser. 1796 — Nov. 14, 1800
        From the press of Green, English & Co. Georgetown . . . 1800.   fol.   semi-weekly.
    Superseded by the daily *Museum and Washington and George-town Daily Advertiser.*
                                    For 1800: LOC.

37116 CHALLONER, R[ichard]   1691–1781
    Think well on't: or, reflections on the great truths of the Christian religion. . . .
    The thirty-second edition, corrected.
        Philadelphia: Printed by John Bioren, for Mathew Carey . . . June 10, 1800.   pp.
    136, [2].   24mo.
    The last two pages contain "A table of the chapters."   AAS, CL.

37117 CHARITABLE lottery. . . .
    See Conant, Stephen.

37118 CHARLESTON Baptist Association.
    Minutes of the Charleston Baptist Association, convened at Deep-Creek, November 1st,
    1800. . . .
        [Charleston?].   pp. 7.   8vo.   AAS, JCB.

37119 THE CHARLESTON Directory for 1801.
    See Nelson's Charleston Directory.

37120 CHARLESTOWN, Massachusetts.
        Proceedings of the Town of Charlestown . . . in respectful testimony . . . of the late
        George Washington.
            [*Charlestown: Printed by Samuel Etheridge.*] *January. M,DCCC.*   pp. 46, 36.
        This contains "A Prayer and Sermon Delivered at Charlestown, December 31, 1799. . . .
        By Jedidiah Morse. . . . To which is prefixed, An Account of the Proceedings . . . Written
        by Hosiah Bartlett." The portion of the imprint in brackets is from the second titlepage.
                        AHTS, BA, BPL, CSL, EI, HC, HEH, LOC, MFM, NYHS, NYPL, NYSL, RU, YC.

37121 —— —— Annexed is the Valedictory Address of the deceased, to his fellow citizens. . . .
            [*Same imprint.*]   pp. 46, 36, 24.
                        AAS, BA, BPL, CSL, HC, HEH, JCB, LOC, NYHS, NYPL, WⁱˢHS.

37122 CHARLESTOWN. Massachusetts. Artillery Company.
        Rules and regulations, for the Charlestown Artillery Company. As revised by a vote of
        the Company. January 30, 1800.
            Charlestown: Printed by Samuel Etheridge. 1800.   pp. 6.   16mo.   WLC.

37123 CHASE, Jeremiah Townley   1748–1828
        [Would it not be an extraordinary thing, in the organization of a national govern-
        ment. . . .
            Annapolis: Printed by Frederick and Samuel Green?   Broadside.]   Minick 566.

37124 CHAUDRON, [Jean] Simon
        Funeral oration on Brother George Washington; delivered January 1st, 1800, before the
        French Lodge L'Aménité. . . . Translated from the French by Samuel F. Bradford.
            Philadelphia: Printed by John Ormrod, no. 41, Chestnut-street. 1800.   pp. 26.   8vo.
                        AAS, BA, BPL, HC, HEH, JCB, LOC, NYHS, NYPL, NYSL, OH&PS, PPL, WLC.

37125 —— Oraison funèbre de Frère Gaspard Shultess. Prononcée le 7 Décembér, 1800. Dans la
        Loge Francaise L'Aménité. . . .
            A Philadelphie: chez Thomas & William Bradford. . . . 1800.   pp. 14.   8vo.   PFM.

37126 —— Oraison funèbre, du Frére George, M. de la Grange, Oncle, prononcée le 18 Novembre, 1798.
        Dans la Loge Francaise L'Aménité. . . .
            Philadelphie: Chez John Ormrod, no. 41, Chestnut-street. 1800.   pp. 44.   8vo.
        The "Oraison Funèbre des FF: Tanguy La Bossiere, Gauvain et Decombaz; Pronouncée
        par Le V. de la Grange . . . dans la Loge Francaise L'Aménité, no. 73, seance du 8 du
        10eme mois, 1799" occupies pp. 15–35, and the "Orasion Funèbre, du Frére R. Jarossay,
        prononcée le 4 Mai, 1800, dans la Loge. . . . Par le F. Simon Chaudron" occupies 37–44.
        Each has a titlepage.   AAS, HSP.

37127 —— Oraison funèbre, du Frére George Washington, prononcée le premier janvier 1800, dans la
        Loge Francaise L'Aménité. . . .
            Philadelphie: Chez John Ormrod. . . . 1800.   pp. 35.   8vo.
                        APS, BA, BPL, HEH, HSP, JCB, LOC, MᵈHS, NYHS, NYPL, NYSL, PFM, PPL, WLC, YC.

37128 (CHEAP repository. [Number 1.]) The Shepherd of Salisbury Plain, Part I. [& The
        Lancashire collier girl.]
            Philadelphia: Printed by B. & J. Johnson, no. 147 High-Street. . . .   pp. 36.   24mo.
        Written by Hannah More.   AAS, HSP, LOC.

37129 —— —— [Number 2.] The Shepherd of Salisbury Plain, Part II. to which is added The sorrows
        of Yamba, a poem.
            Philadelphia: Printed by B. & J. Johnson, no. 147 High-Street. . . .   pp. 36.   24mo.
        Written by Hannah More.   AAS, HSP, LOC.

37130 —— —— [Number 3.] The Parable of the labourers in the vineyard. [The horse race; or, The
        pleasures of the course. The plow boy's dream.]
            Philadelphia: Printed by B. & J. Johnson, no. 147 High-Street. . . .   pp. 36.   24mo.
                        AAS, HSP, LOC, YC.

37131 —— —— [Number 4.] The Wonderful advantages of adventuring in the lottery!!! To which is added The Happy Waterman.
Philadelphia: Printed by B. & J. Johnson, no. 147, High-Street. . . . pp. 36. 24mo.
AAS, LOC, YC.

37132 —— —— (No. V.) The Two wealthy farmers; or, The history of Mr. Bragwell. Part I.
Philadelphia: Printed by B. & J. Johnson, no. 147 High-Street. . . . pp. 36. 24mo.
Written by Hannah More. AAS, HSP, LOC, YC.

37133 —— —— (No. VI.) The Two wealthy farmers; or, The history of Mr. Bragwell. Part II.
Philadelphia: Printed by B. & J. Johnson, no. 147 High-Street. 1800. pp. 36. 24mo.
Written by Hannah More. AAS, HSP, LOC, YC.

37134 —— —— (No. VII.) The Two wealthy farmers; or, The history of Mr. Bragwell. Part III.
Philadelphia: Printed by B. & J. Johnson, no. 147 High-Street. 1800. pp. 36. 24mo.
Written by Hannah More. AAS, HSP, LOC, YC.

37135 —— —— (No. VIII.) The Two wealthy farmers; or, The history of Mr. Bragwell. Part IV.
Philadelphia: Printed by B. & J. Johnson, no. 147 High-Street. 1800. pp. 36. 24mo.
Written by Hannah More. AAS, HSP, LOC, YC.

37136 —— —— (No. IX.) The Two wealthy farmers; or, The history of Mr. Bragwell. Part V. [& a new Christmas hymn].
Philadelphia: Printed by B. & J. Johnson, no. 147 High-Street. 1800. pp. 36. 24mo.
Written by Hannah More. AAS, HSP, LOC, YC.

37137 —— —— (No. X.) Sorrowful Sam; or, The history of two blacksmiths [and a true account of a pious negro].
Philadelphia: Printed by B. & J. Johnson, no. 147 High-Street. 1800. pp. 36. 24mo.
Written by Hannah More. AAS, HSP, LOC, YC.

37138 —— —— Number 11. The History of Tom White, the postilion. Part I.
Philadelphia: Printed by B. & J. Johnson, no. 147 High-Street. 1800. pp. 36. 24mo.
Written by Hannah More. AAS, LOC, YC.

37139 —— —— Number 12. The Way to plenty; or, The second part of Tom White.
Philadelphia: Printed by B. & J. Johnson, no. 147 High-Street. 1800. pp. 36. 24mo.
Written by Hannah More. AAS, LOC, YC.

37140 —— —— Number 13. The Cheapside apprentice; or, The history of Mr. Francis H***. . . .
Philadelphia: Printed by B. & J. Johnson, no. 147 High-Street. 1800. pp. 36. 24mo.
AAS, HSP, LOC, WL.

37141 —— —— Number 14. Husbandry moralized; or, Pleasant Sunday reading for a farmer's kitchen.
Philadelphia: Printed by B. & J. Johnson, no. 147 High-Street. 1800. pp. 36. 24mo.
AAS, HSP, LOC, WL, YC.

37142 —— —— Number 15. Black Giles the poacher; with some account of a family who had rather live by their wits than their works.
Philadelphia: Printed by B. & J. Johnson, no. 147 High-Street. 1800. pp. 36. 24mo.
Written by Hannah More. Appended is "The Gin Shop" in verse.
AAS, HSP, JCB, LOC, NYPL, VªU, WL, YC.

37143 —— —— Number 16. Black Giles, the poacher; with the history of Widow Brown's apple-tree.
Philadelphia: Printed by B. & J. Johnson, no. 147 High-Street. 1800. pp. 36. 24mo.
Written by Hannah More. Appended is "A Hymn." AAS, HSP, JCB, LOC, NYPL, VªU, WL, YC.

37144 —— —— NUMBER 17. THE HISTORY OF TAWNY RACHEL, THE FORTUNE TELLER, BLACK GILES'S WIFE.
Philadelphia: Printed by B. & J. Johnson, no 147 High Street. 1800. pp. 35, [1].
24mo.
Written by Hannah More. Appended is "The Plum Cakes" in verse. The last leaf contains
a list of the Repository Tracts.   AAS, HSP, JCB, LOC, NYPL, V·U, WL.

37145 —— —— NUMBER 18. THE HISTORY OF THE TWO SHOEMAKERS. PART I.
Philadelphia: Printed by B. & J. Johnson, no. 147 High-Street. 1800. pp. 36. 24mo.
Written by Hannah More.   AAS, HSP, LCP, LOC, NYPL, WL, YC.

37146 —— —— NUMBER 19. THE HISTORY OF THE TWO SHOEMAKERS. PART II.
Philadelphia: Printed by B. & J. Johnson, no. 147 High-Street. 1800. pp. 36. 24mo.
Written by Hannah More.   AAS, HSP, LCP, LOC, NYPL, WL, YC.

37147 —— —— NUMBER 20. THE HISTORY OF THE TWO SHOEMAKERS. PART III.
Philadelphia: Printed by B. & J. Johnson, no. 147 High-Street. 1800. pp. 36. 24mo.
Written by Hannah More.   AAS, LCP, LOC, NYPL, WL, YC.

37148 —— —— NUMBER 21. THE HISTORY OF THE TWO SHOEMAKERS. PART IV.
Philadelphia: Printed by B. & J. Johnson, no. 147 High-Street. 1800. pp. 36. 24mo.
Written by Hannah More.   AAS, LCP, LOC, NYPL, YC.

37149 —— —— NUMBER 22. SUNDAY READING. THE HARVEST HOME.
Philadelphia: Printed by B. & J. Johnson, no. 147 High-Street. 1800. pp. 36. 24mo.
Appended are Hannah More's "Hymn of praise for the abundant harvest of 1796" and
"The True heroes."   AAS, HSP, LCP, LOC, NYPL, PPL, YC.

37150 —— —— NUMBER 23. THE HISTORY OF THE PLAGUE IN LONDON, IN 1665.
Philadelphia: Printed by B. & J. Johnson, no. 147 High-Street. 1800. pp. 36. 24mo.
By Daniel Defoe. Appended is "The Honest Miller of Glocestershire. A true ballad."
      AAS, HSP, LCP, LOC, NYPL, YC.

37151 —— —— NUMBER 24. SUNDAY READING. THE STORY OF JOSEPH AND HIS BRETHREN. PART I.
Philadelphia: Printed by B. & J. Johnson, no. 147 High Street. 1800. pp. 36. 24mo.
      AAS, HSP, LCP, LOC, NYPL, YC.

37152 —— —— NUMBER 25. SUNDAY READING. THE STORY OF JOSEPH AND HIS BRETHREN. PART II.
Philadelphia: Printed by B. & J. Johnson, no. 147 High-Street. 1800. pp. 36. 18mo.
      AAS, LCP, LOC, NYPL, YC.

37153 —— —— NUMBER 26. SUNDAY READING. THE STORY OF JOSEPH AND HIS BRETHREN. PART III.
Philadelphia: Printed by B. & J. Johnson, no. 147 High-Street. 1800. pp. 36. 24mo.
Includes "The history of diligent Dick."   AAS, LCP, LOC, NYPL, YC.

37154 —— —— NUMBER 27. THE GAMESTER.
Philadelphia: Printed by B. & J. Johnson, no. 147 High-Street. 1800. pp. 36. 24mo.
Appended are "The Story of Sinful Sally" and "The Trials of Virtue."
      AAS, HSP, LCP, LOC, NYPL, YC.

37155 —— —— NUMBER 28. THE FALL OF ADAM.
Philadelphia: Printed by B. & J. Johnson, no. 147 High Street. 1800. pp. 36. 24mo.
Appended are extracts from the "Book of Martyrs."   AAS, HSP, LCP, LOC, NYPL, PPL, YC.

37156 —— —— NUMBER 29. THE LIFE OF WILLIAM BAKER.
Philadelphia: Printed by B. & J. Johnson, no. 147 High-Street. 1800. pp. 36. 24mo.
By the Rev. Mr. Gilpin. Suffixed are two poems, "The Carpenter; or the Danger of Evil
Company," and "The Execution of Wild Robert."   AAS, LCP, LOC, NYPL, YC.

37157 —— —— Number 30. The History of the beggarly boy.
Philadelphia: Printed by B. & J. Johnson, no. 147 High-Street. 1800. pp. 36. 24mo.
LCP, LOC, NYPL, YC.

37158 —— —— Number 31. The Shopkeeper turned sailor; to which is prefixed, A true story of a good negro woman.
Philadelphia: Printed by B. & J. Johnson, no. 147 High-Street. 1800. pp. 36. 24mo.
Written by Hannah More. LCP, LOC, NYPL, YC.

37159 —— —— Number 32. The Troubles of life. To which is prefixed, Patient Joe, or The New-castle collier.
Philadelphia: Printed by B. & J. Johnson, no. 147, High-Street. 1800. pp. 36. 24mo.
In verse. AAS, HC, LCP, LOC, NYPL.

37160 —— —— Number 33. The History of Mary Wood, the housemaid; or, The danger of false excuses.
Philadelphia: Printed by B. & J. Johnson, no. 147, High-Street. 1800. pp. 36. 24mo.
Contains "The Bad Bargain; or the World set up to sale," in verse, pp. 34–6.
AAS, HC, LCP, LOC, NYPL.

37161 —— —— Number 34. The History of Mr. Fantom, the new fashioned philosopher. And his man William.
Philadelphia: Printed by B. & J. Johnson, no. 147, High-Street. 1800. pp. 36. 24mo.
Written by Hannah More. AAS, LCP, LOC, NYPL.

37162 —— —— Number 35. The Hubub; or, The history of Farmer Russel, the hard-hearted overseer.
Philadelphia: Printed by B. & J. Johnson, no. 147, High-Street. 1800. pp. 36. 24mo.
"The Hubub" is signed by S (Sarah More) and followed by "The Lady and the Pye," in verse, signed Z (Hannah More). AAS, HC, LCP, LOC, NYPL.

37163 —— —— Number 36. Bear ye one another's burdens; or, The valley of tears: a vision.
Philadelphia: Printed by B. & J. Johnson, no. 147, High-Street. 1800. pp. 36. 24mo.
Written by Hannah More. AAS, LCP, LOC, NYPL.

37164 —— —— Number 37. The Black prince, a true story; being an account of . . . Naimbanna, an African king's son. . . .
Philadelphia: Printed by B. & J. Johnson, no. 147, High-Street. 1800. pp. 34, [2]. 24mo.
Contains in verse "The Gravestone," pp. 26–30, "The Day of Judgment," pp. 31–4, signed Z (Hannah More), and "A List of Repository Tracts," pp. [2]. AAS, LCP, LOC, NYPL.

37165 —— —— Number 38. Betty Brown, the St. Giles's orange girl: with some account of Mrs. Sponge, the money-lender.
Philadelphia: Printed by B. & J. Johnson, no. 147, High-Street. 1800. pp. 36. 24mo.
Attributed to Hannah More. Also contains "Dan and Jane," verse signed Z (Hannah More), pp. 26–9, "The History of Richard, a Ballad," pp. 30–4, and reviews, pp. 35–6.
AAS, HC, LCP, LOC, NYPL.

37166 —— —— Number 39. The Cock-fighter. A true history.
Philadelphia: Printed by B. & J. Johnson, no. 147, High-Street. 1800. pp. 36. 24mo.
Includes an "Account of an Affecting Mournful Death, as Related by Dr. Young," pp. 8–11, and "The good Mother's Legacy," pp. 12–36. AAS, HC, LCP, LOC, NYPL.

37167 —— —— Number 40. Onesimus; or, The run-away servant converted. A true story.
Philadelphia: Printed by B. & J. Johnson, no. 147, High-Street. 1800. pp. 36. 24mo.
Contains, in verse, "The Old Man," pp. 30–4, and "The Cuckoo," pp. 35–6.
AAS, HC, LCP, LOC, NYPL, PPL.

37168 —— —— NUMBER 41. THE HISTORY OF CHARLES JONES, THE FOOTMAN; WRITTEN BY HIMSELF.
    Philadelphia: Printed by B. & J. Johnson, no. 147, High-Street. 1800.   pp. 36.   24mo.
    Contains "Verses Supposed to be Written by Alexander Selkirk" (by William Cowper),
    pp. 31–3, and "An Ode to Content," pp. 34–6.   AAS, HC, LCP, LOC, NYPL.

37169 —— —— NUMBER 42. SOME NEW THOUGHTS FOR THE NEW YEAR.
    Philadelphia: Printed by B. & J. Johnson, no. 147 High-Street, 1800.   pp. 36.   24mo.
    "This is the last number of the Cheap Repository — The whole 42 numbers may be had
    either bound or in pamphlets of B. & J. Johnson."   AAS, LCP, LOC, NYPL.

37170 [CHEETHAM, JAMES]   1772–1810
    AN ANSWER TO ALEXANDER HAMILTON'S LETTER CONCERNING THE PUBLIC CONDUCT AND CHARACTER
    OF JOHN ADAMS. . . .
        *New-York: Printed by P. R. Johnson & J. Stryker, at the Literary Printing Office,
    no. 29 Gold-street. 1800. (Copy-right secured.)*   pp. 32.   8vo.
    Also attributed to Uzall Ogden.
            AAS, APS, BPL, EI, HC, HEH, JCB, LCP, LOC, MSL, NL, NYHS, NYPL, NYSL, VᵃU, WLC, YC.

37171 —— A DISSERTATION CONCERNING POLITICAL EQUALITY, AND THE CORPORATION OF NEW YORK. . . .
        New York, Printed by D. Denniston. 1800.   pp. 50.   8vo.
    Some copies have a list of errata pasted on p. [4].
            AAS, BM, BʳU, HC, HEH, HSP, JCB, LOC, NL, NYHS, NYPL, NYSL, YC.

37172 [——] A LETTER TO GENERAL HAMILTON. . . .
    A ghost arising from an advertisement.

37173 CHESTERFIELD, LORD.
    See Stanhope.

37174 [CHESTERFIELD'S IMPENETRABLE SECRET; OR, THE MYSTERIOUS PUZZLE.
        Baltimore: Printed by Warner and Hanna? 1800.]   MINICK 567.

37175 CHILD OF PALLAS.
    See Prentiss, Charles.

37176 THE CHILD'S FIRST PRIMER; OR, A NEW AND EASY GUIDE TO THE INVALUABLE SCIENCE OF A. B. C.
        Philadelphia: Printed for W. Jones. 1800.   pp. 30.   32mo.   PL.

37177 THE CHILD'S GUIDE TO SPELLING AND READING. . . .
    See Carey, Mathew.

37178 THE CHILD'S INSTRUCTOR. . . .
    See Ely, John.

37179 THE CHILD'S SPELLING BOOK: CALCULATED TO RENDER READING COMPLETELY EASY TO LITTLE CHIL-
    DREN. . . . SECOND EDITION. . . .
        Hartford. Printed by John Babcock. 1800.   pp. 112, cuts.   sq. 32mo.
    Attributed by Evans to Elisha Babcock.   AAS, CHS, UOP, YC.

37180 CHOICE TALES; CONSISTING OF AN ELEGANT COLLECTION OF DELIGHTFUL LITTLE PIECES FOR . . .
    YOUNG PERSONS.
        *Philadelphia, printed by Joseph Charless, for Mathew Carey, no. 118, Market Street,
    1800.*   pp. 170, [2].   24mo.
    The last two pages contain the table of contents.   AAS, LOC, PPL.

37181 CHURCH, James
IMPORTANT INFORMATION TO THE AFFLICTED WITH RHEUMATISMS, COUGHS, AND COLDS. . . .
New-York: G. & R. Waite, 1800.   pp. 31.   16mo.   AML.

37182 CHURCHILL, Silas   d. 1854
A SERMON, OCCASIONED BY THE DEATH OF . . . WASHINGTON . . . DELIVERED AT LEBANON, IN THE
TOWN OF CANAAN, FEBRUARY 22D, 1800. . . .
Albany: Printed by Barber and Southwick. . . . M,DCCC.   pp. 31.   12mo.
HEH, LOC, MFM, MSL, NYHS, NYPL.

37183 CHURCHMAN, John   1753–1805
THE MAGNETIC ATLAS; OR, VARIATION CHARTS OF THE WHOLE TERRAQUEOUS GLOBE. . . . THE THIRD
EDITION WITH ADDITIONS. . . .
New York: Printed for the author, and sold by Gaine & Ten Eyck. . . . 1800.
pp. viii, 82, fold. diagrs.   4to.   BM, PʳU, WLC.

37184 CINDERELLA: OR, THE HISTORY OF THE LITTLE GLASS SLIPPER.
Philadelphia: Printed for Mathew Carey, no. 118, Market-Street. 1800.   pp. 32.
32mo.   HEH.

37185 THE CITIZEN AND FARMER'S ALMANAC, FOR THE YEAR OF OUR LORD, 1801. . . . CONTAINING . . . A
GREAT VARIETY OF INSTRUCTIVE AND USEFUL MATTER. . . .
Baltimore: Printed and sold by Bonsall & Niles, no. 173, Market-Street.   pp. [44].
12mo.   AAS.

37186 CITY GAZETTE & DAILY ADVERTISER.   1787–1840
Charleston [S. C.]: published by Freneau & Paine. . . .   fol. daily.
FOR 1800: CLS, [LOC].

37187 THE CLAIMS OF THOMAS JEFFERSON TO THE PRESIDENCY, EXAMINED AT THE BAR OF CHRISTIANITY.
BY A LAYMAN.
Philadelphia: Published by Asbury Dickins. . . . H. Maxwell, printer . . . 1800.
pp. [2], 54.   8vo.
Variously attributed to William Brown, Asbury Dickins, and Joseph Dennie.
APS, HEH, HSP, JCB, LOC, MᵈHS, MHS, NYHS, NYPL, NYSL, PSL, UOC, VᵃU, WL, YC.

37188 CLARK, Joseph
SELECT RELIGIOUS PIECES, PUBLISHED FOR THE BENEFIT OF THE AFRICANS, AND THEIR DESCEND-
ANTS. . . .
Philadelphia: Printed by J. Ormrod, no. 41, Chestnut-street. 1800.   pp. 12.   12mo.
AAS, HSP.

37189 CLARKE, Abraham L[YNSON]   1768?–1810
A DISCOURSE, OCCASIONED BY THE DEATH OF GENERAL GEORGE WASHINGTON . . . DELIVERED BEFORE
THE . . . MOUNT-VERNON LODGE, AND THE CONGREGATION OF ST. JOHN'S CHURCH, IN
PROVIDENCE, ON . . . THE 22D OF FEBRUARY, A. L. 5800. . . .
Providence: Printed by John Carter, 1800.   pp. 26, 18.   8vo.
Affixed is Amos Maine Atwell, *An address, delivered before Mount-Vernon Lodge, on their
anniversary election of officers, February 22, 5800. . . .* Providence: Printed by Brother
John Carter. 5800.   AAS, HC, HEH, JCB, LOC, MFM, NYPL, NYSOC, RIHS, WLC.

37190 CLAYPOOLE'S AMERICAN DAILY ADVERTISER.   1796–1800
Printed . . . by D. C. Claypoole . . . Philadelphia.   fol.
With the issue of Sept. 30 the paper was sold to Zachariah Poulson, Jr., who changed the
title to *Poulson's American Daily Advertiser.*   FOR 1800: AAS, HEH, LCP, LOC, NYHS, WLC.

37191 CLEAVELAND, Moses   1754–1806
AN ORATION, COMMEMORATIVE OF THE LIFE AND DEATH OF . . . WASHINGTON, DELIVERED AT
WINDHAM, (CONNECTICUT,) ON THE 22D DAY OF FEBRUARY, 1800, TO THE BRETHREN OF
MORIAH AND EASTERN STAR LODGES. . . .
Windham: Printed by John Byrne. 1800.   pp. 15.   8vo.
BA, BPL, CHS, HEH, LOC, MFM, NYHS, NYPL, WL, YC.

37192   THE CLERK'S MAGAZINE; CONTAINING THE MOST USEFUL AND NECESSARY FORMS OF WRITINGS. . . .
THE CONSTITUTION OF THE UNITED STATES. . . . TOGETHER WITH A SCHEDULE OF THE WHOLE
NUMBER OF INHABITANTS. . . .
         *Albany: Printed by Charles R. and George Webster, and sold at their bookstore . . .
and by Daniel Steele. . . .*   pp. [4], 310, [6].   16mo.
The Preface is dated Albany, 1st August, 1800.   AAS, HC, MᵈHS, NYSL.

37193   CLEVELAND, CHARLES
TABLES, EXHIBITING AT ONE VIEW THE DIFFERENT DUTIES AS VALOREM ARISING ON THE COST OF
MERCHANDISE. . . . TO WHICH IS ADDED, A LIST OF DUTIES. . . .
         Salem: Printed by Joshua Cushing and sold by Thomas C. Cushing. 1800.   pp. 131.
12mo.   AAS, BPL, BᵣU, EI, HC.

37194   CLIFFTON, WILLIAM   1772–1799
POEMS, CHIEFLY OCCASIONAL, BY THE LATE MR. CLIFFTON. TO WHICH ARE PREFIXED, INTRODUCTORY
NOTICES OF THE LIFE, CHARACTER AND WRITINGS OF THE AUTHOR. . . .
         New-York: Printed for J. W. Fenno, by G. & R. Waite. 1800.   pp. xviii, 82, 85–119,
[1], portrait.   24mo.
The frontispiece was engraved by D. Edwin after Field.
                AAS, BA, BPL, BᵣU, HC, HSP, LOC, NYHS, NYPL, NYSL, PPL, PᵣU, RU, UOP, WC, YC.

37195   [CLINTON, DE WITT]   1769–1828
A VINDICATION OF THOMAS JEFFERSON; AGAINST THE CHARGES CONTAINED IN A PAMPHLET
ENTITLED, "SERIOUS CONSIDERATIONS," &C. BY GROTIUS. . . .
         New-York, printed by David Denniston. 1800.   pp. 47.   8vo.
There are 16 lines of errata on p. 47.   AAS, BPL, HSP, JCB, LOC, MHS, NYHS, NYSL, WLC, YC.

37196   CLOSE, JOHN, *M. A.*
A DISCOURSE ON THE SUPERIOR EXCELLENCIES OF LOVE. . . . AT WATERFORD, AT THE REQUEST . . .
OF ORANGE LODGE NO. 53; ON THE ANNIVERSARY FESTIVAL OF ST. JOHN THE BAPTIST, 1800. . . .
         Lansingburgh: 1800.   4to.   pp. 12.   NYHS.

37197   [CLOWES, JOHN]   1743–1831
REMARKS ON THE ASSERTIONS OF THE AUTHOR OF THE MEMOIRS OF JACOBINISM RESPECTING . . .
EMANUEL SWEDENBORG. . . .
         Philadelphia: Printed for John Ormrod, no. 41, Chestnut Street.—1800.   pp. 37.
8vo.   AAS, APS, BA, BM, HSP, JCB, LCP, LOC, MSL, NYPL, RU, WLC, YC.

37198   [COBBETT, WILLIAM]   1762–1835
THE RUSH-LIGHT. 15TH FEB. 1800 [No. 1, TO 30TH APRIL, No. 5.]. . . . BY PETER PORCUPINE.
         New York: published by William Cobbett, no. 141, Water-Street.   pp. [2], 258,
[2].   8vo.
There are two settings of the titlepage; what is probably the second issue lacks the border
of rule. Numbers 6 and 7 were probably printed in England.
                                    AAS, AML, HEH, JCB, LOC, NYAM, NYHS, NYPL, NYSL.

37199   COE, JONAS   1759–1822
A SERMON, DELIVERED BEFORE THE MILITARY OFFICERS, APOLLO LODGE, AND . . . THE CITIZENS OF
TROY, JANUARY 12, 1800. IN CONSEQUENCE OF THE DEATH OF . . . WASHINGTON. BY JONAS
COE, A. M. MINISTER OF THE PRESBYTERIAN CHURCH IN TROY.
         Troy: Printed at the Budget Office, by R. Moffitt & Co. 1800.   pp. 16.   4to.
                                                                   HEH, NYHS, NYPL.

37200   COFFIN, EBENEZER   1769–1816
A SERMON DELIVERED FEBRUARY 22D 1800, THE DAY OF NATIONAL MOURNING . . . FOR THE DEATH
OF GENERAL GEORGE WASHINGTON. . . .
         Printed at Portland, by Rand & Burdick, 1800.   pp. 16.   8vo.
                                                                 AAS, CL, EI, LOC, NYPL.

37201   COLEMAN, WILLIAM
         See Report of the trial of Levi Weeks. . . .

37202 A COLLECTION OF THE NEWEST COTILLIONS AND COUNTRY DANCES. TO WHICH IS ADDED, A VARIETY OF MODERN SONGS. ALSO, RULES FOR CONVERSATION. . . .
Printed and sold at Worcester: (Massachusetts.) [By Isaiah Thomas & Son] July — 1800. pp. 36. 24mo. AAS, NYPL.

37203 COLLEGE OF NEW JERSEY.
CATALOGUS COLLEGII NAEO-CAESARIENSIS. . . .
Trenton: E typis Sherman, Mershon & Thomas. 1800. pp. 16. 8vo.
NYHS, PrU.

37204 COLLEGE OF WILLIAM AND MARY.
THE CHARTER OF THE COLLEGE OF WILLIAM & MARY.
Richmond. Re-Printed by Thomas Nicholson — 1800. pp. 77. 8vo. AAS.

37205 COLLINS, ALEXANDER
THIS ORATION WAS DELIVERED ON THE 26TH OF DECEMBER 1799 . . . TO ST. JOHN'S LODGE, NO. 2D, IN MIDDLETOWN. . . .
Middletown: Printed by Tertius Dunning January 10, 1800. pp. 21. 8vo.
CHS, LOC, MFM, NYHS, NYPL, WRHS, YC.

37206 THE COLUMBIAN ALMANAC: OR, THE NORTH-AMERICAN CALENDAR, FOR THE YEAR OF OUR LORD 1801. . . .
Printed and Sold by Peter Brynberg, Market-Street, Wilmington. pp. [48].
12mo AAS, HC, HSP, LOC, NYHS, NYSL, WC.

37207 COLUMBIAN CENTINEL AND MASSACHUSETTS FEDERALIST. 1790–1840.
Printed and published on Wednesdays and Saturdays, by Benjamin Russell . . . Boston (Massachusetts.) 1800. fol. semi-weekly.
FOR 1800: AAS, BA, BPL, EI, HC, LOC, MHS, NEHGS, NYHS, NYSL, WLC.

37208 — BOSTON, JANUARY 1, 1800. THE CARRIERS OF THE COLUMBIAN CENTINEL, PRESENT THEIR RESPECTS TO ITS PATRONS. . . .
[Boston.] Broadside. fol. EI.

37209 COLUMBIAN COURIER. 1798–1805
New-Bedford, Massachusetts. Printed and Published by Abraham Shearman Jun. fol. weekly. FOR 1800: NEW BEDFORD PUB. LIB.

37210 COLUMBIAN MINERVA. 1799–1804
Dedham, (Massachusetts) Published every Thursday, by Herman Mann, near the Court-House. weekly. fol. FOR 1800: DEDHAM HIST. SOC.

37211 THE COLUMBIAN MIRROR AND ALEXANDRIA GAZETTE. 1792–1800
Alexandria: Printed . . . by Ellis Price. fol. tri-weekly.
FOR 1800: [AAS], [HC].

37212 COLUMBIAN MUSEUM & SAVANNAH ADVERTISER. 1796–1822
Savannah — published on Tuesday and Friday, by Seymour and Woolhopter. fol.
FOR 1800: [AAS], GHS.

37213 COLUMBIAN PATRIOTIC GAZETTE. 1799–1803
Rome [N. Y.] published by Ebenezer Eaton & Thomas Walker. fol. weekly.
FOR 1800: [AAS].

37214 THE COLUMBIAN PHENIX AND BOSTON REVIEW. CONTAINING USEFUL INFORMATION ON LITERATURE, RELIGION, MORALITY, POLITICS AND PHILOSOPHY. . . . VOL. I. FOR 1800.
Boston: Printed by Manning & Loring, for Joseph Hawkins, no. 39, Cornhill. pp. 451, [1], 3 plates.
With the May issue Daniel Tillotson became associated with the publication and the firm name became Hawkins and Tillotson. The last number was that for July.
AAS, BA, BM, BPL, HC, HEH, LOC, MHS, NL, NYHS, NYPL, NYSL, VaU, WLC, YC.

37215　　—— Boston, Sept. 1800. To the patrons of the Columbian Phenix. It is with extreme
regret. . . . Joseph Hawkins.
　　　　　　[*Boston.*]　　Broadside.　　fol.　　　　　　　　　　　　　　　　AAS.

37216　　COMMERCIAL Advertiser.　　　　　　　　　　　　　　　　　　　　　1797–1879
　　　　　　[*New York:*] *Published . . . by E. Belden.* . . . 　fol.　　daily.
　　　　　　　　　　　　　　　　　　　　　　For 1800: BA, NYHS, NYPL, NYSOC.

37217　　—— [The Embassina: addressed to the patrons of the Commercial Advertiser, by the carriers
— with the complements of the season. January 1, 1800.
　　　　　　New York, 1800.　　Broadside.]
　　　　Reprinted in the above paper on January 2, 1800.

37218　　THE COMMITTEE appointed to draft an address to the citizens of the third election
district of Chester County. . . . September 23, 1800.
　　　　　　Wilmington: Printed at the Franklin Press, by James Wilson.　　Broadside.　　4to.
　　　　　　　　　　　　　　　　　　　　　　　　　　　　　　　　AAS.

37219　　THE COMPLAINT; or Night-Thoughts. . . .
　　　　See Young, Edward.

37220　　CONANT, Stephen
　　　　Charitable lottery. The following scheme is presented to the public in pursuance of
an Act of the General Assembly of the State of Vermont, granting a lottery to
Stephen Conant . . . January, 1800.
　　　　　　[*Windsor?*]　　Broadside.　　fol.　　　　　　　　　　　H. G. Rugg.

37221　　CONDICT, Ira　　　　　　　　　　　　　　　　　　　　　　1764–1811
　　　　A Funeral discourse, delivered in the Presbyterian church of New-Brunswick, on the
31st of December, 1799 . . . paying solemn honors to the memory of Gen. George
Washington. . . .
　　　　　　New-Bbunsiwck [*!*], *New-Jersey: Printed by Abraham Blauvelt. 1800.*　　pp. 23.
　　　　8vo.　　　　　　　　　　HEH, LOC, NJHS, NYHS, NYPL, PPL, PᵣU, RU.

37222　　[CONDIE, Thomas]
　　　　Biographical memoirs of the illustrious Gen. Geo: Washington, late president of the
United States. . . .
　　　　　　Philadelphia: Printed by Charless & Ralston. 1800.　　pp. 243.　　18mo.
　　　　Also attributed to Thomas Childs.　　AAS, BA, BPL, HEH, HSP, JCB, LOC, NYPL, PᵣU, UOP, WLC.

37223　　—— —— *Philadelphia: From the press of R. Folwell. 1800.*　　pp. 217.　　24mo.
　　　　Evans calls for a portrait but there is none in the one located copy, which lacks a leaf.
　　　　　　　　　　　　　　　　　　　　　　　　　　　　　　　　AAS.

37224　　CONGREGATIONAL Church in Connecticut.
　　　　At a meeting of the General Association of the State of Connecticut, at Norfolk, the
third Tuesday of June, 1800. The following system of rules. . . .
　　　　　　Broadside.　　fol.　　　　　　　　　　　　AAS, NYHS, NYPL, YC.

37225　　—— A Specimen of the confession of faith, and covenant engagements, upon which, for
substance, the members of the several consociated churches, in Conneticut, unite
and practice. . . .
　　　　　　Litchfield, [*Printed by Thomas Collier*] *A. D. 1800.*　　pp. 7.　　8vo.　　CHS.

37226　　CONNECTICUT. State.
　　　　Acts and laws. Electors. Acts and laws, made in and passed by the General Court . . .
at New-Haven . . . on the second Thursday of October, A. D. 1800.
　　　　　　[*Colophon:*] *Hartford: Printed by Hudson and Goodwin.*　　pp. 529–46.　　8vo.
　　　　　　　　　　　　　　　　AAS, CHS, HC-L, HEH, LOC, PL, NYPL, RISL.

37227 —— Acts and laws. Shows. Acts and laws passed in and by the General Court . . . at Hartford . . . on the second Thursday of May, A. D. 1800.
[*Colophon:*] *Hartford: Printed by Hudson and Goodwin.* pp. 521–8. 8vo.
AAS, CHS, CSL, HC-L, HEH, LOC, PL, NYPL, RISL, YC.

37228 —— At a General Assembly of the State of Connecticut, holden at Hartford, on the second Thursday of May, A. D. 1800. An Act renouncing the claims of this State to certain lands. . . .
Broadside. 4to. HSP.

37229 —— By his Excellency Jonathan Trumbull, Esquire, Governor . . . of Connecticut. A proclamation. Agreeably to a resolution of the General Assembly, passed . . . in October 1798. . . .
Hartford: Printed by Hudson & Goodwin. Broadside. fol.
This broadside, dated at Lebanon, March 1, 1800, was the first of a series of annual proclamations authorizing the collection of contributions for the Missionary Society of Connecticut.
NYHS, PL.

37230 —— By his Excellency Jonathan Trumbull, Esquire, Governor . . . of Connecticut. A Proclamation. Another revolving year having furnished the people of this State with renewed experience of the continued bounties . . . this twentieth day of October . . . 1800. . . .
New Haven, Printed by Thomas Green & Son. Broadside. fol. YC.

37231 CONNECTICUT. General Association.
See Congregational Church in Connecticut.

37232 CONNECTICUT. Missionary Society of Connecticut.
The Constitution of the Missionary Society of Connecticut: with an address from the Board of Trustees . . . and a narrative on the subject of missions. . . .
Hartford: Printed by Hudson and Goodwin. M,DCCC. pp. 27. 8vo.
AAS, BA, CHS, JCB, LOC, MHS, NL, NYHS, NYPL, PL, UOC, WL, YC.

37233 CONNECTICUT Academy of Arts and Sciences.
New-Haven, Jan. 1, 1800. To. . . . The Connecticut Academy of Arts and Sciences, desirous of contributing to the collection . . . of useful knowledge . . . request you to furnish them with . . . information. . . .
[*New Haven.*] pp. 12. 32mo. AAS, BA, CHS, YC.

37234 THE CONNECTICUT Courant. 1764–1914
Hartford: Printed by Hudson & Goodwin, 1800. fol.
For 1800: AAS, BPL, CHS, [HC], LOC, MHS, [NYHS], NYPL, WLC, YC.

37235 —— The Death of General Washington having filled the hearts of all the virtuous people in the United States with the sincerest affliction, we presume our readers will pardon us for presenting them, instead of the common New-Years address, with the following tribute. . . .
[*Hartford.*] Broadside. fol. B'U, NYHS.

37236 THE CONNECTICUT Evangelical Magazine, volume I. Consisting of twelve numbers, to be published monthly. From July 1800 to June 1801. . . .
Hartford: Printed by Hudson and Goodwin. . . . pp. 482, [6]. 8vo.
The JCB has two different prospectus circulars dated in manuscript April 12, 1800.
AAS, BPL, CHS, HC, JCB, LCP, LOC, MHS, NYHS, NYPL, NYSL, YC.

37237 —— —— Second edition. . . .
This edition differs from the first only in being on thinner paper and having the titlepage reset. AAS.

37238	CONNECTICUT Gazette, and the Commercial Intelligencer.					1773–1823
			New-London: Printed by Samuel Green, adjoining the Bank. 1800.	fol.	weekly.
					For 1800: AAS, CHS, [HC], [LOC], [NYHS], WⁱˢHS.

37239	CONNECTICUT Journal.					1767–1835
			Printed at New-Haven, by Thomas Green & Son, near the College. 1800.	fol.
					For 1800: AAS, [CHS], [HC], LOC, YC.

37240	—— The Trial of time—presented by the carrier of the Connecticut Journal to his customers. . . . New-Haven, January 1, 1800.
			[New Haven.]	Broadside.	4to.					LOC, YC.

37241	CONSTANT, Joseph
		Patent cement. The patentee of the cement for preserving wood and brick from decay. . . . Joseph Constant. Directions. . . . March 15, 1800.
			Broadside.	fol.					NYHS.

37242	THE CONSTITUTIONAL Diary and Philadelphia Evening Advertiser.					1799–Feb. 3, 1800
			Philadelphia: Published by James Carey.	fol.	daily.	For 1800: [AAS].

37243	THE CONSTITUTIONAL Telegraphe.					1799–1802
			Published at Boston by Samuel S. Parker, Jonathan S. Copp, and John S. Lillie successively.	fol.	semi-weekly.	For 1800: AAS, BA, BPL, [MHS], YC.

37244	THE CONSTITUTIONS of the sixteen states which compose the confederated republic of America. . . .
			Newburgh: Printed by David Denniston, for self & H. Craig. 1800.	pp. 288.
		12mo.					AAS, BM, HC, LOC, NYPL.

37245	THE CONSTITUTIONS of the United States . . . to which are prefixed the Declaration of Independence and the federal Constitution. . . .
			Philadelphia: Printed for Robert Campbell, no. 30, Chestnut-street. 1800.	pp. xxiv, [5]–272, 12.	16mo.
		The last twelve pages contain a catalogue of books for sale by the Conrads.
					AAS, HC, HSP, JCB, LCP, LOC, NYPL, PʳU, PSL.

37246	COOK, David, *Jr.*
		Cook's American arithmetic. . . . To which is annexed, by way of a second part, the American surveyor. . . .
			New-Haven: Printed by Thomas Green and Son. M,DCCC.	pp. 107, 9, 3 plates.
		16mo.					AAS, CHS, LOC, YC.

37247	COOLEY, Timothy Mather					1772–1859
		A Sermon delivered in the east society in Granville, January 5, 1800. . . .
			Hartford: Printed by John Babcock. 1800.	pp. 16.	8vo.	CHS, NYHS, NYPL, PL, YC.

37248	[COOPER, Samuel]
		Youth's library. Vol. II. The blossoms of morality. . . . With fifty-one wood cuts.
			New-York. Printed and published by David Longworth. . . . MDCCC.	pp. [8], [7]–258.	12mo.
		There are copies paged ii, 26, 15–258. The colophon cut reads "A. Anderson fecit." For Vol. I see Berquin.					AAS, JCB, NYPL.

37249	COOPER, Thomas					1759–1840
		An Account of the trial of Thomas Cooper . . . on a charge of libel against the President of the United States. . . .
			Philadelphia: Printed by John Bioren, no. 83, Chesnut Street, for the author. April 1800.	pp. 64.	8vo.
		"Erratum. In the title page this trial is said to be printed for the author: this is a mistake: it is not printed for me. T. C."
					AAS, BPL, HC, HEH, HSP, LOC, MHS, NL, NYPL, PPL, PSL, VᵃSL, WⁱˢHS, WLC, YC.

37250 —— POLITICAL ESSAYS, BY THOMAS COOPER, ESQ. OF NORTHUMBERLAND. SECOND EDITION, WITH COR-
RECTIONS AND ADDITIONS.
Philadelphia: Printed for Robert Campbell, no. 30, Chestnut-street. 1800.   pp. [4],
88.   8vo.   AAS, APS, BPL, EI, HC, HSP, LOC, M^{d}HS, MSL, NL, NYHS, NYPL, NYSL, PPL, YC.

37251 COOPER, [W. D.]
THE HISTORY OF NORTH-AMERICA. CONTAINING A REVIEW OF THE CUSTOMS & MANNERS OF THE
ORIGINAL INHABITANTS; THE FIRST SETTLEMENT . . . TO THE TIME OF THEIR BECOMING UNITED,
FREE AND INDEPENDENT STATES. BY THE REV. MR. COOPER.
Bennington, Printed by Anthony Haswell, 1800.   pp. [8], [13]–184.   16mo.
Author unidentified; attributed in the older bibliographies to "Samuel" Cooper.   NYSL.

37252 COPIES OF ORIGINAL LETTERS FROM THE FRENCH ARMY IN EGYPT. PART THE THIRD, CONSISTING OF
THOSE LETTERS TO THE FRENCH GOVERNMENT, INTERCEPTED BY THE BRITISH FLEET. . . .
London, Printed . . . Boston, Re-Printed by John Russell.   pp. 75.   12mo.
The Advertisement is dated Boston, April 22, 1800.   AAS, JCB, MHS, MSL, NYPL, YC.

37253 A COPY OF A LETTER FOUND IN THE STUDY OF THE REVEREND MR. JOSEPH BELCHER. . . .
See Belcher, Joseph.

37254 COPY OF A LETTER FROM A YOUNG MAN. . . .
An English imprint.

37255 A COPY OF THE PETITION OF DOCTORS [DANA] HYDE AND [RUSSEL] FITCH, TO THE HON. THE GENERAL
ASSEMBLY OF THE STATE OF VERMONT. PRAYING FOR A MEDICAL LOTTERY. UNTO WHICH ARE
ANNEXED, THE RECOMMENDATIONS OF SUNDRY GENTLEMEN, AND DOCTOR DUNCAN'S REASONS
WHY THE . . . PETITION OUGHT TO BE GRANTED. . . .
Printed in the year M,DCCC.   pp. 16.   16mo.   V^{t}HS.

37256 CORDERIUS, MATHURIN   1479–1564
CORDERII COLLOQUIORUM CENTURA SELECTA. . . . DESIGNED FOR THE USE OF BEGINNERS IN THE LATIN
TONGUE. BY JOHN CLARKE. LATE MASTER OF THE PUBLIC GRAMMAR SCHOOL IN HULL. A NEW
EDITION . . . COMPARED WITH THE TWENTY-SIXTH LONDON EDITION.
*Printed at Exeter, by H. Ranlet, for I. Thomas & E. T. Andrews . . . Boston; . . .
I. Thomas, Worcester; . . . Thomas, Andrews & Penniman, Albany; and . . . Thomas,
Andrews & Butler, Baltimore. March 1800.*   pp. viii, 170.   24mo.
The 1800 edition by Jacob Halsey of Newark, described from a bookseller's catalogue, is
probably a ghost of his 1801 edition.   AAS, G^{r}L, JCB, NYSL, UOC, YC.

37257 CORNELISON, JOHN   1769–1828
A SERMON, DELIVERED AT HACKINSACK, DECEMBER 15, 1799, AT THE INSTALMENT OF THE
REVEREND JAMES C. V. ROMEYN. . . .
New-York: Printed by T. and J. Swords. . . . 1800.   pp. 31.   8vo.
NYHS, NYPL, NYSOC.

37258 THE COUNTY TICKET. FIRM FRIENDS TO THE CONSTITUTION AND LIBERTY OF THE PRESS, BUT OPPOSERS
OF UNNECESSARY LAND TAXES. THOMAS TILLINGHAST, JOSEPH STANTON, JUN. . . .
Printed by S. J. Williams [Providence, R. I., 1800].   Broadside.   32mo.   B^{r}U.

37259 THE COURIER.   OCT. 14, 1800–1801
Fredericksburg, (Va.) Printed by James Walker.   fol.   semi-weekly.
FOR 1800: [MRS. F. L. W. GREEN, FREDERICKSBURG.]

37260 THE COURIER.   1796–1930
Norwich (Chelsea Society). Printed by Thomas Hubbard, 1800.   fol.   weekly.
FOR 1800: CSL.

37261 THE COURIER, AND NEW-YORK AND LONG ISLAND ADVERTISER.   1799–1803
Brooklyn: Printed by Thomas Kirk.   weekly.   fol.
With the issue of July 3 the title was changed to *The Long Island Courier.* FOR 1800: [LOC.].

37262   COURIER OF NEW HAMPSHIRE.   1794–1805
            [*Concord*] *By George Hough. . . .*   fol.   weekly.   FOR 1800: AAS, BPL, NHHS

37263   COWLES, GILES H[OOKER]   1766–1835
            THE JEWISH AND CHRISTIAN CHURCH THE SAME . . . IN PROOF OF THE DUTY OF INFANT-
            BAPTISM. . . . TO WHICH IS ADDED, AN APPENDIX ON THE MODE OF BAPTISM. . . . BY JONATHAN
            MILLER, A. M. PASTOR OF THE CHURCH IN WEST-BRITAIN. . . .
                Hartford: Printed by Hudson and Goodwin. 1800.   pp. 98.   8vo.
                                                            AAS, CHS, EI, JCB, NYPL, PL, WL.

37264   COXE, JOHN REDMAN   1773–1864
            A SHORT VIEW OF . . . MEDICINE. . . . READ BEFORE THE PHILADELPHIA MEDICAL SOCIETY, ON THE
            7TH OF FEBRUARY, 1800. . . .
                Philadelphia: Printed for Mathew Carey, no. 118, Market-street. February, — 1800.
            pp. [2], 33.   8vo.   AAS, AML, BPL, HSP, LCP, LOC, NYAM, PrU, RU.

37265   [COXE, TENCH]   1755–1824
            STRICTURES UPON THE LETTER IMPUTED TO MR. JEFFERSON, ADDRESSED TO MR. MAZZEI.
                Printed, June, 1800.   pp. 12.   8vo.
            Signed "Greene." The authorship is given in manuscript in Jefferson's own copy.   LOC, NYPL.

37266   —— [TO THE PUBLIC. ADDRESSES FROM INDIVIDUALS, WITHOUT SOME APPOINTMENT FROM A MEETING OF
            THE PEOPLE, OR SOME STATION REQUIRING THE ACT, ARE RARELY NECESSARY. . . . LANCASTER,
            OCT. 27, 1800.
                [*Colophon: Lancaster:*] *Printed by W. & R. Dickson, Nov. 5, 1800.*   Broadside.
            fol.]   Evans.

37267   CRANE, JOHN   1756–1836
            A SERMON, PREACHED AT NORTHBRIDGE, NOVEMBER 27, 1800. ON THE ANNIVERSARY THANKSGIVING
            IN MASSACHUSETTS. . . .
                Printed at Worcester, (Massachusetts,) by Daniel Greenleaf. 1800.   pp. 21.   8vo.
                                            AAS, BPL, CL, JCB, NYHS, NYPL, PL, YC.

37268   CRAWFORD, CHARLES
            AN ESSAY UPON THE ELEVENTH CHAPTER OF THE REVELATION OF ST. JOHN. . . .
                Philadelphia: Published by Asbury Dickins. . . . M. Maxwell, printer, Columbia-
            House. 1800.   pp. 74.   8vo.   AAS, HC, LCP, NHSL, NYPL.

37269   CRAZY JANE. A FAVORITE SONG.
                Boston, printed & sold at P. A. von Hagen's music store, no. 3 Cornhill [*July 1800*].
            And to be had of G. Gilfert . . . New York.   Broadside.   4to.
                                                        J. FRANCIS DRISCOLL, BROOKLINE.

37270   CROES, JOHN   1763–1832
            A DISCOURSE DELIVERED AT WOODBURY, IN NEW-JERSEY, ON THE TWENTY-SECOND OF FEBRUARY
            EIGHTEEN HUNDRED. . . . BEFORE THE CITIZENS OF GLOUCESTER COUNTY, ASSEMBLED TO PAY
            FUNERAL HONOURS TO . . . WASHINGTON. . . .
                Philadelphia, Printed by John Ormrod, no. 41, Chestnut-Street. 1800.   pp. 32.   8vo.
            AAS, BA, HC, HEH, JCB, LCP, LOC, MFM, NL, NYHS, NYPL, NYSL, PL, PPL, PrU, WLC.

37271   CUMINGS, HENRY   1739–1823
            AN EULOGY ON THE LATE PATRIOT WASHINGTON, ADDRESSED TO THE PEOPLE OF BILLERICA, JANUARY
            10, 1800. . . .
                Amherst [*N. H.*]: *Printed by Samuel Preston. Feb. 1800.*   pp. 16.   8vo.
                                                    AAS, HEH, JCB, LOC, NYHS, NYPL.

37272   CUNNINGHAM, WILLIAM   1767–1823
            AN EULOGY DELIVERED AT LUNENBURG . . . THE 22D OF FEBRUARY 1800. . . . TO COMMEMORATE
            THE UNEQUALLED VIRTUES . . . OF GEN. GEORGE WASHINGTON. . . .
                Worcester: Printed by Isaiah Thomas, jun. March — 1800.   pp. 16.   8vo.
                                        AAS, BA, BM, BPL, HC, HEH, JCB, MFM, NYPL, PL, YC.

37273   A CURE FOR CANTING; AN ORIGINAL YANKEE POEM. IN TWO LETTERS. . . .
         Philadelphia: Re-printed from the New-England ed., for the booksellers, 1800.
         pp. 12.   16mo.   LOC.

37274   CURRIE, WILLIAM   1754?–1829
         A SKETCH OF THE RISE AND PROGRESS OF THE YELLOW FEVER, AND OF THE PROCEEDINGS OF THE
         BOARD OF HEALTH, IN PHILADELPHIA, IN . . . 1799. . . .
         Philadelphia: Printed by Budd and Bartram, no. 58, North Second Street.— 1800.
         pp. 112. 8vo.   AAS, AML, BA, BM, BPL, HC, HSP, NYAM, NYHS, NYPL, PᵗU, RIMS, UOM¹, WL, YC.

37275   CURTIS, SAMUEL   1747–1822
         CURTIS'S POCKET ALMANACK, FOR THE YEAR 1801: TO WHICH IS ADDED, A REGISTER OF NEW-
         HAMPSHIRE. . . .
         Printed at Exeter, by H. Ranlet, for the compiler. 1800.   pp. 107, [1].   24mo.
                                                            AAS, NHHS, NL, NYHS.

37276   CUSHING, THOMAS C.
         DISCOURSE FOR THE AGED. . . .
         A ghost of Cushing's 1801 edition of Job Orton's work.

37277   DABOLL, NATHAN   1750–1818
         DABOLL'S SCHOOLMASTER'S ASSISTANT. BEING A PLAIN PRACTICAL SYSTEM OF ARITHMETIC; ADAPTED
         TO THE UNITED STATES.
         New-London: Printed and sold by Samuel Green. 1800.   pp. 194, [3].   12mo. WL.

37278   —— —— THE SECOND EDITION, WITH IMPROVEMENTS.
         New-London: Printed and sold by Samuel Green. 1800.   pp. 228, [3].   12mo.
                                                              AAS, WL, YC.

37279   —— THE NEW-ENGLAND ALMANACK, AND GENTLEMEN AND LADIES' DIARY, ENLARGED, FOR THE YEAR . . .
         1801. FITTED TO THE MERIDIAN OF NEW-LONDON. . . .
         New-London: Printed and sold by Samuel Green.   pp. [36].   12mo.
                                                            AAS, BPL, NYHS, NYSL.

37280   —— [SHEET ALMANACK FOR 1801.
         New-London: Samuel Green.   Broadside.]
         Advertised in the *Connecticut Gazette* of Jan. 7, 1801.

37281   [DAGGETT, DAVID]   1764–1851
         THREE LETTERS TO ABRAHAM BISHOP, ESQUIRE, CONTAINING SOME STRICTURES ON HIS ORATION,
         PRONOUNCED, IN THE WHITE MEETING-HOUSE, ON THE EVENING PRECEDING THE PUBLIC
         COMMENCEMENT, SEPTEMBER, 1800. . . .
         Hartford: Printed by Hudson and Goodwin. 1800.   pp. 36.   8vo.
         Also attributed to Elizur Goodrich and Noah Webster.
                   AAS, BM, CHS, CL, CU, HC, JCB, LOC, MHS, NYPL, WRHS, YC.

37282   —— —— —— *Hartford Printed: Bennington, Reprinted by Collier & Stockwell.*   pp. 36.   8vo.
                                                           JCB, VᵗHS.

37283   —— —— —— [*New-Haven: Printed by Thomas Green & Son. 1800.*]   SABIN 105939

37284   THE DAILY ADVERTISER.   1785–1806
         New-York, printed and published for the proprietor, by Robert Wilson.   fol.
         daily.   FOR 1800: [AAS], BA, LOC, [NYHS], NYSOC.

37285   —— FROM THE OFFICE OF THE DAILY ADVERTISER. THE FOLLOWING INTERESTED DESCRIPTION OF THE
         LATE FUNERAL PROCESSION, IS FROM THE COMMITTEE OF ARRANGEMENT. NEW-YORK, JANUARY
         4. ON THE 31ST DECEMBER, 1799 . . . TO PAY . . . FUNERAL HONORS TO . . . WASH-
         INGTON. . . .
         [*New-York, printed and published by Robert Wilson.*]   Broadside.   fol.
                                               LOC, NYHS, NYPL.

37286   DANA, Daniel   1771–1859
A Discourse on the character . . . of . . . Washington: delivered on the twenty-second
of February, 1800. . . .
Newburyport: from the press of Angier March. Sold at his bookstore, north side of
Market-Square.   pp. 31.   8vo.
Concludes with an original hymn.
AAS, BA, BPL, CL, EI, HC, HSP, JCB, LCP, LOC, MFM, MHS, NL, NYHS, NYPL, NYSL, PFM, PL, PPL, YC.

37287   —— Sermons on John vi. 29. and Ephesians iv. 30. delivered Lord's-Day, March 24th, 1799. . . .
From the press of Angier March . . . Newburyport. — MDCCC.   pp. 53.   8vo.
AAS, BA, CL, HC, HEH, JCB, LOC, MHS, NYPL, NYSL, PL, UOC.

37288   DANA, Joseph   1742–1827
A Discourse on the character and death of General George Washington . . . delivered at
Ipswich on the 22d. February, A. D. 1800. . . .
Printed at Newburyport, by Edmund M. Blunt, 1800.   pp. 28, [1].   8vo.
The last page contains a hymn.
AAS, BA, BPL, BʳU, CHS, CL, HC, HEH, JCB, LOC, MFM, MHS, NL, NYHS, NYPL, NYSL, PL, PTS, WLC.

37289   DANBURY Baptist Association.
Minutes of the Danbury Baptist Association, holden at Suffield, October 1st and 2d, 1800.
Together with their circular and corresponding letters.
[*Suffield?*]   pp. 8.   8vo.
Caption title; no imprint.   CHS.

37290   DARTMOUTH Gazette.   1799–1820
Hanover, New Hampshire. Printed on the College Plain, by Moses Davis.   weekly.
fol.   For 1800: DC.

37291   [DARTON, William]   1747–1819
Little truths better than great fables: containing information on divers subjects, for
the instruction of children. . . .
Philadelphia: Printed for, and sold by, J. and J. Crukshank, no. 87, High-street. 1800.
2 vols.   pp. 56, 6 plates; 64, 6 plates.   32mo.
Illustrated blue paper covers.   AAS, HEH, HSP, LOC, NYPL, PPL, UOP.

37292   DAVENPORT, Ebenezer, *Esq. of Stamford*
An Oration on the Death of General George Washington, delivered at Stamford,
Connecticut, on the 22d day of February, A. D. 1800. . . .
New York: Printed by John Furman. 1800.   pp. 19.   8vo.   HEH, NYHS

37293   DAVIS, John   1761–1847
An Eulogy, on General George Washington, pronounced at Boston, on . . . February
XIX, MDCCC. Before the American Academy of Arts and Sciences. . . .
Boston — printed by W. Spotswood — MDCCC.   pp. 24.   4to.
Reprinted in "Washingtonia," Baltimore, 1800, etc.
AAS, APS, BPL, CL, HC, HEH, JCB, MHS, NYHS, NYPL, NYSL, PFM, PL.

37294   [DAVIS, John]   1774–1854
The Farmer of New-Jersey; or, A picture of domestic life. A tale. By the translator of
Buonaparte's campaign. . . .
New-York, Furman and Loudon's type. 1800.   pp. 70, [1].   24mo.   HC, LOC, PʳU.

37295   DAVIS, M[atthew] L[ivingston]   1773–1850
An Oration, delivered in St. Paul's Church, on the Fourth of July, 1800 . . . before the
General Society of Mechanics & Tradesmen, Tammany Society or Columbian Order,
and other associations. . . .
New-York: Printed by W. A. Davis, Greenwich-Street. 1800.   pp. 21, [3].   8vo.
The appended three pages contain an "Ode for the Fourth of July, 1800. By Samuel
Low [1765-]."   AAS, BʳU, HEH, LOC, NYPL, NYSL, WLC, YC.

37296 THE DAWN OF DAY. . . .
  See Austin, David.

37297 DAYTON, JONATHAN 1760–1824
  PUBLIC SPECULATION UNFOLDED: IN SIXTEEN LETTERS, ADDRESSED TO F[RANCIS] CHILDS &
  J[ONATHAN] H[AMPTON] LAWRENCE, OF NEW YORK. . . .
    New-York: Printed by David Denniston, no. 54, Wall-street. 1800. pp. 18. 8vo.
      LOC, NYHS, PᵃU, WⁱˢHS.

37298 THE DEATH OF GENERAL WASHINGTON HAVING FILLED THE HEARTS. . . .
  See Connecticut Courant.

37299 THE DEATH OF WASHINGTON. HOW SAD ARE THE TIDINGS THAT SOUND IN MY EARS!
    Broadside. 4to. HEH.

37300 THE DEATH OF WASHINGTON: OR, COLUMBIA IN MOURNING FOR HER SON. . . .
    Broadside. 4to. MHS, NYPL.

37301 THE DEATH OF WASHINGTON WITH SOME REMARKS ON JEFFERSONIAN & MADISONIAN POLICY. . . .
  [A POEM.]
    Broadside. 4to. NYHS.

37302 DECKER, I.
  FUNERAL DIRGE. ADOPTED FOR & PLAY'D BY THE ALEXANDRIA BAND AT THE FUNERAL OF GENL. GEO.
  WASHINGTON. . . . ENGR'D BY A. LYNN.
    [*Alexandria: Published by Cottom & Stewart.*] Broadside. 4to.
      MR. LESTER S. LEVY OF BALTIMORE.

37303 [DEFOE, DANIEL] 1661?–1731
  LIFE AND SURPRISING ADVENTURES OF . . . ROBINSON CRUSOE. . . . (FIRST AMERICAN, FROM A
  MUCH ADMIRED LONDON EDITION.)
    Dedham: Printed and sold by Herman Mann. 1800. pp. 136, frontispiece, cuts.
  24mo.
    "Account of the island of Juan Fernandes, and of Alexander Selkirk," and "Verses supposed
    to be written by Alexander Selkirk," pp. 132–6. AAS, LCP.

37304 —— *See* Cheap repository. Number 23.

37305 —— THE WONDERFUL LIFE AND ADVENTURES OF ROBINSON CRUSOE. ORNAMENTED WITH CUTS.
    Hartford: Printed by John Babcock. 1800. pp. 31. 32mo. AAS, BPL.

37306 —— THE WONDERFUL LIFE AND MOST SURPRISING ADVENTURES OF ROBINSON CRUSOE. . . .
    New York, Printed by John Tiebout. . . . June, 1800. pp. 134. 12mo. YC.

37307 —— THE WONDERFUL LIFE AND SURPRISING ADVENTURES OF ROBINSON CRUSOE, OF YORK, MARINER . . .
  WITH A TRUE RELATION HOW HE WAS AT LAST MIRACULOUSLY PRESERVED. . . .
    Philadelphia: Printed and sold by John M'Culloch, no. 1, North Third Street. — 1800.
  pp. 144, illus. 24mo. LOC.

37308 DEHON, THEODORE 1776–1817
  A DISCOURSE, DELIVERED IN NEWPORT, RHODE-ISLAND; BEFORE THE CONGREGATION OF TRINITY
  CHURCH, THE MASONIC SOCIETY, AND THE NEWPORT GUARDS; THE SUNDAY FOLLOWING THE
  INTELLIGENCE OF THE DEATH OF GENERAL GEORGE WASHINGTON. . . .
    Newport: Printed by Henry Barber, M,DCCC. pp. 17, [2]. 4to.
  "A prayer" which preceded the discourse occupies the last two pages.
      AAS, AHTS, BA, BPL, HEH, JCB, LOC, MFM, MHS, NHS, NYHS, NYPL, NYSL, RIHS.

37309 DE LAUNE, THOMAS   –1685
A PLEA FOR THE NON-CONFORMISTS. . . . IN A LETTER TO DR. BENJ. CALAMY. . . . TO WHICH IS
ADDED A NARRATIVE OF THE SUFFERINGS UNDERWENT. . . .
Ballston . . . Re-printed by William Child, at the Printing-Office, north of the Court-
House. 1800.   pp. 211, xx.   12mo.
This work includes, with separate titlepages but continuous signature marks and pagination,
De Laune's "Eikoon" and "Narrative of . . . sufferings." A list of subscribers occupies the
last 20 pages.   AAS, AHTS, BPL, HEH, JCB, LCP, LOC, NYHS, NYPL, NYSL, WⁱˢHS, YC.

37310 DELAWARE. STATE
JOURNAL OF THE HOUSE OF REPRESENTATIVES OF THE STATE OF DELAWARE, AT A SESSION OF THE
GENERAL ASSEMBLY, BEGUN AND HOLDEN AT DOVER, ON TUESDAY, THE SEVENTH DAY OF
JANUARY . . . ONE THOUSAND EIGHT HUNDRED. . . .
New Castle: Printed by Samuel and John Adams . . . 1800.   pp. 85, 114.
DSA, LOC, NYPL.

37311 —— JOURNAL OF THE SENATE OF THE STATE OF DELAWARE, AT A SESSION OF THE GENERAL ASSEMBLY,
COMMENCED AND HOLDEN AT DOVER, ON TUESDAY, THE SEVENTH DAY OF JANUARY, IN THE YEAR
OF OUR LORD ONE THOUSAND EIGHT HUNDRED. . . .
New-Castle: Printed by Samuel and John Adams, nearly opposite the Court-House.
1800.   pp. 59.   fol.   AAS, LOC, NYPL.

37312 —— LAWS OF THE STATE OF DELAWARE, PASSED AT A SESSION OF THE GENERAL ASSEMBLY, WHICH WAS
BEGUN AND HELD AT DOVER, ON TUESDAY THE SEVENTH . . . OF JANUARY . . . ONE THOUSAND
EIGHT HUNDRED. . . .
Dover: Printed by W. Black, 1800.   pp. [2], 119–139.   8vo.   HEH.

37313 DELAWARE AND SCHUYLKILL CANAL COMPANY.
EXTRACTS FROM THE RESOLUTIONS OF THE STOCKHOLDERS OF THE DELAWARE AND SCHUYLKILL
CANAL. . . .
Philadelphia . . . 25th January, 1800.   pp. 12.   16mo.   HSP, NYPL, PPL, PSL.

37314 D'ERES, CHARLES DENNIS RUSOE
See Rouso.

37315 [DESAUSSURE, HENRY WILLIAM]   1763–1839
ADDRESS TO THE CITIZENS OF SOUTH-CAROLINA, ON THE APPROACHING ELECTION OF PRESIDENT AND
VICE-PRESIDENT OF THE UNITED STATES. . . .
Charleston: Printed by W. P. Young, Franklin's Head, no. 43, Broad-Street. 1800.
pp. [2], 34.   8vo.   AAS, BA, CLS, LOC, MHS, NYHS, SCHS.

37316 [——] ANSWER TO A DIALOGUE BETWEEN A FEDERALIST AND A REPUBLICAN; FIRST INSERTED IN THE NEWS-
PAPERS IN CHARLESTON AND NOW REPUBLISHED. . . .
Charleston: Printed by W. P. Young. . . .   pp. 36.   8vo.
Signed, A South-Carolina Federalist. Charleston, August 25, 1800.   BA, BPL, LOC, MHS, SCHS.

37317 DESULTORY REFLECTIONS. . . .
See Fenno, John Ward.

37318 [DEUTSCHE BAUER'S REGISTER.   Nov. 29, 1800–1803
Greensburg, Pa., published by John M. Snowden and William M'Corkle.   weekly.]
FOR 1800: No copy known.

37319 DEWEY, SHERMAN   1772–1813
AN ORATION: DELIVERED AT HARTFORD IN THE STATE OF VERMONT, ON THE 17TH OF OCTOBER, 1799.
PARTICULARLY ADDRESSED TO THE YOUNG PEOPLE OF THAT PLACE. . . .
East-Windsor: Printed for the author, by L. Pratt. 1800.   pp. 24.   8vo.
CHS, NYHS, VᵗHS, WL.

37320 DIALOGUES FOR SCHOOLS, SELECTED, WITH ALTERATIONS, FROM THE WORKS OF VARIOUS DRAMATIC WRITERS. . . .
Hartford: Printed by Hudson and Goodwin for Oliver D. & I. Cooke. . . . 1800. pp. iv, 212. 12mo.
AAS, LOC

37321 DICKINS, ASBURY 1780–1861
AN EULOGIUM ON GENERAL GEORGE WASHINGTON, PRONOUNCED ON THE 22D OF FEBRUARY, 1800, BEFORE THE HERMATHENIAN SOCIETY OF PHILADELPHIA. . . .
[Philadelphia:] Printed by order of the Society by H. Maxwell. pp. 29. 8vo.
BA, NYHS, WL.

37322 DICKINSON, JONATHAN 1688–1747
THE TRUE SCRIPTURE-DOCTRINE. . . . WITH A PREFACE, AND SOME SKETCHES OF THE LIFE OF THE AUTHOR, BY MR. [DAVID] AUSTIN [1759–1831.]
Chambersburg: Printed by Robert & Geo. K. Harper. M,DCCC. pp. 216. 12mo.
A list of subscribers occupies pp. 209–16. AAS, BM, HC, HEH, NYSL, PʳU, UOMᴵ, YC.

37323 DICKINSON, TIMOTHY 1761–1813
A SERMON, DELIVERED AT THE ORDINATION OF . . . DRURY FAIRBANK . . . IN PLYMOUTH, NEW-HAMPSHIRE, JANUARY 8TH, 1800. . . .
Concord: Printed by George Hough. 1800. pp. 27. 8vo.
Affixed, pp. 21–7, are "The Charge. By the Rev. Mr. Woodman, of Sandbornton," and "The Right-Hand of Fellowship. By the Rev. Noah Worcester, of Thornton."
AAS, HC, HEH, JCB, NYPL, PʳU, WC, YC.

37324 DICKSON, JOSEPH 1745–1825
PHILADELPHIA MAY 1ST, 1800. SIR, AS MY FELLOW CITIZENS HAVE DONE ME THE HONOR TO GIVE ME A SEAT IN THE CONGRESS OF THE UNITED STATES. . . .
[Philadelphia?] pp. [2]. fol.
LOC.

37325 DICKSON'S BALLOON ALMANAC, FOR THE YEAR OF OUR LORD, 1801 . . . ADAPTED TO PENNSYLVANIA AND THE NEIGHBOURING STATES.
Lancaster, Printed and sold by W. & R. Dickson. . . . pp. [40]. 8vo.
WINTERTHUR MUSEUM.

37326 DILWORTH, THOMAS
A NEW GUIDE TO THE ENGLISH TONGUE; IN FIVE PARTS. . . . A NEW EDITION. WITH CONSIDERABLE ADDITIONS.
Philadelphia: Printed and sold by Peter Stewart. 1800. pp. 131, [1], front. port. 12mo.
NYPL.

37327 —— THE SCHOOLMASTER'S ASSISTANT; BEING A COMPENDIUM OF ARITHMETIC BOTH PRACTICAL AND THEORETICAL. . . .
New-York: Printed by G. & R. Waite, for T. S. Arden, T. B. Jansen and Co. J. Tiebout, C. Davis, J. Harrison, S. Stephens, P. A. Mesier, B. Gomez, W. Falconer, R. Magill, Bell and Smith, and W. Durell. 1800. pp. xvi, [6], 194, plate. 12mo.
Contains verses to Dilworth by Moses Brown, and by William Deane dated Halifax, 1765.
AAS, GʳL, LOC, NYPL, YC.

37328 DIRECT TAXES! LOANS! FRUITS OF COMMERCIAL RESTRICTIONS! ELECTORS OF WORCESTER COUNTY. . . .
[Worcester.] Broadside. 4to.
WᵒʳHS.

37329 DODDRIDGE, PHILIP 1702–1751
A PLAIN AND SERIOUS ADDRESS TO THE MASTER OF A FAMILY, ON THE IMPORTANT SUBJECT OF FAMILY RELIGION. . . .
Northampton: Printed by Andrew Wright. 1800. pp. 36.
FLN.

37330 —— THE PRINCIPLES OF THE CHRISTIAN RELIGION, DIVIDED INTO LESSONS, FOR CHILDREN. ABRIDGED. . . . ORNAMENTED WITH CUTS. . . .
Hartford: Printed by John Babcock. 1800. pp. 31. 32mo.
AAS, PL.

37331 [DODSLEY, Robert]   1703–1764
      THE ECONOMY OF HUMAN LIFE. TRANSLATED FROM AN INDIAN MANUSCRIPT WRITTEN BY AN
      ANCIENT BRAMIN. . . .
           Philadelphia: Printed by Charles & Ralston, for the booksellers. 1800.   pp. xii,
[2], [1]–4, 19–156.   12mo.   AAS, BM.

37332 DORCHESTER. MASSACHUSETTS.
      PUBLIC EXPRESSIONS OF GRIEF, FOR THE DEATH OF GENERAL GEORGE WASHINGTON, AT DORCHESTER.
      [Charlestown: Printed by Samuel Etheridge, 1800.]   pp. 6, [5]–22, [2], 16, 30.   8vo.
This includes the Eulogy by Oliver Everett, the Discourse by T .M. Harris (with separate
titlepages), and Washington's Farewell Address. Some copies contain also *The Fraternal
Tribute of Respect paid to the Masonic Character of Washington in the Union Lodge,
in Dorchester, January 7th, A. L. 5800,* by T. M. Harris, pp. 14.
                                AAS, BA, BPL, HEH, LOC, MSL, NYPL, NYSL, PPL.

37333 THE DOWNFALL OF PRIDE. ALMIGHTY COCK WAS LATE SET UP, UPON A LOFTY STEEPLE TOP; THE
      OWNER OF THIS COCK AND STEEPLE WERE A PROUD AND SCORNFUL PEOPLE. . . .
           Published at Salem, Massachusetts . . . Feb. 1800.   Broadside.   fol.
      A poem in three parts.   EI.

37334 DUNHAM, Josiah   1769–1844
      A FUNERAL ORATION ON GEORGE WASHINGTON. . . . PRONOUNCED, AT OXFORD, MASSACHUSETTS,
      AT THE REQUEST OF THE FIELD OFFICERS OF THE BRIGADE STATIONED AT THAT PLACE, ON THE
      15TH JAN. 1800. . . .
           *Boston: Printed by Manning & Loring, for Joseph Nancrede, no. 49, Marlbro'
Street. . . .*   pp. 20.   8vo.
Reprinted in "Eulogies and Orations," Boston, 1800.
           AAS, AHTS, BA, BPL, HC, HEH, JCB, LOC, MFM, NL, NYHS, NYPL, NYSL, PL, WᴵˢHS, WLC.

37335 DUNLAP, William   1766–1839
      [THE GERMAN THEATRE. BY WILLIAM DUNLAP.
           New-York: 1800.]
      89th New York District copyright issued to Dunlap as translator and author, March 17,
1800. This was the collective title for the plays which in this bibliography are listed
separately under author. There was probably a general titlepage for the collection, but
no copy of it has been found.

37336 DUPORT, P. Landrin
      [UNITED STATES COUNTRY DANCES WITH FIGURES ALSO ACCOMPANIMENTS FOR THE PIANO FORTE.
      COMPOSED IN AMERICA. BY MR. P. LANDRIN DUPORT, PROFESSOR OF DANCING FROM PARIS &
      ORIGINAL COMPOSER OF CADRIEL'S.
           New York: 1800.]
      102d New York District Copyright, issued to P. Landrin Duport, as author, Nov. 3, 1800.

37337 DUTTON, Warren   1774–1857.
      THE PRESENT STATE OF LITERATURE; A POEM, DELIVERED IN NEW-HAVEN, AT THE PUBLIC COM-
      MENCEMENT OF YALE-COLLEGE, SEPTEMBER 10, 1800. . . .
           Hartford: Printed by Hudson and Goodwin. 1800.   pp. 16.   8vo.
      AAS, BA, BPL, BᴿU, CHS, HC, HEH, HSP, LCP, LOC, MHS, NYHS, NYPL, NYSL, PL, PTS, UTS, WL, YC.

37338 DWIGHT, Nathaniel   1770–1831
      A SHORT BUT COMPREHENSIVE SYSTEM OF THE GEOGRAPHY OF THE WORLD: BY WAY OF QUESTION
      AND ANSWER. . . . THE FOURTH CONNECTICUT EDITION. . . .
           *Hartford: Printed by Hudson and Goodwin. Sold by them. . . . By I. Beers, New-
Haven. By B. Talmadge & Co. Litchfield. By T. C. Green, New-London; and by
Andrew Huntington, Norwich. 1800.*   pp. 214.   12mo.
                                    AAS, HC, JCB, LOC, NYSL, PPL, WL, YC.

37339 DWIGHT, Timothy   1752–1817
       A Discourse, delivered at New-Haven, Feb. 22, 1800; on the character of George
       Washington. . . .
            Printed by Thomas Green and Son, New-Haven: 1800.   pp. 55.   8vo.
       Cover title: "Dr. Dwight's discourse, Feb. 22, 1800. Also, Gen. Washington's Farewell
       address."   AAS, BA, BPL, CHS, CSL, Gᴿʟ, HEH, JCB, LCP, LOC, MFM, MHS, NL, NYPL, NYSL, PL,
                                                                      PʳU, RU, WC, WL, YC.

37340 THE EAGLE, or, Carlisle Herald.   1799–1802.
            Carlisle [Pa.]: Published by John P. Thompson.   fol.   weekly.
                                                                      For 1800: [AAS].

37341 EASTERN Herald and Gazette of Maine.   1796–1800
            Published by Baker & George, Fish Street, Portland.   fol.   weekly.
       Name changed on Dec. 29, 1800, to Russell & George's Eastern Herald & Maine Gazette.
                                                            For 1800: York Inst., Saco, [HC].

37342 EATON & Walker's Oneida, Herkimer, Chenango, Onondaga, Cayuga, Ontario, Steuben &
       Tioga Almanack, with an ephemeris, for the Year . . . 1801. . . .
            Printed at Rome, New-York, by Thomas Walker. . . .   pp. [36].   12mo.
                                                                      AAS, LOC,*NYHS.

37343 EBSWORTH, Daniel
       [The Republican harmonist; being a select collection of republican patriotic and
       Masonic songs, odes, sonnets, &c. American and European. . . .
            Philadelphia: 1800.]
       252d Pennsylvania District copyright issued to Daniel Ebsworth as proprietor May 7, 1800.

37344 THE ECHO: or, Columbian songster, being a large collection of the most celebrated, modern
       poetical writings. . . . Second edition.
            Brookfield: (Massachusetts) from the press of E. Merriam. Sold by him in Brookfield,
       and by Dan Merriam in Worcester. 1800.   HC.

37345 THE ECONOMY of human life. . . .
            See Dodsley, Robert.

37346 EDDY, Zechariah   1780–1860
       Philandrianism: an oration, delivered in . . . Raynham, September 10th, A. D. 1800.
       At the . . . anniversary election of the Philandrian Society. . . .
            Providence: Printed by B. Wheeler. 1800.   pp. 28.   8vo.
       "Ode 1st. To industry. By Brother Moses Noyes" occupies p. 27 and "Ode 2d. To
       sympathy. By Brother Mason Williams," p. 28.   AAS, BʳU, HEH, JCB, LOC, RIHS.

37347 THE EDENTON Gazette.   1800–1801
            Edenton [N. C.]: published by Joseph Beasley.   fol.   weekly.
       A continuation of The Post-Angel, or Universal Entertainment.   For 1800: [NCU].

37348 [ELECTION of President of the United States. To citizens of the United States, and
       particularly to those not born therein. By a Republican.
            n. p., 1800.   8vo.]   Sabin.

37349 AN ELEGIAC poem on the death of General George Washington. . . . Printed by R.
       Aitken. . . .
            See Caldwell, Charles.

37350 ELEGIES, and other little poems. By a student in a college in this State. . . .
            Baltimore, August 7, 1800.   pp. [6].   12mo.   BʳU.

37351 ELIOT, John.   1754–1813
       A Sermon on the propriety of attending public worship, and an attentive serious conduct
       in the house of God. . . .
            Boston. Printed by John Russell, 1800.   pp. 36.   8vo.
                 AAS, BA, BPL, CL, HC, LOC, MHS, MSL, NYHS, NYPL, NYSL, PL, PTS, YC.

37352   ELKHORN Association.
       Minutes of the Elkhorn Association of Babtists [*sic*], held at Bryan's Fayette County, State of Kentucky, August 9th, 10th and 11th, 1800.
           Lexington: Printed by J. H. Stewart.   pp. 4.   8vo.
       Caption title; imprint on p. 4.   WRHS.

37353   ELLIOTT, John   1768–1824
       A Discourse delivered on . . . February 22, 1800, the day recommended by the Congress . . . to . . . pronounce eulogies on . . . George Washington. . . .
           Hartford: Printed by Hudson and Goodwin. 1800.   pp. 23.   8vo.
               AAS, BPL, BᶠU, CHS, HEH, JCB, LOC, MFM, MHS, NYPL, PL, PTS, YC.

37354   —— A Discourse occasioned by the death of the Reverend Amos Fowler . . . of . . . Gilford. . . .
           Middletown: Printed by T. & J. B. Dunning. 1800.   pp. 26.   8vo.
               AAS, CHS, CU, JCB, NYHS, NYSL, PTS, YC.

37355   —— A Selected, pronouncing and accented dictionary. . . . By John Elliott . . . and Samuel Johnson, junr. [1757–1836]. . . .
           Suffield: Printed by Edward Gray, for Oliver D. & I. Cook . . . in Hartford. 1800.
       pp. 16, 223.   obl. 32mo.   HEH, NYHS, NYPL, YC.

37356   —— —— The second edition.
           [*Same imprint.*]   pp. 32, 203.   obl. 32mo.
               AAS, CHS, CSL, HC, LOC, NYHS, NYPL, YC.

37357   ELLIS, Benjamin
       An Address, read before . . . Somerset Lodge [in Norwich], on the festival of St. John the Evangelist, in the year of light, 5779.
           Norwich: J. Trumbull. 1800.   pp. 20.   8vo.   CHS, PTS.

37358   ELLIS, Jonathan   1762–1827
       An Eulogical poem on General George Washington. . . . Pronounced at Topsham, February 22d. 1800. . . .
           Portland, Printed by Elezer A. Jenks.   pp. 24.   8vo.
       The NYHS copy contains Ms. corrections by the author.   AAS, BA, MHS, NYHS.

37359   ELMER, Jonathan   1745–1807
       An Eulogium, on the character of Gen. George Washington . . . at Bridge-Town . . . New-Jersey, January 30th, 1800. . . .
           Trenton, printed by G. Craft, 1800.   pp. 25, front.   8vo.   HEH, LOC, NJHS.

37360   ELMINA; or, the flower that never fades. . . .
       See Masson, Charles Francis Philibert.

37361   [ELY, JOHN]   1758–1847
       The Child's instructor; consisting of easy lessons for children on subjects which are familiar to them. . . . The seventh edition. . . .
           New-York: Printed by G. & R. Waite for Everet Duyckinck. 1800.   pp. 108.
       16mo.   AAS.

37362   —— —— —— *New York, Printed by W. Durell, 1800.*   pp. 108.   36mo.   CU-T.

37363   —— A Plan to render our militia formidable, shewing that the most effectual way to preserve peace in the United States wll be to let military knowledge form a part of the education of boys. . . .
           Philadelphia: Printed [by John Ormrod] at no. 41 Chestnut street, for the author.
       1800.   pp. 22.   8vo.   BPL, HSP, LOC, NL, NYPL, PPL.

37364 —— A Regiment to consist of one thousand boys. Our whole country must, in a few years, become the inheritance of boys. . . . John Ely, Philadelphia, April 9th, 1800.
Broadside. 4to. HSP.

37365 EMBLEMS of mem'ry are these tears; sung by Mrs. Warrell at the New Theatre in commemoration of the first anniversary of General Washington's birthday, after his decease 22d Feby 1800.
Philadelphia. Printed by G. Willig, no. 185 Market St. pp. [4]. fol. HEH.

37366 EMERSON, Samuel 1765–1851
An Oration on music. Pronounced at Portland — May 28th, 1800. . . . (Published by special request.)
From the press of E. A. Jenks, Portland. 1800. pp. 20. 8vo.
AAS, BA, BM, HC, JCB, LOC, MᵉHS, MHS, NYHS, NYPL.

37367 EMERSON, William 1769–1811
A Discourse, delivered before the Roxbury Charitable Society . . . September 15, 1800. . . .
Printed by Samuel Hall, in Cornhill, Boston, 1800. pp. 23. 8vo.
This is apparently the item erroniously attributed by Sabin to Ralph Emerson. The "Constitutional articles of the Roxbury Charitable Society" occupy pp. 19–23.
AAS, BA, BM, CL, HC, JCB, LOC, MHS, NEHGS, NL, NYHS, WⁱˢHS, YC.

37368 EMMONS, Nathaniel 1745–1840
A Sermon, delivered before the Massachusetts Missionary Society . . . in Boston, May 27, 1800. . . . To which is added, an abstract of the proceedings, and fund of the Society. . . .
Charlestown: Printed and sold by Samuel Etheridge. 1800. pp. 44. 8vo.
AAS, BA, BM, BPL, CHS, CL, CSL, Gʳ L, HC, HEH, JCB, LOC, MᵉHS, MHS, MSL, NL, NYHS, NYSL, PTS, WLC, YC.

37369 —— A Sermon, on the death of Gen. George Washington, Preached February 22, 1800. . . .
Printed at Wrentham, Massachusetts, by Nathaniel and Benjamin Heaton. 1800.
pp. 26. 8vo. AAS, BA, BPL, CL, HC, HEH, JCB, LOC, MFM, NHHS, NYPL, NYSL, PPL.

37370 —— Sermons on some of the first principles and doctrines of true religion. . . . Published according to Act of Congress.
Printed at Wrentham, Massachusetts, by Nathaniel and Benjamin Heaton. 1800.
pp. 510. 8vo.
Issues of this edition appear with and without rule enclosing the words "Published according to Act of Congress."
AAS, AHTS, BA, BPL, CL, Gʳ L, HC, JCB, LOC, MHS, NYPL, NYSL, PL, WC, YC.

37371 THE ENCYCLOPEDIAN Instructor, and Farmer's Gazette. 1800
Edenton: Printed by James Wills & Robert Archibald. fol. weekly.
May 21, 1800 at AAS.

37372 ENQUIRIES into the necessity or expediency of assuming exclusive legislation over the District of Columbia. . . .
From the Cabinet office [Georgetown, D. C., 1800.] pp. 27. 16mo. AAS.

37373 ENTERTAINING and diverting stories on various subjects, for the instruction of children. Adorned with cuts.
Printed for, and sold by the booksellers. 1800. pp. 16. 32mo. AAS.

37374 THE ENTERTAINING, moral and religious repository . . . for the amusement and instruction of the youth of both sexes. . . .
Elizabeth-town: Printed by Shepard Kollock, for C. Davis, no. 167 Water-Street, New-York. 1800. pp. [2], 324. 16mo. AAS.

37375 ENTICK, JOHN 1703?–1773
NEW ENGLISH SPELLING DICTIONARY. . . . TO WHICH IS ADDED A CATALOGUE OF WORDS OF SIMILAR
SOUNDS, BUT OF DIFFERENT SPELLINGS AND SIGNIFICATIONS. BY WILLIAM CRAKELET. . . .
London: Printed. Wilmington: Reprinted and sold by Peter Brynberg. 1800.
pp. 460. sq. 16mo. NYPL.

37376 EPISTLE TO PETER PINDAR. . . .
See Gifford, William.

37377 EPITOME OF THE TIMES. 1798–1802
Norfolk [Va.] published . . . by Augustus C. Jordan. fol. semiweekly.
FOR 1800: [HC].

37378 ERNST, JOHN FREDERIC
ORATION . . . BEFORE THE GRAND ROYAL-ARCH CHAPTER FOR THE STATE OF NEW-YORK, ON THE
21ST. DAY OF JANUARY, A. L. 5800. . . .
Printed in Albany, A. D. M.DCCC. pp. 21. 12mo. MFM, NYSL.

37379 —— A SERMON, DELIVERED BEFORE THE CIVIL AND MILITARY OFFICERS, THE MEMBERS OF FRANKLIN
AND ST. PAUL'S LODGES, AND A LARGE AND RESPECTABLE NUMBER OF CITIZENS OF MONTGOMERY
COUNTY . . . IN THE CHURCH AT FORT PLAIN, ON JANUARY 28TH, 1800. IN CONSEQUENCE OF
THE DEATH OF . . . WASHINGTON. . . .
Cooperstown: Printed by Elihu Phinney, 1800. pp. 20. 4to.
NYHS, NYPL, NYSL, PPL.

37380 ERSKINE, EBENEZER 1680–1754
A SERMON. THE STONE REJECTED. . . . PREACHED AT THE OPENING OF THE SYNOD OF PERTH AND
STERLING, AT PERTH, OCTOBER 10, 1732. . . .
Wiscasset: Printed by Henry Hoskins. 1800. pp. 30. 12mo. AAS, CL, LOC.

37381 ESSAY ON POLITICAL SOCIETY. (COPY RIGHT SECURED, AGREEABLY TO ACT OF CONGRESS.)
Whitehall: Printed by William Young . . . N. 52 South 2d-street, Philadelphia. 1800.
pp. [6], 9–234. 8vo.
An inscription on the Eames copy attributes this to the Hon. S. W. Dana (1760–1830),
but Dexter does not.
AAS, BA, HEH, HSP, JCB, LCP, LOC, NYHS, NYPL, NYSL, PTS, UOP, UOTˣ.

37382 ESSAYS ON THE SPIRIT OF LEGISLATION, IN THE ENCOURAGEMENT OF AGRICULTURE, POPULATION,
MANUFACTURES, AND COMMERCE. TRANSLATED FROM THE ORIGINAL FRENCH, WHICH GAINED
THE PREMIUMS OFFERED BY THE OEconomical SOCIETY OF BERNE. . . .
Newark: Printed for William Reid, by Pennington & Gould, M,DCCC. pp. 479,
[1], vii. 8vo.
The last signature contains the table of contents. The authors are Jean Bertrand (1708–
1777), Benjamin Carrard (b. 1740), and Gabriel Seigneux de Correvon (d. 1776).
AAS, BM, BPL, HC, HEH, HSP, JCB, LOC, NPL, PʳU.

37383 EULOGIES AND ORATIONS ON THE LIFE AND DEATH OF GENERAL GEORGE WASHINGTON, FIRST
PRESIDENT OF THE UNITED STATES OF AMERICA. . . .
*Boston: Printed by Manning & Loring, for W. P. & L. Blake . . . and Manning
& Loring. . . . 1800.* pp. 304. 8vo.
Contains a list of subscribers and orations by Henry Lee, George Richards Minot, Jonathan
Mitchel Sewall, Gouverneur Morris, Thomas Paine, John Brooks, David Ramsay, George
Blake, Fisher Ames, Timothy Bigelow, John Davis, William Linn, Jeremiah Smith,
Joseph Blyth, Isaac Parker, John M. Mason, William Jackson, Charles Pinckney Sumner,
Josiah Dunham, and John Thornton Kirkland.
AAS, BA, BM, BPL, BʳU, CL, CSL, EI, HC, HEH, HSP, LOC, MHS, NL, NYHS, NYPL, NYSL, YC.

37384 AN EULOGIUM ON THE LATE GENERAL GEORGE WASHINGTON, DELIVERED ON THURSDAY EVENING,
DEC. 26, 1799. BEFORE THE CICERONIAN SOCIETY: BY A MEMBER APPOINTED FOR THAT PURPOSE.
[Philadelphia.] pp. 15. 12mo. MFM, MHS.

37385 AN EULOGY ON GEORGE WASHINGTON, ESQ. DECEASED. . . .
See Kinloch, Francis.

37386 EVERETT, DAVID   1770–1813
DARANZEL. . . . AN ORIGINAL DRAMA. . . . AS PERFORMED AT THE THEATRE IN BOSTON. . . .
CORRECTED AND IMPROVED BY A LITERARY FRIEND.
Boston, Printed by John Russell. 1800.   pp. 66, [2].   8vo.
An "Epilogue. By a gentleman of Boston" occupies the last leaf.
AAS, BA, BPL, BʳU, HC, LOC, MHS, NYHS, NYPL, UOC, UOP, UOTˣ, YC.

37387 EVERETT, OLIVER   1752–1802
AN EULOGY, ON GENERAL GEORGE WASHINGTON. . . . PRONOUNCED AT DORCHESTER, FEB. 22,
1800. . . .
Charlestown: Printed by Samuel Etheridge. M,DCCC.   pp. 22.   8vo.
Issued also in Dorchester, Massachusetts, *Public Expressions of Grief.*
AAS, AHTS, BPL, GU, HC, HEH, HSP, JCB, LCP, MFM, MHS, NYHS, NYPL, NYSL, PL, RU, WC, YC.

37388 EVERTSON, NICHOLAS
A CERTIFICATE AND A LETTER INCLOSING THE SAME, WRITTEN BY A GENTLEMAN IN NEW-YORK, TO
HIS CORRESPONDENT IN KINGS COUNTY. NEW YORK, APRIL 26TH, 1800.
Broadside.   fol.   LOCᴾʰ.

37389 AN EXAMINATION OF THE OPINION CONTAINED IN THE REPORT OF THE ONONDAGA COMMISSIONERS,
OF THE SEVENTEENTH OF FEBRUARY, 1800, TO HIS EXCELLENCY THE GOVERNOR; AND BY HIM
TRANSMITTED TO THE HONOURABLE THE LEGISLATURE: WITH A VIEW TO ITS REFUTATION. BY
A WESTERN CITIZEN. . . .
Albany: Printed by Barber & Southwick, for the author.   pp. 24.   8vo.
Attributed by Evans to "Mr. Stewart of the Western Country."   LOC, NYPL, NYSL, WⁱˢHS.

37390 THE EXAMINER.   1798–1804
Richmond [Va.]: printed . . . by Meriwether Jones. . . .   fol.   semiweekly.
FOR 1800: [VᵃSL].

37391 EXECUTION OF LA CROIX, BERROUSE, & BAKER, FOR PIRACY. [SECOND TITLE:] THE LAST WORDS AND
DYING CONFESSION OF THE THREE PIRATES, WHO WERE EXECUTED THIS DAY, (MAY 9TH, 1800.)
From Folwell's Press . . . Philadelphia. (Copy-right secured according to law.)
pp. [2], [8].   8vo.   LOC.

37392 EXTRACTS OF THE PROCEEDINGS OF A CONVENTION OF DELEGATES APPOINTED BY THE SYNODS OF THE
REFORMED DUTCH CHURCH OF NEW-YORK AND NEW-JERSEY, OF THE PRESBYTERIAN SYNOD OF
NEW-YORK AND PHILADELPHIA, AND OF THE ASSOCIATE REFORMED SYNOD, WHEN MET IN
NEW-YORK THE 5TH DAY OF OCTOBER, 1785.
[Colophon:] *New-York, May 19, 1800.*   pp. 4.   8vo.   AAS, JCB.

37393 FALCONER, WILLIAM   1732–1769
THE SHIPWRECK. BY WILLIAM FALCONER, AN ENGLISH SAILOR. . . .
New-York: Printed by James Oram, no. 102, Water-Street. 1800.   pp. 170, [1],
4 plates.   16mo.
"Biographical sketch of Falconer from Johnson's lives of the poets" affixed. The illustrations were drawn by Stothard and engraved by Scoles. There are copies with the title
reading "An English seaman." The AAS has both.   AAS, BM, BʳU, HC, NYPL, NYSL, RU, VᵃU

37394 THE FALL OF ADAM. . . .
See Cheap repository. Number 28.

37395 THE FAMOUS HISTORY OF WHITTINGTON AND HIS CAT, SHEWING, HOW FROM A POOR COUNTRY BOY
. . . HE OBTAINED GREAT RICHES. . . . ADORNED WITH CUTS.
New-York: Printed by W. Durell, for John Harrison. 1800.   pp. 31.   48mo.   AAS.

37396 THE FARMER OF NEW-JERSEY. . . .
See Davis, John, 1774–1854

37397 THE FARMER'S ALMANAC, CALCULATED FOR PENNSYLVANIA, DELAWARE, MARYLAND, VIRGINIA AND KENTUCKY, FOR THE YEAR OF OUR LORD, 1801. . . .
Baltimore: Printed and Sold by Warner & Hannah, no. 37, Market street. . . . 1801
[*sic*].   pp. [36].   12mo.   AAS, HSP.

37398 THE FARMERS INSTRUCTOR, AND HARRISBURGH COURANT.   1800–1802
Harrisburgh, Pennsylvania. Published by Benjamin Mayer.   fol.   weekly.
                                                                       FOR 1800: PSL.

37399 FARMERS JOURNAL.   APRIL 7, 1800?–1803
Danbury, Conn., published by Stiles Nichols and Samuel Morse. 1800.   fol.
weekly.   FOR 1800: [AAS].

37400 THE FARMER'S MONITOR.   MAR. 5, 1800–1807
Litchfield, (Con.) Printed by T. Collier. 1800.   fol.   weekly.
A continuation of *The Monitor*.   FOR 1800: [AAS], [HC].

37401 FARMER'S MUSEUM, OR LAY PREACHER'S GAZETTE.   1797–1810
Printed at Walpole, Newhampshire, by David Carlisle, for Thomas & Thomas.
weekly.   fol.
With the issue of Feb. 17 the name was changed to *Farmer's Museum, or Literary Gazette*.
                    FOR 1800: AAS, BPL, CHS, DC, LOC, MHS, NHHS, NYHS, NYSL.

37402 THE FARMERS REGISTER.   1799–1810
Greensburg, (Penn.) Printed and published by Snowden & M'Corkle.   fol.
weekly.   FOR 1800: HSP.

37403 THE FARMER'S WEEKLY JOURNAL.   JULY 25, 1800–1801
Printed . . . in Doylstown, Bucks County (Penn) by Isaac Ralston.   fol.   weekly.
                                                                       FOR 1800: [LOC].

37404 FARNHAM, BENJAMIN
DISSERTATIONS ON THE PROPHECIES. . . . PUBLISHED ACCORDING TO ACT OF CONGRESS.
Printed at East Windsor, by Luther Pratt. 1800.   pp. 155.   16mo.
List of subscribers.   AAS, BM, BPL, CHS, CSL, HEH, MHS, WL, YC.

37405 FATHER ABRAMAM'S ALMANAC. . . .
See Sharp, Joshua.

37406 FATHER TAMMANY'S ALMANAC. . . .
See Sharp, Joshua.

37407 THE FAYETTE GAZETTE.   1798–1805
Uniontown [Pa.]: Printed by Stewart and Mowry. . . .   fol.   weekly.
                                                                       FOR 1800: [NYHS].

37408 FEDERAL CAROLINA GAZETTE.   1800
Charleston: Published by Timothy & Sheppard.   fol.   weekly.
In the latter part of the year Thomas Sheppard retired from the partnership and was
replaced by Andrew M'Farlan.   FOR 1800: [HC], [LOC].

37409 FEDERAL GALAXY.   1797–1803
Published for Windham County, by Benjamin Smead, in Brattleborough, Vermont.
fol.   weekly.   FOR 1800: [AAS], [VᵗSL].

37410 FEDERAL GAZETTE & BALTIMORE DAILY ADVERTISER.
[Baltimore:] Printed and sold by Yundt and Brown, 1800.   fol.   daily.
                                                                       FOR 1800: MᵈHS.

37411 —— FRIDAY, JANUARY 24, 1800. THE FOLLOWING APPEARS TOO IMPORTANT NOT TO BE LAID BEFORE OUR READERS. . . . BUONAPARTE. . . .
[*Baltimore: Printed by Yundt and Brown.*]   Broadside.   fol.   MᵈHS.

37412 FEDERAL OBSERVER.   1798–JUNE 12, 1800
Portsmouth: Printed and published by William Treadwell.   weekly.   fol.
With the issue of May 22 the publishers were given as "W. Treadwell & Co."
FOR 1800: BA.

37413 THE FEDERAL SONGSTER: BEING A COLLECTION OF THE MOST CELEBRATED PATRIOTIC SONGS. . . .
New-London: Printed by James Springer. 1800.   pp. 109, [3].   12mo.   AAS.

37414 THE FEDERAL SPY.   1792–1805
Published by Timothy Ashley. Springfield, Massachusetts.   fol.   weekly.
FOR 1800: [AAS].

37415 THE FEDERALIST: OR NEW-JERSEY GAZETTE.   1798–1829
Printed at Trenton, under the direction of G. Craft. . . .   weekly.   fol.
With the issue of July 8 the *Federalist* was combined with the *New-Jersey State Gazette* to form *The Federalist & New-Jersey State Gazette* which was published by George Sherman, John Mershon, Isaiah Thomas, and Gershom Craft.   FOR 1800: NJSL.

37416 FENELON, [FRANÇOIS] SALIGNAC DE LA MOTHE   1651–1715
THE ADVENTURES OF TELEMACHUS. . . . FROM THE FRENCH OF . . . FÉNÉLON. . . . BY THE LATE JOHN HAWKESWORTH, LL.D. CORRECTED AND REVISED BY G. GREGORY, D.D. WITH A LIFE OF THE AUTHOR. . . .
New York: Printed by T. & J. Swords, no. 99 Pearl Street. 1800.   2 vol.   8vo.
VᵃU.

37417 [FENNO, JOHN WARD]   1778–1802
DESULTORY REFLECTIONS ON THE NEW POLITICAL ASPECTS OF PUBLIC AFFAIRS . . . SINCE THE COMMENCEMENT OF THE YEAR 1799. . . .
New-York, Printed for the author, by G. and R. Waite, and published by J. W. Fenno, no. 141 Hanover Square. 1800.   pp. 62.   8vo.
BA, BM, EI, HEH, JCB, LOC, MHS, NYHS, NYPL, NYSL, RU, WˡᵃHS, WL, YC.

37418 —— —— *New-York, printed: Philadelphia, reprinted: for R. T. Rawle (opposite Christ church), N. Second Street. 1800.* pp. 26. 8vo.   AAS, APS, HEH, HSP, JCB, LOC, MHS, NL, NYSL, UOC, YC.

37419 —— —— PART II. . . .
New-York: Printed for the author, by G. and R. Waite, and published by J. W. Fenno, no. 141 Hanover Square. 1800.   pp. [2], 38.   8vo.   BA, BPL, HEH, HSP, JCB, LOC, NYHS.

37420 THE FESTIVAL OF MIRTH, AND AMERICAN TAR'S DELIGHT: A FUND OF THE NEWEST HUMOROUS, PATRIOTIC, HUNTING, AND SEA SONGS. WITH A VARIETY OF CURIOUS JESTS . . . &C.
New-York; Printed for Thomas B. Jansen & Co. no. 248 Pearl-Street. 1800.   pp. 12, incl. front.   24mo.   BPL, LOC.

37421 A FEW REMARKS ON MR. HAMILTON'S LATE LETTER. . . .
See Pinkney, William.

37422 FIELD, MARTIN
AN ORATION, PRONOUNCED AT WALPOLE, NEW HAMPSHIRE, BEFORE THE JERUSALEM, GOLDEN RULE, AND OLIVE BRANCH LODGES OF FREE AND ACCEPTED MASONS . . . JUNE 24TH ANNO LUCIS, 5,800. . . .
Putney.—Printed by Cornelius Sturtevant. October 1800.   pp. 24.   4to.   CL, YC.

37423   FIELDS, R.
A Practical treatise upon the Bankrupt law of the United States. . . . Copy right secured.
  Boston: Printed by B. Edes & Son. 1800.   pp. 59.   16mo.
                          AAS, BM, BPL, HC, JCB, MᵉHS, MHS, NYPL, UOC.

37424   FISHER, George
Arithmetic, in the plainest and most concise methods hitherto extant: with new improvements. . . .
  London, printed: Wilmington: Reprinted and sold by Peter Brynberg, Market-Street. 1800.   pp. xii, 2, 11–312.   12mo.   AAS.

37425   FISHER, Nathaniel   1742–1812
A Sermon, preached December 29, 1799, in St. Peter's Church, Salem . . . after . . . the death of General Washington. . . .
  Salem: Printed by Thomas C. Cushing, at the Bible & Heart.   pp. 24.   8vo.
                AAS, BA, EI, HC, HEH, JCB, LOC, MFM, MᵈHS, NL, NYHS, NYPL, NYSL, YC.

37426   FISKE, Thaddeus   1762–1855
A Sermon, delivered Dec. 29, 1799. At the Second Parish in Cambridge, being the Lord's Day . . . following the . . . intelligence of the death of . . . Washington. . . .
  Boston, printed by James Cutler, at his printing-office, Quaker-Street. — 1800.   pp. 21.   8vo.   AAS, BA, HC, HEH, JCB, LOC, MFM, NYPL, PL, PTS.

37427   FITCH, John   1770–1827
A Sermon, delivered at Danville, at the request of Harmony Lodge, as a tribute of respect for the memory of the late Gen. George Washington; February 26th, 1800.
  Peacham, Vermont, Printed by Farley & Goss. 1800.   pp. 24.   8vo.
                                              MFM, PTS, VᵗHS.

37428   [FITZSIMMONS, Thomas]   1741–1811
A Brief statement of opinions, given by the Board of Commissioners, under . . . the treaty . . . with Great Britain. . . .
  Philadelphia: Printed by James Humphreys, no. 106, South side of Market-Street. 1800.   pp. viii, 71.   8vo.
Also attributed to Thomas Macdonald.
            AAS, BPL, HC, HEH, HSP, JCB, LOC, MHS, NYHS, NYPL, NYSL, PSL, UOC, WLC.

37429   FLEMING, James
[General rules for country schools.
  Carlisle: Printed by George Kline for Archibald Loudon, 1800.]
Adv. in Kline's *Gazette*, Oct. 15, 1800.

37430   FLINT, Abel   1765–1825
A Discourse, delivered at Hartford Feb. 22, 1800 . . . to pay a tribute of respect to the memory of General George Washington. . . .
  Hartford: printed by Hudson and Goodwin. 1800.   pp. 22.   8vo.
          AAS, BA, BPL, CHS, CL, EI, HC, HEH, HSP, JCB, LCP, LOC, NL, NYPL, NYSL, UTS, VᵃSL, WLC, YC.

37431   FLORIAN, [Jean Pierre Claris de]   1755–1794
A Very entertaining and affecting history of Claudine . . . (from the French of M. de Florian.)
  Whitestown, [N. Y.]: Printed by Warren Barnard, 1800.   pp. 16.   8vo.   NYPL.

37432   FOLSOM, Peter [Lawrence]
An Eulogy on Geo. Washington. . . . Delivered in the Academy, February 22d, A. D. 1800, before the inhabitants of Gilmanton. . . .
  Gilmanton: Printed by E. Russell, for the contractors, March, 1800.   pp. 12.   12mo.
                                              HC, JCB, LOC.

37433 FORBES, Eli   1726–1804
An Eulogy moralized on . . . George Washington. . . . Delivered at Gloucester, on the 22d of February, 1800. . . . To which is added, General Washington's affectionate address . . . declining . . . the presidency. . . .
Printed at Newburyport, by Edmund M. Blunt, 1800. pp. 40. 8vo.
AAS, BA, CL, HEH, JCB, LOC, MFM, MHS, NYHS, NYPL, NYSL.

37434 FORLORN Hope.   Mar. 24–Sept. 13, 1800
Prison, New York [edited by William Keteltas]. fol. weekly.
For 1800: [LOC], [NYHS].

37435 FOSTER, Dan   d. 1810
A Sermon, delivered at Walpole, New Hampshire, before the Jerusalem, Golden Rule, and Olive Branch lodges, of Free and Accepted Masons, at the celebration of the festival of St. John the Baptist, on the 24th June, A. L. 5800. . . .
Putney.—Printed by Cornelius Sturtevant. 1800. pp. 16. 4to. NYSL, YC.

37436 FOSTER, Edmund   1752–1826
Husbandry. . . . An oration delivered before the Western Society of Middlesex Husband-men . . . at Littleton . . . October 28, 1799. . . .
Amherst, N. H. printed by Samuel Preston. 1800. pp. 15. 8vo. AAS, JCB, LOC, MHS.

37437 FOSTER, Joel   1755–1812
The Duties of a conjugal state . . . delivered at Brimfield . . . December 1, 1799; after which, marriage was publicly solemnized between the Rev. Clark Brown, and the amiable Miss Tabitha Moffatt. . . .
Stonington-Port: Printed by Samuel Trumbull. 1800. pp. 19. 12mo.
CL, NYPL, PTS.

37438 FOSTER, John   1763?–1829
A Discourse delivered December 29, 1799; occasioned by the melancholy death of George Washington. . . .
Printed by Samuel Hall, no. 53, Cornhill, Boston. 1800. pp. 22. 8vo.
AAS, BA, BPL, HC, HEH, JCB, LOC, MFM, MHS, NEHGS, NYHS, NYPL, NYSL, PPL, PTS, WⁱˢHS, YC.

37439 FOTHERGILL, Samuel   1715–1772
Discourses delivered extempore at several meeting houses of the people called Quakers. . . .
Philadelphia: Printed by B. & J. Johnson, no. 147 High-Street. MDCCC. pp. xv, [5], 270. 12mo. AAS, HSP, JCB, LOC, NL, NYPL, NYSL, PʳU, RU, WC, YC.

37440 FOWLE, Robert   1765?–1847
An Oration delivered at Plymouth, in New-Hampshire . . . July 4th, 1800. . . .
Concord: Printed by Geo. Hough. 1800. pp. 15. 8vo. AAS, BA, BPL, MHS.

37441 FOX, George   1624–1691
A Journal or historical account of the life, travels, sufferings . . . of . . . George Fox. The fourth edition, corrected. In two volumes. . . .
New-York: Printed by Isaac Collins, no. 189, Pearl-Street. 1800. pp. lxxviii, 440; 464, [15]. AAS, HSP, JCB, LCP, NEHGS, NYPL, WLC, YC.

37442 FRANKLIN, Benjamin   1706–1790
Works of the late Dr. Benjamin Franklin. Consisting of his life, written by him-self, together with essays, humorous, moral and literary; chiefly in the manner of the Spectator. In two volumes. . . .
Huntingdon: Printed for the proprietor, M,DCCC. pp. 156; 119. Portrait. 12mo.
Issued with the two volumes bound in one. The portrait was engraved by J. Bannerman.
AAS, HEH, LOC, UOC, WLC, YC.

37443 THE FRANKLIN Minerva. 1799 — Jan. 18, 1800
 Chambersburg: Printed by Robert Harper for George K. Harper.
biweekly. quarto.   For 1800: RU, LOC.

37444 THE FRANKLIN Repository. 1796–1931
 Chambersburg: Published by George Kenton Harper. fol. weekly.
               For 1800: [LOC].

37445 FRASER, D[onald], *"teacher in New York"*
 An essay on the origin, antiquity. &c. of the Scots and Irish nations, with an impartial sketch of the character of most of the nations of Europe. To which is added, An Oration, lately delivered before the Caledonian Society, in this city. . . .
  New York: Printed by Furman and Loudon. . . 1800 (Copy right secured.) pp. 32.
8vo.   BPL

37446 —— The Mental flower-garden or instructive and entertaining companion for the fair sex. . . .
  Danbury: Printed by Douglas & Nichols. M,DCCC. pp. 208, [4], plate. 16mo.
 The last two leaves are occupied by an index. The plate is by Scoles.
        AAS, B^rU, CHS, HEH, NYHS, NYPL, PL.

37447 THE FRATERNAL Tribute. . . .
 See Harris, Thaddeus Mason.

37448 FRAZER, William Clark
 A Funeral oration. . . . In memory of . . . George Washington . . . delivered at Lancaster, on the 22nd of February last, to Lodge no. 43. . . .
  Wilmington: Printed at the Franklin Press, by James Wilson. 1800. pp. 15.
 8vo.
 The title given is from caption and text.   HEH.

37449 FREE and Accepted Masons. Concordia Lodge, no. 67.
 Rules and Regulations for the government of Concordia Lodge, no. 67.
  Philadelphia: Printed by R. Aitken. . . 1800. pp. 8. 12mo.   PFM.

37450 FREE and Accepted Masons. Grand Lodge of Connecticut.
 Proceedings of the Grand Lodge of Connecticut; holden at . . . New Haven . . . the 15th day of October, anno lucis, five thousand eight hundred. . . .
  [New Haven?] pp. 2. fol.   NYFM.

37451 FREE and Accepted Masons. Grand Lodge of Maryland.
 Constitution and rules for the Grand Lodge of the Free and Accepted Masons. Now working in Maryland.
  [Baltimore.] pp. 15. 12mo.
 Caption title; no imprint.   PFM.

37452 —— Extract of proceedings of the Grand Lodge of Free and Accepted Masons, of the State of Maryland. . . .
  [Baltimore: Printed by Thomas Dobbin?] pp. [3]. 8vo.
 Caption title; no imprint.   M^dFM, PFM.

37453 FREE and Accepted Masons. Grand Lodge of Massachusetts.
 Order of solemnities. . . . Prayer, by the Rev. Dr. Eckley. Anniversary ode, by Rev. Brother Harris: to be sung by Dr. Fay. . . . Eulogy, by the Hon. Brother Timothy Bigelow. Masonic dirge, written by the Rev. Brother Harris . . . to be sung by Brother Bowman. . . .
  Broadside. 4to.
 Program of the exercises held Feb. 11, 1800, in honor of Washington. HEH^ph.

37454 —— Order of the grand Masonic funeral procession, Tuesday, Feb. 11, 5800.
Broadside. 4to.
Arrangements for the procession in honor of Washington. HEHph.

37455 FREE and Accepted Masons. Grand Lodge of New York.
The Grand Lodge of the State of New-York, extraordinarily assembled, June 16, 5800.
[*New York?*] pp. 11. 4to.
Caption title. PFM.

37456 FREE and Accepted Masons. Grand Lodge of North Carolina.
Proceedings of the Grand Lodge of North-Carolina, for tke year A. L. 5800, A. D. 1800.
Raleigh: Printed by Brothers Hodge & Boylan. pp. 16. 12mo. NYFM, PFM.

37457 FREE and Accepted Masons. Grand Lodge of Pennsylvania.
Order of the grand Masonic funeral procession, Tuesday, Feb. 11. (1800) Arrangement
at the Old State House. . . .
Broadside. 8vo. HSP.

37458 FREE and Accepted Masons. Grand Lodge of Virginia.
Extracts from the proceedings of the last annual meeting of the Grand Lodge of
Virginia . . . in . . . Richmond . . . the ninth day of December, A. L. 5799 — A. D.
1799.
Richmond: Printed by John Dixon . . . A. L. 5800. pp. 8. 12mo. NYFM.

37459 —— Proceedings of . . . the Grand Lodge of Virginia . . . held in the Masons' Hall, in . . .
Richmond . . . the eighth day of December . . . A. D. 1800.
Richmond: Printed by Brother John Dixon. . . . 1800. pp. 64. 12mo. AAS.

37460 FREE and Accepted Masons. Loge Francaise l'Aménité, No. 73.
Extrait des régistres de la loge française l'Aménité, no. 73, séante à Philadelphie. . . .
A Philadelphie: par Jacques Carey, 1800. pp. 8. 8vo.
Relative to the memorial service for Washington. LOC, NYPL, PFM.

37461 FREE and Accepted Masons. Union Lodge of Dorchester.
See Harris, Thaddeus Mason

37462 FREEMAN, Samuel 1743–1831
A Valuable assistant to every man: or, the American clerk's magazine. Containing . . .
forms of writings. . . . Fourth edition. . . .
*Printed at Boston, By I. Thomas and E. T. Andrews. Sold by them . . . by I. Thomas,
Worcester; by Thomas, Andrews & Penniman, Albany; and by Thomas, Andrews & Butler,
Baltimore. April, 1800.* pp. 303, [1]. 16mo. AAS, HC-L, JCB, VaU.

37463 [FREEMAN'S Journal. 1796–1800
Cincinnati: published by Edmund Freeman. weekly.]
Removed to Chillicothe early in 1800. For 1800: no copy known.

37464 FREEMAN'S Journal and Chillicothe Advertiser. 1800
[*Chillicothe, Ohio, published by Edmund Freeman.*] weekly.
Freeman moved this paper from Cincinnati to Chillicothe in April, and in October sold
to Winship & Willis who continued it as the *Scioto Gazette.* For 1800: [WRHS].

37465 FREIHEITS Vogel und Sunbury Zeitung. 1800–1802
[*Published at Sunbury, Pa., by Jacob D. Breyvogel.*] For 1800: [CorU].

37466 FRELINGHUYSEN, Frederick 1753–1804
An Oration on the Death of Gen. George Washington: delivered in the Dutch Church,
in New-Brunswick, on the 22d of February, 1800. . . .
New-Brunswick, New-Jersey: Printed by Abraham Blauvelt. 1800. pp. 23, [1].
8vo. AAS, CU, HC, HEH, LCP, LOC, NJHS, NYHS, NYPL, PPL, PrU.

37467 FRENCH, JONATHAN   1740–1809
       A SERMON, PREACHED AT THE ORDINATION OF . . . JAMES KENDALL . . . IN PLYMOUTH, JANUARY
       1, 1800. . . .
               Printed by Samuel Hall, no. 53, Cornhill, Boston. 1800.   pp. 28.   8vo.
       Affixed are "The Charge, given by the Rev. John Howland" and "The Right Hand of
       Fellowship, by the Rev. William Shaw, of Marshfield."
                       AAS, BA, BPL, CL, CU, EI, HC, HSP, LOC, MHS, NYHS, NYPL, NYSL, UOC, WLC, YC.

37468 THE FRIEND OF THE PEOPLE.   APR.–JULY, 1800
               Richmond: published by James Lyon.   fol.   fortnightly.   FOR 1800: [AAS].

37469 [THE FRIEND OF THE PEOPLE, A POLITICAL PAPER.   AUG.–NOV. 1800
               Georgetown: published by James Lyon.   fortnightly.]   NO COPY LOCATED.

37470 A FRIEND TO FAIR PLAY. . . .
               See Key, Philip Barton.

37471 FRIENDS, SOCIETY OF
       THE EPISTLE FROM THE YEARLY MEETING, HELD IN LONDON . . . 1800 . . . TO THE QUARTERLY
       AND MONTHLY MEETINGS. . . .
               [*Philadelphia.*]   pp. [4].   fol.   AAS, HEH.

37472 —— —— *N. Bedford: Re-printed by A. Shearman, jr.*   pp. [4].   8vo.   MHS.

37473 —— FROM OUR MEETING FOR SUFFERINGS, HELD AT PROVIDENCE, FOR NEW-ENGLAND, THE 13TH AND
       14TH OF 5TH MONTH, 1800. TO THE MONTHLY MEETINGS OF FRIENDS IN THE STATE OF
       MASSACHUSETTS. . . .
               [*Providence.*]   Broadside.   fol.   RIHS.

37474 —— RULES OF DISCIPLINE, AND CHRISTIAN ADVICES, OF THE YEARLY MEETING OF FRIENDS FOR THE
       STATE OF NEW-YORK AND PARTS ADJACENT. AGREED ON BY SAID MEETING, HELD IN NEW-YORK,
       IN THE FIFTH MONTH, 1800.
               New-York: Printed by Isaac Collins, no. 189, Pearl-Street. 1800.   pp. v, [3], 141.
       8vo.   AAS.

37475 —— A VINDICATION OF THE RELIGIOUS SOCIETY CALLED QUAKERS: ADDRESSED TO THE EDITORS OF THE
       AMERICAN EDITION OF MOSHEIM'S ECCLESIASTICAL HISTORY.
               Printed by S. C. Ustick, Mount-Holly. 1800.   pp. 8.   8vo.
                       AAS, HC, HEH, HSP, JCB, LOC, NYHS, NYSL.

37476 FRIENDS TO PEACE, AND TO THE CONSTITUTION. GEORGE CHAMPLIN, ESQ. OF NEWPORT. . . .
               [*Newport?*]   Broadside.   16mo.   BrU, NHS.

37477 FRISBIE, LEVI   1748–1806
       AN EULOGY ON . . . WASHINGTON. . . . DELIVERED AT IPSWICH, ON THE 7TH DAY OF JANUARY,
       1800. . . . TO WHICH IS ADDED GENERAL WASHINGTON'S . . . ADDRESS . . . DECLINING THEIR
       FUTURE SUFFRAGES FOR THE PRESIDENCY.
               Printed at Newburyport, by Edmund M. Blunt, 1800.   pp. 61.   8vo.
                       AAS, BA, BPL, CL, HC, HEH, HSP, JCB, LOC, MeHS, MHS, NL, NYHS, NYPL, NYSL, VtU, WisHS, YC.

37478 FROM OUR MEETING FOR SUFFERINGS. . . .
               See Friends, Society of

37479 FRY, JOHN   1699–1775
       SELECT POEMS. . . . TO WHICH IS NOW ADDED, THE HISTORY OF ELIJAH AND ELISHA. . . .
               Stonington port, Connecticut, printed by Samuel Trumbull. 1800.   pp. 144.   16mo.
                       AAS, CHS, JCB, HEH, NYPL, PL.

37480 FULLER, ANDREW 1754–1815
THE GOSPEL . . . CONTRASTED WITH THE IMMORALITY AND ABSURDITY OF DEISM. . . .
New-York: Printed for Cornelius Davis . . . no. 167, Water-Street, New York. 1800.
pp. 288. 8vo. AAS, BPL, HEH, WLC, YC.

37481 FUNERAL DIRGE ON THE DEATH OF GENERAL WASHINGTON, AS SUNG AT THE STONE CHAPEL.
See Boston, Massachusetts, King's Chapel.

37482 FUNERAL EULOGY AND ORATION. . . .
See New London, Connecticut, Presbyterian Church.

37483 FURLONG, LAWRENCE 1734–1806
THE AMERICAN COAST PILOT; CONTAINING THE COURSES AND DISTANCES . . . WITH THE LATITUDES
AND LONGITUDES. . . . THIRD EDITION.
Newburyport (Massachusetts) printed by Edmund M. Blunt . . . 1800. pp. 251, [5].
8vo.
There are two issues, one with the advertisement on the last page dated Sept. 18, 1800,
and the other with a different advertisement dated Nov. 26, 1800.
AAS, APS, BPL, CSL, EI, HC, HSP, JCB, LOC, NYPL, NYSL, YC.

37484 FURMAN, RICHARD 1755–1825
HUMBLE SUBMISSION . . . A SERMON, OCCASIONED BY THE DEATH OF . . . WASHINGTON. . . .
PREACHED IN THE BAPTIST CHURCH, IN CHARLESTON, SOUTH-CAROLINA, ON THE 22D OF
FEBRUARY, 1800, BEFORE THE AMERICAN REVOLUTION SOCIETY, THE STATE SOCIETY OF THE
CINCINNATI, AND A NUMEROUS ASSEMBLAGE. . . .
Charleston: Printed by W. P. Young, Franklin's Head, no. 43, Broad Street. M.DCCC.
pp. [4], 28. 8vo. AAS, BA, BM, BPL, HC, HEH, JCB, LCP, LOC, NYHS, NYPL.

37485 GALLATIN, [ABRAHAM] ALBERT [ALPHONSE] 1761–1849
VIEWS OF THE PUBLIC DEBT, RECEIPTS & EXPENDITURES OF THE UNITED STATES. . . .
New-York: Printed by M. L. & W. A. Davis. 1800. pp. 61, [5]. 8vo.
AAS, BA, BPL, CU, HC, HEH, JCB, LOC, NL, NYHS, NYPL, NYSL, PL, UOP, WL, YC.

37486 THE GAMESTER. . . .
See Cheap repository. Number 27.

37487 GANO, STEPHEN 1762–1828
A SERMON ON THE DEATH OF GENERAL GEORGE WASHINGTON; DELIVERED . . . JANUARY 5, 1800,
BEFORE THE BAPTIST SOCIETY IN PROVIDENCE. . . .
Providence: Printed by John Carter, jun. at the new Printing-Office, Market-Street.
1800. pp. 20. 8vo. AAS, HEH, JCB, LOC, MFM, NYHS, NYPL, NYSL, RIHS.

37488 —— UNDISSEMBLED LOVE . . . DELIVERED BEFORE THE GRAND LODGE OF . . . MASONS . . . OF RHODE-
ISLAND, ON THE 24TH OF JUNE, 1800, IN THE BAPTIST MEETING-HOUSE IN PROVIDENCE. . . .
Providence: Printed by Samuel J. Williams. 1800. pp. 23. 8vo.
AAS, HEH, JCB, MFM, NYHS, RIHS, YC.

37489 GARDENIER, BARENT –1822
AN ADDRESS, DELIVERED BEFORE THE SOCIETY OF FREE AND ACCEPTED MASONS, IN THE TOWN OF
KINGSTON, ON THE 27TH DECEMBER MDCCC. . . .
Kingston: (Ulster County) Printed by Samuel S. Freer. 1800. pp. 28. 8vo. NYPL.

37490 —— AN ORATION, DELIVERED BEFORE THE MEMBERS OF HUDSON LODGE, ON THE ANNIVERSARY OF ST. JOHN
THE EVANGELIST, AND IN COMMEMORATION OF THE DEATH OF GEORGE WASHINGTON. DECEMBER
XXVII, M,DCC,XCIX. . . .
Kingston: Printed by S. S. Freer. pp. 18, [5]. 12mo. NYSL.

37491 —— AN ORATION, DELIVERED BEFORE THE . . . LIVINGSTON LODGE, ON THE ANNIVERSARY OF ST. JOHN
. . . DECEMBER 27, MDCCC. . . .
Kingston [N. Y.]: Printed by S. S. Freer. pp. 21, [4]. 12mo.
The last four pages contain a "Masonic ode, written by . . . Robert Treat Paine" and a
"Masonic song . . . written by the late Robert Burns." AAS.

37492   GARDINER, John S. J.   1765–1830
     Reminiscence of Washington. Hymn. Written by Rev. John S. Gardiner . . . and sung in the Old South Church January 9, 1800. . . .
       [*Boston.*]   Broadside.   4to.   MHS.

37493   GAY, EBENEZER   1766–1837
     An Oration, pronounced at Suffield, on . . . the 22'd of Feb. A. D. 1800. . . . To testify . . . grief, for the death of . . . Washington. . . .
       Suffield, Printed by Edward Gray, 1800.   pp. 16.   8vo.
                      AAS, BPL, CHS, HEH, NYHS, UTS.

37494   GAZETTE of the United States, & Philadelphia Daily Advertiser.   1790–1804
       Printed by J. W. Fenno.   fol.   daily.
       With the issue of May 28, Caleb P. Wayne bought the paper and dropped "Philadelphia" from the title.   For 1800: AAS, HSP, LCP, [LOC], MᵈHS, PPL.

37495   [GEDICHTE, dem andenken des General Waschingtons des Grossen, gewidmet, die bey gelegenheit des treuer-aufzugs in Hagerstaun, den 24 sten Januar, 1800. . . .
       [*Hagerstaun, Gedruckt bey Joh. Gruber.*]   1800.   Broadside.   4to.
       Three hymns.]   MINICK 637.

37496   GEISTLICHES blumen-gartein. . . .
       See Tersteegen, Gerhard

37497   DER GEMEINÜZIGE Americanische Kalender auf das Jahr Christi 1801. . . . Zum erstenmal herausgegeben.
       Reading, gedruckt und zu haben bey Jacob Schneider. . . .   pp. [38].   sq. 8vo.
                      AAS.

37498   [THE GENIUS of Liberty.   1797–1800
       Fredericksburg (Va.) printed . . . by Mercer & Field.   fol.   weekly.]
             For 1800: NO COPY KNOWN.

37499   THE GENIUS of Liberty.   1798–1811
       Morris-Town: Printed and published by Jacob Mann. . . .   Weekly.   fol.
             For 1800: NYPL.

37500   —— A Memorial of the respect paid to the man first in war, first in peace, and first in the affections of the American people.
       [*Morristown: Printed by Jacob Mann.*]   Broadside.   fol.
       Published as an extraordinary sheet of the *Genius of Liberty.*   NYPL.

37501   GENTZ, [Friedrich von]   1764–1832
       The Origin and principles of the American Revolution, compared with the origin and princples of the French Revolution. . . .
       Philadelphia: Published by Asbury Dickins, opposite Christ-Church. H. Maxwell, printer, Columbia-House. 1800.   pp. 73.   8vo.
       Translated by John Quincy Adams.
         AAS, BA, HEH, HSP, JCB, LCP, LOC, NL, NYPL, PʳU, WⁱˢHS, WLC, YC.

37502   THE GEORGETOWN Gazette.   1798–1817
       Georgetown, (S. C.) printed . . . by John Burd. . . .   fol.   semi-weekly.
             For 1800: CLS.

37503   GEORGIA. State.
       Acts of the General Assembly of the State of Georgia: Passed at Louisville, in November and December, 1799.
       Augusta: Printed by John E. Smith, printer to the State. MDCCC.   pp. 81, [3].
       8vo.   DᵉRGL, LOC.

37504 —— An Address and remonstrance of the legislature of the State of Georgia.
[*Savannah?*] pp. 18. 8vo.
Dated Nov. 29, 1800, advocating Georgia's right to the Mississippi Territory. DᵉRGL, LOC.

37505 —— A Digest of the Laws of the State of Georgia . . . the State constitutions . . . and . . .
original charters and documents. . . . By Robert & George Watkins.
Philadelphia: Printed by R. Aitken, no. 22, Market Street. 1800. pp. iv, [2], 837,
[29]. 4to.
The last leaves contain a list of subscribers and two pages of errata.
AAS, CSL, DᵉRGL, HEH, HSP, JCB, LOC, MSL, NYHS, NYPL.

37506 —— [Georgia. By his excellency James Jackson, Governor. . . . A Proclamation. Whereas I
have received substantial information, that William A. Bowles . . . has endeavored
to seduce from their allegiance. . . . Given . . . at the State House in Louisville,
this eighth day of July . . . one thousand eight hundred. . . .
Broadside.] EVANS.

37507 —— Journal of the House of Representatives of the State of Georgia.
[*Augusta: Printed by John E. Smith.*] pp. 55. 4to.
Caption title; imprint on p. 55. This is the Journal for the session of November and
December, 1799. GSL.

37508 —— Journal of the Senate of the State of Georgia.
[*Augusta: Printed by John E. Smith.*] pp. 37. 4to.
Caption title; imprint on p. 37. This is the Journal for the sessions of November and
December. GSL.

37509 GEORGIA Gazette. 1788–1802
Savannah: Printed by N. Johnston and Co. fol. weekly. For 1800: AAS, GHS.

37510 GEORGIA. The Augusta Chronicle and Gazette of the State. 1789–
Augusta: Printed by John E. Smith, printer to the State. fol. weekly.
For 1800: GHS.

37511 EIN GESPRÄCH, betreffend des Sabbaths, zwischen einem Täufer . . . und Kirchen-
mann. . . . Aus dem Englischen übersetzt.
Ephrata: Gedruckt ben J. Baumann. 1800. pp. 32. 24mo. AAS, PSL.

37512 GETCHELL, Dennis 1724–1791
A Testimony concerning acceptable worship to Almighty God. By Dennis Getchell, late
of Vassalborough. . . .
New-Bedford: Printed by Abraham Shearman, jun. 1800. pp. 12. 12mo.
AAS, HC, JCB.

37513 GIFFORD, William 1756–1826
The Baviad and Maeviad, by William Gifford, esquire. . . . A new edition revised.
New-York: Printed by G. and R. Waite, for J. W. Fenno. 1800. pp. xi, vi, xiv,
[xiii]–xx, 145. 12mo.
This volume is also found with the following in a 2 volume in 1 edition of the *Works of
William Gifford, Esquire.* Some copies have half-titles as volume 1 or 2 of the *Works.*
The front matter varies. BA, NYSL, WC, YC.

37514 [——] Epistle to Peter Pindar. By the author of the Baviad. . . . To which is added, the trial
of Mr. Faulder, the bookseller, for publishing a libel on Anthony Pasquin . . . and
a preface to the sixth London edition of the work.
New York: Printed by G. and R. Waite, for J. W. Fenno. 1800. pp. vi, xiv, 128, xi.
2 plates. BA, HC, NYSL, YC.

37515 —— Works of William Gifford, esquire. . . .
See under *The Baviad.*

37516   GILLET, ELIPHALET   1768–1848
        AN ORATION, DELIVERED JANUARY 8, 1800, BEFORE THE CITIZENS OF HALLOWELL . . . IN COM-
        MEMORATION OF THE . . . DEATH OF . . . WASHINGTON. . . .
              Hallowell (District of Maine). Printed by Peter Edes. 1800.   pp. 19.   8vo.
                                                       BPL, HEH, LOC, NYHS, NYPL, NYSL.

37517   THE GILMANTON GAZETTE: AND FARMERS' WEEKLY MAGAZINE.   1800
              Printed and published on Saturdays, by [Dudley] Leavitt & Clough, near the academy,
        Gilmanton, Newhampshire.   weekly.   fol.   FOR 1800: [LOC], [NYHS].

37518   GILMANTON RURAL MUSEUM.   1799–1800
              Gilmanton, New-Hampshire. Printed and published by Elijah Russell.   weekly.
        fol.   FOR 1800: [NHHS].

37519   GILPIN, JOHNNY, *pseud.*
        THE TODDY-MILL, OR THE HUMOROUS ADVENTURES OF DICK BULLY. A CARICATURE: BY JOHNNY
        GILPIN. . . .
              [Baltimore?] September 1, 1800.   pp. 8.   8vo.   BrU.

37520   GLEASON, BENJAMIN   1777–1847
        AN ORATION, PRONOUNCED AT THE BAPTIST MEETING-HOUSE IN WRENTHAM, FEBRUARY 22,
        1800. . . . IN MEMORY OF GEN. GEORGE WASHINGTON. . . .
              Printed at Wrentham, Massachusetts, by Nathaniel and Benjamin Heaton. 1800.
        pp. 31, [1].   8vo.
        The last leaf contains "An occasional ode, sung at the Baptist meeting-house, in
        Wrentham, February 22, 1800."
                                  AAS, BA, BM, BPL, HC, HEH, MFM, MSL, NYHS, NYPL, PPL, WLC.

37521   GLENDY, JOHN.   1755–1832
        AN ORATION, ON THE DEATH OF . . . WASHINGTON, COMPOSED AT THE SPECIAL REQUEST OF THE
        COMMANDANT . . . OF THE CANTONMENT IN THIS VICINITY, AND DELIVERED AT STAUNTON, ON
        THE TWENTY SECOND DAY OF FEBRUARY LAST PAST, 1800. . . .
              Staunton [Va.]: Printed by John Wise. . . . 1800.   pp. 27.   sm. 4to.
                                                       HEH, JCB, LOC, NYPL, VaU.

37522   GLEZEN, LEVI   1774?–1842
        AN ORATION DELIVERED AT LENOX, ON THE TWENTY-SECOND OF FEBRUARY, 1800. . . . [ON THE
        DEATH OF WASHINGTON.]
              Stockbridge. Printed at the office of H. Jones & Co. by H. Willard, 1800.   pp. 20.
        8vo.   HEH, LOC, WC.

37523   GLORIOUS NEWS! A BRIEF ACCOUNT OF THE LATE REVIVALS OF RELIGION IN A NUMBER OF TOWNS IN
        THE NEW-ENGLAND STATES, AND ALSO IN NOVA-SCOTIA, EXTRACTED CHIEFLY FROM LETTERS
        WRITTEN BY SEVERAL GENTLEMEN. . . .
              [Mount Holly] Printed by S. C. Ustick, and sold at no. 79, North Third Street, Phila-
        delphia, Jan. 1800.   pp. 28.   16mo.   NYPL.

37524   ——— ——— *New-York: Printed for L. Seaver and J. Sutton. 1800.*   pp. 28.   12mo.   AAS.

37525   GLOUCESTER. NEW JERSEY.
        AT A MEETING OF THE INHABITANTS OF THE TOWNSHIP OF GLOUCESTER, ON MONDAY THE 4TH DAY
        OF AUGUST, AT THE HOUSE OF MRS. MARY MCCONKEY, IN BLACKWOOD TOWN. . . . DATED,
        AUGUST 6TH, 1800. . . .
              Broadside.   fol.   HSP.

37526   GLOUCESTER COUNTY, STATE OF NEW JERSEY. AT A MEETING OF THE REPUBLICAN COMMITTEE, HELD
        AT THE HOUSE OF ISAAC SMALLWOOD, IN THE TOWNSHIP OF NEWTON . . . THE 6TH OF
        SEPTEMBER, 1800. . . .
              [Philadelphia or Trenton.]   pp. 20.   12mo.
        No titlepage; the title is taken from the caption and text.   HSP, LOC.

37527 GLOVER, Joseph   1770–
    An Attempt to prove that digestion, in man, depends on the united causes of solution and fermentation. By Joseph Glover, of Charleston, South-Carolina. . . .
        Philadelphia: Printed by Way & Groff, no. 48, North Third-street. 1800.   pp. 65.
8vo.
    "An inaugural experimental inquiry, for the degree of doctor of medicine . . . University of Pennsylvania."   AAS, AML, LOC, NYAM, NYPL, RU, UOP, YC.

37528 GOLD, Thomas Ruggles   1764–1827
    To the people of the County of Oneida. . . . Whitestown, December 13, 1800.
        [Utica: Printed by William M'Lean, 1800.]   pp. 28.   4to.
    Caption title. Signed and dated on p. 26. This tract was a reply to that of Jonas Platt, *q. v.*
         BPL, NYHS, NYSL, WᶦˢHS.

37529 GOLDSBOROUGH, Charles W[ashington]   1779–1843
    An Original and correct list of the United States Navy containing a list of the ships in commission. . . . And a digest of the principal laws relating to the Navy. . . .
        City of Washington, November, 1800.   pp. 32.   16mo.
    There is a reprint of about 1873 which is frequently offered as an original. LOC, NYHS, NYPL.

37530 GOLDSMITH, [Oliver]   1728–1774
    Goldsmith's poems. . . . To which is added, The history of Tom Dreadnought.
        Philadelphia: Printed by H. Maxwell, for Mathew Carey, no. 118, Market-Street.
    1800.   pp. 60.   12mo.   AAS, EI, LOC, NYPL.

37531 —— The Grecian history. . . . Two volumes in one. A new edition, improved and corrected.
        Washington [Pa.]: Printed for Mathew Carey, no. 118, Market-Street, Philadelphia.
    Sept. 24, 1800.   pp. 208, 150.   12mo.
    The second volume has its own titlepage and signature sequence. AAS, BPL, HEH, NL, NYPL, YC.

37532 THE GOOD old Virginia Almanack, for the year of our Lord, 1801. . . . The twenty-fifth of American independence. . . .
        Richmond: Printed by Thos. Nicholson, first house below the Capitol.   pp. [48].
24mo.   AAS, LOC.

37533 GOODWIN, Hezekiah   1740–1767
    A Remarkable vision: shewing the sudden . . . appearance . . . of the departed spirit of Mr. Yeamens . . . 2d. ed. . . .
        Amherst, New Hampshire; Printed and sold by Nathaniel Coverly & Son.   pp. 15,
[5].   12mo.   DC, YC.

37534 —— A Vision; showing the sudden . . . appearance . . . of the departed spirit of Mr. Yeamens, late student at Yale College, to, and with Mr. H. Goodwin, his friend and classmate.
        Brattleboro, Vt. 1800.   pp. 11.   12mo.   NYSL.

37535 GOUGH, John   1721–1791
    Practical arithmetick. . . . By John Gough, author of the Practical English Grammar. Carefully revised by Thomas Telfair. . . . With an appendix of algebra, by the late W. Atkinson, of Belfast.
        Dublin, printed: Wilmington: Reprinted, and sold, by Peter Brynberg. 1800.
pp. 348.   12mo.   AAS, NCU.

37536 GOUGH, John Parker   –1829
    An Essay on cantharides . . . their use in diseases. With some remarks relative to the time when they should be employed. By John Parker Gough of Charleston, South-Carolina. . . .
        Philadelphia: Printed by Way & Groff, no. 48, North Third-street. 1800.   pp. 43.
8vo.
    "An inaugural thesis for the degree of doctor of medicine . . . University of Pennsylvania."
        AAS, AML, BM, JCB, LCP, LOC, NYAM, NYPL, RU, UOP, YC.

37537 A GRAMMAR OF THE GREEK LANGUAGE. . . .
    See Camden, William

37538 GREEN, AARON   1764?–1853
    A DISCOURSE, DELIVERED AT MALDEN, JANUARY 8, 1800. . . . PUBLICLY TO RESPECT THE MEMORY
    OF . . . WASHINGTON. . . .
        Medford: Printed by Nathaniel Coverly, near the Bridge.   pp. 23.   8vo.
                                AAS, AHTS, BA, HC, HEH, JCB, LOC, MFM, NYHS, NYPL.

37539 THE GREEN MOUNTAIN PATRIOT.   1798–1810
        Printed at Peacham, Vermont, by Farley & Goss. . . .   fol.   weekly.
                                FOR 1800: AAS, WOODSTOCK PUB. LIB.

37540 GREEN RIVER ASSOCIATION.
    MINUTES OF THE GREEN-RIVER ASSOCIATION OF BAPTISTS. HELD AT TRAMMEL'S CREEK MEETING
    HOUSE, IN GREEN COUNTY . . . NOVEMBER 1ST, 1800. . . .
        [Colophon:] Lexington — Printed by James H. Stewart.   pp. 4.   12mo.
                                MR. HENRY S. ROBINSON.

37541 GREENE, BENJAMIN   1764–1837
    AN EULOGY ON GEORGE WASHINGTON. . . . PRONOUNCED AT BERWICK, JANUARY 4, 1800. . . .
        Portsmouth, New-Hampshire, Printed by J. Melcher. 1800.   pp. 16.   8vo.
                                AAS, HC, HEH, LOC, NYHS, NYPL.

37542 GREENFIELD GAZETTE. A REGISTER OF GENUINE FEDERALISM.   1792–1811
        *Printed and published on Saturdays, by Thomas Dickman, at his printing office in
    Greenfield, Massachusetts.*   fol.   weekly.   FOR 1800: GREENFIELD PUB. LIB.

37543 GREENLEAF'S NEW-YORK, CONNECTICUT, & NEW-JERSEY ALMANACK, FOR THE YEAR OF OUR
    LORD 1801. . . .
        Brooklyn: Printed and sold wholesale and retail by T. Kirk.   pp. [36].   12mo.
    There is a woodcut portrait and an ode to Washington on the last leaf. This almanac is
    sometimes listed under the name of Abraham Shoemaker, of New York, who is said to
    have made the astronomical calculations.   AAS, HEH, LOC, NYHS, NYPL, RU, WᴵˢHS.

37544 GREENLEAF'S NEW YORK JOURNAL, & PATRIOTIC REGISTER.   1794–MAR. 8, 1800
        *New-York — printed and published (on Wednesdays and Saturdays) by Ann Green-
    leaf.* . . .   fol.   semi-weekly.
    This paper was bought out by David Denniston who substituted the *Republican Watch-
    Tower* in its stead.   FOR 1800: NYHS, YC.

37545 GREEN'S ALMANACK AND REGISTER, FOR THE STATE OF CONNECTICUT; FOR THE YEAR OF OUR LORD,
    1801. . . .
        New-London: Printed and sold by Samuel Green.   pp. 153, [3], 22, tables.
                                AAS, CHS, LOC, NYPL, VᵃU.

37546 GREEN'S IMPARTIAL OBSERVER.   MAY 5, 1800–1801
        Natchez: — printed by J[ames] Green.   fol.   weekly.   FOR 1800: UOC.

37547 GREENWOOD, ANDREW   1776–1816
    AN ORATION, COMPOSED AT THE REQUEST OF THE SELECT-MEN, AND DELIVERED BEFORE THE
    INHABITANTS OF THE TOWN OF BATH, ON SATURDAY, 22D FEBRUARY, 1800. . . .
        Hallowell (District of Maine) Printed by Peter Edes. 1800.   pp. 16.   12mo.
                                HEH, LOC, NHHS.

37548 GRIFFITH, WILLIAM   1766–1826
    AN ORATION, DELIVERED TO THE CITIZENS OF BURLINGTON, ON THE 22D OF FEBRUARY, 1800, IN
    COMMEMORATION OF . . . WASHINGTON. . . . TO WHICH IS ADDED, A PRAYER ON THE SAME
    OCCASION. BY CHARLES H. WHARTON. . . .
        Trenton: Printed by G. Craft. MDCCC.   pp. 25.   8vo.
    There are copies which have the words "(At the request of the Committee)" inserted
    between "added" and "a prayer."   AAS, BA, HEH, LOC, NYHS, NYPL, PPL, PʳU, RIHS, YC.

37549 GRISWOLD, Stanley   1763–1815
A Funeral eulogium, pronounced at New-Milford, on the twenty-second of February, 1800 . . . testifying respect to the memory of George Washington. . . .
Printed at Litchfield, by T. Collier.   pp. 24.   8vo.
AAS, BA, Bʳʊ, CHS, HEH, JCB, LOC, MFM, MHS, NL, NYHS, NYPL, NYSL.

37550 —— Truth its own test. . . . A discourse delivered at New-Milford, October 12th, 1800. . . .
Bridgeport: Printed by Lazarus Beach. 1800.   pp. 32.   8vo.
There is an errata slip pasted on the reverse of the titlepage.
AAS, CHS, CL, CSL, HEH, JCB, LCP, LOC, NYHS, NYPL, RIHS, YC.

37551 GROTON Union Conference.
Minutes of the Groton Union Conference held at the meeting-house in Groton occupied by the church of Christ under the pastoral care of Eld. Silas Burrows. June 18 and 19, 1800.
Norwich: Printed by John Sterry, M,DCCC.   pp. 8.   8vo.
Westerly Public Library.

37552 THE GROUND and nature of Christian redemption. . . .
Philadelphia: Edited by John Ormrod, no. 41 Chestnut-Street. 1800.   pp. 42.   12mo.
There was an earlier edition, Philadelphia, 1768.   HSP, LCP, LOC.

37553 GROVE, Henry   1684–1738
A Discourse concerning the nature and design of the Lord's Supper. . . . The second American edition.
Dedham: Printed by Herman Mann. 1800.   pp. 168.   16mo.
AAS, BA, BPL, CL, HC, HEH, LOC, NYPL, WC, YC.

37554 [GUARDIAN of Freedom.   1798–1805
Frankfort (Kentucky): printed by John Bradford & Son.   fol.   weekly.]
For 1800: no copies located.

37555 THE GUARDIAN of Liberty.   Oct. 3, 1800–1801
Newport (Rhode-Island) published weekly, by Oliver Farnsworth. . . .   fol.
For 1800: AAS, NHS.

37556 THE GUARDIAN of Liberty: & Huntingdon Chronicle.   1799–1800
Huntingdon, Pennsylvania. Published by John R. Parrington.   fol.   weekly.
For 1800: [AAS].

37557 GUARDIAN; or, New-Brunswick Advertiser.   1792–1816
New-Brunswick, New-Jersey; printed by Abraham Blauvelt, in Albany-Street.
weekly.   fol.   For 1800: [HC], [LOC].

37558 GUIREY, William
A Funeral sermon on the death of . . . Washington. . . . Delivered . . . before the Methodist Episcopal Church at Lynn, January 7, 1800. . . .
Salem: Printed by Joshua Cushing, for the proprietors. 1800.   pp. 22.   8vo.
AAS, BPL, EI, HEH, JCB, MFM, MHS, NYHS, NYPL, PFM, PPL, WⁱˢHS, WLC.

37559 GUNNING, Bedford
See Bedford, Gunning.

37560 GURLEY, John Ward
An Address on the origin and principles of Masonry. Before St. John's Lodge, 30th Dec. 5800.
Boston, Russell & Cutler, 1800.   pp. 22.   8vo.   BA, BPL, HC, MFM, NYHS.

37561 GWINETT, Ambrose
The Life and adventures of Ambrose Gwinett . . . who for a murder which he never
committed, was tried, condemned, executed, and hung. . . .
Boston: Printed by J. White. 1800. pp. 24. 8vo.
**In a copy at the British Museum the authorship is attributed to Isaac Bickerstaffe
(c.1735–c.1812), the Irish dramatist.** AAS, BA, BPL, EI, NEHGS, NYHS.

37562 HALE, David   1765–1837
An Oration, pronounced before the honorable justices of the Supreme Judicial Court . . .
and the citizens of Portland . . . July 4th. 1800. . . .
From the press of E. A. Jenks, Portland. July, 1800. pp. 28, [1]. 8vo.
BPL, HC, NYHS, NYSL.

37563 HALL, Joseph   1761–1848
An Oration, pronounced July 4, 1800, at the request of the inhabitants of the town of
Boston. . . .
Boston. From the printing-office of Manning & Loring, Spring-Lane. pp. 24. 8vo.
AAS, BʳU, HC, HEH, HSP, LOC, MHS, MSL, NL, NYHS, NYPL, UOC, YC.

37564 HALL, Robert   1764–1831
Modern infidelity considered with respect to its influence on society: in a sermon,
preached at the Baptist meeting, Cambridge. . . .
The third edition. Philadelphia: Printed by John Bioren — for T. Dobson. . . . 1800.
pp. 63. 12mo. APS, BʳU, PPL.

37565 HALSEY, William   1765?–1843
An Oration, delivered the twenty-second of February, MDCCC. Before the brethren
and a select audience, in the hall of St. John's lodge, No. 2, Newark, New-Jersey. . . .
Newark, Printed by Jacob Halsey, 1800. pp. 23. 8vo. LOC, NYHS, NYPL, NYSOC.

37566 HAMILTON, Alexander   1757–1804
Letter from Alexander Hamilton, concerning the public conduct and character of John
Adams. . . .
New-York: Printed for John Lang, by George F. Hopkins. 1800. (Copy-right secured.)
pp. 54. 8vo. AAS, BPL, CSL, CU, HEH, JCB, LCP, LOC, NYHS, NYPL, NYSL, RU, UOC, VᵃU, YC.

37567 —— —— The second edition.
New-York: Printed for John Lang, by John Furman. 1800. pp. 54. 8vo.
AAS, APS, BA, BPL, CL, HC, HEH, HSP, JCB, LCP, LOC, MHS, NYPL, WL, YC.

37568 —— —— The third edition.
New-York: Printed for John Lang, by Furman & Loudon. 1800. pp. 54. 8vo.
The NYPL has an issue of this edition with a different setting of the titlepage and without
the copyright notice. AAS, BA, HC, JCB, LOC, MᵈHS, MHS, NYPL, NYSL, VᵃU, WLC, YC.

37569 —— —— The fourth edition.
New-York: Printed for John Lang, by Furman & Loudon. 1800. pp. 54. 8vo.
AAS, AHTS, JCB, LOC, NYHS, NYPL, YC.

37570 —— —— —— *New-York: Printed for John Lang, by George F. Hopkins. 1800. Philadelphia: Re-
printed [by William Duane] pro bono publico.* pp. 54. 8vo.
AAS, BM, HC, HEH, HSP, JCB, LOC, MHS, NL, NYPL, NYSL, PL, RU, WⁱˢHS, WLC, YC.

37571 —— Observations on certain documents . . . in which the charge of speculation against
Alexander Hamilton . . . is fully refuted. . . .
Philadelphia: Printed [by William Duane] pro bono publico. 1800. pp. 37, [1],
lviii. 8vo.
AAS, BA, HC, HEH, HSP, LOC, MᵈHS, MHS, MSL, NEHGS, NYPL, NYSL, UOC, UTS, WL, YC.

37572 —— —— —— [*Philadelphia: Reprinted pro bono publico.* pp. 37, lviii. 8vo.] SABIN 29970.

37573 —— —— [*New York: Printed for John Lang, by George F. Hopkins. 1800.* pp. 37, lviii. 8vo.] SABIN 29970.

37574 HAMILTON, JOSEPH 1739?–1805
A CERTAIN BAR AGAINST THE APPROACH OF THE YELLOW FEVER, WRITTEN FOR THE GOOD OF THE PUBLIC. . . .
Hudson: Printed by A. Stoddard, M,DCCC. pp. 22. 8vo. LOC, NYAM.

37575 HAMPSHIRE GAZETTE. 1786–1918
Printed at Northampton (Massachusetts,) by William Butler. fol. weekly.
FOR 1800: FLN.

37576 HARDIE, JAMES 1750?–1832
AN IMPARTIAL ACCOUNT OF THE TRIAL OF MR. LEVI WEEKS FOR THE SUPPOSED MURDER OF MISS JULIANNA ELMORE SANDS, AT . . . NEW-YORK, MARCH 31, 1800. . . .
New York, M. M'Farlane, 1800. pp. vii, 34. 8vo. LOC.

37577 HARGROVE, JOHN
A SERMON . . . AT THE OPENING OF THE NEW JERUSALEM TEMPLE, IN THE CITY OF BALTIMORE. ON SUNDAY, THE 5TH OF JANUARY, 1800. . . .
Baltimore: Printed for the acting committee, of the new church. pp. 22. 8vo.
LOC, M^dHS.

37578 HARPER, J. A.
THE UNITED STATES REPOSITORY, AND NEW-HAMPSHIRE REGISTER, WITH AN ALMANACK PREFIXED; FOR THE YEAR 1801. . . .
Portsmouth: Printed by W'm Treadwell & Co. Sold by . . . J. Melcher & C. Peirce, Portsmouth; J. True, Hampstead; Moses Davis & J. Baldwin, Hanover; John Mann, jr., Oxford; S. Bagg, jr., Dover; and by E. & S. Larkin, Boston. pp. [2], 12, [17]–110, [2]. 24mo. AAS, BM, NHHS, NYHS.

37579 HARPER, ROBERT GOODLOE 1765–1825
SPEECH OF THE HON. ROBERT G. HARPER, IN THE HOUSE OF REPRESENTATIVES, OF THE UNITED STATES ON THE REDUCTION OF THE ARMY.
Philadelphia: Printed at the office of "The True American." 1800. pp. 44. 12mo.
AAS, APS, BA, BM, HC, HSP, JCB, LOC, MHS, NYHS, NYPL, P^rU.

37580 HARPER'S ALMANAC, FOR THE YEAR OF OUR LORD, 1801. CONTAINING, BESIDES THE USUAL ASTRONOMICAL CALCULATIONS, A LIST OF STAMP DUTIES. . . .
Chambersburg [Pa.] Printed by R. & G. K. Harper. . . . pp. 22+. 12mo. HEH.

37581 HARRIS, THADDEUS MASON 1768–1842
A DISCOURSE, DELIVERED AT DORCHESTER, DEC. 29, 1799. . . . AFTER HEARING THE DISTRESSING INTELLEGENCE OF THE DEATH OF . . . WASHINGTON. . . .
Charlestown: Printed by Samuel Etheridge. M,DCCC. pp. 16. 8vo.
Issued also in Dorchester, Massachusetts, *Public expressions of grief.*
AAS, BA, BPL, GU, HC, HEH, HSP, JCB, LOC, MHS, NHHS, NYHS, NYPL, NYSL, PFM, PL, PPL, RU, YC.

37582 [——] THE FRATERNAL TRIBUTE . . . TO THE MASONIC CHARACTER OF WASHINGTON, IN THE UNION LODGE, IN DORCHESTER, JANUARY 7TH, A. L. 5800.
Charlestown: Printed by Samuel Etheridge. M,DCCC. pp. 13, [2]. 8vo.
The final pages contain "The Extemporaneous dirge which was sung on the occasion" and the "Masonic dirge, composed by the Rev. T. M. Harris."
AAS, BPL, B^rU, CL, HC, HEH, JCB, LOC, MHS, MSL, NYHS, NYPL, PFM, PL, RU, YC.

37583 —— *See* Sturm, Christoph Christian.

37584 DIE HARRISBURG MORGENRÖTHE ZEITUNG.
See Unpartheyische Harrisburg Morgenröthe Zeitung.

37585 HARRISON, [RALPH]   1748–1810
    HARRISON'S RUDIMENTS OF ENGLISH GRAMMAR; A NEW EDITION, WITH CORRECTIONS AND ADDITIONS,
    BY A TEACHER OF PHILADELPHIA. . . .
        Philadelphia: Printed by Sweeny & Plowman, for John Bioren. 1800. . .   pp. 107.
    24mo.   CU, UOM¹.

37586 HARRISON, WILLIAM HENRY   1773–1841
    (CIRCULAR) PHILADELPHIA, 14TH MAY, 1800 DEAR SIR, THE ARDENT DESIRE I FEEL TO VISIT AGAIN
    MY NATIVE STATE. . . . YOUR VERY HUMBLE SERVANT, WILLIAM HENRY HARRISON.
        [*Philadelphia.*] pp. [2]. 8vo.   OH&PS

37587 HART, LEVI   1738–1808
    RELIGIOUS IMPROVEMENT. . . . A DISCOURSE ADDRESSED TO . . . THE NORTH SOCIETY IN PRESTON
    . . . DEC. 29, 1799, OCCASIONED BY THE DEATH OF . . . WASHINGTON. . . .
        Norwich: Printed by Thomas Hubbard. 1800.   pp. 26. 8vo.
        AAS, BPL, CHS, HEH, JCB, LCP, LOC, MFM, NYPL, WLC.

37588 HARTFORD AND NEW HAVEN TURNPIKE COMPANY.
    WE THE SUBSCRIBERS BEING REQUESTED. . . .
        [*Hartford: Hudson and Goodwin, 1800.*] pp. 5. 8vo.
    A report of a committee regarding alterations, dated November 6, 1800.   HC, YC.

37589 HARVARD COLLEGE
    CATALOGUS EORUM QUI IN UNIVERSITATE HARVARDIANA, CANTABRIGIAE . . . AB ANNO MDCXLII,
    AD ANNUM MDCCC, ALICUJUS GRADUS LAUREA DONATI SUNT. . . .
        Bostoniae: Typus Johannis et Thomae Fleet, MDCCC. . . .   pp. 43. 8vo.
        AAS, HC, JCB, LOC, MᶜHS, MHS, NYPL, NYSL, YC.

37590 —— EXTRACTS FROM THE LAWS OF HARVARD COLLEGE, FOR THE INFORMATION OF THE PARENTS AND
    GUARDIANS OF THE STUDENTS. . . .
        [*Cambridge?*]   pp. [4]. 8vo.
    Caption title. This was an "Admittatur," a leaflet serving both as a circular of information
    and a certificate of admission to be filled out by the president.   AAS, HC.

37591 —— THE FOLLOWING PAGES CONTAIN AMENDMENTS AND ADDITIONS TO THE SEVERAL LAWS OF HARVARD
    COLLEGE; WHICH AMENDMENTS AND ADDITIONS HAVE BEEN ENACTED SINCE THE SUMMER OF
    1798, AND ARE NOW IN FORCE DEC. 1, 1800. . . .
        [*Cambridge.*]   pp. 4. 8vo.
    Caption title. These pages are usually found affixed to copies of the Laws of 1798.
        AAS, BM, HC.

37592 —— HARVARD UNIVERSITY, IN CAMBRIDGE, COMMONWEALTH OF MASSACHUSETTS. THE ORDER OF THE
    EXERCISES OF COMMENCEMENT, JULY 16, M,DCCC. . . .
        Cambridge — printed by W. Hilliard.   Broadside.   fol.   AAS, BA, BPL, HC, MHS.

37593 —— ILLUSTRISSIMO CALEB STRONG, ARMIGERO. . . . THESES HASCE JUVENES IN ARTIBUS INITIATI. . . .
    HABITA IN COMITIS UNIVERSITATIS CANTABRIGIAE, MASSACHUSETTENSIS, DIE JULII XVI, ANNO
    SALUTIS M,DCCC. . . .
        Cantabrigiae: Typis Gulielmi Hilliard.   Broadside.   fol.   AAS, BA, BPL, HC, MHS.

37594 [HASELL, WILLIAM SORANZO]   1780–1815
    ALFRED, AN HISTORICAL POEM. DELIVERED AT THE PUBLIC COMMENCEMENT IN YALE COLLEGE, IN
    NEW-HAVEN, SEPTEMBER 11, 1799. . . .
        Charleston; Printed by T. J. Cox . . . 1800.   pp. 12. 12mo.   BA, CLS, YC.

37595 HASWELL, ANTHONY   1756–1816
    AN ORATION, DELIVERED BY REQUEST OF TEMPLE LODGE, IN BENNINGTON, VERMONT, DECEMBER
    27TH, 1799. BEING . . . IN HONOR OF THE MEMORY OF GENERAL GEORGE WASHINGTON. . . .
        Bennington: From the Press of the Author. A.D. 1800.   pp. 20, [4].   24mo. AAS.

37596 HASWELL'S VERMONT AND NEW-YORK ALMANAC, FOR THE YEAR OF OUR LORD, 1801. . . . CALCULATED
FOR THE MERIDIAN OF BENNINGTON. . . .
Bennington: Printed by Anthony Haswell. pp. [24]. 12mo. AAS.

37597 HAVEN, SAMUEL 1727–1806
THE DISINTERESTED BENEVOLENCE OF GOSPEL MINISTERS. . . . AN OCCASIONAL DISCOURSE . . .
AFTER THE ORDINATION OF . . . TIMOTHY ALDEN . . . IN PORTSMOUTH, N. H. . . .
*Portsmouth, New-Hampshire, printed at the United States' Oracle-office by Charles
Peirce. 1800.* pp. 28. 8vo.
With "The Charge, by the Rev. John Tompson" and the "Right-hand of fellowship, by
Joseph Buckminster." AAS, BA, JCB, NHSL, NYHS, PᵗU.

37598 HAVERHILL. MASSACHUSETTS.
ARRANGEMENTS TO BE OBSERVED ON THE 22D DAY OF FEBRUARY NEXT . . . PAYING A PUBLIC TRIBUTE
OF RESPECT TO . . . GEORGE WASHINGTON. . . .
[Haverhill, Mass.] Broadside. Fol. HEH.

37599 HAY, [GEORGE] 1729–1811
AN ABRIDGEMENT OF THE CHRISTIAN DOCTRINE. BY BISHOP HAY.
Philadelphia: Printed for Mathew Carey, no. 118, Market-Street. 1800. pp. 152.
24mo. GU.

37600 —— THE PIOUS CHRISTIAN INSTRUCTED, IN THE NATURE AND PRACTICE OF THE PRINCIPAL EXERCISES OF
PIETY, USED IN THE CATHOLIC CHURCH. . . .
*Philadelphia: Printed for Mathew Carey, no. 118, Market Street, by James Carey.
Nov. 10, 1800.* pp. xii, 299. 16mo. BPL, GU, VᵗU.

37601 HAYWOOD, JOHN 1762–1826
THE DUTY AND OFFICE OF JUSTICES OF THE PEACE. . . . ACCORDING TO THE LAWS OF THE STATE OF
NORTH CAROLINA. . . .
Halifax [N. C.]: Printed by Abraham Hodge. M,DCCC. pp. viii, 400. 8vo.
AAS, HC, HEH, JCB, NCU.

37602 HELME, [ELIZABETH] D. 1816
THE HISTORY OF LOUISA. . . . TWO VOLUMES IN ONE. . . . BY MRS. HELME. . . . FIRST NEW-
YORK EDITION.
New-York: Printed and sold by John Tiebout, no. 358 Pearl-Street. 1800. pp. 167,
front.
The frontispiece is "A Pastoral Scene" engraved by Scoles. AAS, NYPL, NYSL.

37603 [HELMUTH, JUSTUS HENRY CHRISTIAN] 1745–1825
KLAGEN ÜBER DEN TOD DES GENERAL WASCHINGTONS AM 22STEN FEBRUAR 1800, IN DEM DEUTSCH
EVANGELISCH LUTHERISCHEN ZION, ZU PHILADELPHIA.
[Philadelphia.] pp. [4]. 16mo.
In verse. GTS, LCP.

37604 HEMENWAY, SAMUEL
MEDICINE CHESTS, WITH PARTICULAR DIRECTIONS, PREPARED BY SAMUEL HEMENWAY.
[Salem: Printed by Thomas C. Cushing.] pp. 15. EI.

37605 HEMMENWAY, MOSES 1735–1811
A DISCOURSE DELIVERED AT WELLS, ON THE 22D FEBRUARY, 1800; OCCASIONED BY THE LAMENTED
DEATH OF . . . WASHINGTON. . . .
*Portsmouth, (New-Hampshire,) Printed at the United States' Oracle-office, by Charles
Peirce, 1800.* pp. 16. 8vo. BA, HEH, JCB, LOC.

37606 HERALD AND EASTERN SHORE INTELLIGENCER. 1790–1804
Easton — (Maryland:) published every Tuesday morning, by James Cowan. 1800.
fol. weekly. FOR 1800: [MᵈHS].

37607   [THE HERALD OF LIBERTY.   1798–1802
        Washington, Pennsylvania. Printed by John Israel.   fol.   weekly.]
                                                     FOR 1800: NO COPY KNOWN.

37608   HERALD OF THE UNITED STATES.   1792–1812
        Warren [R. I.]: — published by Nathaniel Phillips.   fol.   weekly.
                                                     FOR 1800: [HC], [RIHS].

37609   THE HERALD OF VIRGINIA, AND FINCASTLE WEEKLY ADVERTISER.   1800
        [Fincastle, Va.] Printed . . . by David Amen.   fol.   weekly.   FOR 1800: [LOC].

37610   THE HERMIT OF THE FOREST, AND THE WANDERING INFANTS, A RURAL FRAGMENT. . . .
        New-York: Printed by W. Durell, for John Harrison. 1800.   pp. 30, front.   32mo.
                                                                                    AAS.

37611   — — — *New-York: Printed by W. Durell, for Stephen Stephens. 1800.*   pp. 30, front.
        32mo.   PECK LIBRARY, NORWICH FREE ACADEMY.

37612   HERRICK, CLAUDIUS   1775–1831
        AN ORATION, DELIVERED AT DEERFIELD, ON THE FOURTH OF JULY, 1800. . . .
        Greenfield, Massachusetts: Printed by Thomas Dickman. 1800.   pp. 19.   8vo.
                                                                    AAS, LOC, NYSL, YC.

37613   HERTY, THOMAS
        A DIGEST OF THE LAWS OF THE UNITED STATES OF AMERICA, BEING A COMPLETE SYSTEM, (ALPHA-
        BETICALLY ARRANGED). . . .
        Baltimore: Printed for the Editor, by W. Pechin. 1800.   pp. iv, [9]–562, [1].   8vo.
        The last leaf contains an advertisement for Herty's *Laws of Maryland.* A second volume
        of the *Digest* was published in Washington in 1802.
                                        AAS, BA, BPL, EPFL, HC, LOC, NYPL, PʳU, YC.

37614   HEWITT, [JAMES]   1770–1827
        THE WOUNDED HUSSAR. COMPOSED BY MR. HEWITT. [SONG WITH ACCOMPANIMENT FOR FLUTE
        AND PIANOFORTE.]
        New York: Printed and sold at J. Hewitt's Musical Repository. . . . 1800.   pp. [2].
        4to.   BPL, LOC, NYPL.

37615   HIBERNIAN SOCIETY.
        [CONSTITUTION OF THE HIBERNIAN SOCIETY FOR THE RELIEF OF EMIGRANTS FROM IRELAND.
        Mount Holly, N. J.: Stephen C. Ustick, 1800.]   GASKILL 97.

37616   HILLIER, RICHARD
        LIBERTY AND EQUALITY: AN ORATION. . . . DELIVERED, JULY 4TH, 1800 AT MOUNT PLEASANT. . . .
        Mount-Pleasant: Printed by Russel Canfield, 1800.   pp. 11.   8vo.   HEH, NYSL.

37617   HIRZEL, HANS KASPAR   1725–1803
        See Vaughan, Benjamin.

37618   THE HISTORY OF AMELIA, OR AN ELEGANT COLLECTION OF DIVERTING STORIES, FOR BOYS & GIRLS.
        Printed for and sold by the Booksellers. 1800.   pp. [16].   32mo.   AAS.

37619   THE HISTORY OF LITTLE KING PIPPIN; WITH AN ACCOUNT OF THE MELANCHOLY DEATH OF FOUR
        NAUGHTY BOYS, WHO WERE DEVOURED BY WILD BEASTS; AND THE WONDERFUL DELIVERY OF
        MASTER HARRY HARMLESS, BY A LITTLE WHITE HORSE.
        Boston: Printed and sold by Samuel Hall [1800?].   pp. 60, illus.   32mo.   NYPL.

37620   — — — *New-York: Printed by Wm. Durell, for Thomas B. Jansen & Co. 1800.*   pp. 63,
        illus.   32mo.   AAS.

37621 —— —— Third Worcester edition.
Printed at Worcester, Massachusetts, by Isaiah Thomas, Jun. . . . MDCCC. pp. 63, illus. 48mo.
The text of this edition differs from that of the two above, particularly in the inclusion of a plug for, and alleged picture of, Thomas' bookstore. At the end are added four hymns, a prayer, and a brief catechism. AAS.

37622 THE HISTORY of Mary Wood. . . .
See Cheap repository. Number 33.

37623 [THE HISTORY of Mr. Tommy Thoroughgood, and Mr. Francis Forward, two apprentices to the same master. . . .
Stonington-Port, Printed by S. Trumbull. 1800. pp. 24. 12mo.] Bates 2252.

37624 HISTORY of modern Europe. . . .
See Russell, William.

37625 HISTORY of the plague in London in 1665. . . .
See Cheap repository. Number 23.

37626 THE HISTORY of the tales of the fairies: newly done from the French. . . .
See Aulnoy, Marie.

37627 HITCHCOCK, Enos   1744–1803
A Discourse on . . . Washington. . . . Delivered February 22, 1800, in the Benevolent Congregational Church in Providence. . . .
Providence: Printed by John Carter, jun. 1800. pp. 35. 8vo.
AAS, BA, CL, HC, HEH, JCB, LCP, LOC, MFM, MHS, NHS, NYPL, NYSL, RIHS, WᴵˢHS, WLC, YC.

37628 —— A Funeral sermon, occasioned by the death of Mrs. Sarah Bowen. . . . Delivered in the Benevolent Congregational Church. . . .
Providence: Printed by John Carter, jun. 1800. pp. 24. 8vo.
AAS, BʳU, HC, HSP, JCB, LCP, NYHS, NYPL, NYSL, RIHS, WLC.

37629 DER HOCH-Deutsche Americanische Calender. Auf das jahr 1801. . . . Zum siebenzehnten-mal heraus gegeben.
Germantown: Gedruckt und zu finden bey Michael Billmeyer. . . . pp. [40]. 8vo.
HSP, LOC, NYSL.

37630 HOCH-Deutsches reformirtes A B C und namen buchlein, fur kinder, welche anfangen zu lernen.
Germanton. Gedruckt und zu haben von Michael Billmeyer. 1800. pp. [30]. 16mo. AAS.

37631 HOCHMANN von Hochenau, Ernst Christoph   1661–1721
Ernst Christoph Hochmanns von Hochenau glaubens-beckanntniss. . . . Nun aum 5ten mal gedruckt. . . .
Germantaun: Gedruckt bey Peter Leibert, 1800. pp. 44, [4]. 24mo.
The last leaves contain "Anhang zweyer lieder, von Johannes Kelpius." AAS.

37632 HODGE & Boylan's North-Carolina Almanack, for the year of our Lord 1801. . . . Calculated for the state of North-Carolina. . . .
Halifax: Printed by Abraham Hodge. pp. 48. 16mo. AAS, Bruce Cotten.

37633 HODGKINSON, [John]   1767?–1805
Let Washington be our boast. Sung with great applause at the theatre at the conclusion of the ode to the memory of Gen'l Washington. The words written & music selected by Mr. Hodgkinson.
New York, printed & sold at J. Hewitt's musical repository, no. 23 Maiden Lane. . . .
pp. [2]. fol. HEH.

37634 HOLCOMBE, Henry   1762–1824
    A Sermon, occasioned by the death of . . . Washington . . . delivered in the Baptist church, Savannah, Georgia, January 19th, 1800. . . .
        [Savannah:] Printed by Seymour & Woolhopter, on the Bay.   pp. 16, [2].   4to.
    The last leaf contains "The Prayer and Concluding Hymn."
                AAS, BA, DᵉRGL, HEH, JCB, NYHS, NYPL, NYSL, VᵃU, YC.

37635 [HOLDEN, Oliver]   1765–1831
    Sacred dirges, hymns, and anthems, commemorative of the death of General George Washington. . . .
        Printed at Boston, by I. Thomas and E. T. Andrews, no. 45, Newbury-Street.   pp. 24, 4, printed wrappers.   obl. 4to.
    There are two issues, one priced 50 cents and one 37½ cents on the covers. Some copies of the former have the final leaves which contain a dirge by Anthony Pasquin (J. M. Williams) with music by Holden. The AAS has both issues.
        AAS, BA, BʳU, CL, HC, HEH, JCB, LOC, MFM, MHS, MSL, NL, NYHS, NYPL, PPL, WC.

37636   —— *See also* Laus Deo *and* Plain Psalmody.

37637 HOLLAND, James
    Strictures upon the letter of General Joseph Dickson of the first of May, 1800. . . .
        Lincolnton [N. C.]: Printed by John M. Slump.   pp. 10.   8vo.   LOC.

37638 HOLLAND Land Company
    Holland Land Company West Geneseo lands — information. The Holland Land Company will open an office. . . .
        [Albany.]   Broadside.   Buffalo Hist. Soc.

37639 HOLLINSHEAD, William   1748–1817
    To live is Christ . . . a sermon preached at Dorchester on the 14th of May, 1800, occasioned by the death of Mrs. Eliza Adams. . . .
        Printed by T. B. Bowen [Charleston, S. C.]   pp. 33.   12mo.   AAS, JCB, YC.

37640 HOLMES, Abiel   1763–1837
    The Counsel of Washington recommended in a discourse delivered at Cambridge, February 22, 1800. . . .
        Printed by Samuel Hall, no. 53, Cornhill, Boston. 1800.   pp. 23.   8vo.
    AAS, AHTS, BA, BPL, CHS, CL, HC, HEH, HSP, JCB, LCP, MFM, MᵈHS, MHS, NL, NYHS, NYPL, PFM, PPL, YC.

37641   —— A Sermon, preached at Cambridge . . . December 29, 1799, occasioned by the death of George Washington. . . .
        Printed by Samuel Hall, no. 53, Cornhill, Boston.   pp. 22, [1].   8vo.
    The last leaf contains "A hymn, composed and sung at Cambridge."
        AAS, AHTS, BA, BPL, CHS, CL, HC, HEH, JCB, LOC, MFM, MHS, NL, NYHS, NYPL, NYSL, PPL, PTS, YC.

37642 HOLYOKE, Samuel   1762–1820
    Hark! from the tombs, &c. And, Beneath the honors, &c. Adapted from Dr. Watts, and set to music. . . . Performed at Newburyport 2d January, 1800, the day on which the citizens unitedly expressed their unbounded veneration for the memory of our beloved Washington. . . .
        Exeter: Printed by H. Ranlet.   pp. 12.   obl. 8vo.   HC, HEH, LOC, NL, YC.

37643   —— The Instrumental assistant, containing instructions for the violin, German-flute, clarionett, bass-viol, and hautboy. . . . Volume I.
        Printed at Exeter, N. H. by H. Ranlet. . . .   pp. 79, [1].   obl. 8vo.
    Goodspeed's had the original agreement between Holyoke and Ranlet for publication, dated November 14, 1800. The copyright entry was made on August 30. Volume II is dated 1807.   AAS.

37644 [HONEYWOOD, St. John]   1763–1798
  A Poem on the President's Farewell Address. With a sketch of the character of his
  successor. Second edition.
    Philadelphia: John Ormood. pp. 8. 8vo.   BPL, HEH, MHS, NYPL, RIHS, YC.

37645 THE HONOURABLE Mr. [Theodore] Sedgwick's political last will and testament. . . .
    From a Republican press. Annoque Domini, [Stockbridge?]. *1800.* pp. 21. 8vo.
                  AAS, BA, MHS, NYHS, NYPL, NYSL.

37646 HOPKINS, Daniel   1734–1814
  A Sermon, preached December 29, 1799, in the South Meeting House, Salem . . . after
  the . . . death of General George Washington. . . .
    Salem: Printed by Thomas C. Cushing, at the Bible & Heart. pp. 28. 8vo.
    AAS, BA, BPL, EI, Gᴿʟ, HC, HEH, JCB, LOC, MᵈHS, MFM, MHS, NL, NYHS, NYPL, NYSL, WLC, YC.

37647 HORATIUS Flaccus, Quintus
  The Works of Horace, translated literally into English prose. . . . By C. Smart, A. M.
  of Pembroke-College, Cambridge. Revised . . . by M. Campbell, A. M. of New-York.
  In two volumes. . . .
    *New-York: Printed by L. Nichols & Co. for Samuel Campbell, no. 124 Pearl-Street.
  1800.* pp. v, [1], 331; [2], 423. 24mo.   AAS, HC, NYSL, YC.

37648 HORNBLOWER, Josiah   1729–1809
  Letter from Mr. Hornblower to Mr. Kitchell, on the subject of Schuyler's copper mine,
  in New-Jersey. April 18th, 1800. . . .
    [*Philadelphia.*] pp. 4. 8vo.   BA, YC.

37649 [HORSLEY,] Samuel   1733–1806
  Critical disquisitions on the eighteenth chapter of Isaiah . . . In a letter to Edward
  King. . . .
    Philadelphia: Re-printed by James Humphreys, from the London copy of 1799. 1800.
  pp. 101, [2]. 12mo.
  The last leaf contains an advertisement. AAS, BPL, BʳU, CL, HC, HEH, HSP, JCB, LOC, NYPL, VᵃU.

37650 HOSMER, A., and Lawton, J.
  A View of the rise and increase of the churches, composing the Otsego Baptist
  Association. . . .
    Whitestown: Printed by Warren Barnard. 1800. pp. 38. 8vo.   AAS, SCBHC.

37651 HOTCHKISS, Frederick W[illiam]   1762–1844
  An Oration delivered at Saybrook on . . . February 22d, 1800 . . . for the death of General
  George Washington. . . .
    New-London: Printed by S. Green. 1800. pp. 32. 8vo.
                AAS, CHS, HEH, LOC, NYPL, NYSL, YC.

37652 —— A Sermon, delivered at the installation of Pythagoras lodge of Free Masons; in Lyme,
  Connecticut, October 7th, 1800. . . .
    New-London, Printed by Samuel Green, 1800. pp. 35. 8vo.   CHS, LOC, YC.

37653 HOUDIN, Michael Gabriel
  Et sicut illud statutum est hominibus. . . . A funeral oration on the death of George
  Washington: delivered in the City Hall of Albany . . . on the twenty-second of
  February, 1800. . . .
    Albany: Printed by Barber & Southwick, Faust's Statue, State-Street. pp. 11.
  front. (portrait). 4to.
      AAS, BA, BPL, HEH, HSP, JCB, LOC, MSL, NYHS, NYPL, PL, UOTˣ, WⁱᵃHS.

37654 HOUGHTON, Asa
  The Gentlemen's and ladies' diary, and Almanac . . . for . . . 1801. . . . Fitted for the
  latitude and longitude of Boston. . . .
    Keene, N. H. Printed by John Prentiss. . . . pp. [48]. 12mo.
                 AAS, LOC, NHHS, NYHS.

37655 THE HOUSE that Jack built, a diverting story for children of all ages. To which is added, some account of Jack Gingle. . . . With a collection of riddles. Adorned with cuts.
New-York: Printed by W. Durell, for Longworth & Wheeler. 1800. pp. 32, including picture covers and frontispiece. 32mo. AAS.

37656 ——— — *New-York: Printed by W. Durell for Evert Duyckinck. 1800.* pp. 32. 32mo. AAS.

37657 HOWARD, Bezaleel 1753–1837
A Sermon preached at the ordination of . . . Benj. R. Woodbridge . . . in Norwich, October 17th, 1799. . . .
Springfield [Mass]: Printed by Timothy Ashley. M,DCCC. pp. 15. 8vo.
AAS, BM, CL, HC, HEH, JCB, NL, PTS, UOC, YC.

37658 HOWE, S[olomon] 1750–1835
The Divine law [eleven verses]. . . . Greenwich, (Mass.) March, 1800. [Second column:] The Beautiful infant [eight verses]. . . .
[Sold by E. Larkin, Cornhill, Boston.] Broadside. fol.
Printed on the same sheet with the item below. AAS.

37659 —— Honoribus laureatus. . . . An elegy on the departure of General George Washington. . . . Greenwich, (Mass.) Feb. 22, 1800. . . .
Sold by E. Larkin, Cornhill, Boston. Broadside. fol. AAS.

37660 [HUDSON Gazette. 1792–1806
Hudson, N. Y. Printed by Ashbel Stoddard. weekly. fol.]
For 1800: no copies known.

37661 HUMPHREYS, Daniel 1740–1827
A Plain attempt . . . shewing . . . that the clergy and their followers in our age and country, are the very antichrist. . . .
Printed at the Republican Press in Portsmouth. 1800. pp. 35. 12mo.
AAS, BA, BM, BPL, CHS, JCB.

37662 DER HUNDERTJÄHRIGE Calender . . . von 1800 bis 1900. . . . Zweyte verbesserte auflage.
Baltimore: Gedruckt und zu haben bey Samuel Saur. pp. 96. 12mo.
AAS, EPFL, WRHS.

37663 HUNTINGTON, Asahel 1761–1813
A Sermon, delivered at Topsfield January 5, 1800. Occasioned by the death of George Washington. . . .
Printed by Joshua Cushing, Salem. 1800. pp. 32. 8vo.
A biographical sketch of Washington occupies pp. 29–32.
AAS, BA, BPL, CL, EI, HEH, JCB, LOC, MFM, MHS, NYPL, NYSL, PL, PTS, W¹ˢHS, YC.

37664 HUNTINGTON, Enoch 1739–1809
An Oration delivered at Middletown, in the State of Connecticut, February 22, A. D. 1800. . . .
Middletown: Printed by Tertius Dunning, 1800. pp. 9. 8vo.
On the death of Washington. CHS, HC, JCB, LOC, MFM, MSL, NL, NYHS, NYPL, UTS.

37665 —— A Sermon occasioned by the death of Mr. Hezekiah Hulbert, who died at Middletown, Jan. 19th, A. D. 1800. . . .
Middletown: Printed by Tertius Dunning. 1800. pp. 19. 8vo.
CHS, JCB, NHHS, NYHS.

37666 HUNTINGTON, Jedidiah 1743–1818
Funeral eulogy [by Huntington] and oration [by Lyman Law, 1770–1842, on George Washington.]
[New-London: Printed by Samuel Green.] pp. 17, [1]. 8vo.
Published without a titlepage. AAS, HEH, LOC, MHS, NYHS, NYPL, NYSL.

37667 HUNTINGTON, Jonathan
The Albany collection of sacred harmony. Containing a plain, and intelligible instruction for learners of church music. . . .
Northampton: Printed by A. Wright, 1800. pp. 91. obl. 24mo. NYPL.

37668 HUSE, Jonathan 1767–1853
A Discourse, occasioned by the death of . . . Washington . . . delivered at Warren, (District of Maine.) on the 22d, of February, 1800. . . .
Wiscasset: Printed by Henry Hoskins. 1800. pp. 12. 8vo. BA, BrU, JCB.

37669 HUTCHINS, John Nathan
Hutchins improved: being an Almanack and ephemeris . . . for the year of our Lord 1801. . . .
New-York: Printed and sold by Ming and Young, (Successors to Hugh Gaine) no. 33, Liberty-Street. . . . pp. [36]. 16mo. AAS, BPL, LOC, NYHS, NYPL, RU.

37670 —— Stoddard's diary: or, the Columbia Almanack, for the year of our Lord 1801. . . .
Hudson: Printed and Sold by Ashbel Stoddard. pp. [36]. 12mo. AAS.

37671 HUTCHINSON, William 1732–1814
The Spirit of Masonry. In moral and elucidatory lectures. . . .
New-York: Printed by Isaac Collins . . . for Cottom & Stewart . . . Alexandria. 1800. pp. [1], vi, [2], 174, 22. 12mo.
The frontispiece was drawn by Hutchinson and engraved by Scoles. The appendix contains a letter by John Locke on Masonry and four Masonic songs.
AAS, BrU, JCB, LOC, NYFM, PFM, VaU, WlsHS.

37672 HYMN, ode, and dirge, to be sung in New-Bedford. . . .
See New Bedford.

37673 A HYMN, on the death of Gen. Washington. What solemn sounds the ear invade!
[Hartford?] Broadside. 12mo. HEH.

37674 HYMN on Washington. O God! thy darkest ways are just. . . .
Broadside. 12mo. HEH.

37675 HYMNS and odes, composed on the death of Gen. George Washington: adapted to the 22d, day of February. . . .
Portsmouth, (N. H.) January, 1800. Printed at the United States' Oracle Office by Charles Peirce, sold by him. . . . pp. 12. 12mo.
Included are verses by the Rev. John S. J. Gardner, of Boston, Mrs. Rowson, of Medford, Mr. Elliot, of Watertown, Mr. George Richards, of Portsmouth, Mrs. Murray, of Boston, and Mr. Holden, of Boston. AAS, BA, BrU, GrL, HEH, JCB, LOC.

37676 HYMNS composed. . . .
See Richards, George.

37677 HYMNS, to be sung on the 22d of Feb'ry, 1800, in Middletown. . . .
See Middletown, Conn.

37678 IMPARTIAL American or, Seneca Museum. 1800–1801
[Geneva, N. Y., published by Ebenezer Eaton for Eaton, Walker & Co.] weekly.
fol. For 1800: [NYSL].

37679 IMPARTIAL Gazette. 1800
[Published by Russel Canfield at Mount Pleasant, N. Y.] weekly. fol.
For 1800: [CHS].

37680   IMPARTIAL JOURNAL.   1799–1804
                 Stonington, (Connecticut;) published by Samuel Trumbull, 1800.   fol.   weekly.
                                                                          FOR 1800: [CHS].

37681   THE IMPARTIAL OBSERVER.   AUG. 4, 1800–1802
                 Providence: — Published . . . by Samuel J. Williams. . . .   fol.   weekly.
                                                                          FOR 1800: BᵣU, [RIHS].

37682   IMPARTIAL OBSERVER THE KNOXVILLE GAZETTE.   1799–1800
                 Knoxville, (State of Tennessee) printed and published . . . by Roulstone and Wilson.
                 fol.   weekly.
                 In November the partnership was dissolved; Wilson removed to Jonesborough and Roul-
                 stone continued the *Knoxville Gazette.*   FOR 1800: UOC.

37683   THE IMPARTIAL REGISTER.   MAY 12–JULY 24, 1800
                 Published on Mondays & Thursdays, by William Carleton . . . Salem, Massachusetts.
                 fol.   semi-weekly.
                 On July 31 the name was changed to *The Salem Impartial Register.*
                                                                          FOR 1800: AAS, BA, EI, HC.

37684   AN IMPARTIAL REVIEW. . . .
                 See Pettit, Charles.

37685   THE INDEPENDENT CHRONICLE: AND THE UNIVERSAL ADVERTISER.   1776–1840
                 Boston, printed by Ebenezer Rhoades for the proprietor, James White. 1800.   fol.
                 semi-weekly.
                 With the issue of May 15 the printers are given as Abijah Adams and Ebenezer Rhoades.
                         FOR 1800: AAS, BA, BPL, CHS, HC, [LOC], MHS, MSL, NYHS, NYSL, YC.

37686   —— TO THE PATRONS OF THE INDEPENDENT CHRONICLE, THEIR NEWS-CARRIER PRESENTS THE
                 COMPLIMENTS OF THE SEASON. . . . BOSTON JANUARY 2, 1800.
                 [*Boston.*]   Broadside.   8vo.   AAS, HSP.

37687   THE INDEPENDENT GAZETTEER.   1800–1801
                 Printed at Worcester, (Massachusetts) by Mower & Greenleaf. . . .   fol.   weekly.
                 With the issue of Oct. 7 Nahum Mower withdrew, and Daniel Greenleaf continued publica-
                 tion.   FOR 1800: [AAS].

37688   THE INTELLIGENCER, & WEEKLY ADVERTISER.   1799–1922
                 Published by William & Robert Dickson . . . Lancaster [Pa.]   fol.   weekly.
                                                                          FOR 1800: AAS, HSP, PSL.

37689   THE INVISIBLE SPY. . . . [No, 1. . . . LETTER VII. TO ALEXANDER HAMILTON. . . . LONDON,
                 SEPTEMBER 16, 1798.]
                 Virginia: Published by a Republican, and supported by the Friends of Liberty.
                 M;DCCC.   pp. 16.   16mo.   LOC.

37690   IRONY, SOLOMON, *pseud.*
                 FASHION; OR, THE ART OF MAKING BREECHES. AN HEROI-SATIRI-DIDACTIC POEM. . . .
                 Philadelphia: Printed by Francis and Robert Bailey. 1800.   pp. 19.   8vo.
                 Attributed to Rembrandt Peale, 1778–1860.   AAS, BPL, BᵣU, HSP, LOC, NYHS, PPL.

37691   ISHAM, JIRAH   1778–1842
                 AN ORATION, COMMEMORATIVE OF . . . WASHINGTON: DELIVERED ON THE 22D OF FEBRUARY, 1800,
                 AT THE MEETING-HOUSE IN THE WEST SOCIETY IN COLCHESTER. . . .
                 New-London, Printed by Samuel Green, 1800.   pp. 16.   8vo.   CHS, HEH, LOC, YC.

37692   J. RUSSELL'S GAZETTE.
                 See Russell's Gazette.

37693 JACKSON, Mrs. J.
JUVENILE ENTERTAINMENT; OR POETICAL MISCELLANY, BY MRS. J. JACKSON.
New-Brunswick: Printed by Abraham Blauvelt. 1800. (Copy right secured.) pp. 69,
[1]. 4to. RU.

37694 JACKSON, WILLIAM 1759–1828
EULOGIUM, ON . . . WASHINGTON . . . PRONOUNCED BEFORE THE PENNSYLVANIA SOCIETY OF THE
CINCINNATI, ON THE TWENTY-SECOND DAY OF FEBRUARY, EIGHTEEN HUNDRED. AT THE GERMAN
REFORMED CHURCH, IN . . . PHILADELPHIA. . . .
Philadelphia: Printed by John Ormrod, no. 41, Chestnut-Street. 1800. pp. 44. 8vo.
Some copies are on thin and some on thick paper.
AAS, BA, BPL, HC, HEH, HSP, JCB, LOC, MFM, MᵈHS, NEHGS, NL, NYHS, NYPL, NYSL, PL,
PPL, RU, WⁱˢHS, WLC, YC.

37695 —— NEW EDITION.
Philadelphia: Printed by John Ormrod, no. 41, Chestnut. 1800. pp. 44. 8vo.
Copies of this edition were issued as an appendix to *Washington's Monuments of
Patriotism*, Philadelphia, 1800. The text also appears in the collection of eulogies published
at Boston in the same year. AAS, BPL, HC, HEH, LOC, MᵈHS, NYPL, NYSL.

37696 [JAMES, JOSEPH, AND MOORE, DANIEL]
A SYSTEM OF EXCHANGE WITH ALMOST ALL PARTS OF THE WORLD. TO WHICH IS ADDED, THE INDIA
DIRECTORY, FOR PURCHASING THE DRUGS AND SPICES. . . .
New-York: Printed by John Furman. 1800. pp. iv. [13]–180. 12mo.
AAS, BA, HC, HSP, JCB, LOC, NYAM, NYSL, WⁱˢHS, YC.

37697 JAMIESON, JOHN
AN ACCOUNT OF THE DISPUTES BETWEEN THE ASSOCIATE REFORMED SYNOD, AND THE REV. JOHN
JAMIESON, IN MATTERS OF DOCTRINE. . . .
Greensburg: From the press of Snowden & M'Corkle, 1800. pp. 176. 12mo. RU.

37698 JAUDON, DANIEL 1767–1826
THE ENGLISH ORTHOGRAPHICAL EXPOSITOR, BEING A COMPENDIOUS SELECTION OF THE MOST USEFUL
WORDS IN THE ENGLISH LANGUAGE. . . . THIRD EDITION.
Philadelphia, printed by D. Hogan, 1800. pp. 223.
PM.

37699 JAY, JOHN 1745–1829
GENTLEMEN OF THE SENATE AND ASSEMBLY, THE GREAT IMPORTANCE OF THE BUSINESS. . . .
[*Albany.*] pp. [2]. fol. NYSL.

37700 JEFFERSON, THOMAS 1743–1826
AN APPENDIX TO THE NOTES ON VIRGINIA RELATIVE TO THE MURDER OF LOGAN'S FAMILY. . . .
Philadelphia: Printed by Samuel H. Smith. M,D,CCC. pp. 51, map. 8vo.
APS, BPL, CLS, HC, HEH, HSP, JCB, LOC, MᵈHS, MHS, NL, NYHS, NYPL, VᵃU, WⁱˢHS, YC.

37701 —— — *Philadelphia: Printed by Samuel H. Smith. M.D.CCC.* pp. 58, map. 8vo.
The additional material in this edition is "The declaration of John Sappington, received
after the publication of the preceding Appendix." HEH, JCB, LOC, MHS, NYHS.

37702 —— JEFFERSON'S NOTES ON THE STATE OF VIRGINIA; WITH THE APPENDIXES — COMPLETE.
Baltimore: Printed by W. Pechin, corner of Water & Gay-streets. 1800. pp. 194,
[2], 53, table. 8vo.
Bound at the end of most copies is a dissertation on Jefferson's religious principles with
titlepage reading: *A Vindication of the religion of Mr. Jefferson. . . . By a friend to real
religion* [Samuel Knox], Baltimore: Printed for the editor of the American, by W. Pechin,
pp. 21. AAS, BA, BPL, HSP, JCB, LOC, MᵈHS, NYHS, NYPL, NYSL, PʳU, UOC, VᵃU, WLC.

37703 —— JEFFERSON'S NOTES, ON THE STATE OF VIRGINIA; WITH THE APPENDIXES — COMPLETE. TO WHICH
IS SUBJOINED, A SUBLIME AND ARGUMENTATIVE DISSERTATION, ON MR. JEFFERSON'S RELIGIOUS
PRINCIPLES.
Baltimore: Printed by W. Pechin . . . 1800. pp. 194, [2], 53, 21, 8, table. 8vo.
HC, HSP, JCB, LOC, MᵈHS, MHS, NL, NYHS, NYPL, NYSL, VᵃU, YC.

37704　　—— A Test of the religious principles, of Mr. Jefferson; extracted (verbatim) from his writings. . . .
　　　　Easton; Re-printed by Thomas Perrin Smith, and presented (gratis) to the patrons of the Republican Star. September 9th, 1800. pp. [2], 6. 8vo. LOC, MᵈHS.

37705　　—— —— —— *Pittsfield [Mass.]: Printed by Phinehas Allen.* pp. 12. 12mo. LOC.

37706　　—— —— —— *Philadelphia [i.e. Suffield, Conn., by Edward Gray], Printed by John Bioren, for Robert T. Rawle. . . . 1800.* pp. [2], ii, 10. 16mo.
　　　　For the printer of this edition see the *Middlesex Gazette*, September 5, 1800.
　　　　　　　　　　　　　　　　　　　　　　APS, CSL, HSP, LOC, NYPH.

37707　　JENKS, Stephen　　　　　　　　　　　　　　　　　　　　　　　1772–1856
　　　　Laus Deo. The New-England Harmonist: containing concise and easy rules of music. . . .
　　　　Danbury: Printed by Douglas & Nicholas, for the author. (Copyright secured.) pp. 64. obl. 8vo.
　　　　Described by Upton-Sonneck from the title to the engraved portion which reads "The Musical Harmonist. . . . Engraved & Printed by Amos Doolittle. New Haven, July 16, 1800." The AAS and NL copies are incomplete. AAS, NL, NYPL, YC.

37708　　JENKS' Portland Gazette.　　　　　　　　　　　　　　　　　　1798–1824
　　　　Published by E. A. Jenks Portland, District of Maine. fol. weekly.
　　　　　　　　　　　　　　　　　　　　　　For 1800: BA, NYPL.

37709　　JOHNSON, John B[arent]　　　　　　　　　　　　　　　　　　1768–1803
　　　　Eulogy on General George Washington. A sermon, delivered February 22d, 1800, in the North Dutch Church, Albany, before the Legislature. . . .
　　　　Albany: Printed by L. Andrews, Printer to the State. 1800. pp. [1], 22. 8vo.
　　　　AAS, BA, BPL, CU, HC, HEH, JCB, LOC, MFM, NL, NYHS, NYPL, NYSL, PFM, PL, PʳU, PTS, RU.

37710　　[JOHNSON, Samuel]　　　　　　　　　　　　　　　　　　　　1709–1784
　　　　The Rambler. In four volumes. Vol. I. . . . A new edition.
　　　　New-York: Printed for Samuel Campbell, no. 124, Pearl-Street. 1800. pp. 309, 296, 309, 254, [28]. 12mo.　　　　　NYPL, NYSL.

37711　　JOHNSON, Thomas　　　　　　　　　　　　　　　　　　　　1732–1819?
　　　　To the freemen of the fourth district. My willingness to serve as your representative in Congress. . . .
　　　　[Elizabeth (Hager's) Town: Printed by Thomas Grieves.] Broadside. fol. MᵈHS.

37712　　JUDSON, Ephraim　　　　　　　　　　　　　　　　　　　　1737–1813
　　　　Advantages of going to the house of mourning. A sermon delivered in Suffield, at the funeral of Major-General John Ashley, Esq. Nov. 7, 1799. . . .
　　　　Stockbridge, Printed at the office of Horatio Jones & Co., by H. Willard, 1800. pp. 32. 16mo.　　　　　BʳA, NYHS, YC.

37713　　—— The Duty of the ministers . . . a sermon, delivered in Durham, at the ordination of the Reverend David Smith: 1799. . . .
　　　　Middletown [Conn.]: Printed by Tertius Dunning. 1800. pp. 23. 8vo.
　　　　　　　　　　　　　　　　　　AAS, CHS, HC, JCB, PL, WL, YC.

37714　　JULIA, and the illuminated baron. . . .
　　　　See Wood, Sarah Sayward Barrell Keating.

37715　　KEITH, Isaac Stockton　　　　　　　　　　　　　　　　　　1775–1813
　　　　National affliction and national consolation! A sermon on the death of . . . Washington . . . delivered on the twelfth of January . . . in the Independent, or Congregational church, in Charleston, South-Carolina. . . .
　　　　Charleston: Printed by W. P. Young, 1800. pp. [2], 30. 8vo.
　　　　　　　　　　　BPL, HC, HEH, JCB, LOC, MFM, NYHS, NYPL.

37716 KEMP, James 1764–1827
A Sermon, delivered in Christ Church, Cambridge, in Maryland; on the twenty-second of February, 1800, being the day of mourning appointed by Congress, for . . . Washington. . . .
Easton [Md.]: Printed by James Cowan. pp. 15, [1], front. 8vo.
The last leaf contains a hymn. BA, LOC, MFM, MᵈHS, NYHS, NYPL, PPL.

37717 KEMPIS, Thomas à 1380–1471
An Extract of the Christian's pattern; or, A Treatise of the Imitation of Christ. . . .
Philadelphia: Printed by Henry Tuckniss for Exekiel Cooper. 1800. pp. 290, [2]. 48mo. RU.

37718 —— The Following of Christ. . . . Translated into English by . . . Richard Challoner, D. D. . . . The ninth edition.
Philadelphia: Printed for M. Carey, no. 118 High Street, by James Carey. 1800. pp. 335. 24mo. NYPL.

37719 —— The Soliloquy of the soul. By . . . Thomas à Kempis. . . . To which are added, Meditations and prayers for sick persons. By George Stanhope, D. D.
Hartford: Printed by John Babcock. 1800. pp. 227, [1]. 24mo.
AAS, CHS, GU, HC, JCB, MHS, NYPL, NYSL, WC, YC.

37720 —— —— —— *Philadelphia: Mathew Carey. 1800.* pp. 335. 12mo. JCB, MHS.

37721 KENDALL, James 1769–1859
The Character and blessedness of the righteous . . . A sermon delivered at Plymouth, September 21, 1800 . . . after the interment of the widow Jane Robbins. . . .
Printed by Samuel Hall, in Cornhill, Boston. 1800. pp. 23. 8vo.
AAS, AHTS, BA, BPL, HC, JCB, MHS, NYHS, NYPL, YC.

37722 —— A Discourse, delivered at Plymouth, February 22d, 1800. At the request of the inhabitants . . . as a testimony of grief for the death of George Washington. . . .
Boston: Printed by John Russell. 1800. pp. 24. 8vo.
AAS, BA, HC, HEH, JCB, LOC, MFM, MHS, NL, NYPL, PPL, WⁱˢHS, YC.

37723 KENDRICK, Ariel 1772–1856
An Eulogy on General George Washington, delivered at the west meeting-house in the town of Boscawen. . . .
Concord: Printed by Geo. Hough. 1800. pp. 16. 8vo. AAS, BPL, NEHGR, NHHS.

37724 KENNEBEC Gazette. Nov. 14, 1800–1810
Published by Peter Edes at Hallowell. fol. weekly. For 1800: HC, MᵉHS.

37725 KENNEBECK Intelligencer. 1795–June 6, 1800
Published by Peter Edes at Hallowell. fol. weekly. For 1800: [HC].

37726 KENTISH Guards.
The Charter and by-laws for the regulation of the Kentish Guards in the towns of East Greenwich, Warwick, and Coventry. . . .
Warren, (R. I.) printed by Nathaniel Phillips. 1800. pp. 15. 16mo.
AAS, BʳU, JCB, NYPL, RIHS.

37727 KENTUCKY. State.
Acts passed at the first session of the eighth general assembly, for the Commonwealth of Kentucky, begun . . . in . . . Frankfort . . . the fourth day of November . . . one thousand, seven hundred, and ninety-nine. . . .
Frankfort: Printed by William Hunter. . . . 1800. pp. 226. 8vo.
HC, HSP, LOC, NYBA, UOC.

37728 THE KENTUCKY ALMANAC FOR THE YEAR OF OUR LORD 1801. . . . WILL SERVE, WITHOUT ANY
         SENSIBLE VARIATION, FOR THE NORTH WESTERN TERRITORY, ST. VINCENNES, STATE OF
         TENNESSEE, AND THE WESTERN PARTS OF VIRGINIA.
              Lexington: Printed by John Bradford, at the office of the Kentucky Gazette.
         pp. [36]. 24mo.   AAS, LOC, OH&PS.

37729 THE KENTUCKY GAZETTE.   1787–1848
              Lexington: — printed by John Bradford.   fol.   weekly.
                                           FOR 1800: LEXINGTON PUBLIC LIBRARY.

37730 THE KENTUCKY POCKET ALMANACK, FOR THE YEAR OF OUR LORD, 1801; BEING THE 5TH AFTER
         BISSEXTILE, OR LEAP YEAR. . . .
              Lexington: Printed by John Bradford. . . .   pp. [24].   32mo.   HEH.

37731 KEY, PHILIP BARTON   1757–1815
         [A FRIEND TO FAIR PLAY.
              Annapolis: Printed by Frederick and Samuel Green?.   Broadside.]   MINICK 593.

37732 KIMBALL, JACOB   1761–1826
         THE ESSEX HARMONY: AN ORIGINAL COMPOSITION, IN THREE AND FOUR PARTS. . . .
              *From the Music-Press of H. Ranlet, Exeter. Printed for T. C. Cushing and B. B.
         Macanulty, and sold at their book-stores in Salem. 1800.*   pp. 111, [1].   obl. 8vo.
         Samuel Holyoke was co-editor with Kimball.   AAS, BPL, BᴿU, CL, EI, HC, MHS, NL, NYSL, YC.

37733 KING, EDWARD   1735?–1807
         REMARKS ON THE SIGNS OF THE TIMES; BY EDWARD KING . . . WITH HIS SUPPLEMENT AND
         APPENDIX.
              *Philadelphia: Reprinted by James Humphreys, from the London copy of 1799. And
         sold by him at no. 106, Market-Street. 1800.*   pp. [1], 144, [2].   12mo.
         Each part has a special titlepage. The last leaf contains the publisher's advertisement.
                                       AAS, BPL, BᴿU, LOC, NYPL, NYHS, NYSL, PTS, VᵃU, YC.

37734 KING, WALTER   1758–1815
         A DISCOURSE DELIVERED IN CHELSEA, IN THE CITY OF NORWICH, JAN. 5, 1800, AS A TOKEN OF
         HUMILIATION . . . ON ACCOUNT OF THE DEATH OF . . . WASHINGTON. . . .
              Norwich [Conn.]: Printed by Thomas Hubbard. 1800.   pp. 22.   8vo.
                                       AAS, CHS, CL, CSL, HC, HEH, JCB, LOC, MFM, MHS, NL, NYHS, NYPL, YC.

37735 [KINLOCH, FRANCIS]   1755–1826
         EULOGY ON GEORGE WASHINGTON, ESQ. DECEASED, LATE COMMANDER IN CHIEF OF THE AMERICAN
         ARMIES. . . .
              Georgetown, S. C.: Printed by John Burd. 1, 800.   pp. 19.   8vo.
                                                             HEH, LOC, MFM, NYPL.

37736 KIRKLAND, JOHN THORNTON   1770–1840
         A DISCOURSE OCCASIONED BY THE DEATH OF GENERAL GEORGE WASHINGTON. DELIVERED DEC. 29,
         1799. . . . TO WHICH IS ADDED, THE VALEDICTORY ADDRESS OF THE LATE PRESIDENT. . . .
              *Printed at Boston, By I. Thomas and E. T. Andrews, Faust's Statue, no. 45, Newbury-
         Street. 1800.*   pp. 22, 22.   8vo.
              AAS, BA, BPL, HC, HEH, JCB, LOC, MFM, MHS, NL, NYHS, NYPL, NYSL, PFM, PL, PPL, WL, WLC.

37737 —— —— SECOND EDITION.
              *Printed at Boston, By I. Thomas and E. T. Andrews, Faust's Statue, no. 45, Newbury-
         Street. April, 1800.*   pp. 22.   8vo.   AAS, HEH, JCB, YC.

37738 —— A SERMON, PREACHED AT TAUNTON, JANUARY 15, 1800; AT THE ORDINATION OF REV. JOHN
         PIPON. . . .
              Cambridge, (Mass.) Printed by William Hilliard. 1800.   pp. 33.   8vo.
         Contains also "The charge by the Rev. Mr. Clark of Lexington" (pp. 23–30) and "The
         right hand of fellowship, by Rev. Mr. Clark of Norton" (pp. 30–3).
                                       AAS, BA, BPL, CL, HC, HEH, JCB, LOC, MHS, NEHGS, NYHS, NYPL, NYSL, YC.

37739 KLAGEN über den tod des General Waschingtons. . . .
See Helmuth, J. H. C.

37740 DER KLEINE catechismus des sel. D. Martin Luthers. Nebst den gewohnlichen morgen-tisch-und abend-gebeten. . . .
Philadelphia: Gedruckt bey Henrich Schweitzer . . . 1800. pp. [1], ii, 143, [1].
24mo. AAS.

37741 KLINE'S Carlisle Weekly Gazette. 1785–1817
Carlisle: (State of Pennsylvania) printed by George Kline. fol. weekly.
For 1800: AAS.

37742 KNOX, Samuel 1756–1832
A Funeral oration commemorative of . . . Washington . . . delivered to a respectable congregation of the citizens of Fredericktown, on Saturday the twenty-second of February, 1800. . . .
Fredericktown, Printed by Matthias Bartgis. . . . pp. [4], 25. 8vo.
HEH, LOC, M^dHS, MFM.

37743 [KNOXVILLE Gazette. 1791–1808
Knoxville: published by George Roulstone. fol. weekly.]
After having been combined for two years with the *Impartial Ovserver, q. v.,* the *Knoxville Gazette* resumed publication under that title in November or December, 1800.
For 1800: NO COPY KNOWN.

37744 KOTZEBUE, [August Friedrich Ferdinand von] 1761–1819
Adelaide of Wulfingen. A tragedy in four acts. . . . From the German of Kotzebue.
New-York; Printed for Charles Smith and S. Stephens. 1800. pp. 67. 8vo.
Translated by Benjamin Thompson. AAS, BPL, B^rU, HC, NYPL, NYSL, RU, UOP, UOT^x.

37745 — Count Benyowsky. . . . Translated from the German, by the Rev. W. Render . . . of Cambridge. First American from the second London edition.
Boston: Printed by Manning & Loring. 1800. 98 pages. 12mo.
AAS, BA, LOC, NYPL, YC.

37746 — The Count of Burgundy: a comedy of Kotzebue. In four acts. Translated from the German, by Charles Smith.
New-York: Printed for Charles Smith and S. Stephens. 1800. (M. McFarlane, Printer, 29 Gold-Street.) pp. vi, [2], 69, front.
Frontispiece portrait of Kotzebue by T. Clarke. The NYPL has an issue with a reset title-page reading *The Count of Burgundy, a Comedy in Four Acts.*
AAS, BPL, HC, LOC, NYHS, NYPL, NYSL, NYSOC, RU, UOP, UOT^x, YC.

37747 — The Dramatic works of Baron Kotzebue. Translated from the German, by Charles Smith. Vol. I [–II].
New-York: Printed for Charles Smith . . . and Stephen Stephens. . . . 1800. 2 vol.
Volume 1 contains a portrait of Kotzebue by T. Clarke, and Volume 2 a portrait of Hodgkinson by C. Tiebout. These volumes consist of the separately-printed plays gathered and bound with or without general titlepages. Volume 3 contains some plays not printed until 1801. AAS, BPL, HC, NYPL, W^{1s}HS, YC.

37748 — The East Indian: a comedy, in three acts. Translated from the German of Kotzebue.
New-York: Printed for Charles Smith and S. Stephens. 1800. pp. 88, front. 8vo.
The frontispiece is an engraving of Hodgkinson by C. Tiebout. The translation is claimed by Charles Smith but attributed to Alexander Thomson.
AAS, BPL, B^rU, HC, HEH, LOC, NYHS, NYPL, NYSL, UOC, UOP.

37749 — False shame: a comedy, in four acts, translated from the German of Kotzebue.
New-York: Printed by M. L. & W. A. Davis. For Thomas S. Arden, no. 186, Pearl-Street. 1800. pp. 80. 16mo.
The translation is attributed to William Dunlap. AAS, BPL, B^rU, HC, WLC, YC.

37750 —— FALSE SHAME: OR THE AMERICAN ORPHAN IN GERMANY: A COMEDY IN FOUR ACTS. FROM THE
GERMAN OF AUGUSTUS VON KOTZEBUE. . . .
Charleston: Printed by W. P. Young, no. 43, Broad-Street, 1800. pp. 16. 8mo.
Translation by William Dunlap. BPL, BʳU, HC, UOC, WLC, YC.

37751 —— THE FORCE OF CALUMNY: A PLAY, IN FIVE ACTS. TRANSLATED FROM THE GERMAN OF KOTZEBUE.
New-York: Printed for C. Smith and S. Stephens, by John Furman. 1800. pp. 124.
8vo.
A translation of Kotzebue's *Die Verläumder* claimed by Charles Smith but also attributed
to Anne Plumptre. AAS, BPL, BʳU, HC, HEH, LOC, NYHS, NYPL, NYSL, NYSOC, RU, UOP, YC.

37752 —— THE HAPPY FAMILY; A DRAMA, IN FIVE ACTS. TRANSLATED FROM THE GERMAN OF KOTZEBUE.
New-York: Printed for C. Smith and S. Stephens. 1800. pp. 84. 8vo.
A translation of *Die Silberne Hochzeit* attributed to both Charles Smith and Benjamin
Thompson. AAS, BPL, BʳU, HC, HEH, LOC, NYHS, NYPL, NYSL, UOC, UOP.

37753 —— ILDEGERTE, QUEEN OF NORWAY. . . . FROM THE GERMAN OF AUGUSTUS VON KOTZEBUE. . . . BY
BENJAMIN THOMPSON, JUN. TRANSLATOR. . . .
Philadelphia: Printed for Robert Campbell, no. 30, Chestnut-Street. 1800. 2 vols. in
one. pp. 103, [1], 94. 12mo. AAS, JCB, LOC, NYSL, PPL, YC.

37754 —— INDIGENCE, AND NOBLENESS OF MIND. A COMEDY IN FIVE ACTS, FROM THE GERMAN OF KOTZEBUE.
New-York: Printed for Charles Smith and S. Stephens. 1800. pp. 64. 8vo.
AAS, BPL, HC, HEH, LOC, NYHS, NYPL, NYSL, UOC, UOP, UOTˣ, WLC.

37755 —— LA PEYROUSE: A COMEDY, IN TWO ACTS. TRANSLATED FROM THE GERMAN OF KOTZEBUE, BY CHARLES
SMITH.
New-York: Printed for Charles Smith and S. Stephens. 1800. pp. 40. 8vo.
AAS, BPL, BʳU, HC, LOC, NYPL, UOC, UOP, UOTˣ.

37756 —— THE PEEVISH MAN: A DRAMA IN FOUR ACTS . . . BY AUGUSTUS KOTZEBUE. TRANSLATED BY C.
LUDGER. . . .
*Philadelphia, printed by John Bioren, for Henry & Patrick Rice; and James Rice,
& Co., Baltimore, 1800.* pp. 99. 16mo. PPL, UOP, WLC.

37757 —— PIZARRO IN PERU; OR, THE DEATH OF ROLLA. A PLAY, IN FIVE ACTS. FROM THE GERMAN OF
AUGUSTUS VON KOTZEBUE. . . .
*New-York: Printed by G. F. Hopkins, for William Dunlap. And sold at . . . T. and
J. Swords . . . Gaine and Teneyck . . . John Black . . . Alex. Somerville. . . . 1800.*
pp. iv, [2], [9]–92, front. 8vo.
Half-title:German theatre, no. III. The frontispiece is a portrait of Hodgkinson.
AAS, BPL, BʳU, HC, LOC, NYPL, NYSL, PPL, YC.

37758 —— PIZARRO; OR THE SPANIARDS IN PERU. A TRAGEDY IN FIVE ACTS. TRANSLATED FROM THE GERMAN OF
KOTZEBUE.
New-York: Printed for Charles Smith, and Stephen Stephens. 1800. pp. [2], 62.
8vo.
Richard Sheridan's translation slightly altered by Charles Smith.
AAS, BPL, BʳA, BʳU, HC, HEH, JCB, NYHS, NYPL, UOC, UOP, WLC.

37759 —— SELF IMMOLATION: OR, THE SACRIFICE OF LOVE. A PLAY IN THREE ACTS. TRANSLATED FROM THE
GERMAN OF KOTZEBUE.
New-York: Printed for Charles Smith and S. Stephens. 1800. pp. 54. 8vo.
A translation of *Der Opfertod* attributed to both Charles Smith and Henry Neuman. This
play is also printed under the title *Family Distress; or Self Immolation.*
AAS, BPL, BʳU, HC, LOC, NYHS, NYPL, UOC, UOP, RU, WLC.

37760 —— SIGHS; OR, THE DAUGHTER; A COMEDY, IN FIVE ACTS. . . . TAKEN FROM THE GERMAN DRAMA OF
KOTZEBUE; WITH ALTERATIONS, BY PRINCE HOARE. . . .
*Charlestown: Printed by Samuel Etheridge, for E. Larkin, no. 47, Cornhill, Boston.
1800.* pp. 71. 12mo.
With a "prologue written by John Taylor." AAS, BA, BʳU, HC, NYPL, UOP.

37761 —— The Sufferings of the family of Ortenberg. A novel. Translated from the German of Augustus von Kotzebue, by P. Will. . . . Two volumes in one.
  Philadelphia: Printed by John Bioren, for Henry & Patrick Rice . . . and James Rice, & Co. Baltimore. 1800.   pp. 154, [2], 160. 16mo.   AAS, HC, LOC, WLC.

37762 —— —— —— *New York: Printed for Hugh M. Griffith, bookseller. . . . 1800.*   2 vol. in 1. 12mo.   HEH, NYPL.

37763 —— The Virgin of the sun. A play in five acts. From the German of Augustus von Kotzebue. With notes marking the variations from the original.
  New York. Printed by G. F. Hopkins for William Dunlap. . . . 1800.   pp. 80, front. 8vo.
  An adaptation by Dunlap of Anne Plumptre's translation of *Die Sonnenjungfrau*; with a second titlepage reading *German Theatre, No. II.*
    BM, BPL, Br U, HC, LOC, NYPL, PPL, UOC, UOP, YC.

37764 —— The Virgin of the sun, a play in five acts. Translated from the German of Kotzebue.
  New-York; Printed for Charles Smith and S. Stephens. 1800.   pp. 96.   8vo.
  A translation attributed to James Lawrence and Anne Plumptre.
    AAS, BPL, Br U, HC, HEH, LOC, NYHS, UOC, UOP, YC.

37765 —— The Widow, and the riding horse. A dramatic trifle, in one act. Translated from the German of Kotzebue.
  New-York: Printed for Charles Smith and S. Stephens. 1800.   pp. 26.   8vo.
  A translation of *Die Wittwe und das Reipferd* attributed to both Charles Smith and Anne Plumptre.   AAS, BPL, Br U, HC, HEH, HSP, LOC, NYHS, NYPL, NYSL, UOC, UOP.

37766 —— The Wild-goose chase: a play, in four acts. With songs. From the German. . . . With notes marking the variations from the original.
  New-York: Printed by G. F. Hopkins, for William Dunlap. And sold at the office of . . . T. and J. Swords . . . Gaine and Teneyck . . . John Black . . . Alex. Somerville. . . . 1800.   pp. x, [3], 10–104, portraits.   8vo.
  The notes are by William Dunlap. There are variations in the text of the front matter. The AAS, LC, and NYPL copies have portraits of Hodgkinson and Kotzebue, but the others reported have one or neither. For a further description of this item see Sonneck-Upton, 471–2.   AAS, BPL, Br U, HC, LCP, LOC, NYHS, NYPL, UOC, UOP, YC.

37767 —— The Wild youth: a comedy for digestion. In three acts. Translated from the German of Kotzebue, by Charles Smith.
  New-York: Printed for Charles Smith and S. Stephens. 1800.   pp. 74.   8vo.
  A translation of *Der Wildfang.*   AAS, BPL, Br U, HC, HEH, LOC, NYHS, NYPL, NYSL, UOC, UOP, YC.

37768 KYD, Stewart   –1811
  A Treatise on the law of bills of exchange and promissory notes. . . . The second American, from the third London, edition. . . .
  Albany: Printed by Loring Andrews, for Thomas, Andrews & Penniman . . . Albany . . . Isaiah Thomas, at Worcester . . . Thomas & Andrews, at Boston, and . . . Thomas, Andrews & Butler, at Baltimore. . . . 1800.   pp. xii, 288.   12mo.
    AAS, BM, HC, HEH, JCB, LOC, MHS, NYBA, NYPL, NYSL, UOP, Va U.

37769 THE LADIES museum.
  Vol. I. No. 1. Saturday, February 15 [to No. 14, Saturday, June 7] 1800.
  Philadelphia: Isaac Ralston, 1800.   4to.   HSP, LCP, YC.

37770 LADY Washington's lamentation for the death of her husband. When Columbia's brave sons sought my hero to lead them. . . .
  Printed and sold by Nathaniel Coverly, Jr. Corner Theatre-Alley, Milk-Street — Boston.   Broadside.   4to.
  There are at least two variant issues.   AAS, BPL, MHS.

37771 A LAMENTATION FOR GEN. WASHINGTON ESQ. COMMANDER IN CHIEF OF THE COMBINED FORCES OF AMERICA AND FRANCE, DURING THE REVOLUTIONARY WAR. . . .
N. Coverly, Jr. Printer, Milk-Street, Boston. Broadside. 4to. AAS.

37772 —— —— —— *Sold wholesale and retail, by L. Deming, no. 1 Market Square Corner, of Merchant's Row, Boston.* Broadside. 4to. HEH.

37773 DER LANCASTER CORRESPONDENT. 1799–1803
Christian Jacob Hütter . . . in Lancaster [Pa.] fol. weekly.
FOR 1800: HSP, LᴬHS.

37774 THE LANCASTER JOURNAL. 1794–1839
Lancaster [Pa.]: Printed . . . by William Hamilton. fol. weekly and semi-weekly.
FOR 1800: [HSP].

37775 LANCASTER COUNTY, PENNSYLVANIA. FEDERALIST PARTY.
TO THE [MUTILATED.] AT A MEETING OF THE FEDERAL CITIZENS HELD AT THE COURT-HOUSE, IN THE BOROUGH OF LANCASTER. . . . SEPT. 22, 1800.
[Lancaster: 1800.] Broadside. fol. AAS.

37776 LA NEUVILLE, M. J.
ELÉGIE SUR LA MORT DE GEORGE WASHINGTON. PAR M. J. LA NEUVILLE, MEMBRE DE LA LOGE L'AMÉNITIÉ.
A Philadelphie: chez Thomas & William Bradford. . . . 1800. pp. 6, [1]. 8vo.
AAS, BʳU, JCB.

37777 LANGDON, CHAUNCEY 1763–1830
AN ORATION ON THE VITRUES AND DEATH OF . . . WASHINGTON . . . DELIVERED AT CASTLETON, FEBRUARY 22D, 1800. . . .
Rutland: Printed by W. Fay. pp. 24. 8vo. AAS, BA, HEH, LOC, MFM, NYPL, YC.

37778 LANGLEY, B[ATTY] 1696–1751
THE BUILDER'S JEWEL, OR, THE YOUTH'S INSTRUCTOR, AND WORKMAN'S REMEMBRANCER. . . . ILLUSTRATED BY UPWARDS OF 200 EXAMPLES, ENGRAVED ON 100 COPPER PLATES. . . . FIRST AMERICAN EDITION.
Charlestown: Printed by S. Etheridge, for Samuel Hill, engraver, no. 2, Cornhill, Boston. pp. 46, 100 plates. sq. 16mo.
This edition can be dated by newspaper advertisements. Thomas Langley, 1702–1751, was joint author. AAS, HC, JCB, MHS, NYHS, PPL.

37779 LANSINGBURGH GAZETTE. 1798–1883
[Lansingburgh, N. Y.] Printed . . . by Gardiner Tracy. weekly. fol.
FOR 1800: TROY PUB. LIB.

37780 LARZELERE, JACOB
A DISCOURSE, ON THE DEATH OF . . . WASHINGTON, DELIVERED IN . . . NORTHAMPTON, BUCKS COUNTY, PENNSYLVANIA, ON THE 22D OF FEBRUARY, 1800. . . .
Printed by Stephen C. Ustick, Mount-Holly [N. J.], 1800. pp. 18. 8vo.
AAS, HEH, JCB, LCP, LOC, MFM, NJHS, NYHS, NYPL, PPL, YC.

37781 THE LAST WORDS AND DYING CONFESSION OF THREE PIRATES WHO WERE EXECUTED THIS DAY, (MAY 9TH, 1800).
From Folwell's Press . . . Philadelphia. (Copy-right secured. . . .) pp. [8], front. 8vo.
Halftitle: Execution of La Croix, Berrouse, & Baker, for piracy. HSP, LOC, WLC.

37782 A LATE LETTER FROM A SOLICITOUS MOTHER TO HER ONLY SON, BOTH LIVING IN NEW ENGLAND. THE TENTH EDITION.
Salem, printed and sold by Nathaniel Coverly, Junr. 1800. pp. 20. 12mo.
AAS, EI, HC, NL, NYPL.

37783 LATHROP, Joseph   1731–1820
A Sermon, preached at Westfield, January 1, 1800. At the dedication of the academy in that town. . . .
Suffield, printed by Edward Gray, M,DCCC.   pp. 15, [1].   8vo.
The last leaf contains a "Dedication speech. By the honorable Samuel Fowler."
AAS, BPL, CHS, HC, HEH, JCB, LOC, MHS, NL, NYHS, NYPL, UTS, YC.

37784 LATHY, Thomas Pike
Reparation: or, the school for libertines. A dramatic piece. . . . As performed at the Boston Theatre. . . .
Boston: Printed by John Russell, 1800.   pp. 46.   12mo.
AAS, BM, BPL, BʳU, HC, JCB, LOC, MHS, NYPL, NYSOC, YC.

37785 [LATROBE, Benjamin Henry]   1764–1820
American copper-mines. To the chairman of the committee of commerce and manufactures. . . .
[Philadelphia.]   pp. 8.   8vo.   AAS, LOC.

37786 LAUS Deo! The Worcester collection of sacred harmony. . . . The seventh edition, altered, corrected and revised, with additions, by Oliver Holden. . . .
Printed, typographically, at Boston, By Isaiah Thomas and Ebenezer T. Andrews: Sold by them . . . by said Thomas in Worcester; by Thomas, Andrews & Penniman, Albany; by Thomas, Andrews & Butler, Baltimore. . . . Dec. 1800.   pp. 143, [1]. obl. 12mo.
AAS, HC, LOC, MHS, NL, NYPL.

37787 LAW, Andrew   1748–1821
The Art of singing; in three parts: viz I. The Musical primer, II. The Christian harmony, III. The Musical magazine. . . . Published according to Act of Congress. . . .
[Printed by William Law] Cheshire; Connecticut: M,DCCC.   pp. 224.   obl. 12mo.
The three parts were published separately, the third being the sixth issue of the *Musical Magazine*, dated November, 1801.   AAS, LOC, WL, YC.

37788 LAW, Lyman   1770–1842
See Huntington, Jedidiah.

37789 LEARNED, Erastus   1775–1824
The Nature and importance of Christian worship . . . preached, July 4th, 1800, at the dedication of the new meeting house in . . . Charlton. . . .
Printed at Worcester, by Isaiah Thomas, Jun. August — 1800.   pp. 21.   8vo.
AAS, BA, CL, LOC, NYPL, NYSL.

37790 LEDYARD, *Dr.* Isaac
An Oration, delivered on Saturday, the 22d of February, 1800, at Newtown . . . on account of the death of George Washington. . . .
Brooklyn, Printed by Thomas Kirk, 1800.   pp. 16.   8vo.
"Ode, composed and set to music, by Mr. Stephen Hoyt," pp. 13–6.   LOC.

37791 LEE, ANDREW   1745–1832
A Sermon, preached at the ordination of . . . David Palmer . . . in Townsend, Massachusetts. January 1, 1800. . . .
Leominster, Massachusetts: Printed by Adams & Wilder. 1800.   pp. 32.   8vo.
AAS, AHTS, CHS, CL, HC, HEH, JCB, NYSL, PL, YC.

37792 LEE, CHAUNCEY   1763–1842
The Tree of knowledge of political good and evil. . . . Delivered at Colebrook [Conn.]. . . . July 4th, 1800. . . .
Bennington: Printed by T. Collier, and Company. 1800.   pp. 31.   8vo.
AAS, BA, CHS.

37793   —— —— —— *Hartford: Printed by Hudson & Goodwin, 1800.*   pp. 31.   8vo.
BA, CHS, HC, JCB, MHS, NYPL, NYSL, WL, YC.

37794   LEE, ELIAS, *of Ballston, N. Y.*
The Christmas dispute revived, in a letter from Mr. William Smith, of Norwalk, Connecticut . . . with a reply by Mr. Lee.
Ballston — printed by W. Child for Elder Elias Lee. . . . 1800.   pp. 12.   12mo.
AAS.

37795   LEE, ELISHA   1757–1835
An Oration, delivered in Sheffield, February the 22d, 1800, in honor of the memory of . . . Washington. . . .
Stockbridge: Printed at the office of Horatio Jones & Co. by H. Willard.   pp. [2], 10.   sq. 12mo.   AAS, BA, MHS, NYPL.

37796   LEE, HARRIET
Arundel. A novel.
Philadelphia: Printed by James Carey. June 1, 1800.   pp. 112.   16mo.   AAS.

37797   [LEE, HENRY]   1756–1818
Funeral oration [on the death of Washington, delivered December 26, 1799, and published by order of Congress].
[*First edition, Philadelphia, 1800.*]   pp. 17.   8vo.
AAS, BM, HEH, HSP, LCP, NYHS, NYPL, PL, YC.

37798   —— A Funeral oration, in honor of George Washington . . . delivered at the request of Congress, at the German Lutheran Church on Thursday, the twenty-sixth of December. . . .
Supplement to The True American, *January 7, 1800.*   broadside.   EBERSTADT.

37799   —— —— —— *Brooklyn: Printed by Thomas Kirk. 1800.*   pp. 16.   8vo.
AAS, BPL, CSL, HEH, JCB, LOC, NL, NYHS, NYPL, NYSL, W¹ˢHS, YC.

37800   —— —— —— *Second edition. Brooklyn: Printed by Thomas Kirk. 1800.*   pp. 16.   8vo.
AAS, BA, BPL, HEH, JCB, LOC, NYHS, NYPL, NYSL, NYSOC, RU.

37801   —— —— —— *Printed at the Minerva Press in Dedham — 1800.*   pp. 15.   8vo.   AAS, JCB, MHS.

37802   —— —— —— *New-Haven: Printed and sold by Read & Morse. 1800.*   pp. 21.   12mo.   HEH, YC.

37803   —— A Funeral oration on the death of General George Washington, delivered at the request of Congress. . . .
Baltimore: Printed by Warner & Hanna, 1800. . . .   pp. 12.   12mo.   LOC.

37804   —— —— —— *Boston: Printed for Joseph Nancrede and Manning & Loring. . . .*   pp. 15.   8vo.
AAS, BA, BPL, HC, HEH, JCB, LOC, MHS, NYPL, NYSL, PʳU, VᵃU, W¹ˢHS, WLC, YC.

37805   —— —— —— *Troy: Printed by R. Moffitt, & Co.*   pp. 11.   sm. 4to.   AAS, NYHS.

37806   —— A Funeral oration, on the death of General Washington. Delivered in Philadelphia. . . . Ornamented with an elegant engraving.
Philadelphia: Printed by John Hoff, 1800.   pp. 20, front.   4to.
BPL, HEH, JCB, NYPL, PPL.

37807   —— A Funeral oration on the death of General Washington, delivered in the German Lutheran church, Philadelphia: at the request of Congress. . . .
Philadelphia: Printed by John Ormrod, 1800.   pp. 17.   8vo.
This is a reissue of the first edition with the Ormrod titlepage added.
BM, HEH, JCB, LOC, MHS, NYPL, PSL, YC.

37808 —— A FUNERAL ORATION, ON THE DEATH OF GEN. WASHINGTON DELIVERED, AT THE REQUEST OF CONGRESS. . . .
Dover [N. H.], printed by Samuel Bragg, Jun. 1800. pp. 15. 16mo. AAS, HEH.

37809 —— THE NATIONAL EULOGY OF THE ILLUSTRIOUS GEORGE WASHINGTON, PRONOUNCED AT THE REQUEST OF THE UNITED STATES IN CONGRESS ASSEMBLED. . . .
Portsmouth, (New-Hampshire,) Printed at the United States' Oracle-Office by Charles Pierce, January, 1800. pp. 16. 8vo. AAS, BA, HC, JCB, LOC, NHSL, NYHS, NYPL.

37810 LEE, JOSEPH   1742–1819
THE RESURRECTION OF THE SAINTS. . . . DELIVERED JUNE 14, 1799, AT THE INTERMENT OF THE REV. BENJAMIN BRIGHAM. . . .
Printed at Brookfield, Massachusetts, by E. Merriam & Co. February, 1800. pp. 51. 8vo. AAS, JCB, NYHS, YC.
Second title: The Blessedness of those who die in the Lord. . . . Delivered April 25, 1793, at the funeral of Mrs. Lucy Brigham. . . .
Printed at Brookfield, Massachusetts, by E. Merriam & Co. February, 1800. pp. [29]–51. 8vo. AAS, JCB, YC.

37811 LEE, RICHARD E.
RICHARD E. LEE'S LETTER, THE ATTORNEY GENERAL'S OPINION, AND THE AFFIDAVITS ACCOMPANYING THE GOVERNOR'S COMMUNICATION TO THE CONDUCT OF DOCTOR JOHN K. READ, A MAGISTRATE OF THE BOROUGH OF NORFOLK.
Richmond: Printed by Meriwether Jones, printer to the Commonwealth. 1800. pp. 32. 8vo. AAS, LOC.

37812 LEGAUX, PETER
TO THE PEOPLE OF THE AMERICAN STATES. ALL WILL AGREE THAT AGRICULTURE CONSTITUTES THE TRUE AND PERMANENT RICHES OF ANY COUNTRY. . . . PETER LEGAUX. SPRING MILLS, 13 MILES. N.N.W. FROM PHILADELPHIA, MARCH 22, 1800.
Broadside. fol. MHS.

37813 LEIB, MICHAEL
DR. LEIB. MUCH HAS BEEN SAID RESPECTING THE CONDUCT OF DOCTOR LEIB IN THE CERTIFICATE BUSINESS. THE FOLLOWING DOCUMENTS WILL, IT IS EXPECTED, SATISFY EVERY CANDID MAN.
[Philadelphia]. pp. [7]. fol. LOC(missing).

37814 LEMPRIERE, WILLIAM   –1834
A TOUR FROM GIBRALTAR . . . OVER MOUNT ATLAS TO MOROCCO. . . . THE THIRD EDITION, WITH ADDITIONS AND CORRECTIONS.
Richmond: Published by William Pritchard. 1800. pp. xii, 330. 12mo.
AAS, CU, GU, LOC, UOP, VᵃSL, VᵃU.

37815 LEONARD, DAVID [AUGUSTUS]   1771–1819
A FUNERAL SERMON, ON THE DECEASE OF A YOUNG MAN, WHOSE DEATH WAS OCCASIONED BY THE EXTRACTION OF A TOOTH. . . . DELIVERED IN THE BAPTIST MEETING-HOUSE . . . IN THE CITY OF NEW YORK, ON FEBRUARY 16TH, 1800. . . .
New-York: Printed by Furman and Loudon . . . 1800. pp. 30. 8vo. LOC, UOC.

37816 —— AN ORATION OCCASIONED BY THE DEATH OF . . . WASHINGTON. PRONOUNCED IN THE FIRST BAPTIST MEETINGHOUSE, IN THE CITY OF NEW-YORK. ON FEBRUARY 22, 1800. . . .
New-York: Printed and sold by M. M'Farlane, 1800. pp. 22, front. 8vo.
The frontispiece is a portrait of Washington engraved by J. White after Joseph Wright.
BA, HEH, LOC, MFM, NYHS, NYPL, UOC.

37817 LESSONS FOR CHILDREN. . . .
See Barbauld, Mrs. Anna Letitia (Aikin).

37818   L'ESTRANGE, ROGER   1616–1704
         SENECA'S MORALS, BY WAY OF ABSTRACT. TO WHICH IS ADDED, A DISCOURSE UNDER THE TITLE OF
            AN AFTER THOUGHT. ADORNED WITH PLATES. . . .
               Boston: Printed for Joseph Bumstead. Sold by him . . . by Thomas and Andrews . . .
         by E. Larkin, W. Pelham. Wm. P. and L. Blake . . . and J. Nancrede. . . . Third American
         edition. 1800.   pp. xvi, [15]–372, 4 plates.   12mo.
                                                            AAS, BPL, HC, JCB, LOC, NYPL, NYSL, UOC.

37819   A LETTER FROM A BLACKSMITH, TO THE MINISTERS AND ELDERS OF THE CHURCH OF SCOTLAND. . . .
               London printed: reprinted, (for Subscribers) by T. Collier, Litchfield [Conn.], — 1800.
         pp. 78.   16mo.
         Attributed to John Witherspoon and Henry Home, Lord Kames.   AAS, CHS, NYPL.

37820   A LETTER FROM MANLIUS, TO JOHN MARSHALL ESQ. MEMBER OF CONGRESS.
               Richmond: Printed for the author, by Samuel Pleasants, Jun. February, 1800.
         pp. 18.   8vo.   NYHS.

37821   A LETTER TO GENERAL HAMILTON, OCCASIONED BY HIS LETTER TO PRESIDENT ADAMS. . . .
               See Webster, Noah.

37822   A LETTER TO MAJOR GENERAL ALEXANDER HAMILTON. . . .
               See Ogden, Uzal.

37823   LEWIS, ELDAD   –1825
         AN EULOGY, ON THE LIFE AND CHARACTER OF . . . WASHINGTON. . . . DELIVERED AT LENOX,
            FEBRUARY 22, 1800. . . .
               Pittsfield: (Mass.), Printed by Chester Smith, March, 1800.   pp. 20.   8vo.
         This eulogy is in verse.   BPL, BʳU, HEH, LOC, MFM, NYPL.

37824   LEWIS, JOHN   1675–1747
         THE CHURCH CATECHISM EXPLAINED. . . . 37TH ED.
               New York, J. Oram, 1800.   pp. 79, [7].   24mo.   GTS.

37825   LEWIS, M[ATTHEW] G[REGORY]   1775–1818
         THE EAST INDIAN: A COMEDY, IN FIVE ACTS. AS PERFORMED AT THE THEATRE-ROYAL, DRURY-
            LANE. . . .
               London — printed. New-York: re-printed by M. L. & W. A. Davis, for H. Caritat,
         bookseller, no. 153 Broad-way. 1800.   pp. 71.   8vo. AAS, HC, JCB, LCP, NYPL, UOC, WC, YC.

37826   LEYDEN ASSOCIATION.
         MINUTES OF THE LEYDEN ASSOCIATION, HELD AT THE BAPTIST MEETING HOUSE, IN RICHMOND:
            M,DCCC. TOGETHER WITH THEIR CIRCULAR. . . .
               Brattleboro', Vermont: Printed by B. Smead, for the Association. 1800.   pp. 10.
         12mo.   AAS.

37827   THE LIFE AND DEATH OF ROBIN HOOD, COMPLETE IN TWENTY-FOUR SONGS.
               New-York: Printed in the year 1800.   pp. 80.   16mo.   AAS, NYPL.

37828   LIFE AND SURPRISING ADVENTURES OF . . . ROBINSON CRUSOE.
               See Defoe, Daniel.

37829   LILLY, WILLIAM, *pseud.*
         LILLY'S ALMANAC FOR THE YEAR OF OUR LORD EIGHTEEN HUNDRED, ONE. . . . FITTED TO THE
            MERIDIAN AND HORIZON OF NEW HAVEN. . . .
               New Haven: Printed and Sold by Read & Morse, 1801 [1800].   pp. [24].   16mo.
         Commonly attributed to David Sanford, 1783–1805.   AAS, LOC.

37830   [LINCOLNTON, N. C., NEWSPAPER.   1800–1802
               Printed by John M. Slump.   fol.   biweekly.]   NO COPY KNOWN.

37831 LINES COMPOSED ON THE DEATH OF GENERAL WASHINGTON. . . .
Broadside. 4to. AAS, EI, NYHS.

37832 LINN, JOHN BLAIR 1777–1804
THE DEATH OF WASHINGTON. A POEM. IN IMITATION OF THE MANNER OF OSSIAN. . . .
Philadelphia: Printed by John Ormrod, no. 41, Chestnut-Street. 1800. pp. 26. 8vo.
AAS, BA, BPL, BʳU, HC, HEH, HSP, JCB, MFM, NYHS, NYPL, NYSL, OH&PS, WLC, YC.

37833 LINN, WILLIAM 1752–1808
A DISCOURSE, DELIVERED APRIL 1ST, 1800, IN THE BRICK PRESBYTERIAN CHURCH, BEFORE THE NEW-YORK MISSIONARY SOCIETY. . . .
New-York: Printed by Isaac Collins, no. 189, Pearl-Street. 1800. pp. 40. 8vo.
Appended is the "Report of the directors."
AAS, CU, HEH, HSP, JCB, NYHS, NYPL, NYSL, PʳU, PTS, RU, YC.

37834 —— A FUNERAL EULOGY, OCCASIONED BY THE DEATH OF GENERAL WASHINGTON. DELIVERED FEBRUARY 22D, 1800, BEFORE THE NEW-YORK STATE SOCIETY OF THE CINCINNATI. . . .
New-York: Printed by Isaac Collins, no. 189, Pearl-Street. 1800. pp. 44. 8vo.
AAS, BA, BPL, HC, HEH, JCB, LCP, LOC, MᵈHS, MFM, MHS, NYHS, NYPL, NYSL, PL, PʳU, PTS, WL, WLC, YC.

37835 [——] SERIOUS CONSIDERATIONS ON THE ELECTION OF A PRESIDENT; ADDRESSED TO THE CITIZENS OF THE UNITED STATES.
New-York: Printed and sold by John Furman, at his blank, stamp, and stationery shop, opposite the City Hall. 1800. pp. 36. 8vo.
AAS, BA, BPL, HEH, HSP, JCB, LCP, LOC, MHS, MSL, NYHS, NYPL, NYSL, WLC, YC.

37836 —— —— *Trenton: Printed by Sherman, Mershon & Thomas. 1800.* pp. 31. 8vo.
LOC, NYSL, PʳU, YC.

37837 LISLE, HENRY MAURICE — 1814
AN ORATION, DELIVERED AT HINGHAM . . . THE 22D OF FEBRUARY, 1800 . . . MOURNING, FOR THE DEATH OF . . . WASHINGTON. . . .
Boston, Printed by John Russell. 1800. pp. 22. 8vo.
AAS, BA, BPL, HC, HEH, JCB, LOC, MFM, MHS, NYPL, NYSL, YC.

37838 LITTLE TRUTHS BETTER THAN GREAT FABLES. . . .
See Darton, William.

37839 LIVINGSTON, ROBERT R. 1746–1813
CATALOGUE OF BOOKS, IN THE LIBRARY OF THE HON. ROBERT R. LIVINGSTON, OF CLERMONT. FEBRUARY, 1800.
Poughkeepsie, State of New-York — printed by John Woods. — 1800. pp. 34. sq. 8vo. AAS, NYHS.

37840 LOGAN, GEORGE 1753–1821
A LETTER TO THE CITIZENS OF PENNSYLVANIA, ON THE NECESSITY OF PROMOTING AGRICULTURE, MANUFACTURES, AND THE USEFUL ARTS. . . .
Lancaster, printed by W. & R. Dickson, north Queenstreet, March 14, 1800. pp. 28. 8vo.
Contains "The constitution of the Lancaster County Society, for Promoting of Agriculture, Manufactures, and the Useful Arts." AAS, HSP, LOC, NYPL.

37841 —— SECOND EDITION.
Philadelphia: Printed by Patterson & Cochran, no. 108, Race-Street. May 1, 1800. pp. 30. 8vo. AAS, APS, HSP, JCB, LOC, MᵈHS, MHS, NYHS, NYPL, PSL.

37842 LONDON. ENGLAND. CADELL & DAVIES
LONDON, DECR. 11, 1800. GENTLEMEN, WE WERE FAVORED WITH YOUR JOINT LETTER OF JUNE 20, ENCLOSING A LIST OF BOOKS FOR THE INTENDED LIBRARY AT WASHINGTON. . . .
[*Washington.*] pp. 8. 12mo.
A printing of the letter transmitting the invoice of the first consignment of books to the Library of Congress. Printed in full in William D. Johnston, *History of the Library of Congress*, Washington, 1904, p. 24. LOC.

37843 THE LONG ISLAND COURIER.
  See The Courier, and New-York and Long Island Advertiser.

37844 LONGWORTH, DAVID   1765?–1821
  LONGWORTH'S AMERICAN ALMANAC, NEW-YORK REGISTER, AND CITY DIRECTORY FOR THE TWENTY-
  FIFTH YEAR OF AMERICAN INDEPENDENCE. . . .
    New-York: Printed and published by D. Longworth, no. 11, Park. 1800.   pp. 390.
  24mo.
  Second title: ASTRONOMICAL CALCULATIONS FOR THE TWENTY-FIFTH YEAR OF AMERICAN INDEPEND-
  ENCE. . . . BY ABRAHAM SHOEMAKER.
    From the press of J. C. Totten, & Co. [New York.]   AAS, HEH, NYHS, NYPL.

37845 THE LOOKING GLASS FOR THE MIND. . . .
  See Berquin, Arnaud.

37846 LOUGHBY, DENNIS, *of Pittsburgh*
  [A LAMENTATION ON THE DEATH OF GENERAL WASHINGTON.
    Pittsburgh, 1800.]
  Advertized in the *Pittsburgh Gazette* of Dec. 5, 1800.

37847 —— [A NEW SONG IN PRAISE OF OUR PRESENT GOVERNOR; COMPOSED BY DENNIS LOUGHBY.
    Pittsburgh, 1800.]
  Advertised in the *Tree of Liberty*, Sept. 6, 1800.

37848 THE LOUISVILLE GAZETTE; AND REPUBLICAN TRUMPET.   1798–1811
  [*Louisville, Georgia. Published by Ambrose Day and James Hely.* fol. weekly.]
  Sometime in 1800 the title was changed from *The State Gazette, and Louisville Journal.*
                  FOR 1800: NO COPIES KNOWN.

37849 [LOUVET DE COUVRAY, JEAN BAPTISTE]   1760–1797
  THE INTERESTING HISTORY OF THE BARON DE LOVZINSKI. WRITTEN BY HIMSELF. WITH A
  RELATION OF . . . THE LIFE OF . . . COUNT PULASKI. . . .
    Hartford: Printed by J. Babcock. 1800.   pp. 142, [2].   24mo.
  Annexed are "The story of Alcander and Septimius," "The romantic shepherdess," and
  two pages of testimonials for Child's Spelling Book.   AAS, CHS.

37850 —— [LOVE AND PATRIOTISM! OR, THE EXTRAORDINARY ADVENTURES OF M. DUPORTAIL, LATE MAJOR-
  GENERAL IN THE ARMIES OF THE UNITED STATES. INTERSPERSED WITH MANY SURPRISING
  INCIDENTS IN THE LIFE OF THE LATE COUNT PULASKI.
    Boston: Samuel Etheridge. 1800.   pp. 59.   12mo.]   SABIN 42357.

37851 LOVE, CHARLES
  A POEM ON THE DEATH OF GENERAL GEORGE WASHINGTON, LATE PRESIDENT OF THE UNITED
  STATES. . . .
    Alexandria, Virginia, A. D. M,DCCC.   pp. 60.   12mo.
  The last four pages contain a list of subscribers.
           BA, BʳU, HEH, JCB, LOC, MFM, NYHS, NYPL, PPL.

37852 [LOVETT, JOHN]   1761–1818
  A TRIBUTE TO WASHINGTON, FOR FEBRUARY 22D, 1800. . . .
    Troy: Printed by R. Moffit & Co. 1800.   pp. 15.   8vo.
  In verse.   BʳU, HEH, LOC, NYHS, NYPL.

37853 LOVZINSKI, BARON DE
  See Louvet de Couvray, Jean Baptiste.

37854 LOW, NATHANAEL 1740–1808
AN ASTRONOMICAL DIARY: OR ALMANACK, FOR THE YEAR OF CHRISTIAN AERA 1801. . . . CALCULATED
FOR THE MERIDIAN OF BOSTON. . . .
Boston: Printed and Sold by John & Thomas Fleet, at the Bible and Heart,
Cornhill. . . . pp. [24]. 12mo. AAS, HEH, LOC, NYPL, NYSL, YC.

37855 LOW, SAMUEL 1765 ———
ODE FOR THE 4TH OF JULY, 1800. COMPOSED BY MR. [SAMUEL] LOW. AGAIN THE SIGNAL DAY,
TO FREEMEN EVER DEAR. . . .
Printed by John Harrisson, no. 3 Peck-Slip [,New York]. Broadside. fol.
Also printed as an appendix to the *Oration* by M. L. Davis. AAS, NYHS

37856 —— POEMS, BY SAMUEL LOW. . . . IN TWO VOLUMES. . . .
New-York: Printed by T. & J. Swords, no. 99 Pearl-Street. 1800. pp. [vi], [9]–147;
[1], 168. 12mo.
A list of subscribers is printed at the beginning of Vol. 2.
AAS, BPL, BʳU, HEH, LOC, NL, NYHS, NYPL, NYSL, UOP, UOTˣ, WLC, YC.

37857 LOWTH, [ROBERT] 1710–1787
A SHORT INTRODUCTION TO ENGLISH GRAMMAR: WITH CRITICAL NOTES. A NEW EDITION. BY DR.
LOWTHE. . . .
Wilmington: Printed and sold by Bonsal and Niles. Also sold at their book-store,
no. 173, Market-Street, Baltimore. 1800. pp. 140. 12mo. AAS, NYPL, WⁱPL.

37858 LUCAS, MARGARET [BRINDLEY] 1701–1769
AN ACCOUNT OF THE CONVINCEMENT AND CALL TO THE MINISTRY OF MARGARET LUCAS, LATE OF
LEEK, IN STAFFORDSHIRE. . . .
Philadelphia: Printed by B. & J. Johnson, no. 147 High Street. 1800. pp. viii, 134,
[1]. 24mo.
The last leaf contains the printer's advertisment. AAS, BPL, HC, UOP.

37859 LUCCA, GAUDENTIO DI, *pseud.*
See Berington, Simon.

37860 LUTHER, MARTIN
See Der kleine catechismus. . . .

37861 LYNCHBURG WEEKLY GAZETTE 1798–1801
[*Lynchburg, Va.*] *Printed by John Carter. . . .* fol. weekly.
FOR 1800: [NYHS].

37862 LYON, ASA 1763–1841
THE MOURNER'S HOPE. A FUNERAL SERMON, DELIVERED AT ST. ALBANS, BEFORE THE . . . FRANKLIN
LODGE. ON THE DEATH OF DAVID HICKOK, ESQ. OF ST. ALBANS; WHO DIED, AT SHEFFIELD,
FEB. 18, 1800. . . .
Vergennes: Printed for Sam Chipman, Jun. 1800. pp. 20. HALL P. MCCULLOCH.

37863 LYTTELTON, GEORGE 1709–1773
OBSERVATIONS ON THE CONVERSION AND APOSTLESHIP OF ST. PAUL. . . . FIRST BOSTON EDITION.
Boston: printed by Manning and Loring. Sold at their bookstore, no. 2, Cornhill. 1800.
pp. 95, [1], 23, [1]. 12mo.
Annexed are "The conversion of a Mahometan" and a poem, "The bird of Paradise. By
the late Rev. Dr. Samuel Stennet." AAS, CL, CSL, JCB, MHS, YC.

37864 M'CALLA, DANIEL 1748–1800
THE ACCEPTABLE YEAR OF THE LORD, OR THE JUBILEE OF THE GOSPEL; A SERMON, PREACHED ON
JAMES ISLAND, JUNE 12, 1799. . . .
Charleston, (South Carolina) Printed by Thomas Bartholomew Bowen, no. 260 King
Street. 1800. pp. 26. 12mo.
Cover title. PʳU.

37865 MACCLINTOCK, SAMUEL   1732–1804
  AN ORATION, COMMEMORATIVE OF . . . WASHINGTON; PRONOUNCED AT GREENLAND, FEBRUARY
  22D, 1800. . . .
    Portsmouth, (New-Hampshire,) printed at the United States' Oracle-office, by Charles
  Peirce, 1800. pp. 16. 8vo.   AAS, LOC, MHS, NL, NYHS, NYPL, PTS.

37866 McCLURE, DAVID   1748–1820
  A DISCOURSE; COMMEMORATIVE OF THE DEATH OF . . . WASHINGTON. . . . DELIVERED AT EAST-
  WINDSOR, CONNECTICUT, FEBRUARY 22, 1800. BY DAVID M'CLURE. . . .
    Printed at East-Windsor, by Luther Pratt. March 24, 1800. pp. 23. 8vo.
    AAS, AHTS, BPL, CHS, HC, HEH, JCB, LOC, MFM, MHS, NYPL, PL, PTS, UTS, WL.

37867 McCORKLE, SAMUEL EUSEBIUS   1746–1811
  TRUE GREATNESS. A SERMON ON THE DEATH OF . . . WASHINGTON . . . DELIVERED AT THYATIRA
  ON SUNDAY, JANUARY 12TH; AND . . . IN SALISBURY, FEB. 11, 1800. . . .
    Lincolnton: Printed, by John M. Slump, at his English and German Printing-Office
  1800. pp. 27, [2]. 8vo.   HC, LOC.

37868 M'CULLOCH'S POCKET ALMANAC, FOR THE YEAR 1801. BEING THE FIRST OF THE 19TH CENTURY. . . .
    Philadelphia: Printed and sold by J. M'Culloch, no. 1, North Third-Street. pp. [32].
  32mo.   AAS, HSP, LOC.

37869 MACDONALD, THOMAS
  See Fitzsimmons, Thomas.

37870 MACGOWAN, JOHN   1726–1780
  THE LIFE OF JOSEPH, THE SON OF ISRAEL. . . . CHIEFLY DESIGNED TO ALLURE YOUNG MINDS TO
  A LOVE OF THE SACRED SCRIPTURES.
    Dover, N. H. Printed by Samuel Bragg, jun. at the Sun Office. 1800. pp. 195.
  12mo.
  "To the public" signed by William Rogers, Philadelphia, 1791.   AAS, BM, JCB.

37871 —— A NEW EDITION.
    Richmond: Published by William Pritchard. 1800. pp. xv, [1], 259. 12mo.
  "To the public" as above.   AAS, JCB, LOC, NYHS, VᵃSL.

37872 M'KEEHAN, DAVID
  AN ADDRESS DELIVERED AT GREENSBURGH . . . PENNSYLVANIA, ON SATURDAY, FEBRUARY, 22D, 1800,
  THE ANNIVERSARY OF THE BIRTH OF . . . WASHINGTON, PUBLISHED IN THE PITTSBURGH
  GAZETTE. . . .
    Washington [Pa.]: Printed by John Colerick, 1800. pp. 15. 16mo.   GTS.

37873 McKEEN, JOSEPH   1757–1807
  A SERMON, PREACHED BEFORE THE . . . COUNCIL . . . OF MASSACHUSETTS, MAY 28, 1800, BEING
  THE DAY OF GENERAL ELECTION. . . .
    Boston: Printed by Young & Minns, State printers. 1800. pp. 30. 8vo.
    AAS, BA, BPL, CL, CSL, HC, HEH, JCB, LOC, MHS, NHSL, NL, NYHS, NYPL, NYSL,
            PL, PTS, UOC, VᵃU, WL, WLC, YC.

37874 McREE, JAMES   1752–1840
  AN EULOGIUM, OR FUNERAL DISCOURSE: DELIVERED AT SALISBURY, ON THE 22ND. FEBRUARY, 1800;
  BY THE REVD. JAMES M'REE: IN COMMEMORATION OF THE DEATH OF . . . WASHINGTON.
    Salisbury [N.C.]: Printed by Francis Coupee. 1800. pp. 20. 24mo. NYPL.

37875 MACWHORTER, ALEXANDER   1734–1807
  A FUNERAL SERMON, PREACHED IN NEWARK, DECEMBER 27, 1799. . . . FOR . . . WASHINGTON. . . .
  TO WHICH IS SUBJOINED, HIS LAST ADDRESS. . . .
    Newark: Printed and sold by Jacob Halsey. MDCCC. pp. [4], iv, 44. 8vo.
    AAS, BA, BPL, HEH, HSP, JCB, LOC, NJHS, NYHS, NYPL, NYSL, RU, WLC.

37876   MADISON, JAMES   1749–1812
         A DISCOURSE, ON THE DEATH OF GENERAL WASHINGTON . . . DELIVERED ON THE 22D OF FEBRUARY,
         1800, IN THE CHURCH IN WILLIAMSBURG. . . .
                 Richmond: Printed by T. Nicolson . . . 1800.   pp. 25.   8vo.
                                                                        BA, HEH, MᵈHS, NYPL.

37877   —— —— SECOND EDITION, CORRECTED.
                 New-York, printed by T. and J. Swords, for W. Prichard, Richmond, 1800.   pp. 42.
         8vo.   HEH, HSP, JCB, LOC, NYHS, NYPL.

37878   MAGAW, JACOB, Jr.   1778–1867
         AN EULOGY ON THE LIFE OF GEN. GEORGE WASHINGTON, DELIVERED AT MERRIMAC, ON THE 22D OF
         FEBRUARY, A. D. 1800. . . .
                 Amherst [New Hampshire]. From S. Preston's Office, 1800.   pp. 16.   8vo.
                                                                        HEH, LOC, MHS.

37879   MAGAW, SAMUEL   1740–1812
         AN ORATION COMMEMORATIVE OF . . . WASHINGTON; PRONOUNCED IN THE GERMAN LUTHERAN
         CHURCH, PHILADELPHIA: BEFORE THE GRAND LODGE OF PENNSYLVANIA. ON THE TWENTY-
         SECOND DAY OF FEBRUARY, EIGHTEEN HUNDRED. . . .
                 Philadelphia: Printed by J. Ormrod, no. 41, Chestnut-Street. 1800.   pp. 45.   8vo.
         "Grand Lodge of Pennsylvania. Grand quarterly communication. Philadelphia, Monday,
         3d March, anno lucis, 5800": pp. [42]–45.
                 AAS, BA, BPL, HEH, HSP, JCB, LOC, MFM, NYFM, NYPL, PFM, PPL, WLC.

37880   —— —— RE-PUBLISHED AT THE REQUEST OF THE PRINCIPAL OFFICERS . . . OF THE GRAND LODGE OF
         CONNECTICUT.
                 Newfield [Conn.]: Printed by Lazarus Beach. 1800.   pp. 23.   8vo.
                                                                        AAS, CHS, HC, NYPL, WLC.

37881   MAGRUDER, WILLIAM B.
         AN ADDRESS TO THE PUBLIC, ACCOUNTING FOR THE LARGE SUM OF MONEY WHICH HAS BEEN SUNK
         IN THE HANDS OF W. B. MAGRUDER. . . .
                 Baltimore, Printed by Samuel Sower, M,DCCC. . . .   pp. 62.   8vo.   BM, MᵈHS.

37882   THE MAN OF REAL SENSIBILITY. . . .
         See Scott, Mrs. Sarah

37883   MANN, JAMES   1759–1832
         AN ADDRESS, DELIVERED DECEMBER 18, 1799. BEFORE THE BRETHREN OF MONTGOMERY LODGE . . .
         IN FRANKLIN; UPON THE EVENING OF THEIR ANNIVERSARY, FOR THE ELECTION OF OFFICERS. . . .
                 Printed at Wrentham, by Nathaniel and Benjamin Heaton. MDCCC.   pp. 19.
         8vo.   AAS, HC, JCB, MFM, PFM, YC.

37884   MANSFIELD, JOSEPH   —— 1830
         HOPE, A POEM, DELIVERED IN THE CHAPEL OF HARVARD UNIVERSITY, AT A PUBLIC EXHIBITION, JULY
         8TH, 1800. . . .
                 Cambridge. Printed by William Hilliard. 1800.   pp. 15.   8vo.
                 AAS, BA, BPL, BʳU, EI, GʳL, HC, HEH, JCB, LOC, MHS, NYHS, NYPL, PTS, WLC, YC.

37885   MANUAL OF THE THEOPHILANTHROPES: OR, ADORERS OF GOD, AND FRIENDS OF MEN.
         CONTAINING THE EXPOSITION OF THEIR DOGMAS, AND OF THEIR RELIGIOUS PRACTICES: WITH INSTRUC-
         TION RESPECTING THE ORGANIZATION AND CELEBRATION OF THEIR WORSHIP. ARRANGED BY
         CERTAIN CITIZENS OF FRANCE: AND NOW TRANSLATED FOR THE USE OF THE AMERICAN THEO-
         PHILANTHROPIC SOCIETIES.
                 Philadelphia: Printed, August 1800.   pp. 47.   8vo.   JCB.

37886   MARSH, EBENEZER GRANT   1777–1803
         AN ORATION, DELIVERED AT WETHERSFIELD, FEBRUARY 22, 1800; ON THE DEATH OF . . . WASHING-
         TON. . . .
                 Hartford: Printed by Hudson and Goodwin. 1800.   pp. 16.   8vo.
                 AAS, BA, BM, BPL, CHS, HEH, JCB, LCP, LOC, NL, NYHS, NYPL, NYSL, WL, YC.

37887 MARSHALL, JOHN   1755–1835
    SPEECH . . . DELIVERED IN THE HOUSE OF REPRESENTATIVES . . . ON THE RESOLUTIONS OF . . .
    EDWARD LIVINGSTON, RELATIVE TO THOMAS NASH. . . .
        Philadelphia: Printed at the office of "The True American." 1800.   pp. 45.   12mo.
        AAS, BA, BPL, HEH, JCB, LOC, MᵉHS, MHS, NYPL, NYSL, PʳU, PSL, WL, YC.

37888 MARTINET, [JOANNES FLORENTIUS]   1729–1795
    THE CATECHISM OF NATURE. FOR THE USE OF CHILDREN. BY DOCTOR MARTINET, PROFESSOR OF
    PHILOSOPHY AT ZUTPHEN. . . .
        Philadelphia: Printed and sold by John M'Culloch, no. 1. North Third-Street.
    M,DCCC.   pp. 108.   24mo.   AAS.

37889 MARYLAND. STATE.
    [THE ACTS OF ASSEMBLY FOR THE REGULATION OF ELECTIONS FOR THE STATE OF MARYLAND. . . .
        Baltimore?]   MINICK 601.

37890 —— ACTS OF ASSEMBLY . . . THE REGULATION OF ELECTIONS. PUBLISHED BY ORDER OF THE HOUSE OF
    DELEGATES.
        Annapolis: Printed by Frederick Green. . . .   pp. 22, [1].   8vo.   NYPL.

37891 —— AT A SESSION OF THE GENERAL ASSEMBLY OF MARYLAND . . . NOVEMBER . . . 1799 . . . JANUARY,
    1800.
        [*Annapolis: Printed by Frederick Green.*]   pp. 80.   4to.   MᵈSL.

37892 —— BY THE HOUSE OF DELEGATES, DECEMBER 9, 1800, RESOLVED . . . THE FOLLOWING AMENDMENTS TO
    THE CONSTITUTION OF THE UNITED STATES. . . . BY THE SENATE, DECEMBER 19, 1800. . . .
        [*Annapolis, Printed by Frederick Green,*]   Broadside.   8vo.   LOC.

37893 —— LAWS OF MARYLAND, MADE AND PASSED AT A SESSION OF ASSEMBLY, BEGUN AND HELD AT THE
    CITY OF ANNAPOLIS ON . . . THE FOURTH OF NOVEMBER . . . ONE THOUSAND SEVEN HUNDRED
    AND NINETY-NINE. . . .
        Annapolis: Printed by Frederick Green. . . .   pp. [81].   4to.
        HEH, JCB, MᵈHS, MᵈSL.

37894 —— THE LAWS OF MARYLAND, TO WHICH ARE PREFIXED THE ORIGINAL CHARTER . . . AND CONSTITUTION
    OF THE STATE. . . . IN TWO VOLUMES. . . . COLLECTED . . . BY WILLIAM KILTY. . . . VOLUME
    II.
        Annapolis: Printed by Frederick Green . . . 1800.   pp. [714].   4to.
    This series was continued in smaller format through Volume seven.
        AAS, BM, EPFL, HC, HEH, HSP, JCB, LOC, NYPL.

37895 —— VOTES AND PROCEEDINGS OF THE HOUSE OF DELEGATES OF THE STATE OF MARYLAND. NOVEMBER
    SESSION, 1799. . . .
        [*Annapolis: Printed by Frederick Green.*]   pp. 112.   fol.
        HEH, LOC, MᵈHS, MᵈSL, NYPL, NYSL.

37896 —— VOTES AND PROCEEDINGS OF THE SENATE OF THE STATE OF MARYLAND. NOVEMBER SESSION, 1799. . . .
        [*Annapolis: Printed by Frederick Green. 1800.*]   pp. 47.   fol.   HEH, MᵈHS, MᵈSL.

37897 THE MARYLAND AND VIRGINIA ALMANAC, FOR THE YEAR OF OUR LORD, 1801. . . . CONTAINING,
    BESIDES THE ASTRONOMICAL CALCULATIONS. . . .
        Baltimore: Printed and sold by Bonsal & Niles. . . .   pp. [48].   12mo.   MᵈHS.

37898 THE MARYLAND GAZETTE.   1745 +
        Annapolis: Printed by Frederick and Samuel Green. 1800.   fol.   weekly.
        FOR 1800: MᵈSL.

37899 THE MARYLAND HERALD, AND ELIZABETH-TOWN ADVERTISER.   1797–1826
    Elizabeth (Hager's) Town: Printed (every Thursday) by Thomas Grieves, 1800.
    fol.   weekly.   FOR 1800: MᵈHS.

37900   MASON, JOHN   1646?–1694
        SELECT REMAINS OF THE REV. JOHN MASON. . . . RECOMMENDED BY THE REV. ISAAC WATTS, D. D.
            WITH A PREFACE GIVING SOME ACCOUNT OF THE AUTHOR.
                Brookfield, printed by E. Merriam, & Co. for G. Merriam.   pp. 15, [5], [17]–237.
            24mo.
            Edited by John Mason, 1706–1763.   AAS, LOC, NYPL.

37901   MASON, JOHN   1706–1763
        SELF KNOWLEDGE. A TREATISE, SHEWING THE NATURE AND BENEFIT OF THAT IMPORTANT SCI-
            ENCE. . . .
                *Printed at Boston, by I. Thomas and E. T. Andrews, sold by . . . I. Thomas, Worces-
            ter; by Thomas, Andrews & Penniman, Albany; and by Thomas Andrews & Butler,
            Baltimore.— May, 1800.*   pp. xiv, [19]–208, front.   12mo.
                                                                   AAS, BPL, CL, JCB, LOC, MHS, NYPL.

37902   MASON, JOHN M[ITCHELL]   1770–1829
        A FUNERAL ORATION, DELIVERED IN THE BRICK PRESBYTERIAN CHURCH IN THE CITY OF NEW-YORK,
            ON THE 22D DAY OF FEBRUARY, 1800 . . . TO TESTIFY . . . GRIEF FOR THE DEATH OF GEN.
            WASHINGTON. . . .
                *New-York: Printed and sold by G. F. Hopkins, at Washington's Head, 84 Maiden-
            Lane. 1800. (Copy-right secured).*   pp. 23.   8vo.
                         AAS, BA, BPL, HC, HEH, JCB, LOC, MHS, NL, NYHS, NYPL, NYSL, RU, WLC, YC.

37903   —— —— A FUNERAL ORATION, ON GEN. WASHINGTON. DELIVERED FEB. 22, 1800. . . . THE 2D ED.
                New-York: Printed and sold by George Folliott Hopkins. . . . 1800.   pp. 32, 48.
            8vo.
            Issued under a common half-title with Fisher Ames, *An Oration on the Sublime Virtues
            of General George Washington,* New York, 1800.
                               APS, BA, BPL, HEH, JCB, LOC, MᵈHS, NYHS, NYPL, NYSL, PPL, WLC.

37904   [—— ——] THE VOICE OF WARNING, TO CHRISTIANS, ON THE ENSUING ELECTION OF A PRESIDENT OF THE
            UNITED STATES. . . .
                *New-York: Printed and sold by G. F. Hopkins, at Washington's head, no. 136, Pearl-
            Street. 1800.*   pp. 40.   8vo.
                         AAS, AHTS, BPL, HEH, HSP, JCB, LOC, MᵈHS, NL, NYHS, NYPL, NYSL, VᵃU, WL, YC.

37905   MASON, WILLIAM   1764–1847
        [FAST DAY SERMON AT CASTINE, 1800.]   WILLIAMSON, II, 100.

37906   MASONIC LAMENT, ON THE DEATH OF WASHINGTON. HOW SAD ARE THE TIDINGS THAT SOUND IN
            MY EAR. . . .
                Broadside.   fol.   HEH.

37907   MASSACHUSETTS. STATE.
        AN ACT TO ENABLE THE PROPRIETORS OF THE CANALS TO COLLECT TOLLS. . . .
                [*Boston.*]   Broadside.   fol.   MHS.

37908   —— AN ACT TO INCORPORATE THE SALEM MARINE INSURANCE COMPANY.
                Salem: Printed by Thomas C. Cushing. . . . 1800.   pp. 13.   16mo.   AAS, BPL, EI.

37909   —— ACTS AND LAWS. PASSED BY THE GENERAL COURT OF MASSACHUSETTS, AT THE SESSION BEGUN AND
            HELD . . . ON WEDNESDAY, THE EIGHTH DAY OF JANUARY . . . 1800.
                [*Boston: Printed by Young and Minns.*]   pp. 341–410.   fol.
                                                                   AAS, HEH, LOC, NJSL, NYPL.

37910   —— ACTS AND LAWS, PASSED BY THE GENERAL COURT OF MASSACHUSETTS, AT THE SESSION BEGUN AND
            HELD . . . ON WEDNESDAY, THE TWENTY-EIGHTH DAY OF MAY . . . 1800.
                [*Colophon:*] *Boston: Printed by Young and Minns, Printers to the honourable the
            General Court.*   pp. 411–438.   fol.   AAS, HEH, LOC, NL, NJSL, NYPL.

37911 —— Acts of the legislature of Massachusetts, incorporating the proprietors of the Middlesex Canal.
[*Boston: Printed by Young and Minns.*]   pp. 14, [1].   8vo.   AAS, CU, LOC.

37912 —— Commonwealth of Massachusetts. An Act in addition to an Act, entitled "An Act to prevent the spreading of contagious sickness. . . ." Passed Feb. 26, 1800.
[*Boston.*]   Broadside.   fol.   HSP.

37913 —— Commonwealth of Massachusetts. By his Excellency Caleb Strong. . . . A proclamation for a day of public thanksgiving. . . . Given . . . in Boston, this twenty-sixth day of September . . . one thousand and eight hundred. . . .
[*Boston.*]   Broadside.   fol.   AAS, LOC.

37914 —— Commonwealth of Massachusetts. By his Honor Moses Gill, Esq. . . A proclamation for a day of solemn fasting, humiliation, and prayer. . . . Given . . . in Boston, this twelfth day of February, one thousand and eight hundred. . . .
[*Boston:*] *Young & Minns.*   Broadside.   fol.   AAS, LOC.

37915 —— Commonwealth of Massachusetts. In the year of our lord one thousand & eight hundred. An Act in addition to an Act entitled, "An Act establishing a Supreme Judicial Court within this Commonwealth."
Printed by Young & Minns [*Boston.*]   Broadside.   pp. 2.   fol.   AAS.

37916 —— Commonwealth of Massachusetts. This twenty fourth day of May . . . one thousand and eight hundred. On the foregoing reference between Henry Knox. . . .
Four page folder, printed on first page only.   fol.   MHS.

37917 —— General orders head-quarters, Boston, July 7, 1800. . . . By order of the Commander in Chief, William Donnison, Adj. Gen.
[*Boston.*]   Broadside.   fol.   LOC, MHS.

37918 —— Laws for regulating and governing the militia of the Commonwealth of Massachusetts. Published by authority.
Boston: Printed by Young & Minns. 1800.   pp. 73, iv.   12mo.   HC, JCB.

37919 —— Militia law. . . . March 4, 1800. By the lieutenant governor approved. Moses Gill.
[*Boston:*] *Young & Minns, printers to the State.*   Broadside.   fol.
Printed in four columns.   NYPL.

37920 —— The Order of the day. For Saturday, Feb. 8, 1800. The marshals, appointed by the committee of the honorable legislature. . . .
Young & Minns, printers.   Broadside.   fol.
Statement of the arrangements and exercises in honor of Washington.   HSP.

37921 —— A Proclamation. By the President of the United States of America. . . . Given . . . at Philadelphia, the sixth day of January . . . one thousand eight hundred. . . . Commonwealth of Massachusetts. In the Senate, January 14, 1800. . . .
Printed by Young & Minns, printers to the State.   Broadside.   fol.
Calling for the observation of the death of Washington.   AAS, BPL, HEH, MHS, NYHS.

37922 —— Resolves, &c. of the General Court of Massachusetts. Passed at the session begun . . . the eighth day of January . . . 1800.
[*Colophon:*] *Boston: Printed by Young and Minns.* . . .   pp. [35]–80, vi.   fol.
                                                            AAS, HEH, LOC, NYPL, YC.

37923 —— Resolves, &c. of the General Court of Massachusetts. Passed at the session begun . . . the eleventh day of November . . . 1800.
[*Colophon:*] *Printed by Young & Minns.* . . .   pp. [29]–36.   fol.   AAS, HEH, NYPL.

37924 —— Resolves of the General Court of . . . Massachusetts. . . . Begun . . . the twenty-
eighth day of May, Anno Domini — M,D,CCC.
Boston: Printed by Young and Minns. . . . pp. 28. fol. AAS, HEH, NYPL, RISL.

37925 —— Tax for the year 1800. . . . An Act to apportion and assess a tax of one hundred and
thirty-three thousand . . . dollars. . . .
[Colophon:] Young and Minns, Printers to the State. pp. 19. fol. AAS, HSP.

37926 —— To the Hon. the Senate and the Hon. the House of Representatives . . . of Massachu-
setts . . . humbly shews the subscribers, inhabitants of the towns of Lewiston. . . .
Supreme Judicial Court, Boston, August 1, 1800. The refferees . . . report. . . .
Broadside. fol. AAS.

37927 MASSACHUSETTS. Ancient and Honourable Company of Artillery.
Commemorative ode. In honor of Washington; — performed on the anniversary choice
of officers of the Ancient and Honourable Company of Artillery, June 2, 1800. . . .
[Boston.] Broadside. 8vo. AAS.

37928 MASSACHUSETTS. Associated Mechanics and Manufacturers.
Constitution of the Associated Mechanics and Manufacturers, of the Commonwealth
of Massachusetts.
Boston, printed by Russell and Cutler. 1800. pp. 24. 24mo. AAS.

37929 MASSACHUSETTS Charitable Fire Society.
Act of incorporation, laws and regulations, catalogue of the members, and state of the
funds of the Massachusetts Charitable Fire Society.
Boston: Printed by Manning & Loring, 1800. pp. 18, [1]. 8vo.
The last leaf contains the "State of the Funds." AAS, CL, HC, HEH, HSP, JCB, MHS, NYPL, RU.

37930 MASSACHUSETTS Historical Society.
Collections of the Massachusetts Historical Society. For the year M,DCC,XCIX.
Printed by Samuel Hall, no. 53, Cornhill, Boston. 1800. pp. xxii, 288. 8vo.
AAS, AHTS, HC, HEH, LCP, LOC, MᵉHS, MHS, NYHS, NYPL, WC, YC.

37931 MASSACHUSETTS Missionary Society
See Emmons, Nathaniel.

37932 MASSACHUSETTS Mercury. 1793–1803
Boston: Printed by Young and Minns. . . . 1800. fol. semi-weekly.
For 1800: AAS, BA, BPL, CHS, EI, LOC, MHS, [NYHS], NYSL, YC.

37933 —— The Carriers of the Massachusetts Mercury, to each of their beneficent customers. . . .
Mercury-Office, January 1, 1800. Broadside. fol. AAS.

37934 THE MASSACHUSETTS Register and United States Calendar; for the year of our Lord
1801 . . . containing civil, ecclesiastical, judicial, and military lists in Massachu-
setts. . . .
Boston: Printed by Manning & Loring. Sold by John West. . . . pp. 180. 18mo.
A continuation of Fleet's Register. Issued with blank pages bound in for notes.
AAS, HC, LOC, NYHS, NYPL, NYSL.

37935 MASSACHUSETTS Society for Promoting Agriculture.
Inquiries by the Agricultural Society.
[Colophon:] Boston: Printed by Young & Minns, printers to the State. MDCCC.
pp. 29. 8vo. AAS, APS, BPL, BʳU, GʳL, HC, JCB, LOC, MHS, NYPL, NYSL, RU, UTS, YC.

37936   [MASSON, Charles Francois Philibert]   1762–1807
        Elmina; or, the flower that never fades. A tale for young people. Embellished with
        elegant cuts.
                Hartford: Printed by John Babcock. 1800.   pp. 31.   32mo.
        Attributed to Masson by the *Biographie Universelle*, which adds the note that Elmina was
        the Princesse Wilhelmine de Courlande.   AAS.

37937   [MATHIAS, Thomas James]   1754?–1835
        The Imperial epistle, and The shade of Alexander Pope. . . .
                Philadelphia: Printed by H. Maxwell, for A. Dickens, bookseller, North Second Street,
        opposite Christ-Church. 1800.   pp. [4], 49, 59, [3].   8vo.
        Each poem has a special titlepage. The last leaf contains Dickens advertising.
                        AAS, BA, BPL, HSP, LOC, NL, NYPL, NYSL, PPL, VᵗU, WC, YC.

37938   [——] Pursuits of literature. A satirical poem in four dialogues, with notes. To which are
        annexed, a vindication of the work. . . .
                Philadelphia: Printed by H. Maxwell, 1800.   pp. 481.   8vo.   NYPL.

37939   —— —— —— Philadelphia: Printed by H. Maxwell, for A. Dickins, bookseller, North Second Street
        opposite Christ-Church. 1800.   pp. 481.   8vo.   AAS, HEH, LOC, NYSOC, UOC, VᵃU, WL, YC.

37940   —— —— —— Philadelphia: Printed by H. Maxwell, for J. Nancrede, Boston; and A. Dickins and
        J. Ormrod, Philadelphia. 1800.   pp. 481.   8vo.
        These three issues are made up from the same sheets with variations in the titlepages.
                        AAS, BA, BPL, GU, HSP, JCB, LCP, LOC, MHS, NYHS, NYSL, UOP, WC.

37941   [——] The Shade of Alexander Pope, on the banks of the Thames. A satirical poem, with
        notes. . . .
                Philadelphia: Printed by H. Maxwell, for A. Dickens. 1800.   pp. 59, [4].   8vo.
                        AAS, BPL, LCP, RU, VᵃU.

37942   MAXCY, Jonathan.   1768–1820
        Reasons of the Christian's triumph. . . . Delivered in the Baptist meetinghouse, in
        Providence . . . December 14, 1800. Occasioned by the decease of Mrs. Mary Gano. . . .
                Providence: Printed by J. Carter.   pp. 19.   8vo.
                        AAS, BA, BʳU, CL, HC, JCB, NYHS, NYPL, NYSL, RIHS.

37943   MAY, ALEXANDER, *of Pennsylvania*
        An Inaugural dissertation on the unity of disease . . . submitted to the . . . Medical
        Faculty of the University of Pennsylvania, on the thirty-first of May 1800. . . .
                Philadelphia: Printed by Way & Groff, no. 48, North Third-Street. 1800.   pp. 26.
        8vo.   AAS, AML, LCP, LOC, RU, UOP, WL.

37944   MEAD, Samuel   1764–1818
        A Sermon, delivered December 29, 1799; occasioned by the death of . . . Washington. . . .
        By Samuel Mead, A. M. Pastor of a church in Danvers. . . .
                Printed by Joshua Cushing, County Street, Salem. 1800.   pp. 24.   8vo.
                        AAS, BA, BPL, EI, HC, JCB, LOC, MFM, NYHS, NYPL, PL.

37945   MEANWELL, Nancy, *pseud.*
        A History of a doll; containing its origin and progress through life, with the various
        calamities that befel it. . . .
                New-York: Printed by William Durell no. 106 Maiden-Lane, 1800.   pp. 31, illust.
        32mo.   AAS.

37946   THE MEDICAL repository. Conducted by Samuel L. Mitchill . . . Edward Miller . . . and
        Elihu H. Smith. . . . Vol. I [–II]. Second edition.
                New-York: Printed by T. & J. Swords, printers to the Faculty of Physic of Columbia
        College, no. 99 Pearl-Street. 1800. Copy-right secured.   pp. 8, 567; 455.   8vo.
                        AAS, AML, HC, JCB, WC, YC.

37947 —— —— Vol. III.
[*Same imprint.*] pp. 8, 428. AAS, AML, BA, HEH, NYAM, NYHS, WC, YC.

37948 THE MEDICAL VADE MECUM. CONTAINING APPROVED DIRECTIONS FOR THE USE, AND A COMPENDIOUS
ACCOUNT OF THE QUALITIES AND DOSES, OF THE MEDICINES MOSTLY WANTED IN FAMILIES AND
ON PLANTATIONS, THAT ARE EITHER TOO DISTANT FROM MEDICAL ASSISTANCE, OR TOO SMALL TO
AFFORD A VERY LIBERAL USE OF IT.
Charleston: Printed by T. C. Cox. . . . MDCCC. pp. [4], 24, [4]. 16mo. CLS.

37949 MEMOIRS OF CHARLES DENNIS RUSOE D'ERES. . . .
See Rouso.

37950 A MEMORIAL OF THE RESPECT. . . .
See Genius of Liberty.

37951 MEMORY OF WASHINGTON: COMPRISING A SKETCH OF HIS LIFE AND CHARACTER; AND THE NATIONAL
TESTIMONIALS OF RESPECT. . . .
Newport, R. I. Printed by Oliver Farnsworth. 1800. pp. 246, [6], portrait. 12mo.
The portrait is an engraving by William Hamlin after the Edward Savage painting. The
last six pages contain a list of subscribers.
AAS, BA, BPL, BᵗU, HC, HEH, HSP, LOC, NHS, NYHS, NYPL, NYSL, NYSOC, VᵗSL, WⁱˢHS, WLC, YC.

37952 MERCANTILE ADVERTISER. 1798–1838
Printed and published, by John Crookes, for the proprietors. . . . fol. daily.
FOR 1800: [NYHS].

37953 MERRICK, PLINY 1755–1814
AN EULOGY ON THE CHARACTER OF . . . WASHINGTON. . . . PRONOUNCED BEFORE THE INHABITANTS
OF . . . BROOKFIELD, ON . . . THE 22D OF FEBRUARY, 1800. . . .
Printed at Brookfield, Massachusetts, by E. Merriam & Co., March, 1800. pp. 14.
8vo. AAS, BA, BPL, HEH, JCB, LOC, MHS, NYHS, NYPL, NYSL.

37954 THE MESSENGER. 1800–1802
New-Haven: printed by Read & Morse, 1800. fol. weekly.
FOR 1800: [AAS], [HC], [YC].

37955 MESSINGER, ROSEWELL 1775–1844
AN ORATION, DELIVERED AT OLD YORK, ON THE DEATH OF GEORGE WASHINGTON. . . . BY THE REV.
ROSEWELL MESSINGER . . . OF THE FIRST CHURCH IN OLD YORK. . . .
Charlestown: Printed by Samuel Etheridge. 1800. pp. 16. 8vo.
AAS, EI, HC, HEH, JCB, LOC, NL, NYHS, NYPL.

37956 —— A SERMON, PREACHED AT THE ORDINATION OF THE REV. JAMES BOYD, AT BANGOR, ON PENOBSCOT
RIVER, SEPTEMBER 10, 1800. . . .
From the press of Angier March, sold at his bookstore, north side of Market-Square,
Newburyport. pp. 28. 8vo. AAS, BM, EI, HC, JCB, MSL, NYHS.

37957 METHODIST EPISCOPAL CHURCH IN AMERICA.
THE ADDRESS OF THE GENERAL CONFERENCE OF THE METHODIST EPISCOPAL CHURCH. . . .
BALTIMORE, MAY 20TH, 1800.
[*Baltimore?*] Broadside. fol. LOC.

37958 —— MINUTES OF THE GENERAL CONFERENCE . . . BEGUN IN BALTIMORE ON THE SIXTH, AND CONTINUED
TILL THE TWENTIETH OF MAY, ONE THOUSAND EIGHT HUNDRED. . . .
Philadelphia: Printed by Henry Tuckniss, for Ezekiel Cooper, no. 118, North Fourth-
Street . . . 1800. pp. 16. 16mo. DREW UNIVERSITY LIBRARY, MADISON, N. J.

37959 —— Minutes taken at the several annual conferences of the Methodist-Episcopal Church, in America, for the year 1800.
   Philadelphia: Printed by Henry Tuckniss, for Ezekiel Cooper, no. 118, North Fourth-Street, near the Methodist church. (Price nine cents.) pp. 24. 12mo. AAS, HSP, JCB.

37960 MIDDLESEX Gazette.   1785–1834
   Middletown — (Connecticut) — Printed and published every Friday, by T. and J. B. Dunning. 1800. fol.   For 1800: [AAS], CHS, [HC].

37961 MIDDLETOWN. Connecticut.
   Hymns, to be sung on the 22d of Feb'ry, 1800, in Middletown; the day appointed by Congress to manifest our grief for . . . Washington. . . .
   [T. & J. B. Dunning, Middletown, Conn?.] Broadside. 4to.   AAS.

37962 MILES, Noah   1752–1831
   A Sermon, delivered at Temple, February 22, 1800, on the death of George Washington. . . . To which is prefixed, an account of the proceedings of the town on the melancholy occasion.
   Printed by S. Preston, Amherst [N. H.]. 1800. pp. 16. 8vo. AAS, JCB, LOC.

37963 MILLER, Alexander
   A Sermon, occasioned by the death of General Washington. Delivered at Greenbush, on the 22d day of February, 1800. . . .
   Albany: Printed by Charles R. and George Webster, at their bookstore, corner of State and Pearl-Street, 1800. pp. 15. 8vo.
        AAS, BA, BPL, BʳU, HEH, JCB, MHS, MSL, NYHS, NYPL, NYSL.

37964 MILLER, Samuel   1769–1850
   A Sermon, delivered December 29, 1799; occasioned by the death of General George Washington. . . . By Samuel Miller, A. M. . . .
   New-York: Printed by T. & J. Swords, no. 99 Pearl-Street. 1800. pp. 39. 8vo.
     AAS, BA, BPL, HEH, JCB, LOC, MFM, MHS, NYHS, NYPL, NYSL, PL, PPL, RU, WLC, YC.

37965 MILTIMORE, James   1755–1836
   A Sermoʳ ʳreached in Newmarket, at the ordination of . . . James Thurston . . . Octoʳ 15, 1800. . . .
   ͻm the press of Henry Ranlet, Exeter, N. H. 1800. pp. 28. 8vo.
   Contains "The Charge, by the Rev'd Curtis Coe, pastor of the church of Christ in Durham," the "Right Hand of Fellowship. By the Rev'd William Pidgin, of Hampton," and the "Rev'd Mr. Thurston's Answer." AAS, JCB, LOC, NHSL, NL, NYHS, NYPL.

37966 MINOT, George Richards   1758–1802
   An Eulogy on George Washington. . . . Delivered before the inhabitants of the town of Boston. . . .
   Boston: from the printing-office of Manning & Loring. pp. 24. 8vo.
    AAS, AHTS, BPL, CL, CLS, HC, HEH, JCB, LOC, MFM, MHS, NL, NYHS, NYPL, PL, PPL, VᵗU, YC.

37967 —— —— Second edition.
   Boston: from the printing-office of Manning & Loring. pp. 24. 8vo.
     AAS, BPL, HC, HEH, JCB, LOC, MᵈHS, MHS, NYHS, NYPL, NYSL, PFM.

37968 MINUTES of debates in council, on the banks of the Ottawa River . . . November ——, 1791, by the chiefs of the several Indian nations, who defeated the army of the United States on the 4th of that month. . . .
   Baltimore: Printed by Warner & Hanna. . . . 1800. pp. 23. 8vo. APS, LOC, WC.

37969 MINUTES of the proceedings of the sixth convention of delegates from the abolition societies, assembled at Philadelphia, June 4, 1800.
   Philadelphia, 1800. pp. 35. 12mo.   BʳU, LOC, MHS, NYHS, NYPL, PPL, WL.

37970 MIRANDA, OR THE DISCOVERY. A TALE. TO WHICH ARE ADDED, CHARIESSA. . . . ALSO, AN ORIGINAL STORY. . . .
    Norwich, printed by J. Trumbull, 1800.   pp. 108.   16mo.   AAS, CHS, YC.

37971 MIRROR OF THE TIMES, & GENERAL ADVERTISER.   1799–1806
    Printed at the Franklin Press, Wednesdays & Saturdays, by James Wilson, south side of the upper market, High-Street, Wilmington, Delaware. 1800.   fol.   semi-weekly.
    FOR 1800: [AAS], DHS, [HC], [NYHS].

37972 [THE MISSISSIPPI GAZETTE.   1799–1801
    Natchez, printed by Benjamin M. Stokes.]   FOR 1800: NO COPY KNOWN.

37973 MISSISSIPPI TERRITORY
    BY WINTHROP SARGENT, GOVERNOR OF THE MISSISSIPPI TERRITORY. IN OBEDIENCE TO THE WILL OF THE GENERAL GOVERNMENT. . . . GIVEN NEAR NATCHEZ, SEPTEMBER 10, 1800. . . .
    [*Natchez: B. M. Stokes?*]   Broadside.   fol.   MᵇA.

37974 —— THE GROVE PLANTATION, M. T. NOVEMBER 16, 1800. SIR, I BELIEVE IT A DUTY TO COMMUNICATE TO THE OFFICERS OF THE TERRITORY, AND THE SLAVEHOLDERS. . . . WINTHROP SARGENT, GOVERNOR, M. T.
    Broadside.   8vo.   MHS.

37975 —— [LAWS OF THE MISSISSIPPI TERRITORY; PUBLISHED AT A SESSION OF THE LEGISLATURE BEGUN IN THE TOWN OF NATCHEZ IN OCTOBER, 1800.
    Natchez: Printed by Benjamin M. Stokes?]   pp. 47.   fol.
    The only known copy lacks the titlepage.   MSL.

37976 —— PROCLAMATION. BY WINTHROP SARGENT, GOVERNOR OF THE MISSISSIPPI TERRITORY. . . . GIVEN AT THE BELLEMONT PLANTATION NEAR NATCHES THIS 24TH DAY OF JUNE, ANNO DOMINI ONE THOUSAND EIGHT HUNDRED. . . .
    [*Natchez: B. M. Stokes?*]   Broadside.   fol.   NA.

37977 MITCHELL, AMMI RUHAMI   1762–1824
    AN EULOGY, ON GENERAL GEORGE WASHINGTON, PRONOUNCED IN THE FIRST MEETING-HOUSE IN NORTH YARMOUTH . . . FEBRUARY 22D 1800. . . .
    Portland. Printed by Elezer A. Jenks.   pp. 20.   8vo.   BA, CL, HEH, MᵉHS.

37978 MITCHILL, SAMUEL L[ATHAM]   1764–1831
    AN ADDRESS TO THE CITIZENS OF NEW-YORK WHO ASSEMBLED IN THE BRICK PRESBYTERIAN CHURCH, TO CELEBRATE THE TWENTY-THIRD ANNIVERSARY OF AMERICAN INDEPENDENCE. . . .
    New-York: Printed and sold by George F. Hopkins, at Washington's Head, 84 Maiden-Lane. 1800.   pp. 27.   8vo.   AAS, HEH, LOC, NYHS, NYPL, NYSL, YC.

37979 THE MITE OF PRAISE. GEORGE WASHINGTON, THE ILLUSTRIOUS OWNER OF MOUNT VERNON . . . FOR HIM A NATION WEEPS.
    Dover; (Delaware) Printed by W. Black, proprietor, 1800.   pp. 11.   8vo.
    In verse.   HEH, LOC, YC.

37980 THE MODERN COLLECTION OF SACRED MUSIC: CONTAINING THE RUDIMENTS OF THE ART, AND A CHOICE COLLECTION OF ANTHEMS. . . .
    Printed, typographically, at Boston, by Isaiah Thomas and Ebenezer T. Andrews: sold by . . . Thomas, Andrews & Penniman, Albany; by Thomas, Andrews & Butler, Baltimore; and by the booksellers in town and country.— Nov. 1800.   pp. viii, 253, [1]. obl. 12mo.
    Sometimes attributed to Oliver Holden.   AAS, BPL, BʳU, HC, LOC, NYSL, UTS.

37981 [THE MODERN PRIMER, OR A NEW AND EASY GUIDE TO SPELLING AND READING. CONTAINING A VARIETY OF LESSONS. . . .
    Elizabeth (Hager's Town): Printed by Thomas Grieves, 1800.]   MINICK 610.

37982   THE MODERN QUAKER. A COMPARATIVE VIEW OF THE PRIMITIVE AND PRESENT STATE OF THE
SOCIETY OF FRIENDS. . . . WRITTEN IN ENGLAND. . . .
Philadelphia: Printed by David Hogan, no. 51, South Third-Street. 1800.   pp. 8.
16mo.
Verse. Imprint from colophon.   AAS.

37983   MONITEUR DE LA LOUISIANE.   1794–1814
Nouvelle Orleans.   4to.   weekly.
Issue of Sept. 4, 1800, is owned by Mrs. T. P. Thompson of New Orleans.

37984   THE MONITOR.   1784–FEB. 26, 1800
Litchfield, (Connecticut): printed by Thomas Collier. 1800.   fol.
The name was changed to *The Farmer's Monitor.*   FOR 1800: [AAS], [HC].

37985   THE MONITOR; OR WILMINGTON WEEKLY REPOSITORY.   FEB. 1, 1800–1802
Wilmington: Published by W. C. Smyth, 1800.   fol.   Weekly until June, 1800,
when it became a semi-weekly with the title *The Monitor, & Wilmington Repository.*
FOR 1800: [HC].

37986   MONTGOMERY COUNTY. NEW YORK.
TWENTY DOLLARS REWARD. BROKE GOAL ON THE FIFTH DAY OF OCTOBER, JACOB SANT. . . . B. VAN
VLECK, SHERIFF. MONTGOMERY COUNTY, OCT. 17, 1800.
Broadside.   12mo.   NYHS.

37987   THE MONTHLY HERALD.   APR. 5–MAY 10, 1800.
Augusta Georgia. Published by Randolph & Bunce, in Washington Street.   pp. 8.
4to.
This was established as a monthly edition of the *Augusta Herald.*   UOG.

37988   THE MONTHLY MAGAZINE, AND AMERICAN REVIEW, FOR THE YEAR 1799 [AND 1800]. . . .
New-York: Printed and sold by T. & J. Swords, no. 99 Pearl-Street. 1800.   3 vol.
pp. vi, 480; iv, 480; viii, 480.   8vo.
Edited by Charles Brockden Brown. Continued as *The American Review.*
AAS, BA, BPL, HC, HSP, JCB, LCP, LOC, NL, NYHS, NYPL, NYSL, UOP, YC.

37989   MOODY, SILAS   1742–1816
A SERMON, PREACHED AT ARUNDEL, JANUARY 12, 1800: ON THE DEATH OF GEORGE WASHING-
TON. . . .
*Portsmouth, (New-Hampshire,) printed at the United States' Oracle-Office, by
Charles Peirce, February, 1800.*   pp. 16.   8vo.   AAS, BA, HEH, HSP, JCB, LOC, NYHS.

37990   MOORE, JOHN, *of Pennsylvania*
AN INAUGURAL DISSERTATION ON DIGITALIS . . . SUBMITTED TO THE . . . MEDICAL FACULTY, OF THE
UNIVERSITY OF PENNSYLVANIA, ON THE THIRTY-FIRST OF MAY 1800. . . .
Philadelphia: Printed by Way & Groff, no. 48, North Third-Street. 1800.   pp. 36,
2 plates.   8vo.   AAS, AML, JCB, LCP, LOC, RIMS, RU, UOP, YC.

37991   MOORE, JOHN HAMILTON   — 1807
THE NEW AND PRACTICAL NAVIGATOR . . . ALSO THE SUBSTANCE OF INFORMATION EVERY CANDIDATE
FOR THE AMERICAN NAVY OUGHT TO BE ACQUAINTED WITH PREVIOUS TO HIS BEING AP-
POINTED. . . . THE FIRST AMERICAN, FROM THE THIRTEENTH ENGLISH EDITION. . . . IL-
LUSTRATED WITH COPPER-PLATES. . . . SECOND EDITION.
*Newburyport: Printed by Edmund M. Blunt (proprietor) 1800. Sold by every book-
seller and ship-chandler in the United States and by Thomas Biggs, no. 85, South Front
Street, Philadelphia.*   pp. 570, [2], 8 plates.   8vo.
AAS, BPL, EI, GU, HC, JCB, MᶜHS, NYPL, WC, YC.

37992   —— THE YOUNG GENTLEMAN AND LADY'S MONITOR, AND ENGLISH TEACHER'S ASSISTANT: BEING A
COLLECTION OF SELECT PIECES FROM OUR BEST MODERN WRITERS. . . .
New-York: Printed by James Oram . . . 1800.   pp. vi, 368, [1].   16mo.   WL.

37993 MOORE, Thomas, *pseud.*
  Gaine's New-York pocket Almanack, for the year 1801. . . . Calculated for this and the neighboring states. . . .
    New-York: Printed by Ming & Young, (Successors to H. Gaine) 33, Liberty Street.
  pp. [96]. 48mo.   AAS, BM, HEH, LOC, NYHS, NYPL, NYSL.

37994 MORAL sketches for young minds. . . .
    Dover, (Delaware) Printed by Wm. Black. 1800. pp. ix, 91. 12mo.
  "Copy-right secured according to law."   W¹PL.

37995 MORE, Hannah   1745–1833
  [Moses in the bulrushes: a sacred drama. In three parts. By Miss Hannah More. . . .
    Reprinted at Litchfield, by T. Collier, M,DCCC. pp. 23. sq. 16mo.]
                     Bates 2864.

37996 —— Strictures on the modern system of female education. With a view of the principles and conduct prevalent among women of rank and fortune. . . .
    Philadelphia: Printed by Budd and Bartram, for Thomas Dobson, at the Stone House, no. 41, South Second Street. 1800. 2 vol. pp. 216; 227. 16mo.
          AAS, BPL, HSP, LOC, NYPL, NYSOC, PPL, UOP.

37997 —— —— *Charlestown, printed by Samuel Etheridge, for E. Larkin, no. 47, Cornhill, Boston, 1800.* 2 vol. pp. 146; [3]–136. 16mo.
        AAS, BPL, CL, HC, HEH, MSL, NHSL, NYSL, PʳU, WC, WLC, YC.

37998 —— *See also* Cheap Repository Tracts.

37999 MORISON, William   1748–1818
  A Sermon, delivered at the . . . Presbyterian Society in the west parish of Londonderry, January 1st, 1800. On the death of . . . Washington. . . .
    From the press of Angier March. Sold at his bookstore, north side of Market-Square, Newburyport. pp. 18. 8vo. AAS, BA, EI, HEH, JCB, LOC, MFM, NYPL, NYSL, PL.
  Second title: An Oration, delivered at the request of the . . . Militia officers, on the 22d of February, 1800, in the west parish of Londonderry, in commemoration of the death of . . . Washington. . . .
    [*Same imprint.*] pp. 19–32.   AAS, BA, CL, EI, HEH, LOC, MFM, NL, NYPL, PL.

38000 MORRELL, Thomas
  A Sermon on the death of . . . Washington. By Thomas Morrell, elder in the Methodist Episcopal Church. . . . Delivered on the 22d of February, 1800, in the city of Baltimore. . . .
    Baltimore: Printed by Warner & Hanna. pp. 29. 12mo.
           BA, EPFL, JCB, LCP, LOC, MFM, NYPL.

38001 MORRIS, Edward   —1815
  The Secret: a comedy. In five acts. As performed at the new theatre, Philadelphia. . . .
    Philadelphia: Printed by John Bioren, for Mathew Carey. 1800. pp. 77, [7]. 24mo.
  Contains a "Prologue" by Charles Morris, an "Epilogue" by George Colman, and a list of "Books for sale at Mathew Carey's store." AAS, HSP, LOC, UOC, YC.

38002 MORRIS, Gouverneur   1752–1816
  An Oration, upon the death of General Washington. . . . Delivered at the request of the corporation of the City of New-York, on the 31st day of December, 1799. . . .
    New-York, Printed by John Furman, opposite the City Hall. 1800. pp. 24. 8vo.
  There are issues with and without Errata on p. 24, and several variants of the former.
    AAS, BA, BPL, HC, HEH, HSP, JCB, LOC, MᵈHS, NL, NYHS, NYPL, NYSL, PL, RU, UOP, WLC, YC.

38003   MORRIS, James   1752–1820
AN ORATION, DELIVERED IN SOUTH-FARMS, IN LITCHFIELD, FEBRUARY 22, 1800, COMMEMORATIVE OF
THE DEATH OF GEN. GEORGE WASHINGTON. . . .
Printed at Litchfield, by T. Collier.   pp. 29.   8vo.
AAS, BPL, CHS, CL, HEH, JCB, LOC, NL, NYPL, PPL, WL, YC.

38004   MORSE, Jedidiah   1761–1826
GEOGRAPHY MADE EASY: BEING AN ABRIDGMENT OF THE AMERICAN UNIVERSAL GEOGRAPHY. . . .
SEVENTH EDITION. . . .
*Printed at Boston, by I. Thomas and E. T. Andrews. . . . Sold by . . . I. Thomas,
Worcester, Thomas, Andrews & Penniman, Albany; and Thomas, Andrews & Butler,
Baltimore. October, 1800.*   pp. 432, 2 maps.   12mo.
AAS, CL, CSL, HC, JCB, NHS, NYPL, UOC, VᵃSL, WL, WLC.

38005   —— A PRAYER AND SERMON DELIVERED AT CHARLESTOWN, DECEMBER 31, 1799. . . .
See Charlestown, Massachusetts.

38006   MORTON, Thomas   1764?–1838
SPEED THE PLOUGH: A COMEDY, IN FIVE ACTS. . . . FIRST AMERICAN EDITION.
*London-printed. New-York: Re-printed by M. L. & W. A. Davis, for H. Caritat,
Bookseller, no. 153 Broadway. 1800.*   pp. 69, [3].   8vo.
With a "Prologue. Written by T. Fitzgerald," and an "Epilogue. Written by Miles Petit
Andrews."   AAS, BPL, BʳU, LOC, NYPL, UOP, WC, YC.

38007   —— —— FIRST AMERICAN, FROM THE THIRD BRITISH EDITION.
*Philadelphia: Printed for John Conrad, & Co. no. 30, Chestnut Street — Michael and
John Conrad, & Co. no. 140, Market Street, Baltimore — and Rapine, Conrad, & Co.
Washington City. 1800.*   pp. 82, [2].   12mo.
With a "Prologue, written by W. T. Fitzgerald," an "Epilogue, written by Miles Petit
Andrews," and two pages of book advertisements.   AAS, CU, HC, HEH, HSP, MᵈHS, VᵗU, WLC.

38008   MOSELEY, Jonathan Ogden   1762–1839
AN ORATION, DELIVERED AT EAST-HADDAM . . . AT THE REQUEST OF THE INHABITANTS OF THE
FIRST SOCIETY IN THAT TOWN, ON THE 22D OF FEB. A. D. 1800.
Hartford: Printed by Hudson and Goodwin. 1800.   pp. 18.   8vo.
A Washington memorial oration.
AAS, CHS, CL, HEH, JCB, MFM, MHS, LOC, NYHS, NYPL, NYSL, PL, WL, YC.

38009   MOSHEIM, Johann Lorenz von   1694–1755
AN ECCLESIASTICAL HISTORY, ANCIENT AND MODERN, FROM THE BIRTH OF CHRIST, TO THE BEGIN-
NING OF THE PRESENT CENTURY. . . . VOL. VI.
[Mount Holly, N. J.:] Printed by Stephen C. Ustick, 1800.   pp. [4], 387, 8, [18].
8vo.   PPL.

38010   MOUNT Pleasant Register.   1797–1800
[Mount Pleasant, N. Y., printed by William Durell].   No COPY KNOWN.

38011   [MURDOCK, John]   1748–1834
THE BEAU METAMORPHIZED, OR THE GENEROUS MAID: AN AFTER-PIECE, IN TWO ACTS. . . . BY AN
AMERICAN CITIZEN OF PHILADELPHIA. . . .
Philadelphia: Printed by Joseph C. Charless for the author. 1800.   pp. 52.   12mo.
HC, PSL, UOC, UOP, WLC.

38012   MURRAY, Lindley   1745–1826
AN ABRIDGEMENT OF MURRAY'S ENGLISH GRAMMAR, WITH AN APPENDIX, CONTAINING AN EX-
EMPLICATION OF THE PARTS OF SPEECH. . . .
*Philadelphia: Printed for J. Ormrod, Joseph & James Crukshank, B. & J. Johnson,
and Robert T. Rawle. 1800.*   pp. 118.   24mo.   HSP, LCP.

38013 —— English grammar, adapted to the different classes of learners. With an appendix, containing rules. . . . First American edition.
  Boston: Printed by Manning & Loring, for Joseph Nancrede, no. 94, Marlbro' Street, Boston. 1800.   pp. 288.   12mo.   AAS, BPL, HC, LOC, MHS, UOP, WC.

38014 —— —— *Boston: Printed by Manning & Loring, for Isaac Beers and Co. New-Haven, and Joseph Nancrede, Boston. 1800.*   pp. 288.   12mo.   AAS.

38015 —— —— *Philadelphia: Published by Asbury Dickins, opposite Christ-Church. H. Maxwell, Printer, Columbia-House. 1800.*   pp. [2], 311.   12mo.   AAS, HC, UOP.

38016 —— —— The third edition. . . .
  New York: Printed and sold by Isaac Collins, no. 189, Pearl-Street. 1800.   pp. xii, 248, [4].   16mo.   HSP, LCP, NYPL, NYSOC.

38017 —— The English reader; or, pieces in prose & poetry, selected from the best writers. . . .
  Philadelphia: Printed for J. Ormrod, B. & B. Johnson, & Joseph & James Crukshank. 1800.   pp. 392, [2].   12mo.   HC, NYHS.

38018 —— —— Second Philadelphia edition.
  Philadelphia: Printed by B. & J. Johnson, no. 147, High Street. 1800.   pp. 392, [3]. 12mo.
The last three pages contain reviews and advertisements.   AAS.

38019 —— —— —— *New-York: Printed and sold by Isaac Collins. . . . 1800.*   pp. 366, [6].   12mo.   NYPL, YC.

38020 —— Exercises, adapted to Murray's English Grammar designed for the benefit of private learners . . . the use of schools; with a key. . . .
  Philadelphia: Published by Asbury Dickins, opposite Christ-Church. H. Maxwell, printer, Columbia-House. 1800.   pp. 168, 124.   12mo.
The Key is separately paged but the signatures are continuous with the Exercises.   AAS, HSP, LCP, UOP, YC.

38021 THE MUSEUM and Washington and George-town Daily Advertiser.   Nov. 18, 1800–1802
  George-Town. From the press of Green & English.   fol.   daily and tri-weekly, with a weekly country issue.
This was a continuation of the *Centinel of Liberty.*   For 1800: LOC.

38022 THE MUSICAL Journal. . . .
 See Carr, Benjamin.

38023 MYCALL, John   1750–1833
  A Funereal address, on the death of . . . Washington. . . . Delivered in the Baptist meeting-house in Harvard, February 22, 1800. . . .
  Boston: Manning & Loring, printers, near the Old South Meeting-House.   pp. 27. 8vo.   AAS, BA, EI, HEH, JCB, LOC, MFM, MHS, MSL, NL, NYHS, NYPL, PPL, WˡˢHS.

38024 NAPOLEON I. Bonaparte, Emperor of the French.   1769–1821
  Military journal of General Buonaparte; being a concise narrative of his expedition from Egypt into Syria. . . .
  Baltimore: Printed by Warner & Hanna, no. 2, North Gay-Street. 1800.   pp. 96. 8vo.
Pages 87–96, containing "references" in the form of serially numbered footnotes, were apparently printed separately, and are not in all copies.   AAS, APS, LOC, MᵈHS, NYSL, YC.

38025 NARRATIVE of the loss of the ship Hercules. . . .
 See Stout, Benjamin.

38026 NATIONAL INTELLIGENCER. Oct. 31, 1800–1869
Washington City, printed by Samuel Harrison Smith, New-Jersey Avenue. fol.
tri-weekly. FOR 1800: AAS, LOC.

38027 NATIONAL MAGAZINE, OR A POLITICAL, HISTORICAL, BIOGRAPHICAL AND LITERARY REPOSITORY. . . .
NUMBER V [TO VIII]. VOL. II . . . BY JAMES LYON.
[*On No. V:*] *Richmond, Virginia.* pp. 102. 8vo.
Number VII has the imprint: District of Columbia. JCB, LOC, VªSL.

38028 [NELSON, DAVID] 1752–1829
AN INVESTIGATION OF THAT FALSE, FABULOUS AND BLASPHEMOUS MISREPRESENTATION . . . BY
THOMAS PAINE, IN HIS . . . AGE OF REASON. BY A DELAWARE WAGGONER. . . .
[*Lancaster: W. & R. Dickson?*] pp. 192. 12mo.
The date of publication is shown by newspaper advertisements. The presswork resembles
that of the Dicksons. AAS, LOC, NYPL.

38029 NELSON'S CHARLESTON DIRECTORY, AND STRANGERS GUIDE, FOR THE YEAR OF OUR LORD 1801. . . .
Charleston: Printed by John Dixon Nelson. . . . pp. 125. 16mo. CLS.

38030 DER NEUE ALLGEMEIN NÜTZLICHE VOLKS-CALENDER, AUF DAS JAHR CHRISTI 1801. . . . ZUM
ERSTENMAL HERAUSGEGEBEN.
Lancaster, Gedruckt und zu finden bey Christian Jacob Hütter. . . . pp. [40].
sq. 8vo. AAS, LOC.

38031 DER NEUE, GEMEINNÜTZIGE LANDWIRTHSCHAFTS CALENDER, AUF DAS JAHR, NACH DER HEILBRINGEN-
DEN GEBURT UNSERS HERRN JESU CHRISTI, 1801. . . .
Lancäster, Gedruckt und zu haben bey Johann Albrecht und Comp. . . . pp. [44].
sq. 8vo.
The cover is a woodcut farming scene with the heading, "Neuer Lancästerscher Calender,
1800." AAS, HSP, LOC, WªªHS.

38032 DER NEUE HOCH DEUTSCHE AMERICANISCHE CALENDER, AUF DAS JAHR CHRISTI 1801. . . .
EINGERICHTET VOR . . . PENNSYLVANIEN UND MÄRYLAND. . . .
Baltimore, gedruckt bey Samuel Saur. . . . pp. [42]. sq. 8vo.
For full imprint see Minick 614. AAS, HSP, LOC, NYPL.

38033 [DER NEUE NORD-AMERICANISCHE STADT UND LAND CALENDER, AUF DAS JAHR 1801. . . . ZUM
FÜNFTENMAL HERAUSGEGEBEN.
Hägerstaun, Md. Johann Gruber. 8vo.] MINICK 615.

38034 NEUE PHILADELPHISCHE CORRESPONDENZ. 1790–1812
Alle Dienstag herausgegeben von Joseph R. Kammerer, und G. Helmbold, jun. fol.
weekly.
This is a continuation of the *Philadelpische Correspondenz.* Kammerer retired with the
issue of Mar. 7, and in April, John Geyer was taken into partnership. FOR 1800: [HSP].

38035 [DER NEUE UNPARTHEYISCHE BALTIMORE BOTE UND MARYLANDER STAATS-REGISTER.
Baltimore: Gedruckt bey Samuel Saur.] MINICK 616.
Possibly the same as 36885.

38036 NEUE UNPARTHEYISCHE READINGER ZEITUNG UND ANZEIGS-NACHRICHTEN. 1789–1802
Reading: Gedruckt bey Gottlob Jungmann und Comp. fol. weekly.
With the issue of Feb. 5, Carl A. Bruckmann was taken into the firm, which took the
name of Jungmann and Bruckmann. FOR 1800: BERKS CO. HIST. SOC., LOC.

38037 NEUER HAUSZWIRTHSCHAFTS CALENDER, AUF DAS GNADENREICHE JAHR . . . 1801. . . . ZUM
VIERTENMAL HERAUSGEGEBEN.
Reading: Gedruckt bey Jungmann und Bruckmann. . . . pp. [44]. 8vo.
The frontispiece shows a view of the "Sudwestlicher Prospect von Reading." HSP.

38038 NEUER HAUSWIRTHSCHAFTS CALENDER, AUF DAS JAHR, NACH DER HEILBRINGENDEN GEBURT UNSERS HERRN UND HEYLANDES JESU CHRISTI, 1801. . . .
[*Philadelphia: Heinrich Schweitzer.*] pp. [40]. sq. 8vo. AAS, HSP, LOC.

38039 NEUER UNPARTHEYISCHER EASTONER BOTHE, UND NORTHAMPTONER KUNDSCHAFTER. 1793–1805
[*Jacob Weygandt und Sohn . . . Easton.* fol. weekly.]
FOR 1800: NO COPY KNOWN.

38040 THE NEW BALTIMORE DIRECTORY, AND ANNUAL REGISTER; FOR 1800 AND 1801. CONTAINING THE NAMES, OCCUPATIONS, AND PLACES OF ABODE OF THE CITIZENS. . . .
[*Baltimore:*] *By Warner & Hanna.* . . . pp. 104; 50, [1]. 12mo. MᵈHS.

38041 NEW BEDFORD. MASSACHUSETTS.
HYMN, ODE, AND DIRGE, TO BE SUNG IN NEW-BEDFORD, THE 22D OF FEBRUARY, 1800, IN COMMEMORATION OF THE DEATH OF . . . WASHINGTON.
[*New Bedford.*] Broadside. 4to. HEH.

38042 NEW, COMPLETE LETTER WRITER, OR, THE ART OF CORRESPONDENCE. CONTAINING LETTERS . . . COMPOSED BY VARIOUS WRITERS. . . .
New York: Printed by John Tiebout, no. 246 Water Street. Nov. 1800. pp. 82. 16mo. LOC.

38043 THE NEW-ENGLAND PRIMER ENLARGED: OR, AN EASY AND PLEASANT GUIDE TO THE ART OF READING. ADORN'D WITH CUTS. TO WHICH ARE ADDED, THE ASSEMBLY OF DIVINES CATECHISM, &C.
Newport: Printed by Oliver Farnsworth, 1800. pp. [72]. 32mo. NYPL, RIHS.

38044 THE NEW-ENGLAND PRIMER, IMPROVED, FOR THE MORE EASY ATTAINING THE TRUE READING OF ENGLISH. TO WHICH IS ADDED, THE ASSEMBLY OF DIVINES CATECHISM.
Hartford: Printed by Hudson & Goodwin. 1800. pp. 80. sq. 32mo. AAS, CHS.

38045 ——— — *New-York: Printed for Thomas B. Jansen & Co. no. 248 Pearl-Street. 1800.* pp. 70. 32mo. AAS.

38046 ——— — [*Windham: Printed by John Byrne. 1800.* pp. [72]. 24mo.] BATES.

38047 ——— WITH OTHER USEFUL AND PLEASING MATTER.
Hartford: Printed by John Babcock. 1800. pp. 64. 32mo. AAS, PPL.

38048 NEW HAMPSHIRE. STATE.
A JOURNAL OF THE PROCEEDINGS OF THE HON. HOUSE OF REPRESENTATIVES. . . . AT EXETER . . . DECEMBER, 1799.
Portsmouth: Printed by John Melcher, printer to the Hon. General Court, 1800. pp. 106. 12mo. AAS, LOC, NYSL.

38049 — A JOURNAL OF THE PROCEEDINGS OF THE HONORABLE SENATE . . . AT EXETER . . . DECEMBER, 1799.
Portsmouth, Printed by John Melcher, printer to the State. 1800. pp. 57 [i.e. 67]. 12mo. AAS, LOC.

38050 — A JOURNAL OF THE PROCEEDINGS OF THE HONORABLE SENATE OF . . . NEW-HAMPSHIRE, AT THEIR SESSION BEGAN . . . AT CONCORD . . . JUNE, 1800.
State of New-Hampshire: Portsmouth, printed by John Melcher, printer to the State. 1800. pp. 48. 12mo. AAS.

38051 — A JOURNAL OF THE PROCEEDINGS OF THE HOUSE OF REPRESENTATIVES OF THE STATE OF NEW-HAMPSHIRE . . . AT CONCORD . . . JUNE, 1800.
State of New-Hampshire: Portsmouth, printed by John Melcher . . . 1800. pp. 71. 12mo. AAS, LOC, NYSL.

38052   —— The Laws of the State of New-Hampshire, passed at a session of the . . . General Court, begun . . . at Exeter, December, 1799. . . .
           Portsmouth — New-Hampshire: Printed by John Melcher . . . 1800.   pp. [4], 542–61.   8vo.   AAS, LOC.

38053   —— The Laws of the State of New-Hampshire, passed at a session of the General Court, begun and holden at Concord, June, 1800. . . .
           Portsmouth — New-Hampshire: Printed by John Melcher, printer to the State. 1800. pp. [3], 562–5.   4to.   AAS.

38054   —— [State of New Hampshire. By the Governor. A Proclamation . . . appoint Thursday the thirteenth day of November next . . . a day of public Thanksgiving. . . . Given at the Council Chamber, in Exeter, the sixth day of October, one thousand eight hundred. . . .
           Broadside.   fol.]   EVANS.

38055   —— [State of New Hampshire. By the Governor. A Proclamation . . . appoint Thursday, the twenty fourth day of April next to be observed as a day of humiliation, fasting and prayer. . . . Given at the Council Chamber in Exeter this twentieth day of March, one thousand eight hundred. . . .
           Broadside.   fol.]   EVANS.

38056   THE NEW Hampshire Gazette.   1756–
           Portsmouth: (New-Hampshire) published . . . by John Melcher.   weekly.   fol.
                                                                        For 1800: AAS, BA, DC, NHHS, YC.

38057   NEWHAMPSHIRE Sentinel.   1799–
           Keene: Printed by John Prentiss.   weekly.   fol.   For 1800: Keene Pub. Lib.

38058   NEW HAVEN. Fenton & Lyon.
           Church bells: of a superior workmanship, far exceeding any from Europe . . . made by Fenton & Lyon, in New Haven & West Stafford. . . . New Haven, January 20th, 1800.
           Broadside.   8vo.   NYPL, YC.

38059   [A NEW history of Blue Beard, written by Gaffer Black Beard, for the amusement of Little Lack Beard, and his pretty sisters.
           Hartford: Printed by John Babcock, 1800.   24mo.]
           Attributed to Charles Perrault 1628–1703.   BATES 2450.

38060   THE NEW instructive history of Miss Patty Proud, or, The downfall of vanity, with the reward of goodnature. . . .
           From Sidney's Press, New-Haven, 1800.   pp. 31.   32mo.   HSP.

38061   —— —— *Hartford: Printed by John Babcock 1800.*   12mo.   pp. 31.   YC.

38062   NEW JERSEY. State.
           Acts of the twenty-fifth General Assembly of the State of New-Jersey. . . . Begun at Trenton, on the twenty-eighth day of October, one thousand eight hundred. . . . Being the first sitting.
           Trenton: Printed by Sherman, Mershon & Thomas. . . . 1800.   pp. 29, [2].   8vo.
                                                                                        LOC, NJSL, PPL.

38063   —— Laws of the State of New-Jersey; revised and published under the authority of the Legislature, by William Paterson.
           Newark: Printed by Matthias Day. M,D,CCC.   pp. [2], 455, xxi, [3], 46, [1].   4to.
           There are two settings of the titlepage most readily distinguished by whether the horse's head faces right or left.   AAS, BPL, JCB, LOC, NJHS, NJSL, NYHS, NYPL, PrU, RU.

38064   —— —— *New Brunswick: Printed by Abraham Blauvelt. M,DCCC.*   pp. [2], xxi, [1], 455, [33].   fol.   AAS, BPL, BrU, HC, HEH, JCB, LOC, NJSL, NYHS, NYPL, PrU, RU.

38065 —— Votes and proceedings of the twenty-fifth General Assembly of the State of New Jersey. . . . Begun at Trenton, on the twenty-eighth day of October, one thousand eight hundred. . . . Being the first sitting.
Trenton: Printed by Sherman, Mershon & Thomas. . . . 1800. pp. 88. 8vo.
LOC, NJSL, PPL.

38066 THE NEW-JERSEY and Pennsylvania Almanac.
See Shoemaker, Abraham.

38067 NEW JERSEY College.
See 37203.

38068 NEW-JERSEY Journal. 1786–1900
Elizabeth-Town: Printed and published by Shepard Kollock. . . . weekly. fol.
For 1800: NJHS.

38069 NEW-JERSEY State Gazette. 1799–July 1, 1800
Trenton, printed by Sherman, Mershon, & Thomas. . . . weekly. fol.
This paper was merged after July 1 with *The Federalist* into *The Federalist & New-Jersey State Gazette, q. v.*
For 1800: NJSL.

38070 NEW LONDON. Connecticut. Presbyterian Church.
Funeral eulogy and oration. . . .
See 37666.

38071 THE NEW Robinson Crusoe, designed for the amusement and instruction of the youth. . . . Translated from the original German. Embellished with cuts.
Hartford: Printed by John Babcock. 1800. pp. 108. 24mo.
This is not the *New Robinson Crusoe* by Joachim Heinrich Campe (1746–1818) whose hero was named Billingsley. The hero of this narrative is a Robinson Crusoe who was born in Hamburg.
AAS, BPL, NYPL.

38072 A NEW system of chemistry, comprehending the latest discoveries and improvements of the science. Illustrated with copper-plates.
Philadelphia: Printed for Thomas Dobson, at the Stone House, no. 41, South Second Street. 1800. pp. [2], 364. 4to.
AAS.

38073 THE NEW Trade Directory for New-York anno 1800. . . .
See under 1799.

38074 THE NEW universal letter-writer: or, complete art of polite correspondence. . . . To which is prefixed, a new, plain, and easy grammar. . . .
Philadelphia: Printed and sold by D. Hogan, no. 51, South Third-Street . . . 1800.
pp. viii, [13]–254, [4], plate. 16mo.
The last four pages contain advertisements.
AAS, HSP, NYPL, UOP.

38075 NEW YORK. State.
An Act, authorizing the comptroller to correct certain errors, committed in the assessment and collection of taxes.
[Albany.] Broadside. fol.
Refers to the taxes of 1799 and 1800. Each line is numbered.
NYPL

38076 —— By his Excellency John Jay, Governor of the State of New York. A Proclamation [with regard to certain presidential electors]. Dated Albany, 7th November 1800.
Broadside.
NYSL.

38077   —— [Census of the State of New York, for 1800. . . .
                   fol.]
               Described by Sabin (53576) as first in a volume of census reports in NYSL before the fire.

38078   —— Collection of Acts concerning the recovery of debts, to the value of ten pounds, in the
               State and City of New-York.
                   New-York: Printed by G. F. Hopkins . . . 1800.   pp. 28.   8vo.   JCB.

38079   —— Court for the trial of impeachments, and the correction of errors. George Arnold . . . vs.
               The United Insurance Company. . . .
                   New-York: Printed by John Furman. . . . 1800.   pp. 316, [1].   8vo.
               This volume also includes Duguet vs. Rhinelander, Goix vs. Low, Livingston vs. Rogers,
               and Ludlows vs. Gracie. The last page contains a table of contents.   NYSL.

38080   —— Court for the trial of impeachments, and the correction of errors. Isaac Gouverneur &
               Peter Kemble, respondents, ads. Louis Le Guen, appellant. Case on the part of
               Gouverneur & Kemble. . . .
                   New-York: Printed by George Forman, no. 64, Water-Street. 1800.   pp. 32.   8vo.
                                                                                                             NYSL.

38081   —— Dr. The State of New-York in account current with Robert McClallen, Treasurer. . . .
               January the 8th, 1800. . . .
                   [*Albany*.]   pp. 3.   fol.   NYSL.

38082   —— Gentlemen, I herewith lay before you a Report from the commissioners for the settling
               the titles to land in the County of Onondagua. . . . John Jay. Albany, February
               17, 1800.
                   [*Albany*.]   pp. 16.   8vo.   HEH, LOC, NYHS, NYPL, NYSL.

38082a —— Gentlemen of the Senate and Assembly. The great importance of the business. . . .
               John Jay.
                   [*Albany*.]   pp. [2].   fol.
               The Governor's speech of Nov. 1, 1800.   NYSL.

38083   —— In the court for the trial of impeachments and the correction of errors. Robert Gilchrist,
               ads. William Armstrong & Geo. Barnewall. Case on the part of the defendant in error.
                   New-York: Printed at the Law Press. . . . 1800.   pp. 11.   8vo.
               Colophon: Geo. F. Hopkins, Printer.   NYSL.

38084   —— Journal of the Assembly of the State of New-York; at their twenty-third session begun
               . . . at . . . Albany, the twenty-eighth day of January, 1800.
                   Albany: Printed by Loring Andrews. . . .   pp. 299, [4].   fol.
                                                              AAS, JCB, LOC, NYHS, NYPL, NYSL, YC.

38085   —— Journal of the Senate . . . at their 23rd session, began . . . the 28th day of January, 1800.
                   Albany: Printed by Loring Andrews. . . .   pp. 131.   fol.   NYHS, NYSL, YC.

38086   —— Laws of the State of New-York, comprising the constitution, and the acts of the legis-
               lature, since the Revolution . . . Volume III. . . .
                   Albany: Printed by Charles R. and George Webster. M,DCCC.   pp. [4], 605.   8vo.
               Volumes I and II were printed in New York City in 1798.   HC, NJSL, NYHS, NYSL.

38087   —— Laws of the State of New York passed at the twenty-third session . . . January, 1800.
                   Albany: Printed by Loring Andrews. . . . 1800.   pp. 294, [8].   8vo.
                                                              HC, HEH, NYBA, NYHS, NYPL, NYSL.

38088   —— Members composing the Senate of the State of New-York, with their respective districts
               and classes. Nov. 4, 1800.
                   [*Albany*.]   Broadside.   fol.   NYPL.

38089 —— MEMBERS OF THE HOUSE OF ASSEMBLY. . . . ALBANY, FEBRUARY 3, 1800. . . .
Printed by Loring Andrews, printer to the State. Broadside. fol. NYHS.

38090 —— STATE OF NEW-YORK. IN SENATE, 28TH JANUARY, 1800. MR. PRESIDENT LAID BEFORE THE SENATE
THE COMPTROLLER'S STATEMENT. . . .
[*Albany.*] pp. 7. fol. NYPL, NYSL.

38091 —— STATE OF NEW-YORK. IN SENATE, MARCH 15TH, 1800. MR. SPENCER, FROM THE JOINT COMMIT-
TEE . . . TO CONSIDER . . . THE PERSONS WHO HOLD LOTS IN THE MILITARY TRACT. . . .
[*Albany.*] pp. [4]. fol.
Contains a list of New York men killed in the Revolution. NYPL.

38092 —— STATE OF NEW YORK. IN SENATE MARCH 22D, 1800. . . . A MESSAGE FROM HIS EXCELLENCY . . .
RETURNS RECEIVED FROM THE ADJUTANT GENERAL.
[*Albany.*] Broadside. fol. NYSL.

38093 —— TITLES OF THE LAWS PASSED BY THE LEGISLATURE OF NEW-YORK, AT THEIR TWENTY-THIRD SESSION,
BEGAN . . . THE TWENTY-EIGHTH DAY OF JANUARY, 1800.
[*Albany.*] Broadside. fol. NYML.

38094 —— TO THE REPRESENTATIVES OF THE PEOPLE OF THE STATE OF NEW-YORK. . . . THE INSPECTORS OF
THE STATE-PRISON . . . PROCEED TO RENDER THE LEGISLATURE THEIR ANNUAL ACCOUNT.
[*Albany: Printed by Loring Andrews.*] pp. 5, 3 folded tables. 4to.
The imprint is from Evans. The pamphlet is dated "New York, 12th Mo. 31st, 1799."
Caption title. JCB, NYHS, NYPL, NYSL.

38095 —— TO THE REPRESENTATIVES OF THE PEOPLE OF THE STATE OF NEW-YORK . . . THE SUPERINTENDENT
OF THE ONONDAGUA SALT-WORKS, PURSUANT TO LAW, RESPECTFULLY REPORTS. . . .
[*Albany.*] pp. [4], 3 folded tables. 4to.
Dated at Salina, March 1st., 1800. NYSL.

38096 NEW YORK. CITY.
AT A COMMON COUNCIL HELD ON MONDAY THE 28TH DAY OF APRIL, 1800. IN ORDER TO PREVENT
IMPOSITIONS BY ANY OF THE CARTMEN. . . .
Broadside. fol. NYHS.

38097 —— (FROM THE OFFICE OF THE DAILY ADVERTISER.) THE FOLLOWING INTERESTING DESCRIPTION OF THE
LATE FUNERAL PROCESSION, IS FROM THE COMMITTEE OF ARRANGEMENT. NEW-YORK, JANUARY 4.
ON THE 31ST OF DECEMBER, 1799 . . . FUNERAL HONORS TO THE MEMORY OF . . . WASH-
INGTON. . . .
[*New-York: Printed by Robert Wilson.*] Broadside. fol. LOC.

38097a NEW YORK. CITY. COLUMBIAN ANACREONTIC SOCIETY.
LAWS AND REGULATIONS OF THE COLUMBIAN ANACREONTIC SOCIETY, AS REVISED, AMENDED, AND
AGREED TO, THE 6TH DAY OF MARCH, 1800.
New-York: Printed by G. F. Hopkins, Washington's Head. 1800. pp. 13. 16mo.
BPL.

38098 NEW YORK. CITY. J. W. FENNO
SUPPLEMENTARY CATALOGUE, CONSISTING OF BOOKS, IMPORTED FROM LONDON. . . . BY J. W.
FENNO, NO. 141, HANOVER-SQUARE. OCTOBER, 1800.
New-York: Printed by John Furman, op. the Fed. Hall. pp. 35. 12mo. AAS.

38099 NEW YORK. CITY. NEW YORK SOCIETY LIBRARY.
A SUPPLEMENTARY CATALOGUE OF THE BOOKS BELONGING TO THE NEW-YORK SOCIETY LIBRARY,
WHICH HAVE BEEN ADDED SINCE THE YEAR 1793.
New-York: Printed by T. & J. Swords, no. 99 Pearl-street, 1800. pp. 46, [1]. 8vo.
The last leaf contains "Bye-Laws, &c." AAS, HC, NYPL, NYSOC.

38100 NEW YORK. City. St. George's Chapel.
An Hymn to be sung by the Episcopal charity children, at St. George's Chapel, on Sunday, November 30, 1800. . . .
[*New York:*] *Printed by Ming and Young.* Broadside. fol. HC.

38101 NEW YORK. City. Society for the relief of poor widows with small children.
Constitution of the ladies society, established in New-York, for the relief of poor widows with small children. Second edition.
New-York, 1800. Printed by J. Oram. pp. 64. 12mo.
AAS, HSP, JCB, LOC, NYPL, NYSOC.

38102 NEW-YORK Baptist Association.
Minutes of the New-York Baptist Association, holden in the city of New-York, May 21st, and 22d, 1800. . . .
pp. 10. sq. 8vo.
Caption title; no imprint. AAS.

38103 THE NEW York Gazette and General Advertiser. 1795–1840
Published (daily) by John Lang. . . . fol. daily. For 1800: NYHS, NYSOCL.

38104 THE NEW-YORK Missionary Magazine, and repository of religious intelligence; for the year 1800. . . . Vol. I.
New-York: Printed by T. & J. Swords, for Cornelius Davis. 1800. pp. vii, [1], 480.
8vo. AAS, BA, NYHS, NYPL, NYSL, YC.

38105 NEW-YORK Price-Current. 1796–1817
New-York: Published weekly by James Oram. 4to. weekly. For 1800: NYHS.

38106 THE NEWARK Gazette. 1797–1804
Newark, printed by Jacob Halsey. . . . weekly. fol. For 1800: NJHS.

38107 THE NEWBERN Gazette. 1798–1804
Newbern, (North-Carolina): Printed by John S. Pasteur. fol. weekly.
For 1800: [LOC].

38108 NEWBURYPORT. Massachusetts. First Church.
Sacred concert. The principal musicians from Boston, respectfully inform the ladies and gentlemen of Newburyport . . . that they will give a concert . . . the 13th instant, at the Reverend Mr. Andrew's meeting-house. . . . Newburyport, June 11, 1800.
Broadside. fol. NYHS.

38109 THE NEWBURYPORT herald and country gazette. 1797–1902
Published by Angier March, at his office, north corner of Market-Square. fol.
semi-weekly.
From Apr. 11 to Oct. 17 the *Herald* was published by Chester Stebbins for the proprietor.
For 1800: AAS, EI.

38110 NEWEST fashion. The jovial songster containing a good collection of songs.
Boston. Printed by J. White, near Charles-river Bridge. 1800. pp. 34. 16mo. AAS.

38111 NEWFIELD. Connecticut.
Act of incorporation of the inhabitants of the village of Newfield; for the purpose of preserving said village from fire. And the ordinances or bye-laws of said corporation.
[*Newfield:*] *Printed by Lazarus Beach.* pp. 16. 8vo. HEH.

38112 NEWPORT, Rhode Island. First Congregational Church.
First Congregational meeting-house lottery. . . . Newport, June 24, 1800.
Broadside. 16mo. RIHS.

38113 NEWPORT. RHODE ISLAND. HENRY BARBER.
NEWPORT, JANUARY 1, 1800. PROPOSALS FOR PRINTING BY SUBSCRIPTION, TWO SERMONS. . . . BY . . . WILLIAM PATTEN. . . . OCCASIONED BY THE DEATH OF . . . GEORGE WASHINGTON. . . . [AND] DR. ISAAC SENTER. . . . TO BE BOUND TOGETHER. . . .
[*Newport: Printed by Henry Barber.*] Broadside. 8vo. RIHS.

38114 NEWPORT. RHODE ISLAND. THEATRE.
THEATRE. NEWPORT. MR. VILLIERS' NIGHT. ON MONDAY EVENING, OCTOBER 6, 1800. WILL BE PRESENTED A TRAGEDY. . . .
[*Newport.*] Broadside. 4to. LOC.

38115 THE NEWPORT ALMANAC, FOR THE YEAR OF OUR LORD, 1801. . . . CALCULATED FOR THE MERIDIAN OF NEWPORT. . . .
Published at Newport, by Oliver Farnsworth. . . . pp. [24]. 12mo.
AAS, LOC, NHS, NYHS, RIHS.

38116 NEWPORT MERCURY. 1758–
Newport (Rhode-Island) published by Henry Barber. . . . fol. weekly.
Barber died on September 11, and with the issue of September 16, the paper was published for his widow, Ann.
FOR 1800: [AAS], [LOC], [NHS], RL.

38117 NILES, SAMUEL 1743–1814
THE VANITY OF MAN CONSIDERED IN A SERMON DELIVERED FEBRUARY 22D, 1800, COMMEMORATING THE DEATH OF GEORGE WASHINGTON. . . .
Boston: Printed by John & Thomas Fleet, Cornhill. MDCCC. pp. 23. 8vo.
There is a list of errata pasted on p. [4] of the AAS copy.
AAS, BA, BPL, HEH, JCB, LOC, MFM, NYHS, NYPL, NYSL, YC.

38118 THE NOBLE SLAVES. . . .
See Aubin, Penelope.

38119 THE NORFOLK HERALD. 1794–1861
Norfolk [Va.]: published . . . by Willett & O'Connor. . . . fol. tri-weekly and daily.
With the issue of Dec. 1 the paper became a daily with the title *Norfolk Herald, and Daily Advertiser.*
FOR 1800: [LOC].

38120 THE NORRISTOWN GAZETTE. 1799–JUNE 6, 1800
Norristown: Printed by David Sower. 4to. weekly.
FOR 1800: BERKS. CO. HIST. SOC.

38121 NORRISTOWN HERALD, AND WEEKLY ADVERTISER. OCT. 10, 1800–1837
Norristown: Printed by David Sower. fol. weekly.
FOR 1800: MONTGOMERY CO. HIST. SOC.

38122 NORTH CAROLINA. STATE.
INDEX TO THE APPENDIX.
[*Raleigh: Hodge & Boylan.*] pp. 8. fol.
A supplement to the Iredell revision of the Laws.
HC, NCU.

38123 — JOURNAL OF THE HOUSE OF COMMONS. STATE OF NORTH CAROLINA. AT A GENERAL ASSEMBLY BEGUN AND HELD AT THE CITY OF RALEIGH, ON MONDAY, THE 18TH OF NOVEMBER . . . ONE THOUSAND SEVEN HUNDRED AND NINETY-NINE. . . .
[*Raleigh: Printed by Hodge & Boylan.*] pp. 68. fol.
Caption title; the imprint is from p. 68. LOC, SUPREME COURT LIBRARY, RALEIGH.

38124 — JOURNAL OF THE SENATE. STATE OF NORTH-CAROLINA. AT A GENERAL ASSEMBLY, BEGUN AND HELD AT THE CITY OF RALEIGH, ON MONDAY THE EIGHTEENTH DAY OF NOVEMBER . . . ONE THOUSAND SEVEN HUNDRED AND NINETY-NINE. . . .
[*Raleigh: Hodge & Boylan.*] pp. 60. 4to.
LOC, SUPREME COURT LIBRARY, RALEIGH.

38125 —— Laws of North-Carolina. At a General Assembly, begun and held at Raleigh, on the eighteenth day of November . . . one thousand seven hundred and ninety-nine. . . .
[*Printed by Hodge & Boylan.*] pp. 41, [3]. fol.
Caption title; imprint from colophon. HC, LOC, NCU, NYBA, NYPL.

38126 —— —— [*Raleigh?*] pp. 20. fol.
Caption title. This edition is the supplement to the Iredell revision. HC, NCU.

38127 THE NORTH-CAROLINA Journal. 1792–1814
Halifax: Printed by Abraham Hodge. fol. weekly.
For 1800: John G. Wood of Edenton.

38128 THE NORTH-CAROLINA Mercury, and Salisbury Advertiser. 1798–1801
Salisbury: Published by Francis Coupee. fol. weekly. For 1800: Duke Univ.

38129 THE NORTH-CAROLINA Minerva, and Raleigh Advertiser. 1799–1803
Raleigh: — Published every Tuesday by Hodge & Boylan. fol. For 1800: [NCU].

38130 NORTH Carolina University.
Laws of the University of North Carolina; established by the Board of Trustees, at their session in December, 1799.
Raleigh: Printed by J. Gales. 1800. pp. 24. 16mo. NCU.

38131 NORTHERN Budget. 1798–1927
Troy: — Published every Wednesday . . . by Robert Moffitt & Co. . . . fol.
weekly. For 1800: Troy Pub. Lib.

38132 NORTHERN Centinel. 1798–1804
Salem, Washington County, State of New York: Published every Tuesday, by Henry Dodd. . . . fol. weekly. For 1800: [AAS].

38133 A NORTHERN light. . . .
See Adgate, Matthew.

38134 NORTHWEST Territory.
Journal of the House of Representatives, of the Territory . . . north-west of the river Ohio, at the first session of the General Assembly, A. D. 1799. . . .
Cincinnati, from the press of Carpenter & Findlay. . . . M,D,CCC. pp. 211, [1].
8vo. OH&PS, OSL.

38135 —— Journal of the House of Representatives of the Territory . . . north-west of the river Ohio, at the second session of the first General Assembly, A. D. 1800. . . .
Chillicothe: Printed by Winship & Willis . . . M,D,CCC. pp. 131. 8vo.
AAS, OH&PS, OSL.

38136 —— Journal of the Legislative Assembly of the Territory . . . northwest of the river Ohio, at their second session, begun and held at Chillicothe, on the third day of November, anno domini, 1800.
Chillicothe: Printed by Winship & Willis. . . . M,D,CCC. pp. 77. 8vo.
OH&PS, OSL, WRHS.

38137 —— Laws of the Territory of the United States, northwest of the Ohio River, passed at the first session of the General Assembly . . . at Cincinnati . . . the 16th day of Sept. A. D. 1799; also certain laws enacted by the governor and judges of the Territory from the commencement of the government. . . .
Cincinnati: From the press of Carpenter and Findley . . . MDCCC. pp. 280.
8vo. HC, LOC, NYBA, NYHS, NYPL, NYSL, OH&PS, WRHS, YC.

38138 —— [The Militia law. Act of December 13, 1799.
        Cincinnati: Carpenter & Findlay, 1800.]
W. P. A. Ohio Imprints, 14

38139 THE NORWICH Packet. 1773–1802
        Norwich (Connecticut). Published by John Trumbull, a few rods west of the meeting-house. 1800. fol. weekly. For 1800: CHS.

38140 NOTES upon Luke XVII. 30. With other texts respecting the Grand Epiphany . . . and present signs that the day is nigh. . . .
        Boston: Printing-office, Union-Street. 1800. pp. 23. 12mo. AAS, JCB.

38141 O'BRIEN, Matthew
        Charity sermon, preached before the congregation of St. Mary's, Philadelphia, on Sunday the 13th of July, 1800, for completing the church of Albany.
        Philadelphia, M. Carey, 1800. pp. 21.
        The author's Washington oration, frequently quoted as an 1800 imprint, is a modern reprint of the newspaper account. PM.

38142 OBSERVATIONS on the commerce of Spain with her colonies, in time of war. By a Spaniard, in Philadelphia. . . .
        Philadelphia. Printed by James Carey. 1800. pp. 63, folded table. 8vo.
        Attributed to the Marquis d'Irujo y Tacon. For authorship see *Monthly Magazine and American Review*, III, 137. APS, BA, BM, HC, HSP, LOC, NYHS, NYPL, NYSL, YC.

38143 OBSERVATIONS on the proposed state road. . . .
        See Williamson, Charles.

38144 THE OBSERVER. Dec. 5, 1800–1804
        Published by Galen H. Fay, at his office, opposite Mr. D. How's store, Haverhill, Massachusetts. fol. weekly. For 1800: LOC.

38145 OCCASIONAL essays on the Yellow Fever, containing a number of remarkable relative facts. . . . By a Philadelphian.
        Philadelphia, printed by John Ormrod, no. 41, Chestnut-Street. 1800. pp. 42. 8vo.
AAS, HSP, LCP, LOC.

38146 OCCASIONAL ode, for February 22, 1800.
        Broadside. 4to. BA.

38147 AN ODE in honor of the Pennsylvania militia. . . .
        See Brackenridge, Hugh Henry.

38148 ODE PERFORMED at the First Church of the Universalists. . . .
        See Boston. Mass. Universalist Church.

38149 OGDEN, John Cosens 1751–1800
        A Excursion into Bethlehem & Nazareth, in Pennsylvania, in the year 1799; with a . . . history of the Society of United Brethren. . . .
        Philadelphia: Printed by Charles Cist, no. 104 North Second-Street, near the Corner of Race-Street. M,DCCC. pp. [2], 167, [1]. 12mo.
AAS, BA, CU, HC, HEH, JCB, LOC, NYHS, NYPL, NYSL, PL, PʳU, PSL, RU, UOPᶦ, WᶦˢHS, WL, YC.

38150 —— A Sermon, upon peace, charity, and toleration: delivered in St. Paul's Church, in Philadelphia, on . . . February 23, 1800. . . .
        Philadelphia: Printed by James Carey, no. 7, South Front-Street. 1800. pp. 23, [1].
        8vo. AAS, EI, HSP, JCB, LOC, NYHS, NYPL, PSL.

38151   —— A Tour through Upper and Lower Canada. . . . Containing, a view of the present state of
religion, learning, commerce. . . . Second Edition.
Wilmington: Printed by Bonsal and Niles, for the author, 1800.   pp. 117.   12mo.
Pages 89–117 contain "A Letter from a Gentleman to his Friend, Descriptive of the Differ-
ent Settlements in the Province of Upper Canada" dated "New York, 20th, Nov. 1794."
AAS, HEH, LOC, MHS, NYPL, NYSL, YC.

38152   [OGDEN, Uzal]   1744–1822
A Letter to Major General Alexander Hamilton; containing observations on his letter
concerning . . . John Adams. . . .
New-York: Printed by G. F. Hopkins, Washington's Head. 1800.   pp. 32.   8vo.
"Copy right secured according to law."   APS, EI, LOC, MSL, NYHS, NYPL, YC.

38153   —— —— —— *Printed by Joshua Cushing, Salem. 1800.*   pp. 28, [1].   12mo.
The last leaf contains a postscript.   AAS, BPL, EI, HC, HEH, LOC, MHS, NL, NYSL.

38154   —— Two discourses, occasioned by the death of General George Washington. . . . By . . .
Uzal Ogden . . . of Trinity Church, Newark. . . . Delivered in that church, and
in . . . Bellville, December 29th, 1799, . . . and January 5th, 1800. . . .
Newark: Printed and sold by Matthias Day, MDCCC. (Copy right. . . .)   pp. 46,
portrait.   8vo.
The portrait was drawn by G. Stewart and engraved by C. Tiebout.
AAS, BA, BPL, HC, HEH, JCB, LCP, LOC, MFM, MHS, NJHS, NYHS, NYPL, PPL, PʳU, YC.

38155   —— —— —— *Philadelphia: Printed by H. Maxwell, for A. Dickins, bookseller, North Second
Street. . . . 1800.*   pp. 40.   8vo.   BA, HEH, HSP, LCP, LOC, MᵈHS, NYPL.

38156   ONE STORY good till the other is heard!
[*Dated*] *City of New York, 27th April, 1800.*   Broadside.   fol.
Relating to the case of Benjamin Coddington and James H. Neilson.   NYHS.

38157   ON THE death of General Washington . . . the Christian's song. By a lady. Love to
Christ. . . . Price twelve and a half cents.
Broadside.   fol.   HEH.

38158   ON WEDNESDAY evening, 1st January, will be presented, the tagedy [sic] of The Roman
Father. . . . After which will be delivered, A Monody on the death of General
Washington written by J. Lathrop. . . .
Broadside.   4to.   BPL.

38159   THE ONTARIO Gazette, & Genesee Advertiser.   1799–1803
Canandaigua published by Lucius Carey.   weekly.   fol.
Some time during the year the title was changed to *The Ontario Gazette, & Geneseo
Advertiser.*   For 1800: [UOIˡˡ].

38160   THE ORACLE of Dauphin. And Harrisburgh Advertiser.   1792–1827
Harrisburgh: Published by John Wyeth.   Weekly.   fol.
[For 1800:] AAS, HSP, NYHS.

38161   ORANGE Patrol.   1800–1802
Goshen, Orange County, State of New York. Printed and published by John G. Hurtin.
weekly.   fol.
This was a continuation of *The Goshen Repository.*   For 1800: [AAS].

38162   AN ORATION, in memory of the virtues of Gen. George Washington. Delivered at Lovett's
Hotel . . . the 22d February, 1800, before a literary society. . . .
New-York; Printed by M. L. & W. A. Davis, for T. S. Arden, 186, Pearl-Street. 1800.
pp. 23.   12mo.   AAS, BPL, HEH, JCB, MFM, MHS, NYHS, NYPL, NYSL, PPL, RU, WˡˢHS.

38163 AN ORATION, PRONOUNCED AT HANOVER, NEW HAMPSHIRE, JANUARY 9, 1800. . . .
Sabin 57444. *See* Evans 39141.

38164 ORDER OF DIVINE SERVICE IN THE NORTH DUTCH CHURCH. . . .
See Albany. New York. North Dutch Church.

38165 ORDER OF PERFORMANCES, AT THE OLD SOUTH MEETING-HOUSE, FEBRUARY 22, 1800. BEFORE THE
MECHANICS OF BOSTON. . . .
See Boston. Mass. Mechanics.

38166 ORDER OF PERFORMANCES. INSTRUMENTAL DIRGE.
See Boston. Mass.

38167 ORDER OF THE FUNERAL PROCESSION, TO BE HAD AT TRENTON. . . .
See Trenton. New Jersey.

38168 ORIENTAL TRUMPET. OR, THE TOWN AND COUNTRY GAZETTE. 1796–1800
Portland — (District of Maine) — published by Rand and Burdick. fol. weekly.
FOR 1800: [HC].

38169 ORR, BENJAMIN 1772–1828
AN ORATION, DELIVERED AT BEDFORD, N. H. ON THE 22D FEBRUARY, 1800, IN COMMEMORATION OF
THE LIFE OF GEN. GEORGE WASHINGTON. . . .
S. Preston, printer, Amherst. 1800. pp. 16. 8vo. AAS.

38170 OSGOOD, DAVID 1747–1822
A DISCOURSE, DELIVERED DECEMBER 29, 1799 . . . FOLLOWING THE . . . TIDINGS OF THE . . .
DEATH OF . . . WASHINGTON. . . . PUBLISHED IN COMPLIANCE WITH A VOTE OF THE TOWN,
TO FURNISH EACH FAMILY WITH A COPY, TOGETHER WITH THE FAREWELL ADDRESS . . . IN ONE
BOOK.
Printed by Samuel Hall, no. 53, Cornhill, Boston. 1800. pp. 40. 8vo.
The Address is contained in pages 21–40.
AAS, BA, BPL, CL, HC, HEH, HSP, JCB, MFM, MHS, NYHS, NYPL, NYSL, PL, PFM, PPL, VᵃSL, WⁱˢHS, WLC, YC.

38171 OSGOOD, JOSEPH
AN ALMANACK, FOR THE YEAR OF OUR LORD, 1801. . . . CALCULATED FOR THE MERIDIAN OF
BOSTON. . . .
Boston: Printed and sold by Joseph White, near Charles' River Bridge. pp. [24].
24mo. AAS, LOC.

38172 OTIS, CUSHING 1768–1837
AN ORATION, PRONOUNCED AT SCITUATE, JULY 4, 1800, AT THE REQUEST OF THE INHABITANTS, IN
COMMEMORATION OF AMERICAN INDEPENDENCE. . . .
Boston: Printed by Manning & Loring. pp. 16. 8vo.
AAS, HC, JCB, LOC, NYPL, YC.

38173 OTSEGO HERALD: OR, WESTERN ADVERTISER. 1795–1821
Cooperstown: Printed and published . . . by Elihu Phinney. weekly. fol.
FOR 1800: OTSEGO CO. HIST. SOC., COOPERSTOWN.

38174 A PACK OF CARDS CHANGED INTO A COMPLETE ALMANACK & PRAYER-BOOK. TO WHICH IS ADDED, — A
VERY LAUGHABLE STORY. . . . TWELFTH EDITION.
Stonington-Port, printed, 1800. pp. 14, [1]. 16mo.
The last leaf contains an advertisement for books offered at the Printing-Office, Stonington-
Port. AAS.

38175 PAINE, ROBERT TREAT (1773–1811)
See Paine, Thomas.

38176 PAINE, Seth
An Eulogy, on General George Washington. Pronounced in the Friendship Lodge . . . on the 22d of February, 1800. . . .
  Charleston, South-Carolina: Printed by Freneau & Paine, no. 47, Bay. 1800.
pp. [2], 28.   8vo.   AAS, BA, HC, HEH, LCP, LOC, MFM, PFM.

38177 PAINE, Thomas   1773–1811
Adams and liberty the Boston patriotic song. Written by Thomas Paine, A. M. Third edition corrected.
      Boston. Printed & sold by P. A. von Hagen & Co. at their pianoforte ware house, no. 3 Cornhill.   pp. [2].   4to.   BPL, HC, LOC.

38178 —— An Eulogy on the Life of General George Washington. . . . Written at the request of the citizens of Newburyport, and delivered at the first Presbyterian Meeting-House in that town, January 2nd. 1800.
      Printed at Newburyport, by Edmund M. Blunt, 1800.   pp. 22.   8vo.
There are copies with and without an urn on the last page.   AAS, APS, BA, BPL, CL, EI,
      HC, HEH, JCB, LOC, MᵈHS, MᵉHS, MFM, NL, NYHS, NYPL, PFM, PL, UOC, VᵃU, WLC, YC.

38179 —— —— —— *Richmond: Henry Pace.*   Broadside.   fol.   VᵃU.

38180 THE PALLADIUM: a literary and political weekly repository.   1798–1816
      Frankfort: Printed and published (weekly) by William Hunter, printer to the Commonwealth.   fol.   For 1800 : [KʸSL], UOC, WⁱˢHS.

38181 PALMER, Elihu   1764–1806
The Political happiness of nations; an oration. Delivered at the city of New-York, on the Fourth of July, twenty-fourth anniversary. . . .
      [New York.]   pp. 23.   12mo.   AAS, CU, LOC.

38182 PANTHER, Abraham, *pseud.*
A Very surprising narrative of a young woman, discovered in a rocky cave. After having been taken by the savage Indians . . . in the year 1777. . . .
      Brookfield, [Printed by Ebenezer Merriam & Co.] December 1800.   pp. 12.   12mo.
                                                                    AAS, LOC.

38183 —— —— —— *Bennington, (Vermont.) Printed by Collier & Stockwell. 1800.*   pp. 12.   12mo.
                                                                    NYSL.

38184 PARISH, Elijah   1762–1825
An Oration, delivered at Byfield, February 22d, 1800, the day of national mourning for the death of General George Washington. . . .
      From the press of Angier March. . . . Newburyport.   pp. 32.   8vo.
There is an elegiac poem on pages 29–32.
AAS, BA, BPL, EI, HC, HEH, JCB, LOC, MᵉHS, MFM, MHS, NYHS, NYPL, NYSL, PPL, WⁱˢHS, WLC, YC.

38185 PARK, *Sir James Allan*   1763–1838
Appendix to a system of the law of marine insurances. . . . Containing all the new cases added to the fourth English edition. . . .
      Printed at Boston, for Thomas and Andrews . . . David West . . . and John West. . . . 1800.   pp. v, [34].   8vo.
The pagination is irregular, following that of the fourth English edition.   AAS, LOC, NYPL.

38186 —— A System of the law of marine insurances. . . . 3d American, from the latest English, ed.
      Printed at Boston, for Thomas and Andrews . . . David West . . . and John West . . . 1800.   pp. xxvii, liv, 516 (i.e. 570).   8vo.   HC, LOC, PPL, YLS.

38187 —— —— THIRD AMERICAN, FROM THE THIRD ENGLISH EDITION. TO WHICH IS ADDED . . . AN AP-
PENDIX. . . .
[*Same imprint and pagination plus*] v. [34].
This consists of the two preceeding items issued together under a revised titlepage.
AAS, HC-L, LOC, MSL, PPL.

38188 PARK, MUNGO   1771–1806
TRAVELS IN THE INTERIOR DISTRICTS OF AFRICA . . . WITH AN APPENDIX, CONTAINING GEOGRAPHICAL
ILLUSTRATIONS OF AFRICA: BY MAJOR [JAMES] RENNELL. . . .
*Philadelphia: Printed from the London quarto edition by James Humphreys: and
sold by him, at no. 106, south side of Market Street. 1800.* pp. 484. Map. 8vo.
AAS, APS, EI, HC, HEH, HSP, LOC, MᵉHS, PʳU, UOC, VᵗU.

38189 —— —— —— *New-York: Printed and sold by J. Tiebout, no. 246, Water-Street. 1800.* pp. 354,
[2], 86. Map. 8vo.   AAS, HC, NYPL, NYSL, PʳU, UOP, WC, WL, WLC.

38190 PARKER, ISAAC   1768–1830
AN ORATION ON THE SUBLIME VIRTUES OF GENERAL GEORGE WASHINGTON . . . BEFORE THE IN-
HABITANTS OF PORTLAND, FEBRUARY 22ND. 1800. . . .
Portland, printed by Elezer Alley Jenks. pp. 24. 8vo.
The Boston edition mentioned in some of the bibliographies is the reprint in the volume
of collected *Eulogies and Orations.*
AAS, BA, CL, HC, HEH, JCB, LOC, MᵉHS, MFM, MHS, NYHS, NYPL.

38191 PARKER, ISAIAH   1752–1848
A FUNERAL DISCOURSE, DELIVERED IN THE BAPTIST MEETINGHOUSE, HARVARD, AT THE INTERMENT
OF MR. JOSIAH BOWLES, WHO DEPARTED THIS LIFE MARCH 29, 1799. . . .
Boston: Printed by Luther Parker, 1800. pp. 21. 16mo.   BM, HEH.

38192 PARSONS, BENJAMIN   1769–1857
AN ORATION, DELIVERED AT CHESTERFIELD, ON THE 4TH OF JULY, 1800, THE ANIVERSARY OF
AMERICAN INDEPENDENCE. . . .
Printed at Northampton, (Massachusetts) by William Butler. MDCCC. pp. 16.
8vo.   AAS, NYHS, NYSL.

38193 PASQUIN, ANTHONY
See Williams, John, 1761–1818

38194 PATRIOTIC GAZETTE.   1799 — JUNE 23, 1800
Northampton, Mass. Published by Andrew Wright. fol. weekly. FOR 1800: NYPL:

38195 PATRIOTIC MEDLEY, BEING A CHOICE COLLECTION OF PATRIOTIC, SENTIMENTAL, HUNTING AND SEA
SONGS, INTERSPERSED WITH ANACREONTIC & CYTHRIAN POEMS. . . .
New York: Printed for Jacob Johnkin, Maiden lane. 1800. pp. 208, [7]. 24mo.
LOC, NL.

38196 PATTEN, WILLIAM   1763–1839
A DISCOURSE, DELIVERED IN THE 2D CONGREGATIONAL CHURCH, NEWPORT, THE SABBATH SUCCEEDING
THE INTERMENT OF DOCTOR ISAAC SENTER. . . .
Newport: Printed by Henry Barber. 1800. pp. 12, iv. 8vo.
"A prayer, suited to the preceeding sermon" occupies pp. iv. This item and that following
were also issued with a common half-title.
AAS, BA, JCB, LOC, MFM, NHS, NYHS, NYPL, PPL, RIHS, YC.

38197 —— A DISCOURSE, DELIVERED IN THE 2D CONGREGATIONAL CHURCH, NEWPORT, DECEMBER 29TH, 1799:
OCCASIONED BY THE DEATH OF GENERAL GEORGE WASHINGTON. . . .
Newport: Printed by Henry Barber, M,DCCC. pp. 19. 8vo.
AAS, BA, HEH, JCB, LOC, MFM, MHS, NHS, NL, NYHS, NYPL, PPL, RIHS, YC.

38198 PATTERSON, Mrs.
The Unfortunate Lovers, and cruel parents: a very interesting tale, founded on fact. . . .
Springfield: Printed and sold by T. Ashley. M,DCCC.   pp. 23.   12mo.   AAS.

38199 PAYNE, John.
New and complete system of universal geography. . . . To which is added, a view of astronomy. . . . In four volumes. Vol. II [–III].
New-York: Printed for, and sold by John Low, book-seller, at the Shakespeare's Head, no. 332 Water-Street. 1800.   pp. 578, [12]; 710, [8], plates and folding maps.   8vo.
The first volume was printed in 1798 and the fourth in 1799. There is an undated 8vo. atlas volume published by Low and Willis. Some of the maps are engraved by A. Anderson and by Doolittle.   AAS, BA, CSL, HSP, LOC, NYSL, YC.

38200 PAYSON, John P.
Masonic oration delivered before the . . . Columbian Lodge, convened at Deerfield: — New Hampshire; December 27th, A.L. 5799. . . .
Portsmouth, printed by John Melcher.   pp. 20.   8vo.   NYHS.

38201 PAYSON, Phillips   1737–1801
A Sermon, delivered in Chelsea, January 14, 1800 . . . on . . . the death of General Washington. . . .
Charlestown: Printed by Samuel Etheridge. 1800.   pp. 15.   8vo.
The half-title has a mourning border.
          AAS, BA, HC, HEH, JCB, LOC, MFM, MHS, NYHS, NYPL, NYSL, WLC, YC.

38202 PAYSON, Seth   1758–1820
A Sermon, at the consecration of the Social Lodge in Ashby, and the installation of its officers, June 24, A. D. 1799. . . .
From Preston's printing-office, Amherst, N. H. 1800.   pp. 16.   8vo. AAS, NYHS, LOC.

38203 PEALE, Charles Willson   1741–1827
Discourse introductory to a course of lectures on the science of nature; with original music. . . . Delivered in the hall of the Universiy [sic] of Pennsylvania, Nov. 8, 1800. . . .
Philadelphia: Printed by Zechariah Poulson, Junior, no. 106, Chesnut-Street. 1800.
pp. 50, 5 plates of music.   8vo.   AAS, BA, HSP, LOC, MHS, NYHS.

38204 —— Introduction to a course of lectures on Natural History. Delivered in the University of Pennsylvania, Nov. 16, 1799. . . .
Philadelphia: Printed by Francis and Robert Bailey, no. 116, High-Street. 1800.
pp. 28.   8vo.   AAS, BA, BPL, HSP, LOC, MHS, YC.

38205 PEIRCE, John, Jr.
The New, American spelling-book, improved. In three parts. . . . The fifth revised edition.
Philadelphia: Printed for, and sold by, Joseph & James Crukshank, no. 87, High-Street. . . . 1800.   pp. [4], 200.   12mo.   AAS.

38206 —— The New American spelling-book — in three parts. Containing, I. Dilworth's tables. . . . The seventh edition.
Wilmington — Printed and sold by Peter Brynberg. 1800.   pp. [6], 198.   12mo.
          WˡPL.

38207 PEIRCE, Proctor   1768–1821
An Eulogy, pronounced on the 22d of February, 1800: before the inhabitants of Greenfield, Massachusetts. Assembled to commemorate the death of . . . Washington.
Greenfield: Printed by Thomas Dickman. 1800.   pp. 16.   8vo.
          BrU, Deerfield Public Library, JCB, YC.

38208   PENNSYLVANIA. STATE.
      ACTS OF THE GENERAL ASSEMBLY OF THE COMMONWEALTH OF PENNSYLVANIA, PASSED AT A SESSION,
      WHICH WAS BEGUN AND HELD AT THE BOROUGH OF LANCASTER, ON TUESDAY, THE THIRD DAY
      OF DECEMBER . . . ONE THOUSAND SEVEN HUNDRED AND NINETY-NINE. . . .
          Lancaster, Printed by Francis & Robert Bailey, in West King-Street — M,DCCC.
      pp. [2], [531]–621.   4to.
      There are copies in which page 620 was omitted in the numbering.   AAS, LOC, PPL.

38209   — ERLÄUTERUDE BEMERKUNGEN ÜBER SEINER EXCELLENZ THOMAS M'KEAN GEGENWÄRTIGEM
      GOUVERNEUR VON PENNSYLVANIEN BEY SEINEM AMTSEINTRITT GEHALTEN. ADDRESSE AN BEIDE
      HAUSER DER GESEZGEBUNG. . . .
          Lancaster: Gedruckt bey Chr. Jacob Hutter. 1800.   pp. 16.   12mo.
                                                              BASSLER-UNGER COLLECTION.

38210   — THE INAGURAL ADDRESS OF THOMAS M'KEAN [1734–1817], GOVERNOR OF PENNSYLVANIA, TO . . .
      THE LEGISLATURE; WITH THEIR ANSWERS, AND HIS REPLIES. TO WHICH ARE ADDED, REMARKS.
          Lancaster: Printed by W. & R. Dickson.   pp. 16.   16mo.   NYPL.

38211   — JOURNAL DES SENATES DER REPUBLIK PENNSYLVANIEN, WELCHES ZU LANCASTER SEINEN ANFANG
      GENOMMEN, MITWOCHS, DEN FÜNFTEN NOVEMBER, IN JAHR UNSERS HERRN EIN TAUSEND
      ACHT HUNDERT. . . .
          Lancaster, gedruckt bey Johann Albreiht und Comp . . . 1800.
      Before this copy was described it was assumed, from the order to print, that the title read
      "Tagebuch des Senate."   LᴬHS.

38212   — JOURNAL OF THE FIRST SESSION OF THE TENTH HOUSE OF REPRESENTATIVES OF THE COMMON-
      WEALTH OF PENNSYLVANIA, WHICH COMMENDED AT LANCASTER, ON TUESDAY, THE THIRD DAY
      OF DECEMBER, IN THE YEAR OF OUR LORD ONE THOUSAND SEVEN HUNDRED AND NINETY NINE. . . .
          Lancaster: Printed by Francis & Robert Bailey, in King Street. 1799 [1800].   pp. 439,
      59, 18.   fol.
      The appendices contain the "Receipts and Expenditures" and the "Report of the Register-
      General." Each has its own titlepage.   APS, HSP, LCP, PPL.

38213   — JOURNAL OF THE FIRST SESSION OF THE ELEVENTH HOUSE OF REPRESENTATIVES OF THE COMMON-
      WEALTH OF PENNSYLVANIA, WHICH COMMENCED AT LANCASTER, ON WEDNESDAY, THE FIFTH
      DAY OF NOVEMBER, IN THE YEAR OF OUR LORD ONE THOUSAND EIGHT HUNDRED. . . .
          Lancaster: Printed by Francis Bailey. . . . 1800.   pp. 474, 67, 21, 6.   fol.
      The appendices contain the "Receipts and Expenditures," the "Report of the Register-
      General," and the "Report of the Comptroller-General." Each has its own titlepage.
                                                              APS, HSP, LCP, LOC, NYPL.

38214   — JOURNAL OF THE SENATE OF THE COMMONWEALTH OF PENNSYLVANIA, WHICH COMMENCED AT
      LANCASTER, ON TUESDAY, THE THIRD DAY OF DECEMBER, IN THE YEAR OF OUR LORD,
      ONE THOUSAND, SEVEN HUNDRED AND NINETY-NINE. . . . VOLUME X.
          Printed by William Hamilton . . . Lancaster.   pp. 281, 19, 59.   fol.
      The appendices are the "Report of the Register-General" and the "Receipts and Expendi-
      tures," each with its own titlepage dated 1800.   APS, HSP, LCP, LOC, NYHS, PPL.

38215   — JOURNAL OF THE SENATE OF THE COMMONWEALTH OF PENNSYLVANIA WHICH COMMENCED AT
      LANCASTER, ON WEDNESDAY THE FIFTH DAY OF NOVEMBER, IN THE YEAR OF OUR LORD, ONE
      THOUSAND, EIGHT HUNDRED. . . . VOLUME XI.
          Printed by William Hamilton . . . Lancaster. 1800.   pp. 356, 66, 6, 21.   fol.
      The appendices contain the "Receipts and Expenditures," the "Report of the Comptroller-
      General," and the "Report of the Register-General," each with its own titlepage.
                                                              APS, HSP, LCP, NYHS, NYSL.

38216   — LAND-OFFICE OF PENNSYLVANIA, SEPT. 13, 1800. THE FIRST DAY OF OCTOBER APPROACHES, WHEN IT
      WILL BE IMPOSSIBLE TO MAKE ANY MORE RELEASES TO THE COMMONWEALTH, OF LANDS OWNED
      UNDER THE PENNSYLVANIA TITLE, WITHIN . . . LUZERNE. . . .
          Broadside.   fol.   LOC.

38217 —— PRINTED BY WILLIAM HAMILTON, LANCASTER, NOV. 22, 1800. GOVERNOR'S MESSAGE. TO THE
SENATE AND HOUSE OF REPRESENTATIVES . . . OF PENNSYLVANIA.
[*Lancaster.*]   pp. 4.   fol.
Signed and dated: Thomas M'Kean. Lancaster, November 21, 1800.   NYPL.

38218 —— RECEIPTS AND EXPENDITURES IN THE TREASURY OF THE COMMONWEALTH OF PENNSYLVANIA, FROM
THE FIRST OF JANUARY TO THE THIRTY-FIRST OF DECEMBER, 1799. . . .
Printed by William Hamilton . . . Lancaster. 1800.   pp. 59.   fol.   LOC, PPL.

38219 —— RECEIPTS AND EXPENDITURES IN THE TREASURY OF THE COMMONWEALTH OF PENNSYLVANIA FROM
THE FIRST OF JANUARY TO THE TWENTY-NINTH OF NOVEMBER, 1800. . . .
Printed by William Hamilton. Lancaster, 1800.   pp. 66.   fol.
The edition with the imprint of Francis Bailey was an Appendix to the *Journal* of the
House.   LOC, NYPL, PPL.

38220 —— REPORT OF THE COMMITTEE APPOINTED TO ENQUIRE CONCERNING THE COMPLAINT OF GEORGE LOGAN
AGAINST SAMUEL W. FISHER, ON A BREACH OF PRIVILEGE; WITH THE DOCUMENTS ACCOMPANY-
ING THE SAME.
Lancaster, Printed by Francis & Robert Bailey, in King-Street.   pp. 56.   8vo.
BPL, LCP, LOC, NYHS, PSL.

38221 —— REPORT OF THE COMPTROLLER-GENERAL OF THE COMMONWEALTH OF PENNSYLVANIA.
Printed by William Hamilton. Lancaster. 1800.   pp. 6.   fol.
Issued also bound in with the *Journal* of the Senate.   LOC, NYPL, PPL.

38222 —— REPORT OF THE REGISTER GENERAL OF THE STATE OF THE FINANCES OF THE COMMONWEALTH OF
PENNSYLVANIA, FOR THE YEAR 1799.
Printed by William Hamilton . . . Lancaster. 1800.   pp. 19 [i.e. 17].   fol.
Issued also bound in with the *Journal* of the Senate.   LOC, NYPL, PPL.

38223 —— RULES, ESTABLISHED FOR REGULATING THE PRACTICE OF THE SUPREME AND CIRCUIT COURTS OF
PENNSYLVANIA. . . .
[*Whitehall: Printed for William Young . . . Philadelphia.*]   pp. 24.   12mo.
LOC, PSL.

38224 PENNSYLVANIA. SOCIETY FOR THE RELIEF OF POOR, AGED AND INFIRM MASTERS OF SHIPS, THEIR
WIDOWS AND CHILDREN. AN ACT FOR INCORPORATING THE SOCIETY FORMED FOR THE RELIEF OF
POOR, AGED AND INFIRM MASTERS OF SHIPS, THEIR WIDOWS, AND CHILDREN, TOGETHER WITH THE
BY-LAWS OF THE SOCIETY, AND A LIST OF THE MEMBERS NAMES.
Philadelphia, Printed by Henry Tuckniss for the Society, 1800.   pp. 37.   8vo.
HSP, JCB, LCP.

38225 THE PENNSYLVANIA ALMANAC, FOR THE YEAR OF OUR LORD, 1801. . . . ALSO A VARIETY OF USEFUL
AND ENTERTAINING MATTER.
Philadelphia: Printed by Francis and Robert Bailey.   pp. [36].   16mo.   AAS, LOC.

38226 THE PENNSYLVANIA GAZETTE.   1728–1815
Philadelphia: printed by Hall and Sellers. . . .   fol.   weekly.
FOR 1800: [AAS], [HC], LCP.

38227 THE PENNSYLVANIA, NEW-JERSEY, DELAWARE, MARYLAND AND VIRGINIA ALMANAC, FOR THE
YEAR OF OUR LORD, 1801. . . .
Philadelphia: Printed and sold by Peter Stewart, no. 34, South Second-Street.
pp. [40].   12mo.   AAS, LOC.

38228 PENNSYLVANIA SOCIETY FOR PROMOTING THE ABOLITION OF SLAVERY.
CONSTITUTION AND ACT OF INCORPORATION OF THE PENNSYLVANIA SOCIETY FOR PROMOTING THE
ABOLITION OF SLAVERY AND THE RELIEF OF FREE NEGROES. . . .
Philadelphia: Printed by J. Ormrod, for the . . . Society. . . . 1800.   pp. 53.   8vo.
AAS, BPL, BrU, HC, HEH, HSP, LOC, MHS, NYHS, NYPL, PrPL.

38229 —— An Address from the Pennsylvania Abolition Society to the free black people . . . of Philadelphia.
Philadelphia, J. Ormrod, 1800. pp. 8. 8vo. NL.

38230 [DIE PENNSYLVANISCHE Correspondenz. 1797–1800
Herausgegeben von Henrich Schweitzer . . . Philadelphia. . . . fol. semi-weekly and weekly.] For 1800: no copy known.

38231 [DIE PENNSYLVANISCHE Wochenschrift. 1797–1805
Hanover, Pa., published by W. D. Lepper and S. E. Stettinius.] weekly.
For 1800: no copy known.

38232 PERCIVAL, Thomas 1740–1804
A Father's instructions; consisting of moral tales, fables, and reflections. . . . The ninth edition.
Richmond: Published by William Prichard. 1800. pp. xii, 219. 12mo.
AAS, BPL, NYSL, PrU.

38233 PERKINS, Nathan 1749–1838
Two discourses on the grounds of the Christian's hope; containing a brief account of the . . . revival . . . in West-Hartford, in . . . 1799. Delivered on the first Sabbath of the year 1800. . . .
Hartford: Printed by Hudson and Goodwin. 1800. pp. 62. 8vo.
AAS, BM, CHS, CL, HC, JCB, LOC, MHS, NYPL, NYSL, WL, YC.

38234 PERRIN, John [i. e. Jean Baptiste] FL. 1786.
Entertaining and instructive exercises. . . . By John Perrin. . . .
New York: E. Duyckinck: 1800. pp. 384. 16mo. JCB, NHSL, NYPL.

38235 —— A Grammar of the French tongue, grounded upon the decisions of the French Academy. . . . By John Perrin. . . . The tenth edition. . . .
New York: Printed by M. L. & W. A. Davis, for E. Duyckinck, T. S. Arden, S. Stephens, P. A. Mesier, and W. Falconer. 1800. pp. xii, 358. 12mo. BA, BPL, LOC, NYPL.

38236 PERRY, William, *of Edinburgh*
The Royal standard English dictionary. . . . To which is prefixed, a comprehensive grammar. . . . The fifth American edition. . . .
Printed at Boston, by Isaiah Thomas and Ebenezer T. Andrews. Sold by them . . . by I. Thomas, in Worcester; by Thomas, Andrews & Penniman, in Albany; and by Thomas, Andrews & Butler, in Baltimore. January, 1800. pp. [4], 596. sq. 24mo.
AAS, LOC, NYPL.

38237 PETERSBURG. Virginia. Ross & Douglas.
A Catalogue of books, &c., now selling by Ross & Douglas, booksellers and stationers, Petersburg.
Petersburg, 1800. pp. 31. NCU.

38238 THE PETERSBURG Intelligencer. 1800–1860
Virginia—Published . . . by William Prentis. . . . fol. semi-weekly.
For 1800: [NYPL].

38239 [PETTIT, Charles] 1736–1806
An Impartial review of the rise and progress of the controversy between the . . . Federalists, & Republicans. . . .
Philadelphia: Printed by John Ormrod, no. 41, Chestnut-street. 1800. pp. 50. 8vo.
AAS, APS, BPL, BrU, HEH, LCP, LOC, MSL, NYPL, NYSL, UOTx.

38240 PFEIFFER, George, M. D.
AN EULOGIUM TO THE MEMORY OF GENERAL GEORGE WASHINGTON. . . .
Natchez: Printed by B. M. Stokes. 1800.   pp. 38.   16mo.
Reprinted in *The Washingtonian,* Baltimore, 1800.   MFM.

38241 [THE PHENIX.   1798–1804
Staunton (Virginia) published . . . by John Wise.   fol.   weekly.]
FOR 1800: NO COPY KNOWN.

38242 PHILADELPHIA. PENNSYLVANIA.
THE ORDINANCES OF THE CITY OF PHILADELPHIA, AND THE SEVERAL SUPPLEMENTS TO THE ACT OF
INCORPORATION. . . .
Philadelphia: Printed by Zachariah Poulson, Junior. . . . 1800.   pp. 46.   8vo.
BPL, LCP, LOC, PPL.

38243 — — — [*Same imprint.*]   pp. 46, [2], 47–70.   8vo.
Pages 47–70 contain the ordinances for 1801.   AAS, BPL, HEH, HSP, LCP, NYPL

38244 PHILADELPHIA. PENNSYLVANIA. BAPTIST ASSOCIATION.
MINUTES OF THE PHILADELPHIA BAPTIST ASSOCIATION, HELD AT PHILADELPHIA, OCTOBER 7TH, 8TH,
9TH, 1800.
[*Mount Holly, N. J.: Printed by Stephen C. Ustick.*]   pp. 8.   sm. 4to.
On p. 6: "Brother Ustick is requested to superintend the printing of the Minutes."
BrU, NJHS.

38245 PHILADELPHIA. PENNSYLVANIA. CHURCHES.
ACCOUNT OF THE BAPTISMS AND BURIALS IN THE UNITED CHURCHES OF CHRIST CHURCH AND ST.
PETER'S. . . . ALSO . . . BAPTISMS . . . IN VARIOUS CONGREGATIONS IN THE CITY AND SUBURBS
OF PHILADELPHIA FROM DEC. 25, 1799 TO DEC. 25, 1800.
Philadelphia, J. Ormrod.   Broadside.   LCP.

38246 PHILADELPHIA. PENNSYLVANIA. CICERONIAN SOCIETY.
THE CONSTITUTION OF THE CICERONIAN SOCIETY.
Philadelphia: Printed by the Society, by R. Aitken . . . 1800.   pp. 23.   12mo.
APS.

38247 PHILADELPHIA. PENNSYLVANIA. COMMITTEE FOR IMPROVING THE CONDITION OF FREE BLACKS.
ADDRESS OF THE COMMITTEE FOR IMPROVING THE CONDITION OF THE FREE BLACKS, TO THE MEM-
BERS OF THE PENNSYLVANIA ABOLITION SOCIETY. . . .
Philadelphia, 1800.   pp. 8.   8vo.
Signed by John Letchworth, vice-president.   APS, CSL, LCP, NL, WⁱˢHS.

38248 PHILADELPHIA. PENNSYLVANIA. FRIENDSHIP FIRE COMPANY.
ARTICLES AND BYE LAWS OF THE FRIENDSHIP FIRE COMPANY.
Philadelphia: Printed by Z. Poulson, Jun. February 22, 1800.   pp. [12], interleaved.
24mo.   HSP.

38249 PHILADELPHIA. PENNSYLVANIA. MAGDALEN SOCIETY.
THE CONSTITUTION OF THE MAGDALEN SOCIETY.
Philadelphia: Printed by Benjamin & Jacob Johnson. . . . 1800.   pp. 11.   12mo.
LOC, MHS, NYPL.

38250 PHILADELPHIA. PENNSYLVANIA. PENNSYLVANIA HOSPITAL.
THE COMMITTEE APPOINTED TO PREPARE AN ACCOUNT OF THE MONIES RECEIVED FROM THE LEGIS-
LATURE OF PENNSYLVANIA, TOWARD ERECTING . . . THE PENNSYLVANIA HOSPITAL. . . . REPORT.
PHILADELPHIA, TWELFTH-MONTH 22D, 1800. . . .
Philadelphia: Printed by Zachariah Poulson, junior, no. 106, Chestnut-Street.
Broadside.   fol.   HSP.

38251 —— State of the accounts of the Pennsylvania Hospital, adjusted by the managers; being a summary of the receipts and payments for the year ending the 25th day of the 4th month, 1800. . . .
 [Philadelphia:] Printed by D. C. Claypoole.   Broadside.   fol.
 Mrs. Joseph Carson.

38252 PHILADELPHIA. Pennsylvania. Philadelphia Fire Company.
 Articles and bye-laws . . . list of members of the Philadelphia Fire Company.
 Philadelphia, 1800.   pp. 24.   HSP.

38253 PHILADELPHIA. Pennsylvania. Philadelphia Medical Society.
 The Act of incorporation and laws of the Philadelphia Medical Society. Arranged and copied by order of the Society, February, 1800. . . .
 Philadelphia: Printed for Mathew Carey, no. 118 Market Street. 1800.   pp. 23.   8vo.
 Includes a list of members.   AAS, AML, LCP.

38254 PHILADELPHIA. Pennsylvania. Samuel Israel.
 [15 Boxes and trunks of new books, just imported. . . . Sold at his auction room, Philadelphia, May 7, 1800.]   McKay 143d.

38255 PHILADELPHIA. Pennsylvania. Samuel Yorke.
 Drugs & Medicine. On Tuesday afternoon, at two o'clock, at the auction store, will be sold. . . . Samuel Yorke, auctioneer.
 Philadelphia, May 26th, 1800. Printed by James Humphreys, no. 106, South side of Market-Street.   Broadside.   4to.   AAS.

38256 PHILADELPHIA. Pennsylvania. Shannon & Poalk.
 [Auction of very select and valuable books. . . . Sold at their vendue store, Market Street, Philadelphia. Apr. 21, 1800.]   McKay 143c.

38257 —— [A Quantity of books, French and English, in good preservation. . . . Sold at their store, 177 Market Street, Philadelphia. May 12, 1800.]   McKay 143f.

38258 —— [Scarce and valuable books; in good preservation. . . . Sold at their auction store . . . Philadelphia. Aug. 27, 1800.]   McKay 143i.

38259 PHILADELPHIA. Pennsylvania. William Birch & Son.
 The City of Philadelphia, in the State of Pennsylvania . . . as it appeared in the year 1800, consisting of twenty eight plates. . . .
 [Philadelphia.]   Engraved t. p., 3 leaves, 29 plates, plan.   obl.   fol.
 The work contains two colored plates not mentioned in the list on p. [2]. The plates were also sold individually, and were later reprinted.   LOC, NYHS, RL.

38260 PHILADELPHIA. Pennsylvania. Zion German Lutheran Church
 Klagen uber den tod des general Waschingtons am 22sten februar 1800, in dem Deutsch evangelisch Lutherianschen Zion zu Philadelphia.
 [Philadelphia.]   pp. [4].   16mo.   LOC.

38261 THE PHILADELPHIA Aurora.   Mar. 10–Nov. 7, 1800
 Published (tri-weekly) for the heirs of Benj. Franklin Bache. . . .   fol.
 A continuation of *Bache's Philadelphia Aurora*, continued as *Aurora, for the Country*.
 For 1800: AAS, NYPL, PSL.

38262 THE PHILADELPHIA Directory.
 See Stafford, Cornelius William.

38263   THE PHILADELPHIA GAZETTE & UNIVERSAL DAILY ADVERTISER.   1794–1802
         [Philadelphia, published] By Brown & Relf.   fol.   daily.
         With the issue of June 18 the word "Universal" was dropped from the title.
                                        FOR 1800: [AAS], HSP, LCP, [LOC], W¹ˢHS.

38264   PHILADELPHIA REPOSITORY, AND WEEKLY REGISTER.   Nov. 15, 1800–1804
                Printed by E[phraim] Conrad. . . .   4to.   weekly.
                                        FOR 1800: AAS, HSP, LCP, LOC, NYHS.

38265   PHILADELPHISCHE CORRESPONDENZ.   1798–1800
                Alle Dienstag herausgegeben von Joseph R. Kämmerer, und G. Helmbold, jun.
                fol.   weekly.
         With the issue of Mar. 7 Kämmerer retired, and in April the old title *Neue Philadelphische*
         Correspondenz was resumed.   FOR 1800: [HSP].

38266   PHILANTHROPHIC LOTTERY.
                A LIST OF ALL THOSE NUMBERS WHICH WERE DRAWN BLANKS AND PRIZES IN THE SECOND CLASS OF
                THE PHILANTHROPIC LOTTERY, NOVEMBER, 1800. . . .
                        pp. [16].   8vo.
         This lottery was drawn at Boston for the benefit of Joseph Hawkins, for whom see Evans
         32239.   AAS.

38267   PIERCE, JOHN   1773–1849
                A EULOGY ON GEORGE WASHINGTON . . . DELIVERED, ON THE ANNIVERSARY OF HIS BIRTH, AT
                BROOKLINE. . . .
                        Boston: Manning & Loring, printers, near the Old South Meeting-House. 1800.
                pp. 24, 24.   8vo.
         "General Washington's farewell address" 24 pp. at end.
                        AAS, BA, BPL, HC, HEH, JCB, LOC, NYHS, NYPL, NYSL, VᵃU, YC.

38268   PIKE, SAMUEL, AND HAYWARD, SAMUEL
                RELIGIOUS CASES OF CONSCIENCE ANSWERED . . . AT THE CASUISTICAL LECTURE, IN LITTLE ST.
                HELEN'S, BISHOPGATE-STREET. . . .
                        Philadelphia: Printed for Robert Campbell. 1800.   pp. viii, 527.   16mo.
                                        AAS, CL, LOC, NYPL, NYSL, PSL, WLC, YC.

38269   [PILKINGTON, MARY (HOPKINS)]   1766–1839
                TALES OF THE HERMITAGE; WRITTEN FOR THE INSTRUCTION AND AMUSEMENT OF THE RISING
                GENERATION.
                        Philadelphia: Published by James Thackara. H. Maxwell, printer. 1800.   pp. 158.
                                                                                EI.

38270   PINCKNEY, CHARLES   1758–1824
                SPEECHES OF CHARLES PINCKNEY, ESQ. IN CONGRESS; ON THE SUBJECT OF HAVING IMPARTIAL
                JURIES, BY LOT, IN ALL THE FEDERAL COURTS. . . .
                        [Philadelphia?] Printed in 1800.   pp. [4], iv, 135.   8vo.
                                        AAS, JCB, LOC, MHS, NYHS, NYPL, YC.

38271   [PINKNEY, WILLIAM]   1764–1822
                A FEW REMARKS ON MR. HAMILTON'S LATE LETTER, CONCERNING THE PUBLIC CONDUCT &
                CHARACTER, OF THE PRESIDENT. BY CAIUS. . . . COPY RIGHT. . . .
                        Baltimore — printed by Warner & Hanna. 1800.   pp. 24.   8vo.
                                        AAS, APS, BA, HEH, HSP, LOC, MᵈHS, MHS, NYPL, NYSL.

38272   PINTARD, JOHN MARSDEN
                [LETTERS TO TIMOTHY PICKERING, SECRETARY OF STATE, AND THE PRESIDENT OF THE U. S.
                        New York: 1800?]   pp. 35.   8vo.
         Letters dated Nov. 15–Dec. 20, 1799, by, or relating to the conduct of, J. M. Pintard
         when consul at Maderia, in a pamphlet without a titlepage.   NYHS.

38273 PITT, WILLIAM 1759–1806
SPEECH OF THE RIGHT HON. WILLIAM PITT, DELIVERED IN THE HOUSE OF COMMONS, MONDAY, FEBRUARY 3, 1800. . . . FROM THE FOURTH LONDON EDITION.
New York: Printed and sold by John Furman. . . . 1800. pp. 68. 8vo.
AAS, APS, BᵣU, CL, LOC, NYHS, NYPL, PPL.

38274 THE PITTSBURGH ALMANACK, FOR THE YEAR OF OUR LORD, 1801. . . . CONTAINING . . . A VARIETY OF INTERESTING AND USEFUL MATTER. . . .
[Pittsburgh: Zadock Cramer]. pp. [34]. 16mo. AAS.

38275 THE PITTSBURGH GAZETTE. 1786–1876
Pittsburgh: printed by John Scull. . . . fol. weekly.
FOR 1800: [CARNEGIE LIBRARY, PITTSBURGH].

38276 PLAIN PSALMODY, OR SUPPLEMENTARY MUSIC. AN ORIGINAL COMPOSITION . . . CONSISTING OF SEVENTY PSALM AND HYMN TUNES. . . .
Printed, typographically, at Boston, by Isaiah Thomas and Ebenezer T. Andrews . . . November, 1800. pp. 71, [1]. obl. 8vo.
Frequently attributed to Oliver Holden, but not so in Isaiah Thomas' Ms. catalogue of his library, in which he was careful to give authors. AAS, BPL, LOC, MHS, MSL, NEHGS.

38277 THE PLAN FOR CORRESPONDENCE AND FRIENDLY INTERCOURSE, PROPOSED BY . . . DELEGATES . . . OF THE PRESBYTERIAN CHURCH . . . THE DUTCH REFORMED CHURCH AND . . . THE ASSOCIATE REFORMED CHURCH, WHEN MET IN NEW YORK . . . JUNE, 1798 . . . APPROVED BY THE GENERAL ASSEMBLY OF THE PRESBYTERIAN CHURCH, IN MAY, 1799. . . .
[New York.] pp. 4. 8vo.
Caption title. Dated May 14, 1800, at end. PPL, JCB, NYPL, RU.

38278 A PLAN FOR THE MORE EFFECTUAL INSTRUCTION OF CHILDREN AND YOUTH, WITH AN ADDRESS TO MINISTERS AND PARENTS ON THE SUBJECT, RECOMMENDED BY THE CONSOCIATION OF THE WESTERN DISTRICT OF NEW HAVEN COUNTY, DECEMBER 3, 1800. IN CONCERT WITH THE ASSOCIATED MINISTERS . . . OF BERKSHIRE, AND THE NORTHERN ASSOCIATED PRESBYTERY OF NEW YORK.
New Haven: Printed for the Consociation, by Read & Morse, 1800. pp. 8. 16mo.
CL.

38279 A PLAN. MORE EFFECTUAL RELIGIOUS INSTRUCTION OF CHILDREN AND YOUTH, WITH AN ADDRESS TO THE MINISTERS AND PARENTS ON THE SUBJECT. BY THE ASSOCIATION OF THE MINISTERS IN THE COUNTY OF BERKSHIRE, AND THE NORTHERN ASSOCIATED PRESBYTERY IN THE STATE OF NEW YORK.
Printed at Stockbridge, 1800. pp. 6. 12mo. BᵣA.

38280 A PLAN OF CONSOCIATION. . . .
See Windham County.

38281 PLATT, JONAS
TO THE PEOPLE OF ONEIDA COUNTY. THE UNFORTUNATE CONTROVERSEY ABOUT A COURT-HOUSE. . . . OCTOBER 1ST, 1800.
[Utica: William McLean?] pp. 23. 12mo.
Caption title. Signed and dated on p. 20. For a reply see Gold, Thomas Ruggles.
NYHS, NYPL.

38282 PLEASING INCITEMENTS TO WISDOM AND VIRTUE . . . CALCULATED TO ENTERTAIN . . . THE JUVENILE MIND. TRANSLATED CHIEFLY FROM THE GERMAN.
Philadelphia: Re-printed by James Humphreys, from the London edition. 1800. pp. iv, [2], 120. 24mo.
AAS, UOC.

38283 [PLUMPTRE, ANNE]
        ANTOINETTE PERCIVAL. A NOVEL. . . .
                Philadelphia: Printed for Mathew Carey, no. 118, High-Street. March 20, 1800.
        pp. 234.   12mo.
        The titlepage is preceeded by two pages describing the "Character of this work." The
        author's name appears on later editions.   AAS, HC, JCB.

38284 PLYMOUTH. MASSACHUSETTS.
        FESTIVAL OF THE SONS OF THE PILGRIMS. ODE FOR THE 22D OF DECEMBER. COMPOSED FOR THE
        ANNIVERSARY FESTIVAL AT PLYMOUTH, IN THE YEAR 1793. . . . ODE. . . . COMPOSED FOR THE
        FESTIVAL . . . 1800. . . .
                Broadside.   fol.   MHS.

38285 A POCKET HYMN-BOOK, DESIGNED AS A CONSTANT COMPANION FOR THE PIOUS. COLLECTED FROM
        VARIOUS AUTHORS. THE TWENTY-THIRD EDITION. . . .
                Philadelphia: Printed by Henry Tuckniss . . . for Ezekiel Cooper . . . 1800. . . .
        pp. 285, [10], 6, [2].   24mo.
        There are at least three combinations of the supplementary pages.   AAS, HSP, UTS, YC.

38286 A POEM ON THE PRESIDENT'S FAREWELL ADDRESS. . . .
        See Honeywood, St. John.

38287 [POLITICAL BANQUET, AND FARMER'S FEAST.   1799–1800
                Exeter, printed by Henry Ranlet.]   FOR 1800: NO COPY KNOWN.

38288 THE POLITICAL GRINDER. A POETIC SATIRE ON CERTAIN CONSPICUOUS CHARACTERS. CONTAINED IN
        AN ADDRESS TO THE FRIENDS OF REPUBLICAN LIBERTY ON THE COMMENCEMENT OF THE NEW
        CENTURY.
                Boston: Press of the Constitutional Telegraphe.   pp. 12.   16mo.   BPL, NYHS.

38289 THE POLITICAL MAGAZINE; AND MISCELLANEOUS REPOSITORY. CONTAINING ANCIENT AND MODERN
        POLITICAL AND MISCELLANEOUS PIECES. . . . FOR OCTOBER [–NOVEMBER] 1800. V.I. — NUMB. I.
        [–II].
                Ballston, Saratoga County: Printed and sold by William Child. 1800.   pp. [2], 96.
        8vo.   NYSL.

38290 POLITICAL MIRROR.   1800–1802
                Staunton, Virginia: Printed by M'Arthur & Courtney for the proprietors. . . .   fol.
        weekly.
        The publisher was James Lyon.   FOR 1800: [AAS].

38291 THE POLITICAL NOSEGAY; OR THE SWINDLER JAMES GEO. SEMPLE REVIVED IN THE PERSON OF HUGH
        WORKMAN, A NATIVE OF IRELAND. COPY-RIGHT SECURED, ACCORDING TO LAW. 1800.
                pp. [10], 20.   12mo.   NYPL.

38292 THE POLITICAL REPOSITORY: OR, FARMER'S JOURNAL.   1798–1802
                Printed at Brookfield, Massachusetts, by Ebenezer Merriam & Co.   weekly.   fol.
                                                                     FOR 1800: AAS.

38293 POLWHELE, RICHARD   1760–1838
        THE UNSEX'D FEMALES; A POEM, ADDRESSED TO THE AUTHOR OF THE PURSUITS OF LITERATURE. . . .
        TO WHICH IS ADDED, A SKETCH OF THE . . . CHARACTER OF P. PINDAR [JOHN WOLCOT, M. D.]
                New-York: Re-published by Wm. Cobbett. 1800.   pp. vi, [3]–68.   16mo.
                                AAS, BPL, HEH, LCP, LOC, MSL, NYPL, PrU.

38294 POMEROY, JONATHAN L[AW]   1768–1836
        THE FOLLY OF DENYING A GOD . . . TWO SERMONS; THE SUBSTANCE OF WHICH WAS PREACHED,
        EXTEMPORE, AT WORTHINGTON. . . .
                Northampton: Printed by William Butler. 1800.   pp. 45.   8vo.
                                AAS, JCB, NYPL, NYSL, YC.

38295 —— Religion a security. . . . Preached . . . at Worthington, October 20, 1799, at the funeral of Mrs. Olive, wife of Mr. Lemuel Pomeroy, Jun. . . .
  Northampton, [Massachusetts] printed by William Butler. 1800. pp. 28. 8vo.
  AAS, JCB, NYPL, NYSL, YC.

38296 POOR Richard revived: or, the Albany Almanack: for the year of our Lord, 1801. . . . By Old Father Richard, mathemat.
  Albany: Printed and sold by John Barber, Faust's Statue, two doors east of the Dutch Church, State-Street. . . . pp. [36]. 12mo. AAS, LOC, NYPL, WⁱˢHS, YC.

38297 POOR Will's Almanack, for the year of our Lord, 1801. . . . Also a variety of essays in prose and verse.
  Philadelphia: Printed for, and sold by, Joseph and James Crukshank, No. 87, High-Street. pp. [36]. 12mo. AAS, LOC, NYPL, WⁱˢHS.

38298 POOR Will's pocket Almanack, for the year 1801; being the fifth after bis-sextile or leap-year. . . .
  Philadelphia: Printed for, and sold by, Joseph & James Crukshank, no. 87, High-Street.
  pp. [48]. 32mo. AAS, HSP, LOC, NYHS.

38299 POPE, Alexander   1688–1744
  An Essay on man; in four epistles. . . . To which is added, the Universal Prayer. . . .
  Boston: Printed and sold by Samuel Hall, no. 53, Cornhill. 1800. pp. 60. 16mo.
  AAS, BPL, HC, JCB, MᵉHS, YC.

38300 —— —— —— *Salem: Printed by Joshua Cushing, for T. C. Cushing. 1800.* pp. 43. 16mo. EI.

38301 POPE, John   1770–1845
  [To the citizens of the electoral district composed of the counties of Nelson and Jefferson. John Pope. October 31st, 1800.]
  Broadside. fol. McMurtrie, *Kentucky*, 134.

38302 POPE, Nathaniel   —— 1809
  A Speech, delivered . . . in support of the resolutions which he prepared and presented to the people of Hanover, at their meeting the 17th day of October, 1798, with which he has incorporated sundry observations . . . intended as an answer to the arguments of a gentleman of Richmond, in favour of the Sedition Act.
  Richmond: Printed by Meriwether Jones, MDCCC. pp. 37. 16mo. HEH, LOC.

38303 PORCUPINE'S Gazette, No. 779.   1800
  New York: Published by William Cobbett, Jan. 13, 1800. pp. 49–72. 12mo.
  This was the concluding number of the newspaper of the same name published by Cobbett at Bustleton. AAS, HC, JCB, LCP, LOC, NYAM, NYPL, NYSOC, WLC.

38304 PORTER, David   1761–1851
  Two discourses: the first occasioned by the death of General Washington, delivered at Spencertown, January 19, 1800. The second, delivered on a thanksgiving occasion, at the same place, December 13, 1799. . . .
  Printed in Hudson, by Ashbel Stoddard. 1,800. pp. 33. 12mo. BA, HEH, LOC.

38305 PORTER, Eliphalet   1758–1833
  An Eulogy on George Washington. . . . Delivered Jan. 14th, 1800, before the inhabitants of the Town of Roxbury. . . .
  Boston: From the printing-office of Manning & Loring, near the Old South Meeting-House. pp. 22, 22. 8vo.
  "The legacy of the father of his country," pp. 22 at the end.
  AAS, BA, BPL, HC, JCB, LOC, MHS, NYHS, NYPL, NYSL, YC.

38306 PORTER, Huntington   1755–1844
A Funeral discourse, delivered at Rye, August, 1800: occasioned by the death of . . .
Samuel Jenness. . . . The widow Catharine Elkins . . . and Miss Apphia Rand. . . .
*Portsmouth, New-Hampshire, printed at the United States' Oracle-office, by Charles
Peirce. 1800.*   pp. 18.   8vo.   AAS, NYHS, YC.

38307 PORTER, Nathaniel   1745–1837
A Discourse on the death of General Geo: Washington, delivered at Conway, January
16th, 1800. . . .
Portsmouth, printed by John Melcher, 1800.   pp. 23.   8vo.   AAS, MHS.

38308 [PORTEUS], Bielby   1731–1808
A Summary of the principal evidences for the truth and divine origin of the Christian
religion. . . . Third edition.
*Charlestown. Printed by Samuel Etheridge, for E. & S. Larkin, no. 47, Cornhill,
Boston. 1800.*   pp. 159.   12mo.   AAS, AHTS, BPL, WC.

38309 PORTSMOUTH, New Hampshire
State of Newhampshire, Rockingham ss. At a meeting of the Selectmen of Portsmouth,
whereas it is of great importance that the fire engines. . . . May 1st, 1800. . . .
Broadside.   fol.   AAS.

38310 PORTSMOUTH. New Hampshire. Charles Peirce.
Valuable medicines, just received from Lee and Co's patent and family medicine store,
Baltimore, and for sale by Charles Peirce. . . . Portsmouth, New-Hampshire, Oct. II,
1800. . . .
Broadside.   fol.   MHS.

38311 THE POST-Angel, or Universal Entertainment.   1800
Edenton [N. C.]: Printed for Robert Archibald, by Joseph Beasley.   fol.   weekly.
In November the title was changed to *The Edenton Gazette.*   For 1800: [NCU].

38312 THE POTOMAK Guardian.   1792–Jan. 8, 1800
Martinsburg, Virginia: printed and published . . . by Armstrong Charlton. . . .   fol.
weekly.   For 1800: [BPL].

38313 THE POUGHKEEPSIE Journal.   1789–1844
Poughkeepsie, (Dutchess County), published by Power and Southwick. . . .   fol.
weekly.
On November 25 Southwick retired.   For 1800: Adriance Lib., Poughkeepsie.

38314 POULSON'S American Daily Advertiser.   1800–1839
Philadelphia: Printed by Zachariah Poulson, Jun.   fol.   daily.
This was a continuation of *Claypoole's American Daily Advertiser*, the change occurring
with the issue of Oct. 1.   For 1800: AAS, BA, HSP, LCP, LOC, NYHS, PSL, WˢHS.

38315 POULSON'S town and country Almanac, for the year of our Lord, 1801. . . . The twelve
constellations . . . and the manner in which they are said to govern the human
body. . . .
*Philadelphia: Printed and sold by Zachariah Poulson, Junior, no. 106, Chestnut-
street. . . .*   pp. [48].   12mo.   AAS, LOC.

38316 PRENTISS, Charles   1774–1820
Child of Pallas: devoted mostly to the belles-lettres. . . .
Baltimore — printed weekly, by Warner & Hanna. 1800.   pp. 288.   16mo.
Eight numbers were published between November, 1800, and January, 1801.
AAS, BM, BPL, BʳU, HC, HSP, JCB, LOC, MᵈHS, NL, NYHS, NYPL, WL.

38317 PRESBYTERIAN CHURCH IN NEW JERSEY.
RULES ESTABLISHED BY THE PRESBYTERY OF NEW BRUNSWICK. . . . TOGETHER WITH A PASTORAL LETTER. . . . DONE AT PRINCETON, APRIL 23D, 1800.
New Brunswick: Printed by A. Blauvelt. 1800. pp. 30. 8vo.
AAS, JCB, NJHS, NYPL, P'U, RU.

38318 PRESBYTERIAN CHURCH IN THE UNITED STATES OF AMERICA.
ACTS AND PROCEEDINGS OF THE GENERAL ASSEMBLY OF THE PRESBYTERIAN CHURCH. . . . IN THE YEAR, 1800.
Philadelphia: Printed by R. Aitken, no. 22, Market Street. 1800. pp. 18. 8vo.
AAS, BM, HSP.

38319 A PRESENT FOR AN APPRENTICE. . . .
See Barnard, Sir John.

38320 THE PRESS. 1800
[Richmond, Va.] Published by Meriwether Jones, Alex. McRae, and John H. Foushee. fol. weekly. FOR 1800: [AAS].

38321 PRESTON, SAMUEL
A CHARGE DELIVERED TO THE GRAND JURY OF WAYNE COUNTY, BY SAMUEL PRESTON, ESQ., FIRST ASSOCIATE JUDGE OF SAID COUNTY.
Easton, printed by Sam. Longcope. 1800. pp. 22. 12mo. HSP, NYPL.

38322 PRIESTLY, JOSEPH 1733–1804
LETTERS TO THE INHABITANTS OF NORTHUMBERLAND. . . . TO WHICH IS ADDED A LETTER . . . RELATING TO MR. LIANCOURT'S TRAVELS. . . .
Philadelphia: John Bioren. 1800. pp. v, 96. 8vo. JCB.

38323 PRINCE, JOHN 1751–1836
PART OF A DISCOURSE DELIVERED ON THE 29TH OF DECEMBER, UPON THE CLOSE OF THE YEAR 1799. . . .
Salem: Printed by Thomas C. Cushing. . . . pp. 24. 8vo.
An eulogy to Washington occupies pp. 16–24.
AAS, EI, HC, HEH, JCB, LCP, LOC, MFM, MHS, NL, NYPL, NYSL, WLC, YC.

38324 [LE PRINCE DE BEAUMONT, MARIE] 1711–1780
THE YOUNG MISSES MAGAZINE: CONTAINING DIALOGUES BETWEEN A GOVERNESS AND SEVERAL YOUNG LADIES OF QUALITY, HER SCHOLARS. . . .
Whitehall, pr. for W. Young, Philadelphia, 1800. 2 vol. 24mo.
FORREST BOWE (VOL. 1), NYPL (VOL. 2).

38325 PRINCETON UNIVERSITY.
See College of New Jersey.

38326 PRINGLE, JOHN J[ULIUS] 1753–1843
AN ORATION, DELIVERED IN ST. PHILIP'S CHURCH . . . CHARLESTON, SOUTH-CAROLINA, ON THE FOURTH OF JULY, 1800. . . .
Charleston: Printed by W. P. Young, Franklin's Head, no. 43, Broad-Street. M,DCCC. pp. [2], 37. 8vo. AAS, JCB, LCP, LOC, MHS, PM, RL, SCHS, W'sHS.

38327 PRISONER OF HOPE. MAY 3–AUG. 23, 1800
New-York: published by William Sing, the conductor. . . . fol. weekly and semi-weekly. FOR 1800: NYPL.

38328 PROCEEDINGS RELATIVE TO THE DANISH BRIG HOPE, AND CARGO.
[Philadelphia?] pp. 13, [1], 32. sq. 12mo.
The introductory statement is signed by William Bingham (1752–1804), in whose behalf the case was being presented. AAS, BPL, HEH.

38329 THE PROMPTER; OR, A COMMENTARY ON COMMON SAYINGS. . . .
 See Webster, Noah.

38330 THE PROSPECT BEFORE US. . . .
 See Callender, James Thomson.

38331 PROTESTANT EPISCOPAL CHURCH IN MARYLAND.
 JOURNAL OF A CONVENTION OF THE PROTESTANT EPISCOPAL CHURCH IN THE STATE OF MARYLAND: HELD AT BALTIMORE, IN WHITSUN WEEK, 1800.
  [*Caption title, no imprint.*] pp. 12. 12mo.   LOC, M^dHS.

38332 PROTESTANT EPISCOPAL CHURCH IN MASSACHUSETTS.
 THE CONSTITUTION AND CANONS OF THE PROTESTANT EPISCOPAL CHURCH IN THE UNITED STATES OF AMERICA: TOGETHER WITH THE ECCLESIASTICAL CONSTITUTION FOR . . . MASSACHUSETTS. . . .
  Boston: Printed by John & Thomas Fleet, Cornhill, 1800. pp. 46. 8vo.
             AAS, BPL, CU, EI, HC, JCB, NYHS, NYPL, YC.

38333 PROTESTANT EPISCOPAL CHURCH IN NEW JERSEY.
 PROCEEDINGS OF A CONVENTION OF THE PROTESTANT EPISCOPAL CHURCH IN THE STATE OF NEW-JERSEY . . . AT BURLINGTON THE FOURTH AND FIFTH DAYS OF JUNE, 1800.
  Trenton: Printed by G. Craft. 1800. pp. 8. 8vo.   AAS, P^rU.

38334 PROTESTANT EPISCOPAL CHURCH IN THE UNITED STATES.
 THE BOOK OF COMMON PRAYER, AND ADMINISTRATION OF THE SACRAMENTS . . . TOGETHER WITH THE PSALTER. . . .
  Printed at Boston, by I. Thomas and E. T. Andrews, sold by them and . . . by I. Thomas, in Worcester; by Thomas, Andrews, & Penniman, in Albany; and by Thomas, Andrews, & Butler, in Baltimore. Oct. 1800. pp. [378], 70, [2]. 12mo.
 "The Whole Book of Psalms" has a separate titlepage and signature series. Later issues have bound in at the end 24 pages of "Hymns, set forth in General Convention, 1808."
      AAS, BPL, CL, HC, JCB, LOC, MHS, NYSL, WL, WLC, YC.

38335 — — — *New-York: Printed by M. I. & W. A. Davis, for E. Duyckinck, and T. S. Arden. . . .
 1800.* pp. [368], 217, [3]. 12mo.   AAS, HC, NYSL, RU.

38336 — — — *Philadelphia: Printed by Hall & Sellers. 1800.* pp. xxxvi, 327. 12mo.
                HSP, LCP, LOC.

38337 — — — *Wilmington: Printed by Peter Brynberg. 1800.* pp. [370], 226, [2]. 16mo.
                HEH, W^tPL.

38338 — THE CATECHISM OF THE PROTESTANT EPISCOPAL CHURCH, WITH AN APPENDIX; PUBLISHED FOR THE USE OF THE PHILADELPHIA ACADEMY. . . .
  Philadelphia: Printed by John Ormrod. . . . 1800. pp. 17. 12mo.   LCP.

38339 PROVIDENCE. RHODE ISLAND.
 SCHEDULE OF THE EXPENSES OF THE TOWN OF PROVIDENCE, FROM AUGUST 1, 1799, TO AUGUST 1, 1800. . . .
  Printed by John Carter. Broadside. fol.   RIHS.

38340 PROVIDENCE. RHODE ISLAND. B. HOPPIN AND CO.
 [CATALOGUE OF A SALE TO BE HELD AT B. HOPPIN AND COMPANY'S AUCTION ROOM, SEPTEMBER 4, 1800.
  Providence, 1800.]   ALDEN, 1675.

38341 PROVIDENCE. RHODE ISLAND. HENRY CUSHING.
 CATALOGUE OF HENRY CUSHING'S CIRCULATING LIBRARY: AT THE SIGN OF THE BIBLE AND ANCHOR, PROVIDENCE. . . .
  Providence: Printed by B. Wheeler, 1800. pp. 39. 16mo.   RIHS.

38342 PROVIDENCE. RHODE ISLAND. JOHN POPE.
CERTIFICATES OF CURES IN CANCEROUS CASES, PERFORMED BY JOHN POPE, OF PROVIDENCE, IN THE
STATE OF RHODE ISLAND, &C.
Printed at Providence, by Bennett Wheeler. M,DCCC. pp. 38. 24mo. BʳU.

38343 PROVIDENCE. RHODE ISLAND. MUTUAL FIRE INSURANCE COMPANY.
THE CONSTITUTION, OR DEED OF SETTLEMENT, OF THE PROVIDENCE MUTUAL FIRE INSURANCE
COMPANY . . . IN THE STATE OF RHODE-ISLAND AND PROVIDENCE PLANTATIONS.
[Colophon:] Printed by J. Carter. pp. 15. 8vo.
The Company was incorporated in 1800, and this is presumed to be the first printing of
the charter. BʳU.

38344 PROVIDENCE. RHODE ISLAND. WASHINGTON INSURANCE COMPANY.
CHARTER OF THE WASHINGTON INSURANCE COMPANY IN PROVIDENCE.
[Providence:] Printed by B. Wheeler. 1800. pp. 12. 16mo. AAS, BʳU, RIHS.

38345 THE PROVIDENCE GAZETTE. 1762–1825
Providence: Printed by John Carter. . . . fol. weekly.
FOR 1800: AAS, BʳU, JCB, LOC, RIHS, [RL].

38346 —— NEW-YEAR VERSES, BY THE CARRIER OF THE GAZETTE. LADIES AND GENTLEMEN, HERE COMES
THE NEWS-BOY. . . .
[Providence: Printed by John Carter, Jr.] Broadside. 8vo.
The verses are by William Gerrish. RIHS.

38347 THE PROVIDENCE JOURNAL, AND TOWN AND COUNTRY ADVERTISER. 1799–1801
Published . . . by John Carter, jun. . . . PROVIDENCE. fol. weekly.
FOR 1800: AAS, BA, BʳU, LOC, RIHS.

38348 PROVIDENCE, NOVEMBER 13, 1800. SIR, THE IMPORTANCE OF THE APPROACHING TOWN-MEETING TO
THE BEST INTERESTS OF THE NATION. . . .
[Providence.] Broadside. 4to. JCB.

38349 PUBLIC EXPRESSIONS OF GRIEF. . . .
See Dorchester, Massachusetts.

38350 PURSUITS OF LITERATURE. . . .
See Mathias, Thomas James.

38351 PURVIANCE, SAMUEL D[INSMORE] 1774–1806
TO THE FREEMEN OF FAYETTEVILLE DISTRICT. THE PARTIALITY OF A CONSIDERABLE NUMBER OF THE
CITIZENS OF OUR DISTRICT, HAD INDUCED THEM FREQUENTLY TO REQUEST THAT I WOULD
BECOME A CANDIDATE FOR THE REPRESENTATION TO CONGRESS. . . . SAMUEL D. PURVIANCE.
FAYETTEVILLE, JULY 1, 1800.
[Raleigh: J. Gales.] Broadside. fol. NCHC.

38352 RADCLIFFE, ANNE [WARD] 1764–1822
THE MYSTERIES OF UDOLPHO, A ROMANCE; INTERSPERSED WITH SOME PIECES OF POETRY. . . . IN
THREE VOLUMES.
Philadelphia: Printed for H. &. P. Rice. . . . MDCCC. 3 vol. 12mo. LCP, PPL.

38353 RALEIGH REGISTER, AND NORTH-CAROLINA WEEKLY ADVERTISER. 1799 ——
Raleigh: Printed by Joseph Gales. fol. weekly.
In December the subtitle was changed to *North-Carolina Gazette.* FOR 1800: NCSL.

38354 RALLING, JOHN
A SHORT ESSAY; ON SCRIPTURAL INSTRUCTIONS FOR THE TIMES, IN RECOMMENDATION OF DR.
MARTIN LUTHER'S COMMENTARY ON ST. PAUL'S EPISTLE TO GALATIANS. . . .
Philadelphia, printed for the author. 1800. pp. 22, [1]. 12mo. HSP, LCP.

38355 A RALLYING POINT. . . .
       See Simons, James.

38356 THE RAMBLER.
       See Johnson, Samuel.

38357 RAMSAY, DAVID   1749–1815
       AN ORATION ON THE ADVANTAGES OF AMERICAN INDEPENDENCE: SPOKEN BEFORE A PUBLIC ASSEMBLY
       OF THE INHABITANTS OF CHARLESTOWN IN SOUTH-CAROLINA, ON THE SECOND ANNIVERSARY
       OF THAT GLORIOUS AERA. . . .
            Charleston: Printed by T. C. Cox. 1800.   pp. [4], 28.   8vo.
       A reprint of the Charlestown [i.e. Charleston] edition of 1778.   JCB, MHS.

38358 —— AN ORATION ON THE DEATH OF . . . WASHINGTON. . . . DELIVERED IN ST. MICHAEL'S CHURCH,
       JANUARY 15, 1800, AT THE REQUEST OF THE INHABITANTS OF CHARLESTON. . . .
            Charleston: Printed by W. P. Young . . . no. 43, Broad Street. M.DCCC.   pp. [4],
       30.   8vo.   AAS, APS, BA, CLS, HC, HEH, JCB, LOC, MFM, MHS, MSL, NYHS, NYPL, PPL, PᵣU.

38359 RATHBUN, REUBEN
       REASONS OFFERED FOR LEAVING THE SHAKERS.
            Pittsfield: (Mass.) Printed by Chester Smith, 1800.   pp. 28.   8vo.   BᵣA.

38360 READ, COLLINSON   1751–1815
       LANCASTER, JANUARY 6, 1800. SIR, A BILL BEING NOW BEFORE THE LEGISLATURE, TO AUTHORIZE HIS
       EXCELLENCY THE GOVERNOR TO SUBSCRIBE FOR A CERTAIN NUMBER OF COPIES OF "AN
       ABRIDGEMENT OF THE LAWS OF PENNSYLVANIA". . . . COLLINSON READ.
            [Lancaster, Pa.?].   folder, 1 page.   12mo.
       The *Abridgement* itself is sometimes listed as an 1800 imprint because of its copyright
       date, but the imprint reads 1801.   UOP.

38361 READ, JOHN K.   1746–1805
       COMMEMORATIVE ORATION, DELIVERED ON THE 22D OF FEBRUARY, 1800, ON THE DEATH OF . . .
       WASHINGTON, BEFORE . . . THE CITIZENS OF NORFOLK . . . AND THE LODGES OF NO. 1, AND
       OF NAPHTALI, NO. 56. . . .
            [Norfolk:] Augustus C. Jordan, printer.   pp. 15.   16mo.   BPL, HEH, LOC, NYPL.

38362 REED, ABNER   1771–1866
       THE FIRST STEP TO LEARNING; OR, LITTLE CHILDREN'S SPELLING AND READING BOOK. DESIGNED TO
       RENDER THE FIRST RUDIMENTS OF LEARNING EASY. . . .
            East-Windsor: Connecticut. Printed for the author, by Luther Pratt. MDCCC.
       pp. 60.   16mo.   CHS.

38363 —— —— THE SECOND EDITION.
            East-Windsor: (Connecticut) Printed for the author, by Luther Pratt. MDCCC.
       pp. 60.   16mo.   MRS. EDNA GREENWOOD, WASHINGTON, D.C.

38364 REES, THOMAS
       A NEW SYSTEM OF STENOGRAPHY, OR SHORT HAND. . . .
            *Philadelphia, re-printed by James Humphreys, from the sixth London edition; and
       sold by him no. 106, South side of Market-Street. 1800.*   pp. 14, 2 plates.   24mo.
                                                            AAS, HC, LCP, NYPL, PSL.

38365 REFLECTIONS ON LOVE: IN A POETICAL EPISTLE TO LYCIAS. . . .
            Printed for the author. 1800.   pp. 12.   16mo.
       Signed D. R. P.   AAS.

38366 REFORMED CHURCH IN THE UNITED STATES.
       ACTS AND PROCEEDINGS OF THE GENERAL SYNOD OF THE REFORMED DUTCH CHURCH IN THE
       UNITED STATES OF AMERICA. IN THE YEAR 1800.
            New York: Printed by George Forman, no. 64, Water-Street. . . .   pp. 40.   8vo.
                                                            AAS, GTS, JCB.

38367 REMARKS ON THE ASSERTIONS OF THE AUTHOR OF THE MEMOIRS OF JACOBINISM RESPECTING. . .
EMANUEL SWEDENBORG. . . .
See Clowes, John.

38368 THE RENOWNED HISTORY OF VALENTINE AND ORSON; THE TWO SONS OF THE EMPEROR OF GREECE.
NEWLY CORRECTED AND AMENDED.
Hartford: Printed by J. Babcock. 1800. pp. 141, [2]. 24mo. AAS, CHS.

38369 RENSSELAERVILLE BAPTIST ASSOCIATION.
THE MINUTES OF THE RENSSELAER-VILLE ASSOCIATION, HELD AT THE MEETING-HOUSE IN
RENSSELAER-VILLE, ON THE FIRST AND SECOND OF OCTOBER, ONE THOUSAND EIGHT HUNDRED.
Albany: Printed by John Barber, Faust's Statue, State Street, 1800. pp. 12. 8vo.
AAS, SCBHC.

38370 A REPLY TO ALEXANDER HAMILTON'S LETTER CONCERNING THE PUBLIC CONDUCT AND CHARACTER OF
JOHN ADAMS. . . . BY A FEDERAL REPUBLICAN. ALSO, A LETTER FROM JOHN ADAMS . . . TO
THOMAS PINCKNEY, ESQ., OF SOUTH-CAROLINA.
New York: Printed by L. Nichols and Co. 1800. pp. 16, 4. 8vo.
BA, BM, LOC, NYHS, NYPL, WL.

38371 A REPORT OF AN ACTION FOR A LIBEL, BROUGHT BY DR. BENJAMIN RUSH. . . .
See Carpenter, Thomas.

38372 REPORT OF THE TRIAL OF LEVI WEEKS, ON AN INDICTMENT FOR THE MURDER OF GULLELMA SANDS,
ON . . . THE THIRTY-FIRST DAY OF MARCH . . . 1800. . . .
New-York: Printed by John Furman, and sold at his blank, stamp & stationary shop,
opposite the City-Hall. 1800. pp. [6], 9–98. 8vo.
Preface by William Coleman. AAS, BPL, HC, LOC, NYHS, NYPL, NYSL, NYSOC, PPL.

38373 REPORT OF THE TRIAL OF RICHARD D. CROUCHER, ON AN INDICTMENT FOR RAPE ON MARGARET
MILLER; ON TUESDAY, THE 8TH DAY OF JULY, 1800. . . .
New York — Printed by George Forman, no. 64, Water-Street, and sold by the
respective booksellers in this city. pp. 28. 8vo. HC, NYHS, NYPL, NYSOC, PPL.

38374 REPRESENTATIVE FOR THE 7TH CONGRESS. — THOMAS NOYES, OF WESTERLY. . . .
Broadside. 24mo. BᵣU.

38375 THE REPUBLICAN. 1799–1827
Petersburg [Va.]: printed by Lyon and Field. fol. weekly and semi-weekly.
FOR 1800: [DUKE UNIV.]

38376 REPUBLICAN JOURNAL. 1796–FEB. 10, 1800?
Danbury (Connecticut): printed by Douglas & Nichols. 1800. fol.
FOR 1800: [AAS], [CHS].

38377 THE REPUBLICAN LEDGER. 1799–1803
Portsmouth, (New-Hampshire). Printed by George Jerry Osborne, jun. weekly.
fol.
Osborne died on June 2, 1800, and the *Ledger* was taken over by Samuel Nutting and
John Whitelock. FOR 1800: [BA], [DC], [HC].

38378 THE REPUBLICAN RUSH-LIGHT.
This is the title of the final number (vol. 1. no. 7 or vol. 2. no. 1) of *The Rush-light*, for
which *see* Cobbett, William.

38379 REPUBLICAN STAR, OR, EASTERN SHORE POLITICAL LUMINARY. 1799–1833
Easton, (Maryland): Printed and published every Tuesday morning, by Thomas
Perrin Smith, 1800. fol. weekly. FOR 1800: [AAS], [LOC].

38380 REPUBLICAN Watch-Tower.   Mar. 12, 1800–1810
New-York: Printed and published (on Wednesdays and Saturdays) by D. Dennis-
ton. . . .   fol.   semiweekly.
This was a continuation of *Greenleaf's New York Journal.*
                                    For 1800: [AAS], [HC], [NYPL], YC.

38381 THE RETURNED captive, a poem. Founded on a late fact. . . .
Northampton: Printed by Andrew Wright. . . . *1800.*   pp. 50.   12mo.   AAS.

38382 RHODE Island. State.
By His Excellency Arthur Fenner . . . governor . . . of the State of Rhode Island. . . .
A proclamation . . . given . . . this third day of November, in the year of our Lord,
one thousand eight hundred. . . .
     [*Newport: Printed by Oliver Farnsworth.*]   Broadside.   fol.
A Thanksgiving proclamation.   RIHS.

38383 —— Charter of the North-Kingstown Academy. State of Rhode-Island, &c. In general
assembly, June session, A. D. 1800. . . .
     [*Providence?*]   pp. 8.   sq. 8vo.   AAS, NYHS, RIHS.

38384 —— October, 1799. At the General Assembly of the State of Rhode-Island . . . begun . . .
at South-Kingstown . . . on the last Monday in October, in the year of Our Lord
one thousand seven hundred and ninety-nine. . . .
     [*Colophon:*] *Newport: Printed by Oliver Farnsworth.* . . .   pp. 29.   4to.
             AAS, BʳU, CSL, HC, JCB, LOC, MSL, NYBA, NYPL, RIHS, RISL.

38385 —— February, 1800. At the General Assembly of the State of Rhode-Island . . . begun . . .
at Providence . . . on the last Monday in February, in the year of Our Lord one
thousand eight hundred. . . .
     [*Colophon:*] *Newport, Printed by Oliver Farnsworth.* . . .   pp. 32.   4to.
             AAS, BʳU, CSL, HC, JCB, MSL, NYBA, NYPL, RIHS, RISL.

38386 —— May, 1800. At the General Assembly of the State of Rhode-Island . . . begun . . . at
Newport . . . on the first Wednesday in May, in the year of Our Lord one thousand
eight hundred. . . .
     [*Colophon:*] *Newport, Printed by Oliver Farnsworth.* . . .   pp. 23.   4to.
             AAS, BʳU, CSL, HC, HEH, JCB, MSL, NYBA, NYPL, RIHS, RISL.

38387 —— June, 1800. At the General Assembly of the State of Rhode-Island . . . begun . . . at
Newport . . . on the second Monday in June, in the year of our Lord one thousand
eight hundred. . . .
     [*Colophon:*] *Newport: Printed by Oliver Farnsworth.* . . .   pp. 32, 3.   4to.
             AAS, BʳU, CSL, HC, JCB, NYBA, NYPL, RIHS, RISL.

38388 —— Ferries. Hogs. Acts made and passed by the General Assembly of the State of Rhode-
Island . . . holden at South-kingstown, on the last Monday in October, A. D. 1799.
     [*Newport: Printed by Oliver Farnsworth.*]   pp. 27–38.   8vo.
Continues the *Public Laws* listed under 1799 and includes the sessions of October, 1799, and
February, 1800.   AAS, CSL, HC, JCB, MSL, RIHS, RISL.

38389 —— Fines. Judgments. Acts made and passed by the General Assembly of the State of
Rhode-Island . . . at Newport, on the first Wednesday in May, A. D. 1800.
     [*Newport: Printed by Oliver Farnsworth.*]   pp. 39–46.   8vo.
The fourth part of the *Public Laws*, including the sessions of May and June, 1800.
             AAS, CSL, HC, JCB, MSL, RIHS, RISL.

38390 —— Ferries. Hogs. Acts made and passed by the General Assembly of the State of Rhode
Island . . . at Providence . . . in October, A. D. 1800.
     [*Newport: Printed by Oliver Farnsworth.*]   pp. 47–9.   8vo.
The fifth part of the *Public Laws.*   AAS, CSL, HC, JCB, MSL, RIHS, RISL.

38391 THE RHODE ISLAND ALMANAC, FOR THE YEAR OF OUR LORD, 1801. . . . CALCULATED FOR THE
MERIDIAN OF NEWPORT. . . .
Published at Newport, by Oliver Farnsworth. . . . pp. [24]. 12mo.
AAS, LOC, NHS, RIHS.

38392 — — — *Published at Newport, by Oliver Farnsworth. . . . Great allowance to those who
purchase quantities.* pp. [24]. 12mo. AAS, LOC, NHS, NYHS, RIHS.

38393 — — — *Printed for Jacob Richardson, and sold at the post-office, Newport. From the press
of O. Farnsworth.* pp. [24]. 12mo. LOC, NHS.

38394 — — — *Printed for William R. Wilder . . . Newport. . . .* pp. [24]. 12mo.
BPL, CSL, RIHS.

38395 RHODE ISLAND COLLEGE.
CATALOGUE OF THE OFFICERS AND STUDENTS OF RHODE-ISLAND COLLEGE, PROVIDENCE, OCTOBER
1800. . . .
[Providence:] Printed by John Carter, jun. Broadside. fol. BrU.

38396 — COMMENCEMENT OF RHODE-ISLAND COLLEGE. SEPTEMBER 3, 1800. ORDER OF THE EXERCISES. . . .
[Providence:] Printed by John Carter, Jun. Broadside. fol.
AAS, BrU, MSL, RIHS.

38397 — ILLUSTRISSIMO JABEZ BOWEN, ARMIGERO . . . HABITA IN SOLEMNIBUS ACADEMICIS . . . DIE TERTIO
SEPTEMBRIS, A. D. M.DCCC. . . .
[Providence:] Typis Johannis Carter, Jun. Broadside. fol. BrU, RIHS.

38398 RICHARD, OLD FATHER.
See Poor Richard.

38399 RICHARDS, GEORGE — 1814
THE ACCEPTED. . . . AN HISTORICAL DISCOURSE, IN TWO PARTS: GRATEFULLY COMMEMORATING THE
UNPARALLELED SERVICES . . . OF . . . WASHINGTON. . . .
[Portsmouth:] Printed and published . . . by Charles Peirce. . . . March, M,DCCC.
pp. 83. sq. 8vo.
Contains hymns and odes by Richards, a dirge by L. M., and a Masonic hymn by C. M.
AAS, BA, BPL, HEH, JCB, LOC, MHS, NYHS, NYPL, NYSL, UOP[1].

38400 [—] HYMNS COMPOSED ON THE DEATH OF GEN. WASHINGTON; AND SUNG, AT THE UNIVERSALIST
MEETING-HOUSE, PORTSMOUTH, N. H., JANUARY, 1800.
[Portsmouth:] Printed at the United States Oracle press, by Charles Peirce. . . . 1800.
pp. [4]. 8vo.
The attribution to Richards is from the printing in *Hymns and Odes,* Portsmouth, 1800.
The so-called eight-page edition is a binder's error. BrU, HEH, JCB, LOC, NYHS.

38401 RICHARDSON, JOSEPH 1778–1871
AN ORATION, PRONOUNCED AT TEWKSBURY, ON THE 22D OF FEBRUARY, 1800. IN HONOR OF GENERAL
GEORGE WASHINGTON. . . .
Printed at Medford, (Massachusetts). 1800. pp. 8. 8vo.
BPL, HC, HEH, JCB, MFM, NEHGS, NYHS.

38402 RICHARDSON, LUTHER 1774–1811
AN ORATION, PRONOUNCED JULY 4, 1800, AT THE REQUEST OF THE INHABITANTS OF THE TOWN OF
ROXBURY. . . .
Boston. Printed by John Russell. pp. 19. 8vo.
AAS, BA, HC, HEH, JCB, LOC, MHS, NL, NYPL, NYSL, YC.

38403 RICHARDSON, SAMUEL   1689–1761
    CLARISSA: OR THE HISTORY OF A YOUNG LADY. COMPREHENDING THE MOST IMPORTANT CONCERNS
    OF PRIVATE LIFE. . . .
        From the Press of William W. Morse. . . . New Haven. M,DCCC.   pp. 138.
    24mo.   AAS.

38404 RICHMOND, AUGUST 9TH, 1800. SIR, WE HAVE TAKEN THE LIBERTY TO ADVISE YOU, TO HAVE THE
    TICKETS FOR ELECTORS OF THE PRESIDENT. . . .
    Broadside.   fol.   LOC.

38405 THE RICHMOND GAZETTE, & GENERAL ADVERTISER.
    See Virginia Gazette.

38406 RIDDEL, WILLIAM   1768–1849
    THE CHRISTIAN DOCTRINES STATED, AND FALSE TEACHERS DISCOVERED, IN TWO SERMONS. . . .
        Wiscasset: Printed by Henry Hoskins, 1800.   pp. 28.   8vo.
                                AAS, CL, JCB, LOC, M•HS, NYPL.

38407 RIGGS, CALEB S.
    TO THE FREE ELECTORS OF KINGS COUNTY. HAVING SEEN A HANDBILL, SIGNED "A KINGS COUNTY
    FARMER," CONTAINING SOME OBSERVATIONS ON MY CONDUCT, AND A SLANDEROUS ACCUSATION
    AGAINST THE GOVERNOR AND COUNCIL OF APPOINTMENT. . . . NEW-YORK, 26TH APRIL, 1800.
    Broadside.   fol.   LOCᵖʰ.

38408 RIGHTS OF MAN.   1794–1800
        Frederick-Town, (Maryland): printed by John Winter . . . 1800.   fol.   weekly.
                                  FOR 1800: [MᵈHS].

38409 THE RIGHTS OF MAN.   1799–1806
        Newburgh [N. Y.] published by Benoni H. Howell, for Elias Winfield.   fol.
    weekly.
    During the year Howell retired and Winfield continued as printer.
                            FOR 1800: [NEWBURGH FREE LIB.]

38410 RIPLEY, EZRA   1751–1841
    LOVE TO OUR NEIGHBOUR . . . DELIVERED AT CONCORD, MASSACHUSETTS, DECEMBER 26, 1799.
    BEING THE DAY ON WHICH SAMUEL SMITH WAS EXECUTED FOR BURGLARY. . . .
        Printed by Samuel Hall, no. 53, Cornhill, Boston. 1800.   pp. 31.   8vo.
                         AAS, BA, JCB, LOC, MHS, NYHS, NYPL, YC.

38411 ROBBINS, THOMAS   1777–1856
    AN ORATION, OCCASIONED BY THE DEATH OF . . . WASHINGTON, DELIVERED AT DANBURY, ON . . .
    JANUARY 2, MDCCC. TO WHICH IS ADDED A SKETCH OF HIS LIFE. . . .
        Danbury: Printed and sold by Douglas & Nichols.   pp. 16.   8vo.
                             CHS, HEH, MFM, NYPL, YC.

38412 ROBERDEAU, ISAAC   1763–1829
    AN ORATION; UPON THE DEATH OF GENERAL WASHINGTON. PRONOUNCED BEFORE THE OFFICERS
    OF THE SECOND BRIGADE, FOURTH DIVISION OF THE MILITIA OF NEW-JERSEY, AT JOHNSONBURY
    SUSSEX COUNTY, ON THE TWENTY SECOND OF FEBRUARY, EIGHTEEN HUNDRED. . . .
        Philadelphia, Printed by William W. Woodward, 1800.   pp. 30.   8vo.
                              BA, HEH, LOC, PPL.

38413 ROBERTSON, WILLIAM   1721–1793
    THE HISTORY OF AMERICA, BOOKS IX AND X. CONTAINING THE HISTORY OF VIRGINIA TO THE
    YEAR 1688; AND OF NEW ENGLAND TO THE YEAR 1652. . . .
        Walpole, Newhampshire, printed for Thomas & Thomas, by David Carlisle. 1800.
    pp. 192.   16mo.   AAS, BPL, HC, JCB.

38414 ROBINSON, *Sir* Christopher 1766–1833
Reports of cases . . . in the High Court of Admiralty . . . commencing with the judgments of . . . Sir William Scott, Michaelmas term 1798. . . . Volume the first.
Philadelphia, re-printed: (From the London copy . . .) and sold by James Humphreys. . . . 1800. pp. xii, [3], 332. 8vo.
Volume 2 was published in 1801. AAS, BA, CSL, HCL, JCB, LOC, PʳU, VᵃU, WLC.

38415 ROCHE, Edward 1754–1821
A Funeral oration, on the death of . . . Washington: prepared at the request of the Society of Cincinnati of the State of Delaware, and pronounced at Wilmington, on the 22d day of February, 1800. . . .
Wilmington: Printed at the Franklin press, by James Wilson. 1800. pp. 15, [1].
8vo.
Contains "Stanzas for the twenty-second February, 1800. By Mr. Coleman."
BA, HEH, HSP, LOC, NYHS.

38416 ROCHE, Regina Maria (Dalton) 1764?–1845
The Children of the abbey, a tale. In four volumes. . . . Second American edition.
Philadelphia: Printed by John Bioren, for Robert Campbell. 1800. pp. 195; 208;
172; 184. 12mo.
Issued bound in two volumes. AAS, HSP.

38417 A ROD for the fool's back. . . .
See Webster, Noah.

38418 ROGERS, Samuel 1763–1855
The Pleasures of memory. In two parts. By Samuel Rodgers.
Wilmington: Printed at the Franklin Press by James Wilson. 1800. pp. 39. 16mo.
AAS, DHS, LOC.

38419 ROGERS, William 1751–1824
The Prayer, delivered on . . . the 22d of February, 1800, in the German Reformed Church, Philadelphia: before the Pennsylvania Society of the Cincinnati. . . .
Philadelphia: Printed by John Ormrod, no. 41, Chestnut-Street. 1800. pp. 12.
8vo.
Occasioned by the death of Washington. AAS, BA, HC, HEH, HSP, JCB, LOC, NYHS, NYPL, NYSL.

38420 ROMAN Catholic Church. Council of Baltimore.
Ordo Divini officii recitandi missaeque celebrandae juxta Breviarium et Missale Romanum. . . . Pro Anno Domini MDCCCI.
Baltimori: Typis Johannis Hayes. pp. [24]. 16mo. GU.

38421 ROMEYN, John Brodhead 1777–1825
A Funeral oration, in remembrance of George Washington; delivered at Rhinebeck Flats, February 22. . . .
Poughkeepsie, State of New York: Printed by John Woods. 1800. pp. 12.
Portrait. 8vo.
The one copy located lacks the portrait called for by Sabin. NYPL.

38422 ROUSO, Charles Dennis D'Eres
Memoirs of . . . a native of Canada; who was with the Scanyawtauragahrooote Indians eleven years. . . .
Printed for, and sold by Henry Ranlet, Exeter. 1800. pp. 176. 12mo.
As to the authenticity of this narrative see Vail 1248.
AAS, BA, CU, HC, HEH, JCB, LOC, NHSL, NL, NYHS, NYSL.

38423 ROUSSEAU, John Baptiste Clement, *of Hispaniola*
An Inaugural dissertation on absorption. Submitted to the . . . Medical Faculty of the University of Pennsylvania for the degree of doctor of medicine. On the 31st of May, 1800. . . .
Philadelphia: Printed by J. Ormrod, no. 41, Chestnut-Street. 1800. pp. 36. 8vo.
AAS, AML, APS, LCP, LOC, NYAM, RU, UOP, YC.

38424 ROWE, Elizabeth (Singer)   1674–1737
Devout exercises of the heart. . . . By . . . Mrs. Elizabeth Rowe. Reviewed and published at her request, by I. Watts, D. D.
Printed by J. Babcock: Hartford. 1800.   pp. [2], 180.   24mo.   AAS, CHS, NYPL, PL.

38425 ROWLANDSON, Mary (White)   1635?–1678?
A Narrative of the captivity, sufferings, and removes, of Mrs. Mary Rowlandson. . . .
Boston: Re-printed and sold by John and Thomas Fleet . . . 1800.   pp. 36.   12mo.
NL, Lancaster, Mass., Town Library, LOC.

38426 ROWLETT, John
[Rowlett's Tables of discount, or interest, on every dollar from one to two thousand. . . .
By John Rowlett, accomptant, Bank of North America.
Philadelphia: 1800.]
257th Pennsylvania District copyright issued to Rowlett July 31, 1800. The AAS and NYHS have copies of these tables with the imprint 1802.

38427 —— [Table of discount or interest (accurately calculated) from 50 cents to 5.000 dollars, from 1 day to 123 days inclusive; at 6 per cent.
Philadelphia: 1800.]
244th Pennsylvania District copyright issued to John Rowlett as proprietor, Jan. 9, 1800.

38428 THE ROYAL convert: or, the force of truth. . . . Written in French by the messieurs of Port-Royal, and now newly translated into English.
Brookfield, Massachusetts, printed by E. Merriam & Co. March 1800.   pp. 124.   24mo.
AAS, LOC, NYPL, YC.

38429 THE RULE of life. Being a collection of select moral sentences; extracted from the greatest authors, ancient and modern. . . .
Springfield: Printed by Ashley & Brewer. M,DCCC.   pp. 192.   16mo.
AAS, HEH, JCB, NYPL, UOC.

38430 THE RULES of work of the carpenters in the town of Boston. . . .
See Boston. Massachusetts. Carpenters.

38431 RURAL Gazette.   Mar. 31, 1800?–1801
Sharon, Connecticut: Published by E. Hopkins, a few rods north of the meeting-house. 1800.   fol.   weekly.   For 1800: [HC].

38432 THE RURAL Socrates. . . .
See Vaughan, Benjamin.

38433 RUSH, Benjamin   1745–1813
A Report. . . .
See Carpenter, Thomas.

38434 THE RUSH-light.
See Cobbett, William.

38435 RUSSELL, John Miller   1768–1840
A Funeral oration, on General George Washington. . . .
Boston, Printed by John Russell, for Joseph Nancrede, no. 49, Marlboro' Street. 1800.
pp. 22.   8vo.   AAS, BA, HC, HEH, LOC, NYHS, NYPL.

38436 RUSSELL, Jonathan   1771–1832
An Oration, pronounced in the Baptist meeting-house, in Providence, on . . . July 4, 1800.
Providence: Printed by Bennett Wheeler. 1800.   pp. 23.   8vo.
AAS, BPL, JCB, LOC, NYHS, NYPL, RIHS.

38437 —— An Oration, pronounced July 4th, 1800, in the Baptist meeting-house, in Providence. . . .
Rhode-Island: Providence, printed; — Warren, re-printed and sold by Nathaniel Phillips. M,DCCC. pp. 38. 12mo. AAS, BA, BPL, HC, HEH, JCB, LOC, RIHS, WLC.

38438 [——] To the freemen of Rhode-Island, &c. . . .
[Providence?] pp. 16. 8vo. HC, LOC, YC.

38439 [RUSSELL, William] 1741–1793
The History of modern Europe. With an account of the decline and fall of the Roman Empire . . . to the Peace of Paris, in 1763. . . . In a series of letters from a nobleman to his son. A new edition. . . . Vol. I[–IV].
Philadelphia: Printed by H. Maxwell, Columbia-House, for William Young Birch and Abraham Small. 1800. 4 vols. 8vo.
Volume V was published in 1801 and Volume VI in 1811. AAS, APS, BA, HC, MᵈHS, PʳU, VᵃU.

38440 RUSSELL'S Gazette. Commercial and political. 1798–1800
Published on Mondays and Thursdays, by John Russell, at his office, in Quaker-Lane, Boston. fol. semi-weekly.
With the issue of Jan. 9 Russell transferred publication to his associate, James Cutler. With the issue of Oct. 9 they changed the imprint of John Russell & James Cutler and changed the name to *Boston Gazette. Commercial and Political,* which see.
For 1800: AAS, BA, CHS, EI, LOC, MHS, NYPL, NYSL.

38441 —— Boston, January 1st. 1800. The carriers' of the Boston Commercial Gazette, as custom dictates, thus addresses its readers and patrons.
Broadside. LOC.

38442 RUSSELL & George's Eastern Herald & Maine Gazette. Dec. 29, 1800–1801
Published by Elijah Russell and Daniel George, Portland. fol. weekly.
The name was changed from *Eastern Herald and Gazette of Maine.*
For 1800: York Inst., Saco, [HC].

38443 THE RUTLAND Herald. 1794–1920
Printed at Rutland, (Vermont) by William Fay, for Samuel Williams. . . . fol. weekly.
For changes in the imprint see Brigham, *Newspaper Bibliography.* For 1800: [VᵗSL].

38444 SACRED concert. . . .
See Newburyport. Massachusetts. First Church.

38445 SACRED dirges, hymns, and anthems. . . .
See Holden, Oliver.

38446 SACRED harmony. . . .
Published by Thomas Lee, Junr. pp. [8], 57–116, [2]. 16mo.
Thomas Lee (1717–1806) was author and editor to an undetermined degree. The year of publication has not been definitely determined. The pagination given above is that of the Yale copy; the AAS copy, which is in contemporary covers, has a section of Ms. music between the eight preliminary engraved pages and the printed ones. AAS, YC.

38447 THE SAILOR'S medley. A collection of the most admired sea and other songs.
Philadelphia, printed for Mathew Carey. 1800. pp. 72, front. 16mo.
BʳU, NYPL.

38448 ST. HUBERT; or, Mistaken friendship. A tale. . . .
District of Columbia: Printed for W. W. Wood, 1800. pp. 36. 8vo. NYPL.

38449 SAINT Pierre, Jacques Henri Bernardin de 1737–1814
Indian Cottage or a search after truth. . . .
New-York: Printed by M. M'Farlane, 1800. pp. [2], 114. 32mo. AAS.

38450 —— PAUL AND VIRGINIA, AN INDIAN STORY. TRANSLATED FROM THE FRENCH OF J. H. B. DE SAINT
PIERRE . . . BY H. HUNTER, D. D. . . .
Baltimore, printed and sold by Bonsal & Niles. . . . 1800. pp. 201. 24mo.
AAS, MᵈHS.

38451 SALEM. MASSACHUSETTS.
SALEM, NOVEMBER, 18, 1800. WHEREAS THERE ARE SEVERAL NOTED FORESTALLERS RESIDING IN THE
NEIGHBOURHOOD. . . . SELECTMEN. . . . BOARD OF HEALTH.
Broadside. 12mo. EI.

38452 —— TRIBUTE TO THE MEMORY OF WASHINGTON. ORDER OF PROCESSION. THE PROCESSION WILL MOVE
FROM COURT STREET PRECISELY AT 11. . . .
[*Salem: Printed by Joshua Cushing.*] Broadside. 4to.
Program for the Salem exercises of February 22, 1800. AAS, EI.

38453 SALEM. MASSACHUSETTS. CUSHING AND CUSHING.
PROPOSAL FOR PRINTING BY SUBSCRIPTION THE FOLLOWING . . . WORK, VIZ DISCOURSES TO THE
AGED . . . BY THE REV. JOB ORTON. . . . SALEM, MAY 15, 1800.
Broadside. fol.
Signed by Thomas C. Cushing and Joshua Cushing. EI.

38454 SALEM. MASSACHUSETTS. EAST INDIA MARINE SOCIETY.
BY-LAWS AND REGULATIONS OF THE EAST INDIA MARINE SOCIETY, MASSACHUSETTS: AN ASSOCIATION
OF MASTERS AND COMMANDERS OF VESSELS . . . ENGAGED IN THE EAST INDIA TRADE FROM
THE TOWN OF SALEM.
Printed by Thomas C. Cushing, Salem. 1800. pp. 13. AAS, EI.

38455 SALEM. MASSACHUSETTS. EDWARD S. LANG.
MEDICINE CHESTS: WITH SUITABLE DIRECTIONS: PREPARED BY EDWARD S. LANG: AT HIS SHOP IN
ESSEX-STREET, CORNER OF LIBERTY-STREET, SALEM.
[*Salem: Printed by Thomas C. Cushing.*] pp. 10. 12mo. EI.

38456 SALEM. MASSACHUSETTS. JOHN DUTCH.
[CATALOGUE OF BOOKS. . . . SOLD AT HIS OFFICE, SALEM, MASS. FEB. 17, 1800.]
McKAY 143.

38457 THE SALEM GAZETTE. 1790–1908
Published on Tuesdays and Fridays, by Thomas C. Cushing . . . Salem, Massachusetts.
fol. semi-weekly. FOR 1800: AAS, BA, BPL, EI, HC, HEH, LOC, YC.

38458 THE SALEM IMPARTIAL REGISTER. JULY 31, 1800–1801
Published on Mondays & Thursdays, by William Carleton . . . Salem, Massachusetts.
fol. semi-weekly.
Name changed from *The Impartial Register.* FOR 1800: AAS, BA, EI, HC.

38459 SAMPSON, EZRA 1749–1823
THE BEAUTIES OF THE BIBLE: BEING A SELECTION FROM THE OLD AND NEW TESTAMENTS . . .
FOR THE USE OF SCHOOLS. . . .
Hudson: Printed by Ashbel Stoddard, M,DCCC. pp. 283, [4]. 12mo.
AAS, BPL, CSL, HC, NYPL.

38460 SANDERS, DANIEL CLARKE 1768–1850
A DISCOURSE PRONOUNCED AT BURLINGTON, VERMONT, IN COMMEMORATION OF GENERAL GEORGE
WASHINGTON. . . .
Burlington, Vermont, Printed by John K. Baker. 1800. pp. 20. 4to.
BA, MFM, MHS, VᵗU.

38461 SANGER, JEDEDIAH
AN ANSWER TO GENERAL JONAS PLATT'S ADDRESS TO THE PEOPLE OF THE COUNTY OF ONEIDA.
OCTOBER 18, 1800.
Broadside. NYPL.

38462 [THE SARATOGA REGISTER: OR, FARMER'S JOURNAL. 1798–1800
    Ballston Spa: published by Increase & William Child. weekly. fol.]
In April, 1800, Increase Child retired from the firm. FOR 1800: NO COPY KNOWN.

38463 SARGENT, WINTHROP 1753–1820
    MAY 28TH, 1800. THE FOLLOWING AUTHENTICATED COPIES OF LETTERS FROM N. HUNTER . . .
WERE RECEIVED LAST EVENING BY THE GOVERNOR. . . .
        [Natchez: J. Green.] pp. [6]. 16mo. NA.

38464 SAUNDERS, RICHARD, *pseud.*
    POOR RICHARD IMPROVED: BEING AN ALMANACK AND EPHEMERIS . . . FOR THE YEAR OF OUR LORD
1801. . . .
        Philadelphia: Printed and Sold by Hall & Sellers — no. 51 — Market-Street.
pp. [36]. 12mo. AAS, HEH.

38465 —— POOR RICHARD REVIVD. BEING AN ASTRONOMICAL DIARY, OR ALMANACK, FOR 1801. BY POOR
RICHARD SAUNDERS.
        Newfield: Printed by L. Beach. pp. [24]. 12mo. CHS.

38466 SAVAGE, EZEKIEL 1760–1837
    AN EULOGY ON GEN. GEORGE WASHINGTON . . . DELIVERED AT ST. PETER'S CHURCH, IN SALEM,
THE 22D OF FEBRUARY, 1800. . . .
        Printed by Joshua Cushing, Salem. 1800. pp. 23. 8vo.
        AAS, BA, BPL, EI, HC, HEH, JCB, LCP, LOC, MFM, MHS, NYPL, NYSL, PPL, WL.

38467 SCHEEL, HENRI OTHON DE 1745–1807
    TREATISE OF ARTILLERY; CONTAINING A NEW SYSTEM, OR THE ALTERATIONS MADE IN THE FRENCH
ARTILLERY, SINCE 1765. . . .
    [SECOND TITLE;] TABLES AND PLATES, REFERED TO IN A NEW SYSTEM OF ARTILLERY. . . .
        *Philadelphia: Printed for the War Office, by John Ward Fenno, no. 119, Chestnut-
Street. 1800.* 2 vols, pp. 154, 6; 8vo. And pp. 12, plates, obl. fol.
The plates are engraved by Thackara and the translation is by Jonathan Williams. There
are two settings of the Treatise in one of which the last word of the second line in the
table inserted after the titlepage is "English," and in the other is "and."
        AAS, APS, BA, BPL, LOC, NYHS, NYSL, WC.

38468 SCHENECTADY. NEW YORK. SOCIAL SOCIETY.
    THE CONSTITUTION OF THE SOCIAL SOCIETY, INSTITUTED AT SCHENECTADY, JUNE 28TH, 1798. . . .
        Schenectady: Printed by John L. Stevenson, 1800. pp. 15. 16mo.
There is a near-facsimile reprint in which the date 1853 appears on p. 4. NYPL, NYSL.

38469 SCHENECTADY GAZETTE. 1799–1802
    Schenectady (State of New-York) printed by John L. Stevenson. fol. weekly.
        FOR 1800: [NYHS].

38470 THE SCHOOL OF WISDOM. . . .
    See Carey, Mathew.

38471 SCIOTO GAZETTE AND CHILLICOTHE ADVERTISER. 1800–1925
    Chillicothe: Winship & Willis. fol. weekly.
This was a continuation of *Freeman's Journal and Chillicothe Advertiser*, the change
being made with the issue of Oct. 10, 1800. FOR 1800: [WRHS].

38472 SCOTT, J[OHN], *of Islington*
    WAR INCONSISTENT WITH THE DOCTRINE AND EXAMPLE OF JESUS CHRIST. . . . BY I. SCOTT.
        New-Bedford: Printed by Abraham Shearman, Jun. 1800. pp. 24. 12mo.
This tract is sometimes attributed to Job Scott, 1751–1793, but the author is identified in
the 2nd London edition, 1817, of tract no. 2 of the Society for the Promotion of Permanent
and Universal Peace. AAS, BM, CL, HSP, LOC.

38473 SCOTT, Joseph
The New and universal gazetteer; or, modern geographical dictionary. . . . With twenty-five maps. . . . In four volumes. Vol. III [and IV].
Philadelphia: Printed by Patterson & Cochran, no. 108, Race-Street. 1800.   pp. [446], 4 maps; [516], 12 maps, 1 table.   8vo.
Volumes 1 and 2 were published in 1799.   AAS, BPL, EPFL, HSP, NYHS, NYSL, PʳU, UOP.

38474 [SCOTT, Sarah (Robinson)]   1723–1795
The Man of real sensibility: or, The history of Sir George Ellison. Founded on fact. . . .
Wilmington: — Printed and sold by Bonsal & Niles — also sold at their book-store, no. 173, Market-street, Baltimore, — 1800.   pp. 72.   24mo.   LOC.

38475 SCOTT, William, *of Edinburgh*
Lessons in elocution: or a selection of pieces, in prose and verse. . . . To this edition are prefixed elements of gesture. Illustrated by four elegant plates. . . . Eighth American edition.
Worcester, (Massachusetts) printed by Mower & Greenleaf, for Isaiah Thomas. 1800.   pp. viii, [13]–436, 4 plates.   12mo.   AAS, NHSL, NYSL.

38476 THE SCOURGE of fashion. A poem by Phylanthus. . . .
New York: Printed by Ming & Young . . . 1800.   pp. 23.   12mo.
AAS, BPL, BʳU, LOC, NYSOC.

38477 SEAMAN, Valentine   1770–1817
The Midwives monitor, and mothers mirror: being three concluding lectures of a course. . . . By Valentine Seaman. . . .
New York, Printed by Isaac Collins. . . . 1800.   pp. 123.   12mo.
AML, LOC, NYAM.

38478 THE SEAMAN'S journal: being an easy and correct method of keeping the daily reckoning of a ship, during the course of her voyage. . . .
New Haven: Printed for Isaac Beers & Co., 1800.   8vo.   pp. [78].   YC.

38479 SEARSON, John, *of Philadelphia.*
Mount Vernon, a poem. . . . With a copper-plate likeness of the General. It was taken from an actual view on the spot by the author. . . .
Philadelphia: Printed for the author by Folwell.   pp. vi, [9]–83, [1], 4, portrait.   8vo.
The last four pages contain Searson's "Elegiac verses on the decease of . . . Washington."
AAS, BA, BM, BPL, BʳU, HEH, LCP, LOC, MᵈHS, MFM, NYHS, NYSL, PPL, UOP, VᵃSL, WLC, YC.

38480 SEDGWICK, Theodore   1746–1813
See The Honourable Mr. Sedgwick's political last will and testament.

38481 SEIP, Frederic, *of Philadelphia.*
An Inaugural dissertation on cataract: submitted to the . . . Medical Faculty, of the University of Pennsylvania, on the thirty-first of May 1800, for the degree of doctor of medicine.
Philadelphia: Printed by Way & Groff, no. 48, North Third-Street. 1800.   pp. 27.   8vo.   AAS, AML, LCP, LOC, NYAM, UOP, YC.

38482 SELDEN, Andrew   1762?–1825
The young child's easy guide to the seats of science, containing the first principles of spelling and reading. . . .
Burlington, Vermont. Printed by Anthony Haswell, with the benefit of copyright. 1800.   pp. 142.   12mo.   BʳA.

38483 A SELECTION of orations and eulogies . . . of . . . Washington. . . .
See Atherton, Charles Humphrey.

38484 SENECA, [Lucius Annaeus] 5 B. C.–65 A. D.
 See L'Estrange, Roger.

38485 SERIOUS considerations on the election of a president. . . .
 See Linn, William.

38486 SERIOUS facts, opposed to "Serious Considerations:" or, the voice of warning to religious
 Republicans. . . .
  October, 1800. pp. 16. 8vo.
 Signed "Marcus Brutus." Sometimes attributed to Benjamin Pollard, 1780–1836.
              AAS, BPL, HEH, JCB, LOC, NYHS, NYPL.

38487 SEWALL, Daniel 1755–1842
 An Astronomical diary, or Almanac, for the year of Christian aera, 1801. Calculated for
 the meridian of Portsmouth, New-Hampshire.
  Portsmouth, New-Hampshire: printed by Charles Peirce. . . . pp. [24]. 12mo.
              AAS.

38488 —— An Eulogy, occasioned by the death of General Washington. Pronounced at the
 middle parish in Kittery, February 22, 1800. . . .
  *Portsmouth, (New-Hampshire,) Printed at the United States' Oracle office, by Charles
 Peirce, 1800.* pp. 20. 8vo. AAS, BA, JCB, LOC, NYHS.

38489 SEWALL, Jonathan Mitchel 1748–1808
 Eulogy on the late General Washington; pronounced at St. John's Church, in Ports-
 mouth, Newhampshire, on . . . 31st December, 1799. . . .
  Portsmouth, N. H. Printed by William Treadwell. pp. 28. sq. 8vo.
     AAS, BA, BPL, HC, HEH, JCB, LOC, MⁱHS, NYHS, NYPL, NYSL, VᵘU.

38490 THE SHADE of Alexander Pope. . . .
 See Mathias, Thomas James.

38491 SHARP, Joshua
 Citizen's and farmer's Almanac, for the year 1801. . . . Containing . . . the death and
 character of G. Washington.
  Philadelphia: Printed and sold by John McCulloch, no. 1, North Third-street.
 pp. [40]. 12mo. LOC.

38492 —— Father Abraham's Almanac, for the year of our Lord, 1801 . . . containing . . . astronomical calculations, by Joshua Sharp. . . .
  Philadelphia: Printed and sold by Peter Stewart, no. 34, South Second-Street.
 pp. [40]. 12mo. AAS, LOC, RU.

38493 —— Father Tammany's Almanac, for the year 1801. . . . Containing, besides the astronomical
 calculations by Joshua Sharp, the death and will of G. Washington.
  *Philadelphia: Printed for Wm. Young, bookseller, no. 51, corner of Chestnut and
 Second streets. 1800.* 12mo. BPL.

38494 SHEPHERD, E.
 The Columbian accountant; or a complete system of practical arithmetic: particularly
 adapted to the commerce of the United States. . . .
  New-York: Printed for the author, by T. & J. Swords, no. 99 Pearl-Street. 1800.
 pp. x, [2], 212. 12mo. AAS.

38495 SHERBURNE, Henry 1741–1825
 The Oriental philanthropist, or true republican. . . . By Henry Sherburne, A. B. Published according to act of Congress.
  Printed for Wm. Treadwell & Co. Portsmouth, N. H. . . . 1800. pp. 215, [1].
 12mo.
 There are copies in which the last signature is in smaller type and the advertisement on
 the last page is omitted. AAS, BA, BPL, HC, HEH, JCB, LCP, LOC, NL, NYPL, NYSL, UOP, YC.

38496 [SHERLOCK, Thomas]   1678–1761
       The Trial of the witnesses of the resurrection of Jesus. . . . Mr. Woolston's objections
       . . . considered. . . .
                 Philadelphia: Printed by H. Tuckniss, for Ezekiel Cooper. . . . 1800.   pp. 128, 15.
       24mo.
       The last section contains [Charles Leslie's] "An Extract of a short and easy method with
       the Deists."   AAS, GU, LOC, UOP, UOT^x.

38497 SHIRTLIFF, Roswell
       See Shurtleff, Roswell.

38498 SHOEMAKER, Abraham.
       The New-Jersey and Pennsylvania Almanac, for the year 1801. . . . Calculated for the
       latitude and meridian of Philadelphia. . . .
                 Trenton: Printed . . . by Sherman, Mershon & Thomas.   pp. [36].   16mo.
                                                                          AAS, HSP, LOC, NYHS.

38499 —— The Town and country Almanac, for . . . 1801. . . . Also, an authentic sketch of the
       life of General Washington. . . .
                 New York: Printed and published by D. Longworth. . . .   pp. [36].   12mo.
                                                                                   BPL, RU.

38500 A SHORT account of the death of a profligate youth, that, by bad company, learned to
       deny . . . the Saviour. . . .
                 Springfield: Printed by T. Ashley — 1800.   pp. 12.   12mo.   AAS.

38501 A SHORT introduction to Latin grammar, for the use of the university and academy of
       Pennsylvania in Philadelphia. . . . Seventh edition. . . .
                 *Wilmington, printed and sold by Bonsal & Niles — also sold at their book-store,
       no. 173, Market-Street, Baltimore — 1800.*   pp. 108.   12mo.
       Attributed by Yale to James Davidson (1732–1809).   AAS, JCB, YC.

38502 [SHORT stories for young people. Contents 1. The little hopper. 2. The white chicken.
       3. Charlotte. 4. The sly child. 5. The untidy girls. 6. The good child. The second
       Windsor edition.
                 Printed at Windsor, Vermont, by Mahum Mower. . . . 1800.   pp. 27.   24mo.]
                                                                                        EVANS.

38503 THE SHORTER Catechism. . . .
       See Westminster Assembly of Divines.

38504 SHURTLEFF, Roswell   1773–1861
       An Oration on . . . Washington. . . . Pronounced before the citizens of Westmoreland
       . . . and the Jerusalem Lodge, February 22d. 1800. By Roswell Shirtliff, A. B. . . .
                 Walpole: Printed for Thomas & Thomas, by David Carlisle. 1800.   pp. 15.   8vo.
       "Lines adapted to the occasion, by B. White," p. 15.   AAS, HEH, NHHS, NYHS.

38505 SIMMONS, Amelia
       American cookery. . . . The second edition. Published according to Act of Congress.
                 Albany: Printed by Charles R. & George Webster . . . for the authoress.   pp. 64.
       12mo.   AAS, NYPL.

38506 [SIMONS, James]
       A Rallying point for all true friends to their country.
                 [*Charleston.*]   pp. 16.   8vo.
       Caption title. Dated, Charleston, October 10, 1800. The tract relates to the economic
       situation of the country and of Charleston in particular.   BA, LOC, MHS.

38507 SITER, Sarah and John
By an order from the Orphan's Court, will be sold, by public Vendue . . . the 27th day of February next . . . the Upper Ferry, on Schylkill. . . . Sarah Siter, administratrix John Siter, administrator. January 23d, 1800. . . .
Printed by Hall and Sellers [Philadelphia] Broadside. 8vo. HSP.

38508 SKETCHES of the history, genius, disposition, accomplishments, employments, customs and importance of the fair sex. . . .
Philadelphia: Printed by Samuel Sansom, Jun. no. 27, Mulberry-Street. pp. viii, 292. 16mo.
"Just received and for sale by Thomas C. Cushing, Salem," 1800. The pages in signatures U-Aa are misnumbered. AAS.

38509 SMALLEY, John 1734–1820
On the evils of a weak government. A sermon, preached on the general election at Hartford, in Connecticut, May 8, 1800. . . .
Hartford: Printed by Hudson and Goodwin. 1800. pp. 51. 8vo.
AAS, AHTS, CHS, CL, HEH, JCB, LOC, MHS, MSL, NL, NYHS, NYPL, PrU, UTS, WL, YC.

38510 SMITH, Amasa
A Short compendium, of the duty of artillerists. . . . Also, an easy method of finding the distance of an object, by a plain table. . . .
Worcester: (Massachusetts.) Published according to act of Congress, by Isaiah Thomas, Jun. . . . Sept. 1800. pp. 56, front. (a folding chart). 12mo.
AAS, EI, GU, LOC, NYPL.

38511 SMITH, Charles 1768–1808
[The Gentleman's political and commercial pocket Almanac for 1801. . . .
New York. pp. 123. 18mo.]
There was a copy in NYSL before the Fire.

38512 SMITH, Charlotte (Turner) 1749–1806
Montalbert. A novel. By Charlotte Smith. In two volumes. . . .
Printed for Mathew Carey, no. 118, Market Street, Philadelphia; by Snowden & M'Corkle, Greensburg. 1800. pp. [2], 270; [2], 244. 12mo. AAS, LCP, LOC, VᵃU.

38513 SMITH, Ebenezer, *of Partridgefield, Mass.*
Remarks on a book, entitled, The nature and design of the baptism of Christ . . . by the Rev. Samuel Whitman of Goshen. . . .
Pittsfield, Phinehas Allen, 1800. pp. 12. 8vo. CL.

38514 SMITH, Edward Darrell 1777–1819
Inaugural dissertation, being an attempt to prove that certain substances are conveyed, unchanged, into the circulation. . . .
Philadelphia: Printed by Way & Groff, no. 48, North Third-Street. 1800. pp. 54. 8vo. AAS, AML, BM, JCB, LCP, LOC, NYAM, RU, UOP, YC.

38515 SMITH, Ethan 1762–1849
A Farewell sermon, delivered at Haverhill, Newhampshire, Sabbath, June 30, 1799. By Ethan Smith, A. B. who had been pastor of the church . . . but was now dismissed for want of support.
Peacham, Vermont, Printed by Farley & Goss. 1800. pp. [5]–27. 8vo.
JCB, NYHS, NYSL, UTS, WˡᵇHS.

38516 SMITH, Isaac 1744–1817
A Sermon preached at the instalment of . . . Ethan Smith . . . in Hopkinton, N. Hampshire, March 12th, 1800: being the same delivered at the ordination of . . . Josiah Prentice, at Northwood, N. H. May 29th, 1799. . . . To which are annexed. the Charge [by Eden Burroughs], and the Right Hand of Fellowship [by Asa M'Farland], and the discourse delivered by . . . Ethan Smith, the next Sabbath. . . .
Printed at Concord, by George Hough — for Francis Mitchel, of Hopkinton, N. Hampshire. 1800. pp. 55. 8vo. AAS, JCB, LOC, NEHGS, NYHS, RU.

38517   SMITH, Isaac, *of New Jersey.*
        A Charge, delivered by the Honourable Isaac Smith, Esq. second justice of the Supreme
        Court, to the grand-jury, Circuit Court, holden at Woodbury, in and for the county
        of Gloucester . . . the seventh day of October, 1800: and the answer of the grand-
        jury. . . .
                Broadside.   fol.   NJHS.

38518   SMITH, Jeremiah   1759–1842
        An Oration on the death of George Washington; delivered at Exeter, February 22,
        1800. . . .
                Exeter: From the press of Henry Ranlet. 1800.   pp. 31.   8vo.
                        AAS, AHTS, BA, BM, BPL, CL, HEH, JCB, LOC, NHHS, NYHS, NYPL, NYSL, PL, YC.

38519   SMITH, John   1681–1766
        A Narrative of some sufferings, for his Christian peaceable testimony by John Smith. . . .
        To which is annexed . . . the sufferings of Richard Seller, of Keinsey, Great
        Britain.
                Philadelphia: Printed by Benjamin & Jacob Johnson, no. 147, High-Street. 1800.
        pp. 48.   8vo.
        Extracts from Besse's *Collection of the Sufferings of the People Called Quakers.*
                        AAS, HC, HSP, LOC, NEHGS, NL, NYHS, NYPL, UOC, YC.

38520   SMITH, Joshua, and others.
        Divine hymns, or spiritual songs, for the use of religious assemblies. . . . A collection,
        by Joshua Smith, and others. The seventh edition — revised.
                *Elizabeth-town: Printed by J. Woods, for John Tiebout, no. 246, Water-Street, New
        York. 1800.*   pp. 171.   12mo.   AAS, BʳU.

38521   — — — *Norwich: Printed by John Trumbull. 1800.*   pp. 187, [5].   12mo.   WL.

38522   — — — *New-London: Printed by James Springer, for John Green, bookseller. 1800.*   pp. 192.
        12mo.   HEH, LOC, NYHS.

38523   — — — *New-London: Printed by James Springer. 1800.*   pp. 192.   12mo.   NYHS.

38524   SMITH, Samuel Stanhope   1750–1819
        An Oration, upon the death of General George Washington, delivered in the State-House
        at Trenton, on the 14th of January, 1800. . . .
                Trenton: Printed by G. Craft. M,DCCC.   pp. 45, [1].   8vo.
                        AAS, BA, BʳU, HC, HEH, JCB, LOC, MᵈHS, MHS, NJSL, NL, NYHS, NYPL, PPL, PʳU, RU, YC.

38525   — — The second edition.
                Trenton: Printed by G. Craft. M,DCCC.   pp. 45, [1].   8vo.
                        BA, HEH, HSP, LOC, MHS, NYHS.

38526   SMITH, William   1727–1803
        A Funeral address, delivered in the German Lutheran church, Lancaster; at the public
        interment of Major-General Mifflin, January 22, 1800. . . .
                [Lancaster.] Printed by W. & R. Dickson, Queenstreet.   pp. 19.   8vo.
                        HSP, NYHS, PSL, WLC.

38527   SNETHEN, Nicholas   1769–1845
        A Reply to an apology for protesting against the Methodist Episcopal government. . . .
                Philadelphia: Printed by Henry Tuckniss. 1800.   pp. 62.   16mo.   LOC.

38528   SOCIETY of the Cincinnati.
        Proceedings of the General Society of the Cincinnati, at the triennial general meeting
        of 1799 . . . in the city of Philadelphia, in May, 1800.
                Philadelphia: Printed by J. Ormrod. . . . 1800.   pp. 15.   4to.   CHS, NYPL.

38529 A SOLEMN ADDRESS. . . .
See Wortman, Tunis.

38530 SOME ACCOUNT OF AN EXISTING CORRESPONDENCE NOW CARRYING ON BETWEEN THE INHABITANTS OF THE MOON, AND THE NATIVES OF OLD ENGLAND. . . .
London. . . . New-York: Re-published by William Cobbett, no. 141, Hanover Square. 1800. pp. 23. 12mo. AAS, LOC.

38531 SOREN, JOHN   1757 ——
THE NARRATIVE OF MR. JOHN SOREN . . . PIRATICALLY CAPTURED ON THE HIGH SEAS, IN REQUITAL FOR AN ACT OF HUMANITY, IN SAVING A BRITISH TRANSPORT. . . . WITH AN APPENDIX, CONTAINING THE DOCUMENTS . . . AND TESTIMONIALS OF MAJOR [J. W.] MANSERGH . . . AND CAPTAIN [WILLIAM] DAVIS.
London, printed. . . . Boston, reprinted, and sold for the relief of Mr. Soren and his family. 1800. pp. 54. 8vo. AAS, BPL, HC, HEH, JCB, LOC, MHS, NYHS, NYPL, NYSL.

38532 SOUTH CAROLINA. STATE.
ACTS AND RESOLUTIONS OF THE GENERAL ASSEMBLY, OF THE STATE OF SOUTH-CAROLINA. PASSED IN DECEMBER, 1798. THE SECOND EDITION.
Charleston: Printed by Freneau & Paine, printers to the State, no. 47, Bay. 1800. pp. 50, [2], 52–83, [1]. fol. HC-L, HEH, LOC, MSL.

38533 —— ACTS AND RESOLUTIONS OF THE GENERAL ASSEMBLY, OF THE STATE OF SOUTH-CAROLINA. PASSED IN DECEMBER, 1799.
Charleston: Printed by Freneau & Paine, printers to the State, no. 47, Bay. 1800. pp. 90. fol. CLS, HC, HEH, LOC, MSL, NYBA, NYHS, SCSL, YC.

38534 —— AT A GENERAL ASSEMBLY BEGUN AND HOLDEN AT COLUMBIA . . . THE TWENTY-FOURTH DAY OF NOVEMBER . . . ONE THOUSAND EIGHT HUNDRED. . . . IN THE SENATE-HOUSE, THE TWENTIETH DAY OF DECEMBER. . . .
Printed by John M'Iver, no. 47, East-Bay, Charleston. Broadside. 8vo.
The Act making it unlawful to import slaves into South Carolina. LOC.

38535 —— [THE RULES AND ORDERS OF THE COURTS OF SESSIONS AND COMMON PLEAS, AS MADE JULY 1, 1800. ALSO THE RULES AND ORDERS OF THE COURT OF EQUITY, UP TO MAY TERM, 1800.
Charleston: W. P. Young. 1800.]
Advertised in the *Charleston City Gazette* of July 8 as "this day published."

38536 —— STATE OF SOUTH-CAROLINA. AT A GENERAL ASSEMBLY BEGUN AND HOLDEN AT COLUMBIA, ON MONDAY THE TWENTY-FOURTH DAY OF NOVEMBER . . . ONE THOUSAND EIGHT HUNDRED. . . . AN ACT TO PREVENT NEGRO SLAVES, AND OTHER PERSONS OF COLOR, FROM BEING BROUGHT INTO OR ENTERING THIS STATE. . . .
[Colophon:] Printed by John M'Iver, no. 47, East Bay, Charleston. Broadside. fol. LOC.

38537 THE SOUTH-CAROLINA GAZETTE, AND COLUMBIAN ADVERTISER.   1795–1830
Columbia; South Carolina. Published by Daniel Faust. fol. weekly.
FOR 1800: [HC].

38538 SOUTH-CAROLINA STATE GAZETTE, AND TIMOTHY'S DAILY ADVERTISER.   1794–1802
[Charleston, printed by Benjamin Franklin Timothy.] fol. daily.
FOR 1800: CLS.

38539 SOUTHWICK, REMINGTON, *of Mendon*
THE COLUMBIAN CALENDAR: OR ALMANAC, FOR THE YEAR OF OUR LORD, 1801. . . . CALCULATED FOR THE MERIDIAN OF BOSTON. . . .
Dedham: Printed and sold by H. Mann. . . . pp. [24]. 12mo. AAS, EI, HSP.

38540   SPALDING, Joshua   1760–1825
    A Sermon, preached at the Tabernacle, in Salem, December 29, A. D. 1799, on the death
      of General Washington. . . .
        Salem: Printed by Thomas C. Cushing, at the Bible & Heart.   pp. 20.   8vo.
    With a slip of errata.
        AAS, BA, BM, BPL, EI, HC, HEH, JCB, LOC, MFM, MHS, NL, NYHS, NYPL, NYSL, PPL, WLC, YC.

38541   SPALDING, Josiah   1751–1823
    The Duty and importance of calling upon God . . . two sermons. . . . at Shelburne,
      September 22d, 1799. . . .
        Printed at Northampton, (Massachusetts) by William Butler. 1800.   pp. 40   8vo.
        AAS, BM, BPL, CL, JCB, MHS, NYPL, YC.

38542   A SPECIMEN of the confession of faith. . . .
    See Congregational Church in Connecticut.

38543   THE SPECTATOR.   1797–1879
        New-York . . . published (Wednesdays and Saturdays) by E. Belden & Co. . . .
    fol.   semi-weekly.   For 1800: AAS, BPL, CHS, MHS, NYHS, NYPL, NYSL, WⁱˢHS, YC.

38544   SPIESS, C[hristian] H[einrich]   1755–1799
    The Mountain cottager; or, wonder upon wonder. A tale. Translated from the German
      of C. H. Spiess. . . .
        Philadelphia: Printed by W. W. Woodward, no. 17 Chestnut Street, for Samuel
    Hyndman. 1800.   pp. 228.   16mo.
    Contains a list of subscribers, pp. 219–25.   AAS, LOC, NYSL, UOP, YC.

38545   [SPIRIT of '76. At a numerous meeting of the young men of Troy, at Bill's Phoenix Hotel,
    April 15, 1800, for the nomination of candidates to represent the county of Rensselaer
    in the House of Assembly, New York, together with an address; Stephen Warren,
    chairman; dated Troy, April 15, 1800.
      Broadside].
    From Henkel's auction catalogue 1378 (1925), item 131. Bought by LOC, but not
    located in 1951.

38546   SPOONER'S Vermont Journal.   1783 ———
        Windsor: Printed and published by Alden Spooner. . . .   fol.   weekly.
            For 1800: AAS, VᵗSL.

38547   SPRING, Samuel   1746–1819
    God the author of human greatness. A discourse on the death of . . . Washington . . .
    at the North Congregational Church in Newburyport, December 29, 1799. . . .
        Printed at Newburyport, by Edmund M. Blunt.   pp. 28.   8vo.
        AAS, BA, HC, HEH, JCB, LOC, MFM, NL, NYHS, NYPL, NYSL, PPL, UOP, UTS, WⁱˢHS.

38548   SPRINGER'S Weekly Oracle.   1796–1801
        Printed and published by James Springer, on the Parade, New-London. 1800.   fol.
    weekly.   For 1800: [AAS], [HC].

38549   STAFFORD, Cornelius William
    The Philadelphia Directory, for 1800 . . . also a register of the executive, legislative,
    and judicial magistrates of the United States . . . with an accurate table of the
    duties on goods. . . . To all of which are added, an account of the post office . . .
    the banks. . . .
        Printed for the editor, by William W. Woodward, no. 17, Chesnut Street. 1800.
    pp. 151, [1], 80.   8vo.   AAS, HSP, LCP, LOC, NYHS, YC.

38550 STAFFORD, H[OSEA], *pseud.*
>> AN ASTRONOMICAL DIARY, CALENDAR, OR ALMANACK, FOR . . . 1801. . . . CALCULATED FOR THE MERIDIAN AND HORIZON OF NEW-HAVEN. . . .
>>> *New-Haven, Printed & sold by T. Green & Son.* pp. [24]. 16mo.
>> Probably the work of Nehemiah Strong (1729–1807). AAS, BM, CHS, LOC, NYSL, YC.

38551 STANCLIFF, JOHN
>> A SERMON ON THE DEATH OF GENERAL GEORGE WASHINGTON, DELIVERED AT CAPE MAY, ON THE 22D OF FEBRUARY 1800. . . .
>>> *Printed by S. C. Ustick, Mount-Holly. 1800.* pp. 23. 12mo. NYPL.

38552 STANFORD, JOHN 1754–1834
>> No. II. CHRISTIAN'S POCKET LIBRARY. EDITED BY JOHN STANFORD, A. M. ASSISTED BY OTHER MINISTERS. VOL. II, No. 1–6.
>>> *New-York, printed for the editor, by T. & J. Swords. 1800.* Engraved title, pp. 286, [2]. 16 mo.
>> The first volume was published in 1796. BM, GTS, LOC, NYHS.

38553 [STANHOPE, PHILIP DORMER, 4TH EARL OF] CHESTERFIELD 1694–1773
>> PRINCIPLES OF POLITENESS . . . BY THE LATE LORD CHESTERFIELD. WITH ADDITIONS BY THE REV. DR. JOHN TRUSLER. . . .
>>> *Philadelphia: Printed for Mathew Carey . . . 1800.* pp. 106, [1]. 24mo.
>> The last leaf contains the Index. AAS, WL.

38554 STANIFORD, DANIEL 1766–1820
>> THE ART OF READING: CONTAINING A NUMBER OF USEFUL RULES EXEMPLIFIED BY A VARIETY OF SELECTED AND ORIGINAL PIECES. . . .
>>> *Boston: Printed by John Russell, for John West, no. 75, Cornhill. 1800.* pp. viii, [7]–232. 12mo. AAS, HC, LOC.

38555 —— A SHORT BUT COMPREHENSIVE GRAMMAR. . . . TO WHICH IS ADDED, AN APPENDIX, COMPREHENDING A LIST OF VULGARISMS. . . . SECOND EDITION ENLARGED.
>>> *Printed at Charlestown, by Samuel Etheridge, for John West, proprietor of the copy right, sold at his bookstore, no. 75, Cornhill, Boston.* pp. 96. 12mo.
>> The preface to this edition is dated Jan. 1, 1800. AAS, CL, MSL, NYSL.

38556 STANLY, JOHN 1774–1834
>> TO THE INDEPENDENT ELECTORS OF THE TENTH DISTRICT [OF] NORTH CAROLINA. . . .
>>> *Newbern, April 25, 1800.* Broadside. 8vo. NYHS.

38557 A STATEMENT OF THE MEASURES CONTEMPLATED AGAINST SAMUEL BRYAN, ESQUIRE, REGISTER-GENERAL OF THE COMMONWEALTH OF PENNSYLVANIA. . . .
>>> *Philadelphia: Printed by Francis and Robert Bailey. 1800.* pp. 62. 8vo.
>>>> AAS, LCP, UOP, YC.

38558 STEARNS, ELISHA
>> AN EULOGIUM, ON GENERAL GEORGE WASHINGTON; SPOKEN AT TOLLAND, ON THE 22ND OF FEBRUARY, 1800. . . .
>>> *Printed at East-Windsor, by Luther Pratt. July 29th, 1800.* pp. 24. 12mo.
>>>> AAS, BPL, CHS, HEH, LOC, NYPL, YC.

38559 STEUBEN, F. W. L. G. A.
>> *See* United States, Regulations. . . .

38560 STEVENS, JAMES WILSON, *of Philadelphia*
>> AN HISTORICAL AND GEOGRAPHICAL ACCOUNT OF ALGIERS: CONTAINING A CIRCUMSTANTIAL AND INTERESTING DETAIL OF EVENTS RELATIVE TO THE AMERICAN CAPTIVES, TAKEN FROM THEIR OWN TESTIMONY. SECOND EDITION. BY JAMES WILSON STEPHENS. . . .
>>> *Brooklyn: Printed by Thomas Kirk, for Alexander Brodie. 1800.* pp. 318, [6], front. 12mo.
>> The end-matter includes a list of subscribers.
>>>> AAS, BA, BPL, HC, JCB, LOC, NL, NYHS, NYPL, NYSL, YC.

38561 STEVENS, JOHN   1750–1799
THE VALEDICTORY ADDRESS OF THE LATE REV. JOHN STEVENS . . . OF . . . NEW-MARLBOROUGH. . . .
DELIVERED TO HIS CHURCH . . . AT THE CLOSE OF HIS FUNERAL. . . . THE SECOND EDITION.
Hartford: Printed by Hudson and Goodwin. 1800.   pp. 24.   12mo.
The first edition was in *A Posthumous Publication,* 1799.

AAS, BʳA, CHS, CL, NYHS, PL, UTS, YC.

38562 STEWART'S KENTUCKY HERALD.   1795–1803
Lexington: Printed by James H. Stewart.   fol.   weekly.   FOR 1800: [AAS].

38563 STILLMAN, SAMUEL   1737–1807
A SERMON, OCCASIONED BY THE DEATH OF GEORGE WASHINGTON. . . . BY SAMUEL STILLMAN,
D. D. MINISTER OF THE FIRST BAPTIST CHURCH IN BOSTON.
Boston: Printed by Manning & Loring, Spring-Lane.   pp. 26.   8vo.

AAS, BA, BPL, BʳU, CL, EI, HC, HEH, HSP, JCB, LOC, MHS, NYHS, NYPL. NYSL, UTS, YC.

38564 STONE, ELIAB   1737–1822
A DISCOURSE, DELIVERED AT READING FEBRUARY 22, 1800 . . . IN . . . MEMORY OF GENERAL GEORGE
WASHINGTON. . . .
Boston: Manning & Loring, Printers, near the Old South Meeting-House.   pp. 23.
8vo.   AAS, BA, BPL, EI, HC, HEH, JCB, LOC, MHS, NL, NYPL, NYSL.

38565 STONINGTON ASSOCIATION [BAPTIST].
MINUTES OF THE STONINGTON ASSOCIATION, HELD AT HAMPTON, OCTOBER 21 AND 22, 1800.
Norwich: Printed by John Sterry. 1800.   pp. 8.   8vo.   SCBHC.

38566 STORM, N., *pseud.*
THE TOWN & COUNTRY ALMANACK FOR THE YEAR OF OUR LORD 1801. . . . CALCULATED FOR THE
MERIDIAN OF NORWICH. . . .
Printed and sold by John Trumbull in Norwich. . . .   pp. [24].   12mo.
AAS, LOC, NYPL, WL.

38567 STORY, ISAAC   1774–1803
AN EULOGY ON . . . WASHINGTON. . . . WRITTEN AT THE REQUEST OF THE INHABITANTS OF
STERLING, AND DELIVERED BEFORE THEM . . . THE 22D OF FEBRUARY, 1800. . . .
Worcester. Printed by Isaiah Thomas, Jun. April—1800.   pp. 23.   8vo.
AAS, BA, BPL, BʳU, HC, HEH, JCB, LOC, MFM, NYHS, NYPL, NYSL.

38568 STORY, JOSEPH   1779–1845
AN EULOGY ON . . . WASHINGTON; WRITTEN AT THE REQUEST OF THE INHABITANTS OF MARBLE-
HEAD, AND DELIVERED BEFORE THEM ON THE SECOND DAY OF JANUARY, A. D. 1800. . . .
Printed by Joshua Cushing, County Street, Salem. 1800.   pp. 24.   8vo.
An "Elegy to the memory of General George Washington" pp. 17–24.
AAS, BA, BPL, CL, EI, HC, HEH, HSP, JCB, LCP, LOC, MFM, MHS, NL, NYHS, NYPL, NYSL, PPL, VᵗU, YC.

38569 [——] THE POWER OF SOLITUDE. A POEM. IN TWO PARTS. . . .
Boston, Printed by John Russell.   pp. 100.   8vo.
184th Massachusetts District copyright issued to Joseph Story, as author, on May 21, 1800.
AAS, BPL, BʳU, HEH, LOC, MHS, NYHS, NYPL, UOTˣ, YC.

38570 STOUT, BENJAMIN
NARRATIVE OF THE LOSS OF THE SHIP HERCULES, COMMANDED BY CAPTAIN BENJAMIN STOUT, ON
THE COAST OF CAFFRARIA, THE 16TH OF JUNE, 1796: ALSO . . . HIS TRAVELS THROUGH . . .
AFRICA. . . .
London, Printed: New-Bedford, re-printed by Abraham Shearman, jun. 1800.
pp. 124.   12mo.   AAS, HC.

38571 —— —— —— *London, Printed: Hudson, re-printed by Ashbel Stoddard. 1800.*   pp. xxxvii, [39]–
118.   24mo.   AAS, HEH, JCB, NYPL, NYSL, YC.

38572 STREBECK, George
A Sermon on the character of the virtuous woman. By George Strebeck: pastor of the English Lutheran Church in New-York.
New-York: Printed for the author. 1800. pp. 26. 12mo. AAS, LCP, NYHS.

38573 STRICTURES upon the letter imputed to Mr. Jefferson. . . .
See Coxe, Tench.

38574 STRONG, Cyprian 1743–1811
Sermon, preached at Chatham, at the request of St. John's Lodge, No. II. in Middletown, on the celebration of the festival of St. John the Baptist.
Middletown: Tertius Dunning. 1800. pp. 20. 8vo. CHS.

38575 —— A Sermon, preached at Hartford. . . . At the ordination of . . . Jedediah Bushnell, as a missionary to the new settlements; January 15th, A. D. 1800. . . .
Hartford: Printed by Hudson and Goodwin. 1800. pp. 19. 8vo.
AAS, BA, BM, BᵣU, CHS, CL, HEH, JCB, LOC, MHS, NL, NYHS, NYPL, NYSL, PᵣU, UTS, YC.

38576 STRONG, Joseph 1753–1834
A Sermon, preached at Norwich, on hearing of the death of General George Washington. . . .
Norwich: Printed by John Trumbull. 1800. pp. 17. 8vo.
AAS, CHS, HC, HEH, JCB, LOC, MHS, NYHS, NYPL, NYSL, UTS, WL, YC.

38577 STRONG, Nathan 1748–1816
A Discourse, delivered on . . . December 27, 1799, the day set apart by the citizens of Hartford, to lament . . . the death of . . . Washington. . . .
Hartford: Printed by Hudson and Goodwin, 1800. pp. 31. 8vo.
There are two issues with different settings of the title-page and p. 7.
AAS, BA, BPL, CHS, HC, HEH, HSP, JCB, LOC, MHS, NL, NYHS, NYPL, NYSL, UTS, YC.

38578 —— A Sermon, delivered at the funeral of Mrs. Sarah Williams, consort of the Rev. Eliphalet Williams, D. D. . . .
Hartford: Printed by Hudson and Goodwin. 1800. pp. 15. 8vo.
AAS, BA, BPL, CHS, HC, JCB, NYHS, NYPL, RIHS, UTS, WⁱˢHS, YC.

38579 —— Sermons, on various subjects, doctrinal, experimental and practical. . . . Vol. II. Published according to Act of Congress.
Hartford: Printed by John Babcock, for Oliver D. & I. Cooke. . . . 1800. pp. 408. 8vo.
Contains an eighteen-page list of subscribers. The first volume was published in 1798.
AAS, BA, BM, BPL, HC, LOC, NL, NYPL, UTS, WC, WⁱˢHS, YC.

38580 —— A Thanksgiving sermon, delivered November 27th, 1800. . . . Published by the desire of the hearers.
Hartford: Printed by Hudson and Goodwin. 1800. pp. 18. 8vo.
AAS, AHTS, BPL, CHS, HC, HEH, JCB, LOC, NYHS, NYSL, WL, YC.

38581 STRONG, Nehemiah 1729–1807
The Connecticut Pocket Almanack, for the year of Our Lord 1801. . . . Calculated for the meridian of Hartford. . . .
Hartford: Printed by John Babcock, for E. & J. Babcock. pp. 47. 24mo.
AAS, CHS, LOC, NYPL, YC.

38582 —— See also Stafford, H.

38583 STURM, [CHRISTOPH CHRISTIAN] 1740–1786
    BEAUTIES OF NATURE DELINEATED. . . . SELECTED FROM STURM'S REFLECTIONS, BY THE REV.
    THADDEUS M. HARRIS. . . .
        Charlestown: Printed and sold by Samuel Etheridge. 1800. pp. [2], 223, [1], front.
    16mo.
    The frontispiece is engraved by S. Hill.
                  AAS, BPL, CL, HC, LCP, LOC, MHS, NYPL, NYSL, PᵣU, WC, YC.

38584 THE SUBSTANCE OF A LATE REMARKABLE DREAM, IN WHICH WERE PRESENTED THE CELESTIAL WORLDS
    AND THE . . . PLOT AGAINST THE UNITED STATES OF AMERICA.
        Hallowell (District of Maine) Printed by Peter Edes. 1800. pp. 16. 8vo.
    In verse form. The introduction is signed "James Shurtleff [1745–1832]. Litchfield,
    February, 1800."   AAS, BᵣU, NYPL.

38585 SULLIVAN, GEORGE 1771–1838
    AN ORATION, PRONOUNCED AT EXETER ON THE FOURTH DAY OF JULY 1800, IN COMMEMORATION OF
    THE ANNIVERSARY OF AMERICAN INDEPENDENCE. . . .
        From the press of H. Ranlet, Exeter, New-Hampshire. 1800. pp. 16. 8vo.
              AAS, BA, BM, HC, HEH, JCB, LOC, MHS, NYHS, NYPL, NYSL.

38586 SUMNER, CHARLES PINCKNEY 1776–1839
    EULOGY ON THE ILLUSTRIOUS GEORGE WASHINGTON, PRONOUNCED AT MILTON, TWENTY-SECOND
    FEBRUARY, 1800. . . .
        Dedham: Printed by H. Mann. 1800. pp. 24. 8vo.
    There are several issues with different tail-pieces (an eagle, a scroll, a setting sun)
    and textual variations. See Sabin 93693.
          AAS, BA, BPL, EI, HC, HEH, JCB, LOC, MHS, NL, NYHS, NYPL, NYSL, UTS, YC.

38587 SUMNER, JOSEPH 1739–1824
    A SERMON, PREACHED AT SHREWSBURY NOVEMBER 28, 1799. ON THE ANNIVERSARY THANKSGIVING
    IN MASSACHUSETTS. . . .
        Printed at Brookfield, Massachusetts, by E. Merriam & Co, February, 1800. pp. 26.
    8vo.   AAS, BA, CHS, HEH, JCB, LOC, MHS, NL, NYHS, YC.

38588 THE SUN. SEPT. 16, 1800–1906
        Pittsfield, Massachusetts. Printed and published by Phinehas Allen. fol. weekly.
                       FOR 1800: BᵣA.

38589 THE SUN. DOVER GAZETTE, AND COUNTY ADVERTISER. 1795–1818
        Published on Wednesdays by Samuel Bragg, jun. at his printing-office, Dover.
    weekly. fol.   FOR 1800: [NHHS].

38590 SUN OF LIBERTY. JUNE 24, 1800?–1801
        [Danbury to Oct. 8; Norwalk thereafter.] Printed by Samuel Morse. 1800. fol.
    weekly.   FOR 1800: [MᵢₙₙHS].

38591 THE SUNBURY AND NORTHUMBERLAND GAZETTE. 1793–1817
        Northumberland — printed by George Schusler. fol. weekly. FOR 1800: [LOC].

38592 SUPPLEMENT TO A MEMOIR CONCERNING THE FASCINATING FACULTY WHICH HAS BEEN ASCRIBED
    TO THE RATTLE-SNAKE. . . .
    See Barton, Benjamin Smith.

38593 SUPPLEMENT TO THE ENCYCLOPAEDIA, OR DICTIONARY OF ARTS, SCIENCES, AND MISCELLANEOUS
    LITERATURE. IN THREE VOLUMES. ILLUSTRATED WITH COPPERPLATES.
        Philadelphia: Printed by Budd and Bartram, for Thomas Dobson. . . . 1803. pp. vi,
    704, 26 plates. 4to.
    Volume 1 part 1 was published in May, 1800; the title-page was issued after the completion
    of the work.   AAS.

38594 SUPPLICATION OF J. R********. TO HIS EXCELLENCY HENRY LAURENS, ESQUIRE, PRESIDENT, AND
    OTHER, THE MEMBERS OF THE HONOURABLE, THE AMERICAN CONGRESS. . . .
        *[On slip pasted on the verso of the last leaf:] Philadelphia: Printed and published
    by William W. Woodward, no. 17, Chestnut, near Front Street. 1800.* pp. [8]. 8vo.
    A satirical attack on James Rivington, the New York printer.   HC.

38595 THE SUPPORTER, OR DAILY REPAST.   1800
          Philadelphia: Published by John Nicholson. Printed by Isaac Ralston.   fol.   daily
      and weekly.
          Ralston was succeeded by Francis & Robert Bailey, and they by Thomas Bedwell.
                                                                   FOR 1800: [HC].

38596 SURR, T[HOMAS] S[KINNER]   1770–1847
          NEW WORK. GEORGE BARNWELL, A NEW NOVEL. BY T. S. SURR. . . . TWO VOLUMES IN ONE.
              *Boston: Printed for Joseph Bumstead. Sold by . . . Thomas and Andrews . . . E.
      Larkin, Wm. P. & L. Blake . . . and J. Nancrede. . . . 1800.*   pp. 300.   12mo.
                                                                   AAS, HC, HSP.

38597 THE SYREN: A CHOICE COLLECTION OF SEA, HUNTING AND OTHER SONGS.
              Philadelphia, printed for Mathew Carey. . . .   pp. 72, front.   16mo.
                                                                   BʳU, LOC, NYPL.

38598 A SYSTEM OF EXCHANGE WITH ALMOST ALL PARTS OF THE WORLD.
          See James, Joseph, and Moore, Daniel

38599 TAGGART, SAMUEL   1754–1825
          A DISCOURSE, DELIVERED AT COLRAIN, FEBRUARY 22, 1800. . . . TO THE MEMORY OF . . . GEORGE
      WASHINGTON. . . .
              Printed at Greenfield, by Thomas Dickman. 1800.   pp. 32.   8vo.
                                            BA, BPL, HC, HEH, JCB, LOC, MFM, NYPL, WRHS, YC.

38600 DIE TÄGLICHEN LOOSUNGEN UND LEHRTEXTE DER BRÜDERGEMEINE, FÜR DAS JAHR 1801.
              Lancaster: Gedruckt bey Johann Albrecht und Comp. . . . 1800.   pp. [126].
          16mo.   MORAVIAN HISTORICAL SOCIETY LIBRARY, NAZARETH, PA.

38601 TALBOT, CATHERINE   1721–1770
          REFLECTIONS ON THE SEVEN DAYS OF THE WEEK. BY MRS. CATHERINE TALBOT. A NEW EDITION.
              Newcastle [Del.]: Printed by S. & Jno. Adams. 1800.   pp. 36.   12mo.   AAS.

38602 TALBOT, SILAS
          EXPLANATORY: EXTRACT OF A LETTER FROM COMMODORE SILAS TALBOT, ADDRESSED TO MR SECRETARY
      STODDERT, DATED MAY 12TH, 1800. . . .
              Broadside.   fol.   MHS.

38603 TALES OF THE HERMITAGE. . . .
          See Pilkington, Mary (Hopkins).

38604 TANSILLO, LUIGI   1510–1568
          THE NURSE, A POEM. TRANSLATED FROM THE ITALIAN OF LUIGI TANSILLO. BY WILLIAM ROSCOE
      [OF LIVERPOOL].
              *London — printed — New-York: re-printed for William Cobbett by John Furman.
      1800.*   pp. 30, 44, 34.   24mo.
          This also appears with separate titlepage but with pagination and signatures continuous
      in the Durell, New York, editions of Thomas Campbell, *The Pleasures of Hope.*
                                            AAS, AML, BPL, HC, HSP, JCB, NYSL, UOP, VᵃU.

38605 TAPPAN, DAVID   1752–1803
          THE BEAUTY AND BENEFITS OF THE CHRISTIAN CHURCH . . . TWO SERMONS . . . IN PLYMOUTH,
      ON JANUARY 5, 1800 . . . FOLLOWING THE ORDINATION OF . . . MR. KENDALL. . . .
              Printed by Samuel Hall, no. 53, Cornhill, Boston. 1800.   pp. 46.   8vo.
                              AAS, BA, BPL, CL, CU, EI, HC, JCB, LOC, MHS, NYHS, NYPL, NYSL, UOC, WLC, YC.

38606 —— A SERMON DELIVERED AT KENNEBUNK, SEPTEMBER 3, 1800. AT THE ORDINATION OF REV. NATHANIEL
      HILL FLETCHER. . . .
              Cambridge, printed by William Hilliard. 1800.   pp. 34.   8vo.
                              AAS, BA, BPL, CL, CU, HC, HEH, HSP, JCB, LOC, MHS, NYHS, NYPL, YC.

38607   TAYLOR, Joshua   1768–1861
        An Answer to the Rev. Jonathan Ward's Brief statement and examination of the
        sentiments of the Weslean [sic] Methodists. . . .
                Hallowell (District of Maine) Printed by Peter Edes, 1800.   pp. iv, 76, [2].   8vo.
                                                                              NYPL.

38608   THE TELEGRAPHE and Daily Advertiser.   1795–1807
                Baltimore — printed by Thomas Dobbin, 1800.   fol.   daily.   For 1800: MᵈHS.

38609   THE TELESCOPE: or, American Herald.   1800–1802
                Published every Thursday, by [Daniel] Adams & [Salmon] Wilder, in Leominster,
        Massachusetts.   fol.   weekly.   For 1800: [AAS].

38610   THE TEMPLE of Reason.   Nov. 8, 1800–1802
                New-York: Published by D. Driscol.   4to.   weekly.
                                                            For 1800: AAS, HC, HSP, LOC, NYHS.

38611   —— The Temple of Reason. A quarto paper. To be published every Saturday morning, in
        New-York. By D. Driscoll. . . . New-York, October 4, 1800.
                Broadside.   fol.   LOC, NYSL.

38612   TENNESSEE. State.
        Laws relative to lands and intestate estates, extracted from the North-Carolina revised
        code, by the last General Assembly of this State, and ordered to be printed as will
        appear on the Journals.
                Knoxville: Printed by Roulstone & Wilson, Printers to the State. 1800.   pp. 86.
        12mo.   JCB.

38613   THE TENNESSEE Company.
        The Tenessee Company to Messrs. Strawbridge Jackson and Dexter. Deed of trusts.
        Dated 20th of June, 1800.
                [Philadelphia.]   pp. 23, [1].   8vo.   AAS, DᵉRGL, JCB, LOC, NL, NYHS, NYPL.

38614   THE TENNESSEE Gazette.   1800–1806
                [Nashville: printed by Bradford & Elam and published by Benjamin J. Bradford.]
        fol.   weekly.
        With the issue of July 30, the paper was printed by Bradford alone.   For 1800: [LOC].

38615   [TERSTEEGEN, Gerhard]   1697–1769
        Geistliches blumen-gartlein inniger seelen; oder kurze schluss-reimen, betrachtungen
        und lieder. . . . Achte und vermehrte auflage.
                Germantaun: Gedruckt . . . bey Michael Billmeyer, 1800.   pp. [12], 564, [12].
        24mo.
        The last twelve pages contain a "Register der Materien in den Liedern."
                                                    AAS, HSP, JCB, LCP, NYPL, NYSL, WLC, YC.

38616–7 A TEST of the religious principles of Mr. Jefferson, extracted (verbatim) from his writ-
        ings. . . .
                See Jefferson, Thomas.

38618   THACHER, Peter   1752–1802
        A Sermon, occasioned by the death of . . . Washington, and preached Feb. 22, 1800 . . .
        before . . . the honorable Senate and House of Representatives of . . . Massachu-
        setts. . . .
                Boston: — Printed by Young & Minns.   pp. 21.   8vo.
                AAS, BA, BPL, HC, HEH, HSP, JCB, LOC, MHS, NYHS, NYPL, NYSL, UTS, WⁱˢHS, WLC, YC.

38619 —— A Sermon preached to the church and society in Brattle-Street, Boston, Dec. 29, 1799, and occasioned by the completion of a century. . . .
> *Boston: Printed by Young & Minns, State-Street MDCCC.* pp. 18. 8vo.

AAS, BA, BPL, CL, HC, HEH, HSP, JCB, LOC, MHS, NL, NYHS, NYPL, NYSL, UTS, W¹ˢHS, YC.

38620 THACHER, Thomas 1756–1812
A Discourse delivered at Boston, before the Humane Society of the Commonwealth of Massachusetts, June 10th, 1800. . . .
> *Boston: Printed by John and Thomas Fleet, Cornhill, 1800.* pp. 31. sq. 8vo.

Contains an appendix of material relating to the Society, including a list of members.

AAS, AHTS, AML, BA, BM, BPL, CU, HC, HEH, JCB, LOC, MHS, NYAM, NYHS, NYPL, NYSL, UTS, W¹ˢHS.

38621 —— A Discourse, delivered at Peterborough October 23, 1799; at the ordination of the Rev. Elijah Dunbar. . . .
> *Printed by Samuel Preston, Amherst, N. H. 1800.* pp. 37. 8vo.

Appended are "The Charge. By the Rev. Stephen Farrar, of New-Ipswich," "The Right Hand of Fellowship. By Henry Cumings, D. D. of Billerica," and "A Sermon, preached at Peterborough . . . October 27th, 1799. . . . By Thomas Thacher."

AAS, AHTS, BA, HEH, JCB, MHS, NHSL, YC.

38622 —— An Eulogy on George Washington. . . . Delivered at Dedham, February 22, 1800, at the request of the inhabitants of said town. . . .
> *Dedham: Printed by H. Mann. 1800.* pp. 22. 8vo.

AAS, BA, BPL, CL, EI, HC, HEH, JCB, MHS, LOC, NYPL, UTS.

38623 THACHER, Thomas Cushing 1771–1849
An Eulogy on the memory of . . . Washington. . . . Pronounced at the request of the citizens of Lynn, Jan. 13, 1800. . . .
> *Boston: Printed by Manning & Loring, Spring-Lane.* pp. 12. 8vo.

AAS, BA, BPL, HC, HEH, JCB, LOC, MHS, NYHS, NYPL, W¹ˢHS, YC.

38624 [THARP, Peter]
An Elegy. On the death of Capt. Annanias Valentine . . . the 12th of December, 1800. . . . Come all you good people. . . .
> *[Kingston, N. Y., printed by S. Freer?]* Broadside. 4to. AAS.

38625 —— —— By Peter Tharp. . . .
> *Kingston, (Ulster County) Printed by Samuel S. Freer, (Copy Right Secured.)*
Broadside. fol. AAS, BʳU.

38626 THEOBALD, John
Every man his own physician. Being a complete collection of efficacious and approved remedies. . . . Eighth edition.
> *Hartford: Printed by J. Babcock. 1800.* pp. 108. 24mo. AAS, AML, BML.

38627 THOMAS, Eliza —— 1799
A Vision . . . experienced by Miss Eliza Thomas. . . . By William Billings & Thomas Pitnam . . . who received the foregoing from Miss Thomas's own mouth. . . . To which is added, a number of excellent hymns.
> *Printed. [Stonington-Port, by Samuel Trumbull.] 1800.* pp. 15. 16mo.

AAS, NYSL.

38628 THOMAS, Isaiah 1749–1831
Isaiah Thomas's Massachusetts, Connecticut, Rhode Island, Newhampshire & Vermont Almanack . . . for . . . 1801. . . .
> *Printed at Worcester, Massachusetts, by Isaiah Thomas, sold by. him, and by I. Thomas, jun. in Worcester; by Thomas & Andrews, S. Hall, West & Greenleaf, E. Larkin, J. Boyle, W. Spotswood, C. Bingham, and at the Boston Bookstore, in Boston; by Thomas and Thomas, Walpole; by T. C. Cushing, Salem. . . .* pp. [48]. 12mo.

Contains a biographical sketch of Washington.

AAS, BPL, CSL, HEH, LOC, MHS, NEHGS, NYHS, NYPL, RU, W¹ˢHS, WL, YC.

38629 THOMAS, John Chew 1764–1836
Fairland, May 28th, 1800. Dear sir, Believing that it will be agreeable to you to receive some account of the most important business which has been acted upon during the late session of Congress. . . .
[*Philadelphia?*] pp. [2]. fol. LOC.

38630 THOMAS, Robert B[ailey] 1766–1846
No. IX. The Farmer's Almanack . . . for 1801. . . . Containing . . . new, useful, and entertaining matter. . . .
Boston: Printed by Manning & Loring, for John West, proprietor of the copy-right, and. . . . sold also . . . by the author at Sterling, and at various other places. pp. [48].
12mo. AAS, HEH, LOC, MHS, NYPL, NYSL, YC.

38631 THOMAS à Kempis
See Kempis, Thomas à.

38632 THOMAS'S Massachusetts Spy: or, the Worcester Gazette. 1775–1904
Printed at Worcester, (Massachusetts) by Isaiah Thomas, Junior, for Isaiah Thomas and Son. fol. weekly. For 1800: AAS, APS, BA, BM, BPL, LOC, MHS, MSL, NYHS.

38633 THOMPSON, Otis 1776–1859
A Sermon, preached on . . . January 26th, 1800 . . . in Rehoboth, on occasion of the funeral of Capt. Jonathan Bliss. . . .
Providence, printed by B. Wheeler, 1800. pp. 16. 8vo.
AAS, BPL, JCB, NYPL, PPL, RIHS.

38634 THOMSON, James 1700–1748
The Seasons. . . . By James Thomson. With the life of the author, by Dr. Samuel Johnson.
Printed at Wrentham, Massachusetts, by and for Nathaniel Heaton, Jun. also for David Heaton, Providence; Oliver Farnsworth, Newport; Henry Cushing, Providence; Thomas C. Cushing, Salem; Ephraim Goodale, Mendon, &c. &c. 1800. pp. 168 12mo.
AAS, BPL, BⁱU, HEH, JCB, LOC, MSL, NL, NYPL, NYSL, WLC, YC.

38635 THOUGHTS, on the subject of the ensuing election, addressed to the party in the State of New-York, who claim exclusively the appellation of Federalists. . . . April 1, 1800.
[*Albany: Printed by Barber & Southwick.*] Broadside. fol. LOC (PHOTOSTAT).

38636 THREE letters to Abraham Bishop. . . .
See Daggett, David.

38637 TILLIER, Rodolphe
Memoire pour Rodolphe Tillier, Commissaire-Gérant de la Compagnie de New-York.
[*Colophon:*] *De l'Imprimerie de J. C. Parisot* [*New York*]. pp. 18. 8vo.
Caption title. Signed and dated on p. 18. JCB.

38638 —— Translation of a memorial of Rodolphe Tillier's justification of the administration of Castorland, County of Oneida, State of New-York.
Rome: Printed by Thomas Walker, October — 1800. pp. 16. 8vo. LOC, NYPL.

38639 THE TIMES; and District of Columbia Daily Advertiser. 1797–1802
Printed daily, by J. & J. D. Westcott . . . Alexandria. fol. For 1800: [WⁱᴿHS].

38640 THE TIMES, and Political and Commercial Evening Gazette. Oct. 6, 1800 ——
Charleston [*S. C.*]. *published by Cox & Sheppard. . . .* fol. daily.
With the issue of Nov. 17 the title was changed to *The Times, City Gazette & Merchants' Evening Advertiser.* For 1800: CLS.

38641 TO BE PERFORMED AT THE BRATTLE-STREET CHURCH. . . .
See Boston. Massachusetts. Brattle Street Church.

38642 TO BE PERFORMED AT THE OLD-SOUTH. . . .
See Boston. Massachusetts. Old South Church.

38643 TO THE CITIZENS OF BURLINGTON COUNTY. . . .
[Burlington?] pp. 16. 12mo.
A defence of the John Adams administration in reply to the *Address to the Federal Republicans of Burlington County.* LOC.

38644 TO THE CITIZENS OF THE COUNTY OF PHILADELPHIA. . . .
See 36422.

38645 TO THE CITIZENS OF THE UNITED STATES, AND PARTICULARLY TO THE CITIZENS OF NEW-YORK, NEW-JERSEY, DELAWARE AND PENNSYLVANIA, MARYLAND AND NORTH-CAROLINA, ON THE PROPRIETY OF CHOOSING REPUBLICAN MEMBERS TO THEIR STATE LEGISLATURES. . . .
[New York?] pp. 6. 8vo.
Caption title. Signed "A Republican Farmer" and dated "State of New-York, March 8, 1800." LOC.

38646 [TO THE CITIZENS OF VIRGINIA. WE HAD PRESENTED TO YOU, FOR YOUR CONSIDERATION, AT THE NEXT CHOICE OF ELECTORS, A TICKET, WHICH WE THOUGHT UNCENSORABLE. . . . PHILIP NORBONE NICHOLAS, CHAIRMAN. RICHMOND, JULY 7TH, 1800. REPUBLICAN TICKET. . . .
Richmond: Printed by Samuel Pleasants, junior. Broadside.] EVANS.

38647 TO THE DETESTABLE AUTHOR OF A SCURRILOUS HAND-BILL UNDER THE SIGNATURE OF APOLLOS. . . . DIO — CASSIUS. JUNE 9TH, 1800.
[Albany, N. Y.: Barker & Southwick.] Broadside. fol. NYSL, WⁱˢHS.

38648 TO THE ELECTORS OF THE STATE OF NEW YORK. FRIENDS & FELLOW-CITIZENS. A REPRESENTATIVE GOVERNMENT CONFERS THE RIGHT. . . .
Broadside. fol. LOC (PHOTOSTAT).

38649 TO THE ELECTORS OF THE TENTH DISTRICT OF THE STATE OF NEW-YORK FOR REPRESENTATIVE IN CONGRESS. . . . BEGS LEAVE TO RECOMMEND TO YOUR SUFFRAGES WILLIAM STUART, ESQ. OF GENEVA. . . . OTSEGO, APRIL 4, 1800.
Broadside. fol. LOC (PHOTOSTAT).

38650 TO THE FEDERAL ELECTORS OF LANCASTER COUNTY. FRIENDS AND FELLOW-CITIZENS. THE COMMITTEE FOR PROMOTING THE ELECTION OF FEDERAL REPUBLICANS. . . .
[Lancaster?] Broadside. fol. AAS.

38651 TO THE FREEMEN OF RHODE ISLAND. . . .
See Russell, Jonathan.

38652 TO THE FREEMEN OF THE STATE OF RHODE-ISLAND AND PROVIDENCE PLANTATIONS. . . . NEWPORT, AUGUST 19, 1800.
Broadside. fol.
In behalf of Asher Robbins, candidate for the House of Representatives of the United States. LOC.

38653 TO THE HONORABLE GENERAL ASSEMBLY, NOW IN SESSION, AT NEW HAVEN. THE PRESENT CLAIMANTS, AND PROPRIETORS OF THE LANDS PURCHASED OF THIS STATE, COMMONLY CALLED THE GORE. . . .
[Hartford.] pp. [3]. fol.
"Dated at Hartford, October 10th, 1800." BM, YC.

38654   TO THE HONORABLE THE SENATE AND HOUSE OF REPRESENTATIVES OF THE UNITED STATES. . . . THE
        MEMORIAL AND PETITION OF THE SUBSCRIBERS, MERCHANTS. . . .
             Broadside.   8vo.
        A petition relating to the French spoliation claims.   EI, LOC.

38655   TO THE PEOPLE OF CECIL. No. I [–III]. . . .
             [*Wilmington, printed at the Franklin Press, by J. Wilson.*]   8vo.
        Three Republican pamphlets of the campaign of 1800, dated at Elkton, Sept. 3, 16, 26, 1800.
                                                                                            LOC.

38656   TO THE PEOPLE OF NEW-JERSEY. FRIENDS, COUNTRYMEN AND FELLOW CITIZENS. . . . SIGNED BY
        ORDER, JOSEPH BLOOMFIELD, CHAIRMAN. . . . SEPT. 30, 1800. . . .
             Broadside.   fol.   HSP, NJHS.

38657   [TO THE PEOPLE OF THE STATE OF NEW-YORK. . . .
             [*Albany?*]   pp. 8.   8vo.
        A denunciation of the administration on President Adams signed "A citizen of Albany."]
                                                                                          EVANS.

38658   TO THE PUBLIC. FELLOW-CITIZENS, OF ALL THE EXTRAORDINARY PERFORMANCES I EVER BEHELD, THE
        LATE HAND-BILL, SIGNED BY EIGHT MEMBERS OF OUR HOUSE OF REPRESENTATIVES, IS THE MOST
        EXTRAORDINARY. . . . NATCHEZ, NOVEMBER 15TH, 1809 [*i. e.*, 1800]. . . .
             Broadside.   fol.   LOC, MHS.

38659   TO THE PUBLIC. THE UNDERSIGNED HAVING OBSERVED IN GREEN'S IMPARTIAL OBSERVER, OF THE
        1ST INST. AN ANONYMOUS PUBLICATION, BY A PERSON STYLING HIMSELF "THE FRIEND OF THE
        PEOPLE". . . . SATURDAY NOV. 8, 1800. . . .
             [*Natchez:*] *From the office of J. Green.*   Broadside.   fol.   LOC.

38660   TO THE REPUBLICAN CITIZENS OF THE STATE OF PENNSYLVANIA. LANCASTER, SEPT. 17, 1800.
        FELLOW-CITIZENS, THE VERY INTERESTING POSTURE OF OUR PUBLIC AFFAIRS. . . .
             [*Lancaster: Printed by W. & R. Dickson.*]   pp. [16].   8vo.
        Issued as a Supplement to *The Intelligencer* for September 24, 1800.   HSP, LCP, LOC, NYPL.

38661   TOLMAN, THOMAS   1756–1842
             AN ORATION, ON THE DEATH OF GEN. GEORGE WASHINGTON; DELIVERED AT DANVILLE, BEFORE
        HARMONY LODGE OF FREE MASONS . . . THE 26TH DAY OF FEBRUARY, A. D. 1800. . . .
             Peacham, Vermont, Printed by Farley & Goss. 1800.   pp. 14.   8vo.
                                                                           HEH, PFM, VᵗU.

38662   TOMB, SAMUEL   1766–1832
             AN ORATION ON . . . WASHINGTON; PRONOUNCED FEB. 22, 1800; IN NEWBURY SECOND PARISH. . . .
        TO WHICH ARE ANNEXED, TWO ODES AND AN ACROSTIC . . . BY THE SAME HAND. . . .
             Printed at Newburyport by Edmund M. Blunt — 1800.   pp. 17, [3].   8vo.
                  AAS, BA, BPL, HC, HEH, HSP, JCB, LOC, MHS, NYHS, NYPL, NYSL, VᵃU, YC.

38663   A TOUCHSTONE FOR THE LEADING PARTYMEN IN THE UNITED STATES. DEDICATED TO MR. SEDGWICK.
             pp. 8.   8vo.
        Caption title. Signed "Washington."   HC, LOC.

38664   THE TRAVELLERS; EXHIBITING A VARIETY OF CHARACTERS, MOUNTED UPON CURIOUS AND WONDERFUL
        ANIMALS.
             New-York: Printed by W. Durell, for Thomas Kirk. 1800.   pp. 31, illus.   32mo.
                                                                                          AAS.

38665   TREE OF LIBERTY.   AUG. 16, 1800–1810
             Pittsburgh: Printed and published by John Israel.   fol.   weekly.
                       FOR 1800: CARNEGIE LIBRARY OF ALLEGHENY, PITTSBURGH.

38666 TRENT, Joseph, *of Richmond, Va.*
An Inquiry into the effects of light in respiration . . . submitted . . . to the . . . Medical Faculty of the University of Pennsylvania, on the thirty-first of May 1800. For the degree of doctor of medicine. . . .
Philadelphia: Printed by Way & Groff, no. 48, North Third-Street. 1800. pp. 38.
8vo. AAS, AML, BML, LCP, LOC, NYAM, NYPL, UOP, YC.

38667 TRENTON. New Jersey.
Order of the funeral procession, to be had at Trenton . . . the 14th day of January, 1800, in commemoration of . . . Washington. . . .
Broadside. fol. NJHS.

38668 —— Verses, composed and sung at Trenton, on the delivering of the funeral eulogium in honor of the memory of General George Washington.
[Trenton: Printed by Gershom Craft.] Broadside. 4to.
There is a dangerously good lithographic facsimile. HEH.

38669 THE TRIAL of the witnesses of the resurrection of Jesus. . . .
See Sherlock, Thomas, 1678–1761.

38670 A TRIBUTE to the memory of Catherine Berrenger, who fell a victim of death on the 4th day of November . . . 1800, by swallowing a potion of arsenic, supposed to be administered to her by John Benner . . . who has been confined in the gaol of Poughkeepsee, Dutchess County. . . .
Broadside. fol. AAS.

38671 A TRIBUTE to Washington. . . .
See Lovett, John.

38672 TRIPP, John 1761–1847
The Bible the word of God. A treatise on the truth and divinity of the Sacred Scripture. . . .
Boston: Printed by J. Bumstead. . . . 1800. pp. 62. 8vo. BPL, SCBHC.

38673 THE TRIUMPHANT Christian. . . . Exemplified in the last experiences and dying words of a private gentleman. The seventh edition.
London: Printed. Hartford: reprinted by J. Babcock. 1800. pp. 47. 12mo.
AAS, CHS, YC.

38674 TROY. New York.
Laws and catalogue of the Troy Library. Incorporated January 15, 1800.
Troy: Printed by Robert Moffitt & Co. For the trustees. 1800. [Colophon:] O. Penniman & Co. Printers. pp. 20. 12mo. BA.

38675 THE TRUE American. 1798–1800
Leesburg, (Virginia) published by Patrick M'Intyre. fol. weekly.
For 1800: [LOC].

38676 THE TRUE American and Commercial Advertiser. 1798–1818
[Philadelphia: Published] By Samuel F. Bradford. . . . fol. daily.
For 1800: [AAS], [HC], HSP.

38677 —— An Elegiac poem on the death of . . . Washington. . . .
See 37080.

38678 [TRUE Republican. 1800–1803
Norristown: Published by Wilson & Palm. fol. weekly.]
For 1800: no copy known.

38679 TRUMBULL, BENJAMIN   1735–1820
THE MAJESTY AND MORTALITY. . . . A FUNERAL DISCOURSE, DELIVERED AT NORTH-HAVEN, DECEMBER 29, 1799. ON THE DEATH OF . . . WASHINGTON. . . .
New Haven: Printed by Read & Morse. 1800.   pp. 31, portrait.   8vo.
Probably sold both with and without the portrait, which was engraved by Amos Doolittle after Joseph Wright.
AAS, BA, BPL, B^rU, CHS, CL, HC, HEH, JCB, LOC, MHS, NL, NYHS, NYPL, NYSL, UTS, WLC, YC.

38680 TUCKERMAN, JOSEPH   1778–1840
A FUNERAL ORATION. OCCASIONED BY THE DEATH OF . . . WASHINGTON. WRITTEN AT THE REQUEST OF THE BOSTON MECHANIC ASSOCIATION, AND DELIVERED BEFORE THEM, ON THE 22D OF FEB. 1800. . . .
Boston: Printed by Manning & Loring.   pp. 24.   8vo.
AAS, BA, BM, BPL, B^rU, CU, HC, HEH, HSP, JCB, LOC, MHS, NYHS, NYPL, NYSL, W^i^sHS, YC.

38681 TUFTS, COTTON   1731–1815
AN ORATION, IN HONOUR . . . OF . . . WASHINGTON . . . DELIVERED BEFORE THE INHABITANTS OF THE TOWN OF WEYMOUTH . . . ON THE 22D DAY OF FEBRUARY, 1800. . . .
Printed by Samuel Hall, no. 53, Cornhill, Boston. 1800.   pp. 19.   8vo.
AAS, BA, BPL, HC, HEH, JCB, LOC, MHS, NYHS, NYPL, NYSL.

38682 TURFORD, HUGH   —— 1713
THE GROUNDS OF A HOLY LIFE. . . . TO WHICH IS ADDED, PAUL'S SPEECH TO THE BISHOP OF CRETIA. AS ALSO, A TRUE TOUCHSTONE OR TRIAL OF CHRISTIANITY. . . . THE TWELFTH EDITION.
Hartford: Printed by J. Babcock. 1800.   pp. 120.   24mo.
Paul's Speech has a separate title-page but is paged continuously.   AAS, CHS, YC.

38683 TYLER, JOHN   1742–1823
AN EULOGY ON THE LIFE OF GEN. GEORGE WASHINGTON. . . . DELIVERED BEFORE . . . THE PARISH OF CHELSEA, IN NORWICH, ON THE 22D OF FEB. 1800. . . .
Norwich: Printed by Thomas Hubbard. 1800.   pp. 32.   8vo.
AAS, BM, CHS, HEH, LOC, NYPL, YC.

38684 TYLER, ROYALL   1757–1826
AN ORATION, PRONOUNCED AT BENNINGTON, VERMONT, ON THE 22D FEBRUARY, 1800. IN COMMEMORATION OF THE DEATH OF GENERAL GEORGE WASHINGTON. . . .
Walpole, Newhampshire, printed for Thomas & Thomas, by David Carlisle. 1800.
pp. 16.   4to.
AAS, HEH.

38685 ULSTER COUNTY GAZETTE.   1798–1803
Published at Kingston [N. Y.], (Ulster County) by Samuel Freer and Son.   weekly.
fol.   FOR 1800: [AAS], [LOC].

38686 UNION BRIGADE.
PROCEEDINGS OF THE UNION BRIGADE . . . ON THE DEATH OF GENERAL WASHINGTON. TOGETHER WITH THE REV. MR. AUSTIN'S PRAYER, AND CAPT. SAMUEL WHITE'S ORATION.
[New York] From [John] Lang's Press. 1800.   pp. 36.   8vo.
AAS, BA, HEH, M^dHS, MHS, NYHS, NYPL, PPL.

38687 UNITED STATES.
ABSTRACT OF CASES TRANSMITTED TO THE SECRETARY OF THE TREASURY PURSUANT TO THE SIXTH SECTION OF THE ACT ENTITLED "AN ACT FURTHER TO SUSPEND THE COMMERCIAL INTERCOURSE. . . ."
[Philadelphia.]   pp. [2], 7 folded plates.   8vo.   LCP, NL, NYSL.

38688 —— ACCOMPANYING THE REPORT OF THE COMMITTEE OF CLAIMS, ON THE PETITION OF OLIVER POLLOCK. MADE THE 18TH OF APRIL, 1800.
[Philadelphia.]   pp. 6.   8vo.   AAS, BA, LOC, NYPL.

38689 —— An Account of the receipts & expenditures of the United States, for the year 1799. . . .
    Washington, Territory of Columbia: Printed and published by order of the House of Representatives.   pp. [4], 7 folded tables, [11]–74, folded table, [10], 2 folded tables. fol.   AAS.

38690 —— An Account of the receipts and expenditures of the United States, for the year 1799. . . . Published by order of the House. . . .
    City of Washington: Printed by Way and Groff, near the Post-Office.   pp. 8, [17]–74, 2 folded tables, [8], 2 folded tables.   fol.   AAS.

38691 —— Accounts of the Treasurer of the United States, of his receipts and expenditures of the public monies, for the quarter ending the 30th of June last. . . . 8th December, 1800. . . . Published by order of the House. . . .
    [*Washington.*]   pp. 143.   8vo.   AAS, BA, LOC, NYPL.

38692 —— An Act, for the better government of the Navy of the United States.
    [*Philadelphia?*]   pp. 23.   12mo.   AAS.

38693 —— An Act further to suspend the commercial intercourse between the United States and France. . . . John Adams. Febr. 27, 1800.
    [*Philadelphia.*]   pp. [3].   fol.   LOC.

38694 —— An Act to amend an Act, intituled, An Act for appointing electors to choose a president and vice-president of the United States. Passed, January 20th, 1800.
    [*Philadelphia.*]   pp. 2.   fol.   LOC.

38695 —— An Act to amend the Act, intituled "An Act providing for the sale of the lands of the United States, in the Territory north-west of the Ohio". . . . May 10, A. D. 1800. . . .
    [*Philadelphia.*]   Broadside.   fol.   W¹·HS.

38696 —— An Act to enlarge the powers of surveyors of the Revenue. . . . [Approved, May 13, A. D. 1800.]
    [*Philadelphia.*]   pp. 4.   8vo.   LOC (PHOTOSTAT).

38697 —— An Act to establish an uniform system of bankruptcy throughout the United States. Enacted April 4, 1800.
    Philadelphia: Printed by H. Maxwell, for A. Dickins, bookseller. . . . 1800.   pp. 33. 8vo.   AAS, BA, LOC, NYHS.

38698 —— An Act to suspend in part, an Act, entitled "An Act to augment the army of the United States. . . ." Passed the House . . . January 24th, 1800.
    [*Philadelphia.*]   Broadside.   fol.   LOC.

38699 —— Acts passed at the first session of the sixth Congress of the United States . . . begun . . . the second of December . . . M,DCC, XCIX.
    Philadelphia: Printed by Richard Folwell.   pp. 352, iv, [22].   8vo.
    This printing has been found only as volume V of *The Laws of the United States of America*, Washington City, Samuel Harrison Smith, 1801.   AAS, NYHS, PʳU.

38700 —— —— —— [*Philadelphia: Printed by Samuel Harrison Smith.*]   pp. 223, vii.   8vo.
                                                                      AAS, HEH, JCB, MHS, VᵃU.

38701 —— —— —— *Halifax: Printed by A. Hodge.*   pp. 28.   fol.
    This edition was issued as a supplement to the *North-Carolina Journal*, no. 409.
                                                                                      AAS, HC.

38702 —— —— —— *Portland, A. D. 1800. Printed by authority, by Elezer A. Jenks. Printer of the laws of the United States, for the District of Maine.*   pp. 223, vii.   8vo.   AAS.

38703 —— —— —— *Richmond: Printed by Meriwether Jones. . . . M.DCCC.* pp. 106, [2]. fol.

V*U.

38704 —— —— —— [*Rutland: Printed by Samuel Williams. 1800.* pp. 223, vii. 8vo.] GILMAN.

38705 —— AN ADDRESS AND REMONSTRANCE OF THE LEGISLATURE OF THE STATE OF GEORGIA. [SENATE DOCUMENT, DEC. 31, 1800.]
[*Washington?*] pp. 18. 8vo. AAS, LOC.

38706 —— AMENDMENT, PROPOSED BY MR. BINGHAM, TO THE BILL, PRESCRIBING THE MODE OF DECIDING DISPUTED ELECTIONS OF PRESIDENT AND VICE PRESIDENT OF THE UNITED STATES. [IN THE SENATE . . . FEBRUARY 28TH, 1800.]
[*Philadelphia.*] pp. 4. 8vo. AAS.

38707 —— AMENDMENTS, &c PROPOSED BY THE HOUSE OF REPRESENTATIVES TO THE AMENDMENTS OF THE SENATE, TO THE BILL, ENTITLED "AN ACT SUPPLEMENTAL TO THE ACT, ENTITLED "AN ACT FOR . . . THE MISSISSIPPI TERRITORY."" PRINTED BY ORDER OF THE SENATE . . . APRIL 28TH, 1800.
[*Philadelphia.*] pp. 4. 8vo. LOC.

38708 —— AMENDMENTS OF THE SENATE, TO THE BILL ENTITLED, "AN ACT SUPPLEMENTAL TO THE ACT FOR AN AMICABLE SETTLEMENT OF THE LIMITS WITH THE STATE OF GEORGIA, AND AUTHORIZING THE ESTABLISHMENT OF A GOVERNMENT IN THE MISSISSIPPI TERRITORY." 17TH. APRIL 1800. . . .
[*Philadelphia.*] pp. 4. 8vo. AAS, BA, LOC, NYPL.

38709 —— AMENDMENTS OF THE SENATE TO THE BILL ENTITLED, "AN ACT TO AMEND THE ACT ENTITLED, AN ACT PROVIDING FOR THE SALE OF LANDS . . . NORTHWEST OF THE OHIO. . . ." 23D APRIL, 1800.
[*Philadelphia.*] pp. 8. 8vo. BA, LOC, NYPL.

38710 —— AMENDMENTS OF THE SENATE TO THE BILL INTITULED "AN ACT IN ADDITION TO THE ACT, INTITLED 'AN ACT REGULATING THE GRANTS OF LAND APPROPRIATED FOR MILITARY SERVICES, AND FOR THE SOCIETY OF THE UNITED BRETHREN FOR PROPAGATING THE GOSPEL AMONG THE HEATHEN.'" 21ST FEBRUARY, 1800. . . . (PUBLISHED BY ORDER OF THE HOUSE. . . .)
[*Philadelphia.*] pp. 6. 8vo. AAS.

38711 —— AMENDMENTS OF THE SENATE TO THE BILL, INTITULED "AN ACT PROVIDING FOR SALVAGE IN CASES OF RE-CAPTURE." 31ST JANUARY, 1800. . . . (PUBLISHED BY ORDER OF THE HOUSE. . . .)
[*Philadelphia.*] pp. 6. 8vo. AAS, WLC.

38712 —— AMENDMENTS OF THE SENATE TO THE BILL INTITULED, AN ACT TO DIVIDE THE TERRITORY OF THE UNITED STATES, NORTH-WEST OF THE OHIO, INTO TWO SEPARATE GOVERNMENTS. 22D. APRIL, 1800. . . .
[*Philadelphia.*] pp. 4. 8vo. AAS.

38713 —— AMENDMENTS PROPOSED TO THE BILL, ENTITLED "AN ACT IN ADDITION TO THE ACT, ENTITLED, 'AN ACT REGULATING THE GRANTS OF LAND APPROPRIATED FOR MILITARY SERVICES, AND FOR THE SOCIETY OF THE UNITED BRETHREN FOR PROPAGATING THE GOSPEL AMONG THE HEATHEN.'" [IN SENATE, FEBRUARY 20TH, 1800.]
[*Philadelphia.*] pp. 4. 8vo. AAS, LOC.

38714 —— [ARTICLES OF AGREEMENT OF THE CONVENTION OF AMITY AND COMMERCE BETWEEN THE UNITED STATES AND FRANCE.
New York: December 20, 1800. Broadside. fol.] EVANS.

38715 —— A BILL TO ESTABLISH AN UNIFORM MODE OF DRAWING JURORS BY LOT, IN ALL THE COURTS OF THE UNITED STATES. . . . [MARCH 11TH, 1800.]
[*Philadelphia.*] pp. 10. 8vo. AAS.

38716 —— A BILL TO ESTABLISH AN UNIFORM SYSTEM OF BANKRUPTCY THROUGHOUT THE UNITED STATES. 6TH JANUARY, 1800. . . . [PUBLISHED BY ORDER OF THE HOUSE. . . .)
[*Philadelphia.*]   pp. 35.   8vo.   AAS, LOC.

38717 —— —— —— *Baltimore: Printed for Campbell Conrad & Co. . . . 1800.*   pp. 32.   8vo.   APS.

38718 —— A BILL TO ESTABLISH AN UNIFORM SYSTEM OF BANKRUPTCY THROUGHOUT THE UNITED STATES. 30TH JANUARY, 1800. . . . (PUBLISHED BY ORDER OF THE HOUSE. . . .)
[*Philadelphia: J. Gales, printer.*]   pp. 34, 2.   8vo.
The last leaf contains Amendments Proposed by Mr. Otis. Probably only this leaf, which has Gales' imprint, was set by him, the rest of the document being typical of the press of William Ross.   AAS, LOC.

38719 —— A BILL TO ESTABLISH AN UNIFORM SYSTEM OF BANKRUPTCY THROUGHOUT THE UNITED STATES. PRINTED BY ORDER OF THE SENATE . . . 11TH MARCH, 1800.
[*Philadelphia.*]   pp. 39.   8vo.   AAS, LOC.

38720 —— A BILL TO PROVIDE FOR THE BETTER ESTABLISHMENT & REGULATION OF THE COURTS OF THE UNITED STATES. 11TH MARCH, 1800. . . . (PUBLISHED BY ORDER OF THE HOUSE. . . .)
[*Philadelphia.*]   pp. 44.   8vo.   AAS, LOC.

38721 —— A BILL TO PROVIDE FOR THE MORE CONVENIENT ORGANIZATION OF THE COURTS OF THE UNITED STATES. 31ST MARCH, 1800, PRESENTED. 1ST APRIL, 1800, READ. . . . (PUBLISHED BY ORDER OF THE HOUSE. . . .)
[*Philadelphia.*]   pp. 40.   8vo.   AAS, LOC.

38722 —— A BRIEF STATEMENT OF OPINIONS. . . .
See Fitzsimmons, Thomas.

38723 —— CIRCUIT COURT OF THE UNITED STATES, MIDDLE CIRCUIT OF THE NEW-JERSEY DISTRICT. THE UNITED STATES (A) WILLIAM BRIGSTOCK. . . . [MARCH 1ST, 1800.]
[*Trenton?*]   pp. 8, [7].   8vo.
Caption title.   AAS, LOC, NYPL, PrU.

38724 —— THE COMMITTEE TO WHOM WAS REFERRED THE BILL AUTHORIZING THE ACCEPTANCE, FROM THE STATE OF CONNECTICUT, OF A CESSION OF THE JURISDICTION OF TERRITORY WEST OF PENNSYLVANIA. . . . REPORT. . . .
[*Philadelphia?*]   pp. [3]–24.   8vo.
The two reported copies of this pamphlet begin with page [3] which has the signature mark B, but they otherwise give no evidence of missing pages.   AAS, LOC.

38725 —— [THE COMMITTEE, TO WHOM WAS REFERRED THE REPORT OF THE SECRETARY OF STATE, TO WHOM WAS REFERRED THE MEMORIAL OF STEPHEN SAYRE, REPORT. . . .
[*Philadelphia?*]   pp. 8, 6.   fol.]   EVANS.

38726 —— CONVENTION, BETWEEN THE FRENCH REPUBLIC AND THE UNITED STATES OF AMERICA; SIGNED AT PARIS, SEPTEMBER 3D, 1800. . . .
[*Salem:*] *Printed and sold by T. C. Cushing. 1800.*   pp. 16.   EI.

38727 —— DEPARTMENT OF STATE. PHILADELPHIA, APRIL 30, 1800. SIR, I INCLOSE "AN ACT PROVIDING FOR THE SECOND CENSUS. . . ."
[*Philadelphia.*]   pp. 15.   8vo.   AAS.

38728 —— DIVISION ORDERS. . . . GENERAL ORDERS. . . . AFTER DIVISION ORDERS. . . . REGIMENTAL ORDERS. . . . JANUARY, 1800. CHARLES COTESWORTH PINCKNEY, MAJOR GENERAL. UNITED STATES. SOUTHERN DIVISION.
[*Richmond.*]   pp. [3].   fol.   LOC.

38729 —— Division orders. January 14, 1800. After the recruits have been instructed. . . . W. Bentley, Lieut. Co. Comdt. 7th U. S. Regt.
pp. [3]. 4to. LOC.

38730 —— 11th February, 1800. Read the first and second time, and committed to a committee of the whole House. . . . A Bill to allow a drawback of duties on goods exported to New-Orleans. . . .
[*Philadelphia.*] Broadside. fol. LOC.

38731 —— Extracts of letters received by J. Jackson, Supervisor of Massachusetts District, from the Treasury Department of the United States, on subjects relative to the Direct Tax. . . .
[*Boston.*] pp. 3. fol. AAS.

38732 —— 4th February, 1800. Read the first and second time, and committed to a committee. . . . A Bill to continue in force an Act concerning certain fisheries. . . .
[*Philadelphia?*] pp. 2. fol. LOC.

38733 —— Further report, in part, of the committee of privileges, on the form of proceedings in the case of William Duane. Printed by order of the Senate. . . . March 25th, 1800.
[*Philadelphia.*] pp. 4. 8vo. AAS, LOC.

38734 —— Further Report, (in part) — of the committee of revisal and unfinished business. . . . 30th December, 1800. . . . Published by order of the House. . . .
[*Washington.*] pp. 4. 8vo. AAS, LOC.

38735 —— Further Report, (in part) — of the committee, to whom was re-committed on the 10th instant, the Bill directing the erection of a mausoleum to George Washington. . . . 19th December, 1800. . . . Published by order of the House. . . .
[*Washington.*] pp. [3]. 8vo. AAS, BPL, BrU, LOC.

38736 —— Further Report, of the committee of revisal and unfinished business. 19th December, 1800. . . . Published by order of the House. . . .
[*Washington.*] pp. [3]. 8vo. AAS, LOC.

38737 —— In Senate of the United States. A Bill, to repeal an Act, entitled, "An Act for the punishment of certain crimes. . . ."
[*Washington:*] *Duane, printer.* Broadside. fol. LOC.

38738 —— In Senate of the United States, January 16th, 1800. The committee, to whom was referred the Bill, entitled, "An Act providing for salvage in cases of recapture". . . .
[*Philadelphia.*] pp. 3. 8vo. AAS, LOC.

38739 —— In Senate of the United States, January 23d, 1800. Ordered, That the Memorial of the Connecticut Academy of Arts and Sciences; also, the Memorial of the American Philosophical Society . . . be printed. . . .
[*Philadelphia.*] pp. 7. 8vo. AAS, LOC, NYPL, WLC.

38740 —— In Senate of the United States, February 7th, 1800. The committee to whom was referred the Bill, passed by the House of Representatives, entitled, "An Act to suspend, in part, an Act, entitled An Act to augment the army". . . . Report. . . .
Broadside. 8vo. NYHS.

38741 —— In Senate of the United States, February 26th, 1800. A motion was made that . . . the committee of privileges be . . . directed to enquire, who is the editor of . . . the General Advertiser, or Aurora. . . .
[*Philadelphia.*] Broadside. 8vo. LOC, NYPL.

38742 —— In Senate of the United States, February 26th, 1800. The following Motion was made, to wit, Whereas the United States, by Act of cession from the State of North-Carolina. . . .
[*Philadelphia*.] pp. [1]. 8vo. AAS, LOC.

38743 —— In Senate of the United States, March 5th, 1800. The committee, to whom was referred the Bill, from the House of Representatives, declaring the assent of Congress to certain Acts of the States of Maryland and Georgia. . . .
[*Philadelphia*.] pp. [1]. 8vo. AAS.

38744 —— In Senate of the United States, March 6th, 1800. Resolved, that the committee of privileges be . . . directed to consider . . . what measures it will be proper for the Senate to adopt, in relation to a publication in . . . the General Advertiser or Aurora. . . .
[*Philadelphia*.] Broadside. 8vo. LOC.

38745 —— In Senate of the United States, March 14th, 1800. The committee, to whom was referred the message of the President of the United States, of the 8th day of January 1800. . . .
[*Philadelphia*.] pp. 7. 8vo. AAS, LOC.

38746 —— In Senate of the United States, April 29th, 1800. A Motion was made as follows: That a committee be appointed to enquire into . . . the expenditure of public money. . . . Printed by order of the Senate. . . .
[*Philadelphia*.] Broadside. 8vo. LOC.

38747 —— In Senate of the United States, May 8th, 1800. The joint committee of both Houses, appointed the 19th December ult. on the receipt of the intelligence of the death of General George Washington. . . . Printed by order of the Senate. . . .
[*Philadelphia*.] Broadside. 8vo. AAS, HEH, NL.

38748 —— Journal of the House of Representatives of the United States, at the first session of the sixth Congress. . . .
Philadelphia: Printed by W. Ross, in Locust-Street. . . . pp. 446, [32]. 8vo.
AAS, BA, LOC, NYPL.

38749 —— Journal of the Senate of the United States of America, being the first session of the sixth Congress. . . .
Philadelphia: Printed by John Ward Fenno, no. 119, Chestnut-Street. 1799 [*1800*].
pp. 336, [2], xx. 8vo. AAS, BA, BPL, B'U, CSL, LOC, MHS, NYSL, WLC.

38750 —— Journals of Congress: containing their proceedings from September 5, 1774, to [August, 1784]. . . . Volume I [–IX].
From Folwell's press. Philadelphia. 1800. 9 vols. pp. 289, [12]; 480, [22]; 468, [16]; 537, [42]; 349, [34]; 176, [22]; 396, [36]; 337, [16]; 227, [11], 29. 8vo.
AAS, APS, BPL, B'U, HC, JCB, MSL, NJSL, NYPL, NYSL, UOC, UOP, V'U, WLC.

38751 —— A Law to establish an uniform system of bankruptcy throughout the United States.
Newport: Printed by Henry Barber.
This is the Act signed on April 4, 1800. Newspaper advertisements suggest that there were printings in other towns, but no copies of these imprints have been found. RIHS.

38752 —— Letter and Report of the Secretary of the Navy, Navy Department, 20th. March 1800. . . .
[*Philadelphia*.] pp. 8. 8vo. AAS, BA, HEH, LOC, NYPL, NYSL.

38753 —— Letter from Arthur St. Clair, Governor of the North-western Territory, on the subject of a division of the said Territory; and the Petition of George Tevebaugh and others. . . . Read the 14th. March 1800. . . . Printed by order of the House. . . .
Philadelphia: Printed by Zachariah Poulson, junior, no. 106, Chestnut-street. 1800.
pp. 8. 8vo. AAS, BA, CU, HSP, JCB, LOC, NYPL, NYSL, P'U, WLC, YC.

38754 —— Letter from Mr. Hornblower to Mr. Kitchell, on the subject of Schuyler's copper mine, in New-Jersey. April 18th, 1800. Printed by order of the House. . . .
[*Philadelphia.*]   pp. 4.   8vo.   AAS, LOC, NYPL.

38755 —— Letter from the Secretary at War, accompanying a Report exhibiting the expenses of the national armory at Springfield, Massachusetts. 7th January, 1800. . . . (Published by order of the House. . . .)
[*Philadelphia.*]   pp. 8.   8vo.   AAS, BA, LOC, NL, NYPL, NYSL.

38756 —— Letter from the Secretary of State, inclosing abstracts of all the returns made to him by the collectors of the different ports, of registered seamen, and of impressed seamen. . . . 12th December, 1800. . . . Published by order of the House. . . .
[*Washington.*]   pp. 16 [i.e. 15], folded table.   8vo.   AAS, BA, LOC, NYPL.

38757 —— Letter from the Secretary of State, inclosing his Report, made in pursuance of a resolution of the House of Representatives of the twenty-eighth ultimo. 1st April, 1800. . . . (Published by order of the House. . . .)
[*Philadelphia.*]   pp. 6.   8vo.   AAS, LOC, NYPL.

38758 —— Letter from the Secretary of the Navy, transmitting a Report of the commissioners of the fund for Navy pensions. . . . 2d December, 1800. . . . Published by order of the House. . . .
[*Washington.*]   pp. 6.   8vo.   AAS, BA, LOC, NYPL, YC.

38759 —— Letter from the Secretary of the Treasury, accompanied with a Report and estimates of the sums necessary to be appropriated for the year 1801: also, a statement of the receipts and expenditures . . . for one year. . . . 11th December, 1800. . . . Published by order of the House. . . .
[*Washington.*]   pp. [1], 99.   8vo.   AAS, BA, LOC, NYSL.

38760 —— Letter from the Secretary of the Treasury, accompanying a Report of the commissioner of the revenue. . . . December 22, 1800. . . . —— Published by order of the House. . . .
[*Washington.*]   pp. [4], 9 folded tables, [8].   fol.   AAS, BA, NYPL, NYSL, YC.

38761 —— Letter from the Secretary of the Treasury, accompanying copies of two letters from the commissioners of the City of Washington. . . . 12th December, 1800. . . . Published by order of the House. . . .
[*Washington.*]   pp. 16.   8vo.
Includes four folded tables numbered as pages.   AAS, LOC.

38762 —— Letter from the Secretary of the Treasury accompanying his Report on the Petition of Benjamin Wells. . . . 2nd. April, 1800. . . .
[*Philadelphia.*]   pp. 21.   8vo.   AAS, NYPL.

38763 —— Letter from the Secretary of the Treasury, accompanying his Reports on the Memorial of David Jones, and the Petitions of Obadiah Scott, and of George Gilbert and Jacob Gilbert. 25th March, 1800. . . . (Published by order of the House. . . .)
[*Philadelphia.*]   pp. 13.   8vo.   AAS, BA, BPL, JCB, LOC, NYPL, NYSL, YC.

38764 —— Letter from the Secretary of the Treasury, to the chairman of the committee, of ways and means, transmitting to him a letter from the commissioners of the valuation of houses and lands in the State of New-York. 10th April, 1800. . . . (Published by order of the House. . . .)
[*Philadelphia: 1800.*]   pp. 7.   8vo.   AAS, BA, JCB, LOC, NYPL, NYSL.

38765 —— Letter from the Secretary of the Treasury, transmitting a Letter from the Comptroller, accompanied with an Abstract of the compensations of the officers of the customs, for the year 1799. 10th March, 1800. . . . Printed by order of the House. . . .
[*Philadelphia.*]   pp. [4], 6 folded tables, [11]–17.   8vo.   AAS, JCB, LOC, NYSL.

38766 —— Letter from the Secretary of the Treasury, transmitting a Letter from the Comptroller of the Treasury, accompanied with sundry statements, prepared in obedience to the Act, entitled "An Act establishing a mint". . . . 25th April, 1800. . . . Printed by order of the House. . . .
[*Philadelphia.*] pp. [4], 3 folded tables, [2], 4 folded tables, [2], 3 folded tables. 8vo. AAS, BA, LOC, NYPL, YC.

38767 —— Letter from the Secretary of the Treasury, transmitting a Report, with two statements, relating to the internal revenue. . . . 5th February, 1800. . . . Printed by order of the House. . . .
[*Philadelphia.*] pp. 8, 8 folded tables, 25–30, 1 table. AAS, BA, LOC, NYPL, NYSL.

38768 —— Letter from the Secretary of the Treasury, transmitting a statement exhibiting the amount of duty on salt. . . . Published by order of the Senate . . . April 3d, 1800.
[*Philadelphia.*] pp. [3], 1 folded table. 8vo. AAS, BA, JCB, LOC, NL, NYPL, NYSL.

38769 —— Letter from the Secretary of the Treasury, transmitting a statement, exhibiting the tonnage of the shipping of the United States. . . . April 12th, 1800. . . . (Published by order of the House. . . .)
[*Philadelphia.*] pp. [3], folded table. fol. AAS, BA, LOC, NYHS, NYPL.

38770 —— Letter from the Secretary of the Treasury, transmitting a statement of goods, wares and merchandize exported. . . . February 10th. 1800. . . . Printed by order of the House. . . .
Philadelphia: Printed by Zachariah Poulson, Junior. no. 106, Chestnut-street. 1800.
pp. [3], folded plate. AAS, BA, HEH, LOC, NL, NYPL, NYSL, PPL.

38771 —— Letter from the Secretary of the Treasury, transmitting two statements, exhibiting the amount of duties and drawbacks on goods, wares and merchandize imported. . . . February 10th. 1800. . . . Printed by order of the House. . . .
Philadelphia: Printed by Zachariah Poulson, Junior. no. 106, Chestnut-street. 1800.
pp. [3], 2 folded tables. 8vo. AAS, BA, HEH, JCB, LOC, NL, NYPL, NYSL.

38772 —— Letter from the Secretary of the Treasury transmitting two statements; one exhibiting the value or quantities of the goods, wares and merchandize, imported. . . . 3d. March, 1800. . . . Printed by order of the House. . . .
— *Philadelphia: — Printed by Zachariah Poulson, Junior. no. 106, Chestnut-street.* . . .
March 12, 1800. pp. [4], 2 folded tables. fol.
AAS, BA, JCB, LOC, NYHS, NYPL, NYSL, UOC, WLC.

38773 —— Letter from the Secretary of War, accompanying his Report on the Petition of John Armstrong. . . . 21st March, 1800. . . . Printed by order of the House. . . .
[*Philadelphia.*] pp. 8. 8vo. AAS, JCB, LOC, NYPL, NYSL.

38774 —— Letter from the Secretary of War, accompanying his Report on the Petitions of William Milton, and others. . . . 14th March, 1800. . . . Printed by order of the House. . . .
[*Philadelphia.*] pp. 41. 8vo. AAS, DᵉRGL, JCB, LOC, NYSL.

38775 —— Letter from the Secretary of War, and the Secretary and Comptroller of the Treasury, transmitting a Report on the claim of Seth Harding. . . . 17th February, 1800. . . .
(Published by order of the House. . . .)
[*Philadelphia.*] pp. 7. 8vo. AAS, BA, LOC, NL, NYPL.

38776 —— Letter from the Secretary of War, to the chairman of the committee, appointed on the 9th of December last, on so much of the speech of the President, as relates to "A system of national defence. . . ." 13th February, 1800. . . .
[*Philadelphia.*] pp. 13. 8vo. AAS, BA, LOC, NYPL, NYSL, YC.

38777 —— [A List of the duties, payable by law, on all goods, wares and merchandise, imported into the United States, from and after the last day of June, 1800.
Baltimore: Printed by Warner & Hanna, 1800.] Minick 627.

38778 —— Message from the President of the United States, accompanying an account of the application of grants, made by Congress for the contingent expenses of government. . . . 20th January, 1800. . . . (Published by order of the House. . . .)
[*Philadelphia.*] pp. 3. 8vo. AAS, BA, JCB, LOC, NL, NYPL, PPL.

38779 —— Message from the President of the United States, accompanying a Report of the Secretary, of State, with a letter to him, from Matthew Clarkson. . . . 23d January, 1800. . . . (Published by order of the House. . . .)
[*Philadelphia.*] pp. 8. 8vo. AAS, JCB, LOC, NL, NYSL.

38780 —— Message from the President of the United States, transmitting an original letter from Mrs. Washington, in answer to a letter . . . requesting her assent to the intirment of the remains of General Washington in the Capitol. . . . 8 January, 1800. . . . (Published by order of the House. . . .)
[*Philadelphia.*] pp. 3. 8vo. HEH, JCB, LOC, NYPL.

38781 —— Message from the President of the United States, transmitting a Report from the Secretary of War, accompanied by a return of the officers who have been appointed. . . . Printed by order of the Senate. . . . April 17th, 1800.
[*Philadelphia.*] pp. 28. 8vo. AAS, BA, LOC, NYPL.

38782 —— Message from the President of the United States, transmitting a Report of the Secretary of State . . . relative to . . . Jonathan Robbins. . . . 7th February, 1800. . . . (Published by order of the House. . . .)
[*Philadelphia.*] pp. 8. 8vo. AAS, BA, JCB, LOC, NL, NYPL, NYSL.

38783 —— Message from the President of the United States transmitting a Report of the Secretary of War, on . . . our military system. 13th January, 1800. . . . Printed by order of the House. . . .
[*Philadelphia.*] pp. 36, 2 folded tables. AAS, BA, JCB, LOC, NYPL, NYSL.

38784 —— Message from the President of the United States, transmitting sundry statements relative to the Mint of the United States. . . . 8th January, 1800. . . . Printed by order of the House. . . .
Philadelphia: Printed by Way & Groff, no. 48, North Third-street. pp. 7. 8vo.
AAS, JCB, LOC, NL, NYPL, NYSL, PPL, YC.

38785 —— [Message from the President of the United States, transmitting two Reports; one from the acting Secretary of War, the other from the Secretary of the Treasury, with details of the expenditure of the monies appropriated by the Acts of the 20th of May and the 6th of July, 1798, and of the 10th of May, 1800.
[*Philadelphia.*] pp. 34. 4to.] Evans.

38786 —— Mr. Abiel Foster's Motion for an amendment to the Constitution of the United States. 4th February, 1800. . . . (Published by order of the House. . . .)
[*Philadelphia.*] pp. [3]. 8vo. AAS, BA, BPL, LOC, NL, NYPL, NYSL, YC.

38787 —— Mr. Bayard's Motion. 17th February, 1800. Committed to the committee of the whole House, to whom is committed the Message of the President, transmitting the papers, relative to . . . Jonathan Robbins. (Published by order of the House. . . .)
[*Philadelphia.*] pp. [3]. 8vo. AAS, JCB, LOC, NL, NYPL, NYSL.

38788 —— Mr. Harper's Motion. 10th March, 1800. Ordered to lie on the table. (Published by order of the House. . . .)
[*Philadelphia.*] pp. 4. 8vo. AAS, BA, JCB, LOC, NYPL, NYSL, YC.

38789 —— Mr. Henry Lee's Motion. 10th March, 1800. Ordered to lie on the table. (Published by order of the House of Representatives.)
[*Philadelphia.*]   pp. [3].   8vo.   AAS, BA, LOC, NYPL, NYSL, YC.

38790 —— Mr. Livingston's Motion. 13th February, 1800. Ordered to lie on the table. (Published by order of the House. . . .)
[*Philadelphia.*]   pp. [3].   8vo.   AAS, BA, LOC, NYPL, NYSL.

38791 —— Mr. Livingston's Motion. 20th February, 1800. Committed to the committee of the whole House, to whom was committed on the 7th instant, the Message of the President, transmitting the papers, relative to . . . Jonathan Robbins. (Published by order of the House. . . .)
[*Philadelphia.*]   pp. 4.   8vo.   AAS, JCB, LOC, NYSL.

38792 —— Mr. Marshall's Motion [relative to decision of disputes relative to the election of president and vice-president. April 24, 1800.]
[*Philadelphia.*]   Broadside.   fol.   AAS, LOC.

38793 —— Mr. Nicholas's Motion, for amending the Bill to provide for the execution of the . . . treaty . . . with Great Britain. [April 2d, 1800.] (Published by order of the House. . . .)
[*Philadelphia.*]   pp. 4.   8vo.   AAS, BA, LOC, NYPL, NYSL, YC.

38794 —— —— (With the Amendments of Mr. Marshall thereto.)
[*Philadelphia.*]   pp. 4.   8vo.   AAS, LOC.

38795 —— Mr. Nicholas's Motion. November 21, 1800. . . . Published by order of the House. . . .
[*Washington.*]   pp. [3].   8vo.   AAS, LOC.

38796 —— Mr. Nicholas's Motion. 13th March, 1800. Ordered to lie on the table. (Published by order of the House. . . .)
[*Philadelphia.*]   pp. [3].   AAS, BA, LOC, NYPL.

38797 —— Motion, made in committee of the whole house, on the President's Speech. November 25th, 1800.
[*Washington.*]   pp. [1].   8vo.   AAS, LOC.

38798 —— National bankrupt law. By authority. Sixth Congress of the United States, at the first session. . . .
[*Philadelphia?*]   pp. 33.   16mo.   AAS, BPL, NYPL.

38799 —— Petition of Cato West, and others, in behalf of themselves and other inhabitants of the Mississippi Territory. . . . 13th January, 1800. . . . (Published by order of the House. . . .)
[*Philadelphia.*]   pp. [2], 27.   8vo.   AAS, HC, JCB, LOC, NYPL, NYSL, YC.

38800 —— Philadelphia, December 21, 1799. Major-General Hamilton has received thro' the Secretary of War the following order. . . . "The President . . . announces to the army the death of . . . Washington. . . ." Daniel Jackson, Major-Commandant. Newport, January 1, 1800.
[*Newport.*]   Broadside.   fol.   HEH.

38801 —— The Post-Office law, with instructions, forms and tables of distances, pub. for the regulation of the post-offices. 1800.
Washington City, printed by Charles Cist.   pp. 64.   8vo.   HEH, LOC.

38802 —— President's speech! On Saturday the 22d November, at 12 o'clock, the President met both houses of Congress. . . .
[*Wilmington: Printed by James Wilson.*]   Broadside.   fol.   DHS.

38803 —— PRINTED BY ORDER OF THE SENATE OF THE UNITED STATES, MAY 1ST, 1800. A BILL SUPPLEMENTARY TO THE ACT, ENTITLED, "AN ACT TO ESTABLISH THE TREASURY DEPARTMENT. . . ."
     Broadside.   LOC.

38804 —— PRINTED BY ORDER OF THE SENATE OF THE UNITED STATES, MAY 9TH, 1800. AN ACT TO PERMIT, IN CERTAIN CASES, THE BRINGING OF SLAVES INTO MISSISSIPPI TERRITORY. . . . PASSED IN THE HOUSE . . . MAY 9TH, 1800.
     Broadside.   LOC.

38805 —— [A PROCLAMATION, BY THE PRESIDENT OF THE UNITED STATES. WHEREAS THE CONGRESS OF THE UNITED STATES HAVE THIS DAY RESOLVED, "THAT IT BE RECOMMENDED TO THE PEOPLE OF THE UNITED STATES TO ASSEMBLE ON THE TWENTY-SECOND DAY OF FEBRUARY . . . TO TESTIFY THEIR GRIEF FOR THE DEATH OF GENERAL GEORGE WASHINGTON. . . ." AT PHILADELPHIA, THE SIXTH DAY OF JANUARY . . . ONE THOUSAND EIGHT HUNDRED. . . .
     [*Philadelphia.*]   Broadside.   fol.]   EVANS.

38806 —— REGULATIONS FOR THE ORDER AND DISCIPLINE OF THE TROOPS OF THE UNITED STATES. PART I.
     Philadelphia: Printed by Charles Cist, no. 104, North Second-Street, M,DCCC.
     pp. [4], 151, [8], 8 folded plates.   12mo.
     This is a reprint of the Regulations prepared by Baron von Steuben and ordered printed by Congress on March 29, 1779.   AAS, BA, BM, BPL, CSL, LOC, MᵈHS, NYPL, RU, YC.

38807 —— REGULATIONS RESPECTING CERTAIN SUPPLIES AND RESPECTING OBJECTS OF SPECIAL AND EXTRA EXPENCE. . . . THE WAR OFFICE OF THE UNITED STATES IN PHILADELPHIA, THIS FIRST DAY OF MARCH, A. D. 1800. . . .
     [*Philadelphia.*]   Broadside.   fol.   LCP.

38808 —— REPORT, &C. THE SECRETARY OF WAR, AND THE SECRETARY AND COMPTROLLER OF THE TREASURY, IN PURSUANCE OF THE ACT, PASSED ON THE SEVENTH DAY OF APRIL 1798 . . . SUBMIT TO CONGRESS, THE FOLLOWING SPECIAL REPORT ON THE CLAIM OF SETH HARDING. . . .
     [*Philadelphia: Feb. 15, 1800.*]   pp. 3.   8vo.   AAS, LOC.

38809 —— REPORT FROM THE COMMITTEE OF REVISAL & UNFINISHED BUSINESS, TO WHOM WERE REFERRED THE AMENDMENTS OF THE SENATE, TO THE BILL, INTITULED "AN ACT TO PROVIDE FOR MITIGATING OR REMITTING THE FORFEITURES. . . ." 23D JANUARY, 1800. . . . (PUBLISHED BY ORDER OF THE HOUSE. . . .)
     [*Philadelphia.*]   pp. [4].   8vo.   AAS, LOC.

38810 —— REPORT FROM THE SECRETARY OF THE TREASURY, ACCOMPANYING AN ESTIMATE FOR AN APPROPRIATION OF MONIES TO CARRY INTO EFFECT "THE ACT RESPECTING QUARANTINES AND HEALTH-LAWS." APRIL 24TH, 1800.
     [*Philadelphia.*]   pp. [3].   8vo.   AAS, LOC, NYPL.

38811 —— REPORT IN PART, OF THE COMMITTEE APPOINTED ON THE 9TH OF DECEMBER LAST, ON SO MUCH OF THE PRESIDENT'S SPEECH, AS RELATES TO "A REVISION AND AMENDMENT OF THE JUDICIARY SYSTEM." 11TH MARCH, 1800. . . . (PUBLISHED BY ORDER OF THE HOUSE. . . .)
     [*Philadelphia.*]   pp. [3].   8vo.   AAS, BA, JCB, LOC, NYPL, NYSL.

38812 —— REPORT, IN PART, OF THE COMMITTEE APPOINTED ON THE 24TH OF DECEMBER LAST, TO ENQUIRE WHETHER ANY . . . ALTERATIONS ARE NECESSARY IN THE LAWS AUTHORIZING THE SALE OF THE LANDS OF THE UNITED STATES NORTH-WEST OF THE OHIO. 18TH FEBRUARY, 1800. . . . (PUBLISHED BY ORDER OF THE HOUSE. . . .)
     [*Philadelphia.*]   pp. 5.   8vo.   AAS, BA, CSL, JCB, LOC, NYPL, NYSL.

38813 —— REPORT, IN PART —— OF THE COMMITTEE OF ELECTIONS, APPOINTED TO EXAMINE THE CREDENTIALS OF MEMBERS RETURNED TO SERVE IN THIS HOUSE. NOVEMBER 26, 1800. . . . PUBLISHED BY ORDER OF THE HOUSE. . . .
     [*Washington.*]   pp. 4.   8vo.   AAS, LOC.

38814 —— Report, in part, of the Committee of Privileges, on the form of proceedings in the case of William Duane. [March 22d, 1800.] Printed by order of the Senate. . . .
[*Philadelphia*.]   pp. 4.   8vo.   AAS, BA, LOC, NYPL, NYSL.

38815 —— Report in part—of the Committee of Revisal and Unfinished Business. November 26, 1800. . . . Published by order of the House. . . .
[*Washington*.]   pp. 7.   8vo.   AAS.

38816 —— Report (in part) of the Committee to whom was referred on the 28th ultimo, so much of the Speech of the President, as respects the District of Columbia. 17th December, 1800. . . . Published by order of the House. . . .
[*Washington*.]   pp. [3].   8vo.   AAS, LOC.

38817 —— Report, in part, of the Committee to whom were referred on the 13th ultimo, a Petition of Cato West, and others, in behalf of . . . Mississippi Territory. 18th February, 1800. . . . (Published by order of the House. . . .)
[*Philadelphia*.]   pp. 14.   8vo.   AAS, BA, LOC, NL, NYPL, NYSL, UOC.

38818 —— Report of the Commissioners of the Sinking Fund, inclosing a report to them from the Secretary of the Treasury. . . . 28th of November, 1800. . . . Published by order of the House. . . .
[*Washington*.]   pp. 9, 1 folded table.   8vo.   AAS, BA, JCB, LOC, NYPL.

38819 —— Report of the Committee appointed on the 5th instant. To enquire into the expediency of authorizing the President of the United States, to appoint an agent to purchase of the Indians, a tract of land on the south-side of Lake Superior which shall include the Great Copper Bed. 17th March, 1800. . . . (Published by order of the House. . . .)
[*Philadelphia*.]   pp. 4.   8vo.   AAS, BA, JCB, LOC, NL, NYPL.

38820 —— Report of the Committee appointed on the 10th December last, to enquire whether any, and what alterations are necessary to be made in the judicial establishment of the Territory north-west of the Ohio, and to divide the said Territory into two distinct and separate governments. 3d March, 1800. . . . (Published by order of the House. . . .)
[*Philadelphia*.]   pp. 4.   8vo.   AAS, BA, LOC, NYPL, NYSL.

38821 —— Report of the Committee, appointed on the twentieth of March last, to examine the accounts of the United States, relative to the public debt. . . . 8th May, 1800. . . . Printed by order of the House. . . .
[*Philadelphia*.]   pp. 11, [1], 9 folded plates, [37]–39.   fol.
AAS, BA, JCB, LOC, NYPL, NYSL.

38822 —— Report of the Committee, appointed on the 22d instant, to prepare an Address, in answer to the Speech of the President. . . . 25th November, 1800. . . . Published by order of the House. . . .
[*Washington*.]   pp. 4.   8vo.   AAS, LOC.

38823 —— Report of the Committee, appointed to enquire into the expediency of making further provision for the relief of the widow and orphan children, of the late Colonel John Hardinge; and for the orphan daughter, of the late Major Alexander Trueman. 9th April, 1800. . . . (Published by order of the House. . . .)
[*Philadelphia*.]   pp. 4.   8vo.   AAS, LOC, NYSL.

38824 —— Report of the Committee appointed to enquire into the operation of the Acts making provision for the establishment of trading houses with the Indian tribes. . . . 22d April, 1800. . . . Printed by order of the House. . . .
[*Philadelphia*.]   pp. 18, 2 folded tables.   8vo.   AAS, BA, LOC, NL, NYPL.

38825 —— REPORT OF THE COMMITTEE APPOINTED TO ENQUIRE WHETHER ANY, AND IF ANY, WHAT ALTERATIONS ARE NECESSARY IN THE LAWS PROVIDING FOR THE SALE OF THE LANDS OF THE UNITED STATES, NORT-WEST [SIC] OF THE OHIO. 19TH FEBRUARY, 1800. . . . (PUBLISHED BY ORDER OF THE HOUSE. . . .)
     [*Philadelphia.*]   pp. [3].   8vo.   AAS, BA, JCB, LOC, NYPL.

38826 —— REPORT OF THE COMMITTEE OF CLAIMS, INSTRUCTED ON THE 13TH OF JANUARY LAST, TO ENQUIRE WHETHER ANY . . . ALTERATIONS OUGHT TO BE MADE IN THE LAW . . . INTITULED, "AN ACT RESPECTING LOAN-OFFICE AND FINAL SETTLEMENT CERTIFICATES. . . ." 28TH MARCH, 1800. . . . (PUBLISHED BY ORDER OF THE HOUSE. . . .)
     [*Philadelphia.*]   pp. 4.   8vo.   AAS, BA, JCB, LOC, NYPL, NYSL.

38827 —— REPORT OF THE COMMITTEE OF CLAIMS, TO WHOM WAS REFERRED, ON THE 6TH OF DECEMBER LAST, THE PETITION OF SETH NELSON, ATTORNEY FOR SAMUEL BROWN. 24TH MARCH, 1800. . . . (PUBLISHED BY ORDER OF THE HOUSE. . . .)
     [*Philadelphia.*]   pp. 5.   8vo.   AAS, JCB, LOC, NYPL, NYSL.

38828 —— REPORT OF THE COMMITTEE OF CLAIMS, TO WHOM WAS REFERRED, ON THE 8TH OF JANUARY LAST, THE PETITION OF STEPHEN SAYRE. 4TH MARCH, 1800. . . . (PUBLISHED BY ORDER OF THE HOUSE. . . .)
     [*Philadelphia.*]   pp. 15.   8vo.   AAS, BA, LOC, MHS, NYPL, NYSL.

38829 —— REPORT OF THE COMMITTEE OF CLAIMS, TO WHOM WAS REFERRED, ON THE 8TH OF JANUARY LAST, THE PETITION OF WILLIAM NICHOLS. 9TH APRIL, 1800. . . . (PUBLISHED BY ORDER OF THE HOUSE. . . .)
     [*Philadelphia.*]   pp. 4.   8vo.   AAS, BA, JCB, LOC, NYPL.

38830 —— REPORT OF THE COMMITTEE OF CLAIMS, TO WHOM WAS REFERRED ON THE 8TH OF JANUARY LAST, THE PETITION OF WILLIAM NICHOLS. APRIL 9TH, 1800. COMMITTED. . . . NOVEMBER 26TH, 1800. COMMITTED. . . . PUBLISHED BY ORDER OF THE HOUSE. . . .
     [*Washington.*]   pp. 6.   8vo.   AAS, LOC, NYSL.

38831 —— REPORT OF THE COMMITTEE OF CLAIMS, TO WHOM WAS REFERRED, ON THE 9TH OF JANUARY LAST, THE MEMORIAL OF DAVID JONES, & WILLIAM ROGERS. 10TH MARCH, 1800. . . . (PUBLISHED BY ORDER OF THE HOUSE. . . .)
     [*Philadelphia.*]   pp. 4.   8vo.   AAS, BA, JCB, LOC, NYSL.

38832 —— REPORT OF THE COMMITTEE OF CLAIMS, TO WHOM WAS REFERRED, ON THE 10TH OF JANUARY LAST, THE PETITION OF TOBIAS RUDOLPH. 6TH MARCH, 1800. . . . 20TH MARCH, 1800. . . . (PUBLISHED BY ORDER OF THE HOUSE. . . .)
     [*Philadelphia.*]   pp. [3].   8vo.   AAS, BA, JCB, LOC, NYPL, NYSL.

38833 —— REPORT OF THE COMMITTEE OF CLAIMS, TO WHOM WAS REFERRED, ON THE 10TH OF FEBRUARY LAST, THE PETITION OF AMEY DARDIN. 18TH MARCH, 1800. . . . (PUBLISHED BY ORDER OF THE HOUSE. . . .)
     [*Philadelphia.*]   pp. 4.   8vo.   AAS, BA, JCB, LOC, NYPL, NYSL.

38834 —— REPORT OF THE COMMITTEE OF CLAIMS, TO WHOM WAS REFERRED, ON THE 11TH OF DECEMBER LAST, THE PETITION OF CAMPBELL SMITH. 21ST FEBRUARY, 1800. . . . (PUBLISHED BY ORDER OF THE HOUSE. . . .)
     [*Philadelphia.*]   pp. 12.   8vo.   AAS, BA, JCB, LOC, NYSL.

38835 —— REPORT OF THE COMMITTEE OF CLAIMS, TO WHOM WAS REFERRED, ON THE 12TH OF DECEMBER LAST, THE MEMORIAL OF JAMES SOMERVELL AND HENRY T. COMPTON, GUARDIANS OF THE ORPHAN CHILDREN OF THE LATE MAJOR ALEXANDER TRUEMAN. 14TH MARCH, 1800. . . . (PUBLISHED BY ORDER OF THE HOUSE. . . .)
     [*Philadelphia.*]   pp. 4.   8vo.   AAS, BA, LOC, NYPL.

38836 —— Report of the committee of claims, to whom was referred, on the 13th instant, the Petition of Moses Gill. 19th February, 1800. . . . (Published by order of the House. . . .)
[*Philadelphia*.] pp. 7, [1]. AAS, BA, JCB, LOC, NYPL, NYSL.

38837 —— Report of the committee of claims, to whom was referred, on the 16th ultimo, the Petition of Oliver Pollock. 18th April, 1800. . . . Printed by order of the House. . . .
[*Philadelphia*.] pp. 6. 8vo. AAS, LOC, NYPL, NYSL.

38838 —— Report of the committee of claims, to whom was referred, on the 17th ultimo, the Petition of Mary Wooster, relict of the late General David Wooster. 28th. April, 1800. . . . (Published by order of the House. . . .)
[*Philadelphia*.] pp. 4. 8vo. AAS, BA, LOC, NYPL, NYSL.

38839 —— Report of the committee of claims, to whom was referred, on the 18th February, 1800, the Petition of Thomas Johnson. 16th April, 1800. . . . (Published by order of the House. . . .)
[*Philadelphia*.] pp. [3]. 8vo. AAS, BA, LOC, NYPL, NYSL.

38840 —— Report of the committee of claims, to whom was referred on the 21st ultimo, the Petition of the Corporation of Rhode-Island College. . . . 17th February, 1800. . . . (Published by order of the House. . . .)
[*Philadelphia*.] pp. 4. 8vo. AAS, BA, Br U, LCP, LOC, NYPL.

38841 —— Report of the committee of claims, to whom was referred, on the 25th ultimo, the Petition of Jane Lynch. 26th April, 1800. . . . (Published by order of the House. . . .)
[*Philadelphia*.] pp. [3]. 8vo. AAS, BA, LOC, NYPL, NYSL.

38842 —— Report of the committee of claims, to whom was referred, on the 25th ultimo, the Petition of John Baptiste Verdier 25th April, 1800. . . . (Published by order of the House. . . .)
[*Philadelphia*.] pp. 21. 8vo. AAS, BA, LOC, NYPL.

38843 —— Report of the committee of claims, to whom was referred, on the 26th ultimo, the Petition of Gilbert Dench. 21st March, 1800. . . . (Published by order of the House. . . .)
[*Philadelphia*.] pp. 4. 8vo. AAS, BA, JCB, LOC, NYPL, NYSL.

38844 —— Report of the committee of claims, to whom was referred, on the 27th of March last, the memorial of Charles Pettit. . . . 29th. April, 1800. . . . (Published by order of the House. . . .)
[*Philadelphia*.] pp. 34. 8vo. AAS, BA, JCB, LOC, NYPL, NYSL.

38845 —— Report of the committee of claims, to whom was referred, on the 28th of February last, the Petition of Ann Elliot. . . . (Published by order of the House. . . .) [April 26, 1800.]
[*Philadelphia*.] pp. [3]. 8vo. AAS, BA, LOC, NYPL, NYSL.

38846 —— Report of the committee of claims, to whom was referred, on the 28th ultimo, the Petition of Moses White. . . . 4th February, 1799. Committed. . . . 15th January, 1800, committed. . . . (Published by order of the House. . . .)
[*Philadelphia*.] pp. 4. 8vo. AAS, BA, JCB, LOC, NL, NYPL, NYSL.

38847 —— Report of the committee of claims, to whom was referred the Petition of Benjamin Wells. . . . 21st. April, 1800. . . . (Published by order of the House. . . .)
[*Philadelphia*.] pp. 4. 8vo. AAS, BA, LOC, NYPL, NYSL.

38848 —— Report of the committee of claims, to whom were referred, several petitions of Thomas Frothingham, of Massachusetts; of sundry citizens ... of the counties of Washington and Allegany; of Andrew Findley, and others. ... 11th March, 1800. ... (Published by order of the House. ...)
  [*Philadelphia.*]   pp. 4.   8vo.   AAS, BA, JCB, LOC, NYPL, NYSL.

38849 —— Report of the committee of claims, to whom were referred, the Petitions of Benjamin Bird; Emory Sudler, junr. and wife; Alexander Roxburgh; Griffith Jones; David Jones; and Thomas Leiper; Philip Bush, and the Bill from the Senate, intituled "An Act for the relief of the legal representatives of Samuel Lapsley, deceased." 22d April, 1800. ... (Published by order of the House. ...)
  [*Philadelphia.*]   pp. 7.   8vo.   AAS, BA, JCB, LOC, NYPL, NYSL.

38850 —— Report of the committee of claims, to whom were referred, the Petitions of Temple Elliot, Simon Sommers, and William Boyce. 25th February, 1800. ... (Published by order of the House. ...)
  [*Philadelphia.*]   pp. 4.   8vo.   AAS, BA, JCB, LOC, NYPL, NYSL.

38851 —— Report of the committee of commerce & manufactures, instructed on the 15th ultimo, to enquire and report in what manner, and to what effect the Act suspending commercial intercourse with France, has been executed. 14th February, 1800. ... (Published by order of the House. ...)
  [*Philadelphia.*]   pp. 7.   8vo.   AAS, BA LOC, NYPL, NYSL, VᵃU.

38852 —— Report of the committee of commerce and manufactures, to whom was referred on the 4th instant, the Petition of Robert Hooper. 9th December, 1800. ... Published by order of the House. ...
  [*Washington?*]   pp. 4.   8vo.   AAS.

38853 —— Report of the committee of commerce and manufactures, to whom was referred on the 5th instant, the Petition of Thomas Jenkins, and Sons. 8th December, 1800. ... 9th December, 1800. ... Published by order of the House. ...
  [*Washington.*]   pp. 4.   8vo.   AAS, BA, LOC, NYPL.

38854 —— Report of the committee of commerce & manufactures, to whom was referred, on the 17th of December last, the Petition of Henry Stouffer, and Andrew Wallace. 10th February, 1800. ... (Published by order of the House. ...)
  [*Philadelphia.*]   pp. 16.   8vo.   AAS, BA, LOC, NYPL, NYSL.

38855 —— Report of the committee of commerce & manufactures, to whom was referred the amendments proposed by the Senate, to the Bill intituled "An Act providing for salvage in cases of re-capture." 11th February, 1800. ... (Published by order of the House. ...)
  [*Philadelphia.*]   pp. 4.   8vo.   AAS, BA, JCB, LOC, NYPL, NYSL.

38856 —— Report of the committee of privileges, on the measures it will be proper to adopt, relative to a publication in the General Advertiser, or Aurora, of the 19th of February last. Printed by order of the Senate. ...
  [*Philadelphia.*]   pp. 7.   8vo.   AAS, BʳU, HC, LOC, WLC.

38857 —— Report of the committee of revisal and unfinished business, to whom were referred the amendments to the Bill entitled "An Act to provide for mitigating ... the forfeitures ... in certain cases. ..." [House document, Jan. 23, 1800.]
  [*Philadelphia.*]   pp. [4].   8vo.   BA, NYPL, NYSL.

38858 —— Report, of the committee of ways and means, instructed on the 17th instant to enquire into the expediency of repealing the Act, intituled, "An Act to provide for the valuation of lands and dwelling houses. ..." 30th December, 1800. ... 31st December, 1800. ... Published by order of the House. ...
  [*Washington.*]   pp. 4.   8vo.   AAS, BA, LOC.

38859 —— REPORT OF THE COMMITTEE OF WAYS AND MEANS, ON CERTAIN APPROPRIATIONS FOR THE DIPLOMATIC DEPARTMENT. 5TH MAY, 1800. . . . PRINTED BY ORDER OF THE HOUSE. . . .
[*Philadelphia.*] pp. 21. 8vo. AAS, BA, JCB, LOC, NYPL, NYSL.

38860 —— REPORT OF THE COMMITTEE OF WAYS AND MEANS, ON CERTAIN APPROPRIATIONS FOR THE INDIAN DEPARTMENT. 5TH MAY, 1800. . . . PUBLISHED BY ORDER OF THE HOUSE. . . .
[*Philadelphia.*] pp. 12. 8vo. AAS, BA, LOC, NYPL, PPL, W¹ªHS.

38861 —— REPORT OF THE COMMITTEE OF WAYS AND MEANS, ON THE SUBJECT OF A LOAN, FOR THE SERVICE OF THE YEAR 1800. 21ST FEBRUARY, 1800. . . . (PUBLISHED BY ORDER OF THE HOUSE. . . .)
[*Philadelphia.*] pp. 24. 8vo. AAS, BA, JCB, LOC, NYPL, PPL, WLC.

38862 —— REPORT OF THE COMMITTEE OF WAYS AND MEANS, ON THE SUBJECT OF FURTHER REVENUE. 30TH. APRIL, 1800. . . . (PUBLISHED BY ORDER OF THE HOUSE. . . .)
[*Philadelphia.*] pp. 58. 8vo. AAS, BA, JCB, LOC, NYPL, NYSL.

38863 —— REPORT OF THE COMMITTEE, TO WHOM WAS RE-COMMITTED THE REPORT ON THE PETITION OF CATO WEST. . . . 13TH MARCH, 1800. . . .
[*Philadelphia.*] pp. 4. 8vo. AAS, BA, LOC, NYPL.

38864 —— REPORT OF THE COMMITTEE, TO WHOM WAS REFERRED, ON THE 4TH INSTANT, THE PETITION OF ISAAC ZANE. 21ST FEBRUARY, 1800. . . . (PUBLISHED BY ORDER OF THE HOUSE. . . .)
[*Philadelphia.*] pp. 3. 8vo. AAS, BA, LOC, NYPL, NYSL.

38865 —— REPORT OF THE COMMITTEE, TO WHOM WAS REFERRED, ON THE 7TH ULTIMO, THE MEMORIAL OF MATTHEW PATTERSON, AND SUNDRY OTHER PERSONS, RESIDING ON THE WESTERN BORDERS OF NORTH AND SOUTH-CAROLINA. 7TH APRIL, 1800. . . . 8TH APRIL, 1800. . . . (PUBLISHED BY ORDER OF THE HOUSE. . . .)
[*Philadelphia.*] pp. 6. 8vo. AAS, BA, JCB, LOC, NYPL.

38866 —— REPORT OF THE COMMITTEE TO WHOM WAS REFERRED, ON THE 7TH ULTIMO, THE MEMORIAL OF MATTHEW PATTERSON. . . . 7TH APRIL, 1800. . . . 8TH APRIL 1800. . . . 23D DECEMBER 1800. . . . PUBLISHED BY ORDER OF THE HOUSE. . . .
[*Washington.*] pp. 7. 8vo. AAS, LOC, NYPL.

38867 —— REPORT OF THE COMMITTEE TO WHOM WAS REFERRED ON THE 7TH ULTIMO, THE PETITION OF WILLIAM HILL AND OTHERS. 4TH APRIL, 1800. . . . (PUBLISHED BY ORDER OF THE HOUSE. . . .)
[*Philadelphia.*] pp. 7. 8vo. AAS, BA, BPL, JCB, LOC, NYPL, NYSL.

38868 —— REPORT OF THE COMMITTEE TO WHOM WAS REFERRED, ON THE 13TH ULTIMO, THE PETITION OF WILLIAM TAZEWELL. 9TH APRIL, 1800. . . . (PUBLISHED BY ORDER OF THE HOUSE. . . .)
[*Philadelphia.*] pp. 9. 8vo. AAS, BA, BPL, JCB, LOC, NYPL, NYSL, PPL.

38869 —— REPORT OF THE COMMITTEE, TO WHOM WAS REFERRED, ON THE 14TH INSTANT, THE MESSAGE OF THE PRESIDENT OF THE UNITED STATES, TOGETHER WITH A LETTER OF JOHN RANDOLPH, JUNR. . . . 20TH JANUARY, 1800. . . . (PUBLISHED BY ORDER OF THE HOUSE. . . .)
[*Philadelphia.*] pp. 28. 8vo. AAS, BPL, JCB, LOC, MᵈHS, NYPL, NYSL, WLC.

38870 —— REPORT OF THE COMMITTEE TO WHOM WAS REFERRED, ON THE 18TH INSTANT, THE PETITION OF JOHN MOUNTJOY. 21ST FEBRUARY, 1800. . . . (PUBLISHED BY ORDER OF THE HOUSE. . . .)
[*Philadelphia.*] pp. 4. 8vo. AAS, BA, JCB, LOC, NYPL, NYSL.

38871 —— REPORT OF THE COMMITTEE TO WHOM WAS REFERRED ON THE 21ST OF FEBRUARY LAST, THE PETITION OF SUNDRY INHABITANTS OF MOUNT-PLEASANT IN THE STATE OF NEW-YORK. 11TH MARCH, 1800. . . . (PUBLISHED BY ORDER OF THE HOUSE. . . .)
[*Philadelphia.*] pp. 4. 8vo. AAS, JCB.

38872 —— Report of the committee to whom was referred on the 21st of February last, the Petition of sundry inhabitants of Mount-Pleasant in the State of New-York. 14th March, 1800. . . . (Published by order of the House. . . .)
     [*Philadelphia.*]   pp. 4.   8vo.
Except for the date, this is identical with the above, even to the typographical errors.
                                       AAS, BA, LOC, NYPL.

38873 —— Report of the committee to whom was referred, on the 26th, ultimo, the consideration of the expediency of accepting from the State of Connecticut, a cession of jurisdiction of the territory west of Pennsylvania. . . . 21st March, 1800. Committed to a committee of the whole House. . . . Published by order of the House. . . .
     [*Philadelphia.*]   pp. 31.   8vo.   BA, HEH, JCB, MHS, LCP, LOC, NYPL.

38874 —— Report of the committee, to whom was referred, so much of the President's Speech, as relates to "A Revision and amendment of the judiciary system." 1st May, 1800. . . . (Published by order of the House. . . .)
     [*Philadelphia.*]   pp. 44.   8vo.   AAS, BA, JCB, LOC, NYPL, NYSL, PPL.

38875 —— Report of the committee to whom was referred so much of the President's Speech as relates to the exercise of the local powers over the District of Columbia. . . . Printed by order of the Senate. . . . December 17th, 1800.
     [*Washington.*]   pp. 4.   8vo.   AAS, LOC.

38876 —— Report of the committee to whom was referred, so much of the speech of the President of the United States, as relates to a "System of National defence. . . ." 13th January, 1800. . . . (Published by order of the House. . . .)
     [*Philadelphia.*]   pp. 4, [2].   8vo.   AAS, BA, LOC, NYPL, NYSL.

38877 —— Report of the committee, to whom was referred the Bill, authorizing Seth Harding to locate certain lands in the territory north-west of the river Ohio. Printed by order of the Senate. . . . March 31st, 1800.
     [*Philadelphia.*]   pp. 4.   8vo.   AAS.

38878 —— Report of the committee to whom was referred the Bill, entitled, "An Act in addition to the Act, entitled An Act regulating the grants of land appropriated for military services, and for the Society of the United Brethren for Propagating the Gospel Among the Heathen." [February 17th, 1800.]
     [*Philadelphia.*]   pp. 7.   8vo.   AAS.

38879 —— Report of the committee, to whom was referred the Bill, entitled, "An Act providing for the enumeration of the inhabitants of the United States. Printed by order of the Senate. . . . [Jan. 21, 1800.]
     [*Philadelphia.*]   pp. 6.   8vo.   LOC.

38880 —— Report of the committee, to whom was referred the Bill, entitled "An Act supplemental to the Act, entitled An Act for the amicable settlement of the limits with the State of Georgia, and authorizing the establishment of a government in the Mississippi Territory." Printed by order of the Senate. . . . April 9th, 1800.
     [*Philadelphia.*]   pp. 4.   8vo.   AAS.

38881 —— Report of the committee, to whom was referred the bill entitled "An Act to alter and establish sundry post roads. . . ." (April 4th, 1800, in the Senate.)
     [*Philadelphia?*]   pp. 6.   8vo.   WLC.

38882 —— Report of the committee, to whom was referred the Bill, entitled "An Act to divide the territory of the United States north-west of the Ohio river into two separate governments." [In Senate . . . April 16th, 1800.]
     [*Philadelphia.*]   pp. 4.   8vo.   AAS.

38883 —— Report of the committee, to whom was referred the Bill, entitled "An Act to extend the privilege of obtaining patents. . . ." Printed by order of the Senate. . . . March 28th, 1800.
[*Philadelphia*.]   pp. 4.   8vo.   AAS.

38884 —— Report of the committee, to whom was referred the Bill, entitled "An Act to make further provision for the removal and accommodation of the government of the United States. Printed by order of the Senate. . . . April 12th, 1800.
[*Philadelphia*.]   pp. [3].   8vo.   AAS, LOC.

38885 —— Report of the committee, to whom was referred the Bill for the relief of Ithamar Canfield. [In the Senate Feb. 17, 1800.]
[*Philadelphia*.]   pp. 4.   8vo.   LOC.

38886 —— Report of the committee to whom was referred the Bill, from the House of Representatives, entitled "An Act to authorize the sale and conveyance of lands. . . ." Printed by order of the Senate . . . April 28th, 1800.
[*Philadelphia*.]   pp. 4.   8vo.   AAS.

38887 —— Report of the committee to whom was referred the Bill sent from the Senate, intituled "An Act prescribing the mode of deciding disputed elections of president and vice-president of the United States." 25th. April, 1800. . . . (Published by order of the House. . . .)
[*Philadelphia*.]   pp. 12.   8vo.   AAS, BA, LOC, NYPL, NYSL.

38888 —— Report of the committee to whom was referred the Bill, supplementary to the laws now in force fixing the compensations of the officers of the Senate and House of Representatives. Printed by order of the Senate . . . April 22d, 1800.
[*Philadelphia*.]   pp. [3].   8vo.   AAS.

38889 —— Report of the committee, to whom was referred the Bill, to amend an Act, entitled "An Act to establish the judicial courts of the United States." Printed by order of the Senate . . . April 28th, 1800.
[*Philadelphia*.]   pp. 2.   8vo.   NYPL.

38890 —— Report of the committee, to whom was referred the Bill to establish a general stamp-office. Printed by order of the Senate. . . . April 2d, 1800.
[*Philadelphia*.]   pp. [3].   8vo.   AAS.

38891 —— Report of the committee, to whom was referred the Bill, "To establish the district of Kennebunk. . . ." Printed by order of the Senate . . . April 28th, 1800.
[*Philadelphia*.]   pp. 4.   8vo.   AAS.

38892 —— Report of the committee, to whom was referred the letter of John Henderson to Winthrop Serjeant, and the extract of a letter from Governor Serjeant. Printed by order of the Senate. . . . April 7th, 1800.
[*Philadelphia*.]   pp. [3].   8vo.   AAS, LOC.

38893 —— Report of the committee, to whom was referred the Memorial of Daniel Smith. Printed by order of the Senate. . . .
[*Philadelphia: Jan. 23, 1800*.]   pp. 8.   8vo.
The "Report of the committee to whom was referred the Petition of Samuel Glass, and others," occupies pp. [5]–8.   AAS, BA, JCB, LOC, NL, NYPL.

38894 —— Report of the committee, to whom was referred the Petition of Thomas Burling, and others, inhabitants of the Mississippi Territory. Printed by order of the Senate. . . . April 7th, 1800.
[*Philadelphia*.]   pp. [3].   8vo.   AAS, LOC.

38895 —— Report of the committee to whom was referred the Report of the Secretary of War, Secretary and Comptroller of the Treasury, on the subject of the refugees from Canada and Nova Scotia. 9th May, 1800. . . . Published by order of the House. . . .
[*Philadelphia.*]   pp. 5.   8vo.   LOC.

38896 —— Report of the committee to whom was referred the Resolution authorising an enquiry into the situation and extent of the vacant and unappropriated lands, claimed by the United States under the cession of the State of North Carolina. . . . Printed by order of the Senate . . . May 9th, 1800.
[*Philadelphia.*]   pp. 13.   8vo.   AAS, BA, LOC, NYPL.

38897 —— Report of the committee, to whom were referred, on the 24th of December, and on the 1st and 13th of January last, the several Petitions, of Thomas Burling . . . John Collier . . . Cato West & others. 2d April, 1800 . . . (Published by order of the House. . . .)
[*Philadelphia.*]   pp. 17.   8vo.   AAS, BA, DᵉRGL, JCB, LOC, NYPL.

38898 —— Report of the committee to whom were referred, sundry Petitions, of persons residing in the North Western Territory . . . on the subject of Judge Symmes's purchase. 16th April, 1800. . . . (Published by order of the House. . . .)
[*Philadelphia.*]   pp. 11.   8vo.   AAS, BA, LOC, NYPL, NYSL, PPL.

38899 —— Report of the committee, to whom were referred the Petitions of Joseph Russel, Junr, Michael Jackson, and others. [March 17th, 1800.] Printed by order of the Senate. . . .
[*Philadelphia.*]   pp. 7.   8vo.   AAS, LOC.

38900 —— Report of the Secretary of the Navy on the Petition of sundry French officers confined in the prison of Burlington. . . . 27th December, 1799. . . . (Published by order of the House. . . .)
[*Philadelphia.*]   pp. 4.   8vo.   JCB, NL, NYSL.

38901 —— Report on the Petition of Abraham Bell, to whom was referred, the said Petition on the twenty-sixth of March eighteen-hundred. 2d April, 1800. . . . (Published by order of the House. . . .)
[*Philadelphia.*]   pp. [3].   8vo.   AAS, BA, NYPL, NYSL.

38902 —— [Reward of $10.00 for the apprehension of a deserter from the Marine barracks at Fredericktown. [Signed by] John Johnson, lieut . . . August 28, 1800.
Frederick-Town: Printed by M. Bartgis. . . .   Broadside.   4to.]   Minick 590.

38903 —— Rules and articles, for the better government of the troops, raised, or to be raised . . . at the expense of the United States of America.
City of Washington: Printed by Way & Groff, North E Street, near the General Post-Office. 1800.   pp. 92.   12mo.   AAS, HC, LOC.

38904 —— —— —— *Lancaster, Printed by C. J. Hutter.*   pp. 56.   16mo.   HEH, LOC, NYPL.

38905 —— Rules for conducting business in the Senate.
[*Philadelphia.*]   pp. 7.   8vo.   AAS.

38906 —— Speech of the President of the United States, to both Houses of Congress. 22d November, 1800. . . . Published by order of the House. . . .
[*Washington.*]   pp. 7.   8vo.   AAS, LOC, NYSL.

38907 2d December, 1800. Read the first and second time, and committed to a committee of the whole House, to-morrow. A Bill, directing the erection of a mausoleum to George Washington.
[*Washington.*]   Broadside.   HEH.

38908 —— Table of post offices and rates of postage of single letters for post offices in the State of Massachusetts, distance computed from Boston to each other office. . . .
[*Dated*], *Philadelphia, April 14, 1800.* Broadside. fol. AAS.

38909 —— 13th February, 1800, read first and second time, and ordered to be committed to a committee of the whole House next Monday week. A Bill more effectually to provide for the national defence by establishing an uniform militia. . . .
[*Philadelphia.*] pp. 10. fol. AAS.

38910 —— Traité d' amitié et de commerce, entre Sa Majesté le roi de Prusse, et les États-Unis de l'Amérique.
[*Philadelphia?*] pp. 19. 8vo.
Proclaimed at Philadelphia on Nov. 4, 1800. BA, LOC, NYPL.

38911 —— Translation of the 11th, 12th and 14th articles of the Treaty with Tunis, as amended.
[*Philadelphia.*] pp. 2. 8vo. LOC.

38912 THE UNITED States Almanac, for the year of our Lord 1801. . . . Highly useful to the lawyer, justice, mechanic and farmer.
Reading: Printed and sold by Jungmann and Bruckmann, in Callowhill-street.
pp. [40]. 12mo. AAS.

38913 THE UNITED States calendar, and gentleman's complete pocket-companion, for . . . 1801. . . .
New-York: Published by John Ward Fenno. Furman & Loudon, printers. 1800.
pp. [120]. HC.

38914 UNITED States Chronicle. 1784–1804
Published by B. Wheeler . . . Providence. fol. weekly.
For 1800: [AAS], [HC], [LOC], RIHS.

38915 THE UNITED States Oracle of the Day. 1800–1803
Printed and published every Saturday morning, by Charles Peirce, no. 5, Daniel Street, Portsmouth, New Hampshire. weekly. fol.
A continuation of *The Oracle of the Day.* For 1800: AAS, BA, DC, MHS, NHHS.

38916 THE UNIVERSAL Gazette. 1797–1800
Philadelphia: Printed by Samuel Harrison Smith. fol. weekly.
After the issue of Sept. 11 the paper was removed to Washington.
For 1800: AAS, BA, HSP, LOC, PPL, UOC, VᵃHS.

38917 THE UNIVERSAL Gazette. Nov. 6, 1800–1814
Washington City, printed by Samuel Harrison Smith, New-Jersey Avenue. fol. weekly.
This was a continuation, without change of numbering, of *The Universal Gazette* of Philadelphia. In Washington it was essentially the weekly edition of the *National Intelligencer.* For 1800: AAS, HSP, LOC.

38918 UNPARTHEYISCHE Harrisburg Morgenröthe Zeitung. 1799–1840
Harrisburgh, Pennsylvania. Gedruckt bey Benjamin Mayer. fol. weekly.
With the issue of August 11, 1800, "Unpartheyische" was dropped from the title.
For 1800: PSL.

38919 DER UNPARTHEYISCHE Readinger Adler. 1796–1913
Herausgegeben von Jacob Schneider and Comp . . . Reading. . . . fol. weekly.
For 1800: AAS, BERKS Co. Hist. Soc., READING.

38920 DIE UNPARTHEYISCHE York Gazette. 1796–1804
[*York, Pa., published by Salomon Mayer and Christian Schlichting.*] weekly. fol.
For 1800: [YORK Co. Hist. Soc.]

38921   VAN PELT, Peter J.   1778–1861
      An Oration, in consequence of the death of . . . Washington . . . delivered . . . in the Reformed Dutch Church of Flatbush . . . 22d of February, 1800. . . .
           Brooklyn: Printed by Thomas Kirk. 1800.   pp. 24.   8vo.
                                     AAS, BA, BPL, LOC, NYHS, NYPL.

38922   VARNUM, Joseph B[radley]   1751–1821
      An Address, delivered to the Third Division of the Massachusetts militia, at a review, on the plains of Concord, 27th August, 1800. . . .
           Cambridge, Printed by William Hilliard, 1800.   pp. 26.   8vo.
                           AAS, BA, BPL, HC, JCB, LOC, MHS, NYHS, NYPL.

38923   [VAUGHAN, Benjamin]   1751–1835
      The Rural Socrates; or an account of a celebrated philosophical farmer, lately living in Switzerland and known by the name of Kliyogg [James Gouyer]. . . .
         Hallowell (District of Maine) printed by Peter Edes . . . 1800.   pp. xii, [4], 203, xiii.   8vo.
      From Arthur Young's version of the original work by Hans Kaspar Hirzel, 1725–1803.
                   AAS, BA, BPL, EI, HC, HEH, LCP, M^cHS, MHS, NYPL, NYSL, P^rU, RU, WLC.

38924   VAUGHAN, John   1775–1807
      The Valedictory lecture delivered before the Philosophical Society of Delaware. . . .
           Wilmington: Printed at the Franklin Press, by James Wilson. 1800.   pp. 36.   12mo.
                                         DHS, NYHS, YC.

38925   DER VEREINIGTEN Staaten Calender, auf das Jahr Jesu Christi 1801. Ein gemeines Jahr von 365 tagen.
           Philadelphia: Gedruckt bey G. Helmbold und J. Geyer. . . . pp. [42].   8vo.
      Cover-title with a cut of Philadelphia.   HSP, NYHS.

38926   THE VERGENNES Gazette and Vermont and New-York Advertiser.   1798–1801
         Vergennes, State of Vermont: printed . . . for Samuel Chipman, jun. . . .   fol.
      weekly.
      With the issue of Aug. 21 William Fessenden was taken into the publishing firm.
                                       For 1800: [DC], [V^tSL].

38927   VERMONT. State.
      Acts and Laws passed by the Legislature of the State of Vermont, at their session holden at Middlebury, in October, M,DCCC.
           Printed [at Bennington] by . . . Anthony Haswell, assignee of the Hon. Samuel Williams, Esq. deceased.   pp. 159.   8vo.
                         AAS, BM, CU, HC, HEH, LOC, NYBA, NYPL, V^tSL, V^tU.

38928   —— An Address of the Council of Censors, to the people of Vermont. Western district, Vermont.
           Bennington: Printed by Anthony Haswell. M,DCCC.   pp. 32, [1].   8vo.
                         AAS, BA, JCB, MHS, NL, NYHS, NYSL, V^tSL, V^tU.

38929   —— [By his excelency Isaac Tichenor, esquire, governor. . . . A Proclamation for a day of solemn fasting, humiliation and prayer. . . . the twenty-third day of April next. . . . Given . . . this nineteenth day of March, 1800. . . .
         Broadside.   fol.]   Evans.

38930   —— General list of the State of Vermont, for the year 1800.
           [Dated: Middlebury, October 29th, 1800.]   pp. [11].   fol.   V^tU.

38931   VERMONT Association of Baptists.
      Minutes of the Vermont Association. Holden at the meeting house, in Wallingford. . . .
           Rutland, printed for the Association.   pp. 6.   8vo.   SCBHC.

38932 VERMONT GAZETTE. 1783–1847
Printed and published at Bennington, by Anthony Haswell. fol. weekly.
FOR 1800: VᵗSL.

38933 VERMONT UNIVERSITY. THE SUBSCRIBERS FOR BUILDING A COLLEGE AT BURLINGTON, ARE INFORMED THAT THE FIRST BUILDING UNDERTAKEN, WAS FINISHED LAST FALL . . . DAVID RUSSELL, AGENT. BURLINGTON, SEPTEMBER 20TH, 1800.
Small broadside. VᵗU.

38934 VERSES, COMPOSED AND SUNG AT TRENTON. . . .
See Trenton. New Jersey.

38935 A VERY SURPRISING NARRATIVE. . . .
See Panther, Abraham.

38936 VIETS, ROGER 1738–1811
A SERMON, PREACHED BEFORE THE LODGE OF FREE AND ACCEPTED MASONS, AT GRANBY . . . CALLED ST. MARK'S LODGE. ON THE 9TH JULY, 1800. . . .
Hartford: Printed by Hudson and Goodwin, 1800. pp. 12. 8vo. CHS.

38937 —— A SERMON, PREACHED IN ST. PETER'S CHURCH IN GRANBY, FORMERLY SIMSBURY IN CONNECTICUT . . . ON THE 29TH DAY OF JUNE, 1800.
Hartford: Printed by Hudson and Goodwin, 1800. pp. 15. 8vo. CHS, NYHS, YC.

38938 THE VILLAGE HARMONY: OR, YOUTH'S ASSISTANT TO SACRED MUSIC. CONTAINING, A CONCISE INTRODUCTION TO THE GROUNDS OF MUSIC, WITH . . . A COLLECTION OF THE MOST APPROVED PSALM TUNES, ANTHEMS, AND OTHER PIECES. . . . FIFTH EDITION, CORRECTED AND IMPROVED. PUBLISHED AGREEABLY TO ACT OF CONGRESS.
Printed at Exeter, New-Hampshire by Henry Ranlet, and sold . . . by Thomas & Andrews, David and John West, and Caleb Bingham, Boston; Thomas C. Cushing, Salem; Edmund M. Blunt, Newburyport; Stephen Patten, Portland; David Howe, Haverhill; William A. Kent, Concord, and Charles Peirce, Portsmouth. . . . 1800.
pp. [2], 205, [1]. obl. 16mo. AAS, LOC, MHS, UOM¹.

38939 VILLAGE MESSENGER. 1796–1801
Samuel Preston, printer — Amherst, New-hampshire. fol. weekly.
FOR 1800: AAS.

38940 THE VILLAGE ORPHAN: A TALE FOR YOUTH. TO WHICH IS ADDED, THE BASKET-MAKER, AN ORIGINAL FRAGMENT.
Philadelphia: Printed by John Thompson, for James Thackara, no. 177, South Second-Street. 1800. pp. 152. 24mo. AAS.

38941 A VINDICATION OF THE CONDUCT AND CHARACTER OF JOHN ADAMS, ESQ. IN REPLY TO THE LETTER OF GENERAL HAMILTON. . . .
New-York: Printed by John C. Totten, & Co. And for sale by D. Longworth . . . Peter Burtsell. . . . 1800. pp. 24. 8vo
AAS, BA, EI, HC, LCP, LOC, MHS, NYHS, NYPL, NYSL, WⁱˢHS.

38942 A VINDICATION OF THE CONDUCT OF THOMAS JEFFERSON WHILST GOVERNOR OF THE STATE OF VIRGINIA. [DATED RICHMOND, APRIL 12TH, 1800.]
[Richmond: Printed by Samuel Pleasants, junior.] pp. [7]. 8vo.
Probably issued only affixed to *A Vindication of the General Ticket Law.* LOC.

38943 A VINDICATION OF THE GENERAL TICKET LAW, PASSED BY THE LEGISLATURE OF VIRGINIA, ON THE 18TH DAY OF JANUARY, 1800. . . .
Richmond: Printed by Samuel Pleasants, junior, March, 1800. pp. 23, [1], 7. 8vo.
Page [24] contains a list of the electors on the Republican ticket, and the last seven pages contain a vindication of the administration of Jefferson as governor. It is attributed to George Hay, 1765–1830. JCB, LOC.

38944 A VINDICATION OF THE RELIGIOUS SOCIETY CALLED QUAKERS. . . .
         See Friends, Society of

38945 A VINDICATION OF THOMAS JEFFERSON; AGAINST THE CHARGES CONTAINED IN A PAMPHLET
         ENTITLED, "SERIOUS CONSIDERATION". . . .
         See Clinton, De Witt.

38946 VINING, JOHN   1758–1802
         EULOGIUM, DELIVERED . . . AT THE STATE-HOUSE, IN THE TOWN OF DOVER, ON THE TWENTY-
         SECOND OF FEBRUARY EIGHTEEN HUNDRED. IN COMMEMORATION OF THE DEATH OF . . .
         WASHINGTON. . . .
                 Philadelphia: Printed by John Ormrod, no. 41, Chestnut-Street. 1800.   pp. 20.
         8vo.   BA, HC, HEH, HSP, JCB, LCP, LOC, NYHS, NYPL, NYSL, WLC.

38947 —— —— —— [*Same*]   pp. 32.   8vo.   AAS, LCP, NYFM, NYPL.

38948 VIRGINIA. STATE.
         ACTS PASSED AT A GENERAL ASSEMBLY OF THE COMMONWEALTH OF VIRGINIA. BEGUN AT THE
         CAPITOL, IN THE CITY OF RICHMOND, ON MONDAY, THE SECOND DAY OF DECEMBER, ONE
         THOUSAND SEVEN HUNDRED AND NINETY-NINE.
                 Richmond, [Va.]: Printed by Meriwether Jones. . . . M,DCCC.   pp. 35.   fol.
                              BM, HC, HSP, LOC, MSL, NYBA, NYPL, VᵃSL, VᵃU.

38949 —— [ARRANGEMENTS OF THE COMMONWEALTH OF VIRGINIA, FOR THE PURPOSE OF TAKING THE SECOND
         CENSUS, UNDER THE LAWS OF THE UNITED STATES. WITH THE NAMES OF SUCH ASSISTANTS
         AS HAVE ALREADY BEEN APPOINTED. . . .
                 [*Winchester, (Virginia): Printed by Richard Bowen, 1800.*]   Broadside.   fol.]
                                                                                        EVANS.

38950 —— A BILL CONCERNING THE HIGH COURT OF CHANCERY.
                 [*Richmond: Printed by Meriwether Jones, 1800.*]   pp. [2].   fol.   LOC.

38951 —— A BILL TO AMEND AN ACT ENTITULED AN ACT FOR EQUALIZING THE LAND TAX.
                 [*Richmond: Printed by Meriwether Jones, 1800.*]   pp. [2].   fol.   LOC.

38952 —— COMMUNICATIONS FROM SEVERAL STATES, ON THE RESOLUTIONS OF THE LEGISLATURE OF VIRGINIA,
         RESPECTING THE ALIEN & SEDITION LAWS. . . .
                 Richmond — Virginia: Printed by Meriwether Jones, printer to the Commonwealth.
         pp. 104.   12mo.
         Ordered printed January 20, 1800.   HC, HEH, JCB, LOC, MSL, NL, NYPL, NYSL, PPL.

38953 —— INSTRUCTIONS FROM THE GENERAL ASSEMBLY OF VIRGINIA, TO STEPHENS THOMPSON MASON,
         AND WILSON CARY NICHOLAS, SENATORS . . . IN CONGRESS. . . .
                 [*Richmond: Davis.*]   pp. [2].   fol.
         This is the item described as Swem 8007.   AAS, BPL.

38954 —— JOURNAL OF THE HOUSE OF DELEGATES OF THE COMMONWEALTH OF VIRGINIA. BEGUN AND HELD
         AT THE CAPITOL IN THE CITY OF RICHMOND, ON MONDAY THE SECOND DAY OF DECEMBER,
         ONE THOUSAND SEVEN HUNDRED AND NINETY-NINE.
                 Richmond: Printed by Meriwether Jones, Printer to the Commonwealth. 1799
         [*i. e. 1800*].   pp. 100.   fol.   LOC, VᵃSL.

38955 —— [JOURNAL OF THE SENATE OF THE COMMONWEALTH OF VIRGINIA, BEGUN AND HELD AT THE
         CAPITOL IN THE CITY OF RICHMOND, ON MONDAY THE SECOND DAY OF DECEMBER, ONE
         THOUSAND SEVEN HUNDRED AND NINETY-NINE.
                 Richmond: Printed by Thomas Nicholson. 1799 [i. e. 1800].]   SWEM 7954.

38956 —— A LETTER FROM GOVERNOR MONROE, TO THE GENERAL ASSEMBLY OF THE COMMONWEALTH OF
         VIRGINIA.
                 Richmond: Printed by Meriwether Jones, printer to the Commonwealth. M,D,CCC.
         pp. 16.   8vo.   YC.

38957 —— [A Letter from Governor Monroe, several documents in the case of J. K. Reade, and a statement of the trials of certain Negros.
  Richmond. Nicholson. Dec. 30, 1800].   Swem 8004.

38958 —— List of pensioners continued by the honourable the Executive, for the year 1799. . . .
Auditor's Office, 7th January, 1800.
  Broadside. fol.   LOC, NYPL.

38959 —— Proceedings of the Virginia Assembly, on the answers of sundry States to their resolutions, passed in December, 1798.
  Albany: Printed by Barber and Southwick, Faust's statue, State-Street. M.DCCC.
  pp. 57. 8vo.   AAS, BPL, HC, NYPL, NYSL, RU, VᵃU, YC.

38960 —— —— —— *Philadelphia: Printed by James Carey, no. 7, South Front-Street. 1800.*   pp. 59, [1].
  8vo.
  AAS, BPL, HC, HEH, HSP, JCB, LCP, LOC, MHS, NYBA, NYHS, NYPL, NYSL, UOP, UOTˣ, VᵃSL, VᵃU, WⁱᵃHS.

38961 —— Report of the committee to whom was committed the proceedings of sundry of the other States, in answer to the resolutions of the General Assembly of the 21st day of December, 1798, . . . [Jan. 7, 1800].
  Richmond, Printed for the General Assembly.   pp. 71. 12mo.
  Swem 7972.   BA, LOC, NL, VᵃU.

38962 —— Richmond, January 30, 1800. Dear Sir, The Legislature of this State, at their last session, deemed it expedient to prescribe a mode of choosing ellectors, to vote for a president . . . of the United States. . . .
  Broadside. 4to.   LOC.

38963 —— Virginia: In the High Court of Chancery, March 16, 1798. Between Robert Pleasants, son and heir of John Pleasants . . . and Mary Logan. . . .
  [*Richmond.*] pp. 18. 8vo.
  Dated Mar. 19, 1800, on last page.   HEH, LCP, LOC.

38964 THE VIRGINIA Argus.   1796–1816
  Richmond: Printed . . . by Samuel Pleasants, junior. . . . fol. semi-weekly.
                    For 1800: [LOC], [VᵃSL].

38965 THE VIRGINIA Federalist.   1799–1800
  Richmond: Printed . . . by W. A. Rind. . . . fol. semi-weekly.
                    For 1800: [HC].

38966 VIRGINIA Gazette, & Petersburg Intelligencer.   1786–June, 1800
  Published . . . by William Prentis and Tarlton W. Pleasants. . . . fol. semi-weekly.   For 1800: [VᵃSL].

38965a VIRGINIA Gazette, & General Advertiser.   1790–1809
  Richmond: — Printed . . . by Augustine Davis. . . . fol. semi-weekly.
                    For 1800: [VᵃSL].

38967 THE VIRGINIA Herald.   1787–1875
  Fredericksburg: Published . . . by T. Green. fol. semi-weekly.
                    For 1800: [LOC].

38968 VIRTUE and vice: or the history of Charles Careful and Harry Heedless. . . . Third Worcester edition.
  Printed at Worcester, Massachusetts, by Isaiah Thomas, Jun. . . . MDCCC. pp. 61,
  [2], cuts.   AAS.

38969 THE VOICE of warning. . . .
  See Mason, John Mitchel

38970 DER VOLKS-BERICHTER; EIN YORKER WOCHENBLATT.   1799–1803
    York [Pa.], gedruckt bey Andreas Billmeyer. . . .   fol.   weekly.   FOR 1800: AAS.

38971 VOYAGES, ADVENTURES & SITUATION OF THE FRENCH EMIGRANTS, FROM THE YEAR '89 TO '99. AND
    WILL SERVE AS AN EPITOME OF THE HISTORY OF THE FRENCH REVOLUTION. TRANSLATED FROM
    THE FRENCH, BY A LADY.
    Lexington: Printed by John Bradford, on Main Street, 1800.   pp. xi, 25, [1].   8vo.
    Attributed to a Mme. Mentelle.   LEXINGTONPL, LOC, TRANSYLVU, UOP¹.

38972 WADSWORTH, BENJAMIN   1750–1826
    AN EULOGY ON THE EXCELLENT CHARACTER OF GEORGE WASHINGTON . . . PRONOUNCED FEBRUARY
    22, MDCCC. . . . IN DANVERS.
    Printed by Joshua Cushing, Salem. 1800.   pp. 32.   8vo.
          AAS, BA, EI, HC, HEH, LOC, MFM, MHS, NYPL, NYSL, WLC.

38973 WALKER, GEORGE   1772–1847
    THE VAGABOND. A NOVEL. . . . FIRST AMERICAN, FROM THE FOURTH ENGLISH EDITION, WITH
    NOTES. . . .
    Boston, printed for West and Greenleaf . . . and John West . . . from the press of
    John Russell. 1800.   pp. xii, 228.   12mo.   AAS, HC, JCB, LOC, MHS, YC.

38974 WALLIS, JAMES.
    AN ORATION ON THE DEATH OF . . . WASHINGTON . . . DELIVERED IN CHARLOTTE, FEBRUARY 22,
    1800, TO THE CITIZENS OF MECKLENBURGH COUNTY. . . .
    Raleigh: Printed by Joseph Gales. 1800.   pp. 16.   8vo.   NYPL.

38975 [WARD, EDWARD   1667–1731
    FEMALE POLICY DETECTED; OR, THE ARTS OF A DESIGNING WOMAN LAID OPEN. TEACHING I. OF HER
    ALLUREMENTS. . . .
    New York: 1800.   pp. 70.   12mo.]   EVANS.

38976 WARD, EPHRAIM   1741–1818
    FIDELITY APPROVED. . . . PREACHED AT THE THIRD PRECINCT IN BROOKFIELD, NOVEMBER 29, 1799:
    AT THE INTERMENT OF . . . NATHAN FISKE, D. D. . . .
    Printed at Brookfield, Massachusetts, by E. Merriam & Co. March 1800.   pp. 26, [1].
    8vo.
    The last leaf contains a funeral dirge sung on this occasion.   AAS, BM, JCB, NYHS, NYSL.

38977 WARE, HENRY   1764–1845
    A SERMON, OCCASIONED BY THE DEATH OF GEORGE WASHINGTON. . . . DELIVERED IN HINGHAM . . .
    JANUARY 6, 1800. . . .
    Printed by Samuel Hall, no. 53, Cornhill, Boston. 1800.   pp. 27.   8vo.
          AAS, BA, BM, BPL, EI, HC, HEH, JCB, LOC, NYHS, NYPL, NYSL.

38978 WARREN, MOSES   D. 1829
    SERMON PREACHED AT THE FUNERAL OF ABDIEL LOOMIS, WHO DEPARTED THIS LIFE JUNE 29TH,
    1800. . . .
    Springfield, Mas. (H. Brewer — Printer.)   pp. 12.   8vo.
    From the imprint and the statement in the Advertisement that this sermon was printed
    "long after it was preached" it is probable that it dates from about 1806.   CVHS.

38979 WARREN ASSOCIATION OF BAPTISTS.
    MINUTES OF THE WARREN ASSOCIATION, HELD AT THE BAPTIST MEETING-HOUSE IN PROVIDENCE,
    SEPTEMBER 9 AND 10, 1800.
    Boston: Printed by Manning and Loring. MDCCC.   pp. 10.   8vo.
          AAS, BʳU, JCB, NYPL, RIHS.

38980 WARREN INSURANCE COMPANY.
    THE CHARTER OF THE WARREN INSURANCE COMPANY IN WARREN (R. I.). ESTABLISHED FOR THE
    PURPOSE OF INSURING ON VESSELS. . . .
    Warren: Printed by Nathaniel Phillips, M,DCCC.   pp. 16.   16mo.   BʳU.

38981 WASHBURN, Azel   1764–1841
The Duty of magnifying the work of the Lord. . . . Delivered at Hanover, New-Hampshire November 16th, 1797: being . . . Thanksgiving Day. . . .
Printed at Hanover, by Moses Davis. 1800.   pp. 25, [1].   8vo.
The last page contains a hymn "adapted to the occasion."   AAS, HEH, JCB, NYHS.

38982 WASHINGTON, George   1732–1799
Address of George Washington, President of the United States, to his fellow citizens, on his declining being considered a candidate for their future suffrages. To which is added, the tribute of respect, paid to his memory, by the Legislature of New-Hampshire, at their late session at Exeter, December 28th, 1799.
Exeter: From the press of Henry Ranlet. 1800.   pp. 36.   12mo.
                                                               BPL, HC, LOC, NYPL.

38983 —— Address of the late General George Washington, to the citizens of the United States, on declining a re-election to the office of President.
Hartford: Printed by Hudson and Goodwin.   Broadside.   fol.
                                         AAS, BPL, HEH, JCB, LOC, MHS, NYPL, WLC, YC.

38984 —— The Address of the late George Washington, when President, to the people of the United States, on declining being considered a candidate. . . .
Printed by Joshua Cushing, County Street, Salem. 1800.   pp. 32.   8vo.
                   AAS, BA, BM, BPL, EI, HC, HEH, LOC, MHS, NL, NYPL, NYSL, PL, PPL, YC.

38985 —— —— [*Charlestown: Printed by Samuel Etheridge. M,DCCC.*]   pp. 30.   8vo.
This edition has no title-page and was perhaps issued only as a part of the volume issued for the observance at Dorchester, *q. v.*   AAS, BA, BPL, NYPL.

38986 —— —— [*Charlestown: Printed by Samuel Etheridge. 1800.*]   pp. 24.   8vo.
This edition was probably issued only as a part of the volume issued for the observance at Charlestown, *q. v.*   BA, HC, LCP, LOC, MᴵⁿⁿHS, NYPL.

38987 —— America's legacy: containing General Washington's farewell orders to the armies of the United States, with the answer. Circular letter to the governors. . . . Address to Congress, on the resignation of his commission, with their answer. Address to the people . . . on declining a re-election. . . .
Charleston: Printed by W. P. Young, Franklin's Head, no. 43, Broad-Street. 1800.
pp. 58.   12mo.   AAS, BPL, HC, HEH, LOC.

38988 —— Columbia's legacy: or, Washington's farewell address. . . . To which is added, his last speech in Congress. . . .
Newburyport: Printed by Angier March. M,DCCC.   pp. 50, [1].   24mo.
The last leaf contains the printer's advertisement.   AAS, BPL, EI, HEH, JCB, LOC, NL, NYPL.

38989 —— The Farewell address of George Washington, President of the United States. Dated September 17th, 1796.
Philadelphia: Printed by Henry Sweitzer, for Mathew Carey . . . 1800.   pp. 46.
12mo.   AAS, BPL, HEH, LCP, NYPL, PʳU, YC.

38990 —— George Washington to the people of the United States, announcing his intention of retiring from public life.
Philadelphia: Printed by H, Maxwell, for A. Dickins and H. Maxwell. . . . 1800.
pp. [2], 40, frontis. portrait.   8vo.
There is a second issue with pp. 17–8 reset. The portrait is signed "D. Edwin."
                                   AAS, BA, BM, HEH, HSP, LCP, NYPL, PʳU, UOP, YC.

38991 —— The Last will and testament of Gen. George Washington.
Boston: Printed for John Russell and Manning & Loring. . . . Feb. 1800.   pp. 24.
8vo.   AAS, BA, BM, BPL, CL, HC, HEH, HSP, LOC, MHS, NYPL, WLC, YC.

38992 —— —— —— *Philadelphia: Printed by H. Maxwell, for A. Dickins. . . . 1800.*   pp. 26.   8vo.
AAS, BA, BPL, EI, HEH, LCP, LOC, NYPL, WⁱˢHS.

38993 —— —— —— *Portland: Printed by Elezer A. Jenks, and sold at his book-store. . . . February 22d,*
1800.   pp. 24.   12mo.   BPL, HEH.

38994 —— —— —— *Worcester: Printed by Isaiah Thomas, Jun. February, 1800.*   pp. 23.   8vo.
AAS, BA, BPL, HC, HEH, HSP, LOC, MHS, NL, NYPL.

38995 —— LEGACIES OF WASHINGTON: BEING A COLLECTION OF THE MOST APPROVED WRITINGS OF THE LATE
GENERAL WASHINGTON, WITH AN APPENDIX, CONTAINING A SKETCH OF THE LIFE OF THIS
ILLUSTRIOUS PATRIOT. . . .
Trenton, Printed by Sherman, Mershon & Thomas. M.DCCC.   pp. 283, portrait.
16mo.
The portrait is an engraving by W. Harrison, Jr., and the biography is by J. M. Williams.
AAS, BA, BPL, HEH, HSP, LOC, NJHS, NL, NYPL, NYSL, PᵣU.

38996 —— PRESIDENT WASHINGTON'S RESIGNATION AND ADDRESS TO THE CITIZENS OF THE UNITED STATES,
SEPTEMBER 17, 1796. . . .
Portsmouth: Printed by John Melcher. 1800.   pp. 22.   8vo.   AAS, BPL, LOC, NYPL.

38997 —— SELECTIONS FROM THE CORRESPONDENCE OF GEORGE WASHINGTON, AND JAMES ANDERSON,
LL.D. . . .
Charlestown: Printed and sold by Samuel Etheridge. 1800.   pp. 79, [1].   8vo.
The last page contains a printer's advertisement.
AAS, BA, BM, BPL, HC, HEH, HSP, JCB, LOC, MHS, MⁱⁿⁿHS, NYHS, NYPL, NYSL, WLC, YC.

38998 —— WASHINGTON'S POLITICAL LEGACIES. TO WHICH IS ANNEXED AN APPENDIX . . . WITH A BIOGRAPHICAL
OUTLINE OF HIS LIFE AND CHARACTER.
Boston, Printed for John Russell and John West. 1800.   pp. 208, xiv.   8vo.
The biography is by J. M. Williams. The last pages contain a list of subscribers. Some
copies contain a portrait.
AAS, BA, BM, BPL, CL, CU, EI, HC, HEH, JCB, LOC, MHS, MSL, NL, NYBA, NYHS, NYPL, YC.

38999 —— WASHINGTON'S POLITICAL LEGACIES. TO WHICH IS ANNEXED AN APPENDIX . . . WITH A BIOGRAPHICAL
SKETCH. . . . AND DR. TAPPAN'S DISCOURSE. . . .
New-York: Printed by George Forman no. 64, for C. Davis, no. 167, Water-Street.
1800.   pp. 292, [8].   16mo.
The biographical sketch is by Jedidiah Morse. The pages at the end contain a list of
subscribers.   AAS, BM, BPL, HEH, HSP, JCB, LOC, MᵈHS, NYHS, NYPL, NYSL, PPL, UOC, YC.

39000 —— THE WILL OF GENERAL GEORGE WASHINGTON: TO WHICH IS ANNEXED, A SCHEDULE OF HIS
PROPERTY, DIRECTED TO BE SOLD.
Alexandria . . . M,DCCC.   pp. 32.   16mo.
AAS, BA, BPL, HC, HEH, HSP, JCB, LOC, MᵈHS, MHS, NYHS, NYPL, NYSL, VᵃSL, VᵃU, WLC.

39001 —— —— —— *Baltimore: Printed by Thomas Dobbin, at . . . no. 36, Market-Street. M,DCCC.*
pp. 26.   12mo.   AAS, HEH, LOC.

39002 —— —— —— *[Georgetown, South-Carolina: Printed by John Burd, 1800.*   pp. 19.   4to.]*
This edition was furnished to the subscribers to *The Georgetown Gazette* in sheets the
size of the newspaper, paged for folding in quarto form.   EVANS.

39003 —— —— —— *Hudson: Printed by Ashbel Stoddard, and sold at his book-store. M,DCCC.*   pp. 47.
24mo.   HEH, NYSL.

39004 —— —— —— *New-York: Printed and published by J. Furman, opposite the City Hall. 1800. (Price*
two-shillings.)   pp. 23, [1].   12mo.
Woodcut portrait on both covers.   HEH, NYHS, NYPL.

39005 —— —— —— *[Philadelphia:] Printed by Freneau & Paine.*   pp. 16.   8vo.
The imprint is from the half-title.   BA, BPL, HEH.

39006 —— —— —— *Stonington-Port, (Connecticut,) printed at the press of S. Trumbull, for Peter Crary. February, 1800. Copied from the 1st edition, printed at Alexandria. . . .*   pp. 35, [1]. 16mo.   AAS, BA, CHS, YC.

39007 —— THE WILL OF GENERAL GEORGE WASHINGTON: TO WHICH IS ANNEXED A SCHEDULE OF HIS PROPERTY, DIRECTED TO BE SOLD; ALSO, AN INTERESTING CORRESPONDENCE BETWEEN LORD BUCHAN AND OUR ILLUSTRIOUS FELLOW-CITIZEN.
Frederick Town: Printed and sold . . . by Matthias Bartgis. . . .   pp. 26.   12mo.   HEH.

39008 WASHINGTON, MARTHA
See Lady Washington.

39009 WASHINGTON. DISTRICT OF COLUMBIA. UNITED STATES' THEATRE.
ON FRIDAY EVENING, AUG. 29TH 1800, WILL BE PRESENTED A CELEBRATED COMEDY, CALLED THE WHEEL OF FORTUNE. . . .
Printed by Way & Groff. . . .   Broadside.   fol.
Facsimile in *The Month at Goodspeed's,* Sept. 1935, p. 21.

39010 WASHINGTON ADVERTISER.   Nov. 20, 1800
City of Washington: Printed by Brown & Snowden.   4to.   daily and tri-weekly.
FOR 1800: AAS, BPL.

39011 THE WASHINGTON ALMANAC, FOR THE YEAR OF OUR LORD, 1801. . . . CALCULATED FOR PENNSYLVANIA, DELAWARE, MARYLAND, VIRGINIA AND KENTUCKY. . . .
Baltimore: Printed and sold by George Keatinge. . . . 1801 [i. e. 1800].   pp. 32 plus. 12mo.   LOC.

39012 THE WASHINGTON CITY GAZETTE.   JULY 25, 1800.
[Washington City,] published daily, by Charles Cist, printer for the general Post Office. 1800.   4to.
There was probably only one issue.   LCP.

39013 —— WASHINGTON CITY, JULY 21ST 1800. SIR, HEREWITH YOU WILL RECEIVE A SPECIMEN OF THE WASHINGTON CITY GAZETTE. . . . CHARLES CIST. . . .
[Washington, Charles Cist, 1800.]   Broadside.   8vo.   AAS.

39014 WASHINGTON FEDERALIST.   SEPT. 25, 1800–1809
Georgetown: Printed by William Alexander Rind, for himself and John Stewart.
fol.   tri-weekly and daily.   FOR 1800: [AAS].

39015 [WASHINGTON GAZETTE.   1800–1801
Washington, Georgia. Published by Alexander M'Millan.]   NO COPIES LOCATED.

39016 WASHINGTON INSURANCE COMPANY.
See Providence, Rhode Island.

39017 WASHINGTONIANA: A COLLECTION OF PAPERS RELATIVE TO THE DEATH AND CHARACTER OF . . . WASHINGTON, WITH . . . HIS LAST WILL AND TESTAMENT. . . .
From the Blandford Press, and sold by Ross & Douglas, Petersburgh, and by all the booksellers in Virginia. 1800.   8vo. pp. xvi, 95, [1].
The last page contains a publisher's advertisement.   AAS, HEH, LOC, MFM, NYHS, NYSL, PPL.

39018   THE WASHINGTONIANA: CONTAINING A BIOGRAPHICAL SKETCH OF THE LATE GEN. GEORGE
        WASHINGTON, WITH VARIOUS OUTLINES OF HIS CHARACTER. . . .
                Baltimore: Printed and sold by Samuel Sower, no. 190, Market-Street, M,DCCC.
        pp. viii, [7]–258, 271–98, [6], portrait.   12mo.
        List of subscribers at the end. For variants see Sabin 101,900.
                        AAS, BPL, HSP, LCP, LOC, MᵈHS, NYHS, NYSL, WLC, YC.

39019   —— —— —— *Baltimore.* . . .   pp. viii, [7]–258, 271–98, [7], portrait.   12mo.
                                HEH, LOC, NYHS, NYPL, UOP.

39020   WASHINGTONS ANKUNFT IN ELISIUM, EINE DIALOGISIRTE SKIZZE, VON EINEM BEWUNDERER DES
        ERBLASSTEN HELDEN. . . .
                Lancaster, bey Christian Jacob Hütter, 1800.   pp. 36.   16mo.   LOC.

39021   WASHINGTON'S MONUMENTS OF PATRIOTISM. BEING A COLLECTION OF THE MOST INTERESTING
        DOCUMENTS. . . . TO WHICH IS ANNEXED, AN EULOGIUM OF . . . WASHINGTON, BY MAJOR
        WILLIAM JACKSON.
                *Philadelphia: Printed for J. Ormrod, 41 Chestnut-street, By Francis & Robert
        Bailey. 1800.*   pp. 338, 44, portrait.   8vo.
        The frontispiece is an engraving by James Fittler after the Stuart portrait of Washington,
        with the imprint of Richard Phillips of London.
                        AAS, BA, BM, BPL, HC, HEH, HSP, NYHS, NYPL, NYSL, PʳU, VᵃU.

39022   WATERHOUSE, BENJAMIN   1754–1846
        A PROSPECT OF EXTERMINATING THE SMALL-POX; BEING THE HISTORY OF THE VARIOLÆ VACCINÆ,
        OR KINE-POX. . . .
                *Printed for the author, at the Cambridge Press, by William Hilliard, and sold by
        him.* . . . *1800.*   pp. 40.   8vo.
                        AML, BA, BM, BML, BPL, EI, HC, LCP, LOC, MHS, NYAM, NYHS, NYPL, RIHS, YC.

39023   WATERMAN, NEHEMIAH   —— 1802
        AN ORATION, DELIVERED AT BOZRAH, FEBRUARY 22D, 1800. . . . TO THE MEMORY OF GENERAL
        GEORGE WASHINGTON. . . .
                Wyndham, Printed by John Byrne. 1800.   pp. 16.   8vo.
                        BA, BPL, CHS, LOC, NHSL, NYPL, YC.

39024   WATKINS, ROBERT AND GEORGE
        See Georgia, A Digest of the laws. . . .

39025   WATTS, ISAAC   1674–1748
        DIVINE SONGS. ATTEMPTED IN EASY LANGUAGE FOR THE USE OF CHILDREN. BY I. WATTS, D. D. . . .
                Salem: Printed by Joshua Cushing, for T. C. Cushing. 1800.   pp. 48.   24mo.
                                                                        AAS, EI.

39026   —— —— —— *New-Haven: Printed by Read & Morse. 1800.*   pp. 64.   24mo.   BPL.

39027   —— HYMNS AND SPIRITUAL SONGS. IN THREE BOOKS. . . .
                *Albany: Printed by Charles R. and George Webster, and sold at their bookstore,
        corner of State and Pearl-Streets. 1800.*   pp. 247, [17].   24mo.
        Issued bound with *Psalms of David imitated.*   AAS.

39028   —— —— —— *New-York: Printed by William Durell. no. 106, Maiden-Lane. 1800.*   pp. 254, [9].
        24mo.
        Issued bound with *Dr. Watts's Imitation of the Psalms of David,* with and without a
        picture of David.   AAS.

39029   —— —— —— *New York: Printed by William Durell, for T. S. Arden. 1800.*   pp. 254, [9].
        24mo.
        Issued as above.   AAS, NYPL.

39030 —— [PSALMS OF DAVID IMITATED. . . .
    Albany: C. R. and G. Webster, 1800.]   pp. 323, [1].   24mo.
Issued bound with Watts' *Hymns and Spiritual Songs.*   AAS.

39031 —— A WONDERFUL DREAM. BY DR. WATTS. WITH A SURPRISING AND VISIONARY ACCOUNT OF HIS
    TRIUMPH OVER SATAN. . . .
    Leominster, (Massachusetts.) Printed at the press of the Telescope. April, 1800.
pp. 12.   12mo.   AAS, MHS.

39032 WEATHERWISE, ABRAHAM, *pseud.*
    AN ALMANACK . . . FOR . . . 1801. . . . BY ABRAHAM WEATHERWISE. . . .
    Portsmouth: Printed and sold by William Treadwell & Co. . . .   pp. [24].   12mo.
       NHHS.

39033 —— THE TOWN AND COUNTRY ALMANACK, FOR THE YEAR OF OUR LORD 1801. . . . CALCULATED FOR THE
    MERIDIAN OF BOSTON. . . .
    *Boston: Printed for . . . E. & S. Larkin, S. Hall, Thomas and Andrews, W. P. & L.
Blake.*   pp. [24].   12mo.   AAS, LOC, NYPL.

39034 —— WEATHERWISE'S ALMANAC, FOR THE YEAR OF THE CHRISTIAN AERA, 1801. . . . CALCULATED FOR
    THE FOUR NEW-ENGLAND STATES.
    Printed for . . . the Booksellers in Boston, Salem, Newbury-Port, Portsmouth. . . .
pp. [24].   12mo.   AAS.

39035 WEBSTER, DANIEL   1782–1852
    AN ORATION, PRONOUNCED AT HANOVER, NEW-HAMPSHIRE, THE 4TH DAY OF JULY, 1800. . . .
    Printed at Hanover, by Moses Davis. 1800.   pp. 15.   8vo.
There are two facsimile reprints.
    AAS, BA, BPL, HEH, HSP, JCB, LOC, MHS, NHSL, NL, NYPL, PᵣU, WC.

39036 WEBSTER, NOAH   1758–1843
    AN AMERICAN SELECTION OF LESSONS IN READING AND SPEAKING. . . . BEING THE THIRD PART OF
    A GRAMMATICAL INSTITUTE. . . . THOMAS AND ANDREWS' ELEVENTH EDITION. . . .
    *Printed at Boston, by Isaiah Thomas and Ebenezer T. Andrews. . . . Sold . . . at
their bookstore; by said Thomas in Worcester; by Thomas, Andrews & Penniman in
Albany; and by Thomas, Andrews & Butler, in Baltimore. 1800.*   pp. 240, portrait
front.   12mo.   AAS, BM, BPL, HC, NYHS, NYPL, UOP, YC.

39037 —— —— THOMAS AND ANDREWS' TWELFTH EDITION.
       AAS, EI, JCB, LOC, NYPL, WL.

39038 —— —— THE THIRD ALBANY EDITION.
    Albany: Printed by Charles R. and George Webster. . . . 1800.   pp. 236, [4].
12mo.   NYPL.

39039 —— —— THE FOURTH ALBANY EDITION.
    Albany: Printed by Charles R. and George Webster. . . . MDCCC.   pp. 236, [2].
12mo.   HEH.

39040 —— THE AMERICAN SPELLING BOOK: CONTAINING AN EASY STANDARD OF PRONUNCIATION. BEING THE
    FIRST PART OF A GRAMMATICAL INSTITUTE OF THE ENGLISH LANGUAGE. . . . THOMAS &
    ANDREWS' TWENTY SECOND EDITION. . . .
    *Printed at Boston, by Isaiah Thomas and Ebenezer T. Andrews. . . . Sold . . . by
said Thomas in Worcester; by Thomas, Andrews & Penniman in Albany; and by
Thomas, Andrews & Butler, in Baltimore. 1800.*   pp. 156, portrait front.   12mo.
       AAS.

39041 —— —— THE THIRD ALBANY EDITION.
    Albany: Printed by Charles R. and George Webster. . . .   pp. 168, illus.   12mo.
       NYPL.

39042 —— —— The twenty-second Connecticut edition.
   Hartford: Printed by Hudson & Goodwin. pp. 165, [1]. 12mo.
  This edition can be dated by the table of numbers on p. 119.   NYPL.

39043 —— A Grammatical institute of the English language. . . . Part second. Containing a
  plain and comprehensive grammar. . . . Sixth Connecticut edition. . . .
    Hartford: Printed by Hudson and Goodwin. 1800. pp. 131. 12mo.
       AAS, BPL, BʳU, CHS, HC, JCB, MA, NYHS, NYPL, NYSL, UOC, WL, WRHS, YC.

39044 —— —— Thomas & Andrews' sixth edition. . . .
   *Printed at Boston, by Isaiah Thomas and Ebenezer T. Andrews . . . sold . . . by
  said Thomas at his bookstore in Worcester; by Thomas, Andrews & Penniman, in Albany;
  and by Thomas, Andrews & Butler, in Baltimore. June, 1800.* pp. 116, portrait front.
  12mo.   BM, NYPL.

39045 [——] A Letter to General Hamilton, occasioned by his letter to President Adams. By a
  Federalist. . . .
    [New York.] pp. 8. 8vo.
  Signed "Aristides." There are several eight-page editions without imprint, with and
  without "finis," and with like minor variations.
       AAS, BA, BPL, HC, HEH, HSP, JCB, LCP, LOC, NYHS, NYPL, NYSL, WLC, YC.

39046 —— —— —— *[Philadelphia, printed by William Duane.]* pp. [3]–10. 8vo.
              AAS, BA, LOC, MHS, NYPL, VᵃU.

39047 —— —— —— *New-York: Printed by E. Belden. & Co. 1800.* pp. 15. 8vo. MHS.

39048 —— —— —— *Published in New York. Reprinted in Salem, by Joshua Cushing, 1800.* pp. 29.
  A ghost of 38153.

39049 [——] An Oration, "On the extent and power of political delusion," has lately been
  re-printed and issued from the press of Citizen Haswell: the public are in turn
  presented with A Rod for the Fool's Back; or, Abraham Bishop Unmasked. . . .
    Reprinted at Bennington, by Wm. Stockwell. . . . pp. 15. 16mo.
           AAS, BPL, JCB, NL, NYPL, VᵗU.

39050 [——] The Prompter: or, a commentary, on common sayings and subjects, which are full of
  common sense. . . .
    *Printed in Albany, by Charles R. & George Webster. . . . State and Pearl-Streets.
  1800.* pp. 95, [1], cuts. 24mo.   AAS, NYPL, NYSL.

39051 —— —— —— *Alexandria: Printed and sold by J. & J. D. Westcott, Royal Street. . . . 1800.*
  pp. 102. 16mo.   LOC, NYPL.

39052 [——] A Rod for the fool's back. . . .
    New Haven: Printed by Read and Morse, Broadway, 1800. pp. 10. 8vo.
                  WL, YC.

39053 —— —— —— *[n. p.] 1800.* pp. 12. 8vo.   YC.

39054 —— —— —— *[n. p. 1800].* pp. 11. 8vo.   LOC, YC.

39055 —— —— —— The Bennington edition of this work is 39049.

39056 —— Ten letters to Dr. Joseph Priestly, in answer to his letters to the inhabitants of
  Northumberland. . . .
    New Haven: Printed by Read & Morse. 1800. pp. 29. 8vo.
    AAS, APS, BA, BM, BPL, CHS, HC, HSP, LCP, LOC, MHS, NL, NYHS, NYPL, WL, YC.

39057   THE WEEKLY ADVERTISER, OF READING, IN THE COUNTY OF BERKS.   1796–1816
        Published . . . by Gottlob Jungmann and Company in . . . Reading.   4to.
        weekly.
        With the issue of Feb. 1, Carl A. Bruckmann was taken into the firm which took the
        name of Jungmann and Bruckmann.   FOR 1800: BERKS CO. HIST. SOC.

39058   WEEKLY MUSEUM.   1788–1817
        New-York: Printed and published by John Harrisson. . . .   4to.   weekly.
                                            FOR 1800: AAS, HC, LOC, NYHS, NYPL, NYSL.

39059   —— THE CARRIER OF THE WEEKLY MUSEUM, BEGS LEAVE TO PRESENT THE FOLLOWING NEW YEAR'S
        ADDRESS TO HIS KIND CUSTOMERS. . . . NEW-YORK, JANUARY 1, 1800.
        [New York: Printed and published by John Harrison.]   Broadside.   fol.   NYHS.

39060   [WEEKLY WANDERER.   1800–1810
        Randolph, Vermont: printed by Sereno Wright.   fol.   weekly.]
                                                     FOR 1800: NO COPY KNOWN.

39061   WEEMS, MASON LOCKE   1759–1825
        A HISTORY, OF THE LIFE AND DEATH, VIRTUES, AND EXPLOITS OF . . . WASHINGTON: DEDICATED TO
        MRS. WASHINGTON. . . .
                Printed for the Rev. M. L. Weems. . . . By Green and English. Georgetown.
        pp. [4], 80.   12mo.   BA, HEH, HSP, JCB, NYPL.

39062   —— —— A SECOND EDITION. . . .
                Philadelphia: Re-printed by John Bioren, no. 83 Chestnut Street, for the author. . . .
        pp. [2], 82, portrait.   8vo.
        The portrait is a bust engraved by Tanner.
                              AAS, APS, BPL, EI, HC, HEH, HSP, LOC, NYHS, NYPL, YC.

39063   —— —— A THIRD EDITION. . . .
                [Same imprint.]   pp. 84, portrait.   8vo.
                         AAS, APS, BA, EI, HC, HEH, HSP, LOC, MdHS, NYHS, NYPL, PrU, UOP, WLC.

39064   —— HYMEN'S RECRUITING-SERJEANT; OR, THE NEW MATRIMONIAL TAT-TOO, FOR THE OLD BACHELORS. . . .
        WITH SOME ELEGANT SONGS. . . .
                Philadelphia: Printed by H. Maxwell, for the author. 1800.   pp. 19, [1], front.
        4to.   MdHS, NYPL.

39065   [——] THE LIFE AND MEMORABLE ACTIONS OF GEORGE WASHINGTON GENERAL AND COMMANDER OF THE
        ARMIES OF AMERICA.
                [Baltimore:] Printed by and for George Keatinge, no. 207 Market-Street.   pp. [5], 2,
        [1], 1, 5–10, [1], 5, 18–96, portrait.   24mo.   HEH, HSP, LOC, MHS.

39066   WELCH, MOSES COOK   1754–1824
        A SERMON, PREACHED AT THE FUNERAL OF MRS. PEGGY POND, WIFE OF THE REV. ENOCH POND,
        OF ASHFORD, JANUARY 27, 1800. . . .
                Hartford: Printed by Hudson and Goodwin. 1800.   pp. 27.   8vo.
                                      AAS, CHS, CL, HC, JCB, NL, NYHS, UTS, YC.

39067   WELLS, AMOS
        THE EQUAL RIGHTS OF MAN. . . . BEING A DISCOURSE DELIVERED AT WOODSTOCK, APRIL 1799, TO
        THE FREEMEN OF THE TOWN, AT THEIR ANNUAL MEETING. . . .
                Norwich: Printed by John Sterry. M,DCCC.   pp. 13.   8vo.   AAS, CHS.

39068   WESLEY, JOHN   1703–1791
        SERMONS ON SEVERAL OCCASIONS. IN FOUR VOLUMES. . . . VOL. III.
                Philadelphia: Printed by Henry Tuckniss, for Ezekiel Cooper. . . . 1800.   pp. 263,
        [1].   12mo.
        Volume 1 was printed in 1794 and volume 4 in 1801.   AAS.

39069   *See also* Baxter, Richard.

39070 WEST, Samuel   1738–1808
 Greatness the result of goodness. A sermon, occasioned by the death of George Washington. . . . By Samuel West, D. D. Pastor of the church in Hollis Street, Boston.
  Boston: From the printing-office of Manning & Loring. pp. 40. 8vo.
 "Address of George Washington, on declining being considered a candidate for the presidency," pp. 19–40.
  AAS, BA, BPL, EI, HC, HEH, HSP, JCB, LCP, LOC, MHS, NYHS, NYPL, NYSL, VªU, WLC, YC.

39071 THE WESTERN calendar: or, an Almanack for the year of our Lord, 1801. . . . With . . . a correct list of the roads.
  Pittsburgh: Printed by John Scull. . . . pp. [36]. 12mo. AAS.

39072 [WESTERN Centinel.   1794–1800
  Whitestown, N. Y. Printed by Warren Barnard. fol. weekly.]
    For 1800: no copy known.

39073 WESTERN Constellation.   May 26, 1800–1804
  Catskill: Published by Mackay and Harry Croswell. weekly. fol.
    For 1800: Greene Co. Hist. Soc., Coxsackie.

39074 THE WESTERN Spy, and Hamilton Gazette.   1799–1822
  Cincinnati: Published by Carpenter & Findlay. weekly. For 1800: OH&PS.

39075 [THE WESTERN Star.   1800–1812
  Lewistown, Pennsylvania. Published by Edward Cole. fol. weekly.]
    For 1800: no copy known.

39076 THE WESTERN Star.   1789–1806
  Printed at Stockbridge, (Mass.) by H[eman] Willard, for Horatio Jones & Co. fol. weekly.   For 1800: [HC].

39077 THE WESTERN Telegraphe, and Washington Advertiser.   1795–1811
  Washington (Pennsylvania): Printed by John Colerick. fol. weekly.
    For 1800: [Washington Co. Hist. Soc., Washington, Pa.]

39078 [DIE WESTLICHE Correspondenz.   1795–1825
  Hagerstaun, Maryland. Gedruckt bey Johann Gruber, 1800. fol. weekly.]
    For 1800: no copy known.

39079 WESTMINSTER Assembly of Divines.
 The Shorter Catechism. Composed by the reverend assembly of divines. . . . Carefully revised and corrected. By a minister of the Gospel.
  Castine, (Maine), Printed by David J. Waters. 1800. pp. 66. 16mo. MᶜHS.

39080 WETMORE, Robert G[riffith]   1774–1803
 A Feeble attempt to promote the felicity of Campbell's Mark Master's Lodge, in Duanesburgh: being Worshipful Wetmore's valeditory address . . . on the 17th day of June, A. L. 5800. . . .
  Albany: Printed by Charles R. & George Webster. . . . 1800. pp. 22. 12mo.
    JCB, YC.

39081 —— An Oration, occasioned by the death of . . . Washington. Delivered at the Lutheran church, in Schoharie, on the 15th of January, 1800. . . . To which is added the order of procession, and a number of elegiac odes.
  Cooperstown: Printed and sold by Elihu Phinney. 1800. pp. 23. 12mo.
    HEH, LOC.

39082 WETMORE, ROBERT G., AND HANMER, JOHN
[OBSERVATIONS ON MASONARY HUMBLY TENDERED TO THE CONSIDERATION OF THE ROYAL ARCH
MASONS IN THE UNITED STATES OF AMERICA. BY ROBERT G. WETMORE AND JOHN HANMER,
ROYAL ARCH MASONS IN THE STATE OF NEW YORK.]
91st New York District copyright issued Apr. 2, 1800.

39083 WETMORE, WILLIAM   1749–1830
AN ORATION ON THE DEATH OF GENERAL GEORGE WASHINGTON, DELIVERED AT . . . CASTINE, ON
THE 22D FEBRUARY, A. D. 1800. . . .
Castine: Published by David J. Waters.   pp. 30.   8vo.
AAS, BA, BM, BPL, HC, HEH, JCB, LOC, MHS, NYPL.

39084 WEYLIE, JOHN V.
A FUNERAL SERMON, IN COMMEMORATION OF . . . WASHINGTON, DELIVERED . . . ON THE TWENTY-
SECOND OF FEBRUARY, AT THE PARISH OF FREDERICK, AND COUNTY OF FREDERICK. . . .
[Frederick, Md?]   pp. 18.   8vo.   HEH, LOC, PPL.

39085 WHALLEY, THOMAS SEDGWICK   1746–1828
EDWY AND EDILDA, A TALE, IN FIVE PARTS. . . . EMBELLISHED WITH SIX FINE ENGRAVINGS . . .
BY A YOUNG LADY.
London printed: Albany: Reprinted by Loring Andrews. 1800.   pp. 175, 6 plates.
16mo.   AAS, BPL, JCB, LOC, NYPL, NYSL, PPL.

39086 WHEATON, HANNAH
[POEM ON WASHINGTON].
This item, Wegelin 442, is probably Evans 36710.

39087 WHELAND, WILLIAM
A NARRATIVE OF THE HORRID MURDER & PIRACY COMMITTED ON BOARD THE SCHOONER ELIZA, OF
PHILADELPHIA. . . .
From Folwell's Press [Philadelphia], no. 63, North Front-Street.   pp. 16.   8vo.
AAS, HSP, PSL, WLC, YC.

39088 WHITE, DANIEL APPLETON   1776–1861
A EULOGY ON GEORGE WASHINGTON. . . . DELIVERED AT THE REQUEST OF THE INHABITANTS OF
METHUEN, IN THE MEETING HOUSE OF THE FIRST PARISH. . . .
Haverhill: Printed by Seth H. Moore, for the subscribers, Feb. 1800.   pp. 18.   8vo.
BA, BʳU, CL, EI, HC, HEH, JCB, LOC, MFM, MHS, NYPL.

39089 WHITESTOWN GAZETTE. AND CATO'S PATROL.   1798–1803
Utica [N. Y.]: published by William M'Lean.   fol.   weekly.   FOR 1800: [AAS].

39090 WHITING, SAMUEL   1670–1725
See Adams, Eliphalet.

39091 WHITMAN, LEVI   1748–1838
A SERMON, PREACHED AT WELLFLEET, MARCH 9, 1800 . . . AFTER . . . THE DEATH OF CAPT.
WILLIAM CHIPMAN, WHO WAS INHUMANLY MURDERED BY A PARTY OF RIGAUD'D PIRATES IN
THE WEST-INDIES. . . . PUBLISHED AT THE EXPENSE OF ADAMS' LODGE.
Boston: Printed by Manning & Loring. 1800.   pp. 20.   8vo.
AAS, BM, HC, JCB, MFM, NYHS, NYPL.

39092 WHITMAN, SAMUEL   1752–1827
THE NATURE AND DESIGN OF THE BAPTISM OF CHRIST: ILLUSTRATED IN A SERMON. . . .
Printed at Northampton, (Massachusetts) by William Butler. 1800.   pp. 31.   8vo.
AAS, AHTS, BA, CL, JCB, LOC, NYHS, NYSL, UOC, WLC, YC.

39093 WHITNEY, Josiah   1731–1824
       A Sermon, addressed to a military company belonging to the 13th regiment of infantry
       in the army of the United States . . . in Brooklyn . . . August 25, 1799. . . .
              Windham, [Conn.]: Printed by John Byrne, 1800.   pp. 15.   8vo.
                                                               CHS, LOC, MHS, NYHS.

39094 WHITNEY, Peter   1744–1816
       Christ's ambassadors. . . . A sermon preached February 5th, 1800, at the ordination of
       . . . Peter Whitney, Jr. . . . in Quincy. . . .
              Printed by Young & Minns, Boston. 1800.   pp. 26.   8vo.
                                     AAS, BA, BM, CL, HC, JCB, LOC, MHS, NYPL, NYSL, UTS, YC.

39095 —— Weeping and mourning. . . . A sermon, delivered at Northbough February 22d, 1800. . . .
       On account of the death of General George Washington. . . .
              Printed at Brookfield, Massachusetts, by E. Merriam & Co. April, 1800.   pp. 28.
       8vo.
       "An elegy on the death of General Washington. Set to music by Capt. Abraham Wood,
       of Northborough, which being printed, was sung on the 22d of February, 1800," pp. 27–8.
                                     AAS, BA, HC, HEH, JCB, LC, MHS, NL, NYPL, NYSL, RIHS.

39096 WHITNEY, Phineas   1740–1819
       A Sermon, delivered January 1st, 1800, at the ordination of . . . Nicholas Bowes Whitney
       . . . in Hingham. . . .
              Boston: Printed by Manning & Loring. . . . 1800.   pp. 32.   8vo.
       Appended are "The Charge. By the Rev. David Barnes, D. D. Pastor of the Second
       Church in Scituate" and "The Right Hand of Fellowship. By the Rev. Henry Ware,
       A. M. Pastor of the First Church in Hingham."
                                     AAS, BA, CL, HC, HEH, JCB, LCP, LOC, MHS, NL, NYPL, NYSL, PL, YC.

39097 WHITWELL, Benjamin   1772–1825
       An Eulogy, on . . . Washington . . . delivered before the inhabitants of the town of
       Augusta. . . .
              Hallowell (District of Maine): Printed by Peter Edes. 1800.   pp. 18.   12mo.
                                               BA, HC, HEH, LOC, MFM, NYHS.

39098 WIGGLESWORTH, A.
       An Extract from an eulogium on the late Gen. Washington, delivered on the 22d of
       February 1800. . . .
              Albany: Printed by Barber & Southwick . . . M,DCCC.   pp. 7.   8vo.
                                               AAS, BA, HEH, NYSL.

39099 WILKESBARRE Gazette, and Luzerne Advertiser.   1797–1801
              Wilkesbarre: published for the proprietor, T. Wright.   fol.   weekly.
       With the issue of May 20, Joseph Wright became the printer, and with that of Nov. 10,
       the title was changed to *Wilkesbarre Gazette, and Republican Centinel.*
                                     For 1800: Wyoming Hist. Soc., Wilkes-Barré.

39100 WILLARD, Joseph   1738–1804
       An Address in Latin, by Joseph Willard . . . President; and a discourse in English, by
       David Tappan . . . Hollis Professor . . . before the University in Cambridge, Feb. 21,
       1800. In solemn commemoration of General George Washington.
              E. typis. Samuel Etheridge [Charlestown]. M,DCCC.   pp. 44.   8vo.
       AAS, BA, BM, BʳU, CL, EI, HC, HEH, JCB, LOC, MHS, MSL, NHHS, NL, NYHS, NYPL, VᵃU, WLC, YC.

39101 ——— —— [*Same imprint.*]   pp. 31.   4to.
       AAS, BA, BM, BPL, HC, HEH, JCB, LOC, MᶜHS, MHS, NHSL, NYPL, NYSL, PPL, WⁱˢHS, WLC.

39102 WILLIAM and Mary College.
              See College of William and Mary.

39103   WILLIAM Riley's courtship to Collian Band, shewing how he was persecuted by her father; — also how she was confined in her chamber until she was crazy; sent to Bedlam, where she was kept in close confinement until Riley came with the Lord Lt. of Ireland, &c rescued her from out of the hands of his enemies, & made her perfectly happy by marriage. To which is added The Shoemaker's favorite. Together with Contentment.
New-Haven, printed: Suffield, re-printed, 1800.   pp. 8.   8vo.   NL.

39104   WILLIAMS, John   1664–1729
The Redeemed captive. . . . Annexed to which is. . . . An appendix by the Rev. Mr. Williams, of Springfield. An appendix, by the Rev. Mr. Taylor, of Deerfield. Some observations by the Rev. Mr. Prince, of Boston. Subjoined to this is, a sermon, delivered in . . . Springfield, on the 16th of October, 1775. . . . By Robert Breck. . . . The sixth edition. . . .
Printed and sold at Greenfield, Mass. by Thomas Dickman. MDCCC.   pp. 248. 16mo.
This publication has been dated 1802 on the basis of the date on p. 198, but an error would be more likely there than on the titlepage.
AAS, BM, HC, JCB, LCP, LOC, NL, NYPL, PSL, WC, YC.

39105   [WILLIAMS, John Mason]   1761–1818
The Curate of Elmwood. A tale. Edited by Anthony Pasquin, Esq.
Boston: Printed by John Russell. 1800.   pp. 82.   16mo.   LOC.

39106   [——] A Dirge, or sepulchral service, commemorating . . . Washington. Composed at the request of the Mechanic Association of Boston. — (Words by Anthony Pasquin, Esq.)
[Boston: Printed by Thomas & Andrews.]   pp. 4.   obl. 8vo.
See Sabin 104278.
AAS, NYPL.

39107   WILLIAMS College.
Catalogue of students in Williams' College, November 1800. . . .
[Pittsfield: Chester Smith.]   Broadside.   fol.   AAS, LOC, WC.

39108   —— Commencement at Williams College, September 3, 1800. Order of exercises. . . .
[Colophon:] Printed at Stockbridge.   Broadside.   4to.   WC.

39109   [WILLIAMSON, Charles]   1757–1808
Observations on the proposed State road, from Hudson's River . . . to Lake Erie. . . .
New York: Printed by T. & J. Swords. . . . 1800.   pp. 18, folded map.   8vo.
See the bibliographical note under Sabin 104444.
LOC, NYHS, NYPL, NYSL, WC, WᵐsHS, WLC.

39110   WILLIAMSON, J[ohn] B[rown]   D. 1802
Preservation; or the hovel of the rocks: a play, in five acts; interspersed with part of Lillo's drama . . . "Fatal curiosity". . . .
Charleston: Printed by T. C. Cox, no. 137, Tradd Street. . . . M.DCCC.   pp. vii, [1], 75.   8vo.   AAS, BPL, BʳU, CU, HC, HSP, LCP, LOC, PʳU, UOP.

39111   WILLICH, A[nthony] F[lorian] M[adinger]
Lectures on diet and regimen . . . together with physiological and chemical explanation. . . . The first Boston, from the second London, edition. . . .
Boston: Printed by Manning & Loring, for Joseph Nancrede, no. 49, Marlbro' Street. 1800.   2 vols.   pp. xxxii, 304; [2], [13]–334.   12mo.
AAS, AML, BPL, CL, JCB, MHS, NYPL, NYSL, YC.

39112   —— —— Two volumes abridged in one.
Boston: Printed by Manning & Loring, for Joseph Nancrede, 1800.   pp. xxiv, 381, [3].   8vo.   AML, BPL, NYPL, WC.

39113 WILLISTON, Seth   1770–1851
    The Agency of God . . . a discourse, delivered at Scipio, on the twenty-second day of February 1800 . . . at the death of General Washington. . . .
        Printed at Geneva, New-York, at the press of Eaton, Walker, & Co. By Ebenezer Eaton.   pp. 24.   8vo.   AAS, BPL, CL, HEH, JCB, LOC, NYHS, NYPL, YC.

39114 THE WILMINGTON Gazette.   1799–1816
        Wilmington, N. C. Published by Allmand Hall.   fol.   weekly.   For 1800: [HC].

39115 THE WILMINGTONIAD or a touch at the times. A Dialogue. . . .
        Wilmington: Printed at the Franklin Press by James Wilson.   pp. 19.   16mo.
    A reprint from the *Mirror of the Times* of a verse satire attributed to both John Vaughan and James Wilson.   DHS, LOC.

39116 WILSON, James   1760–1839
    Substance of a discourse on . . . Washington, delivered extempore, February 9th, 1800, before the military officers of Providence. . . .
        Printed at Providence, by B. Wheeler. 1800.   pp. 16.   8vo.
        AAS, B⁺U, HC, HEH, JCB, LOC, MFM, NYHS, NYPL, RIHS.

39117 WINCHESTER, Elhanan   1751–1797
    A Course of lectures on the prophecies that remain to be fulfilled. Delivered in the borough of Southwark. . . .
        Walpole, printed, for Thomas & Thomas, by David Carlisle. . . . 1800.   2 vols. pp. plate, 524; 524.   8vo.
    In some copies the plate is signed "J Purves 1788" and in others, "A. Doolittle 1800."
        AAS, HC, NYHS, V⁰U, WC, YC.

39118 —— The Three woe trumpets. . . . Two discourses . . . delivered in Parliament, on February 3, and 24, 1793. . . . From the second London edition.
        Brookfield, printed by E. Merriam & Co. January, 1800.   pp. 87.   12mo.
        AAS, LOC, NYPL.

39119 WINCHESTER Gazette. The Centinel.   1788–1825
        Winchester (Virginia) printed and published . . . by Richard Bowen. . . .   fol. weekly.   For 1800: UOC.

39120 [WINCHESTER Triumph of Liberty.   1799–1803
        Winchester, Va., published by Trisler & Haff.   fol.   weekly.]
        For 1800: NO COPY KNOWN.

39121 WINDHAM County. Connecticut. Congregational Churches.
    A Plan of consociation, adopted and recommended by a convention of churches in Windham County, November, 1800.
        Windham: Printed by John Byrne, 1800.   pp. 16.   8vo.
        AAS, AHTS, BM, CHS, CSL, HEH, PTS, WL, YC.

39122 WINDHAM Herald.   1791–1816
        Windham: Printed by John Byrne, in the lower room of the Court-House. 1800.   fol.   weekly.   For 1800: AAS, CHS, [HC], [NYHS].

39123 WINKFIELD, Unca Eliza, *pseud.*
    The Female American, or, the extraordinary adventures of Unca Eliza Winkfield. Compiled by herself.
        Newburyport: Printed for & sold by Angier March, north-corner of Market-Square.   pp. 213, front.   12mo.
    Advertised as "in the press and to be published in ten days" in the *Newburyport Herald* of July 8, 1800, and as "just published" on August 26, 1800.   AAS, HC, LOC, NYPL, UOC.

39124 WIRT, WILLIAM   1772–1834
AN ORATION DELIVERED IN RICHMOND ON THE FOURTH OF JULY, 1800; THE ANNIVERSARY OF AMERICAN INDEPENDENCE. . . .
> *Richmond: Printed by Meriwether Jones. MDCCC.*   pp. 19.   12mo.   JCB, LOC.

39125 WISDOM IN MINIATURE: OR THE YOUNG GENTLEMAN AND LADY'S MAGAZINE. BEING A COLLECTION OF SENTENCES. . . .
> *Hartford: Printed by John Babcock. 1800.*   pp. 30.   32mo.   LOC.

39126 WISDOM IN MINIATURE: OR THE YOUNG GENTLEMAN AND LADY'S PLEASING INSTRUCTOR. . . . INTENDED NOT ONLY FOR THE USE OF SCHOOLS, BUT AS A POCKET COMPANION. . . . THIRD EDITION.
> *Brooklyn: Printed by T. Kirk. 1800.*   pp. 208.   16mo.   CU, NYHS, PPL, YC.

39127 WISEMAN, BILLY, *pseud.*
"PUZZLING CAP: A CHOICE COLLECTION OF RIDDLES, IN FAMILIAR VERSE." BY MASTER BILLY WISEMAN. . . . ADORNED WITH CUTS.
> *New-York, Printed by William Durell for John Low. 1800.*   pp. 32.   48mo.
>   D'ALTE A. WELCH.

39128 WITHERSPOON, JOHN   1723–1794
THE WORKS OF THE REV. JOHN WITHERSPOON. . . . TO WHICH IS PREFIXED AN ACCOUNT OF THE AUTHOR'S LIFE . . . BY THE REV. DR. JOHN RODGERS, OF NEW YORK. . . . IN THREE VOLUMES. . . .
> *Philadelphia: Printed and published by William W. Woodward, no. 17, Chestnut near Front Street. 1800.*   pp. 36, [4], 37–604; 632; [4], 9–611, [12].   8vo.
> List of subscribers at the end of volume 3.
>   AAS, BPL, HEH, JCB, LOC, NYHS, NYPL, NYSL, PʳU, RU, WⁱˢHS, YC.

39129 A WONDERFUL ACCOUNT OF A LITTLE GIRL . . . IN THE TOWN OF JERICO . . . VERMONT, WHO WAS CONVERTED. . . . LIKEWISE AN ACCOUNT OF THE VISION OR TRANCE OF A YOUNG WOMAN WHO LIVES ON THE WEST-SIDE OF LAKE CHAMPLAIN. . . .
> *Printed for the Purchaser. 1800.*   pp. 12.   12mo.   HAROLD G. RUGG.

39130 THE WONDERFUL LIFE AND ADVENTURES OF ROBINSON CRUSOE.
See Defoe, Daniel.

39131 WOOD, ABRAHAM   1732–1804
A FUNERAL ELEGY ON THE DEATH OF GENERAL GEORGE WASHINGTON. ADAPTED TO THE 22D OF FEBRUARY. . . .
> *Printed at Boston, by Thomas & Andrews. Jan. 1800.*   pp. 8.   obl. 8vo.
>   AAS, BPL, BʳU, HC, HEH, JCB, LOC, NYHS, NYPL.

39132 WOOD, BENJAMIN   1772–1849
A SERMON, DELIVERED AT UPTON, AUGUST 8TH, 1800. OCCASIONED BY THE DEATHS OF SIMON FORBES, AND ABNER HIS SON. . . .
> *Printed at Worcester, Massachusetts, by Daniel Greenleaf. 1800.*   pp. 22.   8vo.
>   AAS, CL, MHS, NYHS, YC.

39133 WOOD, SAMUEL   1752–1836
A DISCOURSE, DELIVERED AT BOSCAWEN, ON SATURDAY THE 22D OF FEBRUARY, 1800, IN COMMEMORATION OF . . . WASHINGTON.
> *Concord [N. H.]: Printed by George Hough.*   pp. 15.   8vo.   LOC.

39134 [WOOD, SARAH SAYWARD (BARRELL) KEATING]   1759–1855
JULIA, AND THE ILLUMINATED BARON. A NOVEL: FOUNDED ON . . . THE LATE REVOLUTION . . . IN FRANCE. . . . BY A LADY OF MASSACHUSETTS. . . .
> *Portsmouth, New-Hampshire, Printed at the United States' Oracle press, by Charles Peirce, (proprietor of the work.) June, 1800.*   pp. 288.   12mo.
> There is an erratum notice on p. 288.
>   AAS, BA, BʳU, CU, NYSOC, YC.

39135 WOOD, Silas   1769–1847
       Letters addressed to the electors of representatives to Congress for the First Election
       District in the State of New-York. . . .
              New-York: Printed by T. & J. Swords, no. 99 Pearl-Street. 1800.   pp. 22.   8vo.
                                                                                 NYHS, NYPL.

39136 WOODBRIDGE, William   1755–1836
       A Plain and concise grammar of the English language; containing large exercises of
       parsing and incorrect English. . . .
              Middletown: Printed by T. Dunning. 1800.   pp. 72.
       Bound at the end of the NYPL copy is a 22 page *Short Introduction to the Study of
       Geography*, but it is printed on a different paper.   CU, JCB, NYPL, YC.

39137 —— The Plain spelling-book, and easy guide to reading: wherein all the syllables in the
       English language are selected and so arranged . . . as to avoid perplexity. . . .
              Middletown: Printed by Tertius Dunning. 1800.   pp. 143.   12mo.   HC, NYHS.

39138 —— A Sermon delivered at Middlefield, on the Lord's day, April 1799. At the funeral of
       Phineas Lyman, son of Col. David Lyman. . . .
              Middletown: Printed by Tertius Dunning. 1800.   pp. 14, [1].   8vo.
       The last leaf contains a biographical appendix.
                                   AAS, BA, BʳU, CHS, HEH, HSP, JCB, LOC, MHS, NYHS, NYSL, WC.

39139* WOODRUFF, Hezekiah [North]   1763–1833
       A Sermon, occasioned by the death of . . . Washington. . . . Preached December 29,
       1799. . . . To which is added, an appendix, giving a particular account of the behaviour
       of Gen. Washington, during his distressing illness. . . . By Doctors James Craik
       and Elisha C. Dick. . . .
              *Stonington Port, Printed by Samuel Trumbull, for Messrs. Edward & Nathan Smith.
       January, 1800.*   pp. 16.   8vo.
                                   AAS, BPL, BʳU, CHS, HEH, LOC, MHS, NYHS, NYPL, NYSL, YC.

39140 WOODRUFF, Merit N.   1780–1799
       Devotional harmony: a posthumous work of Merit N. Woodruff, late of Watertown.
       (Connecticut) deceased. Published by his relatives and friends, under the inspection
       of Asahel Benham. A short narrative of the life and death of the author, may be
       found in the introduction.
              pp. 60.   long 8vo.
       The author died in 1799 and the AAS copy is dated in Mss. 1801.   AAS, CHS, YC.

39141 WOODWARD, William [Henry]   1774–1818
       An Oration, pronounced at Hanover, Newhampshire, January 9, 1800; at request of
       Franklin Lodge, No. 6, in memory of . . . Washington. . . .
              Printed at Hanover, (N. H.) by Brother Moses Davis, Jan. 1800.   pp. 17.   8vo.
                                                          AAS, BA, HC, HEH, LOC, NYHS.

39142 WOOLMAN, John   1720–1772
       The Works of John Woolman. In two parts. The third edition.
              Philadelphia: Printed by Benjamin & Jacob Johnson, no. 147, High-Street. 1800.
       pp. 448.   12mo.   AAS, BM, BPL, CU, HEH, HSP, NYPL, RU, UOP, WLC, YC.

39143 WOOLSEY, Melancton L[loyd]
       [Address delivered at Plattsburg, N. Y., January 1, 1800 . . . upon a funeral occasion in
       honor of General Washington.
              Lansingburgh: Office of the Lansingburgh Gazette, January 28, 1800.]   Sabin 105214.

39144 WORCESTER, Leonard   1767–1846
       An Oration, pronounced at Peacham, in commemoration of the death of the late Gen.
       George Washington, February 22d, 1800. . . .
              Peacham, Vermont, printed by Farley & Goss. 1800.   pp. 20.   8vo.
                                                   AAS, BA, HEH, LOC, NHHS, NYSL, VᵗU.

39145 WORCESTER, Noah 1758–1837
An Election sermon, delivered at Concord, June 4, 1800. . . . Printed by order of the honorable General Court.
Printed at Concord, June 13, by Elijah Russell. pp. 28. sq. 12mo.
AAS, BPL, EI, NHHS, NHSL, NYHS, NYPL, RU.

39146 WORCESTER, Samuel 1770–1821
An Oration, sacred to the memory of Gen. George Washington. Pronounced at Fitchburg . . . Feb. 22, 1800. . . .
Leominster, (Mass.) Printed by Adams & Wilder. 1800. pp. 21. 8vo.
There are two settings of the titlepage, one with "Adams & Wilder" in roman and one with it in italics. AAS, BPL, HC, HEH, JCB, LOC, NYPL, NYSL, PL, WLC, YC.

39147 —— Six sermons, on the doctrine of future punishment. By Samuel Worcester, A. M. Pastor of the church in Fitchburg. . . .
Printed at Worcester, Massachusetts. By Daniel Greenleaf. 1800. pp. 156. 12mo.
AAS, LOC, NHHS, NYPL.

39148 WORCESTER. Massachusetts. John Nazro.
Public auction, — at Worcester. To be sold, one of the best stands for business in the Commonwealth . . . Worcester, April 18th, 1800. . . .
Printed by Mower & Greenleaf [Worcester]. Broadside. 4to. AAS.

39149 [WORTMAN, Tunis] —— 1822
A Solemn address, to Christians and patriots, upon the approaching election of a president of the United States: in answer to a pamphlet, entitled, "Serious considerations," &c.
New-York: Printed by David Denniston. 1800. pp. 36. 8vo.
AAS, BA, HEH, HSP, JCB, LOC, NYHS, NYPL, NYSL, VᴬU, YC.

39150 —— A Treatise, concerning political enquiry, and the liberty of the press. By Tunis Wortman, counsellor at law. . . .
New-York: Printed by George Forman . . . for the author. 1800. pp. 296. 8vo.
AAS, BA, BʳU, HC, HEH, LOC, MHS, NYHS, NYPL, YC.

39151 THE WRETCHED slave. Sung in the new opera of Paul and Virginia.
New York Printed & sold at G. Gilfert's music store . . . and to be had of P. A. Von Hagen . . . Boston. pp. [4]. 4to. JCB.

39152 YALE College
Catalogue of the members of Yale College, in New Haven, November, M,DCCC. . . .
New Haven: Printed by Read & Morse. Broadside. fol. AAS, YC.

39153 —— The Laws of Yale-College, in New-Haven, in Connecticut, enacted by the President and Fellows, the sixth day of October, A. D. 1795.
New-Haven: Printed by Thomas Green and son. 1800. pp. 40. 8vo.
AAS, BA, BM, CHS, HC, NYHS, YC.

39154 —— Scheme of the exhibitions at the public commencement in New-Haven, September 10, 1800.
[New Haven:] Printed by T. Green & son. Broadside. YC.

39155 YATES, Peter Waldron 1747–1826
An Oration on the death of George Washington — delivered on the 22d of February, 1800, in Temple Lodge, in the City of Albany. . . .
Albany: Printed by Barber & Southwick. 1800. 12mo. BPL.

39156 THE YORK Recorder. 1800–1830
York [Pa.]: printed . . . by Edie & M'Clellan. fol. weekly.
For 1800: [AAS], York Co. Hist. Soc.

39157 [Young, Edward] 1683–1765
The Complaint; or, Night-Thoughts on Life, Death, and Immortality. With the Life of the Author. . . .
Philadelphia: Printed for H. & P. Rice, no. 16 South Second Street. And James Rice, & Co. Market Street, Baltimore. 1800. pp. x, 266, front. 16mo. HSP, UOM¹.

39158 Young, Joseph 1733–1814
A New physical system of astronomy; or an attempt to explain the operations of the powers which impel the planets. . . . To which is annexed, a Physiological treatise. . . .
New York: Printed by Geo. F. Hopkins. . . . pp. 188, [1], diagrams, plates.
96th New York District copyright issued May 30, 1800. AAS, NYAM, NYHS, NYPL, YC.

39159 THE YOUNG misses magazine.
See Le Prince de Beaumont, Marie.

39160 THE YOUTHFUL jester, or repository of wit and ioncent [sic] amusement: containing: moral and humourous tales. . . .
Baltimore: Printed by Warner & Hanna, corner of Market and South Gay streets. 1800. pp. 108. 24mo.
Pages 73 ff. contain songs. AAS.

39161 YOUTH'S Library. Vol. II. The blossoms of morality. . . .
See Cooper, Samuel.

39162 EINE Zuschrift an die Deutschen in Friedrich, Waschington und Allegheny Counties. . . .
[Dated] Friederichtaun, den 23sten October, 1800.
Broadside. fol. AAS.

AUTHOR INDEX

RHODE ISLAND, cont.

May, 1799, laws	36218
May, 1800, laws	38386
June, 1799, laws	36219
June, 1800, laws	38387
Oct. 1798, laws	36220
Oct. 1799, laws	38384
Public laws, 1799	36221
1799 . . . Fenner . . . Brown	36222
1799 . . . Fenner . . . Potter	36223
1799 . . . Brown . . . Hazzard	36224
Supreme Judicial Court, laws	36225

RHODE ISLAND ALMANAC, 1801 38391–4

RHODE ISLAND COLLEGE

Catalogue, 1800	38395
Commencement, 1799	36226
Commencement, 1800	38396
Illustrissimus, 1799	36227
Illustrissimus, 1800	38397

RHODES, JOHN
Surprising adventures 36228

RICHARD, OLD FATHER
See Poor Richard

RICHARDS, GEORGE, D. 1814

Accepted	38399
Hymns	38400
Solemn Dirge!	36229
Verses	37675

RICHARDSON, JOSEPH, 1778–1871
Washington 38401

RICHARDSON, LUTHER, 1774–1811
Oration, July 4, 1800 38402

RICHARDSON, SAMUEL, 1689–1761

Clarissa	38403
Pamela (Norristown)	36230
Same, Fairhaven	36231

RICHARDSON, WILLIAM, 1742–1814
The Cacique 36232

RICHARDSON, WILLIAM, OF BOSTON
Imports 37023

RICHMOND, AUG. 9, 1800 38404

RIDDEL, WILLIAM, 1768–1849
Christian doctrines 38406

RIGGS, CALEB S.
To the free electors 38407

RIGHTS OF MAN (FREDERICK-TOWN), 1799 .. 36233
Same, 1800 38408

RIGHTS OF MAN (NASHVILLE), 1799 36234

RIGHTS OF MAN (NEWBURGH), 1799 36235
Same, 1800 38409

RIPLEY, EZRA, 1751–1841

Charge	36409
Love	38410

ROBBINS, THOMAS, 1777–1856
Washington 38411

ROBERDEAU, ISAAC, 1763–1829
Washington 38412

ROBERTSON, JOHN, 1712–1796
Tables 36236

ROBERTSON, WILLIAM, 1721–1793
History of America, 1799 36237
Same, 1800 38413

ROBINSON, CHRISTOPHER, 1766–1833
Reports 38414

ROBINSON, JAMES
Philadelphia Register 36238

ROBISON, JOHN, 1739–1805
Extracts 36239

ROCHE, EDWARD, 1754–1821
Washington 38415

ROCHE, REGINA MARIA, 1764–1845
Children of the abbey 36240
Same, 2nd ed. 38416

ROD FOR THE FOOL'S BACK 39052–5

RODGERS, JOHN, 1727–1811
Life of Witherspoon 39128

RODGERS, JOHN, 1773–1838
Glorious victory 36241

ROGERS, SAMUEL, 1763–1855
Pleasures of memory 38418

ROGERS, WILLIAM, 1751–1824
Prayer 38419
To the public 37870–1

ROMAN CATHOLIC CHURCH
Ordo divini, 1800 36242
Same, 1801 38420

ROMEYN, JOHN BRODHEAD, 1777–1825
Washington 38421

ROOT, ERASTUS, 1773–1846
Arithmetic 36244

ROSCOE, WILLIAM
Translation 38604

ROSS, JAMES, 1744–1827
Latin vocabulary 36245

ROUSO, CHARLES DENNIS D'ERES
Memoirs 38422

ROUSSEAU, JOHN BAPTISTE CLEMENT
Absorption 38423

SARGENT, WINTHROP, 1753–1820
Letters from Hunter 38463

SASSE, BERNHARD HENRICH
Geistliche lieder 36276

SAUNDERS, RICHARD, *pseud.*
Poor Richard improved, 1800 36277
    Same, 1801 38464
Poor Richard revised, 1801 38465

SAVAGE, EZEKIEL, 1760–1837
Washington 38466

SAY, BENJAMIN, 1756–1813
Annual oration 36278

SCHEEL, HENRI OTHON DE, 1745–1807
Treatise of artillery 38467

SCHENECTADY, APR. 13, 1799 36279

SCHENECTADY GAZETTE, 1799 36280
    Same, 1800 38469

SCHENECTADY SOCIAL SOCIETY
Constitution 38468

SCHOOL OF WISDOM 37099

SCIOTO GAZETTE, 1800 38471

SCOTS' CHARITABLE SOC.
Rules 37018

SCOTS THISTLE SOCIETY
Constitution 36108

SCOTT, FRANCES
Remarkable narrative 36199

SCOTT, JOB, 1751–1793 36281

SCOTT, JOHN
War, 1799 36281
    Same, 1800 38472

SCOTT, JOSEPH
New Gazetteer, vol. 1–2 36282
    Same, vol. 3–4 38473

SCOTT, SARAH (ROBINSON), 1723–1795
Man of real sensibility 38474

SCOTT, WILLIAM
Elocution (New Haven, 1799) 36283
    Same, New York 36284
    Same, Whitehall 36285
    Same, Worcester, 1800 38475

SCOURGE OF FASHION 38476

SEAMAN, VALENTINE, 1770–1817
Midwives monitor 38477

SEAMAN'S JOURNAL 38478

SEARSON, JOHN
Mount Vernon 38479

SECRET HISTORY OF ELIZABETH 36286

SEDGWICK, THEODORE, 1746–1813
Political Last Will 37645

SEIGNEUX DE CORREVON, GABRIEL
Essays 37382

SEIP, FREDERIC
Cataract 38481

SELDEN, ANDREW, 1762–1825
Young child's easy guide 38482

SELECT PAMPHLETS RESPECTING YELLOW FEVER 36287

SELECTION OF ORATIONS ON WASHINGTON .. 36859

SELLER, RICHARD
Sufferings 38519

SENECA, LUCIUS ANNAEUS
Morals 37818

SERIOUS CONSIDERATIONS 37835–6

SERIOUS FACTS 38486

SERLE, AMBROSE, 1742–1812
Christian Remembrancer 36288
Horae Solitariae 36289

SERMONS ON VARIOUS IMPORTANT DOCTRINES . 36290

SEVEN CHAMPIONS OF CHRISTENDOM 36291

SEWALL, DANIEL, 1755–1842
Astronomical diary, 1800 36292
    Same, 1801 38487
Washington 38488
Weatherwise's almanac, 1800 36681

SEWALL, JONATHAN M., 1748–1808
Washington 37383, 38489

SEWALL'S SHEET ALMANAC, 1800 36294

SHADE OF ALEXANDER POPE 37941

SHAFTSBURY BAPTIST ASSOCIATION
Minutes 36295

SHARP, JOSHUA
Citizen Almanac, 1800 36296
    Same, 1801 38491
Father Abraham's Almanac, 1801 38492
Father Tammany's Almanac, 1800 36297
    Variant 36298
    Same, 1801 38493

SHAW, ROBERT G.
Catalogue, Sept. 19, 1799 36299
    Same, Dec. 9, 1800 37012
    Same, Dec. 24, 1800 37013
    Same, Feb. 27, 1800 37014

SHAW, WILLIAM, 1741–1816
Resurrection 36300
Right hand 37467

SHEPHERD, E.
Columbian accountant 38494

SUBJECT INDEX

AGRICULTURE: 35935, 36041, 36052, 37436, 37812, 37935

ALIEN *and Sedition Laws*: 36000–1, 36205, 36431, 36434, 36457, 36560, 36581, 36583, 36631–40, 36760–2, 38302, 38952–3, 38959–61

ALMANACS

ALMANACS, cont.

BIBLIOGRAPHY

BIOGRAPHY

CATECHISMS

CHURCH HISTORY

DRAMA

EDUCATION

ELECTION SERMONS

CONNECTICUT

MASSACHUSETTS

NEW HAMPSHIRE

FICTION

FOURTH OF JULY ORATIONS

GEOGRAPHY AND TRAVELS, cont.

HISTORY

HISTORY, cont.

LANGUAGES

ENGLISH LANGUAGE

FRENCH LANGUAGE

GERMAN LANGUAGE

GREEK LANGUAGE

LATIN LANGUAGE

NEWSPAPERS

NEWSPAPERS, cont.

NEWSPAPERS, cont.

POETRY, cont.

ELLIS, J. Washington 37358
EXECUTION of Wild Robert 37156
FALCONER, W. Shipwreck 37393
FRY, J. Select poems 37479
THE GIN shop 37142
GOLDSMITH, O. Poems 37530
THE GRAVESTONE 37164
HASELL, W. S. Alfred 37594
HELMUTH, J. H. C. Waschington 37603
HONEYWOOD, S. Farewell Address 37644
HOWE, S. Divine law 37658
　　Honoribus laureatus 37659
IRONY, S. Fashion 37690
JACKSON, MRS. J. Juvenile entertainment . 37694
LADY Washington's lamentation 37770
LAMENTATION for Gen. Washington 37771-2
LEWIS, E. Washington 37823
LINES composed on Washington 37831
LINN, J. B. Death of Washington 37832
LOVE, C. Washington 37851
LOVETT, J. Washington 37852
LOW, S. Poems 37856
MANSFIELD, J. Hope 37884
MILLER, J. R. Poems 36625
MORE, H. Day of Judgment 37164
MORE, H. Lady and the pye 37162
　　Dan and Jane 37165
MATHIAS, T. J. Imperial epistle 37937
　　Pursuits of literature 37938-40
　　Shade of Pope 37941
MITE of Praise 37979
MODERN Quaker 37982
NEW YEAR VERSES: 35909, 35956-8, 35961, 35965,
35996, 36004, 36273, 36362, 36453, 36693, 36818,
37026, 37114, 37208, 37217, 37240, 37686, 37933,
38346, 38441, 39059
NISBET, R. Numbers 35975
ODES: 36004, 36265, 36376, 36436, 37008, 37031,
37295, 37299-301, 37346, 37491, 37520, 37790, 37855,
37927, 38146-8, 38284, 38399-400, 39081
THE OLD man 37167
THE PLUM cakes 37144
POETICAL flower basket 36129
POLWHELE, R. Unsex'd 38293
REFLECTIONS on love 38365
RETURNED captive 38381

RUSSELL, J. M. Pastoral songs 36256
SCOURGE of fashion 38476
SEARSON, J. Mount Vernon 38479
SMITH, W. M. Flowret 36326
SOUTHEY, R. Poems 36345
STENNET, S. Bird of paradise 37863
STORY, J. Elegy to Washington 38568
　　Power of solitude 38569
SUBSTANCE of a late dream 38584
TANSILLO, L. Nurse 38604
THARP, P. Elegy on Capt. Valentine 38624-5
THOMSON, J. Seasons 38634
TROUBLES of life 37159
TRUMBULL, J. M'Fingal 36456
VERSES COMPOSED and sung at Trenton ... 36620
VERSES ON Benjamin Tubbs 36621
WHEATON, H. On Washington 36710
　　On taking farewell 36711
WHITE, B. Washington 38504
WILMINGTONIAD 39115
YOUNG, E. Resignation 36746
　　Complaint 39157

POST OFFICE 36476, 36489
PSALMODY: 35861, 36331, 36365, 36660, 36836, 38276
SLAVERY: 36110, 36765, 36916, 37188, 37969, 38228-9,
38804
SONGS: 36033, 36246-8, 36330, 36335, 36375, 36462,
36625, 36662, 36747, 36822, 36834, 36840, 36909,
37150, 37165, 37269, 37343, 37344, 37365, 37413,
37420, 37614, 37633, 37671, 37827, 37847, 38110,
38157, 38177, 38195, 38447, 38597, 39064, 39151,
39160

SPELLERS. *See* Languages, English

SOCIETIES: 35968, 36108, 36183, 36278, 36795, 37018,
37067, 37229, 37232, 37233, 37346, 37367-8, 37615,
37833-4, 37840, 37885, 37928, 37935, 37969, 38097a,
38101, 38162, 38224, 38228, 38246, 38249, 38253,
38454, 38468, 38528, 38620, 38710, 38713, 38739,
38874, 38924

TAXATION 37328, 37485, 37925

THANKSGIVINGS AND FASTS: 36369, 36373, 36381,
36497, 36699, 36713, 36738, 36755, 37267, 37553,
37905, 37913-4, 38382, 38580, 38587, 38929, 38981

THEATRE: 36084, 36101-3, 36269, 37335, 37386,
38114, 38158, 39009
　　See also Drama

THEOLOGY

WASHINGTON EULOGIES

WASHINGTON EULOGIES, cont.

John Elliott	37353
Jonathan Elmer	37359
Nathaniel Emmons	37369
John Frederic Ernst	37379
Eulogium	37384
Oliver Everett	37332, 37387
Nathanial Fisher	37425
Thaddeus Fiske	37426
John Fitch	37427
Abel Flint	37430
Peter Lawrence Folsom	37432
Eli Forbes	37433
John Foster	37438
William Clark Frazer	37448
Frederick Frelinghuysen	37466
Levi Frisbie	37477
Richard Furman	37484
Stephen Gano	37487
Barent Gardenier	37490
Ebenezer Gay	37493
Eliphalet Gillet	37516
Benjamin Gleason	37520
John Glendy	37521
Levi Glezen	37522
Aaron Green	37538
Benjamin Greene	37541
Andrew Greenwood	37547
William Griffith	37548
Stanley Griswold	37549
William Guirey	37558
William Halsey	37565
Thaddeus Mason Harris	37332, 37581–2
Levi Hart	37587
Anthony Haswell	37595
Moses Hemmenway	37605
Enos Hitchcock	37627
Henry Holcombe	37634
Abiel Holmes	37640–1
Daniel Hopkins	37646
Frederick W. Hotchkiss	37651
Asahel Huntington	37663
Enoch Huntington	37664
Jedidiah Huntington	37666
Jonathan Huse	37668

Jirah Isham	37691
William Jackson	37383, 37694–5, 39021
John Barent Johnson	37709
Isaac Stockton Keith	37715
James Kemp	37716
James Kendall	37722
Ariel Kendrick	37723
Walter King	37734
Francis Kinlock	37735
John Thornton Kirkland	37383, 37736–7
Samuel Knox	37742
M. J. La Neuville	37776
Chauncey Langdon	37777
Jacob Larzelere	37780
Lyman Law	37666
Isaac Ledyard	37790
Elisha Lee	37795
Henry Lee	36859, 37383, 37797–809
David Leonard	37816
Eldad Lewis	37823
William Linn	37383, 37834
Henry Maurice Lisle	37837
Samuel Macclintock	37865
David McClure	37866
Samuel Eusebius McCorkle	37867
David M'Keehan	37872
James McRee	37874
Alexander Macwhorter	37875
James Madison	37876–7
Jacob Magaw	36859, 37878
Samuel Magaw	37879–80
Ebenezer Grant Marsh	37886
John M. Mason	37383, 37902–3
Samuel Mead	37944
Pliny Merrick	37953
Rosewell Messinger	37955
Noah Miles	37962
Alexander Miller	37963
Samuel Miller	37964
George Richards Minot	36859, 36990, 37383, 37966–7
Ammi Ruhami Mitchell	37977
Silas Moody	37989
William Morison	37999
Thomas Morrell	38000
Gouverneur Morris	37383, 38002